A THEODORE DREISER
ENCYCLOPEDIA

Theodore Dreiser in 1926
Courtesy University of Pennsylvania Rare Book and Manuscript Library

A THEODORE DREISER ENCYCLOPEDIA

Edited by Keith Newlin

Greenwood Press
Westport, Connecticut • London

Library of Congress Cataloging-in-Publication Data

A Theodore Dreiser encyclopedia : edited by Keith Newlin.
    p.   cm.
    Includes bibliographical references and index.
    ISBN 0-313-31680-5 (alk. paper)
    1. Dreiser, Theodore, 1871-1945—Encyclopedias. 2. Novelists, American—20th
century—Biography—Encyclopedias. 3. Journalists—United
States—Biography—Encyclopedias. I. Newlin, Keith.
    PS3507.R55Z459   2003
    813'.52—dc21   2003040841

British Library Cataloguing in Publication Data is available.

Library of Congress Catalog Card Number: 2003040841
ISBN: 0-313-31680-5

First published in 2003

Greenwood Press, 88 Post Road West, Westport, CT 06881
An imprint of Greenwood Publishing Group, Inc.
www.greenwood.com

Printed in the United States of America

The paper used in this book complies with the
Permanent Paper Standard issued by the National
Information Standards Organization (Z39.48–1984).

10 9 8 7 6 5 4 3 2 1

Copyright Acknowledgments

The author and publisher gratefully acknowledge permission for use of the following material:

Excerpts from *An American Tragedy, Chains: Lesser Novels and Stories, Moods: Cadenced and Declaimed,* and *A Gallery of Women* are by permission of the Dreiser Trust.

Excerpts from *Letters of Theodore Dreiser: A Selection,* 3 vols., edited by Robert H. Elias. Copyright © 1959 by the University of Pennsylvania Press. Reprinted with permission of the publisher.

Excerpts from *Dreiser-Mencken Letters: The Correspondence of Theodore Dreiser and H. L. Mencken, 1907–1945,* 2 vols., edited by Thomas P. Riggio. Copyright © 1986 by the University of Pennsylvania Press. Reprinted with permission of the publisher.

Excerpts from unpublished manuscripts and letters and a photograph of Dreiser in the Theodore Dreiser Papers, Rare Book and Manuscript Library, University of Pennsylvania, are by permission of the Trustees of the University of Pennsylvania.

Excerpts from a letter by Mary Pyne to Hutchins Hapgood are courtesy of the Yale Collection of American Literature, Beinecke Rare Book and Manuscript Library, Yale University. Every reasonable effort has been made to trace the copyright owner for this source but this has proven impossible. The author and publisher will be glad to receive information leading to more complete acknowledgments in subsequent printings of the book and in the meantime extend their apologies for any omissions.

Contents

List of Entries

Preface

Perhaps more than most writers, Theodore Dreiser's reputation has waxed and waned dramatically over the last century. From the 1910s through the 1930s, he embodied for many rebellious modernists an absolute artistic integrity. He was much admired for writing courageously and honestly from the heart of his own experience, for attacking a stifling "puritanism," and for extending his pity to common men and women in the grip of vast social forces. With the coming of the Cold War and the triumph of a conservative New Criticism, Dreiser often seemed a quaint curiosity whose simple-minded determinism and clumsy style characterized what Lionel Trilling condescendingly termed the "liberal imagination." With the 1960s, however, a younger generation of critics initiated a Dreiser renaissance that continues to this day. At one time a seeming shoe-in for the Nobel Prize, Dreiser continues to engage readers a half century after his death. Indeed, Dreiser has an international following, with scholars teaching and writing about his work in Algeria, Canada, the Czech Republic, China, Germany, France, Italy, India, Israel, Japan, Portugal, Russia, Switzerland, and the United Kingdom. All eight of his novels continue to be reprinted, with new editions of his writing appearing regularly, and there is a lively scholarly community represented by the thirty-three-year-old journal *Dreiser Studies* and the decade-old International Theodore Dreiser Society. In the United States, Dreiser is widely taught in both undergraduate and graduate classrooms, with *Sister Carrie* one of the most widely assigned works in courses on the American novel and several of his short stories standards in literature anthologies.

Although there is no lack of books about Dreiser, their very number suggests the need for an encyclopedia. For students and scholars interested in Dreiser, many aids exist: two full-scale biographies—W. A. Swanberg's *Dreiser* (1965) and Richard Lingeman's two-volume *Theodore Dreiser* (1986, 1990)—a three-volume collection of his letters, a two-volume collection of his letters to H. L. Mencken, and a primary and secondary bibliography, last revised in 1991. The University of Pennsylvania Dreiser Edition has for more than twenty years been issuing scholarly editions of his books, diaries, and unpublished manuscripts. In addition, there are many critical books, monographs, and collections of essays devoted to the man and his works. While Philip Gerber's *Plots and Characters in the Fiction of Theodore Dreiser* (1977) is a valuable resource, there has not been, until now, a one-volume guide to the essential

Dreiser—his work, his life, and the influences that shaped him.

A Theodore Dreiser Encyclopedia is necessarily selective. Dreiser lived to be seventy-four and was incredibly prolific over the fifty-three years of his professional life. In addition to his twenty-four books, he published more than 870 magazine and newspaper pieces—stories, poems, essays—the most important of which he collected in such books as *Free and Other Stories*, *Hey Rub-a-Dub-Dub*, *Twelve Men*, *Chains: Lesser Novels and Stories*, *Moods*, and *A Gallery of Women*. At the core of the encyclopedia are entries in an alphabetical sequence on each of his books and short stories and on those magazine and newspaper pieces he collected during his life, with two exceptions. His poems, many of which appeared first in magazines, are treated selectively under the entry for the collection *Moods*. Of the thirty-eight brief sketches collected in *The Color of a Great City*, most are treated the same way as the poems, though twelve of the more significant have individual entries. Noteworthy uncollected and posthumously collected works are accorded separate entries, as are major characters in the novels, family members, friends, and other persons important to understanding his work. There are also entries on Dreiser's publishers, on his major influences, on the places and events important to his life, and on the literary and social contexts of his work. Bold-faced terms within entries refer readers to other entries in the encyclopedia, though frequently mentioned terms—members of Dreiser's immediate family, H. L. Mencken, Chicago, New York City, Indiana, the characters Carrie Meeber, George Hurstwood, Charles Drouet, Clyde Griffiths, and the titles of his works—are not so marked.

To assist in the further exploration of Dreiser's work and life, many contributors have added to their entries a list of works for further reading directly related to the topic. To avoid duplication, I have listed several standard works only in the selected bibliography. Readers interested in Dreiser's thirty-one published short stories should assume the need to consult Joseph Griffin's *The Small Canvas: An Introduction to Dreiser's Short Stories* (1985); those interested in his daily routine, the various editions of his diaries; and those interested in a broader understanding of his life, the biographies by Swanberg and Lingeman. Readers seeking publication details for all of Dreiser's works or wanting to trace his reputation through contemporary reviews should consult, respectively, *Theodore Dreiser: A Primary Bibliography and Reference Guide*, edited by Donald Pizer, Richard W. Dowell, and Frederic E. Rusch (1991) and *Theodore Dreiser: The Critical Reception*, edited by Jack Salzman (1972).

Citations within entries have been kept to a minimum. There are no page references for Dreiser's works, though contributors have generally supplied enough context for readers to locate quotations, which, given the lack of a standard edition of Dreiser's works, are from the first American book edition or periodical publication. Page references to scholarly or other works are keyed to the list that follows the entry or to the selected bibliography. The few cited works not listed in those places are fully described within the entry. Throughout, a number of frequently cited titles are abbreviated; a list of abbreviations appears at the front of the encyclopedia.

I am pleased that nearly seventy contributors, ranging from well-known and influential Dreiserians to younger scholars just entering the profession, agreed to take part in this project. Their contributions represent a variety of critical approaches and styles of writing; I have sometimes edited entries for consistency, accuracy, and clarity and have occasionally cut matter duplicated elsewhere, but I have tried not to interfere with an individual's style or approach. *A Theodore Dreiser Encyclopedia* therefore represents a cross-section of current Dreiser scholarship in addition to providing the factual information one comes to an encyclopedia to find.

I have incurred many debts in the course of this project, which I acknowledge with pleasure. I wish especially to thank my contributors, who graciously interrupted their other work to make this volume possible. I am deeply grateful not only for their generosity in agreeing to participate in this project but also for their cooperation in meeting deadlines, responding promptly and fully to queries, and making revisions when necessary. For advice, encouragement, and many other courtesies, I am indebted to Thomas P. Riggio, Stephen C. Brennan, and Jerome Loving. For financial support, I am grateful to the University of North Carolina at Wilmington, College of Arts and Sciences Summer Initiative Program. I thank my department chair, Christopher Gould, whose tangible support and encouragement greatly aided this project. The staff of the interlibrary loan department of Randall Library, especially Sophie Williams and Madeleine Bombeld, rendered indispensable aid. I thank Gregory Neubauer for his assistance with proofreading. My greatest debt is to Robin Briggs Newlin, whose patience and encouragement remain beacons in the night.

Abbreviations

D-M Letters	*Dreiser-Mencken Letters*, 2 vols., ed. Thomas P. Riggio	*Letters*	*Letters of Theodore Dreiser: A Selection*, 3 vols., ed. Robert H. Elias
Dreiser Papers	Theodore Dreiser Papers, Rare Book and Manuscript Library, University of Pennsylvania	Lingeman 1	*Theodore Dreiser: At the Gates of the City, 1871–1907*, by Richard Lingeman
Griffin	*The Small Canvas: An Introduction to Dreiser's Short Stories*, by Joseph Griffin	Lingeman 2	*Theodore Dreiser: An American Journey, 1908–1945*, by Richard Lingeman
SMA 1	*Selected Magazine Articles of Theodore Dreiser: Life and Art in the American 1890s*, vol. 1, ed. Yoshinobu Hakutani	Salzman	*Theodore Dreiser: The Critical Reception*, ed. Jack Salzman
SMA 2	*Selected Magazine Articles of Theodore Dreiser: Life and Art in the American 1890s*, vol. 2, ed. Yoshinobu Hakutani	Swanberg	*Dreiser*, by W. A. Swanberg

Chronology

1871   Herman Theodore Dreiser born on 27 August in Terre Haute, Indiana, the ninth of ten children of (John) Paul and Sarah Schänäb Dreiser.

1879   The Dreiser family separates, with Sarah Dreiser and the three youngest children (Claire, Theodore, and Edward) moving to Vincennes and then to Sullivan, Indiana.

1882   Eldest son Paul (Dresser) arranges for the family to live in Evansville, Indiana, with his mistress Annie Brace (alias Sallie Walker, the madam of the city's best brothel) contributing to the family's support.

1884   Paul leaves for New York after Sallie Walker ends her relationship with him, and the family moves briefly to Chicago and then to Warsaw, Indiana.

1887   Dreiser travels to Chicago and works in a series of unskilled jobs.

1889   He attends Indiana University for one year when a former Warsaw teacher, Mildred Fielding, offers to pay his expenses.

1890   Death of Dreiser's mother on 14 November at age fifty-seven.

1892   Becomes a reporter for the *Chicago Daily Globe* in June and then the *St. Louis Globe-Democrat* in November, inaugurating a three-year career in newspaper journalism.

1893   Meets Sara Osborne White when he is assigned to accompany a group of schoolteachers to the World's Columbian Exposition in Chicago.

1894   Leaves St. Louis and works for newspapers in Toledo, Cleveland, and Pittsburgh before moving to New York in November, where he works briefly for the *New York World*.

1895   In March, Dreiser leaves newspaper journalism and becomes editor of *Ev'ry Month*, which he edits for two years before becoming a freelance magazine journalist.

1898   Marries Sara White on 28 December.

1899   Begins writing fiction during the summer at Arthur Henry's home in Maumee, Ohio, which leads to the composition of his first novel, *Sister Carrie*.

1900   *Sister Carrie* is published and then suppressed by Doubleday, Page & Co. in November; father Paul dies, 25 December, at age seventy-nine.

1901   Begins *Jennie Gerhardt* but becomes incapacitated by neurasthenia; for two years, Dreiser battles the effects of depression before brother Paul sends him to William Muldoon's sanitarium for treatment.

1904   Is hired as an assistant editor at Street and Smith publications in August.

1905   Becomes editor of *Smith's Magazine* in April.

1906   Brother Paul dies, 30 January, at age forty-seven. Becomes editor of *Broadway Magazine* in April.

1907   *Sister Carrie* is republished 18 May by B. W. Dodge & Company. Becomes editor of *The Delineator* in June, which he edits until October 1910.

1908   Meets H. L. Mencken in the spring, when Mencken agrees to ghost-write a series of articles on child care for *The Delineator*.

1910   Separates from Sara White Dreiser permanently; forced to leave *The Delineator* after an infatuation with eighteen-year-old Thelma Cudlipp.

1911   *Jennie Gerhardt* is published in October by Harper & Brothers. In November, Dreiser travels to Europe to research the career of Charles Yerkes for *The Financier*.

1912   *The Financier*, the first volume of *A Trilogy of Desire*, is published in October by Harper's, which also republishes *Sister Carrie*.

1913   Meets Kirah Markham in Chicago and then lives with her in Greenwich Village. *A Traveler at Forty* is published in November by the Century Company.

1914   *The Titan*, the second volume of *A Trilogy of Desire*, is rejected by Harper's and is published in May by the John Lane Company.

1915   With Franklin Booth, Dreiser takes an automobile trip to Indiana. In October, *The "Genius"* is published by John Lane.

1916   *Plays of the Natural and Supernatural* is published by John Lane in February. Ends his relationship with Kirah Markham when he meets Estelle Kubitz, with whom he is involved until 1919. In July, John Lane withdraws *The "Genius"* after obscenity charges are filed against it. *A Hoosier Holiday* is published in November by John Lane.

1918   *Free and Other Stories* is published in August by Boni & Liveright.

1919   *Twelve Men* is published in April and *The Hand of the Potter* in September by Boni & Liveright. Dreiser meets Helen Richardson on 13 September and then, on 8 October, moves to Los Angeles with her.

1920   *Hey Rub-a-Dub-Dub* is published in January by Boni & Liveright. Begins writing *An American Tragedy* in August.

1922   Dreiser moves to New York in October to continue work on *An American Tragedy*. *A Book about Myself* is published in December by Boni & Liveright.

1923   Boni & Liveright reissues *The "Genius"* in September and publishes *The Color of a Great City* in December.

1925   *An American Tragedy* is published in December by Boni & Liveright to good reviews and brisk sales (over 13,000 copies in December alone).

1926   A limited edition of *Moods: Cadenced and Declaimed* is published in July by Boni & Liveright. In October, the first stage adaptation of *An American Tragedy* is produced.

1927   *Chains: Lesser Novels and Stories* and a revised version of *The Financier* are published by Boni & Liveright, both in April. In November, Dreiser travels to Russia to observe the tenth anniversary celebration of the October Revolution.

1928   *Dreiser Looks at Russia* is published in July by Boni & Liveright.

1929   *A Gallery of Women* is published in November by Boni & Liveright.

1931   *Dawn* is published in May and *Tragic America* in December, both by Horace Liveright. The Paramount film of *An American Tragedy* is released. In November, Dreiser goes to Harlan County, Kentucky, to interview striking coal miners.

1932   In November, Dreiser becomes coeditor of the *American Spectator*, until January 1934.

1936   In March, the Erwin Piscator adaptation of *An American Tragedy* is produced by the Group Theater under the title *Case of Clyde Griffiths*.

1941   *America Is Worth Saving* is published in January by Modern Age Books.

1942   Sara White Dreiser dies 1 October.

1944   Accepts Award of Merit on 19 May from the American Academy of Arts and Letters. Marries Helen Richardson 13 June.

1945   On 20 July Dreiser writes a letter to William Z. Foster applying for membership in the Communist Party of the United States. On 28 December, Dreiser dies in Hollywood.

1946   *The Bulwark* is published in March by Doubleday.

1947   *The Stoic* is published in November by Doubleday.

1948   *Theodore Dreiser, Apostle of Nature*, by Robert H. Elias, the first critical biography of Dreiser, is published by Knopf.

1970   *The Dreiser Newsletter*, renamed *Dreiser Studies* in 1987, begins publication at Indiana State University.

1981   *Sister Carrie*, the first volume in the Pennsylvania Dreiser Edition, is published.

1991   The International Theodore Dreiser Society is formed.

A

ADAMS, WILLIAM B. (1818–1900). Dr. William B. Adams, a physician, was a family friend of Dreiser's wife Sara and her parents, the Whites of Danville, Missouri. Born in St. Louis County in October 1818, he was a graduate of the Missouri Medical College in St. Louis. From 1846 to 1881, he practiced medicine in Danville. In 1881 he moved his practice to Montgomery City, where he remained until his death in March 1900 at the age of eighty-one. Following the publication in the December 1901 *McClure's* of "A True Patriarch," the sketch about his father-in-law, **Archibald Herndon White**, Dreiser was requested by Dr. Adams's daughter, Dollie, to write a similar biographical essay about her deceased father. In February 1902, Dreiser received a packet of handwritten notes from Dollie Adams, containing anecdotes about her father. Unable to write effectively about someone he hardly knew, Dreiser incorporated this material into a sketch about his own family physician, Dr. **Amos Woolley** of Warsaw, Indiana, completed by July 1902 and titled "A Samaritan of the Backwoods." This sketch was included in *Twelve Men* as "The Country Doctor."

The first half of the sketch, told from the perspective of a young boy, is based on Dreiser's childhood memories of Dr. Woolley. The anecdotes in the second half are from the point of view of an adult who has heard these stories, as told to him by the doctor's daughter. Much of this material in the second half is taken verbatim from the notes supplied by Dollie Adams. Because the sketch became a composite based on the lives of two different physicians, Dreiser gave his subject the fictitious name of Dr. Gridley.

Robert Coltrane

ADAPTATIONS, FILM. Film adaptations of Dreiser's works include six major motion pictures and a notoriously aborted screenplay. The first of his works to attract intense Hollywood attention was *An American Tragedy.* When it was published in 1925, it immediately attracted a corps of enthusiastic reviewers, and it soon became a runaway bestseller. Hard on this success, Dreiser's publisher, **Horace Liveright**, sold the film rights to Lasky's Famous Players, the company that was later renamed Paramount. After a half-decade hiatus, the firm lured the famed Soviet director **Sergei Eisenstein** (*Strike,* 1924; *The Battleship Potemkin,* 1925) to Hollywood to make *An American Tragedy.* Eisenstein, with Ivor Montagu, developed a promising screenplay that included several innovations including "sound montage." Their interpretation of the novel, however, emphasized Clyde Griffiths's lack of culpability for the death of **Roberta Alden** and transferred responsibility in near totality to the American capitalist system. The Paramount executives, while praising the artistic achievement of Eisenstein's work, decided it could not be filmed because its Soviet take on Dreiser's novel would be offensive to American audiences.

Its contract with Eisenstein was rescinded, and Paramount retained the German director Josef von Sternberg (*The Blue Angel*, 1931) to film *An American Tragedy* based on a new screenplay by Samuel Hoffenstein. The film was released in 1931. Hoffenstein's and von Sternberg's interpretation was in many ways the opposite of Montagu's and Eisenstein's. So was their degree of artistic success. The film downplays Clyde's impoverished background and generally portrays him as a scheming villain. A few contrasting elements seemingly inserted to do some justice to Dreiser's complex characterization of his victimized protagonist, as well as a number of gratuitous additions, bring about a fundamental incoherence in the product. For example, von Sternberg sandwiches his portrayal of Clyde as an irredeemable criminal type between an opening dedication that calls for a better social environment for youth and a closing scene in which Clyde's mother laments her culpability in not giving her son "the right start."

Two decades after the von Sternberg film, *An American Tragedy* was remade at Paramount by director George Stevens. The 1951 adaptation (by Michael Wilson and Harry Browne) was retitled *A Place in the Sun*, and its main characters' names were changed. (Clyde Griffiths to George Eastman played by Montgomery Clift; Roberta Alden to Alice Tripp played by Shelley Winters; and **Sondra Finchley** to Angela Vickers played by Elizabeth Taylor). Stevens's directorial tack was to reimagine Dreiser's novel as a sentimental, if ultimately tragic, love story featuring a highly sympathetic George and an irresistible Angela, but in a late death row cell scene, an unctuous minister leads George to silently signal his murderous intent in Alice's drowning. This admission tends to undermine the audience's sympathy for George so carefully crafted by Stevens earlier in the film. Nevertheless, the director won an Academy Award for his work. It should be remembered that Stevens's original plan to make a more authentic adaptation of *An American Tragedy* was derailed by fear of trouble from the House Un-American Activities Committee, then in the full flush of its power.

A year after the release of A *Place in the Sun,* William Wyler directed Lawrence Olivier, Jennifer Jones, and Eddie Albert as George Hurstwood, Carrie Meeber/ Madenda, and Charlie Drouet in *Carrie,* using a screenplay by Ruth and Augustus Goetz. Like George Stevens's strategy in adapting *An America Tragedy*, Wyler and the Goetzes reconceived *Sister Carrie* as a story of romantic love and frequently sacrificed the novel's gritty **naturalism** for a sunnier surface. The most unrecognizable character in this Paramount film version compared with the novel is Carrie herself. Dreiser's self-absorbed, dreaming drifter who uses as well as she is used becomes a model of virtue and "wifely" devotion. Wyler's selection of Olivier to play Hurstwood was controversial when it was made, and he comes across as far more sophisticated than the bar manager of the novel. Again the looming specter of the House Un-American Activities Committee may have had something to do with the transformation of the more or less morally neutral novel into an exposition of what one critic called "suburban" values.

The other Dreiser novel adapted for the screen was *Jennie Gerhardt*, a Paramount production directed by Marion Gering and released in 1932. The film starred Sylvia Sidney as **Jennie Gerhardt** with supporting roles played by Mary Astor as Letty Pace and Edward Arnold as Senator Brander. It updates the action of Dreiser's novel to the 1930s. This episodic picture (it is broken into a number of short scenes) rounds the one-dimensional title character of the novel into a more worldly woman, while at the same time highlighting her poverty-stricken background. Inexplicably, Gering inserted several jarring scenes apparently in an attempt to provide the audience with some comic relief. On the other hand, the adaptation is generally more faithful here than is the case with the other "Dreiser movies." Though it is true that there is little else to recommend the film version of *Jennie Gerhardt* artistically, Dreiser nonetheless found it "moving" and "beautifully interpreted." His response at this time may have had something to do with his highly negative reaction to von Sternberg's *An American Tragedy*, which he believed had insensitively portrayed Clyde as a "drugstore cowboy."

Two of Dreiser's short works also made it to the screen. In 1942 his sketch "My Brother Paul" was transformed into a lavish Twentieth Century-Fox musical entitled *My Gal Sal*, with Victor Mature as Paul and Rita Hayworth as the Sal of the title. Little of Dreiser's memoir survived the transformation; only six of Paul's songs were deemed still current enough to interest audiences, and Hayworth's singing voice was dubbed. In 1951, Universal-International released *The Prince Who Was a Thief*, based on Dreiser's story, designed to capitalize on Tony Curtis's matinee-idol reputation and costarring Piper Laurie.

Further Reading

Eisenstein, Sergei M., C. V. Alexandrov, and Ivor Montagu. *"An American Tragedy:* Scenario." *With Eisenstein in Hollywood.* By Ivor Montagu. New York: International, 1967. 208–341.

Cohen, Keith. "Eisenstein's Subversive Adaptation." *The Classic American Novel and the Movies.* Ed. Gerald Peary and Roger Shatzkin. New York: Ungar, 1977. 239–56.

Geduld, Carolyn. "Wyler's Suburban Sister: *Carrie*, 1952." *The Classic American Novel and the Movies.* Ed. Gerald Peary and Roger Shatzkin. New York: Ungar, 1977. 152–64.

Hayne, Barrie. "Sociological Treatise, Detective Story, Love Affair: The Film Versions of *An American Tragedy.*" *Canadian Review of American Studies* 8 (1977): 131–53.

Hussman, Lawrence E. "Squandered Possibilities: The Film Versions of Dreiser's Novels." *Theodore Dreiser: Beyond Naturalism.* Ed. Miriam Gogol. New York: New York University Press, 1995. 176–200.

Morsberger, Robert W. "Dreiser's Frivolous Sal." *Dreiser Newsletter* 7.1 (1976): 9–14.

Lawrence E. Hussman

ADAPTATIONS, STAGE. To capitalize on the success of *An American Tragedy*, its publisher, **Horace Liveright**, suggested a play adaptation. He would act as producer, and thirty-three-year-old Patrick Kearney, who had only one produced play (*A Man's Man*, 1925), would write the script. Dreiser signed a contract on 16 March 1926. After a tryout at the Shubert Theater in New Haven, Connecticut, on 5 October, the play opened on 11 October at the Longacre Theater in New York, under the direction of Edward T. Goodman. The cast included Morgan Farley as Clyde Griffiths, Katherine Wilson as **Roberta Alden**, and Miriam Hopkins as **Sondra Finchley**. Because the well-regarded Theater Guild was opening Franz Werfel's *Juarez and Maximilian* on the same night, Liveright's manager, Louis Cline, was afraid of a lukewarm response from the critics, and so he hired seventy-five people to applaud and shout, "Bravo, Dreiser!" The critics were taken in by the deception; the *Herald Tribune* described "an ovation the like of which is seldom seen in a theater," and the *Graphic* reported, "They went mad. They yelled" (Swanberg 315). Nonetheless, the play was a hit, grossing $30,000 per week before tapering off to $9,000 per week in April (Lingeman 2: 287). After 216 Broadway performances, it went on the road (Swanberg 318).

In his adaptation of Dreiser's 840-page novel, Kearney necessarily needed to compress the action, and he chose to focus on Clyde's triangle with Roberta and Sondra, the death of Roberta, and the subsequent trial in a prologue and four acts, in eleven scenes. Kearney largely omitted Dreiser's sketching of the social circumstances that created the conditions for Clyde's actions. Reviewers were mixed in their evaluation of the play: they noted the episodic nature of the play and inevitable gaps caused by the need to compress the novel's bulk, but that same selection of details also simplified Dreiser's characterization, with the effect, as Stark Young wrote in a review for the *New Republic*, of making the characters "more appealing and their reactions more moving than they are in the novel" (3 November 1926: 298). Brooks Atkinson commented in the *New York Times*, "Nearly every scene testifies to the sheer impossibility of telescoping this two-volume novel into a single drama," although he praised the characterization of Roberta, Clyde, and Sondra as "pure Dreiser" (24 October 1926, sec. 8: 1). Dreiser went to a performance with Donald Friede, the co-owner of the Liveright firm, and was so enthralled he wouldn't get up for the intermission. "The poor boy!" he said to Friede. "The poor bastard! What a shame" (qtd. in Swanberg 315). The play was later revived on 20 February

1931 at the Waldorf Theater and played for 137 performances.

In early 1929 Dreiser began corresponding with a German friend, Lina Goldschmidt, to arrange a new adaptation of *An American Tragedy*, with noted German director Erwin Piscator preparing the script from Goldschmidt's scenario. Piscator staged plays in the "epic" style, a method employing such nonrealistic devices as narrators, symbolic and expressionistic stage effects, and other techniques adapted from film; moreover, he was a communist who in his adaptations tended to convey the communist point of view. Dreiser therefore charged Goldschmidt to act as his intermediary, and the script would be subject to his approval. Dreiser had good reason to be concerned, for while Kearney had largely followed the plot and themes of the novel, Piscator introduced a number of changes, the most important of which is the creation of a "Speaker" who functions as a one-man chorus, commenting on the action, addressing the audience and characters, and generally explaining the significance of the action while not directly taking part in it. Thematically, the Piscator script, like Dreiser's novel, indicts society for creating Clyde Griffiths, but it goes beyond Dreiser's intent in suggesting that a Marxist restructuring of society could prevent such a tragedy. When Dreiser received a draft of the script, he asked **Louise Campbell** to translate it and then wrote to Goldschmidt on 25 August 1930 with his response. He thought that the play was "decidedly original and arresting" but complained that "it certainly runs counter to some of my Economic and Sociological principles. I am by no means as final in my conclusions in regard to the ills of society and government or the way out as the text of this dramatization would indicate." He then made some corrections and asked

Goldschmidt to incorporate them into the German production (Dreiser Papers).

The play was scheduled to debut in 1930 but was postponed a number of times because of the unsettled political conditions, and the Piscator adaptation apparently never made it to any European stage prior to World War II; the play that finally opened on 16 April 1932 in Vienna at the Deutsches Volkstheater under the direction of Rudolf Beer was apparently a German-language performance of the Kearney script. In the meantime, Dreiser was exploring other options. On 20 April 1935 the Piscator adaptation, translated by Louise Campbell, opened at the Hedgerow Theater, then the country's best-known repertory theater, under the direction of Jasper Deeter, in Rose Valley, Pennsylvania, and the company gave 110 performances between 1935 and 1948 (Wentz 373). Dreiser attended a performance at the Hedgerow and in an article comparing dramatizations for the *New York Times* wrote that he "was enormously impressed by this [Piscator] version," for it was able to surpass the "semi-melodramatic" Kearney version, which emphasized the "from-rags-to-riches-and-back formula, really dear to the American heart" (1). New York's Group Theater became interested in the Hedgerow production and brought the play to the Ethel Barrymore Theater on 13 March 1936 under the title *Case of Clyde Griffiths* to avoid confusion with the Kearney version. Directed by Lee Strasberg, the cast included Morris Carnovsky as the Speaker, Alexander Kirkland as Clyde, Phoebe Brand as Roberta Alden, Margaret Barker as Sondra Finchley, and Elia Kazan, Sanford Meisner, and John Garfield in minor roles; the play closed after nineteen performances.

The next dramatization to appear was a musical adaptation of a Dreiser short story, "St. Columba and the River," under the title *Sandhog*, by Earl Robinson and Waldo Salt and directed by Howard Da Silva, at New York's Phoenix Theater on 23 November 1954. Robinson, a member of the Young Communist League, and Salt, a member of the Communist Party, were Hollywood screenwriters who had been blacklisted. Their adaptation of Dreiser's story emphasizes the class struggle of the sandhogs digging the Holland Tunnel versus their exploitation by corrupt companies. Much of the action is narrated through songs with such titles as "Johnny's Cursing Song," "Work Song," "Sweat Song," and "Fugue on a Hot Afternoon in a Small Flat." Though Robinson and Salt had difficulty in finding backers for the play, they eventually interested Da Silva, who had also been blacklisted but who had a recent hit (*The World of Sholem Aleichem*), to bring the play to the Phoenix for forty-eight performances. Interestingly, reviewers tended to praise the acting, dancing, and singing but mostly ignored the theme of class struggle, perhaps because by 1954 labor issues were old hat, having been a staple of the Federal Theater era of the 1930s. As Mark Farrelly concludes, "The mainstream critics saw the class struggle as, at best, a dramatic device and, at worst, an annoying diversion from the 'real' human issues of the play" (88).

Two adaptations of *Sister Carrie* appeared after Dreiser's death. On 27 March 1991 the People's Light and Theater Company, under the direction of Ken Marini (with Elizabeth Meeker as Carrie Meeber, Stephen Novelli as Drouet, and Tom Teti as Hurstwood), staged the play in Malvern, Pennsylvania. Resident playwright Louis Lippa's script is a full adaptation taking six hours to perform (in two parts on consecutive nights or a weekend marathon). The ninety-two scenes employ Brechtian epic theater techniques—scenes employ mime and tableaux and blend into one another. Reviewers commented on Lippa's success in conveying Dreiser's characters, though they also pointed out the inevitable updating necessary for contemporary audiences: whereas in the novel Carrie's passivity dominates, in the play she is more sexually aware, more vocal in opinions, and more self-aware.

On 9 January 2002 the Indiana Repertory Theater (IRT) debuted a new adaptation of *Sister Carrie* in Indianapolis under the direction of Janet Allen, with Emma Bowers as Carrie, Rob Breckenridge as Drouet, and Craig Spidle as Hurstwood. Unlike Lippa's adaptation, playwright Charles Smith presented a more truncated script able to be performed in the customary two-hour time slot. In doing so, he necessarily had to exclude much of the texture of the novel. To update Carrie's story for the modern audience, Smith focuses on the Drouet-Carrie-Hurstwood triangle, with characters mentioning in dialogue some events that Dreiser presents more fully in the novel (such as the trolley-car strike, which Hurstwood never takes part in). Carrie's personality has also shifted: she is a modern material girl driven by the desire to accumulate fine clothes, and she is far more cognizant of her seduction than in the novel. Into Hurstwood's mouth Smith places some of Dreiser's philosophizing, which has the effect of developing more clearly the motivation for Carrie's attraction to him. In one radical shift, Hurstwood deliberately plans the robbery of his employer's safe rather than vacillating when confronted by temptation. Hurstwood's decline is greatly compressed, and most of the subplots and observations on New York's poor have been eliminated. As in the earlier production, the IRT staging employs some ninety short scenes that flow into one another, with some simultaneous action on multiple levels, including time shifts in which

Carrie addresses people from her past, and minimal props and sets to facilitate scene changes.

Further Reading

Barber, X. Theodore. "Drama with a Pointer: The Group Theatre's Production of Piscator's *Case of Clyde Griffiths*." *Drama Review* 28.4 (1984): 61–72.

Bates, Laura Raidonis. "*Sister Carrie* at the Indiana Repertory Theatre." *Dreiser Studies* 33.1 (2002): 76–82.

Cassuto, Leonard. "From the 1890s to the 1990s: *Sister Carrie* on the Modern Stage." *Dreiser Studies* 22.2 (1991): 26–32.

Dreiser, Theodore. "Four Cases of Clyde Griffiths." *New York Times,* 8 March 1936, sec. 9: 1, 2.

Farrelly, Mark. "Rising from the Ashes of the Blacklist: *Sandhog* by Earl Robinson and Waldo Salt, a Worker's Musical." *American Drama* 7.2 (1998): 73–91.

Wentz, John C. "*An American Tragedy* as Epic Theater: The Piscator Dramatization." *Modern Drama* 4 (1962): 365–76.

Keith Newlin

"ALBERTINE." In Theodore Dreiser's two-volume work *A Gallery of Women*, "Albertine" is the final sketch of the first volume. Unlike other narratives in this volume, Dreiser begins "Albertine" with a brief Foreword, attributing the tale to an American sculptor who died six years earlier. Dreiser claims the story is true but admits that he "disguised" names and places to conceal the identities of those involved. Unlike the other sketches in *A Gallery of Women* that are narrated by the author, "Albertine" is narrated by the unnamed sculptor who told Dreiser the story. The sculptor begins by referring to Albertine as "[a] girl of the Diana rather than the Hebe or Aphrodite type," claiming that she interested men "not only by her statuesque, reserved and apparently remote beauty, but also by a certain quiescence."

Not unlike Carrie Meeber in *Sister Carrie,* Albertine rises from humble beginnings, working briefly in a factory before attracting men who wish to assist her. After receiving a promotion and a proposal from an elderly employer, Albertine marries an ambitious young interior designer, Phillip Millerton, who remains loyal to Albertine but who devotes his life to his growing business. As a successful interior designer and art dealer, Millerton supplies wealthy New Yorkers with treasures from Europe, but he ignores Albertine, so she pursues relationships with other men.

While married to Philip Millerton, Albertine begins an affair with the narrator: "The thing [affair] did come to pass, and lasted, with changes of mood and periods of regret, even quarrels and temporary dismissal for nearly three years, ending finally in a warm and durable friendship." The narrator fathers Albertine's second child, Joan, but Albertine remains married to Philip Millerton, who continues to accumulate wealth. Eventually, the narrator learns that Albertine, while traveling through Europe with her husband, has had an affair with another man, an architect, Stetheridge. Several times in the narrative, abortion and birth control are discussed as options available to Albertine and as methods that she has employed in the past. Albertine is thus a liberated woman who has affairs while her husband remains faithful. Despite her relationships with other men, Albertine values her marriage to Millerton, and when her husband is charged with fraud, a charge that destroys his business, the couple's relationship strengthens. In the end, the married couple grow old and stout together.

"Albertine" resembles other sketches from *A Gallery of Women* in two ways. First, in other sketches and in "Albertine," Dreiser traces the vicissitudes of male–female relationships, and in all sketches, monogamous relationships fail. Second, in "Albertine" and other sketches, the characters are torn between their careers and their personal relationships—characters must choose between a successful career and a successful relationship and cannot have both. Albertine stops working when she marries, and Albertine's husband ceases to notice her when he concentrates on his career; only when the business fails does the marriage succeed. But "Albertine," as a sketch, is unique. Albertine's marriage does not ultimately fail, and Albertine, not her husband, is sexually adventurous.

Albertine marries, has affairs, becomes pregnant by a lover while still married, considers abortion, and contemplates divorce. For Dreiser, Albertine is a libertine, a woman who finds happiness when her husband is preoccupied with business. In his characterization of Albertine, Dreiser depicts a woman's power, her potential to soothe or to disrupt. As a distant beauty who has a calming effect on men, Albertine may seem to some to be a passive woman, but she is far more liberated than other women in the gallery.

Further Reading

Fishkin, Shelley Fisher. "Dreiser and the Discourse of Gender." *Theodore Dreiser: Beyond Naturalism.* Ed. Miriam Gogol. New York: New York University Press, 1995. 1–30.

Gammel, Irene. "Sexualizing the Female Body: Dreiser, Feminism, and Foucault." *Theodore Dreiser: Beyond Naturalism.* Ed. Miriam Gogol. New York: New York University Press, 1995. 31–54.

Roark Mulligan

ALDEN, ROBERTA, in *An American Tragedy,* is intriguingly both the victim of protagonist Clyde Griffiths's burningly materialistic desires and a kind of female alter ego. Since Roberta is the poor lover of whom Clyde must rid himself to be free to embrace and pursue a future with his dream-girl, the rich **Sondra Finchley**, many readers of the novel have tended to note only her victimization, yet a key element of the book's artistic achievement actually concerns complexities of Roberta's characterization, including ways in which she has a sort of complicity in Clyde's "murder" of her at Big Bittern Lake. Indeed, Roberta is not merely the unfortunate girl in the rowboat with the confused, ambition-driven youth in the climactic scene on a lonely lake but also a character whose own story creates a subplot that expands the *Tragedy*'s exposure of the cruel costs of the "success-dream."

Long before this lower-class girl drowns in the hauntingly ambiguous episode that culminates Clyde's quest for wealth, pleasure, and beauty, she has shown herself to be motivated by values and desires quite like his. Each is full of desires for material "success" and worldly pleasures; each has ironically similar attitudes about *what* is worth desiring and *how* to define "success" in both love and life. One of the powerfully poignant ideas emerging from this novel about modern America's compulsive quest for wealth and status is that these two characters from comparably impoverished backgrounds are ultimately divided, rather than united, by their society's dream-shaping values. In an insight long established by Dreiser scholarship, the novel turns upon a "worlds-within-worlds" theme in which a reader sees a kind of ratio of differing desires, as Roberta is to Clyde as Clyde is to Sondra, for in each relationship, crucially, one partner is or seems to be the socially and materially superior one, while the other aspires to the world of, and is led by desire for, that elevated person promising such a successful attainment of happiness. Even as he

openly ignores and seeks to shun her, Roberta continues, in her own "American tragedy" story, to admire and yearn for Clyde. Thus, the stage is set for her own movement toward that moment on a lake—her fear of water as a nonswimmer submerged by her need to trust in him and his love—where her hunger for life leads instead to her death, in turn assuring the subsequent death of *his* dreams and of Clyde himself, the two of them enmeshed in that poignant drama of the failure of belief in "Success" it was Dreiser's purpose to portray.

Paul A. Orlov

AN AMATEUR LABORER is Dreiser's unfinished account of his three-year struggle with extreme depression, diagnosed as **neurasthenia**, which debilitated him physically and emotionally, severely limited his ability to concentrate and write, and ultimately reduced him to complete destitution. This personal narrative was undertaken early in 1904, immediately after his recovery, but remained unpublished until 1983, when it was issued by the University of Pennsylvania Press.

Though always something of an insomniac and previously under a doctor's care for a tension-related illness, Dreiser began to experience major neurasthenic symptoms in early 1901, shortly after **Doubleday, Page's** reluctant publication of *Sister Carrie* and that novel's subsequent commercial failure. Over the next three years, he struggled against health problems variously identified as headaches, muscular pains, constipation, dizziness, skin irritation, reduced appetite, indigestion, weight loss, feverishness, listlessness, irritability, hallucinations, and an incapacity to sustain mental activity, including a loss of imagination and the diminished ability to reason. He might well have added "paranoia," for by mid-1901 he was convinced that the *Sister Carrie* debacle had caused him to be blacklisted by editors, who in reality found him peevish and his work careless.

For a time, Dreiser made progress on *Jennie Gerhardt*, but after forty chapters he was stymied by what he termed "an error in character analysis." Faced with this impasse, Dreiser and Jug, his wife, left New York and traveled to Dumpling Island, near Noank, Connecticut, to visit **Arthur Henry**, who had shepherded him through the composition of *Sister Carrie*. This time, however, Dreiser's irascibility resulted in an abbreviated visit and a gloomy return to New York, where financial straits forced him and Jug into a dreary apartment overlooking Blackwell's Island. There he did little more than brood until Rutger B. Jewett of J. F. Taylor and Company offered him a monthly advance of $100 to complete *Jennie Gerhardt*. With this hedge against poverty, the Dreisers moved in November 1901 to Bedford City, Virginia, where Theodore hoped to work productively in that tranquil mountain setting. That was not to be. Within a month, the self-doubt and restlessness had returned, and, despite Jewett's urging, all meaningful progress on the novel had ceased. The Christmas holidays found the Dreisers in Missouri, visiting Jug's parents, who were shocked by their son-in-law's emotional distress. By January, Theodore and Jug had settled briefly in Hinton, West Virginia, but soon thereafter embarked on a nomadic existence that Dreiser's friend **Richard Duffy** termed "a one-night stand regime" (qtd. in Dowell xv). By April, Jug had returned to Missouri, and a month later, Dreiser, after a brief stay in Charlottesville, Virginia, set out on a 300-mile walking tour that took him northward through Maryland and Delaware before bringing him to Philadelphia by mid-July 1902.

Dreiser spent seven sterile months in Philadelphia, where Jug again joined him to serve as his nurse and editorial assistant, but her support was to no avail. He could not write; his health, both physical and emotional, continued to deteriorate; and his finances dwindled. In October, he put himself under the care of a doctor, and in December, he informed the disgruntled Jewett that he was abandoning *Jennie Gerhardt*, thereby forfeiting his only means of subsistence, but nothing could arrest the downward spiral. In late January, Dreiser again sent Jug back to Missouri. By the middle of the next month, he could pay neither his doctor nor his landlord and was dependent on the University of Pennsylvania's Free Dispensary for health care. Thus, homeless and virtually destitute, he returned to New York to face what he later described as the lowest state of existence "this side of suicide or death."

At this point, in medias res, *An Amateur Laborer* picks up Dreiser's desperate odyssey, narrating his fifty-six dark days in a run-down section of Brooklyn, where he first found a room that rented for $2.50 a week, then transferred to one for $1.25. His menu ultimately consisted of milk and bread, supplemented by any fruit or vegetable he could find on the ground in Wallabout Market. Through friends, he did secure writing assignments but could not fulfill them. Then, Hurstwood-like, he walked the streets in search of menial labor, only to lose his nerve or be humiliatingly turned away by insolent functionaries. Through it all, his pride prevented his accepting aid from charity organizations or family members living in the area. On 18 April 1903, his self-exile in Brooklyn ended. With less than a dollar in his pocket and no idea what he was to do, he took the ferry to Manhattan. Yet, as he wrote in *An Amateur Laborer*, "I felt rather a feeling of relief as if the worst were over."

Indeed the worst was over. Within hours, he had secured the promise of a laboring position with the New York Central Railroad and had pawned his watch for twenty-five dollars. Then, as he strolled up Broadway, Dreiser chanced to meet his oldest brother, Paul Dresser, currently at the height of his fame and prosperity as a popular songwriter and partner in a successful music-publishing firm. The brothers had been estranged, but one look at Theodore's impoverished condition brought Paul to tears. He forced money on the reluctant Dreiser and eventually extracted the promise that he would rehabilitate at Muldoon's sanitarium, at Paul's expense. Concluding this episode, Dreiser wrote, "The good brother. The best of sons. The only man I ever knew who was wholly and absolutely swayed by the tenderest of sentiments."

For the weekend, while Paul was away on business, Dreiser stayed at the Mills Hotel, a philanthropic institution that provided inexpensive food and shelter to the indigent. He was surrounded, he recorded in *An Amateur Laborer,* by "such a company of wretched patrons as might have served to stock the alms house of almost any community." The following week, he entrained to Olympia, near White Plains, New York, a "repair shop" operated by former champion wrestler **William Muldoon** to restore the health of a wealthy clientele victimized by their own excesses. The six weeks Dreiser spent at Olympia were difficult. He quailed before the bullying intimidation of Muldoon and found the condescension of his fellow-patients annoying, but the Spartan regimen and intense exercise bore fruit. He gained weight; his depression began to lift; and his literary interests and skills were somewhat revived.

Despite these encouraging results, Dreiser left Olympia fully aware that he

was not ready to resume his writing career. Thus, he accepted the position with the New York Central that had previously been offered and embarked on the enterprise that gave *An Amateur Laborer* its title. That manuscript describes Dreiser's successful search for compatible lodging in Kingsbridge, New York, and his first day's work in the carpentry shop at Spuyten Duyvil, located on a peninsula at the juncture of the Harlem and Hudson Rivers. Then the continuous narrative breaks off. Apparently, Dreiser had decided to tell his "laborer" story in the form of shorter, more immediately marketable pieces. His stay at Olympia had already yielded "Scared Back to Nature" (*Harper's Weekly,* 16 May 1903: 816), published while he was still a patient, and "The Toil of the Laborer" was circulating. Soon to be making the rounds also were "The Cruise of the 'Idlewild,' " set in the carpentry shop, and "The Mighty Burke," based on Dreiser's later association with **Mike Burke's** masonry crew. Also written in 1904 was "A Wayplace of the Fallen," a retelling of Dreiser's experiences at the Mills Hotel. For more than five years, other interests diverted him from the "laborer" material, but in 1910, during the composition of his most autobiographical novel, *The "Genius,"* he devoted Chapters 9 through 30 of Book 1, "Struggle," to his battle against neurasthenia. Some episodes were highly fictionalized, but others followed *An Amateur Laborer* closely enough to suggest that the manuscript was being regularly consulted. In 1919, Dreiser published *Twelve Men,* which includes three sketches that draw upon his neurasthenic experiences: "The Mighty Rourke," "Culhane, the Solid Man," and "My Brother Paul." "The Mighty Rourke" is a revision of "The Mighty Burke," but the other two were being published for the first time. "Culhane, the Solid Man" is an admiring portrait of William Muldoon that depends heavily on *An Amateur Laborer*, whereas "My Brother Paul," which includes Paul's rescue of Theodore on Broadway, deviates considerably from the details as they were initially presented.

For the rest of his life, Dreiser made plans for, and tried to stimulate interest in, the "laborer" material, most notably in 1924, when he sent *Hearst's International* a seventy-three-page typescript titled "Down Hill and Up." Ultimately, the second half of this condensed and radically altered version of *An Amateur Laborer* was published as "The Irish Section Foreman Who Taught Me How to Live" (*Hearst's International*, August 1924: 30–21, 118–21), which focuses on Mike Burke's salutary influence during Dreiser's recovery. That sketch was to be the last of the published material mined from Dreiser's struggle with neurasthenia, though as late as 1943 Dreiser was still planning to include those experiences in an autobiographical volume tentatively titled *A Literary Apprenticeship*.

An Amateur Laborer remains the fullest and most verifiably accurate account of a tragic and humiliating period to which Dreiser returned over and over for literary coin. As the years passed, however, his attitude toward those experiences changed, his memory perhaps faded, and the narrative demands of each derivative piece necessitated deletions, additions, and changes in detail. Thus, *An Amateur Laborer* exists not only as a compelling narrative of courage and perseverance but also as a measure of the degree to which Dreiser the storyteller would stretch a fabric of fiction over a framework of truth.

Further Reading

Brennan, Stephen C. "Theodore Dreiser's *An Amateur Laborer*: A Myth in the Making." *American Literary Realism* 19.2 (1987): 66–84.

Dowell, Richard W. Introduction to *An Amateur Laborer*. Philadelphia: University of Pennsylvania Press, 1983. xi–xlix.

Richard W. Dowell

AMERICA IS WORTH SAVING. Dreiser's final book-length work of nonfiction, published in January 1941 by Modern Age Books, documents Dreiser's pro-communist, anti-British political leanings toward the end of his life. In June 1940, Dreiser's agent, **William Lengel**, inquired whether Dreiser would be interested in writing a short book, between 70,000 and 100,000 words, arguing that America should not enter the war. Oskar Piest, the head of the newly established publishing house Veritas Press, wanted to publish the book and proposed such titles as "Keep Out, America" and "Let's Be Pro-American" to suggest the import of his project. Piest offered a flat $5,000 fee to write the book, and Dreiser accepted. To capitalize on the public's interest in the war, Piest asked that Dreiser produce a draft in three months, a pace considerably quicker than that to which Dreiser was accustomed. Therefore, at Lengel's urging, Dreiser sought and, with the help of his erstwhile research assistant Lorna Smith, found an editorial assistant, **Cedric Belfrage**, an English journalist and author working in Los Angeles as a film reviewer. Belfrage received $1,000 for his work with the book. Dreiser and Belfrage tackled the book, meeting three times a week at Dreiser's home and submitting the final chapter on 9 September.

The picture that Belfrage paints of Dreiser during this period is unflattering. In interviews with both W. A. Swanberg and Richard Lingeman, Belfrage recounted that Dreiser managed to work for a few hours in the morning but soon went out for a pint of whiskey and, utterly unable to hold his liquor, quickly thereafter was incapable of work. Dreiser, who seemed to

Belfrage to be "one of the loneliest men I ever knew," would urge Belfrage to stay and chat, but Belfrage would instead return to his own home and continue to work on the manuscript (Swanberg 469). Indeed, Belfrage claims that Dreiser did not write the book at all: "He couldn't have possibly written the book by himself, so in fact I wrote the book" (qtd. in Lingeman 2: 424). Although Belfrage's influence can be discerned in the "occasional Anglicisms" such as "up a gum tree" and "like a Girl Guides' Field Day" (Lingeman 2: 424), the form and content of *America Is Worth Saving* is similar enough to *Tragic America* to convince the reader that the ideas contained in the book are Dreiser's own. For example, Dreiser's angry views of **capitalism** as wasteful and degrading are identical to those expressed in *Tragic America*, as is his support for the Soviet experiment; in both *Tragic America* and *America Is Worth Saving*, Dreiser's enthusiasm for Russia far exceeds the zeal he felt directly after returning from his visit in 1927–1928, as documented in *Dreiser Looks at Russia*. Furthermore, *America Is Worth Saving* amply reflects the influence of Ferdinand Lundberg's *America's 60 Families* (1937), a book that Dreiser had recently read (Swanberg 468).

However, one strikingly new element to be found in *America Is Worth Saving* is Dreiser's strident anti-British sentiment. Chapters such as "Does England Love Us As We Love England?" and "Has England Done More for Its People than Fascism or Socialism?" are filled with angry denunciations of England as a nondemocratic, tyrannical, and imperialistic society, one that oppressed both its own citizens and its colonies. At one point, Dreiser suggests that the English government is not significantly preferable to that of Nazi Germany: "Whether it is better to die quickly by torture or slowly by hunger—and unem-

ployment in England means nothing less— is a question on which there will be difference of opinion." This is the core of Dreiser's argument in *America Is Worth Saving*: because neither England nor Germany is appreciably better than the other, Dreiser argues, America should not enter the war on either side. This stance, however, occasioned Dreiser some trouble in the ensuing years, for an anti-British stance could quite reasonably be interpreted as a pro-Nazi one; Dreiser was forced to explain to the America First Committee, a pro-Nazi group that wanted to distribute extracts from *America Is Worth Saving*, that he opposed imperialism but did not support Hitler.

As perhaps was to be expected given the unpopularity of his ideas, Dreiser encountered some publishing difficulties after he submitted the manuscript. Piest was dissatisfied with what Dreiser had produced, as was Lengel, who wrote to Dreiser after receiving the draft: "Considering the fact that the book was designed to show the futility of America getting into the war . . . you have wandered pretty much afield at times and the book indicates that you believe our salvation rests in communism rather than in the development of democracy within the frame-work of the Constitution" (qtd. in Lingeman 2: 424). Piest, a German émigré, was worried that his citizenship application would be denied if he printed Dreiser's book, and as a result he withdrew from publishing the book after rumors circulated that he was "part of the covert Nazi propaganda effort in America" (Lingeman 2: 425). Lengel turned to Modern Age Books, which agreed to publish the book, but another obstacle arose when two printing houses refused to handle the book, then titled *Is America Worth Saving?* for its apparent anti-Americanism.

After the title was changed to its more positive statement *America Is Worth Saving* and the book went to press, Dreiser sent one of the first copies to Constantine Oumansky, the Soviet ambassador in Washington, who rewarded Dreiser with a book about Stalin and who likely urged the American Council on Soviet Relations to invite Dreiser to speak at an upcoming conference in New York (Swanberg 474). Also supporting his book was the leftist antiwar organization American Peace Mobilization, which promoted the book's sale and which invited Dreiser to speak at rallies in Washington, D.C., and Chicago.

Apart from these friendly responses, however, the book received poor notices. The *New York Herald Tribune* called it "loosely organized, crudely written, ill-proportioned" (rpt. in Salzman 651–52); the *New York Times* called it "not so much a book to be read as a long soap-box speech to be listened to" (rpt. in Salzman 652); and the *New Yorker* termed it a "bitterly sincere but loose-minded Leftist analysis, written in the author's now-familiar substitute for the English language" (rpt. in Salzman 654). For the interested scholar, however, the book provides an insight into Dreiser's philosophy and politics in the last years of his life; F. O. Matthiessen writes that *America Is Worth Saving* provides evidence of Dreiser's "further re-education in the potentialities of American democracy" (*Theodore Dreiser* 228). In addition, the poor public reception of the book helps to explain Dreiser's diminished reputation in the period of his death and why the press, which considered him a "crank, a bore and a Red," ignored him on his seventieth birthday (Swanberg 477). Ultimately, the book's value lies not in its literary merits but in its ability to convey Dreiser's later political ideas, which would otherwise be unknown, and in its documentation of American antiwar sentiment in the months before Pearl Harbor.

Stephen Brain

AMERICAN DIARIES. The American diaries are a series of "private" literary documents that were composed intermittently from 1902 to 1926 and were published by the University of Pennsylvania Press in 1983 as *American Diaries, 1902–1926,* edited by Thomas P. Riggio. They have been preserved in the Dreiser Collection at the Lilly Library, Indiana University; in the Dreiser Papers at the University of Pennsylvania; and in the New York Public Library. Together with correspondence and other documents, they are of importance as a major source for the interpretation of crucial phases in Dreiser's career and for the genesis of many of his works. The entries vary considerably in length and style, from fully developed passages in the manner of vignettes and careful daily narratives to the hurried telegraphic accounts and aide-mémoires also characteristic of his European diaries of 1911–1912, 1926, and 1927, which remain in manuscript. As candid, unadulterated records, they offer insights into Dreiser's personal life at different periods, the organization of his workday, and his social activities. In particular, they shed light on his initial difficulties as a writer, the gradual formation of his work style, and the gestation of some of his literary compositions.

The "Philadelphia Diary, 1902–03" seems to mark the beginning of Dreiser's diary keeping. It originated as a medical record at the behest of Louis Adolphus Duhring, M.D., a dermatologist and neurologist at the University of Pennsylvania, who diagnosed Dreiser with a nervous disorder (**neurasthenia**). The daily entries center on the author's physical state, the effect of different medications on his body, his inability to do any sustained creative work, and his shrinking funds. When the treatment breaks off and his wife Sara leaves him to return to Missouri, the entries provide a more detailed analysis of the condition of his psyche. Probing his position in life, he concludes that in spite of his present miserable situation, he cannot take up other work "simply because I feel or felt that I was cut out and called upon to do literary and socialistic work and that very shortly I would be able to do it."

"Savannah and the South, 1916" shows Dreiser leaving New York and staying alone in Savannah, where he finishes the manuscript of *A Hoosier Holiday* and begins revising *The Bulwark*. It is also a prelude to his separation from **Kirah Markham**. The extended descriptions of the daily routine contain more introspection and also incipient work notes such as lyrical pieces like "The Sea," "Gulls," "Clouds," "Life Moods," and overheard bits of conversation like "A Ship Conversation" or social Darwinistic reflections on society.

"Greenwich Village, 1917–18" discloses Dreiser's intense life in **Greenwich Village**, a period marked by his effort to negotiate his commitment to his literary work with his passionate needs and bohemian lifestyle. Dreiser here describes the minutiae of his extremely active life. He depicts his socializing with such authors, artists, editors, publishers, and producers as H. L. Mencken, Abraham Cahan, Ludwig Lewisohn, Hutchins Hapgood, Douglas C. Doty, Arthur Hopkins, Richard Ordynski, and Samuel L. Rothapfel, and he chronicles his encounters with his various female friends, married and unmarried or divorced, on which he depended or who depended on him. The diary describes the often troubled relationship with his constant partner of this period, **Estelle Kubitz**, as well as the continuing friendships and irregular meetings with other

women, foremost among them **Lillian Rosenthal**, Rella Abell Armstrong, Petronelle Sombart, and **Louise Campbell**. The diary shows the transition and mingling of the daily affairs and the writerly record, an idea for a story springing more than once from a casual encounter or a tale told by a friend. Here Dreiser is at work almost every day and energetically juggling his many obligations, composing new stories ("Love," "Free," etc.), and revising old pieces for his two collections, *Free and Other Stories* and *Twelve Men*. At other times he is minding his autobiographical projects, writing *Newspaper Days* and directing the revision of *Dawn* by Louise Campbell. The entries also reflect his growing interest in the theater and his connection with the Washington Square Players, the success of the opening performance of *The Girl in the Coffin*, and the making of *The Hand of the Potter*.

"Home to Indiana, 1919" is the record of a trip to Indiana from 15 June to 2 July 1919. Dreiser visits May Calvert Baker, his old teacher in Warsaw, who now lives in Huntington; the two sit up together late at night exchanging memories and talking about his work. He then moves on to Indianapolis, where he stays with the Addison Parry family and meets John Milo Maxwell, former editor of the *Chicago Daily Globe*, who had helped Dreiser enter the world of **journalism**.

"A Trip to the Jersey Shore, 1919" covers a weekend trip with Estelle Kubitz to Belmar, the excursion partly spoiled by a sprained ankle.

"Helen, Hollywood, and the *Tragedy*, 1919–24" covers the period from 19 July 1919 to 2 July 1924. It begins with Dreiser's analysis of a dream that presages his future, Helen Richardson's unexpected visit to his studio, his love for her, and his decision to move to Los Angeles. The diary reports both the transports of his intense feelings for Helen and his gradual settling down to a new work routine with longer working days and greatly reduced social contacts, while keeping up with his usual extensive correspondence. Despite several changes of address with the particulars of new landladies and the transportation of his small household, the diary reflects a comparatively stable life, plagued occasionally by money problems but relieved from time to time by unexpected windfalls of checks from magazines, publishers, or theater directors. Within the span of one year, after forcing and then discarding work on *The Bulwark*, he finishes several short stories (among them "Fulfillment") and *Newspaper Days*, and is pleased by the favorable reviews of *Hey Rub-a-Dub-Dub*, and, in a 6 September 1920 entry, he mentions for the first time, "I work on 'An American Tragedy' till 4 P.M."

The diary contains descriptions of the world of actors and studios in Hollywood as reported by Helen, who obtained small roles in various films, ample material that Dreiser used for such magazine pieces as "An Overcrowded Entryway" (unpublished) and "Hollywood Now," published in *McCall's* in September 1921. It also covers in rich detail his Sunday outings and several extended tours to Tijuana, San Francisco, and Portland. The California years end on a note of bitter frustration. Although he had completed numerous short stories and finished some sketches for *A Gallery of Women* and had also written a 175-page manuscript, "Mea Culpa," which he then discarded, he is despondent over the reaction of magazine editors: "At the moment see no clear way out of money troubles or that I am making any real artistic headway with work."

The diary resumes in January 1923 after Dreiser's return to New York, where he again enters the familiar social scene, meeting with his agent **William Lengel** as well as with such editors and publishers as Fulton Oursler, Bernarr MacFadden, and Art Young. He sees **A. A. Brill**, psychiatrist and translator of Freud's work. He records his investigations of the **Grace Brown/Chester Gillette** case, describes a trip to Big Moose Lake, and talks with witnesses to the case. While work on *An American Tragedy* proceeds to his satisfaction, he admits to his increasing difficulties with Helen owing to his involvement with other women, including his secretaries **Sallie Kusell** and May Brandstone, and acquaintances from the stage like Maud Guitteau and Magdalen Davis.

"Motoring to Florida, 1925–26" is Dreiser's last American diary from 8 December 1925 to 25 January 1926. Together with Helen, he leaves New York nine days before the publication of *An American Tragedy* to inspect the new land developments in Florida. En route he briefly records the visit to Mencken in his Baltimore home, which ended the close friendship between the two men because of what Mencken regarded as Dreiser's insensitivity to his mother's fatal illness. Via Richmond and Savannah they reach St. Augustine by Christmas, then proceed to Ft. Lauderdale, from whence they make prospecting trips to the surrounding country. While the diary offers impressive descriptive images of the tropic flora and aquatic fauna, it also catches a historic moment in the state's transition from a neglected swamp land to a booming tourist country. The diary closes with the incoming news of the critical and financial success of *An American Tragedy*, his decision to buy a lot, and his return to New York.

Further Reading

Bardeleben, Renate von. "Dreiser's Diaristic Mode." *Dreiser Studies* 31.1 (2000): 26–42.

Renate von Bardeleben

"THE AMERICAN FINANCIER." First published in *Hey Rub-a-Dub-Dub*, "The American Financier," whether intended to do so or not, clarifies Dreiser's purpose for his character **Frank Cowperwood** in the *Trilogy of Desire*, who embodies the Nietzschean Übermensch. Dreiser's assessment of financiers is paradoxical in that he finds them to be "the coldest, the most selfish, and the most useful of all living phenomena." Drawing upon the social theories of **Herbert Spencer**, he argues that "the individual and the mass are interdependent facets" and that despite such "religious and copy-book maxims" as "all men are created equal" and have "the right to life, liberty, and the pursuit of happiness," brilliant individuals must somehow rise above this impractical ideology to best use their genius not only for their own profit but also to benefit society. In other words, society cannot reduce individuals with gifts that can potentially benefit humankind to the level of those citizens who have nothing to offer. Such an egalitarian belief impedes progress. Using Gustavus Myers's *History of the Great American Fortunes* (1910), Dreiser refers to such robber barons as J. P. Morgan, J. D. Rockefeller, John Astor, and Cornelius Vanderbilt, noting that though their egos may have led to brutal and oppressive acts, their vision and brilliant commercial triumphs opened up remote areas of the country and paved the way for roads and railroads.

Dreiser's primary criticism of modern-day financiers, as opposed to powerful individuals of the past such as Cosimo I of the Medici family, is that their economic exploits are based not upon any artistic or intellectual interest, but rather "to further the most material financial aims: railroads, butcher-companies, electricity, gas, typewriter and other purely mechanical or material organizations." Since Dreiser believed that men of insight, power, and imagination could best recognize the beauty in life, his admonition of modern financiers may explain his reason for choosing **Charles Tyson Yerkes**, an avid art collector, as a model for Frank Cowperwood.

Though Dreiser instructs us to "either keep out of their [financiers'] way or unite firmly to oppose them in whatever way we can, unless we choose to be promptly eaten," he appears to prefer a more Spencerian approach and concludes the essay by suggesting that a place exists for both individuals, with their vices and destruction, and the masses, with their virtues and social mores. Society need not worry about the robber barons since they will be checked, at some point, by an equal and balancing force.

Kevin Jett

THE AMERICAN SPECTATOR. Not to be confused with the nineteenth-century domestic science monthly or the neoconservative journal of opinion organized in 1977, both of the same name, *The American Spectator* with which Dreiser was associated billed itself as "a literary newspaper" with a decidedly left-radical bent. Conceived in 1932 by **George Jean Nathan** and Ernest Boyd, the paper offered its first issue in November 1932, continued monthly publication until October 1936, then lingered on as a bimonthly for another half year before folding.

Beginning with the planning and writing of the first four-page issue, Dreiser, along with Eugene O'Neill and James Branch Cabell, worked as unpaid contributing editors; **Sherwood Anderson** joined them the following year at Dreiser's urging. Dreiser severed connections with the monthly in January 1934; his name last appeared on the masthead in the February issue. The paper was notable for its short articles (contributors were limited to a maximum of 2,000 words and were paid only one cent per word), its refusal to fund itself through selling advertising, and for its immediate success. Despite its relatively high newsstand price of ten cents, the first issue sold out so quickly that an additional 20,000 copies had to be ordered from the printer.

Dreiser, whose social conscience and taste for activism had bloomed along with his improved financial prospects during the 1920s, allied himself, though with idiosyncratic divergences, with various social-justice causes and radical political movements and threw himself into his editorship. He solicited articles widely and with varying success from the likes of Joseph Stalin, Diego Rivera, and Albert Einstein and from liberal and left-leaning literary acquaintances such as John Dos Passos and Lincoln Steffens. Articles by Dreiser on topics ranging from "The Great American Novel" to "Birth Control," as well as several poems and sketches, appear in all but three issues during his tenure as contributing editor. The September 1933 issue featured an editors' roundtable on Jews and the ongoing movement for a Jewish homeland. This "Editorial Conference (With Wine)" was presented as humorous but fell flat with readers. Boyd's, Nathan's, O'Neill's and Cabell's contributions were distinctly anti-Semitic, ridiculing Jewish culture and dismissing the need for a homeland as ridiculous. Dreiser's contribution to the discussion is characteristically idiosyncratic. Himself in favor of a Jewish homeland, his defenses of Jews and Jewish culture bespoke an unconscious anti-Semitism: he praised Jews for their "shrewdness" in money matters but noted that in a Jewish state only one-tenth of 1 percent of Jews could continue as lawyers. The rest would have to farm. The roundtable caused considerable ruckus in subse-

quent issues of *The American Spectator* and was even carried over to the pages of *The Nation* and *The New Masses*.

Despite Dreiser's energetic work soliciting contributions and offering his own, editors Nathan and Boyd rejected many of these, which Dreiser considered an affront and a sign of the two editors' political cowardice. This rejection, along with increasing financial pressures brought on by the depression's impact on publishers at home and world politics' effect on his publishers overseas, together with the increasing burden his other political projects were putting on his time, contributed to Dreiser's resigning his editorship. Dreiser did not contribute to the paper after his resignation.

Complete paper holdings of *The American Spectator* are difficult to find, and no comprehensive index exists. A 1968 reprint of the complete run of issues, with an introduction by **James T. Farrell**, is currently out of print. Microfilm and microform holdings are more commonly, but not universally, available. *The American Spectator Yearbook*, edited by Nathan and published in 1934, includes three Dreiser articles, including his contribution to the "Editorial Conference."

Further Reading

The American Spectator. Introduction by James T. Farrell. 3 vols. New York: Greenwood Reprint, 1968.

Nathan, George Jean, ed. *The American Spectator Yearbook.* New York: Stokes, 1934.

Carol S. Loranger

AN AMERICAN TRAGEDY, published in December 1925, is widely regarded as Dreiser's masterpiece, the culmination of his artistic achievement in fiction. Dreiser labored on this vast novel in various ways for many years. Between 1914 and 1920, he began work on several manuscripts that would eventually evolve into the *Tragedy*, and then, by the early 1920s, he spent several years developing and finally finishing the story of Clyde Griffiths he had decided to tell. When the novel was published, it brought Dreiser a true triumph—great commercial as well as critical success of the kind he had awaited for twenty-five years. Indeed, despite its two volumes and relatively high price of five dollars, sales of the book were soon so excellent that the writer was, for the first time in his life, wealthy, and the majority of reviews brought him a long-sought fame and adulation. Thus, one of the essentially ironic facts about *An American Tragedy* is that in offering it as an ultimate portrayal of the *failure* of those materialistic ambitions driving many individuals' lives in modern America, Dreiser achieved his own very greatest success. Another major irony is that after the novel's publication gave the novelist a wide readership and critical appreciation never before accorded him, he published no other novels in his lifetime, though he lived another twenty years.

The principal stimulus to the novel was Dreiser's observation of a pattern in a number of news stories between the 1890s and the early 1920s: a series of poor, ambition-driven young men had murdered lower-class girls they had made pregnant, seeking to free themselves for potential marriage to rich girls as means of fulfilling dreams of materialistic success. Dreiser describes the evolution of his compelling interest in these real-life stories and offers searching analysis of their significance in "I Find the Real American Tragedy," an essay he wrote a decade after his novel's publication as a result of a newspaper's request for his reports on a real-life trial resembling that toward which the quest of Clyde fatefully leads. Of the nearly twenty actual "American tragedy" cases that caught Dreiser's attention, the one with

greatest impact on his imagination and eventual writing of the book was the case in upstate New York of **Chester Gillette**, who in 1906 killed a "poor" sweetheart for the sake of his ambitions.

Dreiser did not merely recount details of the Gillette case; in a number of crucial ways the novelist altered the facts to create a fully realized, powerful fiction. Two of the characters in this novel most critically affecting the fate of its protagonist, Clyde Griffiths—his wealthy, look-alike cousin, Gilbert, and **Sondra Finchley**, the epitome of wealth and beauty embodying all his desires—had no real-life counterparts in the story of Gillette. Moreover, as masterfully detailed by Donald Pizer and Shelley Fisher Fishkin, Dreiser made the character of Clyde much more sympathetic and poignant than Gillette had been, both in his personal nature (inept, indecisive, and dreamily yearning rather than cold, scheming, and brutally assertive) and in his socioeconomic circumstances, with Clyde's own poverty and deprivations played off, in cruel irony, against his relatives' great wealth and privilege. Furthermore, one of Dreiser's most important innovations lies in the narrative technique of "indirect discourse" by which the author leads a reader toward immersion in, and sympathy toward, the lived experiences of the protagonist—despite one's disapproval of many of Clyde's characteristics, thoughts, and actions. In a further irony, Dreiser's own sense of the limitations of newspaper accounts of any real murder case—including those of the Gillette case—as means of meaningfully grasping the truth of individuals' lives and of the "American tragedy pattern" is in fact suggested dramatically by the last section of Clyde's harrowing story, where the youth is victimized by newspapers' excessive influence complementing those political and legal forces that are indifferent to his identity but that are cruelly ready to denounce and destroy him.

When the story starts, Clyde is about twelve years old, the child of poor, nondescript religious fanatics who run missions and preach on the streets and who have moved their children to a series of cities in pursuit of their spiritual calling. Preparing us to understand his protagonist's alienation from his family and their unworldly values, Dreiser uses the second chapter to suggest two points of future importance about Clyde. The narrator tells us that even at age twelve—inspired by both self-consciousness and envy before the urban crowds largely ignoring or mocking his family on the streets—Clyde "was constantly thinking of how he might better himself" and "how differently he might live if only this, that and the other things were true," for in this boy's eyes, there is a sense of shame "that the calling or profession of his parents was the shabby thing that it appeared to be in the eyes of others." Such narrative comments immediately convey ideas crucial to the entire characterization of Clyde Griffiths—that his tendency to follow the modern world's "religion" of wealth, status, and pleasure derives from a youthful need to rebel against the restrictive morality of traditional religiousness, a propensity Dreiser knew from his own family experiences. Moreover, Clyde will always care excessively about others' views of him as he strives to *look like* a socially approved and significant person. Later in this chapter comes a narrative report that will prove a great portent of a major plot element: Clyde's awareness that "somewhere in the east" lives "an uncle, a brother of his father's, who was plainly different from all this. That uncle—**Samuel Griffiths** by name—was rich." For Clyde, that uncle represents a seemingly magical benefactor who might offer the youth an easy, too-

tempting means of reaching a gloriously higher world.

Having had his schooling disrupted many times by his parents' multiple moves and yearning to begin his movement into the material world they so shun, Clyde quits school at age fifteen to seek jobs that will give him the more meaningful, worldly education of paramount value to all major characters in Dreiser's fiction. After a brief novitiate in hedonism as a soda-fountain hand, Clyde lands a crucially formative position as a bellhop in a luxurious Kansas City hotel, where he becomes exposed for the first time—both excitingly and dangerously—to the world of the wealthy revered as well as idealized by society. Studying the impressive hotel catering to such people, as well as their lives of comfort and great privilege, Clyde learns a momentous lesson shaping his growing goals: "This, then, most certainly was what it meant to be rich, to be a person of consequence in the world—to have money. It meant that you did what you pleased." Clyde soon attains more money than he has ever had in the form of "wondrous" tips, which encourages him to indulge in unchaperoned freedom, with too much money to spend, to pursue very adult activities, far too early.

This sort of unsupervised pursuit of pleasure results in a disastrous car crash that kills a little girl, wrecks the vehicle illegally "borrowed" by another bellhop, and brings to an abrupt end all of the protagonist's prospects in Kansas City, as Clyde flees town to evade punishment for his part in this joyriding escapade. From this terrible scene, at the close of Book 1 of the novel, Clyde goes forward, under assumed names, toward Chicago and months of menial jobs combined with fear of police pursuit, until some chance events enable him to resume the name "Clyde Griffiths" at a place and time when it will do him most good—at the prestigious Union League Club, where he has gained a new bellhop post just when, fatefully, his rich uncle Samuel is staying there while on a business trip.

One of the dreadfully disappointing effects shatteringly caused by this car crash is his sudden, total loss of Hortense Briggs. This shop-girl, whom he had met through his bellhop companions, is an intensely materialistic, narcissistic, and heartless sexual tease as well as gold digger—the first true object of his romantic yearnings as well as his hot lust for feminine beauty—who thrills, yet frustrates, Clyde, always promising him more than she yields. Only the car crash, sending this girlfriend running one way while he seeks escape in another direction, brings to a halt his helpless, ill-fated quest for sexual satisfaction with this lower-class, fatally good-looking temptress. The enormous frustration as well as resentment felt by Clyde in this relationship will prove fatefully formative later, for Clyde's sense of having been duped and mocked by this assertive "bitch" even as his lusts were thwarted leads, in Book 2, to his angry determination that **Roberta Alden**, physically attractive but his supposed social inferior, will either sleep with him or lose him. In this secret relationship with his factory-girl sweetheart, Clyde, no longer meek, drives toward a kind of substitute for the sexual fulfillment he had been denied by Hortense; this shapes his ultimatum to Roberta, crucially leading to the cruel complications and dire turns of plot that will then result from her pregnancy.

A famous hallmark of Dreiser's fiction is its unsparing, stark **realism** in the treatment of human nature and experience that is infused with emphasis on determinism, the belief that individual destinies are shaped in large part by fateful forces of heredity and/or environment as well as by chance events. Such an outlook particularly and powerfully informs the story in Books 2 and 3. For example, once Clyde has settled (under a pseudonym) into work in Chicago, he has a chance reunion with a bellhop friend from his Kansas City days who fatefully enables him to gain a position at the prestigious Union League Club, where he chances to encounter his very rich uncle Samuel Griffiths, whom he had long hoped to meet and to find favor with. Then the chance circumstance of Clyde's great resemblance to this rich manufacturer's own son, **Gilbert Griffiths**, along with some aspects of Samuel's nature and family history, lead him to invite his nephew to Lycurgus, New York.

An intricate set of circumstances shapes Clyde's destiny from the outset of his life in Lycurgus, when he pursues an apparent new opportunity for success by going to work in his Uncle Samuel's shirt-and-collar factory and becoming a member of a community where the Griffiths name symbolizes preeminent wealth and status. As the complex yet very credible plot unfolds—with Clyde's enactment of the "American tragedy" pattern diagnosed by Dreiser slowly but ominously emerging—the novel causes us to question the essential meaning and import of "**chance**," "fate," and individual "will" as formative factors in this tragic protagonist's history.

From the start of his life in Lycurgus, Clyde suffers from confusing, conflicted views of his own identity and possibilities for a future, as a result of his ambiguous position in this small city where (fatefully) he "looks like" a "somebody"—his cousin Gilbert Griffiths—even while actually remaining in financial and social terms a "nobody." At their factory, Samuel and Gilbert condescend to Clyde and relegate him to a menial, aptly named "shrinking-room" job involving low wages and manual labor, while the other employees, who assume the youth will later advance to a position of power, show him striking deference based on his famous name as well as face. In his nonworking hours, Clyde experiences an even more anomalous, socially difficult situation: while his wealthy kin show little interest in him and leave him neglected as their "inferior," the ordinary citizens of this very class-conscious community clearly see him as a "superior" young man worth cultivating and flattering for his family's importance. This fundamentally ironic predicament of conflicting signals about his status as an individual takes on more menacing implications once Clyde—having been promoted on the basis of appearances to a foreman's post in the factory—is simultaneously forbidden to socialize with other employees and, since he is still ignored by his uncle's family, prevented from consorting with *their* respected class of people. Leaving him in a social limbo, dangerously unsponsored and unsupervised, these strange circumstances soon prove especially fateful—and fatal—as they intertwine with Clyde's own internal conflicts.

A double life of conflicting aims develops because Clyde is drawn into a secret romance with "poor girl" Roberta Alden, for companionship and sex alone, while he waits for some way to attract the notice of "rich girl" Sondra Finchley, the consummate beauty who embodies his higher dreams of fulfillment in her elevated socioeconomic sphere. As if to signify that his dreams of success are inevitably to turn nightmarish, Clyde discovers that Roberta is pregnant, just as Sondra begins to love this handsome, pleasingly reverential youth so satisfying to her vanity. Clyde is thus presented with an insoluble dilemma: whether to run away to escape the demands of Roberta to marry her—thus ending all his chances of wedding Sondra in fulfillment of his quest—or to risk

Roberta's exposure of him as the baby's father to all of Lycurgus society by shunning that poor girl in a continuing wait for wondrous, potential marriage to Sondra. The narrative's chapters marking this climactic part of the story show Clyde unable to obtain an abortion for his lower-class, secret sweetheart or otherwise end her claims upon him while, in intensely ironic counterpoint, he spends moments of amorous joy and apparent dreams-become-real with the encouraging socialite he has no means of marrying in time. In this ever more excruciating predicament—of the very kind Dreiser's "I Find the Real American Tragedy" essay would later analyze—Clyde finds no solution, except, at last, an ill-conceived and ominous idea of taking Roberta on a supposed prenuptial trip to a lonely lake from which he, alone, will return.

At Big Bittern Lake, neither willing to marry Roberta nor to murder her or even to speak to persuade her to free him to wed Sondra, Clyde does not dramatically do anything in the rowboat in which his story finds its haunting, defining moment, yet, somehow, the boat capsizes and Roberta drowns, as he had hoped she would, while Clyde remains meaningfully inert, watching her death as if from afar. Dreiser's entire depiction of this famous episode is so skillfully presented, in all its causative and psychological ambiguities, that most readers remain unable to resolve whether Clyde is essentially "guilty" or "innocent" of the death of Roberta— though her death is the seeming necessary condition for his freedom to live and achieve the dreams offered by the other girl of the love-triangle entrapping him. Indeed, in the year after the novel's publication, its great success and this episode's troublingly ambiguous details led the publisher to sponsor an essay contest on the question of Clyde's "legal" guilt, adding to the national enthusiasm for the novel and its author's unique achievement in it. At the same time, Dreiser manages—through his complicated, crucially ambiguous portrayal of the "crime" his protagonist commits in pursuit of wealth and beauty—to make Clyde an object of readers' sympathy and pity, himself clearly an ultimate victim of his dreams, longings, and confused state.

In the aftermath of the drowning scene, Roberta's victimization by the values of the success-dream is followed quickly by Clyde's own victimization, as all his dreams are turned into nightmarish reality: he is arrested, he loses Sondra forever, and he becomes a pawn for political, legal, and journalistic powers to exploit for their diverse, covert purposes—distorting the facts of his life and his identity to support their scapegoating, condemning and finally executing of him for official "justice."

Indeed, in the searching criticism of American life and values that *is* the *Tragedy*, Dreiser dramatizes through the last section's exhaustive treatment of crime and punishment the clear ways in which power and privilege determine the sort of justice diverse citizens may experience. While Clyde is essentially railroaded via unfair legal tactics, publicity, and political influence to a guilty verdict and death in the electric chair, his rich relatives and the upper-class girl who has motivated all his actions and distorted his dreams are protected with anonymity—not even called upon to testify to facts about the youth needed to understand his history in Lycurgus, with its tragic culmination at a lonely lake. It is clear from public responses to the trial that even Roberta, the "poor" girl whose murder society seeks to avenge, is not accorded the actual respect or dignity of those with money or rank.

Ultimately, then, *An American Tragedy* offers a haunting critique of the failure of the so-called American Dream of success for a representative, lower-class seeker, a variation on the very different portrayal of that dream's betrayal and bankruptcy given us (through an intriguing coincidence in our literary history) in *The Great Gatsby* in the same year, 1925. In the process, Dreiser's epic novel of America becomes a masterwork, in part through its detailed depiction of the morals and mores, the new customs as well as entrenched institutions, of our society in the early 1920s. In the over seventy-five years since its original publication, *An American Tragedy* has demonstrated both its endurance and its evident meaningfulness as a classic novel by being translated into more than twenty languages to be read by millions around the world, reissued in many editions and printings in America, made into two different Hollywood film versions (in 1931 and 1951), given life in diverse stage adaptations, and defined by generations of critics and readers as a great work worthy of a permanent place in any list of milestones of modern fiction.

See also Adaptations, Film; Adaptations, Stage.

Further Reading

Bloom, Harold, ed. *Modern Critical Interpretations: Theodore Dreiser's* An American Tragedy. New York: Chelsea, 1988.

Fishkin, Shelley Fisher. *From Fact to Fiction: Journalism and Imaginative Writing in America.* Baltimore: Johns Hopkins University Press, 1985. 85–134.

Lehan, Richard D. *Theodore Dreiser: His World and His Novels.* Carbondale: Southern Illinois University Press, 1969. 142–69.

Moers, Ellen. *Two Dreisers.* New York: Viking, 1969. 209–305.

Orlov, Paul A. An American Tragedy: *Perils of the Self Seeking "Success."* Lewisburg, Pa.: Bucknell/Associated University Press, 1998.

———. "The Subversion of the Self: Anti-Naturalistic Crux in *An American Tragedy*." *Modern Fiction Studies* 23 (1977): 457–72.

Phillips, William L. "The Imagery of Dreiser's Novels." *PMLA* 78 (1963): 572–85.

Pizer, Donald. *The Novels of Theodore Dreiser: A Critical Study*. Minneapolis: University of Minnesota Press, 1976. 203–89.

Riggio, Thomas P. "American Gothic: Poe and *An American Tragedy*." *American Literature* 49 (1978): 515–32.

Salzman, Jack, ed. *Merrill Studies in* An American Tragedy. Columbus, Ohio: Merrill, 1971.

Warren, Robert Penn. *Homage to Theodore Dreiser: On the Centenary of His Birth*. New York: Random House, 1971.

Paul A. Orlov

AMES, ROBERT, is the young "genius" inventor from Indianapolis who *aims* Carrie Meeber toward exalted artistic goals in *Sister Carrie*. He possesses the wholesome idealism of Sara White Dreiser and the commitment to hard work and intellectual development of Thomas Edison, whom Dreiser had interviewed for *Success* magazine in 1897. His "preachments" paradoxically mix Tolstoyan humanitarian aesthetics with an emphasis on desire that strikes some readers as an implicit endorsement of capitalistic ideology. A cousin of Mrs. Vance, Carrie's fashionable neighbor, Ames joins Carrie and the Vances for an evening of theater and dining just when Carrie is beginning to have "fine visions" stirred by the high-steppers on Broadway and the heroines in the theatrical "drawing-room concoctions" she attends with Mrs. Vance. Ames impresses Carrie with his intelligence and his disdain for conspicuous consumption and mass culture. While she is awed by the "glow and shine" of Sherry's restaurant, he is repelled by the "shame" of waste. While the Vances praise a recent "pretty good" popular novel by Robert Ross, he judges it "nearly as bad" as Bertha Clay's pulp *Dora Thorne*. More importantly, he legitimates Carrie's dramatic ambitions by agreeing with her that it is "rather fine to be an actor," at least "a good one." Ames also impresses Carrie with his boyish good looks and "quick and warm" sympathies, so much so that she finds being with the indifferent, slovenly Hurstwood "disagreeable" when she returns home that night, but Ames has "nothing of the lady's man about him" and seems "innocent and clean." Consequently, Carrie, who thinks herself married, sublimates her obvious physical responsiveness. She thinks of him as "an ideal to contrast men by," a kind of aesthetic superego that replaces her conventional conscience, that ineffective and bothersome "drag of habit." "If she were a fine actress," she now thinks, "such men as he would approve of her." Even after she leaves Hurstwood and becomes a Broadway star, she holds herself aloof from stage-door johnnies because they lack "the superiority of a genius like Ames." Four years after their first meeting, Ames, having opened his own laboratory in New York, meets Carrie at the Vances' and again sounds the "old call of the ideal." He has seen her onstage and out of friendly concern lets her know he does not approve her waste of talent. A "genius," he tells her, expresses the "desires" of the inarticulate masses; since nature has made her face "representative of all desire," she has a "burden of duty" to turn from frothy comedies to "good, strong comedy-drama." In the original and longer version of this final meeting, found in the **Pennsylvania Dreiser Edition** version, a love match between two geniuses is in the offing. Ames now has something of Carrie's response to physical beauty and her emotionalism; she, "the perfect Carrie in mind and body," something of his intellectual drive. As their conversation proceeds, powerful undercurrents of feeling create a "bond between them [that] was drawn closer than they knew." Sometime before publication, Dreiser decided that Ames's function was not to provide Carrie with a fitting marriage partner but to emphasize her essentially desirous nature. The physical responsiveness between them is virtually eliminated, and Ames's efforts "to stir her up" leave her feeling "slightly guilty of neglect" but unable to "change" in the way he thinks she ought: "The effect of this was like roiling helpless waters." Largely owing to this revision, which deprives him of much human complexity, Ames has generally been viewed as a stick, a thinly disguised and glorified spokesman for his author.

Further Reading

Brennan, Stephen C. "*Sister Carrie* and the Tolstoyan Artist." *Research Studies* 47 (1979): 1–16.

———. "The Two Endings of *Sister Carrie*." *Studies in American Fiction* 16 (1988): 13–26.

Humphries, David T. " 'The Shock of Sympathy': Bob Ames's Reading and Re-reading of Sister Carrie." *Dreiser Studies* 32.1 (2001): 36–55.

Hussman, Lawrence E., Jr. *Dreiser and His Fiction: A Twentieth-Century Quest.* Philadelphia: University of Pennsylvania Press, 1983. 30–32.

Michaels, Walter Benn. "*Sister Carrie*'s Popular Economy." *The Gold Standard and the Logic of Naturalism.* Berkeley: University of California Press, 1987. 29–58.

Stephen C. Brennan

ANDERSON, SHERWOOD (1876–1941).

American novelist and short-story writer, Anderson left a life as a prosperous businessman in Ohio in 1913 to go to Chicago to write and to live a more bohemian and literary life. He became known as one of the major figures in the cultural "revolt from the village" and along with Dreiser was an important part of the Chicago Renaissance. His most important book, *Winesburg, Ohio* (1919), is considered a classic of modern American literature and describes the longings of small-town Americans for larger, more liberal, and less puritanical lives. A lifelong friend and champion of Dreiser's since their early days in Chicago, Anderson saw Dreiser as a towering literary presence and pathfinder who lit the way to the establishment of a vital and genuine American literature, praising him in an article on *An American Tragedy* in the *Saturday Review of Literature* in 1926 as the "biggest, most important American of our times" (rpt. in Salzman 447). Dreiser also enthusiastically advanced the cause of Anderson's literary career and was instrumental in getting his first novel, *Windy McPherson's Son* (1916), published. Each saw the other as part of a new breed of American writers who would liberate the country's fiction from a genteel tradition that indicated a continuing colonial deference to Britain.

Anderson was particularly inspired by Dreiser's determination to write fiction that was frank and fearlessly critical of the flaws in American society. There is no doubt that Anderson was encouraged in his work toward greater freedom of expression and toward more controversial topics than would have been the case without Dreiser's influence. In addition, he was influenced by Dreiser politically, following him in championing various left-wing causes. In 1933, Anderson was even prevailed upon to work as a part-time editor on *The American Spectator* in order to strengthen Dreiser's own editorial policies.

The most interesting incident involving Dreiser and Anderson concerns the publication of a prose poem by Dreiser called "The Beautiful" (*Vanity Fair*, September 1926: 54). It soon became clear that this poem echoed the short story "Tandy," which Anderson wrote earlier as part of his *Winesburg, Ohio* collection. Although Dreiser's adaptation of "Tandy" was very likely unconscious, the incident caused a small literary scandal. Anderson himself defended Dreiser as a man who had no need to borrow from others, and their friendship continued. Although Dreiser and Anderson saw each other socially though the years, these occasions cannot really be described as successes. Anderson and his wife saw Dreiser for the last time in 1939, when they dined with Dreiser and Helen Richardson in Los Angeles. By this time Dreiser had become increasingly withdrawn, and Anderson had become more critical of Dreiser's politics and his failure to concentrate on fiction. Their correspondence ended soon afterward.

Despite this late break between them, however, Anderson's record of supporting Dreiser in the cause of new literary **realism** and as a champion of individual freedom remains. Anderson's sentiments can be summed up in his comments in his short story collection *Horses and Men* (New York: B.W. Huebsch, 1923), when he commends Dreiser as a groundbreaking pioneer: "Because of him, those who follow will never have to face the road through the wilderness of Puritan denial, the road that Dreiser faced alone" (xii).

Further Reading

Howe, Irving. *Sherwood Anderson*. New York: William Sloane, 1951.
Townsend, Kim. *Sherwood Anderson*. Boston: Houghton Mifflin, 1987.

Margaret Boe Birns

"ASHTORETH." A short essay in *Hey Rub-a-Dub-Dub* that first appeared in *Reedy's Mirror* in July 1919. Ashtoreth, Astarte in Greek and Roman mythology, is the Phoenician goddess of fertility and sexual love. In the essay, Dreiser ponders life and Nature and their relationship with both the young and the old. He writes in the opening sentence that what impresses him most about life "is the freshness and newness of everything." Dreiser remarks on how old the world is and that human beings, like all creatures, grow old and die, yet life itself does not show death or decay; instead, life is always fertile, and its newness is everywhere. In "Ashtoreth" Dreiser contemplates the ability of Nature to make and keep life fresh and new as the years go by. He questions whether Nature herself is cruel, for youth and vigor are in charge of the world while the aged, the sick, and the maimed are put away in asylums and institutions. He argues that Nature does not care for individuals but only fashions each of us as a tool to do her job, keeping life new and maintaining vigor. We are all, in essence, life's victims and Nature's prey, for Nature fashions only a few to succeed while the rest of humankind withers away under the illusion of novelty that life possesses. However, like most of the essays in *Hey Rub-a-Dub-Dub*, Dreiser does not limit himself to these conclusions. He ends "Ashtoreth" by calling Nature wise, tender, and practical. After all, she knows what she is doing.

Reneé D. McElheney

AUTHORS' LEAGUE OF AMERICA. Founded in 1912 as a union of playwrights and book and magazine authors, the league worked to secure and strengthen copyright protection and freedom of expression for writers. The league continues to be a resource for writers, compiling information on such diverse topics as taxation, wills and estates, libel, and the art of interviewing. Perhaps its most visible work has been its activism on First Amendment issues, particularly in fighting **censorship** through filing amicus curiae briefs in state, federal, and Supreme Court cases and in testifying before congressional and state legislative committees on free speech issues.

Founding members included Booth Tarkington, Kate Douglas Wiggin, Arthur Train, and Will Irwin. The league's first president and vice president were Winston Churchill and Theodore Roosevelt. In 1919, in response to the differing problems, such as contract terms and subsidiary rights, facing print and dramatic writers, the organization split into two allied guilds, the Authors' Guild and the Dramatists' Guild. As new markets for writers opened during the twentieth century, additional allied groups were formed for writers for radio, television, and screen. Each guild functions under the umbrella of the Authors' League, with membership in a guild conferring membership in the parent organization.

Dreiser was never a member of the Authors' League, which he dismissed as the "pink tea and chocolate bon bon brotherhood of literary effort" (qtd. in Swanberg 207), but when *The "Genius"* was declared obscene and suppressed by the **New York Society for the Suppression of Vice** in 1916, H. L. Mencken enlisted the league on the novel's behalf. Although most of the league's executive committee agreed with Mencken that *The "Genius"* lacked literary merit, the league began a petition and editorial- and letter-writing campaign, largely out of its commitment to fighting literary censorship. W. A. Swanberg, whose account of the league's efforts on behalf of

The "Genius" remains the most extensive, describes the league's efforts as "halfhearted" due to the membership's reservations about Dreiser's novel (207). Certainly, the campaign had ceased before the case came to trial two years later, and the league's highly visible officers, Churchill and Roosevelt, remained silent on the matter. Many of the league membership also deplored Dreiser's own more combative personal efforts on behalf of his novel. League efforts focused on enlisting the support of the respectable literary establishment—soliciting signatures and statements from the likes of Robert Frost, Arnold Bennett, and H. G. Wells—and on placing articles in similarly respectable publications such as the *Saturday Evening Post* and *Pearson's*. Dreiser, on the other hand, sought assistance from the more bohemian **Liberal Club** and radical *New Masses* and gave numerous, angry interviews in the mainstream press, activities that league members considered crass. Dreiser was denounced in private correspondence among league members as a publicity hound and a fool, suggesting that the author's taste and breeding were as much at issue for some as his book's relative obscenity.

Further Reading

Swanberg, W. A. *Dreiser*. New York: Scribner, 1965. 203–28.

Carol S. Loranger

B

BALZAC, HONORÉ DE (1799–1850), was the French novelist who, Dreiser said, showed him "how a book should be written" (*Uncollected Prose* 186). Balzac is most known for his *La Comédie Humaine*, a cycle comprising some ninety novels and stories that document all the variety and decadence of French society. In his rejection of idealism and his massing of factual details, Balzac anticipates literary **realism**, though his static characters, melodramatic plots, and intrusive moralizing belong to an older, more romantic tradition.

Dreiser began reading deeply in Balzac in 1894, when he was a reporter in Pittsburgh. In Balzac's typical hero—what Dreiser would call "the brooding, seeking, ambitious beginner in life's social, political, artistic and commercial affairs" (*A Book about Myself,* Chapter 62)—he saw his own image, one that would reappear in Carrie Meeber, Clyde Griffiths, and numerous other characters throughout his career. *Sister Carrie* is his most Balzacian work from its title, which echoes such Balzac titles as *Père Goriot* and *Cousine Bette*, to its saccharine coda. Like Balzac, Dreiser painstakingly details speech, manners, and material culture both to document life in a particular place and time and to reveal character. Balzac's Paris is a vast ocean, and many of his characters, such as Father Goriot, are castaways who die alone amid an indifferent city. Hurstwood is such a castaway, and the irony and pathos of his death are intensified when Carrie is reading *Père Goriot* in the comfort of her Waldorf suite the moment he gasses himself in his Bowery flophouse. But whereas Balzac's Paris is a thoroughly corrupting environment, Dreiser's Chicago and New York are not, even though Carrie is at first Balzacian in her attaching moral worth to clothes and in using sex to climb the social ladder. In America's great cities, Carrie evolves from selfishness to altruism and seeks always to satisfy her yearnings for ideal beauty. (In the **Pennsylvania Dreiser Edition**, based on the novel's holograph, **Robert Ames** criticizes Balzac for identifying happiness with love and possessions rather than with knowledge.)

For modern readers who prefer showing to telling, it was unfortunate that Dreiser mistook Balzac's frequent philosophizing and moralizing for "the true method of the seer and the genius" (*A Book about Myself,* Chapter 62). In *Sister Carrie,* he reflects on all manner of subjects, from women's clothes to morals and humankind's place in the universe, often interrupting the action and creating a jarring contrast with the reportorial objectivity of such scenes as Hurstwood's suicide. Yet some readers excuse the method for contributing to the uniquely Dreiserian authorial presence that permeates most of the novel.

Further Reading

Ahnebrink, Lars. "Dreiser's *Sister Carrie* and Balzac." *Symposium* 7 (1953): 306–22.

Barrineau, Nancy Warner. "Dreiser's Debt to Balzac." *American Literary Realism* 24.2 (1992): 70–80.

Brennan, Stephen C. "Dreiser and Balzac: A Literary Source for Hurstwood and Carrie." *American Notes & Queries* 17 (1978): 21–24.

Hakutani, Yoshinobu. "Dreiser and French Realism." *Texas Studies in Literature and Language* 6 (1964): 200–12.

Stephen C. Brennan

BARNES, ETTA, is the most thematically significant of the five children of the Quaker banker and strict father, **Solon Barnes**, in *The Bulwark*. Etta, the dreamy romantic of the family, turns away from her father's narrow discipline and embarks on a relatively adventurous life as a student and then as the mistress of a New York painter. When a series of calamities including the suicide of one of her brothers nearly breaks her father's spirit, she returns home and ministers to him. In the process, she becomes Dreiser's spokesperson for his end-of-life affirmation and an ethic of love and service.

Lawrence E. Hussman

BARNES, SOLON, is the protagonist of Dreiser's posthumously published novel, *The Bulwark*. A pious Quaker banker and strict father, Solon endures a Jobian series of setbacks including the suicide of one of his sons, the falling away from the teachings of the Inner Light by several of his other children, the death of his beloved wife, and his own losing battle with cancer. At the end of the novel, however, Solon, who was originally projected by Dreiser to be an example of a broken "religionist" when the novel was begun in 1914, ends a paragon of compassionate faith. This profound change in the character's conception was inspired by the novelist's own religious affirmation in the late 1930s, a few years before *The Bulwark* was finally finished.

Lawrence E. Hussman

BARNES, STEWART, is the youngest child of Quaker protagonist **Solon Barnes** in *The Bulwark*. Eager for the kind of life his strict father denies him, Stewart rebels at the first opportunity. As a teenager in school he joins several friends on an outing during which they unknowingly administer a lethal drug to a young woman with a weak heart. Stricken with remorse for his betrayal of his father's trust and the Friends' Inner Light, Stewart takes his own life, precipitating a series of culminating tragedies in the novel.

Lawrence E. Hussman

BELFRAGE, CEDRIC. (1904–1990). British author, screenwriter, journalist, and translator, Belfrage assisted Dreiser with the composition of *America Is Worth Saving*, published in 1941. Born to a wealthy family in England, Belfrage began his professional career as a journalist in London in the 1920s. Offended by what in *Away from It All* (1937) he called a "fake society" and the "antics of the maggots on a decaying corpse" (7), he left Great Britain, first embarking upon an around-the-world trip and eventually settling in the United States. Belfrage then worked as a public relations officer for Samuel Goldwyn and as a Hollywood-based film critic for the British press, positions that allowed him to make the transition into screenwriting. While living in Los Angeles, Belfrage was introduced to Dreiser by Lorna Smith, a "Glendale housewife who contributed to the local newspaper," who had once interviewed Dreiser and who occasionally helped Dreiser with research (Swanberg 460). For $1,000, Belfrage agreed to act as editorial assistant for Dreiser's upcoming book, *America Is Worth Saving*. According to Richard Lingeman, who interviewed Belfrage, Dreiser was "good for [only] about two hours of work in the morning" and was otherwise incapacitated by liquor; as a result, Belfrage took on a substantial portion of the composition of the book himself (Lingeman 2: 424). As Belfrage recounts, he met with Dreiser at Dreiser's home three mornings per week and then continued the work at his own home, for after one or two drinks, Dreiser "began to ramble and could not organize any thoughts" (Swanberg 469). The occasional British locutions, including phrases such as "up a gum tree," reveal that Belfrage wrote at least parts of *America Is Worth Saving*, although the major themes of the book correspond closely with Dreiser's ideas during the period directly before the war.

Soon after the publication of *America Is Worth Saving*, World War II broke out, and Belfrage joined the effort as a member of the Allied psychological warfare division. According to Nigel West, recently released documents identify Belfrage as not only a British agent but also a Soviet operative during the 1940s. Toward the end of the war, Belfrage's assignment involved working to reduce the Nazi influence in the German press. While working in this capacity, he met Jim Aronson, later an accomplished journalist and New York University professor; in 1948, the two cofounded the *National Guardian*, a left-wing independent newspaper published in New York. The environment of the ensuing Cold War was a difficult one for Belfrage, for he was a British citizen with communist leanings. After refusing to appear before the House Un-American Activities Committee, Belfrage was deported from the United States in 1955. Several years later, Belfrage's experiences during the McCarthy era led him to write a book about the American anticommunist movement, *The American Inquisition, 1945–1960* (1973). The book met with considerable acclaim, and Belfrage was invited by Harvard University to speak at the Harvard Law School commencement in 1973.

After being deported, Belfrage settled in Mexico, where, after becoming fluent in Spanish, he found employment as a translator. Belfrage's translating credits include such significant leftist works as Eduardo Galeano's *Open Veins of Latin America* (1973) and his *Memory of Fire* trilogy (1985). He also maintained ties with the *National Guardian* until editorial differences led him to resign in 1967. In addition, Belfrage's publications include *They All Hold Swords* (1941), *My Master Columbus* (1961), and *Something to Guard* (1978). Belfrage died in 1990 in Cuernevaca, Mexico.

Further Reading

Belfrage, Cedric. *Away from It All: An Escapologist's Notebook*. New York: Simon and Schuster, 1937.

West, Nigel. *Venona: The Greatest Secret of the Cold War*. New York: HarperCollins, 1999.

Stephen Brain

BEST SHORT STORIES OF THEODORE DREISER. An anthology of four stories from *Free and Other Stories*, eight from *Chains*, and two sketches from *Twelve Men* published in 1947 by World Publishing. Shortly after Dreiser's death, World hired Howard Fast to select a volume of Dreiser's short fiction and write an Introduction. After the printing sold out in 1956, World asked **James T. Farrell** to write a new Introduction. At the time, the country was gripped by the mania of the

Red Scare, and Fast no longer seemed a marketable property, for he was a member of the Communist Party, had been blacklisted for refusing to name names, and had been awarded the Stalin Peace Prize in 1954. The collection was reissued in 1956 with Farrell's Introduction and no trace of Fast's prior association. Contents: "Khat," "Free," "St. Columba and the River," "McEwen of the Shining Slave Makers," "The Shadow," "A Doer of the Word," "Nigger Jeff," "The Old Neighborhood," "Phantom Gold," "My Brother Paul," "The Lost Phoebe," "Convention," "Marriage—for One," "The Prince Who Was a Thief."

Further Reading

Fast, Howard. "Petty Villainy." *Daily Worker,* 21 May 1956.
Griffin, Joseph. "Howard Fast, James T. Farrell, and *The Best Short Stories of Theodore Dreiser." International Fiction Review* 14 (1987): 79–83.

Keith Newlin

BIOGRAPHIES. Several excellent studies of Dreiser interpolate biographical information to support their critical arguments, but there are only four biographies, defined as studies that primarily tell the story of the author's life in chronological order. It has been said that Dreiser's close friend, H. L. Mencken, was the "first" biographer for his seminal essay in *A Book of Prefaces* (1917), but that work belongs to the critical studies that buttress their critical arguments with biographical facts. Moreover, Mencken was too close to his subject to be objective and is indeed part of the Dreiser story. Other such candidates for biographies are F. O. Matthiessen's *Theodore Dreiser* (1951), Carl Shapiro's *Theodore Dreiser: Our Bitter Patriot* (1962), Philip Gerber's *Theodore Dreiser* (1964, 1992), Ellen Moers's *Two Dreisers* (1969),

and Richard Lehan's *Theodore Dreiser: His World and His Novels* (1969).

The first full-fledged biography is *Forgotten Frontiers: Dreiser and the Land of the Free* (1932), reprinted as *Dreiser and the Land of the Free* in 1946, by **Dorothy Dudley**. The Chicago friend of **Edgar Lee Masters** befriended Dreiser in the 1910s, helped to edit some of the sketches in *Twelve Men,* and like many of his female typists and editors may have been intimate with him. Dudley apparently interviewed him extensively for the biography, as well as many who knew him personally. Her biography also employs materials from Dreiser's personal files of correspondence and manuscripts between 1900 and 1931 as well as reviews of his books written during this period. Although it is not formally documented, it is important as a biographical source of information not available elsewhere. For example, it quotes Dreiser's statement about the possibly mystical origin of *Sister Carrie* (160). It echoes Dreiser directly on several issues and tends to embrace his political view of America in the 1920s. It is sweeping in its judgments to the point that Dudley is more impressionistic than analytical and factual. In this regard, its content is sometimes suspect or unreliable. Yet, as her biographical successor, **Robert H. Elias**, once wrote, while she is "not always accurate, sometimes gullible or misled," she is "usually worth verifying" (*Apostle* 361).

The second biography as well as the first and thus far only critical biography (which both tells the life in detail and interprets the work) is Elias's *Theodore Dreiser: Apostle of Nature* (1949, 1969). Elias met Dreiser while writing his master's thesis on the novelist at Columbia University and knew him for the last eight years of his life. His biography was groundbreaking as to facts and basic information now housed at the University of Pennsylvania, but today it is out-of-date in terms of recent scholarship (though a revised edition with an annotated bibliography was issued in 1970) and brief (at around 110,000 words) for either a scholarly or trade biography. It was also important for tapping Dreiser's professional correspondence, a selection of which Elias subsequently edited in three volumes. The major complaint against the book appears to be that the discussion of Dreiser's art tends to be factual or biographical rather than aesthetic. In a review of the first edition in the *New Yorker*, Alfred Kazin complained that Elias "does not even touch on that which is still so moving in a Hurstwood, a Sister Carrie, a Jennie Gerhardt, a Clyde Griffiths. By stressing Dreiser's 'philosophy' rather than his sensibility . . . Mr. Elias has managed to bypass Dreiser's art as effectively as those liberals who think they honor him by praising a social consciousness that was not always in the liberal tradition" (26 February 1949: 91–92). It must be said that Elias's book came out when Dreiser's reputation had gone into eclipse, most of his books had gone out of print, and it was not taken fully for granted that his work was relevant to the postwar era of the New Criticism (where Dreiser's historical bent and penchant for realistic detail were unappreciated). In spite of its relatively brief treatment of the works, *Theodore Dreiser: Apostle of Nature* was almost singularly responsible for reviving critical interest in Dreiser. Even today it is indispensable as the quickest and easiest biographical reference. The basic facts of this pioneering work have gone almost wholly unchallenged in the critical and biographical studies that followed in its wake.

The Elias biography was originally published by a trade press (Alfred A. Knopf), but today it would be considered a "university press" biography because of its emphasis on Dreiser's "ideas." The first

"trade" biography to appear was W. A. Swanberg's *Dreiser* (1965), which upon its publication was almost universally hailed as the fullest Dreiser biography for its narrative drive and extensive research, including not only the letters but interviews with those still living who knew Dreiser (including Elias) and public records. It was the most definitive study of Dreiser to date, but unfortunately it also dwelled excessively on its subject's perceived personal weaknesses. Swanberg, whose earlier biographies had been of rogues such as William Randolph Hearst and Jim Fisk (subtitled "The Story of an Improbable Rascal"), never misses an opportunity to characterize the author of *Sister Carrie* and *An American Tragedy* as suspicious, superstitious, contentious, lecherous, greedy, and egotistical. The original dust jacket advertised the biography as "The Story of a Tormented Life." Swanberg was no literary critic, and thus one tends to come away from the life wondering how such a dysfunctional individual could have written, among other unique contributions to U.S. literature, two of the last century's best 100 novels as ranked by a Random House panel of leading American writers in 1999. The biography distorts Dreiser's personal reputation by not only exaggerating his weakness but often describing them out of context of the full story. The emphasis on his superstitious nature, for example, ignores the ubiquity of such beliefs in the last third of the nineteenth century (and especially the 1890s) when the author came of age as a writer. Dreiser is seldom given the benefit of the doubt, nor is he credited for the friendship he showed the many women—none of them ever complained of mistreatment in their memoirs—whom in the Swanberg view he is merely supposed to have exploited. The Dreiser of Swanberg's industry is finally (in the words of Mark Van Doren) the writer "who lacked everything but genius" (qtd. in Kazin 91), yet even Dreiser's genius goes largely unexplained in the biographer's 526 printed pages.

Unfortunately for Dreiser's reputation today, Swanberg's life is still the most influential and the best single-volume life we have. The next one by Richard Lingeman consists of two volumes. It is imaginatively narrated and more detailed than Swanberg's. It is also fairer and more evenhanded in its treatment of Dreiser's various social crises. Volume 1 is superior to volume 2 in terms of the art of biography. In the second, Dreiser occasionally fades into the mass of minutiae that feeds its narrative. Part of the challenge to Lingeman or any biographer is that Dreiser essentially abandons his art for social and political issues after *An American Tragedy*. In *Theodore Dreiser: At the Gates of the City, 1871–1907* (1986) and *Theodore Dreiser: An American Journey, 1908–1945* (1990), Lingeman uses an "American studies" approach to highlight the cultural influences on the act of literary creation. While his documentation is occasionally difficult to verify because of the lack of clear and exact endnotes, the research for both volumes was exhaustive, and the result is the filling out of important nooks and crannies in the celebrated author's life. Like Swanberg, Lingeman builds on Elias, but his pyramid is higher. No other biography is both so exhaustive and appreciative of Dreiser's genius. Lingeman's two volumes were subsequently abridged into one under the title *Theodore Dreiser: An American Journey* (1993).

Jerome Loving

"BIRTH AND GROWTH OF A POPULAR SONG."

First published in the magazine *Metropolitan* in November 1898 and later reprinted in *SMA* 2, this article is most often read as the earliest source of Dreiser's claim to joint authorship of brother Paul Dresser's 1898 hit song "**On the Banks of the Wabash, Far Away.**" Certainly, the groundwork for the claim appears in nascent form; it would later be significantly altered and extended in *A Hoosier Holiday* and "My Brother Paul," but the three-sentence anecdote about "Wabash" functions here to establish Dreiser's credentials as a commentator on the business of music publishing during the early growth years of Tin Pan Alley and, more importantly, to help dismiss the notion that artistry, rather than promotion, is responsible for any popular song's commercial success. Glossing over how a song is born with "that indefinable shade of sentiment in melody and words which make for popularity," Dreiser focuses instead on the serial steps taken by successful publishers to awaken a popular appetite for a new song, from flogging complementary "professional copies" of the sheet music to popular singers, to offering music dealers deep discounts and thus higher profits on sheet music sales of the new song, in comparison to older sheet music dealers routinely stock. Other techniques of "booming" the song include packing music halls with enthusiastic shills during the new song's debut and delicate financial arrangements made with city street-organ concessionaires.

The seven photographs accompanying this short article likewise focus on the mechanics of popular song promotion rather than the mysteries of composition. Above the title is a photograph of a hand-organ player and his East Side audience. A similar photograph, captioned "The automatic piano with its grist of melodious agonies," ends the piece. Four serial photographs depict distinctly inartistic laborers constructing, marking, and punching pinholes in barrels for streetorgans and player pianos, which are finally tested in a debris-strewn factory. A final photograph shows a banjoist and singer separately making a phonograph recording. A tangle of wires depends from the recording equipment at the singer's elbow and snakes down a wall covered with tattered wallpaper. Both musicians stare into the middle-distance and appear dislocated, unlike the factory workers in the preceding photographs who appear involved with, and focused on, their work.

"Birth and Growth" bears a logical relation to Dreiser's extensive corpus of journalistic treatments of American business and businessmen. Much of its subject is amplified a year later in "Whence the Song" for *Harper's Weekly*. Its focus on the popular song industry and to a lesser extent on songwriting craft, rather than on popular song as an art form and song's meaning for its audience, is, moreover, typical of the era in which it was written, when songs were bought outright for as little as five dollars from songwriters typically regarded as nuisances by publishers who, likewise, viewed audience taste as created solely by marketing.

Carol S. Loranger

BISSELL, HARRIET (1914–). Harriet Bissell graduated from Smith College in 1935, following a family tradition that began with her maternal grandmother, who had been a member of the college's first class. In October 1935 she answered an anonymous ad in the *New York Times* for an author's secretary. Dreiser responded to her application with a phone call to her home in Stamford, Connecticut; shortly afterward, her mother drove her to an interview at his country home at Mt. Kisco, New York. Within weeks, she began work as Dreiser's secretary and research assistant. Her salary was twenty-five dollars per week, from which fifteen dollars was subtracted for room and board. She generally arrived on Sunday night and left for home on Friday evening. Her work consisted of organizing Dreiser's files and managing his finances and legal records. She would also take dictation of his letters and his writing. In addition, she served as his chauffeur and hostess when his longtime companion Helen Richardson was not available. Dreiser asked her to read philosophy and science to help him with the philosophical book on which he was working, portions of which were published posthumously as *Notes on Life*. He provided her with chapter subjects—among others, "free will," "illusions," "the origins of science," "good and evil"—and she would copy out passages on these topics from classical philosophers and scientists. From these and his own readings, Dreiser wrote commentaries that he attempted (with little success) to organize into coherent chapters. In the spring of 1938, after Dreiser received a contract to gather and introduce a selection of Thoreau's writing, Bissell undertook to read the transcendentalist's complete works, from which she made generous selections. Dreiser took these passages, retained those that interested him, wrote a Preface, and sent the book to the publisher, which issued the book as *The Living Thoughts of Thoreau*. Her time with Dreiser came to an end later in 1938, when he left New York to live in California. She later married twice, the second time to the Arctic explorer Charles Hubbard—and has lived since then under the name of Harriet Bissell Hubbard.

Thomas P. Riggio

BLUE, ANGELA. From Blackwood, Wisconsin, lover and eventual wife of **Eugene Witla** in The "*Genius.*" Based largely on how he saw his first wife, Sara White (also known as "Jug"), Dreiser depicts Angela as combining innate sensuality with a conservative, even puritanical streak. These conflicts make her a difficult spouse for Witla but a fascinating character. Practical and a good homemaker, her strong sex drive drains Witla of his talent while fueling her jealousy at his dalliances with other women. She dies after giving birth to their child by caesarean section. Witla names the baby Angela.

Clare Eby

THE BLUE SPHERE. A one-act play written in July 1914 and first published in the December 1914 *Smart Set* before being collected in *The Plays of the Natural and Supernatural*. The play depicts the plight of the Delavan family, whose youngest child, Eddie, "the Monstrosity," is deformed and destined to remain a burden to his family. Both parents secretly wish to be free of this burden but chide themselves for their "unchristian" thoughts. The Shadow, a supernatural entity seen only by Eddie, lures him with a blue sphere and the promise of happiness. The Shadow intrudes into the thoughts of other characters, trying to persuade them to leave the gate open so that Eddie can escape the safety of his yard. After several abortive attempts, the Shadow is successful: Eddie's older brother leaves the gate open, and Eddie follows the blue sphere to his death on the railroad tracks.

This play is referred to as a "reading play," due no doubt to the difficulty of staging a piece that includes a locomotive as a character and the constant anti-Aristotelian shifting from indoor to outdoor settings. On the page or on the radio, where the play was performed in 1930, the device of cutting to the approaching train creates suspense and momentum. However, it would be nearly impossible to put on the stage. *The Blue Sphere* reflects Dreiser's deepening fascination, due to a near-fatal operation in 1914, with man's helplessness in the face of the immutable natural and supernatural forces in life. The choice of the locomotive as the instrument of Eddie's demise portrays scientific and industrial progress as an inexorable and relentless force at odds with the frailties of humanity. The Shadow emerges as an abstract construct representing the unspoken wishes of Eddie's family. This supernatural force, by luring the deformed child to his death, functions to ensure that only the "fittest" beings survive—a dramatic application of **Herbert Spencer's** comment that the poor and malformed have a duty to die. The ultimate irony of the play is that in the end only Eddie, the unfit, is happy, having attained the blue sphere. The surviving characters, those more fitted for life, who gather around the body of the dead child, are devastated. Helene Keyssar states that in his plays Dreiser attempts to "capture the material and the ethereal; indeed, his plays might better be called projections than reflections or creations of the world" (376). *The Blue Sphere* attempts to synthesize the forces of the natural world with those of a psychological and **supernatural** world to explore the interplay of human desire, determinism, and the unknowable forces beyond the realm of scientific and empirical certainty.

Further Reading

Keyssar, Helene. "Theodore Dreiser's Dramas: American Folk Drama and Its Limits." *Theatre Journal* 33 (1981): 365–76.

Debra Niven

BOHEMIAN MAGAZINE. In July 1909 Dreiser bought for $1,000 the bankrupt *Bohemian*, a slim monthly that had formerly catered to the theater crowd. Since he was at that time the editor of *The Delineator* and wanted to keep his involvement secret, he installed as nominal editor

Fritz Krog, a friend from Missouri. In an 8 August 1909 letter to H. L. Mencken, Dreiser outlined his plans: "I want to make it the broadest, most genial little publication in the field. . . . I don't want any tainted fiction or cheap sex-struck articles but I do want a big catholic point of view, grim or gay, and an apt realistic perception of things as they are" (*D-M Letters* 1: 28–29). He created a new editorial department, "At the Sign of the Lead Pencil," through which he could comment on topical issues. Mencken contributed a number of editorials under such titles as "In Defense of Profanity," "The Gastronomical Value of the Knife," and "The Psychology of Kissing" (Elias, *Apostle* 147), and Dreiser published other material by such writers as Clare Kummer, Homer Croy, and O. Henry. To preserve his anonymity, Dreiser published nine brief, unsigned sketches on such topics as organized charities, the life of the down-and-out, the docks and piers of New York, the job of the butcher, spiritualism, and one story under his own name, "The Cruise of the 'Idlewild.' " Dreiser's management of the magazine began with the September issue; he closed the *Bohemian* after the December number because of a decline in advertising and circulation.

Keith Newlin

BONI & LIVERIGHT. Albert Boni (1892–1981) and **Horace Liveright** (1886–1933) met in 1916 and agreed to enter a publishing partnership that would include a series of reprints comprising only modern classics by European writers. In the spring of 1917 Boni and Liveright announced the first volumes of the Modern Library. Both men, however, were eager to expand the company's list of publications, and in 1917 Liveright, prompted by Boni, met with Dreiser and secured the rights to reissue *Sister Carrie*, which became the company's

sixth publication. Thus began a sometimes strained, but ultimately successful, thirteen-year partnership between Dreiser and Liveright, in which most first editions of Dreiser's works from 1918 to 1931 were published by the firm and many previously published works were reissued. Liveright always remained committed to keeping Dreiser. Aware of this fact, Dreiser used his power over Liveright repeatedly: he would threaten to leave for another publisher unless certain demands were met, including increases in royalty percentages and advertising budgets and the publication or reissue of certain works by Dreiser as well as the works of friends such as **Charles Fort**.

Although the dynamic between Liveright and Dreiser remained the primary relationship, Dreiser corresponded with many of the company's executives and staff, often complaining about, or questioning, financial arrangements and accounts, as well as editorial issues. The company's short history entails many staff changes. Within the first year of the firm's existence, Boni's uncle, Thomas Seltzer, bought a one-third interest in the company, Liveright served as president, Boni as treasurer, and Seltzer as vice president; but the firm was constantly plagued by editorial disputes and financial disagreements. Having reached an impasse where neither one was willing to sell out to the other, Boni and Liveright tossed a coin to decide. Liveright won the toss and in July 1918 became the majority owner (Seltzer left the company four months later). Liveright then sold one vice presidency to Julian Messner, who had been the firm's sales manager, and another to Leon Fleischman, who took on the added responsibilities of secretary and treasurer. In 1919 Liveright hired Edward Bernays, a young public relations counsel and the brother-in-law of Fleischman. Together

Liveright and Bernays created a show-business approach to book publishing and promotion; a series of circulars was sent to major bookstores each week; newspaper editors were offered free books and articles on the firm's books and authors; and Bernays wrote feature articles (1,000 to 1,500 words) about authors the company was promoting.

In 1921 T. R. Smith was hired as editor in chief, and Arthur Pell was hired as a bookkeeper, although he gradually took charge of all accounting and company records. After the departure of Fleischman in 1920, Liveright sold a vice presidency to Bennett Cerf. In 1925 Cerf talked Liveright into selling him the Modern Library. Liveright then sold half the firm to Donald Friede in 1925. Friede spearheaded the battle in Boston over the banning of *An American Tragedy*, although Liveright eventually bought him out in 1928, the same year that the name of the business was changed from Boni & Liveright to Horace Liveright, Inc. But the business declined, and Liveright was ousted as president in 1930. Following Liveright's departure, Arthur Pell became a partner in the company and soon head of the business, since he owned most of the stock. The removal of Liveright from his firm had little effect on the fortunes of the house. In 1933 it became Liveright, Inc., but it was never able to regain its former standing. Later that year, an involuntary petition in bankruptcy was filed against the company. By July the entire assets of Liveright, Inc. were sold to Victor Gold for $18,000. Pell later took over the firm and called it the Liveright Publishing Corporation.

Beginning in 1918 and continuing through 1931, Boni & Liveright and its subsequent incarnations published the following first and revised or expanded editions of Dreiser's works: *Free and Other Stories* (16 August 1918); *Twelve Men* (14 April 1919); *The Hand of the Potter* (20 September 1919); *Hey Rub-a-Dub-Dub* (15 January 1920); *A Book about Myself* (15 December 1922); *The Color of a Great City* (6 December 1923); *An American Tragedy* (17 December 1925); *Moods: Cadenced and Declaimed* (1 July 1926); *The Financier*, revised edition (16 April 1927); *Chains* (30 April 1927); *The Hand of the Potter*, revised edition (17 November 1927); *Moods: Cadenced and Declaimed*, expanded edition (30 July 1928); *Dreiser Looks at Russia* (1 November 1928); *A Gallery of Women* (30 November 1929); *My City* (16 December 1929); *Dawn* (8 May 1931); and *Tragic America* (30 December 1931). From 1917 to 1932 it reissued the following titles: *Sister Carrie* (1917 and 1929); *The "Genius"* (1923 and 1931); *Jennie Gerhardt* (1924 and 1932); *The Financier* (1925); *The Titan* (1925); *A Hoosier Holiday* (1925); *Plays of the Natural and the Supernatural* (1926); and *A Traveler at Forty* (1930).

Further Reading

Dardis, Tom. *Firebrand: The Life of Horace Liveright*. New York: Random, 1995.
Gilmer, Walker. *Horace Liveright: Publisher of the Twenties*. New York: D. Lewis, 1970.

Nancy M. Shawcross

A BOOK ABOUT MYSELF. See *Newspaper Days*.

BOOTH, (JAY) FRANKLIN (1874–1948), American book and magazine illustrator. Booth first developed an interest in drawing at an early age while growing up on his parents' Indiana farm, and though essentially self-taught as an illustrator, he studied briefly at the Chicago Art Institute and the Art Students League in New York. Following a series of brief stints on the art staffs of various newspapers in Indianapolis, New York, Boston, and Washington, Booth, best known for his evocative and precisely detailed pen-and-ink drawings, eventually established himself as one of America's leading book and magazine illustrators. Beyond his affiliation with such publishers as Bobbs-Merrill, **Harper & Brothers**, and Collier's, Booth's illustrations appeared in such popular magazines as *Scribner's, McClure's, Good Housekeeping, Collier's, Harper's Monthly*, and *The Saturday Evening Post*. Booth's reputation was further augmented with his advertising illustrations for such prominent commercial firms as Montgomery Ward, Paramount Pictures, Proctor & Gamble, Underwood Typewriters, General Electric, and Victor-Victrola, for which he also drew album covers. Though Booth spent a good deal of his professional life in New York City, he never lost a sense of nostalgic affection for his native state, a fondness shared by his fellow Hoosier Theodore Dreiser, with whom, following their first meeting as colleagues on the *New York Daily News* in 1904, he maintained a lifelong friendship.

In the summer of 1915 Booth and Dreiser undertook a 2,000-mile road trip from New York to Indiana in Booth's new Pathfinder touring auto. Dreiser's account of it was published the following year as *A Hoosier Holiday*, notable as the first American "road book" and containing thirty-two charcoal sketches by Booth on subjects ranging from small-town Americana and Indiana scenes from Dreiser's youth to industrial landscapes and various roadside attractions. In 1923, at the age of forty-nine, Booth married one of his models, Beatrice Wittmack, and later in 1925 he cofounded the Phoenix Art Institute in New York, where he taught over the next twenty-one years. Incapacitated by a stroke in 1946, Booth died two years later in his New York studio. Among the collections of his work are *Franklin Booth: Sixty Reproductions from Original Drawings* (1925)

and *20 Franklin Booth Masterpieces* (1947). Booth's own writings on the art of illustration include the Introduction to Arthur Guptill's *Drawing with Pen & Ink* (1928) and a series of articles in *Professional Art Quarterly* (1934–1935).

Further Reading

Fuderer, Laura S. "Franklin Booth." *Dictionary of Literary Biography*. Vol. 188: *American Book and Magazine Illustrators to 1920*. Ed. Steven E. Smith, Catherine A. Hastedt, and Donald H. Dyal. Detroit: Gale Research, 1998. 37–47.

Michael Wentworth

"THE BOWERY MISSION." In this short sketch from *The Color of a Great City*, a description of a Christian mission house leads to philosophical speculation about Christianity and the possibility of redemption. A textbook example of Dreiser's penchant for holding two opposing ideas and refusing to endorse either wholeheartedly, the piece vacillates between a condemnation of Christian "love" and a condescending, grudging admiration. The latter view tends to surface when the narrator is able to view the mission and its inhabitants "entirely disinterestedly" as pleasing aesthetic phenomena. In Dreiser's hands the whole affair takes on a theatrical air, with missionaries and those who would be "saved" playing their respective roles—a charming, if ultimately meaningless, activity. Or does it have meaning after all? The question is repeatedly reopened. After recounting an improbable "Prodigal son" story involving the founder of the mission and his fallen—then saved—child, Dreiser quotes a Christian hymn in its entirety and considers two opposing conceptions of a supreme being: the loving Christian God of the Mission, and the "vast forces that shift and turn in their mighty inscrutability." While momentarily tempted by the Christian Scientist idea of "divine goodness speaking in and through matter and man" (Dreiser's first wife, Sara White, was a Christian Scientist), the author ends by affirming the idea of an ambivalent, uncaring Nature. The meliorist tendencies and increasing fascination with mysticism that Dreiser would exhibit in the 1930s (and continue to the end of his life) are not yet evident in this 1923 essay; the piece, however, will be of interest to students of Dreiser's views on Christianity and the improvability of humankind.

Jon Dietrick

"BRIDGET MULLANPHY." This portrait of a spirited scrubwoman was published as the concluding sketch of *A Gallery of Women*. A "gray-haired, burly, squarish rather than rotund" inhabitant of New York's lower West Side, Mrs. Mullanphy fascinates the narrator-author with her "outspoken Irish realism," her indomitable will, and the shrill-voiced violence of her speech ("Shut me jaw, is it? Yer own mother, and me that took ye back when ye had no one, when ye couldn't get a man to look at ye! It's me that's to shut me jaw, is it?"). She is the strong, no-nonsense center of a disreputable family that includes her drunken, out-of-work husband, Jabez, her unmarried daughter, Cornelia, and Cornelia's illegitimate daughter, Delia. He is fascinated, too, with Mrs. Mullanphy's professed religiosity that not only tolerates petty theft but profits from, and therefore encourages, it. She takes in two nieces who support themselves by stealing household goods, which she then diverts to her impoverished family. When a neighbor is evicted for failing to pay her rent, Mrs. Mullanphy coaches her about how to make herself appear more pitiable and so play upon the judge's sympathies for a stay of eviction.

Unlike the other sketches in *A Gallery of Women*, "Bridget Mullanphy" is not about the sexual tensions or artistic achievements of the New Woman; rather, in it Dreiser records Mrs. Mullanphy's tribulations as an example of "the vague, blundering, I might even say fantastic, and reasonless pother and ado that *is* life." Such lives lead him to question "the meaning or purpose of the creative force when it could descend to such fol-de-rol and nonsense as this." Nonetheless, he admires Mrs. Mullanphy's strength of will, her audacity, her persistence despite repeated misfortune.

Keith Newlin

BRILL, A. A. (1874–1948). As a resident of **Greenwich Village**, Theodore Dreiser attended parties where the intellectual and artistic elite of New York City gathered. In the fall of 1918, at the home of **Edith De Long Jarmuth** and **Edward Smith**, Dreiser met Dr. Abraham Arden Brill, a psychoanalyst who studied with Carl Jung and who translated **Freud** into English. In America, Brill's translations popularized the new science of psychology. Before meeting Brill, Dreiser was aware of Freud's ideas, but after their encounter, Dreiser read Brill's *Psychoanalysis: Its Theories and Practical Applications* (1913), which introduced him to psychoanalysis and prompted him to write several letters to Brill. In these letters Dreiser asked questions and described his own depression, which seemed to worsen after he discovered abnormal psychology.

Throughout the 1920s and 1930s, Dreiser and Brill communicated and visited regularly. Their relationship was both social and professional, and although Dreiser was never Brill's patient, the two men discussed Dreiser's anxiety, depression, and dreams. In the winter of 1922–1923, Dreiser visited Brill numerous times, discussing the psychology of a murderer, so he could accurately portray Clyde Griffiths in *An American Tragedy*. In 1932, at a time when Dreiser had shifted his attention from fiction to nonfiction, Dreiser arranged to have a series of twelve conversations with Brill, and each conversation was recorded by a stenographer. Brill understood that these conversations would be published as a book on life and happiness, a book that he would coauthor with Dreiser. Two years later, Dreiser seemed to forget this agreement, and he published portions of their conversations in essays: "The Myth of Individuality" (*American Mercury*, March 1934: 337–42) and "You, the Phantom" (*Esquire*, November 1934: 25–26). In addition, Dreiser included their conversations in *Notes on Life*, without giving Brill credit.

Brill's psychological discussions with Dreiser influenced *An American Tragedy* in several ways. At one point, Clyde Griffiths dreams that a woman transforms into a black dog and chases him into a cave, which reveals Dreiser's knowledge of dream theory. In other places, Brill's psychological theories influence Dreiser's descriptions of characters, such as when he describes Clyde's contemplation of murder. In addition, Dreiser and Brill discussed fables, myths, and fairy tales that contained archetypes, and in *An American Tragedy*, Dreiser included allusions to archetypal images, such as the Efrit and the bird that appear only at the lake where **Roberta Alden** is killed.

Born in 1874, three years after Dreiser, Brill and Dreiser shared generational ties, but Brill was a European-born doctor, an intellectual, and a scientist, so it may seem surprising that the two men remained friends from the time Dreiser met Brill in 1918 until Dreiser's death in 1945. Dreiser's intellectual curiosity and his own psychological fears prompted him to contact Brill repeatedly, and Dreiser's fame as an author must have fascinated Brill. Although they were from drastically differ-

ent intellectual and social backgrounds, Dreiser's and Brill's common interest in the human psyche sustained their friendship, a friendship that enhanced Dreiser's writing.

Further Reading

Moers, Ellen. "Chemism and Freudianism." *Two Dreisers*. New York: Viking, 1969. 156–270.

Roark Mulligan

BROADWAY MAGAZINE. Founded in 1898 as a sensationalist publication, *Broadway Magazine* for its first seven years specialized in pictures of bathing beauties, reproductions of artistic female nudes, gossip about New York society, and notes on the theater. By 1905, however, the circulation of the magazine had dropped substantially, and it was sold to new owners who wished to remake it. To accomplish this, they offered the editor's post to Dreiser, then the editor of *Smith's Magazine*. He accepted, proposing to improve *Broadway* in part by incorporating some of the successful elements of *Smith's*: a department on "What Americans Are Thinking," feature articles on important trends and individuals in New York City (one later published in *Broadway*, "The Luxury of the Modern Hotel," surveyed the most lavish establishments Manhattan had to offer), and fiction that was "well told" and could "hold the interest keenly." Later that year, advertising executive Benjamin B. Hampton purchased *Broadway*, leaving Thomas H. McKee (the **Doubleday** lawyer involved in the *Sister Carrie* dispute) as publisher and Dreiser as editor. Dreiser relished what he could do with the money Hampton provided to improve the magazine and during his tenure published fiction by such esteemed authors as Carl Van Vechten, James L. Ford, O. Henry, and **Harris Merton Lyon**. Dreiser saw elements of himself in the young Lyon and so was aghast when the formerly bohemian author fell under the influence of the materialistic Hampton. (Dreiser wrote of these events in "De Maupassant, Jr.," one of the sketches in *Twelve Men*.) Although Dreiser succeeded in raising *Broadway*'s circulation above 100,000, he had growing disputes with Hampton and McKee over his management of the magazine and its future direction, for Hampton wanted cleaner stories and a profitable muckraking profile for the magazine. With his editorial control weakening, Dreiser in June 1907 accepted a position as editor of **The Delineator** and two other women's magazines produced by the **Butterick Publishing Company**. After Dreiser's departure, Hampton directed *Broadway Magazine* himself, attracting strong writers, publishing many exposés, and enjoying increased circulation; however, financial overextension forced him to sell the magazine in 1911, and after further transformations it published its last issue in May 1912.

Christopher Weinmann

BROWDER, EARL RUSSELL (1891–1973). Writer, editor, labor organizer, political leader, and veteran of numerous midwestern radical movements, Earl Browder served as the general secretary of the Communist Party (CPUSA) from 1934 to 1945, the period during which the party enjoyed its widest influence in the United States. This was also more or less the time of Browder's acquaintance with Dreiser, with whom he shared a respectful, but somewhat distant, relationship.

Leaving school after the third grade, Browder helped to support his family of ten children as an errand boy, a telegraph clerk, and a bookkeeper. In 1906 he joined the Socialist Party, and by 1912 he was associated with **William Z. Foster's** Syndicalist League of North America. Late in

1914, Browder organized the League for Democratic Control to oppose the United States' entry into World War I. He was arrested in 1917 and sentenced to a year for draft evasion and two years for conspiracy to block the draft. In 1921 Browder attended the first congress of the Red International of Labor Unions in Moscow. For the next five years, he edited *Labor Herald*, the paper of the Trade Union Educational League, and worked with the Workers Party of America, a political organization that agitated for trade unionism. In 1926 he went to China, where he organized communist labor unions and edited the publication of the Pan-Pacific Trade Union Secretariat.

Shortly before the 1929 stock market crash, Browder returned to America to find the party rife with sectarianism. His distance from factional strife made him an attractive candidate for party leadership, and in 1930 Browder was appointed, along with Foster and William Weinstone, to a three-man ruling secretariat. From his capacity as the administrative secretary Browder began to call upon Dreiser to lend his reputation and energies to various communist-supported causes.

In June 1931, in part at Browder's and Foster's urging, Dreiser investigated conditions outside Pittsburgh where the communist-led National Miners' Union had organized a strike against the wishes of the American Federation of Labor (AFL)-affiliated United Mine Workers Union. Appalled by what he found there, Dreiser accused the AFL of, among other things, coziness with capital and called for its "disestablishment." When William L. Green, the president of the AFL, challenged the validity of Dreiser's charges, the novelist relied upon Browder and Foster for most of the finer points of his published response. In September 1931, Dreiser once again solicited Browder's opinion, in this instance, about a manuscript called "A New Deal for America," published the following year as *Tragic America*. Browder responded with suggestions, some of which Dreiser seems to have accepted, for revising two chapters and the Preface.

Dreiser had undertaken the Pittsburgh fact-finding junket as chairman of the liberal **National Committee for the Defense of Political Prisoners** (NCDPP). In October 1931, when Dreiser was preparing another committee to travel under the auspices of the NCDPP—this time to bloody **Harlan** and Bell Counties in southeastern Kentucky, where striking miners were suffering even more horribly than those in western Pennsylvania—Browder warned the novelist that liberal attorney Arthur Garfield Hays, whom Dreiser had invited along, was trying to link his name to the National Association for the Advancement of Colored People (NAACP) for publicity. Hays declined the invitation, and in November Browder congratulated Dreiser and his Kentucky delegation for "a job well worth doing and well done" and for "smash[ing] through the news boycott" surrounding the oppression of the miners (Browder to Dreiser, 24 November 1931). But when Dreiser asked to join the party early in 1932, Browder turned him down, feeling that the novelist, while a useful friend, might prove an undisciplined party member.

Dreiser was hurt by Browder's rejection, but however cool their relationship had become, the give-and-take between the two men continued apace. In December 1932, Browder invited Dreiser to Chicago for the upcoming Student Congress against War; the novelist claimed to be unavailable but sent a message of support instead. In return, Dreiser asked Browder to recommend "a good resume of the works of Marx" and also solicited some

Communist Party-related manuscripts for publication in *The American Spectator* (Dreiser to Browder, 16 December 1932).

The most ardent of Dreiser's intercessions was on behalf of the artist Hubert Davis. As he did with other influential people he knew, Dreiser approached Browder about this "temperamental radical" sympathetic to the communist struggle and a "man of genius" whose "symbolic art" had, according to Dreiser, "no chance in America." Dreiser asked Browder to arrange a free trip to the Soviet Union for Davis (Dreiser to Browder, 28 September 1934); Browder assured Dreiser that he was "much interested" in Davis and would do everything possible to support his work (Browder to Dreiser, 8 November 1934).

In late March 1941, Browder began to serve a four-year sentence in federal prison for passport violations, but in September, when the party asked Dreiser to make a personal appeal to the president on Browder's behalf, the novelist begged off, claiming he didn't know "enough of the details of Browder's life and political activities" (Dreiser to Joe Pass, 24 September 1941). Roosevelt pardoned Browder in May 1942.

In 1944, badly misreading both Stalin's dissolution of the Comintern and the 1943 Teheran agreements between the United States, Britain, and the Soviet Union, Browder replaced the CPUSA with the Communist Political Association, an independent leftist lobby group designed to contribute to "national unity." For disbanding the CPUSA, Browder was attacked publicly by Jacques Duclos, a leading French communist, replaced as general secretary by William Z. Foster when the CPUSA was reestablished in 1945, and expelled from the party in 1946. Browder died on 27 June 1973, no longer a Marxist and largely remembered by his former comrades as a "right deviationist." In August 1945, Foster finally accepted Dreiser's application to become a member of the party, only four months before the novelist himself passed away.

Further Reading

Dreiser–CPUSA Correspondence. Dreiser Papers, University of Pennsylvania Rare Book and Manuscript Library.
Jaffe, Philip J. *The Rise and Fall of American Communism.* New York: Horizon Press, 1975
Ryan, James Gilbert. "The Making of a Native Marxist: The Early Career of Earl Browder." *Review of Politics* 39 (1977): 332–62.

Arthur D. Casciato

BROWN, GRACE (1887–1906). The character of **Roberta "Bobby" Alden** in *An American Tragedy* is based in part on Grace "Billy" Brown, who was murdered by **Chester Gillette** in 1906. Brown and Gillette both worked at the Gillette Skirt Factory in Cortland, New York. Like many young women of her time, Brown had moved from the farm to a factory job in the city. Gillette came to Cortland a year later to work in his uncle's business, and the two had an affair. When Brown discovered she was pregnant, she went back to her family's farm and wrote several letters to Gillette pleading for him to come for her and threatening suicide if he did not. A few months later, he took her to Big Moose Lake in the Adirondacks for what she thought was to be a wedding trip. Instead, they went out in a boat and he killed her, allegedly by hitting her with a tennis racket and throwing her overboard.

The story depicted in both the trial and local legend was of an innocent young farm girl who was first ruined and then murdered by a predatory villain. Prosecutors presented Grace Brown's letters as evidence supporting this view of the case. Although Dreiser incorporates many of the details of Brown's life and death in *An American Tragedy* and even quotes directly from her letters, he uses these pieces to build a very different picture of the crime. For example, whereas the Brown letters were introduced in the trial to create sympathy for the victim, in the novel the letters underscore Clyde Griffith's growing sense of entrapment. Whereas Chester Gillette was generally viewed as a heartless killer who coolly dispatched his victim, Dreiser's description of the murder scene makes Clyde's actions and intentions in the boat ambiguous, and by adding a social and economic motive for murder that was not present in the original case, Dreiser presents both Roberta Alden and Clyde Griffiths as victims in a larger American tragedy.

Further Reading

Brandon, Craig. *Murder in the Adirondacks:* An American Tragedy *Revisited.* Utica, N.Y.: North Country Books, 1986.
Castle, John F. "The Making of *An American Tragedy*." Diss., University of Michigan, 1952.
Donovan, Nancy. "Representing Grace Brown: The Working Class Woman in 'American Tragedy' Murder Narratives." *Dreiser Studies* 31.2 (2000): 3–21.

Kathryn M. Plank

THE BULWARK, Dreiser's penultimate novel, was published posthumously by **Doubleday** in 1946. It had much earlier become a work in extended "progress," since it was begun in 1914. It was originally conceived as a fictionalized version of a story about her family told to Dreiser by a young Quaker woman, **Anna P. Tatum,** whom he had met in 1912 and with whom he had a brief relationship. At various times between 1914 and the 1940s he worked on or intended to work on the novel, projected to demonstrate the ineffectuality of religious faith in the face of American materialism's tragic lure. By the time he summoned his sympathetic assistant, **Marguerite Tjader**, to help him finish *The Bulwark* in 1942, Dreiser had undergone significant changes in his attitude toward **religion**, especially nondogmatic Quakerism, which he admired for its antimaterialist emphasis on living simply. Consequently, the finished product became a testimony to the power of religion, absent moral rigidity, to provide meaning and solace amid personal tragedies.

The novel opens as its protagonist, **Solon Barnes**, exchanges wedding vows with his sweetheart, Benecia Wallin, in the Friends' meetinghouse at Dukla, Pennsylvania. Dreiser immediately emphasizes in this short wedding section labeled "Introduction" the contrast between the religion's ideal of simplicity spurred by the Inner Light and the manifestations of wealth and worldliness evident among some of the assembled Quaker guests. The Friends' struggle, the Barnes family's in particular, to strike a "rough" if "imperfect balance between many things" indeed proves to be the major theme of the novel.

Part One begins with a flashback focusing mostly on Solon's family history prior to his marriage. Benecia had come from wealthy Quaker stock, while Solon's parents, Rufus and Hannah Barnes, were far less privileged Friends. The death of Hannah's brother-in-law, however, leads Rufus and his family from Maine to New Jersey and then to Dukla and an impressive sixty-acre estate, called Thornbrough, on which the deceased relative had foreclosed a mortgage. Rufus decides, at his widowed sister-in-law's urging, to move his family into a section of the mansion while the whole is being restored for resale, but circumstances lead to Rufus's ownership of the entire estate.

Solon grows up at Thornbrough, coming to love its natural setting, including especially Lever Creek, which runs through the property. Several incidents from Solon's youth are narrated to demonstrate its deeply religious context and his developing sense of personal responsibility. The former is signaled by an accident with an ax, resulting in a life-threatening infection in the boy's ankle. A mystical epiphany assures his mother that Solon will recover, and he immediately does. Solon's profound sense of accountability is foreshadowed by his extreme remorse over accidentally killing a bird while testing another boy's slingshot. A further spur to his moralistic bent comes with his Quaker education, which condemns novels, dancing, and other amusements. His father begins to prepare young Solon for practical affairs, and he eventually secures a position for him at the Traders and Builders Bank. Meanwhile, he and Benecia fall in love, and their planned marriage ends Part One.

Part Two begins by documenting Solon's rise among the administrators of the bank. His mother dies, seriously testing his faith for the first time. Five children are born to Solon and Benecia at two-year intervals: Isobel, Orville, Dorothea, **Etta**, and **Stewart**. On taking over Thornbrough at his father's death, Solon assumes the role of ultra strict disciplinarian with his children, making sure that the spiritual cocoon he fashions for them is not sullied by books, music, or newspapers. Much of the narrative shifts at this point to the unfolding lives of the children. Isobel is bright but homely and socially ignored. Orville is materialistic, conventional, and set on marrying money. Dorothea is beautiful but much aware of it and therefore given to putting on airs. Etta and Stewart, however, are the two that bear the reader's watching, for they will play major roles in the story by rebelling in different ways against their father's discipline, much to his bewilderment. Etta personifies the typical Dreiserian dreamer, given to "romantic flights of fancy" from her earliest years and later displaying a highly developed eagerness for experience. Stewart begins as a "little rebel" and becomes the familiar Dreiser male, obsessed by the lure of sex. After a brief time as a student at the University of Wisconsin, Etta goes to New York and embarks on a love affair with an artist named Willard Kane.

Part Three begins with Stewart and his school chums plotting what they hope will be sexually satisfying excursions with young female acquaintances, an activity that triggers the novel's culminating tragedy. On one of their outings, the boys administer a drug to a girl with a weak heart, and she dies. Stewart's unbearable grief over the girl's death as well as his betrayal of his father's love and the Inner Light lead the lad to take his own life. The stricken Solon, in the throes of his great sorrow, begins to doubt the efficacy of the harsh moral training he had meted out to his children, a reconsideration that will lead him eventually to a more compassionate stance, but his sufferings are not yet over. He resigns from the bank on discovering the dubious ethics of his fellow administrators. Overcome by her own grief at Stewart's suicide, Benecia swiftly weakens and dies. Isobel and Etta, whom Isobel has induced to return from New York to help care for her father, marvel at the profound peace he has found despite his troubles and thanks to his renewed faith in the Inner Light. Here Dreiser transfers, while slightly altering, two of his own late spiritual experiences to Solon. While studying science at the Woods Hole marine biology laboratory in the late 1930s, Dreiser had been struck by the design apparent in a patch of flowers growing by a walkway

and its similarity to the order displayed in the specimens he had earlier been observing through a microscope. In the last section of *The Bulwark*, Solon, walking near Lever Creek, observes a gorgeous green fly feeding on a blossom and wonders at the Creative Purpose behind all beauty. In addition, Dreiser had confronted a puff adder on a walk in the woods and believed he had successfully conveyed his lack of ill intent to the snake. This "mystical" experience is also assigned to Solon. A little later, the Quaker "bulwark" is diagnosed with cancer but remains secure in his faith and comforted by Etta's reading to him from John Woolman's *Journal*.

Construing the meaning of the novel for the reader now falls to Etta. Her experience ministering to her father in his hour of need has taught her that the greatest happiness comes not from the romantic indulgence of the self but rather through the art of giving. In it she has found, as she expresses through the novel's most poignant paragraph, "nothing fitful or changing or disappointing—nothing that glowed one moment and was gone the next." At Solon's funeral, the event that ends *The Bulwark*, Etta cries not for herself nor for her father but rather for *"life."*

Further Reading

Brennan, Stephen C. "Humanism in Dreiser's *The Bulwark*." *Dreiser Studies* 27.2 (1996): 22–38.

Gogol, Miriam. "Dreiser's Search for a 'Religion of Life': A Psychoanalytic Reading." *Dreiser Studies* 21.1 (1990): 21–30.

Hochman, Barbara. "Dreiser's Last Work: *The Bulwark* and *The Stoic*—Conversion or Continuity?" *Dreiser Newsletter* 14.2 (1983): 1–15.

St. Jean, Shawn. "Mythology, Religion, and Intertextuality in Theodore Dreiser's *The Bulwark*." *Christianity and Literature* 48 (1999): 275–93.

Lawrence E. Hussman

"BUMS." One of the thirty-eight sketches of New York City life between 1900 and 1915 that make up *The Color of a Great City*, this brief essay takes up the subject of those figures variously called bums, tramps, hoboes, or the homeless. The essential image of the essay is that of the bum as a kind of burlesque performer reveling in a role he did not choose for himself. Dreiser's bum is no victim of society; rather, he stands heroically—and comically—outside society, thus highlighting the blind adherence to social conventions of those "solid citizens" who would look down upon him. The bum recognizes the ephemeral, inessential nature of social conventions and defies those conventions. He represents "not poverty or want but a kind of devil-may-care indifference and even contempt for all that society as we know it prizes so highly." The bum is no one's social inferior precisely because he stands *outside* society. If he happens to gaze at the shop windows of our materialistic society, it is not with desire but with the disinterested curiosity of a tourist in an exotic locale. At the same time, the bum does not choose to play the role he does; he simply is what he is, the result either of hereditary or circumstantial factors.

Several of Dreiser's most frequently visited themes intersect in this short essay, most notably that of the heroic spectator who stands outside the social and moral conventions of American life. In this respect the bum resembles Dreiser's conception of the artist in his capacity of dispassionate onlooker. In keeping with the naturalistic worldview of Dreiser's major works, the bum's strength lies not in his choosing to throw off social conventions—for he has as little choice in his manner of living as the followers of convention have in theirs—but in his almost joyful acceptance of who he is and the absence of desire to be anything else. Like the other characters that make up the "color" of city life, the bum has his role to play. What seems to distinguish him from these others are the relish with which he accepts this role and his refusal to deceive himself into believing he could play any other. Bums "were as they were, unsocial, unconventional, indifferent to the saving, grasping, scheming plans of men, and in accord with moods if not plans of their own."

Jon Dietrick

BURKE, MICHAEL (?–?). Burke was a masonry foreman for the New York Central Railroad, which employed Dreiser to work ten-hour days at fifteen cents an hour. Dreiser's employment as an "amateur laborer" ran from 5 June 1903 until 24 December of that same year, when he returned to the world of letters as an assistant feature editor for the *New York Daily News*. Dreiser had sought work on the railroad in the hope that manual labor would help him overcome a neurasthenic condition that had set in after the problems attending the publication of *Sister Carrie* and eventually threatened his career as a writer. Unfortunately, Dreiser's early experiences in the carpentry shop at Spuyten Duyvil proved humiliating and too demanding physically, resulting in numerous requests for a transfer. Finally, on 1 September, Dreiser was assigned to Burke's crew, where he remained until the end of his employment with the New York Central. The outdoor work raised Dreiser's spirits, and his role as a requisitions clerk gave him some status while relieving him of the manual labor he found so debilitating. It also relieved Burke of a task he had neither the education nor diplomacy to perform effectively. All reliable evidence suggests that Dreiser's most significant rehabilitation came during the four months he worked with the masonry crew.

An Amateur Laborer, Dreiser's autobiographical account of his struggle with **neurasthenia**, breaks off before narrating his association with Burke; however, over the years, the blustery Irish foreman was destined to play recurring roles in Dreiser's works, the characterization varying with the dramatic or philosophical demands of the individual piece. Dreiser's first literary use of Burke, a polemical essay titled "The Toil of the Laborer," was making the rounds by January 1904, though it was not published until 1913 in the *New York Call* and later revised for *Hey Rub-a-Dub-Dub*. The unnamed Burke appears as a sullen pawn of management who drives his men relentlessly and without mercy. Burke next appears as "The Mighty Burke," published in *McClure's* in 1911 and revised as "The Mighty Rourke" for *Twelve Men*. At the conclusion of this humorous, sentimentalized sketch, the contentious but tenderhearted foreman suffers a fictional death that underscores his nobility and devotion to his men. Dreiser next drew upon his masonry crew experiences for *The "Genius,"* in which Burke was cast as Deegan, whose insensitivity and pedestrianism contribute to **Eugene Witla's** determination to resume his career as an artist. Finally, in 1924, Dreiser submitted an essay titled "Down Hill and Up" to *Hearst's International*. It, too, was the story of his struggle with, and recovery from, neurasthenia. Ultimately, a much-abridged version was published as "The Irish Section Foreman Who Taught Me How to Live" in *Hearst's International* (August 1924: 20–21, 118–21). In this essay, Dreiser paid tribute to Burke (again called Rourke) for the inspirational effect of his fortitude, compassion, and zest for life. In this final characterization, Burke received Dreiser's greatest tribute: "He was so cheerful and amusing and semi-affectionate and considerate, without appearing to be, that I began to love him."

Further Reading

Dowell, Richard W. "Will the Real Mike Burke Stand Up, Please!" *Dreiser Newsletter* 14.1 (1983): 1–9.

Richard W. Dowell

BURRIDGE, ELIHU. *See* Potter, Elihu H.

BUTLER, AILEEN. Mistress and second wife to financier **Frank Cowperwood** in Dreiser's *Trilogy of Desire*: *The Financier*, *The Titan*, and *The Stoic*. Loosely based on **Mary Adelaide Moore**, the second wife of businessman **Charles T. Yerkes** (the model for Cowperwood), Aileen is beautiful, temperamental, showy, and finally unable to satisfy her husband's voracious desire for other women. Not always a sympathetic character, she nevertheless remains a loyal counterpoint to her ruthless and unfaithful husband.

Aileen first appears in *The Financier* as the daughter of political boss Edward Malia Butler. Cowperwood, who is ten years older and married, thinks that he has never met a women with as much "innate force." However, their affair proves to be the first in a series of bad choices in women for Cowperwood, as Aileen's father makes it his business to ruin and imprison him. Aileen supports Cowperwood through the trial and visits him in prison, where for the first time in the novel he breaks down, leaving Aileen "delighted, eager, crazy to make a sacrifice of herself" for him. After his release, Frank and Aileen marry and leave Philadelphia for Chicago.

In *The Titan*, Aileen's loyalty to her new husband is severely tested. Although they make a splash on the Chicago social scene, their financial and marital scandals haunt them, and they are snubbed by local society. This causes Cowperwood to notice the intellectual and social differences between them, which he uses to justify his numerous affairs. Aileen is at first stunned by his betrayals but then recovers sufficiently to nearly choke one woman to death and then to begin an affair of her own. Always on the lookout for young, forceful women, Cowperwood takes an interest in fifteen-year-old **Berenice Fleming** (he is in his fifties), who, after Aileen, is his most serious conquest. Frank's womanizing eventually becomes too much for Aileen, and she drowns her sorrows in alcohol and attempts suicide. The novel ends with the marriage in shambles.

The Stoic concludes their story. Cowperwood plans to move Berenice to England and take Aileen, who will not grant him a divorce, to Europe as a cover. In order to be free to visit Berenice, Cowperwood hires a down-at-the-heels Charleston socialite to distract Aileen, but she finds out about the financial arrangement and returns home furious. Soon after, Frank is taken ill, and husband and wife have a final amicable conversation, where Frank realizes he owes Aileen "a reasonable degree of consideration in return for the kindness and affection which she had displayed at a time when he most needed them." Although Berenice's untimely appearance at Frank's bedside angers Aileen, she is mollified by a final apologetic note and tries to carry out his last wishes, only to be thwarted by Frank's unresolved financial obligations. Aileen dies a year later and asks to be buried beside her husband, as he had intended.

Not exactly the stereotypical devoted wife, Aileen still remains true to the emotional commitment that caused her to abandon the security of her family and remain with her husband in the face of his betrayals and humiliations. Her mesmerizing presence in the three novels, consid-

erably enhanced from that of her real-life counterpart, could be seen as Dreiser's way of showing the high cost—for one woman at least—of Frank Cowperwood's financial and sexual acquisitiveness.

Further Reading

Gerber, Phillip. "Jolly Mrs. Yerkes Is Home From Abroad." *Theodore Dreiser and American Culture: New Readings*. Ed. Yoshinobu Hakutani. Newark: University of Delaware Press, 2000. 79–103.

Lehan, Richard. *Theodore Dreiser: His World and His Novels*. Carbondale: Southern Illinois University Press, 1969. 97–116.

Pizer, Donald. *The Novels of Theodore Dreiser: A Critical Study*. Minneapolis: University of Minnesota Press, 1976. 171–200.

Caren J. Town

BUTTERICK PUBLISHING COMPANY. Publisher of *The Delineator*, *Designer*, and *New Idea Woman's Magazine*, three women's magazines of which Dreiser served as general editor from 1907 to 1910. The company traced its origins to E. Butterick and Company, a producer of sewing patterns founded in 1863 by Ebenezer Butterick. Butterick had published magazines to promote his patterns since 1867; in 1881 this part of the business was so important that the organization was renamed Butterick Publishing Company, Limited, and Ebenezer Butterick handed the responsibility of running the firm to his associates. In the following decades, the company began other publications related to fashion, such as *Tailor's Review* and *Ladies' Review*. In 1902 the company reorganized into two units, with the Butterick Company focusing on patterns and the Butterick Publishing Company dedicating itself to the production of periodicals. (Ebenezer Butterick sold out his remaining holdings in 1899.) When it combined with the Ridgway Company, the publisher of *Everybody's Magazine*, in 1909, the Butterick Publishing

Company became one of the largest producers of magazines, with thirty-two periodicals under its command. In the following years, the company also published cookbooks and other homemaking guides associated with its flagship magazine, *The Delineator*. The decline of the magazine industry during the next few decades brought about the demise of most of its magazines, but at the beginning of the twenty-first century, Butterick Company, Incorporated, still published patterns and a number of magazines in which to market them.

Christopher Weinmann

C

CAMPBELL, LOUISE (?–?). One of the most important of Dreiser's relationships began in February 1917, when Campbell wrote to Dreiser to complain about a disparaging reference to Pennsylvanians in *A Hoosier Holiday*, confided her literary ambitions, and predicted that one day they would meet. She was surprised when Dreiser replied to invite her to meet with him when she was next in New York. One month later, she responded to his invitation, and he astounded her by giving her a manuscript to critique. A passionate affair soon commenced, amply recorded in his *American Diaries*. Soon after they met, Dreiser gave her the manuscript of his autobiography to type and edit, which was eventually published as *A Book about Myself* and *Dawn*. Dreiser found Campbell to be a congenial romantic partner. Born Louise Heym, she had made an early marriage to Donald Campbell and was living in Philadelphia. The intermittent nature of their liaisons meshed well with Dreiser's other entanglements, and he found it easy to put off her desire for marriage. Her account of her marital difficulties inspired the story "Chains" (*American Diaries* 232). Dreiser encouraged her writing, and Campbell sold stories to various magazines; in the late 1920s she became an associate editor for *Ladies' Home Journal*. After their initial passion waned, Dreiser increasingly relied upon Campbell for typing, editing, research, and advice. With **Sallie Kussel**, she cut and edited *An American Tragedy*; and she did much of the editing of the 1927 revision of *The Financier*, as well as editing *Chains* and the sketches of "This Madness" and *A Gallery of Women*. Her translation of Erwin Piscator's adaptation of *An American Tragedy* was staged by the Group Theater as *Case of Clyde Griffiths*. She was partly responsible for the plagiarism scandal attendant upon the publication of *Dreiser Looks at Russia*, for the ever-busy Dreiser had instructed her to pad out the book with excerpts from **Dorothy Thompson's** series of articles published in the *New York Post* (Swanberg 343). In Dreiser's final years, she edited the manuscripts of *The Bulwark* and *The Stoic*. In 1959 Campbell published a valuable memoir, *Letters to Louise: Theodore Dreiser's Letters to Louise Campbell*.

Keith Newlin

CAPITALISM. Was Theodore Dreiser an opponent or supporter of capitalism? Did Dreiser's fiction expose the excesses and abuses of the marketplace, or did his novels employ the evolutionary theories of Darwin to justify robber-baron practices? As a member of the Communist Party, as a social critic in works such as *Tragic America*, and in fictional depictions of factory life, Dreiser appears to be entrenched in the camp of capitalism's critics. But as the author of the **Cowperwood** trilogy (three novels about an American millionaire) and as a businessman who attempted to collect every royalty payment owed him, Dreiser might be characterized as one of capitalism's advocates. For Dreiser's readers, this apparent contradiction is not easily resolved. Literary critics, such as Fredric Jameson, have declared that Dreiser exposes the excesses of capitalism, but other readers of Dreiser, such as Walter Benn Michaels, have claimed that Dreiser is one of capitalism's most ardent supporters, a supporter who reduces art and human relationships to monetary exchange.

In a "Reflections" column for *Ev'ry Month* (February 1896), Dreiser, in response to the financial crisis that occurred during the winter of 1895–1896, criticizes a silent Eastern oligarchy of financiers who control the economy and the government of the United States by controlling gold. In the novel *Sister Carrie*, the narrator advances a Marxist definition of money: "[T]his thing [money] primarily stands for and should only be accepted as a moral due—that it should be paid out as honestly stored energy." In his philosophical and scientific work *Notes on Life*, however, Dreiser describes gold and money as media that allow a financier or an artist to satisfy spiritual, not physical, longings, and Dreiser argues that value is a relative notion: "A discovered diamond may weigh an ounce or twenty carats and be of a certain clarity and radiance. But its value is something else. . . . There are no fixed values or value measures." Dreiser's apparently contradictory pronouncements demonstrate his complex attitude toward money and capitalism, an attitude that is not easily reduced to either anti- or pro-capitalism.

In his writing Dreiser attacks the excesses of capitalism and calls for reform, but he also participates in, and justifies, capitalism. This is the contradiction of Dreiser, but it is also the contradiction of all who try to criticize a structure of which they are a part. In Dreiser's novels, capitalism is a powerful economic force that can help some and hurt others. Dreiser does not necessarily lament the injustices of a market economy; rather, he exposes and condemns individuals who are unwilling to express openly the values inherent in a capitalist society. Dreiser attributes the greatest harm done by capitalism, or the oligarchy of the wealthy, not to the marketplace but to silence and to absent power. When depicting financial transactions, Dreiser portrays gold and money not as absolutes but as *media* of abstraction, and while these symbol systems are often governed by natural laws, they often dangerously depart from natural law, as is evidenced by the "gold standard" itself, which Dreiser associated with all genteel standards that were unnatural in that they froze certain values or abstractions in order to benefit those with power. Dreiser's art counters genteel fiction that he believed failed to depict adequately the money motive at work within American society. In an unpublished essay entitled "American Tragedies" (Dreiser Papers), Dreiser argues that the wealthy of America achieved their fortunes by graft, perjury, political dishonesty, and murderous cruelty, yet the popular fiction of his time depicted young men and women achieving wealth by marriage, a method that worked only if one was already wealthy. Dreiser participates in capitalism, in consumer lust, but he also exposes the money motive that popular nineteenth-century fiction typically ignored or depicted unrealistically.

What were Dreiser's intentions, and what were his assumptions when writing *Sister Carrie, The Financier,* and *An American Tragedy*? Why would Dreiser write three of his eight major works of fiction with an American millionaire as the main character? Why, to some extent, do Dreiser's other novels, *Jennie Gerhardt, The Bulwark,* and *The "Genius,"* explore the motives and lifestyles of the rich? Dreiser was unable to separate himself from capitalism, but Dreiser was not purely a product of capitalism; he was influenced by religious, agrarian, barter, and labor ideologies that have increasingly succumbed to consumer forces. Dreiser and other realists were in a unique position to describe these conflicting and contradictory beliefs because they experienced them. In *An American Tragedy,* Clyde Griffiths is obviously motivated by a desire for money, but this motivation is developed and revealed by contrasting it with conflicting desires that disclose antithetical familial, Christian, and agrarian values. By means of this multifarious play of motivations, this shifting of points of view and value systems, the power of a monetary motive is revealed. If we consider the climactic act of the novel, Clyde's murder of **Roberta Alden** (his first lover and the bearer of his unborn progeny), this act, from a monetary point of view, is intelligent. If Clyde had been successful and had not been caught and had married **Sondra Finchley**, he, judged by a monetary value system, would have been a pillar of the community. The power of *An American Tragedy* is derived from Dreiser's ability to depict the pro-social aspects of what most would consider a deviant action—a murder. Dreiser explores the extent to which capitalism has entered all aspects of our lives. In short, Dreiser realistically portrays capitalism and its effects on both the rich and the poor. For his wealthy characters, such as Frank Cow-perwood, money is a medium for social change, but for poor characters, such as Clyde Griffiths, capitalism is deadly, and in these contrasts Dreiser reveals the power and excesses of a capitalist economy.

Further Reading

Michaels, Walter Benn. *The Gold Standard and the Logic of Naturalism: American Literature at the Turn of the Century.* Berkeley: University of California Press, 1987.

Roark Mulligan

CENSORSHIP. Theodore Dreiser's literary path was littered with more rocks and brambles than that of any other twentieth-century American author. By far the bulk of the obstacles derived from censorship in all its forms—moral, religious, political, commercial—even self-censorship, when he—or his wife or friends—tried to purge his novels of objectionable material. (There was also self-censorship of intimate family material in Dreiser's autobiographical works, *Dawn* and *Newspaper Days*.) It is perverse tribute to Dreiser's massive honesty that these prepublication efforts rarely succeeded in averting some kind of complaint, but for the most part Dreiser refused to compromise with those seeking to suppress his books. He exhibited great courage and integrity throughout his long battle for artistic freedom, though his livelihood, even his health, was at risk.

Dreiser's censorship battles were in part attributable to his stubbornness, prickly temper, and combative nature, but they were far more often a reflection of his times. He came along in the twilight of the genteel age and was thrust into the role of a pathbreaker who cleared the way for a freer American literature. He never harbored an aesthetic program of *epater le bourgeois*; nor did he write controversial or sexually frank novels in hopes of boosting sales.

It is true that his attitude toward organized **religion**, particularly the Catholic Church, and religious morality was hostile. His rebellion against religion had psychological roots in childhood resentment against his fanatical German-Catholic father, who sought to impose a rigid, Old World morality on his children. His reaction against paternal authority was to become a fierce foe of religious authority, which he regarded as the inveterate enemy of free thought and sexual freedom. Later, during his newspaper career, he saw the workings of another form of censorship. There were, he learned, certain stories a reporter didn't touch, and most of these concerned sexual scandal among the wealthy, the powerful, and the politically connected. Few newspaper publishers wanted to risk offending the powerful church-business establishments in their city.

His rude exposure to hypocrisy, vice, and corruption as a reporter laid a tough veneer of cynicism over his attitude toward life. It wasn't, he discovered, what the sanitized popular fiction of the day said it was. This perceived gap between literature and life set him to dreaming of creating novels that told the truth, like those of Europeans like **Balzac** and Zola, and so, after half a decade of newspaper and magazine hackwork, writing articles that were factually accurate but false to the deeper reality of life, he composed his first novel, *Sister Carrie*, in 1900, inspired by his sister Emma's illicit affair with a fast-talking clerk named **Hopkins**.

His manuscript soon ran afoul of publishers' timidity. Most publishers feared legal action by the **New York Society for the Suppression of Vice** under **Anthony Comstock**, who was empowered by New York state law to bring complaints against publishers of books he considered obscene; the publisher could be prosecuted. Moreover, an 1873 federal statue known popularly as the Comstock Law, because he had helped write it, empowered Comstock and his minions to impound and destroy allegedly obscene material that was or would be sent through the U.S. mails. But it was not only fear of the law, personified in the fierce smut-smiter Comstock. The gentlemanly publishers of the day were respectable family men who took pride in serving as moral sentinels. Women were the main buyers of novels, and it was believed that they—particularly innocent, young, unmarried women—must be protected from "immoral" literature, which might inflame their innocent minds.

Young novelists like Stephen Crane, who wrote of a prostitute in *Maggie: A Girl of the Streets* (1893), began to chafe at the ban on dealing with the "sex question." One of the most outspoken objectors was **Frank Norris**, whose novel *McTeague* (1899) the critic and realistic novelist **William Dean Howells** had identified as a test case of whether "the old-fashioned ideal of a novel as something which may be read by all ages and sexes" should give way to "the European notion of it as something fit only for age and experience, and for men rather than women" (qtd. in Franklin Walker, *Frank Norris* [New York: Russell & Russell, 1963] 226). Howells, the champion of **realism** in America, supported censorship to protect young women's virtue. By the turn of century, even the genteel realism Howells had fought for was being pushed out of the literary marketplace by flamboyant romances.

In this cultural context Dreiser composed his first novel. While he wrote it, he said, an inner censor was ever admonishing him to be less frank, less truthful, but then something urged him to write sincerely: "I would come to strange, hard, bitter sad facts in my story . . . and I would say shall I put that down, and something in the very centre of my being would say, "You must! You must! You dare not do otherwise!" ("Attack on Grant Richards," unpub. ms., Dreiser Papers).

After the first publisher Dreiser sent the manuscript to, **Harper & Brothers**, rejected its story line about an unmarried young woman who has sexual liaisons and goes unpunished as unsuitable for young readers, Dreiser, with the help of his wife, Sara, and his friend **Arthur Henry** excised some of the sexual allusions. The novel was then accepted by **Walter H. Page** of **Doubleday, Page & Co**, but the head of the firm, **Frank N. Doubleday**, judged the book immoral when he read it and in effect buried the novel with a small printing and no advertising.

This failure haunted Dreiser for years, and fear of censorship created a psychic block that kept him from finishing his second novel, *Jennie Gerhardt*, and led to a nervous breakdown. In 1902, during a low point in his fortunes, Dreiser wrote a little essay protesting censorship, "True Art Speaks Plainly." In it Dreiser defended truth-telling in art as the highest morality. He questioned the motives of censors, who he charged feared books that challenged the status quo with subversive truths. He contended that the charge of "immorality" in literature would "become a house of refuge to which every form of social injustice hurries for protection . . . . [T]he objection to the discussion of the sex question is so great as to almost prevent the handling of the theme entirely." Here Dreiser was prescient in recognizing that censorship could be a political as well as a moral act. It was a technique used by social elitists to block any questioning of the moral order that underpinned their power. Thus, Dreiser charged, censorship served to conceal the crimes of sexual repression, patriarchy, and economic inequity.

He did not finish *Jennie Gerhardt* until 1911. By then literary Victorianism was fading. *Sister Carrie* had been republished to critical accolades, and Harper & Brothers, which had rejected it in 1900, agreed in 1910 to publish *Jennie Gerhardt*, but not without some qualms. It was turned over to **Ripley Hitchcock**, an editor known for his staunch morality. Before publication the head of the firm sent out a copy for vetting to Hamilton Wright Mabie of the *Christian Outlook*. Mabie approved, though he thought Dreiser was developing a dangerous obsession with the sex theme.

In manuscript the novel had undergone minor censorship—a veiled reference to contraceptives was excised, for example, and impieties and animadversions to religion were jettisoned. Almost as restrictive were editorial changes that transformed Dreiser's flat, ironic style into something closer to the twitterings of popular fiction, and so a novel examining the impact of class and social mores on human freedom became a love story against a realistic backdrop. It was not censorship per se, but it was a way of making the social truths in the book less threatening. Dreiser had gone along with the changes for economic reasons—he was resuming the precarious career of novelist after working as an editor for most of the decade. He wanted the novel to be a commercial success because he badly needed the money; he also wanted to remain with the prestigious house of Harper.

His publisher stuck by him through his next novel, *The Financier*, with its womanizing robber-baron hero, **Frank Cowperwood**. But the second volume in Dreiser's projected *Trilogy of Desire*, *The Titan*, went too far. Dreiser told H. L. Mencken that the publisher found his realism "too hard and uncompromising" (*D-M Letters*, 1: 132).

Dreiser's superman hero seduced too many women, but the muckraking aspect of the novel, the exposures of Cowperwood's unabashed financial chicanery, may also have made Harper executives nervous. That, at least, was the theory of Dreiser's secretary and sometime lover, **Anna Tatum**, who had picked up the gossip along Publisher Row. Harper was deeply in debt to the Morgan Bank and would not publish anything critical of it.

Even before *The Titan* affair Dreiser had had another brush with editorial censorship. A nonfiction book he wrote for the Century Company, *A Traveler at Forty*, was heavily bowdlerized. This was drawn from a trip Dreiser made to Europe ostensibly to research the travels of Cowperwood's real life prototype, **Charles T. Yerkes**. Several love affairs with professional and amateur ladies were described too graphically and had to go.

After the blowup with Harper, Dreiser found a more liberal publisher, the American branch of the British house **John Lane**, but his next novel, *The "Genius,"* ran afoul of the Society for the Suppression of Vice, now headed by **John Sumner**. This worthy had received complaints that the book was riddled with lewdness, profanity, and blasphemy and paid a call on John Lane, with a list of the offending passages and words. Rather than risk prosecution, the publisher withdrew all copies from the stores.

Dreiser was ready to sell the book himself and go to jail; he adamantly refused to cut the offending material, as H. L. Mencken advised him. The latter then mounted a campaign to obtain signatures of prominent American writers on a petition protesting the banning of *The "Genius."* The drive was a great success, with 458 signatures obtained, the first time American authors (many of whom disliked Dreiser and his books) had united in protest against censorship. The **Authors' League** executive council supported him after Dreiser appeared before it and warned about "a literary reign of terror" (Harold Hersey's notes, box 89, Dreiser Papers).

All of this had little effect on the de facto ban. Dreiser cursed Lane for not challenging Sumner and finally brought a friendly suit against his publisher for breach of contract, on the ground that the book was not legally obscene and was thus being wrongly withheld from the stores. The case went all the way up to New York's highest appellate court, which ducked the issue of whether the book was obscene, and so Sumner's ban stood. *The "Genius"* remained an under-the-counter item until 1923, when Dreiser's new publisher, **Horace Liveright**, a foe of censorship, fresh from leading a successful fight against passage of a "clean books" bill before the state legislature, issued it without objection from Sumner.

During the *"Genius"* campaign Mencken almost came to blows with Dreiser over the latter's play *The Hand of the Potter*, about a child molester. Mencken called the play pornographic and said its production would set back the *"Genius"* effort. Dreiser countered that he had handled the touchy subject discreetly, almost clinically. A writer, he said, must not choose his subjects to placate the Sumners of this world.

The de facto banning of *The "Genius"* had hurt Dreiser financially and psychologically. He had lost a fair sum in royalties. His fears of being banned (compounded by the atmosphere of wartime repression) had kept him from completing the *Trilogy of Desire* and stalled him on a new novel, *The Bulwark*, which, as then conceived, had a strong antireligious, anticensor message.

He did not have another battle with the censors until 1926, when his masterpiece *An American Tragedy* was taken off the shelves by Boston's Watch and Ward Society. Liveright challenged the ban, hiring two famous legal talents, Clarence Darrow and Arthur Garfield Hays, for the defense, but the predominantly Catholic jury needed only to find certain passages obscene, whatever the artistic context, and the case was lost. This time, the publicity helped make the *Tragedy* Dreiser's biggest-selling novel to date.

Then a new source of censorship promptly reared up—Hollywood. The producer Jesse Lasky had purchased the motion picture rights to *An American Tragedy* for a record $90,000, but objections by church people and the studio's uneasiness with Dreiser's portrayal of his young hero as not responsible for the murder of his girlfriend—a violation of the Hollywood code—delayed filming until 1931. (The Russian director **Sergei Eisenstein** had written an earlier script in which **capitalism** was the guilty party; it was rejected as communist propaganda.) In the 1940s Dreiser ran into similar problems after selling the film rights to *Sister Carrie*. The Breen Office objected to the story line in which a young woman sins and goes unpunished.

Dreiser's declining productivity as a novelist kept him out of any further censorship battles. His political activism in behalf of radical causes in the 1930s resulted in some controversial nonfiction books and made him a target of an ongoing Federal Bureau of Investigation (FBI) probe. In 1940 he published a strident, isolationist polemic titled *America Is Worth Saving*. It had been mainly ghostwritten by the radical journalist **Cedric Belfrage**, and its pro-communist, anti-British slant made the publishing house nervous. Eventually, another, more radical house brought it out

to damningly negative reviews. It was Dreiser's last battle, ending not with a bang but a sigh.

Further Reading

Kendrick, Walter. *The Secret Museum: Pornography in Modern Culture.* New York: Viking, 1987.

Robins, Natalie. *Alien Ink.* New York: Morrow, 1992.

West, James L. W., III. "The Composition and Publication of *Jennie Gerhardt*." *Jennie Gerhardt.* Philadelphia: University of Pennsylvania Press, 1992. 420–60.

Ziff, Larzer, *The American 1890s.* New York: Viking, 1966.

Richard Lingeman

"CHAINS." Experimental in its form and risqué in content, "Chains" was originally published as "Love" on 18 May 1919 in the *New York Tribune* after having been rejected by at least ten magazines. In December 1920 the story was published as "Chains" in the monthly *Live Stories*, and it reappeared in 1927 as the title story in *Chains: Lesser Novels and Stories* and was reprinted in 1992, with supplementary passages drawn from typescripts in the Dreiser Papers, in *Fulfilment and Other Tales of Women and Men*. Although its content challenged the conventional perceptions of love and marriage, the story's form completely defied traditional narrative techniques. As Joseph Griffin explains, the longer paragraphs provide insight into the protagonist's character and inner turmoil and thus supply the "story" of "Chains." The shorter, italicized sections briefly interrupt the internal narrative and allow the reader to observe the protagonist's interactions with the surrounding physical environment; at the same time, these sections advance the plot, demonstrating movement and charting the protagonist's progression toward his final destination (77).

On the train home from a business conference, forty-eight-year-old Upham Brainerd Garrison contemplates the painful presence of love in his life. Fourteen years before, he had been married to Jessica, but after a few weeks of marriage Jessica "seemed to realize that she had made a mistake" and eventually divorced Garrison. Years pass, and Garrison stumbles upon Idelle, a young woman half his age. Garrison is overcome by her beauty and seeks to possess her, but Idelle is not a woman easily possessed by any man: "She was too interested in other men, and always had been." After Garrison concedes that he will not "interfere" with her comings and goings, they marry, elevating Idelle's social status and granting Garrison a "showpiece," "something wherewith to arouse envy in other persons." These thoughts possess Garrison as he returns home to Idelle, who promised that she would be awaiting his arrival. Now seeing his situation as unbearable and as potentially damaging to his social position, Garrison determines that Idelle must learn to curb her appetite for "variety in life" and settle into a more appropriate role. When Garrison arrives home, he finds a note informing him that Idelle is at a party and that he should join her there. In a fury Garrison packs a bag, determined to leave his wayward wife. Once in the car, though, Garrison hesitates as he becomes aware of the reality of life without Idelle; he is ensnared by the "eternal lure of beauty and vitality" and knows that he is unlikely to attract another young woman at his age. Wearily defeated because he cannot abandon his pride, Garrison directs the driver to take him to the party.

Like many of the stories in the collection, "Chains" seems a cautionary tale. As the title suggests, love and marriage are chains that unnaturally bind two people together. Love leads to agony; and marriage, likewise, can bring only heartache. Garrison is shackled by his desire to possess the ideal woman, Idelle, and he believes that if he could harness his young wife's vivacity, he could effectively save the marriage and secure his position in society. While marriage to Garrison does not hinder Idelle's proclivity for varietism or individual freedom, the story does demonstrate Dreiser's philosophy that marriage is antithetical to happiness and suggests that those who are bound by marriage suffer.

Donna Packer-Kinlaw

CHAINS: LESSER NOVELS AND STORIES. Published on 30 April 1927 by **Boni & Liveright** and followed two weeks later by a special signed and numbered edition, *Chains* was Dreiser's second short story collection and one that enjoyed moderate success, selling 12,000 copies in the first year.

A brief and enigmatic Foreword introduces the dominant theme of the book, namely, that human beings are "chained" by external and internal forces and therefore limited in their ability to effect change and liberate themselves. Indeed, the first story, "Sanctuary," traces how economic and social constrictions lead Madeleine Kinsella into prostitution and eventually into the self-imposed seclusion of a convent. Although she finds a seemingly idyllic sanctuary, the cost is the loss of her autonomy; and, in this way, Dreiser undercuts the notion that choice necessarily equals freedom.

Such an illusory escape is not possible in "The Hand," in which a prospector is haunted, assaulted, and eventually strangled to death by the ghostly hand of the business partner he murdered years earlier. The doctors conclude, however, that his **supernatural** claims were delusional and that he actually murdered himself. By complicating this seemingly straightforward ghost story, Dreiser leads readers to question the cause of Davidson's condition—is it really spirits or merely repressed guilt? A similar tactic occurs in "St. Columba and the River," in which a worker digging a tunnel under the Hudson River credits his survival after three cave-ins to St. Columba's intervention, a conclusion that Dreiser challenges, implying instead that **chance** or indifferent nature is actually in control of one's fate. This theme continues in "The 'Mercy' of God," in which the narrator is troubled by the story of a young woman whose ugliness and desire to feel special lead to her belief that she has exquisite beauty. The narrator tries to believe, but cannot commit to, his friend's explanation that nature spared the woman pain by giving her this delusion.

Although characters may resolve to liberate themselves, that determination does not last, especially in the title story, in which a jealous, forty-eight-year-old businessman debates leaving his younger, more active wife. In the end, however, his fear of being alone and his submissive attachment to her do not allow him to extricate himself. In "Convention," an adulterous newspaper reporter abandons his affair when it becomes public knowledge. Consumed by his desire for social approval, he returns to his wife in order to save face. In "Fulfilment," a wife laments her marriage to her current husband, whom she married largely for money and security; but, in spite of her regrets, she resolves to accept her situation. Lastly, the dissatisfied wife of a suspicious, narrow-minded clerk in "The Shadow" dreams of, but ultimately does not achieve, the happy ending promised in the novels of a writer with whom she enters into a brief affair.

"Khat" and "The Prince Who Was a Thief," the only stories in the collection not previously published in magazines, both depict elderly and poor wandering storytellers ridiculed and abandoned by their people. For Ibn Abdullah, the scorn he receives and his inability to obtain the drug khat lead him to walk out into the desert and lay himself down to die. For Gazzar-al-Din, the telling of his magical tale brings him very little monetary compensation. The fate of the artist, in Dreiser's eyes, is to be at the mercy of a fickle public, a not-so-surprising position for the man who had gone in a quarter century from the failure of *Sister Carrie* to the success of *An American Tragedy*.

Like *An American Tragedy*, "Typhoon" presents a protagonist who is unfit to make wise decisions because of restrictive, overprotective parents. In this case, Ida Zobel ends up seduced, impregnated, and abandoned by the son of a well-to-do family. After fatally shooting him, she is absolved by the law and by public sympathy; but, confused by the absence of punishment, she drowns herself. The successful, middle-aged factory owner of "The Old Neighborhood" struggles as well with the consequences of poor decisions as he strolls through a run-down part of town where years earlier he had abandoned his devoted, but unambitious, wife. He reminisces and attempts to justify his actions but finds only dissatisfaction with the high cost of his wealth. Much of the same applies as well to J. H. Osterman, the ruthless financier of "Victory," who in old age attempts to atone for his past business dealings by establishing a nationwide system of homes for orphans. Before he can put this into action, though, he dies, his plan thwarted by forces larger than himself.

A similar pattern of poetic justice occurs in "Phantom Gold," in which a poor farmer is secretly offered a large sum of money for his zinc-rich land. Because of his own backstabbing and deception, though, he himself is cheated, receiving far less than what the land is worth. Likewise, the ambitious clerk of "Marriage—for One" seeks to intellectually "emancipate" his conventionally minded wife but finds the tables turned when she becomes a deeper and more well-rounded thinker than he.

After publication, several reviewers found the stories in the collection weak and indeed "lesser," while others, such as Carl Van Doren, claimed that they were powerful, describing several as miniature American tragedies. In some cases, Dreiser's stylistic experiments do fall flat, particularly in "Chains" and "Fulfilment," where his use of italicized breaks to illustrate a character's passing thoughts does more to upset the continuity of the narrative. Similar criticism could be made of the overuse of detail in "Khat," the awkward intrusion of dramatic form toward the end of "The Hand," and the various perspectives on J. H. Osterman in "Victory." Nonetheless, even though he may fall short at times, we see at least a Dreiser willing to take chances creatively and who does succeed in such powerful stories as "Sanctuary" and "Typhoon" in bringing the narratives and the themes to life without reducing them to thinly veiled illustrations of his theories.

Monty Kozbial Ernst

CHANCE. Whether one accepts Dreiser's critical reputation as a naturalist writer or his own self-image as a realist, both modes often subtly rely on chance to advance plot and to comment more subtextually on the interaction of character with the fictional world. Traditional definitions of literary **naturalism** usually enumerate forces that influence the lives of characters; heredity and environment are the most common, but the wills of stronger human agents, the power of Nature itself, and perhaps even one's own unconscious fears and desires

could be added. Chance is essential to any comprehensive list. It may be broadly defined as any random occurrence, but perhaps a more useful understanding may be reached by eliminating what it is *not*, that is, happenstance or coincidence that is not the direct result of a character's willful action *or* determined by other external forces. Three examples should suffice to demonstrate the pattern of Dreiser's lifelong incorporation of chance at the most basic levels in his major works, initiating events as crucial and diverse as Carrie Meeber's decision to leave her sister **Minnie Hanson** to become a traveling salesman's mistress in Chapter 7 of *Sister Carrie*, the discovery of **Frank Cowperwood's** misuse of city loan funds late in *The Financier*, and Clyde Griffiths's murder of his pregnant lover **Roberta Alden** at the end of Book 2 of *An American Tragedy*:

In the store they found that shine and rustle of new things which immediately laid hold of Carrie's heart. Under the influence of a good dinner and Drouet's radiating presence, the scheme proposed seemed feasible. She looked about and picked a jacket like the one she had admired at The Fair. When she got it in her hand, it seemed so much nicer. The saleswoman helped her on with it, and *by accident* it fitted perfectly. . . .

"That's the thing," said Drouet. "Now pay for it."

"It's nine dollars," said Carrie.

"That's all right—take it," said Drouet.

She reached in her purse and took out one of the bills. (emphasis added)

Carrie, an eighteen-year-old and inexperienced country girl, has fallen into the guiding hands of "masher" Drouet during the train ride to Chicago and reencountered him while eking out a miserable existence as factory worker and boarder with her indifferent sister and brother-in-law. Her spending of part of the twenty dollars he has given her signals a far more significant decision than the casualness of the scene implies; indeed, Carrie has entered an unspoken agreement to his "scheme" of subsidizing her in her own apartment as a kept woman. Her judgment has been impaired—"under the influence"—not only by the glitter of worldly objects and Drouet's exploitation of their appeal but by her willingness to go along with the sweep of circumstance, becoming what Dreiser calls a "wisp in the wind."

[T]he moment you introduce the elements of chance, accident, or fate into any human situation such as this you immediately arouse human curiosity to the fullest. Fate, chance, accident in the guise of the Chicago fire had made Cowperwood and Stener alleged felons. The newspapers had already freely commented on how strange it was, and yet how true to life that a fire in Chicago, nearly a thousand miles away, should have made a criminal of a man here in Philadelphia.

Frank Cowperwood, in stark contrast to Carrie Meeber of the earlier novel, is a financier with an overdeveloped sense of his own free agency, so much so that he imagines the societal rules that bind other people cannot touch him. His illegal brokering methods literally come to light in a way he could never have anticipated, as a result of the fire and resulting widespread financial calamity and subsequent insurance investigations. Perhaps Dreiser's narrator conflates chance and fate here because the distinction hardly matters. In either case, the fire has erupted as the countering force to hubris, the overreliance on one's own will to power.

[A]s she drew near him, seeking to take his hand in hers and the camera from him in order to put it in the boat, he flinging out at her, but *not even then with any intention* to do other than free himself of her—her touch—her pleading—consoling sympathy—her presence forever—God!

Yet (the camera still unconsciously held tight) pushing at her with so much vehemence as not only to strike her lips and nose and chin with it, but to throw her back . . . [and he] rising and reaching half to assist or recapture her and half to apologize for the unintended blow—yet in so doing completely capsizing the boat—himself and Roberta being as instantly thrown into the water. (emphasis added)

In his acknowledged 1925 masterpiece, Dreiser shows how choice is available only through windows of opportunity, while external forces operate with progressive force when one refuses to choose. Clyde Griffiths, in his attempt to move onward and upward in American society by abandoning factory-girl Roberta Alden for heiress **Sondra Finchley**, has responded to the former's announcement of her pregnancy by delaying action over and over again. Spurred on by base impulses, he plans her elaborate murder and actually drifts to the crucial moment of decision. However, a paralysis sets in on Big Bittern Lake, and Roberta's wonder at his anguished countenance sets the preceding events in motion. Following the girl's drowning, Clyde's evil "Efrit" voice even announces to him that "despite your fear, your cowardice, this—this—has been done for you."

A commonality in the preceding examples is the *mixing* of the forces of human choice, "fate," and chance, a metaphysical amalgam that novelist Dreiser, himself a onetime newspaperman, considered the ultimate verisimilitude: "true to life."

Shawn St. Jean

"CHANGE." Appearing as the second essay in his collection of philosophical inquiries, *Hey Rub-a-Dub-Dub*, "Change" was first published in the February 1916 issue of *Revolt* before being reprinted in *Pagan* (September 1916), the *New York Call* (26 January 1918), and the *Chicago Exam-*

iner (30 March 1918). "Change" may be read as Dreiser's concise exposition of his view about the nature of change in the world. Though several reviewers claimed the entire collection exhibited "nothing startlingly new in his analyses" (*Philadelphia Press*) and that "[Dreiser] is both dull and repetitious" (*New York Evening Post*), others played up Dreiser's "matured thought" and his "iconoclastic theories that really shock by their frankness if not their novelty" (*Detroit News*). Many considered "Change" to be "one of the most significant contributions . . . a composite of question and answer" (*Brooklyn Eagle*; rpt. in Salzman 372–75). Though Robert Elias notes that the title *Hey Rub-a-Dub-Dub* "mean[s] nothing in itself and hence suggested that life was without meaning" (*Apostle* 211), the subtitle, "A Book of the Mystery and Wonder and Terror of Life," points to the unknowability of life, and the thesis in this essay is captured in his statement, "All we can know is that we cannot know."

Having moved with Helen Richardson from New York to California, where he lived from 1919 to 1922, Dreiser entered a new intellectual phase, and critics have noted several books that influenced his thinking: George W. Crile's *Man: An Adaptive Mechanism* (1916); H. W. Frink's *Morbid Fears and Compulsions: Their Psychology and Psychoanalytic Treatment* (1918); John Watson's *Psychology from the Standpoint of a Behaviorist* (1919); and Jacques Loeb's *The Organism as a Whole: From a Physiochemical Viewpoint* (1916). In *Hey Rub-a-Dub-Dub*, Dreiser takes on perennial themes of justice, truth, values, art, economics, politics, and ideology without firmly resolving any debates. Nor does he assume any one privileged epistemology; teleological, eschatological, and cosmological topics are rather "deconstructed," deemed relative. According to "Change," one of his early

speculations, the universe is inscrutable and one need only go along for the ride rather than resist or fight it. Indeed, "[t]he caution, sprung from somewhere, to keep an open mind is well-grounded in Nature's tendency to change. Not to cling too pathetically to a religion or a system of government or a theory of morals or a method of living, but to be ready to abandon at a moment's notice is the apparent teaching of the ages—to be able to step out free and willing to accept new and radically different conditions. This apparently is the ideal state for the human mind."

Kathy Frederickson

CHAPMAN, FREDERIC (?–?). English reader for the **John Lane Company**, Chapman ranked Dreiser as "the leading American novelist" in recommending publication of *The Titan* as the "most important chance" to enhance Lane's reputation in the United States since establishment of its New York branch. Based on his sense of literary freedom in England, Chapman next recommended that Lane publish *The "Genius,"* but Chapman's more influential service to Dreiser was as an editor of works Lane accepted for publication.

In carrying out his responsibility of editing style, Chapman deleted passages of "woman stuff" from *The Titan*. In editing *The "Genius,"* Chapman played a more shaping role. On the typescript edited for publication of the first edition, Dreiser's was the initial revisory hand (his alterations made in black or blue pencil and blue crayon), followed by Chapman's (uniformly in red ink), then **Floyd Dell's** (in green ink, black pencil, and typewriting). Even were it not for his trademark red ink, the content of many Chapman comments identifies them as his: "incomprehensible, to an Englishman," "simile meaningless to an English ear," for example.

In May 1914, Chapman wrote Dreiser to place at his disposal a considerable "knowledge of minutiae" useful for depicting details of the period. By the end of July, Chapman returned the typescript, with the assurance that he had touched no expression Dreiser put into the mouth of any character but had concentrated his editing on ensuring that the narrator's style conveyed an appropriate tone and, "with the fewest possible changes," conformed to standard usage.

Chapman's revisions appear on nearly every page of the extant portion of the typescript (Chapters 32–104). He corrected spelling—usually typist's errors, as comparison with the holograph makes clear; substituted more suitable diction; changed passive voice of verbs to active; deleted sentences, paragraphs, and series of paragraphs. Sometimes Chapman recast a passage to provide smoother texture to Dreiser's prose. Though urging greater selectivity in development, Chapman appreciated Dreiser's need to document character and event with a full measure of supporting details. In a letter to Dreiser praising the "complete realization" of major characters, Chapman explained that he had pruned both excess elaboration of subsidiary figures and also authorial rumination and interpretation, so that the characters' actions and words could better speak for themselves.

The typescript as revised first by Dreiser, then by Chapman, next by Floyd Dell, and again, finally, by Dreiser was the fair copy for the galleys. Chapman's and Dell's combined cutting amounted to approximately 20,000 words; the bulk of Dell's deletions consisted of paragraphs Chapman had already marked for removal. Following publication, Chapman paid Dreiser the compliment, "You could teach most of your contemporaries to observe, to co-ordinate, and to deduce" (1 March 1916, Dreiser Papers).

Further Reading

Oldani, Louis J. "Dreiser's 'Genius' in the Making: Composition and Revision." *Studies in Bibliography* 47 (1994): 230–52.

Louis J. Oldani

CHICAGO. Among the various cities Dreiser lived in—St. Louis, Toledo, Cleveland, New York, Pittsburgh, and Buffalo—none had a more enduring impact on his writings than Chicago. Chicago was for Dreiser what Paris was for **Balzac**—a source of inspiration and a vital subject for literature. This modern industrial city served Dreiser as a form of shorthand for a number of themes. Dealing with stock brokerage, the railroad system, urban architecture, and wolfish competition was one way of getting to the heart of the subject of Chicago and to capture this new city in its full complexity. Dreiser's observation of, and experience in, Chicago gave him a good knowledge of the modern city, although his discovery of what the city meant would change and would become tinged with disillusionment.

Dreiser's keen interest in the capital of the Midwest was typical of this period of rapid growth. As a boy, he recalled in his autobiography *Dawn*, he read with eagerness Eugene Field's column about Chicago in the *Chicago Daily News* and was "fascinated by descriptions . . . in the Chicago daily papers of . . . city life." Dreiser refused to be trapped in an impoverished Roman Catholic family in the small Indiana town of Evansville and longed for the miraculous big city as an escape. He was only one of thousands of hopeful young Americans who migrated from small towns to Chicago in pursuit of the American Dream and in search of new frontiers.

Frederick Jackson Turner's famous "Frontier Thesis" signaled the closing of the frontier and the inauguration of an era of urban development. Rather than the Wild West, it is the city that began to capture the American imagination. Chicago, in particular, promised fabulous success and, as he noted in *Dawn*, Dreiser saw in it "the land of promise, a fabled realm of milk and honey." The reconstruction of Chicago after the fire that consumed it in 1871 gave it a new character, while the World's Columbian Exposition of 1893 brought it to the attention of the nation. At the turn of the century, Chicago's population exceeded 1 million and was growing faster than any other city in America. Chicago was not just the up-and-coming center of the Midwest but the quintessential American City. It was the example par excellence of the rise of the modern industrial city. As Dreiser described it in *Sister Carrie*, Chicago was "a giant magnet drawing to itself, from all quarters, the hopeful and the hopeless—those who had their fortune yet to make and those whose fortunes and affairs had reached a disastrous climax elsewhere."

Dreiser was only twelve years old when his mother first took him to Chicago. His initial encounter with the big city had a long-lasting effect on him, so much so that it became a motif in several of his novels. When we encounter **Frank Cowperwood** in *The Titan*, he is on a business trip from Philadelphia to Chicago, seeking to become the titan of Chicago's financial world. This same scene is repeated in *The "Genius"* as **Eugene Wilta** boards a train to Chicago looking forward to a new life in the city. The extended entrance to Chicago by train at the beginning of *Sister Carrie* reproduces even more forcefully Dreiser's first impressions of the city: "To the child, the genius with imagination, or the wholly untraveled, the approach to a great city for the first time is a wonderful thing." Chicago is in many ways an unreal city. It is a dream world. As a small-town boy, Dreiser was taken by the energy and glamour of the big city. In *Dawn*, he describes his initial uncritical wonder in front of the extraordinary spectacle of the city: "In Evansville there was no such congestion, no such moving tide of people, no such enthusiasm for living. I was lost in a vapor of something so rich that it was like food to the hungry, odorous and meaningful like flowers to those who love. Life was glorious and sensate, avid and gay, shimmering and tingling." Dreiser's sense of helplessness in front of Chicago's awe and force is powerfully depicted in *Sister Carrie* as the adventuresome young girl from Columbia City discovers the city and falls prey to its seductive powers. Chicago is a "wonder," Drouet tells Carrie, who soon becomes a victim of the city's hypnotic influence. "The life of the streets continued for a long time to interest Carrie. She never wearied of wondering where the people in the cars were going or what their enjoyments were. Her imagination trod a very narrow round, always winding up at points which concerned money, looks, clothes, or enjoyment." Carrie is infatuated with the city and enchanted with its marvels—its shops and windows, its looming buildings and endless streets, its hotels and restaurants, its theaters and halls, its vitality and its enthusiasm, and its sounds and movements. Chicago is a tumultuous city that throbs with life and teems with people; Chicago is a "great sea of life" filled with "warm-blooded humanity," so much so that to "join in the great hurrying throng becomes a desire which the mind can scarcely resist."

As a journalist and as a novelist, Dreiser had a keen eye for details and a deep interest in everyday scenes and situations—in fact, life as it unfolds in the metropolis. Chicago appealed to him both as a place and as a condition. He tried to capture the verities of the city and to make sense out of his urban environment. However, Chicago was not only a subject of wonder and excitement but also a source of anxiety and disappointment. Dreiser's optimistic view of the modern metropolis was tempered partly by his own financial insecurities. The various jobs he held—dishwasher, laundry-driver, rent-collector—led him to see Chicago from the perspective of the underprivileged and the poor. It opened his eyes to the darker and unhappy side of the American urban reality. His career as a newspaper reporter put him in even closer contact with the sordidness of Chicago. Dreiser became interested in the cruelty, ugliness, and enigma of life in the city. For instance, his article on Chicago's vilest slum—"Cheyenne, Haunt of Misery and Crime"—describes the ways in which the poor, mostly immigrant families are trapped in a horrible life of vice and degradation, and many of his characters are reduced to a life of poverty, struggle, and misery (*Chicago Globe* 24 July 1892; rpt. *Journalism* 4–7). Dreiser was most disenchanted with the social and economic differences he observed in the city, namely, the disparity between the opulent world of the wealthy and the ordeals of those dying in the slums, between the social ideals of rural America and the social practices in the city. The startling contrasts between wealth and poverty that Dreiser witnessed in the city shook his certitude about a moral order, and he soon realized that the chaotic world of Chicago can't be rationalized, at least not by the conventional ideals he held as a small boy. In *Dawn*, Dreiser distances himself from his youthful idealization of Chicago in a way that dramatizes the urban condition: "The city of which I am now about to write never was on land or sea; or if it appears to have outlines of reality, they are but shadow to the glory that was in my own mind. . . . The city of which I sing was not of land or sea or any time or place. Look for it in vain! I can scarcely find it in my own soul now." The Chicago Dreiser came to know and write about is a city that was dominated by irrational forces; it is a city that left its dwellers baffled about their urban experience and their place in a new, but uncertain, world that often denied understanding.

Further Reading

Lehan, Richard Daniel. *The City in Literature: An Intellectual and Cultural History.* Berkeley: University of California Press, 1998.
Smith, Carl S. *Chicago and the American Literary Imagination, 1880–1920.* Chicago: University of Chicago Press, 1984.
Tandt, Christophe Den. *The Urban Sublime in American Literary Naturalism.* Urbana: University of Illinois Press, 1998.

Mohamed Zayani

CHRISTIAN SCIENCE. In 1905, Theodore Dreiser's wife Sara, who had been a Methodist, became a Christian Scientist and encouraged her husband to explore the **religion.** And Dreiser, interested in any religion, philosophy, or science that might offer answers to life's mysteries, studied the teachings of Mary Baker Eddy. Christian Science would have appealed to Dreiser for two reasons. First, it offers a scientific or logical approach to metaphysical issues. Second, the Christian Science religion asserts a monistic view of existence that parallels the teachings of Eastern religions—Christian Scientists believe that the physical or corporeal world is an illusion; thus, illness and suffering are illusions. Christian Scientists and Christian Science practitioners heal ailments by recognizing that humans are spiritually perfect beings. Not only would

Dreiser have been fascinated by its metaphysical beliefs, but he would also have appreciated the possibility that the religion might cure his many ailments.

In the concluding chapters of Dreiser's autobiographical novel The "Genius," the influences of Christian Science are particularly noticeable, and these passages offer insight into Dreiser's attitude toward the religion. When artist **Eugene Witla** faces the loss of his wife, Angela, he and Angela turn to a Christian Science practitioner, Mrs. Johns, but the practitioner cannot save Angela, who dies because she "had no real faith in it." After losing his wife and after his lover **Suzanne Dale** leaves him, Witla battles depression, and he personally turns to Mrs. Johns, but he admits to himself that he has "no faith in religious conclusions of any kind"; still, he cannot overcome a "metaphysical urge." The narrator summarizes Witla's attitude toward Christian Science beautifully: "He went from what might be described as almost a belief in Christian Science to almost a belief that a devil ruled the world." Finally, Witla admits that he visited Mrs. Johns because she had a "motherly soul" that reminded him of his childhood. That Dreiser ends The "Genius" with an exploration of the Christian Science religion demonstrates his interest in metaphysical matters, an interest that did not please literary critics such as H. L. Mencken, who, in his essay "A Literary Behemoth" (Smart Set, December 1915), attacks the novel, especially the role of the Christian Science practitioner.

Near the end of his life, Dreiser's second wife, Helen, also studied the Christian Science faith (and other religions), attempting to develop Dreiser's spirituality. Helen convinced Dreiser to attend several Christian Science readings, a sign that Dreiser's "metaphysical urges" continued until his death. For Dreiser, the Christian Science monism that dismisses the world of the senses, the corporeal world, as only an illusion would have delighted him, but these spiritual principles seldom guided his behavior. Dreiser was drawn to the teachings of Mary Baker Eddy, as he was drawn to the ideas of **Sigmund Freud**, Karl Marx, **Charles Fort** and **Jacques Loeb**, because he wanted answers to life's mysteries, and he was happy to explore all possibilities.

Further Reading

Eddy, Mary Baker. Science and Health with Key to the Scriptures. 1875. Boston: First Church of Christ, Scientist, 1994.

Roark Mulligan

"CHRISTMAS IN THE TENEMENTS." Unlike Dreiser's other sketches of tenement life, such as "The Tenement Toilers" and "The Transmigration of the Sweat Shop" (Puritan, July 1900; rpt. in SMA 2), this article celebrates the poor's enjoyment of the Christmas season despite the wretchedness of their lives. The poor labor for an "illusion of pleasure" and "endure a hard, unnatural existence." Dreiser is particularly interested in a section of tenement streets where people of all ages and nationalities throng, selling and buying Christmas paraphernalia. A crowd of Italians, Jews, and Bohemians swarms over the sidewalks to buy meats and other foods at modest prices. After six o'clock, hordes of factory and shop workers, as well as an army of shop girls and boys, pour into the brightly lit street. "It is a shabby throng at best, commonplace in garb and physical appearance," Dreiser observes, "but rich in the qualities of youth and enthusiasm, than which the world holds nothing more valuable." Dreiser was struck, in particular, by the demeanor of the poor, "that lightness of spirit and movement which is the evidence of a long strain of labor suddenly relaxed."

Dreiser's portrayal focuses on two families, Bohemian and Italian. The Bohemian family spends three of their twelve dollars' weekly income on rent and six dollars on food, clothing, and utilities. They struggle to save the remaining three dollars, but illness or other misfortunes invariably claim it, leaving little to invest in the celebration of Christmas. The Italian family lives crowded in a two-room tenement. In a corner of the combination kitchen, dining room, workshop, and bedroom, occupied by a bench and table on other days, has been set up a crib in which a doll-like impersonation of the Infant Christ reposes. Several candles, a broken plaster-of-paris lion, a cheap china dog, and a few other pieces of statuary accompany this poor representation of the Nativity.

In the late evening the tenement district is enlivened by a Christmas dance at a Bowery dancing-hall. The male participants all look ambitious: "all designing; the highest conception of life being not marriage, but a vain cavalierlike success with women." The maidens, variously called "goils" or "rags," are eagerly awaiting pleasure and excitement. On such a night, young men and women of the tenements, forgetting the oppressive world of drudgery and firmly believing that "joy is a tangible, obtainable thing," come out and dance away the waning hours of the evening. "Unloose, then, the chains of your misery," Dreiser apostrophizes. "Fling hence the habiliments of your woes. East, drink, and be merry, for to-morrow you must die."

"Christmas in the Tenements" first appeared in *Harper's Weekly* (6 December 1902) before being reprinted, in considerably shortened form, in *The Color of a Great City*. The *Harper's Weekly* version is included in *SMA 2*.

Yoshinobu Hakutani

CLARK, CLARA (1909–). Born in the Germantown section of Philadelphia, Clara Clark came from a prosperous Pennsylvania Quaker family whose origins in America are in the seventeenth century. She attended the Germantown Friend's School and later graduated from Wheaton College in Norton, Massachusetts. In 1931, after reading the newly published *Dawn* and then *An American Tragedy*, she wrote Dreiser to tell him how much the books had moved her. She had identified with his quest to find beauty and his revelations of the pain and shame he had felt at her age. When he invited her to visit him in New York, she accepted. This first meeting began her four-year relationship with the sixty-year-old novelist. Acting primarily as his secretary, she also eventually worked as editor and sounding board for what Dreiser thought was to be his next book, *The Stoic*. In addition she edited his articles and a book of poems. In 1941 she encountered the Oxford Group, a small, but worldwide, society that advocated personal spiritual growth as a way of building a better society. There she met her future husband, William Jaeger, whom she married in 1946. William Jaeger is known internationally for his work with the Moral Re-Armament Association. He helped expand the mission of the Oxford Group by focusing attention on the labor union movement in America and England. In 1988 under her married name, Clara Jaeger, she published *Philadelphia Rebel: The Education of a Bourgeoisie*, which includes a detailed account of her time with Dreiser. In 1995 she published *Never to Lose My Vision: The Story of Bill Jaeger*, a biography of her husband. At this time she lives a short distance outside London in the village of Knebworth.

Thomas P. Riggio

COAKLEY, ELIZABETH (1903–1985). Dreiser first met Elizabeth Kearney Coakley at the 1933 funeral of her brother, Patrick Kearney, the actor turned playwright whom Dreiser and **Horace Liveright** chose to dramatize *An American Tragedy*. Shortly afterward, her husband died, and Coakley moved to Hollywood, hoping to find work writing for the film industry. She renewed her acquaintance with Dreiser after he moved to Hollywood in late 1938, became his secretary in 1940, and, according to Helen Dreiser, was also his "unofficial driver." Helen was jealous of Dreiser's attentions to the younger woman, and **Robert Elias** argues that his involvement "disturb[ed] his creative mood and involv[ed] him in complications and resentments, ruses and inner turmoil, which destroyed [his] concentration," particularly toward the completion of *The Bulwark* (*Apostle* 291). As he did for many of his women friends, Dreiser encouraged Coakley's literary ambitions, and she published an article entitled "Sugar Babies" in the December 1940 issue of the magazine *Hygeia*. In turn, Coakley worked with Dreiser on a series of screen adaptations of some of his short stories, such as "Arda Cavanaugh," "Box Office" "Cinderella the Second," "Solution," and "The Tithe of the Lord." Coakley married Robert Stanley Hicks in September 1944, and, as was his habit, Dreiser remained concerned and involved after her marriage took place. In 1945, just five days before his death, Dreiser spent Christmas Eve with Elizabeth and her children, watching her children decorate their Christmas tree and listening to Elizabeth play the harp.

John W. Reynolds

THE COLOR OF A GREAT CITY. These thirty-eight sketches of New York City as Dreiser experienced it between the years of 1900 to approximately 1915 combine his skills as a reporter with his growing awareness of the vast social contrasts in America that that city exemplified for him. Published by **Boni & Liveright** on 6 December 1923 and illustrated with brown ink drawings by C. B. Falls, this collection was greatly overshadowed by the much brisker sales of a recently reissued novel, *The "Genius,"* at a time when Dreiser was publishing almost a book a year. The timing of its publication and the greater critical and popular attention given to Dreiser's major novels undoubtedly diminished the recognition this work deserves. Some twenty of the sketches in this volume had previously been published in newspapers and magazines; the remainder either existed in draft or were composed for this volume. In his Foreword Dreiser explains that as a young man in the 1890s he spent much time walking through the ethnic neighborhoods and the railroad yards and along the waterfronts of the city, lacking the means to observe first-hand the more glamorous pursuits New York had to offer. Not until approximately 1904, however, when the editor of a New York newspaper asked Dreiser for "some small local stuff" to fill in between the paper's more lurid feature articles, did he begin some of the sketches. After World War I, Dreiser recalls, when he realized how fast the New York of his first acquaintance was vanishing, he felt compelled to complete the sketches and collect them into one volume. "[T]he city, as I see it, was more varied and arresting and, after its fashion, poetic and even idealistic then than it is now," Dreiser writes in the Foreword. For Dreiser the color of the great city is sepia, somber hues contrasted by patches of light, as in an old photograph. The sketches take the reader to "astounding areas of poverty and of beggary" but also impel one to stop and marvel at the architectural wonders at Fifth Avenue ("The City Awakes") and at Broadway and Forty-Second Street ("The City of My Dreams"), at the hopes and aspirations of the working poor ("Six O'clock," "The Realization of an Ideal"), and at the loss of those dreams ("The Rivers of the Nameless Dead").

The Color of a Great City spends little time on the glitter of New York, however, beyond the two opening sketches, "The City of My Dreams" and "The City Awakes," both "panoramic shots," to use a cameraman's terms. The book opens and closes with images of death. "The City of My Dreams" evokes New York before it has awakened in the morning. In the first paragraph Dreiser writes, "It was an amazing city, so far-flung, so beautiful, so dead." The last sentence of the book, describing those who have drowned or committed suicide in New York's waters, reads, "They have proved the uncharitableness of the island of beauty." In between are thirty-six sketches that are, Dreiser explains, "the very antithesis, I think, of that glitter and glister that made the social life of that day so superior. Its shadow, if you will, its reverse face." The sketches are marked by a certain detachment from his subjects. Yoshinobu Hakutani suggests this detachment may be the result of **Spencer's** influence: "Dreiser could now theorize in the light of Spencer's concept that man's existence is a balance between opposing forces and interests. Dreiser's interpretation of this idea was that without contrast there is no life. . . . He could see life whole, yet now without the personal involvement of his previous years" (*Young Dreiser* 125–26). Dreiser's detachment serves another purpose, however, and this is to bring to the foreground the injustices of what are usually considered the everyday circumstances of life in the city. From "The Toilers in the Tenements," in which Dreiser notes that the sons and daughters of the hardworking poor are taught from the cradle to value wealth above all—a philosophy Dreiser condemned in more detail later in *An American Tragedy*—to "The Track Walker," in which he calls into question the pitiful wages that are often paid to the human beings who hold our lives and safety in their hands, Dreiser frequently keeps his own emotional response in the background in order to foreground his social critique. The voice in many of the sketches is reportorial, factual, uninvolved, yet through the use of carefully selected details Dreiser evokes an emotional response in the reader. Two of the sketches, "On Being Poor" and "A Wayplace of the Fallen," describe Dreiser's own descent into depression and poverty in 1903. Unspoken but ever present are Dreiser's own fear of failure in the Darwinian struggle he chronicles, of perhaps becoming one of the "nameless dead" who float on New York's waters and eventually are washed out to sea.

Critical reception of *The Color of a Great City* was generally good, with New York critics somewhat more mixed in their praise than the out-of-state newspapers. "No writer has as yet done justice to New York, probably none ever will," stated the *New York Times Book Review*. "It may be that many readers—since the book is a picture and not a tract—will feel that the author concerns himself too much with the bread line, the unemployed, the pushcart peddlers, the frequenters of the park benches. But it is a book that makes excellent reading; and it is immensely humane. And the illustrations by C. B. Falls are excellent" (rpt. in Salzman 125–26). H. L. Mencken, in the *Baltimore Evening Sun*, opined, "Dreiser, as everyone knows, is not much interested in gilded revelries. It is the life of humble folk that attracts him. Here he presents it in his patient, painstaking manner, as it was at the turn of the century. It is not a very exciting book, but there is something of the glamour and something of the poetry of the New York that is no more" (rpt. in Salzman 428). David Karsner, in the *New York Tribune*, wrote that "there is everything in *The Color of a Great City* to please the Dreiserians and nothing to annoy the Watch and Ward Society" (rpt. in Salzman 430). More enthusiastic reviews appeared in the *Christian Science Monitor, Dallas News, Austin Statesman, Davenport Times*, and the *Liberator*, which wrote in its July 1924 edition, "It was a young Dreiser who wrote the series of sketches, character studies and mood impressions, gathered between the covers of this book. But it was a Dreiser with an ear delicately attuned to the song of the city, an eye expressive to its many varied colors, and a youthful soul, leaping and buoyant in its reactions to the poetry and music and tragedy found everywhere within a great city" (rpt. in Salzman 434). Perhaps Dreiser's most ardent supporters were Russian. Gosizdat, the state publishing house, was favorably impressed with *The Color of a Great City* and its indictment of **capitalism**. Richard Lingeman notes that an abridged edition of this book and *Twelve Men* appeared in Russia without Dreiser's consent, but he later worked out an agreement with the publisher (Lingeman 2: 229).

However overshadowed by his major novels, *The Color of a Great City*, in its humanity and detail, as well as in Dreiser's articulation of his social critique, still deserves attention at the turn of the twenty-first century, a photo album among the novels.

See also separate entries on "The Bowery Mission," "Bums," "Christmas in the Tenements," "The Log of a Harbor Pilot" (as "The Log of an Ocean Pilot"), "On Being Poor," "The Pushcart Man," "The Rivers of the Nameless Dead," "The Toilers of the Tenements" (as "The Tenement Toilers"), "The Track Walker," "A Wayplace of the Fallen," "When the Sails Are Furled," and "Whence the Song."

Nancy McIlvaine Donovan

"THE COLOR OF TO-DAY." This article about Dreiser's friendship with the painter **William Louis Sonntag** first appeared in *Harper's Weekly* (14 December 1901), before being republished, with many stylistic revisions, as "W. L. S." in *Twelve Men*. The *Harper's Weekly* version was reprinted in *SMA 1*.

Dreiser's acquaintance with Sonntag began when, as editor of *Ev'ry Month*, Dreiser paid a visit to Sonntag's studio to inquire whether the artist would do an illustration of city life for the Christmas issue of the magazine. He had earlier been attracted to Sonntag not only by reputation but also by his colored drawings depicting the night scenes of New York that appeared in one of the Sunday newspapers. These pictures, in Dreiser's recollection, "represented the spectacular scenes which the citizen and the stranger most delight in—Madison Square in a drizzle; the Bowery lighted by a thousand lamps and crowded with 'L' and surface cars; Sixth Avenue looking north from Fourteenth Street."

Dreiser's first impression of Sonntag was of "a small, wiry, lean-looking individual arrayed in a bicycle suit, whose countenance could be best described as wearing a perpetual look of astonishment. . . . His forehead was high, his good eye alert, his hair sandy-colored and tousled, and his whole manner indicated thought, feeling, remarkable nervous energy, and above all, a rasping and jovial sort of egotism." Like Dreiser himself, Sonntag "knew he had talent." Sonntag struck Dreiser as "slightly affected," and, like Dreiser, he "was altogether full of his own hopes and ambitions." Sonntag was versatile and well-read, an architect, designer, painter, and illustrator who conversed easily and informedly upon literature, art, music, drama, politics, and history. Dreiser was surprised to learn that Sonntag had constructed several model warships and model cars called "The Great Pullman Line." His association and friendship with Sonntag inspired Dreiser to write several magazine articles, including "Where Battleships Are Built" (*Ainslee's*, June 1898: 433–39), "Scenes in a Cartridge Factory" (*Cosmopolitan*, July 1898: 321–24), "Electricity in the Household" (*Demorest's*, January 1899: 38–39), and "The Town of Pullman" (*Ainslee's*, March 1899: 189–200).

Above all, what Dreiser learned from Sonntag was a commitment to capture an incisive vision of the changing world at the turn of the twentieth century. As Dreiser was convinced, good coloring was the first element of a successful painting after idea, form, or purpose. What was to become his own use of color in portraying urban scenes—streetlights, carriages, department stores, restaurants, luxurious garments— was indeed acquired through his contact with Sonntag. One drizzly autumn night Sonntag took Dreiser to such a scene on their way to the theater while they were involved in a serious discussion of art and life. The scene was truly spectacular with "the blend of the lights and shadows in there under the L." "The broad, converging walks were alive with people," Dreiser noted in silent admiration. "A perfect jam of vehicles marked the spot where the horse and cable cars intersected. Overhead was the elevated station, its lights aug-

mented every few minutes by long trains of brightly lighted cars filled with truly metropolitan crowds." Sonntag urged Dreiser to look at a pool of water. "Now," Sonntag told him, "that isn't silver-colored, as it's usually represented. It's a prism. Don't you see the hundred points of light?" Dreiser at once acknowledged the variety of color, which he realized he had scarcely observed before. "You may think one would skip that in viewing a great scene," Sonntag noted, "but the artist mustn't. He must get that all, whether you notice or not. It gives feeling, even when you don't see it."

Further Reading

Kwiat, Joseph J. "Dreiser and the Graphic Artist." *American Quarterly* 3 (1951): 127–41.

Yoshinobu Hakutani

COMSTOCK, ANTHONY (1844–1915). American reformer whose crusades against sex education, vice, and obscenity in literature and the fine arts made his name a byword for **censorship**. George Bernard Shaw is widely credited with coining the noun "Comstockery" after Comstock's state-chartered organization, the **New York Society for the Suppression of Vice** (founded 1873), led particularly vigorous campaigns against his plays *Mrs. Warren's Profession* and *Man and Superman*.

During the same year that he founded the New York Society for the Suppression of Vice, Comstock lobbied the U.S. Congress to pass strict obscenity laws. The resulting "Act of the Suppression of Trade in, and Circulation of, Obscene Literature and Articles of Immoral Use," also known at the Comstock Act, criminalized publication and distribution of any literature pertaining to abortion and banned the importation and distribution through the U.S. mail of any material, including serious literature and art, deemed to be of a sexual nature. Penalties for violators were stiff, including fines of up to $2,000 and imprisonment with hard labor. Portions of the Comstock Act, particularly those pertaining to information about abortion, remained U.S. law well into the 1990s.

From the passage of the Comstock Act until 1906, Comstock served without pay as a special agent of the U.S. Postal Service and published numerous admonitory books with titles such as *Frauds Exposed; or, How the People Are Deceived and Robbed, and Youth Corrupted* (1880) and *Traps for the Young* (1883). In the latter, he warned readers about obscene books old and new, observing characteristically, "You cannot handle fire and not be burned, neither can the black fiend Lust touch the moral nature without leaving traces of defilement," and asking, "Is there any argument that can be advanced, consistent with morals or common decency, why the filthy side of life, of the reeking imaginings of ancient or modern writers, should be served up[?]" (169, 182).

Comstockery, rather than Comstock himself, had the strongest impact on the public reception and distribution of Dreiser's works. Fear that the book would be seized certainly contributed to **Doubleday's** cold feet about *Sister Carrie* in 1900; Dreiser and Mencken corresponded in 1914 about the likelihood of *Jennie Gerhardt's* catching Comstock's eye, but neither book was targeted by him. However, in 1915 *The "Genius"* was declared obscene and removed from Cincinnati bookstores by the Western Society for the Suppression of Vice, an offshoot of the New York Society. The New York Society, under the leadership of **John S. Sumner**, brought suit against Dreiser's publisher, effectively delaying the book's issuance until 1923. Dreiser's anger at Comstock and Comstockery over the suppression of

The "Genius"—though that event is not specifically mentioned—is evident in several of the essays included in *Hey Rub-a-Dub-Dub*, particularly in "Life, Art, and America" and "Neurotic America and the Sex Impulse."

Further Reading

Comstock, Anthony. *Traps for the Young*. 1883. Cambridge: Harvard University Press, 1967.

Carol S. Loranger

"CONVENTION." First published in *American Mercury* in December 1925, the story later appeared in Dreiser's second volume of short fiction, *Chains*. It was also included in Howard Fast's *Best Short Stories of Theodore Dreiser* (1947) and was the representative Dreiser piece in a 1944 anthology of "distinguished" writings from *American Mercury*. "Convention" is framed as a first-person narration told by a newspaper cartoonist to the author, who desires to set down as an "American social document" a story that makes "rather clear the powerfully repressive and often transforming force of convention." The cartoonist recalls the notorious and unlucky life of a reporter named Wallace Steele with whom he once worked on a city newspaper somewhere in the Midwest. Steele's affair with a young, passionate, and romantic woman, Mrs. Davis, is exposed to the public when the "homely" and "faded" Mrs. Steele accuses the woman of sending her poisoned candy. The newspapers and public are enthralled by the story and by the mystery surrounding what actually happened, inventing numerous plots and narratives to suit their notions of convention, morality, and truth. Arrested and jailed, Mrs. Davis is at first viewed sympathetically as "the more interesting woman . . . helpless because she was desirous," but in a turn of events, Mrs. Steele is shown to have poisoned herself in order to indict her rival. As a result, public sympathy shifts toward the wife. Steele then abandons his lover because he has apparently been "terrorized by convention." "That finally fixed Steele's position in G— as a bounder," and he never again finds work there. In a brief *envoi*, the narrator encounters Steele seven years later in another city, still married to Mrs. Steele "and rightly so." Reflecting upon how he had once envied Steele "the love, the music, the moonlight," the narrator now feels "about all such miscarriages of love and delight— cold and sad."

"Convention" is one of a cluster of stories in *Chains*, including the title story, to focus upon marriage as a contradiction to the life force, sexual happiness, or artistic temperament. Indeed, the title "Convention" embodies a recurring theme in Dreiser's work, the conflicted and deadening marriage, with key narratives including the title story of Dreiser's earlier collection *Free and Other Stories*, as well as *Sister Carrie*, the **Cowperwood** novels, and *The "Genius."* But the story is also interesting as an "American social document" of the mechanics and force of mass culture, in this case the process whereby newspapers collaborate with readers to *fix* individuals into familiar narratives. Convention is therefore the media's and public's "repressive" and "transforming," as well as transient and distorting, construction of truth and morality. Thus, for example, Mrs. Steele's "broken confession . . . lay at the bottom of the public's mood, and caused it to turn sympathetically to that one who had been most willing to murder in the cause of love." As well, genuine sexual desire must be repressed because in America "public opinion compelled it."

Scott Zaluda

CORRESPONDENCE, DREISER'S. It is estimated that Dreiser wrote over 20,000 letters between his first known correspondence, 25 August 1888, and his death in late December 1945. Of these, some 1,300 have been published, principally in volumes edited by **Robert H. Elias, Louise Campbell**, and Thomas P. Riggio. In addition, a small number have appeared in articles, biographies, and critical studies. Since 1970, the *Dreiser Newsletter* (retitled *Dreiser Studies* in 1987) has been especially receptive to the publication of articles devoted to Dreiser's correspondence.

As is true of most authors, much of Dreiser's correspondence is devoted to such personal and literary "business" as making appointments, rejecting proposals, replying (usually briefly) to letters from admirers, and handling permissions, rights, and translations. A sizable number of Dreiser's letters, however, deal fully and directly with his central ideals and beliefs, whether these are related to his literary credo early in his career or to his many social and political concerns later in his life. Dreiser was not shy in making his position known, whoever his correspondent, and his letters thus serve as an important introduction to the values, beliefs, prejudices, and assumptions that underlie his novels and prose works. In his letters to the many women who aided him in his work, he tended to be especially open in expressing his ideas and often as well their source in the deepest recesses of his emotional life. All in all, Dreiser's letters reveal the central role that he played during the early twentieth century in the struggle for artistic freedom and economic and social justice in America.

The first collection of Dreiser's letters appeared in 1959, Robert H. Elias's *Letters of Theodore Dreiser*. Elias was ideally positioned to offer a major edition of Dreiser's correspondence. He had known Dreiser since 1937; he was his official biographer and had published the first reliable biography, *Theodore Dreiser: Apostle of Nature* (1949); and he had played an important role in bringing Dreiser's manuscript collection, which included his massive letter files, to the University of Pennsylvania Library. Although limited by his need to be highly selective (the edition contains 560 letters), to rely largely on carbons in the Dreiser Papers, and (because many of Dreiser's correspondents were still alive) to omit Dreiser's most personal letters, Elias's sure sense of the significant in Dreiser's life and work and his excellent annotation have made the edition an invaluable resource for Dreiser scholars since its publication. Almost every phase of Dreiser's life and work receives representation: his difficulties with publishers, his close reliance on friends for editorial assistance, his many activities in aid of social and political causes, and above all his willingness to explore, often in a series of letters with a congenial correspondent, his basic beliefs. Since roughly a quarter of Dreiser's letters selected for inclusion by Elias were to H. L. Mencken, the edition also documents the centrality of this relationship in Dreiser's career.

Almost thirty years after Elias's groundbreaking collection, Thomas P. Riggio published the only other large-scale edition of Dreiser's correspondence, *Dreiser-Mencken Letters* (1986). Except for 168 brief notes, Riggio includes the complete correspondence (some 1,036 letters) between these two giants of early-twentieth-century American literary life. Especially in the initial years of their relationship, when Dreiser and Mencken were engaged in a joint assault on American narrowness and provinciality, the correspondence offers a valuable insight (aided by Riggio's full annotation) into the early-twentieth-century American literary scene, including the literary politics necessary to maintain an independent career within an inhospitable cultural environment. In addition, Mencken's sharp and often ribald wit stimulated Dreiser to efforts of a like kind—not always successful efforts but of value nevertheless in illuminating a side of Dreiser's nature not often apparent elsewhere in his writing.

The large number of letters Dreiser wrote to the many women in his life are scarcely represented in these collections. This correspondence spans his career from his courtship letters in 1896–1898 to his fiancée, Sara White, to his extensive correspondence with **Marguerite Tjader**, who aided him in writing *The Bulwark*, during the last years of his life. Although some of Dreiser's relationships with women were entirely personal, he had as well an extraordinary capacity to attract and be attractive to women who could also help him in his work. His letters to women therefore often express the nuts and bolts of a writer's life—what he was working on and what he was thinking—as well as his frequent calls upon his correspondents for aid in such basic tasks as the typing and editing of his manuscripts.

Two volumes devoted entirely to Dreiser's relationships with women have been published. In 1959, Louise Campbell, who had a brief affair with Dreiser in 1917 and who aided him in various editorial capacities for the following twenty-eight years, published *Letters to Louise*. Less a scholarly edition than a personal reminiscence based on Dreiser's letters, the volume nevertheless prints 114 letters by Dreiser to Campbell, of which thirty-two also appear in Elias's edition. In 1995, **Yvette Eastman** published her *Dearest Wilding: A Memoir*, to which Thomas P. Riggio appended 111 previously unpublished letters by Dreiser to Eastman from 1929, when they began their relationship, to his death.

A new major edition of Dreiser's correspondence is in progress. Edited by Donald Pizer and Thomas P. Riggio, it is to be published by the University of Illinois Press and is scheduled to appear in 2005. Volume 1 will supplement Elias's edition in that it will contain significant letters bearing on Dreiser's literary career and social activism that were not available to Elias. Volume 2 will be devoted to Dreiser's correspondence with women.

Donald Pizer

"A COUNSEL TO PERFECTION." An essay first published in *Hey Rub-a-Dub-Dub* in which Dreiser ponders the role of humanity in the greater scheme of the universe, Nature, and God. As with most of the essays in the collection, "A Counsel to Perfection" does not come to a definite answer; instead, Dreiser wonders how we should perceive ourselves and our connection to this world.

Dreiser begins the essay by looking at the small pleasures in life such as love, victory, happiness, and success, all of which are the basis for human hope and ambition. However, Nature does not consider these wonderful occurrences in life to be an essential part of human welfare. Therefore, they take place infrequently, and one must reflect upon them and savor them to gain hope and ambition. Dreiser suggests that despite our studies in chemistry, biology, philosophy, and art, we are not fit creatures to contemplate supreme intelligence, Nature, or God, for our "Creator apparently is either unable or unwilling to endow [us] with such equipment as might make for great knowledge." Dreiser compares Hebrew and Greek fables concerning humanity's access to knowledge and shows that in both, our gift of knowledge and awareness is merely an accident and was never meant to be given to us by Nature. With no help in understanding the greater meaning of life, Dreiser remarks that since we are given only about seventy years of life, we should live it to the utmost. Since we cannot depend on help from Nature or from a Supreme Creator, we should reject the notion of the hereafter and strive to live a better and more fulfilling life on earth. People, Dreiser concludes, should help each other live in joy and happiness, strive for perfection on earth, and not depend upon a Supreme Being for a meaningful life.

Reneé D. McElheney

"THE COUNTRY DOCTOR." Written in 1902, this sketch was originally titled "A Samaritan of the Backwoods" and remained unpublished until Dreiser revised it for *Twelve Men* as "The Country Doctor." It was then published by *Harper's Monthly* in July 1918. The sketch began as a favor for a friend of his wife's family, Dollie Adams, who asked Dreiser to write a biographical essay about her recently deceased father, Dr. **William B. Adams**. After attempting to write a sketch about someone he hardly knew, Dreiser gave up and began composing instead a memoir about his own family doctor, Dr. **Amos Woolley**. Based on his childhood memories, this sketch recalls the many times when the kindly Dr. Woolley provided medical assistance to Dreiser's family while they were living in Warsaw, Indiana. After the material from his boyhood was exhausted, Dreiser continued to develop the sketch by incorporating into it the more interesting of the anecdotes from the material that Dollie Adams had provided Dreiser about her father. Because this sketch is a composite of two physicians, Dreiser gave his subject the fictitious name of Dr. Gridley.

The Dreisers moved to Warsaw in 1884, when Theodore was thirteen, and for the next three years until they moved to Chicago, they were provided medical treatment by Dr. Woolley, a man noted for his generosity. By the time the Dreisers arrived in Warsaw, Dr. Woolley was fifty-five years old and had been practicing medicine there for fifteen years. "The Country Doctor" begins with an anecdote illustrating the doctor's practical, humanitarian nature: he prescribes a remedy for Dreiser's very ill father that costs the family nothing, a tea brewed from fresh peach tree sprigs. Also included is a description of the doctor's medical assistance provided for one of Dreiser's sisters.

Dreiser then enlarges the scope of the portrait by describing the doctor's relationship with several other members of the community and including anecdotes that reveal the doctor's kindly personality. Most of this material comes from the life of Dr. Adams. Dreiser emphasizes throughout the sketch that his country doctor's most important characteristic is his Samaritan-like personality, a trait he shares with several of the other subjects in *Twelve Men*.

Robert Coltrane

THE COURT OF PROGRESS. Composed in July 1918, this one-act closet drama was first published in *Hey Rub-a-Dub-Dub*. In 1918 Dreiser was reeling from his battle with the **New York Society for the Suppression of Vice** over *The "Genius,"* which its publisher, **John Lane**, had withdrawn rather than risk a trial on obscenity charges. In the play Dreiser indulges in a wicked satire about a future time when all offensive forms of art have been eliminated. The chairman of the Court of Progress, one Noxus Podunkus, convenes a gathering of Boy Scouts, antisaloon leaguers, anticontraceptionists, watch and ward society guards, women magazine editors, and others to report on the "present state and progress of the world." After recount-

ing the history of "progress"—the elimination of all forms of literature, art, vice, intellectual curiosity, and scientific investigation—Noxus Podunkus, while periodically engorging himself from a pannier of soufflé, catechizes his followers by posing twelve "sacred questions," among which are "Is it not true that all men are now honest, kind, true, moral, virtuous, and wise?" and "All is well with the world, is it not?" To each question, the thousands of followers dance and chant their agreement in unison. Podunkus concludes by announcing, "The one message of this great Court to you is to go and do as you have always done: think no more than is absolutely necessary."

Keith Newlin

COWPERWOOD, FRANK ALGERNON, JR. Modeled after **Charles Tyson Yerkes**, a Chicago traction tycoon of the 1890s, Cowperwood is the central figure in Dreiser's *Trilogy of Desire*. A combination of Machiavellian prince, Nietzschean Übermensch, and Algerian hero, Cowperwood uses his intelligence, thrift, wit, subtlety, and insight to succeed in the veritable jungle of late-nineteenth-century finance. Dreiser integrates many details from the life of the financier Jay Cooke to develop Frank's childhood, but thereafter, Cowperwood parallels Yerkes. This life includes hypothecating funds from the Philadelphia city treasury to speculate in street railways, facing a prison sentence for embezzlement, emerging from prison to profit via the manipulation of the stock market during the Jay Cooke failure of 1873, relocating to Chicago to take control of its streetcar system by bribing local politicians, being driven out of the city after failing to renew his streetcar franchises, and finally settling in London to finance a new subway system. Critics often point out that, unlike most of the characters in

Dreiser's novels such as Carrie Meeber, George Hurstwood, **Jennie Gerhardt**, or Clyde Griffiths, Cowperwood remains superior to his environment; he always maintains a calm, resourceful, opportunistic disposition, regardless of the obstacles thrust before him. Armed with an "I satisfy myself" attitude, a Darwinian philosophy, and an amoral outlook on society, Cowperwood outwits his political and business adversaries while amassing his sizable fortune and pursuing young women.

From the time he witnesses a lobster devour a squid in an aquarium at ten, Cowperwood recognizes the difference between how life actually is and how Christian moralists and reformers idealistically wish it to be: "The incident made a great impression on him. It answered in a rough way that riddle which had been annoying him so much in the past: 'How is life organized?' Things lived on each other—that was it." In other words, he discovers the insignificant role that morality plays in the struggle between the weak and the strong. Such a personal philosophy later causes Cowperwood to view with disdainful eyes the hypocritical moralism of the Catholic, Edward Butler, and the pathetically weak and self-pitying city treasurer, George Stener. Through Cowperwood, Dreiser exposes the impracticality of social conventions grounded in puritanical and dogmatic platitudes, and, in fact, Cowperwood's brutal honesty, along with his interest in art and young women, may help explain why Dreiser modeled his hero after Yerkes rather than better-known robber barons of the time. Yerkes himself collected art, pursued several young women, and never hid behind a veil of sanctimony; instead, he often scoffed at Victorian mores.

Literary scholars often compare Cowperwood to the Nietzschean Übermensch, pointing out that Cowperwood's interests—wealth, art, and women—all require him to undergo a self-transformation and self-transcendence, or what Nietzsche would call a "Will to Power." Regarding wealth, Cowperwood moves from resilient stockbroker to polished financier; regarding women, he moves from the placid and diffident **Lillian Semple** to the artistic and aesthetic **Berenice Fleming**; and regarding art, his taste increases proportionally with his wealth, as evident from his modest home in Philadelphia to his lavish mansion in New York.

Cowperwood further illustrates Dreiser's belief in what he termed "equation inevitable": that for every rising power in society, an equal power will curb it, resulting in a balance. Cowperwood, for example, suffers defeat at the hands of political and business adversaries in Chicago, and in London, death foils his manipulative endeavors. Nonetheless, Cowperwood, like Yerkes, benefits society with his genius and philanthropic pursuits, as evident by a more efficient streetcar system in Chicago and his donation of an observatory to the University of Chicago.

See also "Equation Inevitable."

Further Reading

Fienberg, Lorne. "Dreiser's Frank Cowperwood: The Apotheosis of the Fictional Businessman." *A Cuckoo in the Nest of Culture: Changing Perspectives on the Businessman in the American Novel, 1865–1914.* Ed. Lorne Fienberg. New York: Garland, 1988. 298–367.

Gerber, Philip. "Financier, Titan, Stoic: *A Trilogy of Desire.*" *Theodore Dreiser Revisited.* New York: Twayne, 1992. 47–63.

———. "Frank Cowperwood: Boy Financier." *Studies in American Fiction* 2 (1974): 165–74.

Hughson, Lois. "Dreiser's Cowperwood and the Dynamics of Naturalism." *Studies in the Novel* 16 (1984): 52–71.

Pizer, Donald. *The Novels of Theodore Dreiser: A Critical Study.* Minneapolis: University of Minneapolis Press, 1976. 160–200.

Roulston, Robert. "The Libidinous Lobster: The Semi-Flaw in Dreiser's Superman." *Rendez-vous* 9 (1974): 35–40.

Schöff, Joseph C. "Cowperwood's Will to Power: Dreiser's *Trilogy of Desire* in the Light of Nietzsche." *Nietzsche in American Literature and Thought.* Ed. Manfred Putz. Columbia, S.C.: Camden House, 1995. 139–54.

Kevin Jett

"A CRIPPLE WHOSE ENERGY GIVES INSPIRATION." This is the third sketch Dreiser produced about residents of Noank, Connecticut, based on his stay there during the summer of 1901. The other two, "A Doer of the Word" and "The Village Feudists," were included in *Twelve Men.* This sketch, published in *Success* (February 1902), shows that Dreiser still had the ability to produce an inspirational character study acceptable to the editor of a popular magazine. However, his subversive distortion of the "success story" formula suggests the growing discontent that eventually would make this kind of writing impossible for him. He was having increasing difficulty in promoting the American ideal that hard work would eventually lead to success, a recurring theme in his earlier pieces about famous men.

In this sketch about Harry the Cripple, originally titled "The Noank Boy," Dreiser followed the formula by implying that Harry would become successful because he was so willing to work hard. The narrative pattern is similar to that of the other two Noank sketches: the narrator repeatedly sees this person working about the village, and his interest is aroused, so he talks to the boy about what he is doing and questions other villagers. He discovers that even though crippled, Harry is the only young man in the village willing to

work hard. The other boys are lazy or indifferent. He then describes how he and a friend are lounging about, observing the inefficiency of the villagers: four adults watch while a twelve-year-old boy slowly breaks up a wooden box for kindling. Even though assuming an attitude of superiority, the narrator and his friend must also be counted among the loafers. The reader identifies with the narrator as a superior being, but in doing so also assumes the role of a do-nothing. When Harry energetically begins to sweep out the firehouse, the subversive contrast is established. Only Harry is depicted as industrious.

Like the young Dreiser, Harry is ambitious but young and ignorant of the difficulties he will encounter when he ventures beyond the protective environment of his village. When questioned by the narrator, Harry betrays his ignorance of the business world and its challenges. His knowledge of "large" cities extends no farther than New London, six miles from Noank. Dreiser by this time knew from his own recent experience with *Sister Carrie* that talent and hard work would not automatically lead to success. However, he chose to stop his narrative where the reader could conclude with the positive assumption that Harry would fulfill the American Dream of becoming a success in life.

Robert Coltrane

"THE CRUISE OF THE 'IDLEWILD.' " First published in the October 1909 *Bohemian,* "The Cruise of the 'Idlewild' " was thoroughly revised before it was reprinted in *Free and Other Stories.* This story grew out of Dreiser's experience working on the New York Central Railroad in 1903 as a form of recuperative labor. Unlike other Dreiser writings that deal with experiences from this period, "The Cruise of the 'Idlewild' " does not take a serious or philosophical tone but playfully presents a central conceit. The workers of a railroad machine shop, which is surrounded on three sides by the waters of the Hudson and Harlem Rivers, imagine it to be an imaginary ship, the *Idlewild*, so that they, their instruments, and tasks are all given nautical titles and terms, with the result of making their monotonous work more agreeable. The limited plot centers on how they sustain this idea and concerns three principal characters: John, who is the engineer or captain; Ike, who is the blacksmith's helper or bos'n's mate; and the speaker, who carries wood shavings and is the mate. After the imaginary ship has "cruised" for a month or more, the captain and mate tease the diminutive and ragged Ike until he is alienated from their company. Without another person to order around, the two have a falling-out over who is in charge of the *Idlewild*, which then sinks. At the end of the story, however, the captain and the mate become reconciled with Ike and each other and decide to set sail on another imaginary ship, *Harmony*.

The limited scope and humorous tone of the story nonetheless reveal Dreiser's underlying concerns. Like Melville's "Bartleby, the Scrivener," Dreiser's story takes place entirely at work and his narrator remains shadowy—we know little of him other than his diction is more correct and elevated than the other workers' and he is working in the railway shop only for his health. Yet such limits, along with such playful practices as the narrator's referring to himself in the third person, point to more serious matters than the fanciful idea being described. For example, when the narrator states that "some of us, one in particular, were mortal tired of the life we were leading," the joke of indirectly referring to himself is belied by the adjective "mortal." Similarly, the humorous contrast between the narrator's repeated initial as-sertion that he does not know how the idea of the *Idlewild* started and his later claim that "the whole affair, ship, captain, mate and all, was declared by the mate to be a creation of his brain" reveals a strong need to believe in the power of his imagination. That his imagination has created not just the ship but an identity for himself is particularly telling. The undertone of the story thus suggests a narrator who feels particularly vulnerable, with his emotional need to work as a laborer matched by his need to stake his identity on his imagination. "The Cruise of the 'Idlewild,'" while brief and seemingly light, suggestively describes the world of work as well as these other issues that were important to Dreiser at a key moment in his professional and emotional life.

Further Reading

Graham, D. B. "'The Cruise of the "Idlewild"': Dreiser's Revisions of a 'Rather Light' Story." *American Literary Realism* 8.2 (1975): 1–11.

David T. Humphries

CUDLIPP, THELMA (1892–1983). Born in Richmond, Virginia, Thelma Cudlipp came to New York City in her early teens to study art. Her mother was an assistant editor at *The Delineator*, a prestigious woman's fashion magazine edited by Dreiser. In 1910 Dreiser became infatuated with Miss Cudlipp. Although the involvement was platonic, Cudlipp's family objected because Dreiser was married and twenty years her senior. Her mother sent her abroad to study art in England. This ended her liaison with Dreiser, whose indiscretion cost him his job at the magazine. In the autobiographical novel Dreiser completed in 1911 (heavily revised and published in 1915 as *The "Genius"*), Cudlipp is the original for the character of **Suzanne Dale**. In England she continued her training in art, winning but not accepting a Royal Academy scholarship. When she returned to America, she took lessons from Kenneth Hayes Miller, one of Dreiser's closest friends among painters. Cudlipp became well known as an illustrator for various newspapers and magazines, many of which—*Harper's, Century, McClure's, Saturday Evening Post*—also published Dreiser's work. She and Dreiser developed a friendship in this period, but it was not of a romantic nature. In 1918 she married Edwin Grosvenor, a cousin of ex-president Taft. After Grosvenor's death, she married Charles Seymour Whitman, who had been governor of New York from 1915 to 1918. Dreiser would meet with them socially in New York. In addition to her own work, Cudlipp developed an interest in pre–Columbian sculpture, which she collected and promoted through lectures. In their correspondence she confided to Dreiser the details of her problematic marriage to Whitman, and she told him of a diary she had kept of their unhappy marital relations. Her account fascinated Dreiser, and he toyed with the idea of writing fiction based on her stories. Although she did not object, he never did use the material. They remained at a geographical distance from each other but on good terms, exchanging letters until Dreiser's death.

Thomas P. Riggio

"CULHANE, THE SOLID MAN." This sketch was placed fifth in *Twelve Men*, among those about men Dreiser admired for having achieved some degree of success. It is based on Dreiser's experiences at the health spa run by a former professional wrestler named **William Muldoon**. Dreiser changed the name to Culhane to avoid controversy, but Muldoon was too well known not to be recognized, especially since he was famous for being "the

solid man." When Dreiser was suffering from **neurasthenia** in 1903, his brother Paul sent him to Olympia, Muldoon's sanitarium near White Plains, New York, from 21 April to 2 June, to recover his health. While there, Dreiser produced a short sketch about his experiences, which was published in the 16 May 1903 issue of *Harper's Weekly* and called "Scared Back to Nature." In 1904, he developed a lengthier version for *An Amateur Laborer*, which he never published. His most extensive portrayal of this experience was the one in *Twelve Men*, which incorporated wording verbatim from both earlier versions but was modified to present a more favorable image of the subject. "Culhane" becomes the positive representative of the physical ideal, in contrast to the railroad foreman **Michael Burke** ("The Mighty Rourke"). Internal evidence in the conclusion suggests that Dreiser had completed a rough draft of this sketch around 1907.

When Dreiser began developing material for *Twelve Men*, the sketches about Muldoon and Burke were selected to represent man's physical nature. The difference between these two physically oriented men is that the railroad foreman is shown to be ultimately a failure, while Culhane becomes someone whose disciplined way of life has produced an unaging specimen of manliness. The narrator begins with a brief biographical summary of Culhane's earlier activities and his own negative attitude toward Culhane. Emphasis is then given to describing Culhane's training regimen for the other guests, but without the authorial commentary of the preceding sketches in *Twelve Men*. Dreiser instead provides mostly dialogue and scenes to reveal Culhane's character. Two years later, when the narrator pays a return visit, his attitude has become more admiring. He is astonished to discover that Culhane appears not to have aged at all.

The sketch was republished under the title "Muldoon, the Solid Man" in *Fulfillment and Other Tales of Women and Men.*

Further Reading

Frederickson, Kathy. "Working Out to Work Through: Dreiser in Muldoon's Body Shop of Shame." *Theodore Dreiser and American Culture.* Ed. Yoshinobu Hakutani. Rutherford, N.J.: Fairleigh Dickinson University Press, 1980. 115–37.

Robert Coltrane

"CURIOUS SHIFTS OF THE POOR." This sketch of four scenes of New York in the depth of winter begins with an epigraph that announces the point of these vignettes: "Strange ways of relieving desperate poverty—Last resources of New York's most pitiful mendicants." At the outset, Dreiser portrays a night scene of the crossing of Fifth Avenue and Broadway, which has a feeling of "pleasure and exhilaration, the curious enthusiasm of a great city, bent upon finding joy in a thousand different ways." He finds some of the homeless "leading toward sociability." Surprisingly, they talk about politics, religion, and the problems of city government. He then encounters a self-styled philanthropist called "Captain," who solicits money so that he can provide the homeless men with a night's sleep in a nearby hotel. The Captain, Dreiser remarks, is blessed with a sense of duty and determination to take "this means of fulfilling his own destiny." On Fifth Avenue several blocks away, a convent house of the Sisters of Mercy gives the hungry a free meal around noon every day. Elsewhere, a group of homeless wait impatiently amid falling snow for the door of a shelter to open. The last scene is about the Fleischmann restaurant on the corner of Broadway and Ninth Street, known for a quarter of a century for giving anyone over thirty

a free loaf of bread. These poor, Dreiser remarks, never mention wretchedness, poverty, or distress; instead, the talkative are concerned about the latest murder trial, their prize-ring favorites, the latest engineering innovations of automobiles, the chance of war in Africa, and the economic boom or depression in foreign lands. Some men discuss the Dreyfus affair. Pondering the poor and homeless, Dreiser observes that "society is no better than its poorest type. . . . Wealth may create an illusion, or modify a ghastly appearance of ignorance and error, but it cannot change the effect. The result is as real in the mansions of Fifth Avenue as in the midnight throng outside a baker's door."

The Captain's story was so striking that Dreiser used it in Chapter 45 of *Sister Carrie* (as well as incorporating the Sisters of Mercy and Fleischmann sections into Chapter 47). While the Captain is soliciting money from the passersby to secure beds for the homeless, Hurstwood walks by on Fifth Avenue. At first Hurstwood ignores the Captain's words, for he sounds like a street preacher, but Hurstwood, after noticing a line of men whose beds are already secured by the Captain, decides to join the line of those waiting for their beds. Finally his chance arrives. The Captain begins talking for Hurstwood: "Twelve cents, gentlemen—twelve cents puts this man to bed. He wouldn't stand here in the cold if he had any place to go." When a stranger donates money to the Captain, Dreiser writes, "He [Hurstwood] felt as if the world were not quite so bad with such a good man in it."

"Curious Shifts of the Poor" was originally published in November 1899 in *Demorest's.* Dreiser then reconstructed the story of the Captain and published it under the title "A Touch of Human Brotherhood" in *Success* (March 1902). Dreiser also republished the third and fourth scenes in "Curious Shifts of the Poor" as "The Men in the Storm" and "The Bread-Line" in *The Color of a Great City*. The article has been reprinted in several collections, among which are the Norton critical edition of *Sister Carrie*, edited by Donald Pizer, and in *SMA* 1.

Further Reading

Moers, Ellen. " 'Curious Shifts of the Poor.' " *Two Dreisers*. New York: Viking, 1969. 57–69.

Yoshinobu Hakutani

D

DALE, SUZANNE. Teenaged love object of **Eugene Witla** in Book 3 of *The "Genius."* Based largely on how Dreiser saw his affair with **Thelma Cudlipp**, daughter of a coworker at the **Butterick Publishing Company**, Suzanne is, along with **Berenice Fleming** in *The Titan* and *The Stoic*, one of Dreiser's Lolita figures. The character, called "Flower Face" by her lover, does not successfully bear the large philosophical burden that Dreiser places on her. Witla (and Dreiser) attempt to cast her as the personification of abstract "beauty" in a curious, though typically Dreiserian, erasing of what strikes most readers as a strong sexual pull.

Clare Eby

DARWINISM. *See* Evolution.

DAWN. Dreiser first began writing his autobiography around 1912, soon after completing the manuscript of his autobiographical third novel, *The "Genius."* His original intention was to write separate autobiographies for each twenty-year period of his life and publish them under the collective title *A History of Myself.* However, he completed only two of the anticipated four autobiographies. In 1916 he finished the first volume, *Dawn*, but chose not to publish it because he felt its frank-

ness might embarrass members of his family. Instead, he took the last ten chapters and incorporated them into his second autobiography, *Newspaper Days*, which was published in 1922 under his publisher's preferred title, *A Book about Myself.* Only after the publication and literary success of *An American Tragedy* did Dreiser feel confident enough to revisit and perhaps even publish *Dawn.* Dreiser updated the manuscript, changed the names of several family members to protect their privacy, and wrote a new last chapter. *Dawn* was published by **Horace Liveright** on 8 May 1931.

Dawn is not a conventional autobiography. Instead, it is the product of Dreiser's personal and literary maturity. His intent was to record and analyze "the net of flesh and emotion and human relationship into which [I] was born and which conditioned [my] early . . . life." The work is therefore a careful blending of his more mature philosophy with a chronology of his first nineteen years, but as a whole, *Dawn* is a multilayered work that goes beyond analytical autobiography. Dreiser's vivid and frank descriptions of his parents, siblings, childhood friends, girlfriends, employers, educators, and acquaintances transform the work into a moving and realistic portrait of American society at the close of the nineteenth century, a blueprint, perhaps, for the realistic fiction Dreiser would later write. *Dawn*, as Albert Mordell wrote in a review for the *Philadelphia Record*, "makes the reader forget whether he is really seeing life or reading literature, for here they both merge" (rpt. in Salzman 596).

At the center of Dreiser's autobiography is the constant poverty in which his family lived. Although the family was not always dirt-poor, much of the first half of the book emphasizes the family's constant attempts to "keep from starving." As a young child Dreiser recalls his brothers being sent home from school because they had no shoes. He writes of his mother's begging for credit at local grocery stores and having to make "fried mush" for dinner because there was no food. The children's clothes were "so old and so made over and patched that they were a joke." Dreiser himself, like the Gerhardt boys in *Jennie Gerhardt*, was forced to steal coal from train yards and fence posts from neighboring yards to heat the home, and then there was the "Christmas that passed with scarcely a toy worth mentioning." Early in life, Dreiser remembers feeling the pangs of "isolation" and loneliness" that accompanied such poverty. By the time Dreiser was an adolescent, he well understood that "not to want to be rich or to be willing and able to work for riches was to write yourself down as a nobody." The entire Dreiser clan, with the exception of the father, spent much of their time and energy searching for a life of social prominence and material wealth. Some members of the family were successful, while others failed miserably. Brother Paul became a prominent songwriter and performer, while Rome became a drunk and a thief. Sister Mame (Eleanor in *Dawn*) married into a "new-rich Irish Catholic family," while Sylvia (Amy) became pregnant by a wealthy cad whom Dreiser names Don

Ashley who promised marriage but disappeared shortly thereafter.

Dreiser's experiences with poverty, however, also left him emotionally and psychologically scarred. Even into his forties, for instance, the beginning of the winter season would bring "indefinable and highly oppressive [feelings] of dread." At times, he would even succumb to feelings that were close to "physical pain" whenever he saw people who were wretched and poor, and yet his experiences with poverty also made him extremely sensitive to the "struggles and fortunes" of all people, "the whole cruel as well as kind, rough, as well as smooth, working schemes of life."

In the midst of this poverty Dreiser's mother, Sarah, whom Dreiser adored, stands as a centering force. Throughout the book, he lauds her for keeping the family together despite its incredible hardships and for encouraging all her children to strive for a better life. He continually reiterates her power over her children. She had, he states, a "curiously binding spirit which . . . bound us all." It was a spirit that was "moving . . . powerful . . . compelling." Although at times she would cruelly threaten to leave her children, she was, as Dreiser remembers, a "personage . . . to be reckoned with: strong, patient, understanding, sympathetic, creative, humor-loving, and helpful." Her unwavering love for her children drew them to her like "hooks of steel," and her dreamy, almost mystical way of looking at the world helped keep them optimistic when poverty and social exclusion threatened them.

In opposition, however, stood Dreiser's father, Paul, for whom Dreiser could muster little respect. Dreiser explains that numerous business and personal calamities left his father a broken man unable to find the energy or motivation to make it financially. He was, Dreiser states, "so clear an illustration of the beaten or at least physically depressed man." Probably in an effort to cope with his financial failure, Paul Dreiser immersed himself in his Catholic faith. Dreiser describes many episodes of his father's fanatical, overly moralistic, and rigid behavior, such as forcing the children to go to parochial schools and making them attend mass on Sundays. Such experiences, however, only served to confuse Dreiser.

As a child, he followed church teaching without question. As an adolescent and young adult, however, Dreiser could find nothing emotionally, mentally, or spiritually persuasive about the church and stopped going. In his early adulthood, he admits that he was "confused" about **religion**, and *Dawn* clearly expresses such confusion. On the one hand, we see him leaning toward a more romantic view, wherein God is most readily seen in the sensitive and caring acts of people. On the other hand, there are numerous occasions wherein he clearly lashes out against the parochial schools and Catholicism in general. Religion, he states several times, is nothing more than an "old wives' tale" and religious education a detriment to the intellectual development of young minds, and yet, at the end of the book, he is still not "ready to believe as yet that Christianity and religion in general use were wholly an illusion. . . . God was still some kind of entity somewhere—the devil another." His religious upbringing also served to confuse him on issues of morality. Throughout, we see him "speculat[ing] constantly on what is right and wrong in connection with human wishes and human conduct." For instance, he became extremely "melancholy" when "Amy's" pregnancy "scandalized" the family and "thwarted" their "dreams" for a better life, but he was also deeply aware of the hypocritical treatment the family received from the Ashley family, the local doctor, and the attorney his mother hired to sue the family.

These early seeds of moral confusion became even more troublesome when Dreiser himself began feeling the "pangs" of sexual desire. He wanted sex, but he knew it was wrong, and his attempts to deal with what he felt were natural, even physiological human desires, in the face of his traditional moral upbringing, become an almost consuming theme in the latter half of the autobiography. What we end up with is an almost overwhelming obsession on Dreiser's part with the issue of sex. Some reviewers believed that this overemphasis rendered *Dawn* unrealistic, vulgar, and tedious. Others, like Isabel Peterson in a review for the *New York Herald Tribune*, however, thought that it made the work more "painfully truthful" (rpt. in Salzman 589). At first, Dreiser describes incidents that are much like any other teenager's, such as his first childhood crush and his first sexual experience. As the book continues, however, Dreiser's notions about his own sexuality become increasingly neurotic. Overly shy, thoughts of asking a girl out give him the "shakes," at times so severe that he would be forced to stop whatever he was doing and recuperate. Attempts to have sex with girls always end in disaster and leave him humiliated and depressed, vowing to "retreat to a safe distance" and "never emerge again."

Sexual problems and poverty do not solely define Dreiser's early life, however. *Dawn* is also filled with compelling, even comical anecdotes of childhood play, adolescent growth, and early adult learning. These are, perhaps, the more important moments in the book. They show us a Dreiser who is far different from the naturalist he is reputed to be. "For all my modest repute as a realist," Dreiser states, "I seem, to my self-analyzing eyes, somewhat more of a romanticist than a realist." As a matter of fact, he often refers to himself in *Dawn* as "moonshiny and dreamy." He was also frail, nervous, and prone to hypochondria. As a result, he found himself unsuited for just about every job he took, from farm hand to railroad worker to dishwasher. He was even fired from his position as a photographer's assistant because he talked too much. Instead, he liked to read. By the time he was a teenager, he had already read many of the English and American classics. His earliest experiences with literature, he noted, "gave me a new outlook on life, and . . . aided me better to formulate myself to myself." He loved reading because books were about life, and he was fascinated by life: "the metaphysical and mystic impulses which project life and which were suggested [in literature] appealed to me strongly." These early reading experiences also planted a creative seed in him, for in reading he found "something" he "should like to imitate." Later, he states that the only academic disciplines that interested him were "English literature and the study of words."

Dreiser developed his interest in observing life early. He states that his one "gift" was the desire to "stare about and admire the world so wide." As a child, he loved to look out the window and watch the world go by, and in school he studied his teachers in the same way he studied his lessons. He remembers lingering at an "old potter's" store to watch him work and "speculating" about the "thoughts of others, their homes, pleasures, means, travel." Although he did not yet understand what drew him to people, he did recognize "a sense of something of the scintillations of a world or universe or mystery which could not be dark." At seventeen years old, he describes himself as "burning with desire, yearning for everything and anything which my eyes or my mind could contem-

plate." When the family moved to Chicago, Dreiser was thrilled because it was filled with lights, colors, sounds, and an assemblage of diverse people to study. "All I really cared for," he explains, "was the beauty of life, its spectacles and pleasures." Academics were of little use to him. His education, he contends, came not from the classroom but from life "outside," and from these "direct observations" come numerous fascinating stories about American people.

"Experience," he concludes at the end of his book, "is the only true teacher." Dreiser's early life is sometimes strange, sometimes pathetic, and sometimes beautiful. It is tragic, romantic, even comical. At over 600 pages, it can be a long, occasionally tedious, and sometimes repetitive read, but it is the truth of his experience, warts and all. As Dreiser explains, "One does not make one's relatives or oneself or the world. The most interesting thing one can do is to observe or rearrange or explain, if possible." This is what *Dawn* is about. It is Dreiser's life, and as such it is an important part of Dreiser studies.

Further Reading

Nostwich, T. D. Preface to *Dawn: An Autobiography of Early Youth*. Ed. T. D. Nostwich. Santa Rosa, Calif.: Black Sparrow Press, 1998. N.p.

Annemarie Koning Whaley

DE CAMP, CHARLES B. (?–1915?). A writer and magazine editor, De Camp served as assistant editor at *Everybody's Magazine* from 1904 to 1905 until he was fired for drinking. He then served as Dreiser's assistant at **Broadway Magazine** from 1906 to 1907 and by 1914 was the editor of *Metropolitan Magazine*. In letters to H. L. Mencken, Dreiser described De Camp as "so wise, so sensitive, so esthetic and kind," and counted him as both "genial and sociable" as well as one of the most "grim critically" of his early readers (*D-M Letters* 2: 684). According to Dreiser, De Camp showed promise as a writer and published "six really good short stories," including "Boy and the Law" in *Harper's Magazine* (February 1911) and a poem, "Moral Ballad of the Botts" in *Harper's Weekly* (16 October 1909). Dreiser blamed De Camp's lack of greater publishing success on the "curse" of a lifetime allowance of $100 per month from his "well-to-do" father.

Dreiser valued De Camp's advice and sent him the manuscripts of *Jennie Gerhardt* and several plays for comment. De Camp's experience as an editor of popular magazines must have influenced his critical comments about Dreiser's work, which have to do with decreasing the "depressing effect" he found in Dreiser's **realism**. At De Camp's suggestion, Dreiser added several lines to *Jennie Gerhardt*, including the scene in which Lester tells Jennie that he loves her (West 6), but Dreiser did not make the larger change of cutting "the funeral & depot scenes" that De Camp advised. Though often critical, De Camp's letters always include praise and admiration for Dreiser's writing, as he wrote about the manuscript of *Jennie Gerhardt*: "I don't know any one who has so depicted American life in the broad terms of human nature, with so much objective sincerity and absence of prejudice" (qtd. in West 4). De Camp's untimely death from pneumonia brought an end to his friendship with Dreiser.

Further Reading

West, James L. W., III. "C. B. De Camp and *Jennie Gerhardt*." *Dreiser Studies* 23.1 (1992): 2–7.

Mandy See

"DE MAUPASSANT, JR." This sketch about **Harris Merton Lyon** served as the first of the second six in *Twelve Men*, men Dreiser admired who ultimately were failures. In the first six sketches, the narrator is depicted in a youthfully subservient relationship with each subject; this seventh sketch served to establish the older Dreiser's relationship of equality with the remaining six men. When Dreiser first met Lyon in 1906, their age difference was not so great—Lyon was twenty-four and Dreiser thirty-four. When Dreiser wrote this sketch sometime in 1917–1918, shortly after Lyon's death in June 1916, the age difference had grown—Lyon was still the twenty-four-year-old that Dreiser remembered, but the narrator was now in his mid-forties. The narrative assumes a paternal attitude in which Lyon is depicted as a wayward son whose refusal to listen to his wise father's advice had caused him to fail.

The difference in temperaments is established in the opening paragraph: Lyon is young and outspoken, with a forceful attitude, while the narrator describes himself as merely "an older man than he" who was "editor of an unimportant magazine." In the previous six sketches, the narrator remains inferior in some way to the subject, but this sketch establishes a new pattern in which the narrator increases in importance as the subject declines in importance. The narrative situation is thereby reversed, with Dreiser becoming the older man, at first unimpressive, whose attributes the younger Lyon comes to admire.

Dreiser admired Lyon because he saw many similarities to himself at a young age. The first half of the sketch provides a series of episodes depicting Lyon's personality and skills. Lyon is able to produce the kind of material the narrator needs—sophisticated sketches of urban life and ironic short stories. Soon he becomes a permanent member of the magazine staff. Lyon seeks to emulate the French writers, de Maupassant in particular for his "unbiased outlook on life, his freedom from moral and religious and even sentimental predisposition." The narrator nurtures Lyon's talent, serving as a mentor, but when the narrator moves on to a better position, Lyon chooses to remain behind, ceasing to develop his talent. By the end, Lyon has been reduced to surviving on the kind of hackwork he had earlier disparaged, becoming a failed artist who had not lived up to the "promise of his genius."

Robert Coltrane

THE DELINEATOR. Edited by Dreiser from June 1907 to October 1910, this women's magazine was the flagship publication of the **Butterick Publishing Company**, with a circulation of 480,000 in 1900. *The Delineator* had its origins in the 1873 merger of two magazines, the *Ladies' Quarterly Review of Broadway Fashions* and *Metropolitan Monthly*, both of which had been founded by Ebenezer Butterick to sell his sewing patterns and provide fashion news. Over the next thirty-four years, *The Delineator* widened its scope to include articles on subjects related to the domestic sphere; motherhood, interior decorating, embroidery, and etiquette were some of the matters discussed regularly. In the 1890s, broader series on "Employments for Women," "The Women's Colleges of the United States," and "The Social Code" appeared; *The Delineator* also began to publish short stories. By the time Dreiser became editor, fashion news no longer constituted most of the material in the magazine, although it still had a large place, and public affairs were rarely, if ever, discussed.

Dreiser worked to expand *The Delineator*'s social critique. In his editorial columns, Dreiser discussed, among other topics, the sad but sometimes necessary remedy of divorce for a troubled marriage; the prevalence of nervous breakdowns; the poor state of children's health; the dangerous temptation of materialism; the responsibility of the wealthy to assist the poor; the vulgarity of moving pictures shown in penny arcades and nickelodeons; and the weakening quality of stage plays. Articles by other authors on the decline of the churches, woman suffrage, and troubled public schools also appeared during his tenure. Given the tenor of the times, such writings were by no means radical, but Dreiser's columns and the articles he published did draw his readers' attention to issues relevant to domestic life and women's interests with a stronger dedication to reform than had existed previously in *The Delineator*.

The centerpiece of that reform effort was "The Delineator Child-Rescue Campaign," which began in November 1907 and continued until early 1911. The goal was to place orphaned and homeless children in childless homes, either through foster care or formal adoption. Under Dreiser's direction, each month the magazine published stories of children in need of care. Testimonials by adoptive mothers and prominent reformers such as Jacob Riis argued the benefits of a positive environment in a child's development. *The Delineator* distributed pamphlets warning of the dangers to society of an unloved child growing to become an unloving man. He also attained the endorsement of the program from noteworthy or well-to-do women, such as Mrs. William Jennings Bryan and Edith Rockefeller McCormick, in the hope of influencing his middle-class readers to participate. By 1909, Dreiser could boast that he had met personally with President Theodore Roosevelt to discuss the plight of dependent children. The campaign placed approximately 21,000 children in homes.

Under Dreiser's tenure, *The Delineator* continued to publish fiction by many notable authors of the time, including Rudyard Kipling, Zona Gale, Mary E. Wilkins Freeman, Dorothy Canfield, Francis Marion Crawford, and James Oppenheim. As a whole, this work was palatable to the domestic audience; they were "clean stories." Still, Dreiser would on occasion point out that a contributor had written a story that avoided the trap of "much writing and little thinking" (March 1909), and he applauded an experimental piece by Richard Le Galliene about the author's life as a tramp because it "ignore[d] the supposed demands of the literary marketplace" (May 1909). H. L. Mencken also contributed regularly to the humorous "Man's Magazine Page."

Dreiser's zenith as *The Delineator*'s editor came in 1909. By the end of that year, the Butterick Publishing Company decided to merge with the Ridgway Company, which produced the muckraking *Everybody's Magazine*. The merger placed Erman J. Ridgway in "general charge" of the editorial departments of the new company, so that although Dreiser was nominally in control of *The Delineator*, he was in effect demoted. Under the reorganization, *Everybody's* was considered the main vehicle for social and political critique. His autonomy gradually diminishing throughout 1910, Dreiser grew restless. He was well under way with *Jennie Gerhardt*, and his romantic interest in **Thelma Cudlipp** had continued for some months. By October 1910, Dreiser and *The Delineator* management mutually agreed that, for all these reasons, he should leave the editor's chair.

In the years immediately following Dreiser's departure, *The Delineator* continued reformist causes; child welfare and the legal rights of women and children were

among them. However, the magazine stayed true to its original interest in fashion and domestic concerns. Cookbooks and other homemaking guides were published under *The Delineator* name. The magazine's progressivism declined during World War I and the Red Scare of 1919–1922. *The Delineator* stayed in print until April 1937, when it merged with another women's magazine, the Hearst Corporation's *Pictorial Review*.

Further Reading

Berebitsky, Julie. "Rescue a Child and Save the Nation: The Social Construction of Adoption and *The Delineator*, 1907–1911." *Like Our Very Own: Adoption and the Changing Culture of Motherhood, 1851–1950*. Lawrence: University Press of Kansas, 2000. 51–74.

Christopher Weinmann

DELL, FLOYD JAMES (1887–1969). Journalist, editor, essayist, book reviewer, novelist, playwright, and cultural critic, Dell began his career as an Iowa reporter with a socialist skew. In 1908 he moved to Chicago, where he helped transform the *Chicago Evening Post*'s *Friday Literary Review* into an influential voice. By 1911, as editor of the *Literary Review*, he advocated innovation and championed controversial writers such as Dreiser, whose *Jennie Gerhardt* he reviewed as "a great novel." Dell was also a leader of the Chicago Renaissance. Relocated to New York in 1913, he helped edit the *Masses* and from 1918 to 1921 served on the editorial board of its successor, the *Liberator*.

Dell's belief in the interaction of literature and life paralleled Dreiser's "true picture of life." During the second decade of the twentieth century, Dell maintained ties with Dreiser, despite the fact that Dreiser won out in their rivalry for the love of **Kirah Markham** (Elaine Hyman). Dreiser fictionalized Dell as

Gardner Knowles, one of the Garrick Players in *The Titan*. On 20 December 1912, Dreiser visited Chicago to conduct research for *The Titan*. There he met Dell. When Dreiser departed on 10 February 1913, he left a copy of *The "Genius"* typescript for Dell and others to read. Dell soon responded that, with extensive cuts and rewriting, it could become an estimable novel, but early in 1914, Dell's *Masses* review of *A Traveler at Forty* belittled Dreiser's pessimism about social change.

In June 1914, commenting to H. L. Mencken that he must soon edit *The "Genius"* typescript, Dreiser remarked, "I am such a poor editor." In November, he added that with his editing under way, it would soon be "better written" (*D-M Letters* 1: 144, 164). Part of Dreiser's customary practice entailed multiple revisions, his own and others', a method stemming from that learned as a young reporter of turning over one's writing to be reworked by a newspaper's assistant city editor and later from his own wide experience as a magazine editor. Dell's revisory hand is identifiable on the typescript edited for publication of the first edition of *The "Genius."* The extant typescript lacks Chapters 1–31, but the remaining chapters (32–104) permit one to eavesdrop on a group effort in revision. Least extensive are Dreiser's changes, in blue or black pencil and blue crayon. Those of **Frederic Chapman**, the **John Lane Company's** English reader, are in red ink. Dell's appear in separate instances in green ink, black pencil, and typewriting, his handwriting matching that in his letters to Dreiser.

In claiming that he crossed out many passages that he judged to be needless but that Dreiser rescued, Dell seems not to have accurately recalled the editing task for which Dreiser hired him. Collation of the revised typescript with galleys and with the published edition of *The "Genius"* shows that Dreiser accepted nearly all of Dell's cuts, many of which Chapman had first suggested. Dell seconded most of Chapman's other revisions as well, sometimes noting an extra paragraph for removal but here and there retrieving one of Chapman's bracketed passages. Dell's principal contribution consisted in cutting or reshaping passages to give the story, which Dreiser had written in a spontaneous flow, more exact meaning or more graceful form. Like Chapman, Dell was skilled at paring flab without impairing meaning, but whereas Chapman concentrated on the deletion of otiose passages or on substituting more serviceable diction, Dell also altered structural elements. Together, Dell and Chapman deleted about 20,000 words from the typescript.

Though a contributor to the final form of *The "Genius,"* Dell was its least complimentary admirer in a review for the *New Review*. Noting that Dreiser "has exposed the depths of the human soul with a kind of relentless awe" yet failed to discern that "his hero is an ass," Dell concluded that "the result shows that Mr. Dreiser possesses superhuman energy, if not superhuman taste" (rpt. in Salzman 247–48). In 1916 Dell signed the **Authors' League of America** protest leaflet opposing the ban brought by the **New York Society for the Suppression of Vice** on further publication of the novel. Four years later, Dell published his own first novel, *Moon-Calf*.

Further Reading

Dell, Floyd. *Homecoming*. New York: Farrar & Rinehart, 1933. 268–70, 290–94.

Oldani, Louis J. "Dreiser's 'Genius' in the Making: Composition and Revision." *Studies in Bibliography* 47 (1994): 230–52.

Louis J. Oldani

DESHON, FLORENCE (1894–1922). Stage and silent film actress Florence Deshon (born Florence Danks) met Max Eastman at a *Masses* ball in December 1916. Eastman was smitten by what he described as her "ravishing" beauty, and soon after he left his wife, Ida Rauh, and child to conduct an intense, but tumultuous, romance with her. Eastman describes Deshon as a "wonder child . . . who was . . . so quick-minded, so unconscious of her astounding beauty" (44) but who was also an "ardent feminist" who was "proud" and "incapable of ingratiation toward people whom she did not respect" (102). Dreiser first met Deshon during his **Greenwich Village** years and met with her occasionally after he moved to Hollywood. Dreiser loosely based the *Gallery of Women* sketch "Ernestine" on Deshon's relationship with Eastman (who appears as Varn Kinsey in the sketch). Both Eastman and Dreiser portray Deshon as an ambitious woman whose chief asset was her beauty; Eastman's portrait differs from Dreiser's principally in its emphasis on the effects of the tribulations of their love lives upon her career. In 1920 Deshon entered into an affair with Charlie Chaplin, became pregnant, and suffered a severe infection when the fetus died. While she remained involved with both Chaplin and Eastman for a time, eventually she cut them both off, returned to New York, but found few opportunities to practice her craft. In February 1922 Deshon committed suicide by gas. Upon her death, suffragist and Heterodoxy Club founder Marie Jenney Howe wrote to Eastman to allay his guilt that Deshon had killed herself over their breakup: "Finally she faced herself—a girl with youth and beauty and no trained ability for the important position in the world that her soul craved. She saw no future. Instead of the glittering success she had expected, there was nothing but blackness" (qtd. in Eastman 281).

Further Reading

Eastman, Max. *Love and Revolution: My Journey through an Epoch.* New York: Random, 1964.

Keith Newlin

DETERMINISM. *See* Evolution; Mechanism; Naturalism.

DINAMOV, SERGEI SERGEEVICH (1901–1939). Muscovite author, critic, literary historian, editor, translator, and Soviet bureaucrat. Although Dinamov and Dreiser met only briefly in Moscow late in 1927, their friendship was unusually warm and durable, sustained in letters over the next decade, lasting beyond even the young Soviet writer's disappearance into Stalinist darkness. Dinamov figures prominently in the diary Dreiser kept that recorded, with the help of his secretary **Ruth Kennell**, the details of his two-month sojourn to discover "the real, unofficial Russia." Indeed, Dinamov introduced the American novelist to Kennell, an expatriate from Oklahoma who not only was Dinamov's lover but also would almost immediately become Dreiser's as well. Dinamov appears in the early pages of *Dreiser Looks at Russia* as the unnamed "Russian friend" with whom Dreiser, the "incorrigible individualist," occasionally argues.

The son of a laborer and a textile worker, Dinamov began working as a butcher's helper at the age of twelve and two years later followed his mother into Moscow's textile mills. One of the first Bolshevik deputies to the Moscow Soviet, Dinamov gained membership in the Communist Party in 1919, having served in the Red Army during the revolution. Married with a son and daughter, Dinamov rose steadily in the party bureaucracy, and in 1935 he was named head of the Arts Section of the Culture and Propaganda Department of the Central Committee and appointed editor of *International Literature*, the official journal of the International Union of Revolutionary Writers.

In October 1927, Dinamov had been among the "Moscow personages," along with **Eisenstein**, Stanislavsky, and Mayakovsky, to whom Dreiser was supplied introductions as he prepared to travel to the Soviet Union for the celebration of the tenth anniversary of the October Revolution. Dreiser and Dinamov's acquaintance, however, began nearly a year earlier when the young Marxist critic had written directly to the man he called "the greatest writer in the world," and after Dreiser finally arrived in Russia in November 1927, a slightly overheated Dinamov was the first to present himself at the novelist's suite in Moscow's Grand Hotel.

For the next decade Dinamov plumped for Dreiser however and wherever he might: as the head of the Anglo-American section of Gosizdat, the State Publishing House, for which he edited and wrote prefaces to the first Soviet edition of Dreiser's collected works; as the director of the Institute of Red Professors, where he often championed "Drayzer" to his colleagues; as the general editor of Moscow's *Literary Gazette*, in which he published his translations of several of Dreiser's essays and of literary criticism about Dreiser's novels by Carl Van Doren, Gorham Munson, **Burton Rascoe**, and others. A tall, gaunt man whose bad eyesight and poor health worsened as his efforts on behalf of Western writers increased, Dinamov also published works on, among others, Hawthorne, Poe, Galsworthy, and

Shakespeare, but it was for the reputation of his "dear genius" Dreiser that he always labored most strenuously.

For his part, Dreiser was flattered by the younger man's attention and appreciative of having so earnest an advocate in the Soviet Union. Whatever Dinamov asked for in his letters, Dreiser tried to supply—copies of his own books and those of authors that the struggling critic must have for his studies, American magazines and newspapers then scarce in Russia, even neckties and a yellow fountain pen. In return, Dreiser asked that Dinamov act as his literary agent in the Soviet Union, so that he might not continue to go uncompensated for unauthorized translations of his writing. Here, too, Dinamov succeeded, negotiating a deal with Gosizdat more or less to Dreiser's liking. Only in September 1932, when a somewhat thickheaded Dreiser asked that the young Soviet extract a signed statement from Stalin for the first issue of *The American Spectator*, did Dinamov unavoidably fail him. Three years later, when Dreiser chided Dinamov that he was better at asking things *of* him than at doing things *for* him, the two men quarreled briefly, but neither stopped writing, and Dreiser shortly announced, "I think we will go on as before" (Dreiser to Dinamov, 19 November 1935).

But sadly not much longer. By August 1935, the party line had begun to drift rightward; the anticapitalist International Union of Revolutionary Writers of which Dinamov was a prominent member had dissolved itself in favor of the antifascist International Association of Writers for the Defense of Culture. Despite the shift, Dinamov marched forward evenly, expressing to Dreiser his "confidence in our Party" and his "immeasurable and supreme love [for] Comrade Stalin" (Dinamov to Dreiser, 17 September 1935).

After June 1937, no more correspondence arrived from Russia, and in December, a concerned Dreiser wrote his last letter to Dinamov: "I haven't heard from you for so long that I wonder what has become of you. . . . I'd like to know how the world looks to you from where you are. From here everything seems dark and threatening indeed" (10 December 1937). In 1944, Dreiser was still asking their former lover Kennell about Dinamov's whereabouts and well-being, but he was never to hear another word from his dear friend. Dinamov had been arrested by the secret police during the purges and reportedly died in prison on 20 November 1939. He has been rehabilitated posthumously.

Further Reading

Kennell, Ruth Epperson. *Theodore Dreiser and the Soviet Union, 1927–1945: A First-Hand Chronicle.* New York, International, 1969.
Dreiser-Dinamov Correspondence, Dreiser Papers, University of Pennsylvania Rare Book and Manuscript Library.

Arthur D. Casciato

DODGE, B. W., & Co. After the "suppression" of *Sister Carrie* by **Doubleday, Page & Co.** in 1900, Dreiser resolved to have the novel reprinted so that it might have a second chance. It took him several years, however, to make good on his plan. He tried in 1902 to have *Sister Carrie* reissued by J. F. Taylor, a remainder house, but this effort failed. He attempted in 1905 to have the novel reprinted by Charles MacLean, a personal friend; this effort, too, came to nothing. In 1906 Dreiser himself acquired the back stock and the printing plates of *Carrie* for the sum of $550. He then put $1,000 of his own money into a fledgling book-publishing operation called B. W. Dodge & Co., which agreed to reissue *Sister Carrie* in a fresh print run, with a color frontispiece (showing Carrie in her "Quaker Maid" costume) and with a new binding. Dreiser publicized the reissue, which appeared in 1907, by creating newsworthy copy for the reviewers; much of the apocrypha about the 1900 edition, in fact, originates in these press releases. Dreiser made two changes in the text of the Dodge reprint: he dropped the dedication to **Arthur Henry**, with whom he was no longer on good terms, and he rewrote a passage on page 5 in which he had borrowed freely from the journalist George Ade. Dreiser's promotional efforts worked well. The Dodge reprint of *Sister Carrie* was seriously reviewed, and the firm sold some 8,500 copies. The unsold stock went to Grosset & Dunlap, a large reprint house, which disposed of these copies and in 1908 manufactured its own fresh impression. The B. W. Dodge reissue of *Sister Carrie* was by nearly all measures a success, giving second life to the novel and preparing the way for the publication of *Jennie Gerhardt* in 1911 by **Harper & Brothers**.

Further Reading

West, James L. W., III. "Dreiser and the B. W. Dodge *Sister Carrie*." *Studies in Bibliography* 35 (1982): 323–31.

James L. W. West III

"A DOER OF THE WORD." While spending the summer of 1901 in Noank, Connecticut, with **Arthur Henry**, Dreiser searched out material for articles he could sell to magazines. Upon hearing repeatedly of a local resident famous for being a "truly contented man," Dreiser traveled to nearby Norwich, where he interviewed this man, **Charles Tilden Potter**. The result was "A Doer of the Word," first published in *Ainslee's* in June 1902 and then collected in *Twelve Men*. Dreiser describes his efforts to seek out and talk to Potter, afterward recognizing the reports were true. Although unable himself to adopt Potter's fanatical faith in Christian charity, the narrator does develop a strong admiration for Potter as someone who has discovered at least one answer to the question of how to find contentment in life.

In the original sketch, written in 1901 and called "The Disciple of Noank," Dreiser had depicted Potter as a completely selfless man whose life was devoted to helping others. When he revised the sketch for *Twelve Men*, Dreiser reinforced the impression of Potter as an example of someone living according to the principles of Christian charity by adding new material to emphasize the contrast between the materialistic villagers and the selfless Charlie Potter. He also added several more sentences of dialogue to the interview to reinforce the positive aspects of Potter's character, such as: "Anything I earn or take is for the Lord, not me. I never keep it." Other revisions served to emphasize that, even though devoutly religious, Potter was a nonconformist like the other eleven men in the collection: the only religious authority he recognized was the Bible itself. Dreiser admired Potter as a nonconformist determined to live life on his own terms, rather than according to the traditional rules of organized **religion**.

Robert Coltrane

DOUBLEDAY, FRANK (1862–1934). The publisher Frank N. Doubleday is a minor villain in Dreiser studies since he caused the "suppression" of *Sister Carrie* in 1900. In American book-trade history, however, Doubleday is a much-admired figure. He began in the business in 1877, at the age of fifteen, working as a stock boy and messenger at Charles Scribner's Sons. He learned the trade from the Scribner family, then departed in 1897 to form a short-lived publishing partnership with S. S. McClure, whose news syndicate had become a powerful force in the American newspaper business. In 1899 Doubleday teamed with **Walter Hines Page** to form **Doubleday, Page & Co.**, the imprint that would publish *Sister Carrie*. Doubleday got on well with most of his authors, including Henry George, Joseph Conrad, **Frank Norris**, and especially Rudyard Kipling. He understood the dynamics and potential of the trade better than did most of his peers and saw that the publisher must not be a passive figure, waiting for manuscripts to come to him. Doubleday believed to the contrary that publishers should themselves conceive the ideas for books, find authors to write them, and then create reading audiences by vigorous promotion. By 1910 he had built a publishing empire and had moved his operations to Garden City, New York, in order to escape the expense and noise of the city. He acquired the London firm of Heinemann in 1920 and attempted, with mixed success, to apply American book-publishing methods to the British trade. With his son Nelson he was an early pioneer in book club publishing, helping to found the Literary Guild in 1927, the same year that he merged his list with that of the publisher George H. Doran. Doubleday died in 1934: ironically Doubleday & Co. published Dreiser's final two novels—*The Bulwark* and *The Stoic*—both issued after Dreiser's own death.

Further Reading

Madison, Charles A. *Book Publishing in America.* New York: McGraw-Hill, 1966. 272–91.

James L. W. West III

DOUBLEDAY, PAGE & CO. Publishing company for the first edition of *Sister Carrie*. Over the years a myth has flourished, encouraged by H. L. Mencken, biographer **Dorothy Dudley**, and Dreiser himself (among many others), concerning the suppression of the novel. According to the legend, after Dreiser signed a contract with the firm to publish his work, the prudish wife of the publisher read the manuscript and, in Dreiser's words, was "horrified by its frankness" and demanded that her husband refuse to publish it. In this version of events, Dreiser perseveres, in spite of active opposition to the manuscript and deliberate suppression of the published book, and brings his revolutionary novel to the public, suffering a nervous breakdown afterward due to the strain of resisting conformity.

The reality appears to be both less sensational and more complicated. Dreiser first sent the novel to **Harper & Brothers** in April 1900, where it was rejected because of its uneven style and indelicate content. After cutting more than 30,000 words and toning down the sexual explicitness, Dreiser sent the typescript to the new (and he hoped more adventurous) publishing house of Doubleday, Page in May 1900. There the novel was read by **Frank Norris**, author of the recently published *McTeague*, who enthusiastically recommended it for publication. Senior editor Henry Lanier liked the novel as well, but he was concerned about its use of actual place-names and personal names. Junior partner **Walter Hines Page**, who may—or may not—have read the manuscript, wrote to Dreiser expressing his approval of the book and requesting a meeting in June. The senior partner, **Frank Doubleday**, was in Europe at the time of this meeting, which may have contributed to the ensuing drama. It is also important to note that while there was a verbal agreement to publish the book at the meeting, no contract was signed at that time.

After the meeting, a confident and cheerful Dreiser promptly left New York for a vacation in Missouri, an unfortunate decision given the events that followed. Had he been nearby, he might have been able to answer the publisher's objections and defuse the situation. As it was, his friend and fellow writer **Arthur Henry** negotiated in his stead. Soon after Dreiser's departure, Doubleday returned from Europe and, for reasons that remain unclear, asked that Dreiser release Doubleday, Page from its unwritten obligation to publish the novel. Doubleday's wife *may* have read and disliked the novel, although Doubleday consistently denied her involvement in events. It is more likely that she was added to the story by those wishing to deflect accusations of censorship or failure to honor a contract from Doubleday.

Nevertheless, several attempts over the summer of 1900 to get Dreiser to send the book elsewhere failed, although his early correspondence with Henry suggests he might have been willing to consider another publisher. Henry strongly discouraged this capitulation, although he may have been motivated by his own publishing difficulties ten years earlier. A contract was finally signed on 20 August 1900, with the title "The Flesh and the Spirit" listed on the document (and "Sister Carrie" penciled in the margin). Following the signing, Doubleday, Page insisted that Dreiser change several proper names. Hannah and Hogg's, where the real-life model for Hurstwood works, became Fitzgerald and Moy's, contemporary actors' names were changed, and several concessions were made to popular morality (e.g., "dingy lavatory" became "dingy hall," and Carrie and Hurstwood don't sleep together until their "marriage"). On 8 November 1900 the book was published. One thousand eight sets of sheets were printed, with 450 left unbound and the price set at $1.50.

At this point what can justifiably be-called neglect—if not exactly suppression—begins. Apparently, Doubleday, Page was advised by its lawyers that although they were obligated to publish the novel, they were not obligated to promote the book in any way. Consequently, the book was unattractively bound in a dull red with black lettering. There was no listing for the novel in the Doubleday, Page catalog or any advertisements in bookstores or literary magazines. Frank Norris did send 100 copies to newspaper reviewers, and although many of them liked the novel, there were objections to the frankness of the story and the amorality of the heroine. However, no major literary magazines or well-known writers reviewed it. Between November 1900 and February 1902, the book sold a mere 456 copies. Following the debacle with Doubleday, Page, in July 1901 an abridged *Sister Carrie* was published in England by William Heinemann, who contributed to the myth of Mrs. Doubleday's role in the suppression, perhaps for economic reasons. With support from its new publisher and adequate publicity, the book sold 1,000 copies of the first printing of 1,500 and went into a second printing, and it has remained in print, through various publishing houses, ever since.

Given this troubled relationship with the firm, it is somewhat puzzling that Dreiser contracted to publish his last two novels—*The Bulwark* and *The Stoic*—with Doubleday & Co., the successor to Doubleday, Page. Perhaps Dreiser's return to Doubleday signals his increasingly desperate desire to secure a place for his final novels. Both had been started decades before (*The Bulwark* had three publishers contract for it over the years), and Dreiser had considerable difficulty putting both into their final form, soliciting the guidance of **Marguerite Tjader** and the detailed advice of novelist **James T. Farrell**. The novels were published after his death in 1945, and in a final irony, *The Bulwark* sold well, making over $15,000 in royalties and one

imagines a considerable amount for the firm that seemed determined to prevent the financial success of *Sister Carrie*.

Still, Dreiser's return to Doubleday does little to diminish the mythic power of the *Sister Carrie* story, which derives its strength from **gender** and class conflicts, both in Dreiser's time and in our own. While the real story doesn't quite offer the mythic resonance of a struggle between genteel female **censorship** and working-class artistic integrity, the fact remains that Dreiser's novel had the power to offend even those publishers and readers familiar with the stark **realism** of Frank Norris. The story also serves as testimony to the consequences of Dreiser's stubborn refusal to compromise, which resulted in, at the very least, a delay in the critical and popular acclaim due to *Sister Carrie*. Finally, it reminds us of the power publishing houses had—and still have today—over the fortunes and reputations of authors.

Further Reading

"Backgrounds and Sources II: Composition, Publication, and Legend." *Sister Carrie: An Authoritative Text, Backgrounds and Sources, Criticism.* Ed. Donald Pizer. 2nd ed. New York: Norton, 1991. 436–77.

Berkey, John C., James L. W. West III, and Alice M. Winters. "*Sister Carrie*: Manuscript to Print." *Sister Carrie.* Philadelphia: University of Pennsylvania Press, 1981. 503–41.

Dreiser, Theodore. "The Early Adventures of *Sister Carrie*." Preface to the Modern Library Edition of *Sister Carrie*. New York: Random, 1932.

Moyer, Marsha S. "Dreiser, *Sister Carrie*, and Mrs. Doubleday: Gender and Social Change at the Turn of the Century." *Theodore Dreiser and American Culture.* Ed. Yoshinobu Hakutani. Rutherford, N.J.: Fairleigh Dickinson University Press, 1980. 39–55.

Pizer, Donald. Introduction. *New Essays on Sister Carrie.* Ed. Donald Pizer. Cambridge and New York: Cambridge University Press, 1991. 1–22.

Caren J. Town

DOUGLAS, GEORGE (?–1936). Australian-born newspaperman whose intellect and personality thrilled Dreiser and, apparently, everyone he knew. Helen Dreiser recalls his warmth and generosity, his "brilliance of mind and spirit" in *My Life with Dreiser* (247). While living in San Francisco, he served for ten years as the literary editor for the *San Francisco Chronicle*, served for another ten years at the *San Francisco Bulletin*, and associated with a wide range of artists and intellectuals. His social life waned in Los Angeles, where he worked as an editorial writer in 1929 for William Randolph Hearst's *Los Angeles Examiner*. He longed for intellectual companionship and stimulation, which he found with Dreiser, who relied upon Douglas' expertise in poetry and philosophy, as well as his sound reasoning and sharp criticism, to mold his "Formulae Called Life," posthumously published as *Notes on Life*.

In Dreiser's scientific and philosophical quest to find some cosmic link through humankind, he found what he called a "psychic osmosis" with Douglas. During the summer of 1935, Dreiser moved into a suite in the Douglas home in Los Angeles while Margaret "Molly" Douglas was away in San Francisco and their two young adult daughters were absent. Dreiser and Douglas guarded their privacy, enjoying long evenings of quoting poetry (Douglas could spout lines appropriate for any occasion), discussing current events, and arguing about Dreiser's scientific and philosophical interests. They explored the Mount Wilson Observatory, the California Institute of Technology, and the Huntington Library at San Marino. They entertained several nights a week, assembling what Dreiser called "a fascinating group," or joined Helen (who had rented a room nearby) for dinner.

Douglas wasn't entirely happy with newspaper work, but he felt his obligations to his family wouldn't allow him to risk his income by freelancing or moving to New York, even when Dreiser offered him a job working at *The American Spectator*. George and Molly had two daughters: Halley, who wrote scripts for motion-pictures, and Dorothy, who eventually became a dancer. At Dreiser's request, Douglas published several pieces, including "The God Standard," in the *American Spectator* under the alias John Adam Smith, since he was forbidden to publish outside of his job at the *Los Angeles Examiner*.

Douglas especially enjoyed Dreiser's company and intellectual stimulation, which gave Douglas a renewed interest in life. Dreiser found Douglas an immensely helpful and dear collaborative friend. Shortly after their summer together and while Dreiser was still at work on his "Formulae," Douglas died suddenly of a heart attack on 10 February 1936. Dreiser wired Donald McCord, "GEORGE'S DEATH HURTS BEYOND BELIEF. WILL YOU PERSONALLY SELECT FOUR DOZEN ROSES. SEND WITH CARD SAYING FROM DREISER TO GEORGE" (qtd. in Lingeman 2: 397).

Mandy See

"DOWN HILL AND UP" is a quasi-autobiographical account of Dreiser's neurasthenic decline in early 1901 and his ultimate recovery by 1904. In contrast to the incomplete *An Amateur Laborer*, an exploration of those troubled years written in 1904, "Down Hill and Up" traces Dreiser's illness from breakdown to recovery, though the detail is more selective and less authentic. In fact, Dreiser drew more directly on earlier fictionalized versions of his neurasthenic experiences, specifically

"The Mighty Burke" and *The "Genius,"* than he did on the more verifiable *An Amateur Laborer.*

In 1924, seeking to support himself during the composition of *An American Tragedy*, Dreiser submitted "Down Hill and Up" to *Hearst's International*, which in August published the second half of that manuscript as "The Irish Section Foreman Who Taught Me How to Live." "Down Hill and Up" in its entirety was not published until 1988/1989, when it was issued in two installments by *Dreiser Studies.*

Although Dreiser in "Down Hill and Up" attributed his delicate health to "a malignant appendix," he opened the narrative with a discussion of the puritanical turn-of-the-century literary climate that had doomed *Sister Carrie* and turned him into "a social pariah." The shock of failure—after such great expectations—left him in a debilitatingly depressed state. The events between his hopeful departure from New York in November 1901 and his unceremonious return in early 1903 were briefly treated in two paragraphs focused on his inability to make progress on *Jennie Gerhardt* and his fitful odyssey through the Virginias. Notably omitted were his seven-month stay in Philadelphia and the efforts of Mrs. Dreiser to provide aid and comfort during this period.

In the Brooklyn portion of the narrative, Dreiser emphasized his despair, exaggerated his isolation, and introduced his contemplated suicide toward the end of that ordeal. In *An Amateur Laborer*, he had stressed his indomitable spirit at this crucial juncture: "Low as my condition was physically, mentally and financially I never once truly yielded. People rejected me and I thought I was like to die but I would not give in." In "Down Hill and Up," however, Dreiser spoke of the lure of the East River as a solution to his despair and of the drunken Scotch sailor who had

lifted his spirits from their "requiem" state—episodes that have become staples of Dreiser **biography**.

Maintaining his theme of isolation, Dreiser moved the narrative directly to his employment by the New York Central, omitting thereby Paul Dresser's assistance and his own rehabilitation at **Muldoon's** Olympia. This "up hill" portion is the richest in development, particularly Dreiser's tenure with **Mike Burke** (again identified as "Rourke"). Parts of that section were lifted verbatim from "The Mighty Burke," but the humor of that earlier sketch was largely stripped away. The focus was instead placed on the foreman's fortitude and joy in life, which inspired Dreiser to probably exaggerated feats of manual labor and contributed to his recovery. In conclusion he wrote, "This is the attitude and this is the man—and his policy and his viewpoint are mine from this day forth."

See also Neurasthenia.

Further Reading

Riggio, Thomas P. " 'Down Hill': A Chapter in Dreiser's Story about Himself." *Dreiser Studies* 19.2 (1988): 2–21.
———. " 'Up Hill': A Chapter in Dreiser's Story about Himself." *Dreiser Studies* 20.1 (1989): 2–32.

Richard W. Dowell

THE DREAM. First published in the *Seven Arts* for July 1917, this one-act play was reprinted in *Hey Rub-a-Dub-Dub*. In July 1915 the eccentric writer **Charles Fort** sent Dreiser the manuscript of "X," a book that, according to Dreiser, demonstrated that human beings and the world they inhabit were nothing more than the emanations of some cosmic mind. "And it did this," Dreiser writes in an unpublished memoir, "quite as we, by the means of light and photography, throw a moving picture on a screen, the sensitive chemicals of a photographic film and the light that causes the film first to receive an impression of something and later to retransmit it as seemingly the very substance of reality. Only to X, the earth is the sensitive film and its speeding rays the light of the modern camera film." *The Dream* is a dramatization of "X" written, Dreiser says in his memoir of Fort, as the result of a dream "which seemed in no indefinite way to confirm it. And arising from that dream, some months or weeks after I had read the book, I immediately sat down and wrote out a one-act interpretation of it, using Fort's theory as the thesis or backbone of the action" (qtd. in Helen Dreiser 220–22).

In dramatizing "X," Dreiser structures the play along lines suggested by **Freud's** dream theory, with which he probably became acquainted through **Floyd Dell**, Max Eastman, and other **Liberal Club** habitués who were earnest enthusiasts and popularizers of Freud. The symbolically named George Syphers, a professor of chemistry, discusses with more skeptical professors the possibility that "we were all a part of some invisible psychic body, force body, in the mechanism of which we function in some way, just as the cells do in ours." This "psychic body"—Fort's "X"—has "worked out beforehand" all life, which "is now being orthogentically or chemically directed from somewhere, being thrown on a screen, as it were, like a moving-picture, and we mere dot pictures, mere cell-built-up pictures, like the movies, only we are telegraphed or telautographed from somewhere else." After being dismissed as "a terrible bore" by the others, Syphers returns home and falls asleep; his last thoughts are that "Life is really a dream. We are all an emanation, a shadow, a moving picture cast on a screen of ether. I'm sure of it."

As he begins to dream, the argument with his fellow scientists and the sounds of a storm raging outside become distorted and manifest as incidents in his dream. Syphers discovers himself in the midst of a battle, pursued by soldiers as he tries to hide. The battle, of course, represents his previous argument with his colleagues, and the pursuing soldiers his skeptical associates. Outside it begins to rain, and Syphers's dream thoughts distort the sound into the fire of machine guns. Thunder becomes cannon fire; a telegram messenger rings the bell, and its sound becomes distorted into the rush of artillery and men. The messenger kicks at the door, and Syphers perceives soldiers attacking him. Syphers thinks that if life really is a dream, if we are all emanations in some cosmic mind, then the soldiers cannot kill him. "I defy you!" he says to the soldiers. "Do your worst! You're not real! I'm not real! This whole thing is a dream!" As a soldier prepares to fire at him, Syphers loses faith; shot, he feels the pain and believes he is dying. At this point he begins to awaken and tells the soldiers that while they are mere shadows, he is real. A soldier counters by posing an existential dilemma: "Are we? Well, you're a fool! Wait! You may be waking into another state, but you'll be dead to this one. But we won't. Ha! Ha! We'll still be here alive." Syphers's answer indicates his confusion and reflects Dreiser's sense of the inscrutability of life, the impossibility of arriving at final answers: "What is this? Am I dying, or waking up? Which is it? Are there various worlds, one within the other?" The dramatic conflict is thus whether Syphers can ever realize whether he awakens into a "real" state of being or whether he will always remain as a dream character in someone's mind.

Like all of his philosophical plays, *The Dream* records Dreiser's quest to comprehend a person's place in the cosmos. Prior to *The Dream*, Dreiser had concentrated on depicting—especially in *Laughing Gas*—the random, purposeless chaos of the universe. Whereas Dreiser had formerly seen little besides the great clash of "conflicting forces" in a universe that operated without purpose, in *The Dream* he depicts a "controlling force" that governs the "equation" that this clash ultimately produces. As Syphers remarks, "Why, snow crystals, tree and flower forms, everything, gives us a hint, sometimes instantaneously . . . [that] the controlling impulse is certainly artistic." Despite the craziness of his ideas, Fort appears to have enabled Dreiser to reconcile his essentially pessimistic **mechanism** with his emotional desire to discover an organizing principle behind the mystery of life.

Further Reading

Dreiser, Helen. *My Life with Dreiser*. New York: World, 1951. 219–24.

Keith Newlin

DREISER, ALPHONS JOACHIM (AL) (1867–?). In his autobiography *Dawn*, Dreiser writes that his brother Al "was intended to be a better writer than I could ever hope to be" and that he had a "natural intelligence thwarted by untoward conditions." Dreiser turned to his older brother for companionship, considering him to be the most intellectual member of the family. His respect for his brother lasted until Al dropped from sight after 1906. In 1934 Dreiser again heard from Al, who was seeking his share of brother Paul Dresser's estate, but Al again disappeared before Dreiser's reply could reach him.

While they were young, Al was sent to their mother's half sister's farm in northern Indiana. The hope that he would become a farmer was dashed when he returned home two years later much

stronger than when he left but with no intention to return to a pastoral life. His new strength was a boon to the other Dreiser children who were being terrorized by neighborhood bullies.

Dreiser characterized Al as a good-spirited individual who liked to make friends and enjoy himself, despite his role as bodyguard to the rest of the brood. Al held a variety of jobs before he finally became an electrician. He spent time selling candies and magazines aboard trains, worked in a chair factory, and launched and briefly ran a small-town minstrel show that visited four or five towns but failed to prove profitable. While he never realized his potential as a writer, their niece, Vera Dreiser, quotes some of Al's poetry in her book, *My Uncle Theodore*.

Jennifer Marie Raspet

DREISER, CACILIA (SYLVIA) (1866–1945). Born in Sullivan, Indiana, in 1866, Cacilia, known as Sylvia, was one of Dreiser's sisters. According to Dreiser's comments in *Dawn*, she was sensual and selfish and lacked intelligence, even though she perceived herself as having a superior intelligence. Sylvia shared many of the same life experiences with her sisters Emma and Mame, who spent much of their time trying to meet wealthy young men who would help them reach wealth and high status to escape the poverty of their family.

When Dreiser was fifteen, Sylvia had an affair with a man Dreiser pseudonymously refers to as Don Ashley, who was from one of the more prominent families in Warsaw. She became pregnant and believed Ashley would move away with her and marry her. When Ashley left town, leaving Sylvia behind to deal with the pregnancy herself, Dreiser's mother, Sarah, became embarrassed and wanted to hide Sylvia's mistake. Sylvia was sent to live in

New York with her sister Emma for the duration of her pregnancy. On 16 October 1886 she gave birth to a boy named Carl, who was sent to live first with Sarah and then with Mame, and then, like Al, he disappears from family records after 1908. Sylvia had nothing to do with her baby after the delivery. Dreiser was appalled by his sister's attitude about her own son. Even though Mame was the primary inspiration behind the plot in *Jennie Gerhardt*, Sylvia's experience remained close to Dreiser's heart as he depicted the illegitimate birth of Vesta in this novel.

Sylvia's relationship with men and especially with her father became an inspiration for Dreiser's story "Old Rogaum and his Theresa." While creating this plot, Dreiser reflected upon their father's reaction to Sylvia's and Emma's attempt to leave town with some men they had met. In this story, Old Rogaum is infuriated with Theresa's developing interest in boys and locks his daughter out of the house in an attempt to force her to obey him, just as Sylvia's father threatened to do.

In Dreiser's autobiography *Dawn*, Sylvia is referred to as "Amy" to protect her identity. Dreiser completed this book in 1916, but he did not want to publish it because he was afraid of making his family angry with him. However, because some of his family members, including Sylvia, were financially supported by him and he needed the money, he published the volume in 1931. Dreiser provided financial support for Sylvia until her death in September 1945.

Dana Stolte Koller

DREISER, CLARA CLOTHILDE (CLAIRE)

(1868–1918). Claire was the sister closest to Dreiser in age and therefore the one with whom he spent much of his time during his youth. They attended the same schools and had the same chores while Claire oc- casionally defended him from bullies, but they quarreled frequently. In *Dawn*, where he refers to her as "Trina," Dreiser describes her as "intelligent and practical but lacking in warmth and sympathy." In *Newspaper Days*, he describes her as "hard, narrow, and selfish, a most unattractive type." For a time, during one of the many family dislocations, Dreiser lived with her in Chicago but found her self-absorption and inefficient housekeeping unpalatable, and the living arrangement dissolved. Claire seems to have escaped the sexual peccadilloes that plagued her sisters, instead inclining to a doctrinaire religiosity, and she married Harry V. Gormely, having with him a son, Paul, named after her brother. Despite misgivings about her family's moral behavior, she remained committed to them. After a struggle with tuberculosis, which involved taking a cure in Arizona, she succumbed to cancer.

Jennifer Marie Raspet

DREISER, EDUARD MINEROD (ED)

(1873–1958). Ed and Theodore held similar responsibilities toward the rest of the family. Though they were the two youngest children, both took on the responsibility for caring for their other siblings and parents. Through all the ups and downs of their family's finances, Ed was the only member of the family never to rely on Dreiser for financial support. He was also one of the most stable of the Dreiser siblings. In 1899 he married Mai Skelly; their daughter, Vera, was born in 1908.

As a child Ed was the sibling least interested in school and, according to Dreiser, had to be carried kicking and screaming into the schoolhouse. He was fun-loving and good at sports but was never interested by the books that always intrigued Dreiser. Dreiser often considered Ed as a contrast to himself and found their close relationship surprising. In *Dawn*,

Dreiser describes Ed as "ambitious and emotional, the actor type but without sufficient luck or daring to forward himself."

Although he held a number of jobs, Ed was most successful as an actor. He appeared on Broadway, under the name Edward Dresser, in such plays as *The Climbers* (1901), *Soldiers of Fortune* (1902), *The School for Husbands* (1905), and *Paid in Full* (1908). His daughter, Vera, recalls him as a "matinee idol" until an unfortunate accident blinded him for two years and ruined his career. He also created a publishing business based upon his brother Paul's musical scores, the Paul Dresser Publishing Company. This failed enterprise is detailed in his correspondence with Dreiser.

Jennifer Marie Raspet

DREISER, EMMA WILHELMINA (1863–1937).

Dreiser's favorite sister, "Em" provided him unintentionally with the life material that he would fictionalize in *Sister Carrie* and recount later in *Dawn* (where he referred to her as "Janet"). Rebelling against her father's conventional ideas about women and marriage, Emma dreamed of a life filled with fine clothes provided by wealthy, handsome men. Indeed, by twenty-one, in Chicago, she was involved with an older man, a prominent architect, who set her up in style at a hotel on South Halsted Street. Her apparent prosperity and happiness in such an "immoral" situation initially confused Dreiser but led him in *Sister Carrie* and *Jennie Gerhardt* to highlight the fraudulence of conventional morality. By the fall of 1885, she found herself in another affair, this time with a forty-year-old clerk named **L. A. Hopkins** who worked at Chapin and Gore, a chain of saloons, and who had a wife and an eighteen-year-old daughter living on the West Side. By winter, Mrs. Hopkins suspected adultery. On 11 February 1886, she, a private detective, and

some friends entered a South Side apartment at 1:00 A.M. and found Hopkins and Emma asleep together. Hopkins begged forgiveness. Three days later, though, he stole $3,500 in cash and $200 in jewelry from his employers' safe. Like Hurstwood and Carrie, he and Emma absconded to Montreal, where after a change of heart he returned all but $800 of the money. His employers did not press charges, and the two lovers went on to New York, where Hopkins was able to procure a job through Tammany Hall. By 1894, though, Dreiser found Emma much changed—her beauty faded after having two children, George and Gertrude—and unhappy with Hopkins, who had lost his job after the Lexow Committee's investigations into political corruption. Since then, he had deteriorated in appearance and morale and was pressuring her to rent their rooms to "transient lovers" (i.e., prostitutes). Dreiser's experience there influenced his sympathetic portrayal of Hurstwood's decline. Eventually, Dreiser was able to convince Emma to leave Hopkins, and she did so through a ruse in which she claimed to be joining Dreiser in Pittsburgh when she was actually moving to a new apartment in the city. They never saw each other again. It should be noted finally that Carrie and Emma's personalities and situations are not identical. Dreiser makes Carrie less sexually experienced, less nurturing, and much more naive than Emma. Newspaper accounts of the incident indicate that, unlike Carrie with Hurstwood, Emma was aware of Hopkins's marriage and knew about the premeditated theft ahead of time. After leaving Hopkins, she married John Nelson in 1898, was widowed by 1930, and was dependent on Dreiser for financial help even after being angered by his depiction of her experiences in *Dawn*. (Surprisingly, she did not have the same reaction in 1901 regarding *Sister Carrie*, about which she said simply, "I liked the book very much.")

Monty Kozbial Ernst

DREISER, HELEN RICHARDSON (1894–1955). Helen Patges Richardson's grandmother (Esther Schänäb Parks) and Dreiser's mother (Sarah Schänäb Dreiser) were sisters. Helen visited Dreiser's Manhattan apartment on 13 September 1919, and they were instantly attracted to each other. At the time, she was twenty-five and he forty-eight. They began a long, often tempestuous relationship that culminated in their marriage nearly twenty-five years later. Helen had been in vaudeville, and she had her mind set on a career as an actress in Hollywood. A month after their meeting, Dreiser abandoned the familiar New York associations of over two decades and accompanied Helen to Los Angeles, planning himself to write movie scripts while she made the rounds of the studios. She soon began appearing in films, always in minor roles, but at times she worked with celebrities such as Rudolph Valentino and Bebe Daniels. Helen would subsequently abandon her career, and for many years she lived unofficially as "Mrs. Dreiser." The couple experienced periods of separation, and many of Dreiser's letters to her during these times survive. They contain not just personal matter but reflections on his writing, as, for example, during the period in 1924, when she visited her family in Oregon and Dreiser wrote about his progress and difficulties with *An American Tragedy*. Over the years, Helen was his constant companion, and she was present during major junctures in his life. The best record of these occasions and their relationship is in her memoir, *My Life with Dreiser* (1951), an indispensable primary source. She had become his second wife on 13 June 1944, and she was living with Dreiser in Hollywood when he died

in 1945. In the years after his death, Helen worked to get his final novel, *The Stoic*, ready for publication and helped to administer his literary estate. She suffered a cerebral hemorrhage in 1951 and afterward lived in Greshham, Oregon, in the care of her sister **Myrtle Patges** Butcher. She and Dreiser had chosen burial plots at Forest Lawn Cemetery in Los Angeles, and after her death on 22 September 1955 she was buried beside him.

Thomas P. Riggio

DREISER, JOHANN PAUL (PAUL) (1821–1900). Theodore Dreiser's father, known as Paul, was born in Germany in 1821 and immigrated to America in 1844. He first lived in Massachusetts, where he worked as a weaver, and later moved to Indiana, where he worked in the woolen business. In 1851 he married Sarah Mary Schänäb, and together they had thirteen children, three of whom died in infancy. While in Indiana, Paul made a successful living as a manager and then owner of a woolen mill. He sold the mill at a loss in 1870. At this point, Paul Dreiser's income began to dwindle steadily, and for the rest of his life he was forced to work as a menial laborer to make ends meet. He died at the age of seventy-nine on 25 December 1900.

Theodore Dreiser's relationship with his father was always strained. Dreiser resented his father's strict German business ethics, patriarchal authoritarianism, and emotional weakness. Dreiser especially despised his father's intense religious fanaticism. A Roman Catholic, Paul Dreiser's ritualistic legalism alienated him from his wife and children. He insisted that the children go to parochial schools and was harsh and unwavering when it came to their moral behavior. In his autobiography *Dawn*, Dreiser describes his father's attitude toward the family as being fraught with "Catholic dogma [and] wholly unyielding directive ritual and precept, as to quite sicken not only his wife but all his children." Ironically, he lived out his last years with his daughter, Mame, who, as a young woman, had brought down her father's wrath by taking up with an older man and giving birth to his illegitimate child.

In Dreiser's fiction, subtle references to Paul Dreiser can be seen any time that a staunchly religious character appears. However, the clearest representation of this is found in Dreiser's second novel, *Jennie Gerhardt*. **William Gerhardt**, Jennie's father, a German immigrant, makes his living as a glassblower, but because of an accident is forced to work odd jobs to keep house and home together. His Lutheran fanaticism forces him to banish his young daughter, **Jennie**, from the home when she becomes pregnant with an older man's child. Eventually, they are reunited, and she cares for him until his death. Unlike Dreiser's own father, however, Gerhardt becomes less legalistic in his old age and eventually asks for his daughter's forgiveness: "I understand a lot of things I didn't. We get wiser as we get older," he tells her. This ending to Gerhardt's life represents the growing sympathy Dreiser felt toward his father later in life. Although he never had the same love for him as he did for his mother, he eventually learned to respect his father's struggle to find a place in a world that offered few opportunities.

Further Reading

Cassuto, Leonard. "Dreiser's Idea of Balance." *Dreiser's* Jennie Gerhardt: *New Essays on the Restored Text.* Ed. James L. W. West III. Philadelphia: University of Pennsylvania Press, 1995. 51–62.

Annemarie Koning Whaley

DREISER, JOHANN PAUL, JR. *See* Dresser, Paul.

DREISER, MARIA FRANZISKA (MAME) (1861–1944). Dreiser's oldest sister, "Mame" was perhaps the most similar in temperament to him—domineering and vain as well as given to dramatic extremes of sympathies, enthusiasms, and rages. Her experiences rather than her personality, though, would inspire Dreiser to write *Jennie Gerhardt*. At sixteen, Mame became involved with an older man—a wealthy and prominent Terre Haute attorney referred to in *Dawn* as "Colonel Silsby"; his real identity remains unknown. Like Senator Brander with Jennie, Silsby provided Mame with money, helped get a brother out of jail, and ultimately impregnated her. After attending a finishing school to which Silsby had sent her, she returned home in late 1879, unmarried and with fifty dollars from Silsby to procure an abortion from a country doctor. (Her unsuccessful pilgrimage to the doctor was most likely similar to **Roberta Alden's** in *An American Tragedy*.) Like Jennie, Mame was kept out of sight by her mother during her pregnancy. Unlike her fictional counterpart, however, the resulting baby was stillborn and then buried that night in the yard. By 1884, while living in Chicago, Mame became involved with another older man, Austin Brennan, a casketware salesman born into a socially prominent family from Rochester, New York. Doted on by him but not accepted by his family, she strove to emulate the airs of his class and, in the following years, angered the other siblings with her sometimes haughty demeanor. Mame had been critical as well of Sylvia's failings, and Dreiser felt that, given her own past behavior, Mame had acted hypocritically. Certainly, Mame was not the humble, nurturing Jennie, but she and Brennan did take her father into their home the last years of his life. Shortly after his father's death in 1900, Dreiser began *Jennie Gerhardt*, struck by the idea of a stern, dogmatic father who had disowned his daughter but had later, under her care, presumably forgiven her. Living by 1903 in an apartment on Washington Square, the Brennans provided a meal and comfort to a broken-down Dreiser shortly before brother Paul's intervention. Later, in 1923, while working on *An American Tragedy*, Dreiser stayed at an apartment building, the Rhinelander Gardens, which they were managing. (He would return there in 1937 during a momentary break from Helen.) Like the remaining sisters, Mame was infuriated by *Dawn* but was financially dependent upon her brother. In 1930, two years after Brennan's death and with financial assistance from Dreiser, she provided a home for her confused and destitute brother, Rome. By early 1944, Mame was hospitalized with cancer of the bladder. With royalty money from Paul's songs, the remaining siblings, particularly Dreiser, were able to cover her funeral expenses. He had sought in *Jennie Gerhardt* and through Mame's experiences to demonstrate that a woman's instinctive generosity carries its own moral truth, regardless of conventional social and moral attitudes. By the time of her death, his own affection for, and instinctive generosity to, her had certainly evinced a similar moral affinity.

Monty Kozbial Ernst

DREISER, MARKUS ROMANUS (ROME)
(1860–1940). Dreiser both feared his brother Rome's temper and tendency toward meanness and admired his wanderlust, describing him in his autobiography *Dawn* as "handsome, selfish, indifferent, at times cruel," yet "a lover of life" whose spirit of adventure played to "a responsive chord" in the young Theodore. Rome gained some notoriety as a local drunk when he was home, borrowing money against his brother Paul's reputation be-

fore squandering it and forcing Paul to repay his debts.

Dreiser considered Rome's lengthy absences, at times as long as four years, to be a blessing to the family, for Rome was a source of embarrassment and never contributed to the household expenses. His mother, however, favored her most wayward son and was always eager for his return. Rome did not arrive in time to see his mother before her death. He reported that she had visited him in a dream, prompting his return with the hope of arriving before her demise. Rome was acutely distraught over his mother's death, displaying a degree of emotion few expected considering his normally distant behavior. Dreiser describes Rome's repeated return to alcohol despite repeated vows to quit drinking in memory of his mother. While Dreiser claimed in *Dawn* that Rome had disappeared and died and that "[s]ome mystery of temperament doomed him from the beginning," in fact in 1930 Dreiser retrieved a weak and bewildered Rome from a Chicago hotel and brought him to live with sister Mame, where Dreiser supported him until his death in 1940.

Rome's unpredictable behavior and contrasting personality affected Dreiser deeply. Ellen Moers finds Rome to be at root of Dreiser's depiction of unpredictability and wildness, ranging from the character of the swaggering and thieving Sebastian in *Jennie Gerhardt* to the depiction of emotion inherent in the drowning incident in *An American Tragedy*, which Moers suggests is "the culmination of Dreiser's attempts to dramatize his feelings about being a brother to Rome" (217).

Further Reading

Moers, Ellen. "Mr. Badman." *Two Dreisers*. New York: Viking, 1969. 215–26.

Jennifer Marie Raspet

DREISER, MARY THERESA (THERESA)
(1864–1897). Very little is known about
Theodore Dreiser's sister, Theresa, and her
early years in the Dreiser house. In 1879,
when the family split up and some moved
to Sullivan because of financial difficulty,
Theresa stayed in Terre Haute with her
father and two of her sisters, Sylvia and
Emma. Their father, Paul, assumed they
could find work as governesses, wait-
resses, or clerks in five-and-ten cent stores,
but this lasted only briefly.

Theresa, an independent and adventurous young woman, would leave home
for long periods of time, staying at home
for only brief intervals. This drifting finally
ended when, in 1882, Theresa moved to
Chicago amid rumors of having found
many male friends. Theodore would later
state in Chapter 32 of *Dawn* regarding
Theresa and Emma (referring to Theresa as
"Ruth") "that men . . . were using them as
mere playthings; but most of the time I
had a feeling that they were their own
masters, or might be if they would. Also
that perhaps they enjoyed being playthings." While living with her sister,
Emma, Theresa became caught up in a
scandal. Emma was caught having an affair with the married **L. A. Hopkins** and
fled the city when it was discovered that
Hopkins had stolen from his employers.
Theresa, left to answer reporters' questions, attempted to cover for Emma by
providing false names (Lingeman 1: 67).

Theresa later married Ed Davis, a scen-
ery painter for the stage and photographers, but the stable home life Theresa had
hoped for would not occur. Because of
Theresa's questionable reputation, her
mother-in-law hated Theresa and made
her life very difficult. According to Dreiser
in *Dawn*, Theresa's mother-in-law became
jealous of the fact that Davis left home and
lived with Theresa. This jealousy fueled

animosity for Theresa, ultimately straining
her marriage.

Theresa, although a drifter and a
woman of questionable reputation, was a
sensible woman and devoted to her family. As described by Dreiser, she was
blessed with the common sense her other
sisters lacked. Dreiser had affection for her
he didn't have for the rest of his siblings
because of her devotion to their mother.
He writes in *Dawn*, "Of all the girls she
was the one who, as I observed, carried
her mother's necessities and interests most
closely at heart." In 1890, upon the news
that her mother had fallen ill, she quickly
returned home, ran the house for the rest
of the family, and was a devoted nurse to
her mother. After her mother's death,
Dreiser says in *Dawn* that she condemned
their priest for refusing to give her mother
a proper funeral.

In 1897, while wheeling her bicycle
across the tracks of the Lake Shore and
Michigan Southern Railroad in Chicago,
Theresa was struck by a train and killed.
Theresa was buried in the plot of land next
to her mother-in-law.

David Blamy

DREISER, SARA WHITE (1869–1942).
Sara Osborne White was one of seven sisters and three brothers in the village of
Danville, near Montgomery City, Missouri. Her father, **Archibald Herndon
White**, was a prominent farmer and local
politician whom Dreiser memorialized in
"A True Patriarch," one of the finest
sketches in *Twelve Men*. Sara was fond of
brown clothes, which earned her the nickname "Jug," after the brown jug of a popular song. She was teaching grade school in
a suburb of St. Louis when she traveled
with a small set of schoolteachers to visit
the World's Columbian Exposition of 1893.
Dreiser was then a reporter on the *St. Louis
Republic*, the newspaper that was sponsor-

ing the trip. His editor chose him to accompany the party and to write a feature story on the group's reactions to the fair. On the train to Chicago, Dreiser was immediately attracted to Sara's auburn hair, serene, almond-shaped eyes, and calmly alert demeanor. He quickly found romance in the possibility of courting the genteel Sara. For over four years he did so mainly at a distance; by 1894 he had left the Midwest for New York, where he quickly gave up **journalism** to edit *Ev'ry Month*, a sheet music publication that was subtitled "The Woman's Magazine of Literature and Music." He would often use Sara's name as a pseudonym and occasionally published something she wrote.

Only after this protracted engagement (which Dreiser later claimed weakened their relationship) did they wed on 28 December 1898. Dreiser was then earning a good living as a freelance writer in New York. He was also beginning to seriously devote himself to fiction, and within a year of his wedding day he began writing *Sister Carrie*. Along with her husband's friend and fellow author **Arthur Henry**, Sara encouraged Dreiser and edited his work. She helped with grammar and spelling and at times added words of her own to the manuscript. When editors—first at **Harper's** and then more famously at **Doubleday, Page & Co.**—objected to the book's **realism** on both aesthetic and moral grounds, Sara worked carefully to cut the large manuscript and to domesticate the novel to meet the conservative publishing standards of the day.

Sara gave Dreiser what he wanted in the way of traditional marital comforts. During the dozen years that the marriage lasted, she took charge of his domestic needs, edited his writing, cared for him through periods of depression, and served as a genial hostess in his prosperous editorial days at *The Delineator* (1907–1910).

Dreiser would conceal much of this in later autobiographical works. Sara appears as **Angela Blue** in *The "Genius,"* a novel that portrays her character with an odd mixture of honesty and distortion. In *A Book about Myself*, Dreiser also attempts to explain the failure of their marriage in ways that are at once self-serving and faithful to their problems. In these books, Dreiser both captures Sara's conventional nature and underplays his own early desire for the domestic stability that she provided him. His years at *The Delineator* did nothing to help their relationship. Although Dreiser was ensconced in a position of middle-class respectability, he was restless. Sara had recurrent bouts of bad health in this period; nevertheless, she wanted to have children. Dreiser sensed correctly that he was not suited for fatherhood. He had already sublimated his creative powers in the tiring routine of editorial administration, and a family would not have provided him with sensible outlets for his untapped energies. When the break with Sara came, it was on the heels of his infatuation with **Thelma Cudlipp**, the teenage daughter of a member of his staff. Although the affair remained platonic, he lost his job, and he and Sara began to live separately. He soon recommitted himself to writing and completed *Jennie Gerhardt*, a novel that had remained unfinished for nearly a decade.

Sara slowly learned to live independently, while Dreiser assumed a life of nonconformity that would become his trademark. She never sought a formal divorce, and it wasn't until he made a financial success with *An American Tragedy* that she received financial support. As Dreiser's niece, Vera Dreiser, relates in her memoir *My Uncle Theodore* (1976), Sara remained until her death close to members of the Dreiser family, particularly the novelist's sisters and his brother Ed. For most of her life she stayed in New York City, remaining active, often living with one of her sisters, and supporting herself with various low-paying jobs and monthly payments of $200 from Dreiser. Although she retained her married name and status, she had no direct contact with him after 1926. At her death she was still legally married to Dreiser.

Thomas P. Riggio

DREISER, SARAH SCHÄNÄB (1833–1890). The mother of Theodore Dreiser, Sarah Maria Schänäb was born on 8 May 1833 to Henry Schänäb and Esther Shaub of Pennsylvania Dutch origin. She was raised in the Mennonite faith near Dayton, Ohio. Sarah eloped with John Paul Dreiser and married on New Year's Day 1851, when she was not yet eighteen years old and John Paul twenty-nine. It would be the last time she saw her father, a prosperous Mennonite farmer. Sarah left home poorly educated but possessing a great deal of charisma and charm, although lacking sophistication in the ways of the world. As Dreiser recounts in the opening chapter of his autobiography *Dawn*, his earliest memories are of a deeply superstitious but nurturing mother who was "thoughtful, solicitous, wise, and above all, tender and helpful," a gentle, quiet woman who was the source of endless strength and patience for her children. Her enthusiasm for life was disrupted only when the threat of poverty loomed. He describes her in *Dawn* as "[a] strange and dreamy woman, who did not know how life was organized; who was quick to forget the miseries of the past and contemplate the comforts of the present, or, those wanting, the possibilities of the future."

A devoted son, Dreiser remembers only the most endearing sentiments for his mother. A woman who lavished attention on all her children, Sarah did everything in her power to provide for them and was a source of comfort when their father, a deeply religious and authoritarian parent, was angry. Growing up, Dreiser felt rejected and inferior but sought and found salvation in his mother's arms. To him, she represented "the silver tether of affection, understanding, sweetness, sacrifice"; she was the rock that held the family together. Dreiser describes his mother as adoring him and sacrificing a great deal for him. When Dreiser announced to his mother that he wanted to go to Chicago, she tearfully scraped six dollars from her savings to send him on his way. He describes this event in *Dawn*: "Possibly she saw in my state of mind a precursor of better things for me, and so for herself. . . . And when I kissed my mother good-bye, I did not do so with any great regret; I did not feel for some reason that we were to be parted for long."

In 1889, Sarah Dreiser fell ill, and her health steadily deteriorated. Twice a week Dreiser would take his mother riding in a buggy around the neighborhood. In 1890 she took to her bed. On 14 November 1890, as Dreiser was helping his mother to the bathroom, she died in his arms. Her death was so traumatic to Dreiser—"the most profound, psychologic shake-up I ever received"—that, he would later remark, even years after her death he still felt alone. Sarah had drifted away from the church, and at first their priest refused a funeral or burial in a Catholic cemetery, thereby confirming in young Dreiser a deep-seated antipathy to Catholicism. Her son, Al, captured the importance of Sarah within their family when he said after her death, "Well, that's the end of our home."

In contrast to Theodore's adoring memory of his mother as a picture of sacrifice and concern for others, Vera Dreiser (brother Ed's daughter and a psychoanalyst) portrays her as a "controlling mother" who "could be gentle and lovely" but who could also be "cruel" (33). On occasion, for example, when Sarah was at the end of her patience with the boys, she would threaten to leave home. Once she did so and hid in a nearby cornfield for hours. Theodore, distraught at his mother's absence, fainted and would dream of the incident into adulthood. Vera Dreiser speculates that Sarah's "emotional needs were so great that she used all of her children to fulfill them, but Theo, because of his sensitivity and shyness, emerged as the object of her especial attention" (32). As a result, "his mother's behavior did great damage to his masculinity. . . . His identification with her was such that in later life he was in competition with women, resentful of them, disappointed in them while under the pretext of being in love with them" (33).

While the nature of Sarah's influence continues to be a matter of dispute, no one denies that she had a profound influence on all her children and managed to raise two children who gained considerable acclaim in their respective professions.

Further Reading

Douglas, George H. "The Revisionist Views of Sarah Dreiser." *Dreiser Studies* 18.1 (1987): 22–30.

Dreiser, Vera. "Sarah Schnepp Dreiser." *My Uncle Theodore*. With Brett Howard. New York: Nash, 1976. 29–46.

David Blamy

DREISER, VERA (1908–1998). The niece of Theodore Dreiser, she was the daughter of his younger brother Ed and the former Mai Skelly. A young singer and a protégée of Paul Dresser, Mai quickly turned to the younger and handsomer Ed, an actor, and they were married in June 1899. Vera, their only child, was born in New York on 11 May 1908. Her father gave up acting for a successful career as a textile executive, and Vera grew up in the Far Rockaway section of New York. She rebelled against her mother's strict Catholicism and left the church. She did graduate work at New York University, receiving an Ed.D. in 1944. In 1939 she had married Alfred E. Scott, a newspaperman. Encouraged by a mentor, Dr. Shailor Lawton, she became a psychologist and practiced successfully in New York from 1947 through 1961 and then became administrator of the psychiatric treatment unit at the California Institution for Women, where she worked with prisoners until her retirement in 1972. She and Alfred Scott had one child, a daughter; he died in 1948. She later married Ali Ariana, from whom she eventually separated.

Vera Dreiser first met her uncle Theodore as a young girl when he visited her parents, but she became close to him in 1944, when he returned to New York for a visit. With his usual interest in energetic young women, he had conversations with her on many matters, such as his compulsive womanizing. He proposed that she work with him on *The Bulwark*, which he was then writing, but the collaboration never came about. When she visited him in Hollywood in 1945, she found him depressed and suffering from sagging self-esteem because of age and various personal setbacks. She attended his funeral in 1945 and afterward stayed in touch with his wife, Helen. In 1973 she moved to Terre Haute to research a book on her uncle and her family. The result, *My Uncle Theodore*, published in 1976, is a rich source of Dreiser family lore, with firsthand stories and psychological insights into her subject. She writes, for example, that Dreiser's attachment to his mother "dwarfed his capacity to love, leaving him forever in a state of arrested emotional development," explaining his subconscious hostility toward women (103). She said she was partly driven to write her book as a corrective of previous **biographies**, and she remained the family griot, the keeper of the flame, who was always accessible to Dreiser scholars. In the 1980s she donated papers and Dreiser memorabilia to Emory University in Atlanta, where she moved in 1975 and lived, off and on, until her death on 18 November 1998. She was a large, intelligent, vibrant, strong-willed woman who inherited her uncle's impatience with conventional people. Her daughter, Tedi Dreiser Godard, pursued a singing career on the West Coast and in Atlanta and now lives in New York City with her husband, Joel Godard, a television announcer and performer on the Conan O'Brien Show. Tedi is the reigning interpreter of Paul Dresser's songs, which she has performed and recorded.

Richard Lingeman

DREISER EDITION. *See* Pennsylvania Dreiser Edition.

DREISER LOOKS AT RUSSIA. Published on 1 November 1928 by **Horace Liveright**, *Dreiser Looks at Russia* is an account of Dreiser's visit to the Soviet Union from November 1927 to January 1928. Dreiser had become interested in the Soviet experiment through association with radicals such as John Reed during his years in **Greenwich Village** and was invited by the Soviet government for an all-expense paid visit to celebrate the tenth anniversary of the October Revolution. *Dreiser Looks at Russia*'s origins lay, in part, in a series of newspaper articles for the North American News Alliance (NANA), which appeared in the *New York World*, 18–28 March 1928. After NANA expressed interest in publishing the articles in book form, Dreiser, with the assistance of **Louise Campbell**, ex-

panded them to a length more suitable for a hardcover volume. Dreiser's secretary and guide during his Russian tour, **Ruth Kennell**, claimed that this conversion was too rapid, which adversely affected the quality of the book. At times, the book contradicts both itself and the diary Dreiser kept while in Russia, producing what Kennell called "a carelessly thrown together conglomeration of impressions, facts and evaluations" (220). Amid Dreiser's sometimes inconsistent reflections upon Soviet society just before the Stalin era, however, lie philosophical passages in which Dreiser, attempting to explain his sympathy for the Soviet Union, reveals valuable insights into his thinking in the late 1920s.

All but the final three of *Dreiser Looks at Russia*'s eighteen chapters discuss a salient aspect of Soviet society under such titles as "The Present-Day Russian Peasant Problem," "The Current Soviet Economic Plan," and "Communism—Theory and Practice." Many chapters, including the three previously mentioned, suffer from Dreiser's lack of expertise in the respective subjects. Dreiser's unfamiliarity about these topics may be the cause of some of the book's internal inconsistencies, such as when Dreiser, despite a claim that graft had been eliminated in the Soviet Union because the economic incentives for it had also been eliminated, writes that "when you begin to look into things you may and do find waste and graft"; and later: "But never doubt that there are still in Russia both greedy and cunning men, with their various brands of graft and trickery." Dreiser's uncertainty also extended to America's fate, for while Dreiser explicitly disagreed with the Soviet Union's philosophy and techniques, he nevertheless predicted that America would be "Sovietized," possibly before his own death. Indeed, Dreiser himself acknowledged this tendency to vacillate between extremes, which may partially account for the internal contradictions: "And yet, by turns, and according to what one is looking at or thinking about at the time, one can become either abnormally optimistic or deeply depressed." Dreiser appears to have forced his ambivalence about the Soviet Union into tidy conclusions, which resulted in frequent doubling-back and inconsistency.

This is not to say, however, that all of Dreiser's conclusions are confused or lack insight. Dreiser's chapters on "Propaganda Plus" and "The Tyranny of Communism" are quite unambiguous in their criticism of Soviet propaganda. Dreiser recognized clearly the politicization of nearly all aspects of Soviet life, and he felt that Soviet art and journalism suffered from this politicization. *Dreiser Looks at Russia* also contains occasional moments of striking clarity. For example, although the Soviet government arranged many meetings with satisfied labor representatives from local factories, Dreiser still insisted that the Soviet government "employs labor just as might a capitalist trust," apparently interpreting those meetings as further examples of the Soviet propaganda machine.

Chapters 16 and 17 mark a return to more comfortable territory for Dreiser, for he leaves behind the impulse to make authoritative judgments regarding the Soviet Union and instead relates small episodes from his journey. These chapters, entitled "Three Moscow Restaurants" and "Some Russian Vignettes," resemble Dreiser's other forays into travel literature in *A Traveler at Forty*, *A Hoosier Holiday*, and *The Color of a Great City*.

The final chapter, entitled "Random Reflections on Russia," is the most philosophical section of the book and revisits a recurrent theme in *Dreiser Looks at Russia*: Dreiser's view that, as a matter of course, "big brains" rule society. Dreiser states, "I

know quite well, of course, that thought and brains, especially distinguished ones, are not common, but when they do appear their effect on the mass is astounding and hence to be celebrated and cherished." This statement, combined with sentiments found elsewhere, suggests that, despite his explicit sympathy for the underdog, Dreiser felt that social classes and thus social oppression have their basis in natural or biological differences, that weak or dumb individuals invariably constitute the poorer classes, and that the ruling class is made up of the strong and the smart. As Dreiser asks, "Is Edison to be paid the same as a swineherd? Rockefeller or Gary no more than a steelpuddler?" He then answers his own question: "[T]here are and will remain social discriminations. And the same not based on wealth but power or mental ability."

Yet Dreiser does not unequivocally defend social differentiation; his many criticisms of conditions in the United States make clear that he disapproves of a society dominated by "big brains" commanding economic might. At times Dreiser even strikes a despondent note about American life: "Once I used to think [that] . . . we [Americans] were going somewhere. . . . I have even of late, tended to abandon the thought, for we are so wholly materialistic, so, in the main, utterly puerile, mentally." Thus *Dreiser Looks at Russia*, which also includes frequent pejorative references to dogmatic **religion** and the Catholic faith, suggests that Dreiser's support of the Soviet Union, which was to intensify in later years, arose more from alienation from America than affection for communism.

The publication of *Dreiser Looks at Russia* was beset by controversy. **Dorothy Thompson**, a correspondent for the *New York Evening Post*, filed suit against Dreiser, charging that Dreiser plagiarized sections of her book on Russia, *The New*

Russia, published on 7 September. The lawsuit was eventually dropped after Dreiser's lawyers found similarities between Thompson's book and another. The controversy, however, failed to generate significant interest in the book; it sold only 4,000 copies, and critical reception was cool, yet *Dreiser Looks at Russia* may have had one profound effect upon Dreiser's career. Ruth Kennell, for one, alleged that the plagiarism dispute cost Dreiser the 1930 **Nobel Prize**, which went instead to **Sinclair Lewis**.

See also Dreiser's Russian Diary.

Further Reading

Kennell, Ruth Epperson. *Theodore Dreiser and the Soviet Union, 1927–1945: A First-Hand Chronicle*. New York: International, 1969.

Stephen Brain

DREISER NEWSLETTER. See Dreiser Studies.

DREISER SOCIETY, INTERNATIONAL THEODORE. Formed on 25 May 1991 at the second annual conference of the American Literature Association in Washington, D.C., the International Theodore Dreiser Society's purposes, as stated in its constitution, are (1) to perpetuate Dreiser's name and literary reputation; (2) to publish Dreiser scholarship; (3) to provide forums for the formal and informal exchange of ideas among Dreiser scholars; (4) to meet regularly for the furtherance of our common interests; and (5) to develop an international network of communication among societies of kindred aims and interests.

The society fulfills many of its goals through its affiliation with the American Literature Association, a coalition of societies devoted to the study of American authors that holds an annual conference on the West Coast during the weekend following Memorial Day on even-numbered years and on the East Coast during Memorial Day weekend on odd-numbered years. In addition to holding its annual business meeting at the conference, the society sponsors forums on Dreiser that allow scholars to present papers on his life and works and frequently provides informal gatherings with the **Norris**, London, and Crane societies.

During the academic year, the society publishes a biannual journal entitled *Dreiser Studies* that focuses on scholarship about Dreiser and his circle. From the fall of 1991 through the spring of 1997, the society also published a newsletter that included announcements, interviews, brief scholarly notes, and reviews. In recent years, the society has sponsored a monetary prize to be awarded annually to the graduate student or untenured faculty member who submits the best previously unpublished essay on any aspect of Dreiser's work. Information on this prize and on society membership plus copies of the early newsletters, checklists of publications by and about Dreiser since 1990, a list of Dreiser archives and Web sites, and announcements of current and future society activities can be found on the society's Web site at <http://www.uncw.edu/dreiser/>.

Frederic E. Rusch

DREISER STUDIES is a scholarly journal "dedicated to stimulating, coordinating, publishing, and reporting scholarship about Dreiser and those in his circle." Issued twice a year, the journal was launched in 1970 as the *Dreiser Newsletter* by the English Department at Indiana State University and remained a newsletter until 1987, when it became *Dreiser Studies*. In 1992 the journal became an official publication of the International Theodore **Dreiser Society**, and in 1997, its editorial office moved from Indiana State University to the English Department at the University of North Carolina at Wilmington.

During its years as a newsletter, the journal focused on interviews with Dreiser scholars, such as Ellen Moers, and acquaintances, such as **Ruth Kennell**; brief critical notes, many of which were source and influence studies; descriptions of library holdings; previously unpublished letters to and from Dreiser; book reviews; and news and notes on the activities of Dreiser scholars. Also, beginning with the second issue, the newsletter published an annual checklist of works by and about Dreiser. The change in name to *Dreiser Studies* was made in 1987 in conjunction with the journal's decision to increase its length in order to include longer critical analyses of Dreiser's works in addition to critical notes, book reviews, and the annual checklist. Since this change, the editors have also included in many of the journal's issues the texts of previously unpublished manuscripts of essays and stories by Dreiser along with commentary on the texts.

Over its long history the newsletter/journal has published notes and essays by most of the primary Dreiser scholars in the United States plus a number of contributions from Dreiser scholars in Europe, India, and Japan. In addition, it has promoted the work of younger scholars, many of whom are now contributing major studies of Dreiser's works. Indexes to the first thirty volumes plus the table of contents of current issues can be found on the Web site of the International Theodore Dreiser Society at <http://www.uncw.edu/dreiser/studies/>.

Further Reading

Dowell, Richard W. "The *Dreiser Newsletter* to Become *Dreiser Studies*." *Dreiser Newsletter* 17.2 (1986): 17–19.

Frederic E. Rusch

DREISER'S RUSSIAN DIARY, published in 1996 as part of the **Pennsylvania Dreiser Edition**, is the record of Dreiser's travels in the Soviet Union, which he visited from 4 November 1927 to 13 January 1928. His notes served as an aide-mémoire on which he later based his book *Dreiser Looks at Russia*. While his book is organized by themes and subjects for the instruction of the reader unfamiliar with the life, politics, and commerce of the Soviet Union, the diary is a faithful daily transcript of Dreiser's unfiltered experiences. More than the official account published in 1928, it mirrors the challenges, inconveniences, and hardships arising from traveling in a country struggling with poverty and a harsh climate. Dreiser's personal response to these frequently adverse conditions provides insight into the living conditions of the average Soviet citizen as well as the writer's own personality. It illustrates Dreiser's dedication to his task against all possible odds; it also reveals Dreiser's unwillingness to play the part of the grateful visitor. Ignoring the danger signals of a repressive political system and unimpressed by the political rhetoric of wish fulfillment, he studies and describes the conditions as he sees them, thus producing an important source document on American–Soviet encounters.

Invited originally by International Workers Aid to attend the celebration of the tenth anniversary of the October Revolution from 3 November to 10 November, Dreiser, interested not in the official pageant but in the actual workings of the "experiment," asked to take an extended tour "to see the real, unofficial Russia." While his request was quickly granted by the Russian government, Dreiser nevertheless had to exert pressure to gain access to the persons and institutions he hoped to see. More than once he strategically used his stature as an internationally renowned writer to overcome the slow, distrustful bureaucracy of VOKS, the Society for Cultural Relations with Foreign Countries.

The diary entries begin in New York on 3 October with the telephone call informing Dreiser of the free trip and show Dreiser boarding the *Mauretania* on 23 October and traveling via Paris, Berlin, and Warsaw by train before arriving in Moscow on 4 November, where he stays until 8 December, except for a visit on 20 November to Yasnaya Polyana to see Tolstoy's home and a trip to Leningrad from 26 November to 2 December. On 9 December the journal depicts him en route first to Nizhny Novgorod, after that to Kiev, the capital of the Ukraine, from whence he proceeds via Kharkov, Stalino (Donetsk), and Rostov to Baku, the capital of Azerbaijan, on the Caspian Sea. On 30 December the travelogue describes his arrival in Tiflis, the capital of Georgia, which he then leaves on New Year's Day to board the train for Batum on the Black Sea. The final days of the journey he spends on the steamer *Pestel*, which, on its way to Odessa, docks at several port towns such as Socchi, Navorossisk, Feodosia, Yalta, and Sebastopol. Delayed by the lack of a Polish visa and special permission to take printed matter or manuscripts out of the USSR, Dreiser waits five more days in Odessa before he can finally head home via Poland and Paris.

On his tour he was accompanied by a private secretary, **Ruth Epperson Kennell**, an American expatriate who worked as a translator and editor for Gosizdat, the government publishing house. Dreiser later portrayed Ruth as "Ernita" in *A Gallery of Women*. She was not a party member and was not financed by the Soviet government, which, for its part, selected his official guides, first an interpreter, Trevis, and later, for his travels in the Ukraine, Azerbaijan, and Georgia, a woman physician, Dr. Devedovsky ("Davi").

The diary starts with lively, fully developed scenes in the manner of *A Traveler at Forty*, which may be an indication of Dreiser's original conception for the travel book. The style then quickly changes into Dreiser's characteristically rapid note taking and recording of names and data, all mixed with casual impressions and arranged within the framework of the day's routine of meals, taxi rides, and bedtimes. As of 8 November the diary is transformed into a collaborative production, partly handwritten by the author, partly typed by Kennell, who more and more becomes Dreiser's persona. The composite diary seems to have had its origin in Kennell's faithful transcriptions of Dreiser's interviews, which then led to her adding further descriptions that occasionally parallel Dreiser's, until near the end she seems to have taken over completely.

Dreiser's devotion to his task is evident; he is unnerved when he fails to obtain interviews or has an otherwise idle day. The diary features Kennell's neat transcriptions of Dreiser's official talks with Nikolai Bukharin, a member of the Politburo; Platon, the archbishop of the Russian Reformed Church; Vladimir Mayakovsky, the Russian revolutionary poet; Konstantin Stanislavsky, the director of the Moscow Art Theater; and **Sergei Eisenstein**, the film producer; whereas unauthorized meetings such as his private encounter with Karl Radek, the personal friend of Lenin and Trotsky, are carefully rendered by Dreiser himself. Although Dreiser does the usual round of sightseeing and attends several operas and social events, his diary reveals that his true interest lies in the impact of communism on the lives of workers. Although in Russia he prefers to define himself as an individualist, his trip to the Soviet Union seems to have produced a lasting effect on him and further raised his interest in social and political issues, as is reflected in his activities in the 1930s and such books as *Tragic America* and *America Is Worth Saving*.

Further Reading

Bardeleben, Renate von. "Late Educations: Henry Adams and Theodore Dreiser Look at Russia." *Ars transferendi*. Festschrift for Nicolai Salnikow. Ed. Dieter Huber and Erika Worbs. Frankfurt am Main: Peter Lang, 1997. 417–31.

Casciato, Arthur D. "Dictating Silence: Textual Subversion in Dreiser's Soviet Diary." *Papers on Language and Literature* 27 (1991): 174–90.

Kennell, Ruth. *Theodore Dreiser and the Soviet Union, 1927–1945: A First-Hand Chronicle.* New York: International, 1969.

Riggio, Thomas P. "Letter from Russia: Following Dreiser, Seventy Years Later." *The American Scholar* 65 (1996): 569–77.

Renate von Bardeleben

DRESSER, PAUL (1858–1906). Singer, songwriter, and comedic actor, Dreiser's brother John Paul Dreiser Jr. took the professional name of Paul Dresser. Born in Terre Haute, Indiana, on 22 April 1858, he was the oldest of ten surviving children. It was the dream of Paul's devoutly Catholic father that this firstborn son should enter the priesthood, and to this end, Paul at an early age was sent to St. Meinrad Seminary in southern Indiana. That environment, however, proved uncongenial to the mischievous, fun-loving Paul, and soon he had rejoined the family in Terre Haute, where his troubled teenage years were marked by conflicts with his martinet father and occasionally the law. Eventually, while still a teenager, he left town with a medicine show to launch a theatrical career during which he performed solo as "the Sensational Comique," as an end man for minstrel companies, and as the star of

melodramas. By age twenty, he had published his first song, and by the 1890s he was one of America's foremost balladeers, his signature composition being "the mother song." Among his biggest hits were "Just Tell Them That You Saw Me" (1895), **"On the Banks of the Wabash"** (1897), and "My Gal Sal" (1905). In 1913, "On the Banks of the Wabash" was named Indiana's state song.

Paul's junior by thirteen years, Theodore had his first memorable contact with his oldest brother during the winter of 1882, when Sarah, his mother, and her three youngest children, including ten-year-old Theodore, were facing destitution in Sullivan, Indiana. One dreary day, after an absence of several years, Paul melodramatically appeared, his nearly 300-pound frame adorned by a silk hat and an expensive fur coat. With hugs and humorous stories, he raised their spirits; with money, groceries, and clothes, he saw them through the immediate crisis. The following spring, Paul moved them to Evansville, where he was the headliner at the Opera House and a humor columnist for the *Evansville Argus*. He was also the paramour of local madam Annie Brace (alias Sallie Walker, later immortalized as "My Gal Sal"). For two years, through Sallie and Paul's largesse, Sarah and her brood led a halcyon existence, basking in Paul's reflected glory and insulated from the gossip generated by his relationship with Sallie. Eventually, however, the two separated over Paul's infidelity, and he left Evansville with a minstrel company, while the Dreisers decamped for Chicago. Speaking of Paul during this period, Dreiser wrote in *Dawn* that "he was like the sun, or a warm, cheering fire. He beamed upon us all."

Over the next ten years, Theodore rarely saw his oldest brother, only when Paul was "in town" performing with his current road company. Such was the case in late 1893, when he arrived in St. Louis with his latest sexual conquest in tow to star in a farce, *The Danger Signal*. Theodore, at the time, was a reporter for the *Republic*. During their week together, Theodore began to realize that his unqualified admiration for Paul had waned. As he recalled this experience in *Newspaper Days*, Theodore was taken by Paul's tenderness and good nature, so reminiscent of their mother, but other traits were disturbing. Onstage, his "silly" ballads and "lowbrow" humor seemed embarrassing, even vulgar, and in conversation he proved himself naive and intellectually barren. Theodore pronounced him "middle-class."

One pivotal effect of Paul's stopover in St. Louis was that Theodore was infected by his brother's great enthusiasm for New York and soon began working his way toward that city, arriving in November 1894. Almost immediately he failed both as a reporter and as a freelance writer and turned to Paul for assistance. Paul, at that time near the zenith of his popular and financial success, was a partner in Howley, Haviland & Co., a music publishing firm. Theodore approached them with the proposal that he edit a promotional journal to be titled **Ev'ry Month**, which would feature the firm's latest songs surrounded by items of entertainment value. This proposal was accepted, and for over two years, Paul was one of Theodore's employers. For a time, it was a harmonious relationship. *Ev'ry Month* was a modest success, while Theodore enjoyed participating in Paul's Broadway celebrity and even contributed to the composition of "On the Banks of the Wabash." Soon, however, his literary ambitions for the magazine began to clash with the firm's more utilitarian views, and he saw himself as little more than a lackey in a dead-end position. Fueled by this frustration, Theo-

dore's annoyance with Paul's pedestrian qualities and indiscriminate womanizing grew. Paul's songs, on which his "tawdry" acclaim rested, seemed to the success-starved Theodore "pale little things . . . mere bits and scraps of sentiment and melodrama . . . most asinine sighings over home and mother," as he remarked in his memoir, "My Brother Paul." They quarreled frequently, until Theodore eventually left the firm, beginning a six-year period of estrangement.

In April 1903, Paul encountered Theodore on the streets of New York and was shocked by his shabby appearance. Ill and homeless, Theodore was in the midst of an extended battle with **neurasthenia**. All previous antagonisms were immediately forgotten as Paul pressed money on his reluctant brother and made arrangements for Theodore to spend six weeks at **William Muldoon's** Olympia sanitarium, at Paul's expense. When that rehabilitation ended and Theodore turned to therapeutic day-labor for the New York Central Railroad, Paul was his most ardent cheerleader and a willing source of financial aid. When Theodore felt ready to return to the literary world, Paul secured him a position on the *New York Daily News*.

Soon, however, Paul would need moral and financial support. On the American music scene, ragtime had supplanted Paul's stock-in-trade, the sentimental ballad, contributing to the dissolution of his partnership with Haviland and eventually Howley. Notoriously inept as a businessman, Paul tried to continue alone and failed, wiping out a financial reserve already compromised by a lifetime of generosity. Late in 1905, he was forced to abandon the luxury hotels along his beloved Broadway and move in with his sister Emma. There, in a back bedroom, abandoned by his friends, he sat at a portable organ and tried to revive his moribund career. These efforts, however, were doomed by depression and a physical condition undermined by years of dissipation. Ironically, "My Gal Sal," published in 1905, did not become a hit in time to alleviate his emotional or financial woes. Paul Dresser died of a heart attack on 30 January 1906. He was forty-seven.

During Paul's final days, Theodore visited him frequently and took notes while Paul reminisced about his early years in the hope that Theodore would "write a story some time, tell something about him." The story Theodore promised to write is "My Brother Paul," published in *Twelve Men* in 1919. In 1942, that story served as the genesis of Twentieth Century-Fox's *My Gal Sal,* a movie loosely based on Paul's life.

Richard W. Dowell

DROUET, CHARLES, is the good-natured "drummer," or traveling salesman, who becomes Carrie Meeber's first lover in *Sister Carrie.* He very nearly seduces her on the train to Chicago in the first chapter; he succeeds some weeks later when by chance he sees her roaming the streets down on her luck and vulnerable to a man with a warm heart and "fat purse." Drouet's French name ("It's pronounced Drew-eh," he tells Carrie) suggests his essentially amorous nature; he is a roué, in 1880s American slang a "masher" well practiced in the art of picking up pretty girls, yet his "keen desire for the feminine" is natural and thus inherently moral. This "merry, unthinking moth of the lamp" is "evil and sinning" only to the extent that his "rudimentary" and socially constructed conscience gives him an occasional twinge. In rescuing Carrie from the cold streets of Chicago, he is "the essence of sunshine and good-humour" who makes the wilting "daisy" bloom. "Drouet is so good," Carrie thinks later as she primps before the mirror in her new clothes. Still, Drouet's destiny is "fixed," virtually scripted, by his "innate desire to act the old pursuing part." Despite his "daring and magnetism," the "Magnet Attracting" of the first chapter title is Chicago itself, with its vastly superior "cunning wiles" and "large forces." Drouet lacks the intellect, taste, and sensitivity to hold a girl like Carrie, and if he were deprived of his job and subjected to the city's "baffling forces," he would be "as helpless, as non-understanding, as pitiable, if you will, as she." Among the forces already acting on him are pressures to play various parts before an audience of other men. On the one hand, he wants to display his sexual prowess; he thus frequents all-male watering holes like Hurstwood's "truly swell saloon," where he drinks, mingles with celebrities, and boasts of the "little peach" he has met on the train. On the other hand, he is one of the "boys" in the Elks lodge, that fraternal association of successful, middle-class family men. When he invites Hurstwood to "my house" (a rented flat) to meet "Mrs. Drouet" (the "little peach," now his mistress), he is playing the paterfamilias for the kind of man he wants to be, a "very acceptable individual of our great American upper class." In his simple-minded resilience, Drouet contrasts with Carrie and Hurstwood, who rise and fall with the turning of Fortune's wheel. In the last chapter, after a futile try at getting back with Carrie the Broadway star, he is blithely preparing for a "dandy time" on the town with a new "dead swell" the moment Hurstwood waits in the snow outside the Bowery flophouse where he will lie down on a grimy cot in the dark and end it all. Serving to intensify the pathos of Hurstwood's tragic end, Drouet is a comic embodiment of the enduring pleasure principle, the "old butterfly . . . as light on the wing as ever."

Further Reading

Moers, Ellen. "The Finesse of Dreiser." *American Scholar* 33 (Winter 1963): 109–14.

Zaluda, Scott. "The Secrets of Fraternity: Men and Friendship in *Sister Carrie*." *Theodore Dreiser: Beyond Naturalism*. Ed. Miriam Gogol. New York: New York University Press, 1995. 77–94.

Stephen C. Brennan

DUDLEY, DOROTHY (1884–1962). The daughter of Emelius Clark Dudley, a wealthy Chicago gynecologist, Dorothy Dudley graduated from Bryn Mawr in 1905 and returned to Chicago, where she became part of the coterie surrounding Harriet Monroe and *Poetry* magazine. As part of the renaissance of young intellectuals rebelling against conservative standards, she contributed poems, essays, and reviews to *Poetry, Dial, Nation,* and *American Magazine of Art*. She married Henry Blodgett Harvey, an advertising executive, and bore two children, Anne and Jason, both of whom became artists. In 1925 the Harvey family moved to France to further the education of their daughter Anne, who at age nine was showing signs of being a prodigy in art, and there Dudley expanded her circle to include Matisse, Brancusi, and other modernists.

She met Dreiser in New York during the fall of 1916, and a friendship developed that endured until Dreiser's death. Correspondence between the two in the Dreiser Papers at the University of Pennsylvania suggests that Dudley, always respectful and at times worshipful, made the greater effort. Dreiser was apparently flattered by her attention and suggested she write about him. In an undated letter, Dudley indicated her approach—"Shall I take your isolate position in American letters—a man who has made huge excavations alone with no one over you and never in a gang?" (Dreiser Papers). *Forgotten Frontiers: Dreiser and the Land of the Free* appeared in 1932 (rpt. in 1946 as *Dreiser and the Land of the Free*). This first biography draws upon extensive interviews with Dreiser and his acquaintances, access to his papers, and the experience of editing six of the sketches in *Twelve Men*; her task is to portray Dreiser in the context of his times, with the writer standing as a titan among his contemporaries. As the book neared publication, the publisher sent him galleys of the volume. Dreiser apparently read only parts of the book, delegating to three assistants the task of examining proofs of the book for any objectionable material. "[R]egardless of my own part in it," he wrote to the publisher, "it is a very interesting reaction to and interpretation of the American scene" (*Letters* 2: 609). Dudley was disappointed by the poor reviews of the book but continued writing, moving to the left, politically, as did many writers during the difficult years of the 1930s, writing, for example, for *Vanguard*, billed as "A Libertarian Communist Journal." Dudley died in Paris in 1962.

Keith Newlin

DUFFY, RICHARD (1873–1949). Richard Duffy began his long friendship with Dreiser in 1898, when, working as a freelance writer in New York, Dreiser submitted stories to *Ainslee's Magazine*, where Duffy was an editor. Dreiser became a contributing editor at *Ainslee's* in 1899, a more secure position than that of a freelancer, at a salary of $150 a month. In the same year, Dreiser wrote "Nigger Jeff," a short story that he told Duffy was based on a lynching he witnessed while a reporter. Through Duffy's influence, the story was published in *Ainslee's* in 1901, after being rejected by more prominent literary magazines.

In addition to his professional support, Duffy became a close confidant of Dreiser, providing both encouragement and financial support during Dreiser's battle with severe depression from 1900 to 1903 after the disappointing reception of *Sister Carrie*. During his work on *Sister Carrie*, Dreiser had confidently bragged to Duffy of his incredible productivity, yet by 1903, the confidence had changed to despair, and Duffy faced the task of consoling the despondent writer. He reminded Dreiser of the positive letters the author had received praising *Sister Carrie* and encouraged him to disregard the negative reviews. As Dreiser's depression deepened, Duffy and other friends offered uplifting reading suggestions, including Emerson, Kant and the *Bhagavad-Gita*, vastly different from Dreiser's favored **Spencer**. Duffy also encouraged the author to write a lighter story with a humorous character for his next book. Dreiser didn't take the advice and instead began writing *Jennie Gerhardt*.

Their friendship continued as Dreiser's fame grew, with Duffy offering creative encouragement and personal support. After leaving *Ainslee's*, Duffy became managing editor at *Watson's Magazine* in 1904. Four years later, Duffy's first novel, *Author: An Adventure in Exile*, was published. Duffy contributed essays and stories to magazines in the following years, but his most prominent literary work came much later. In 1939, Duffy's English translation of Edouard Herriot's *The Wellsprings of Liberty* was published. He approached his old friend Dreiser, requesting a comment for an advertisement, but while Dreiser praised Duffy's achievement, he declined to promote the book because he disagreed with its political stance. The slight did not affect the friendship, and the two continued exchanging letters until Dreiser's death.

Blythe Ferguson

E

EASTMAN, YVETTE SZEKELY (1912–).
Yvette Szekely was born in Budapest,
Hungary, and came to America in 1919
with her mother and younger sister Suzanne. Her mother was a foreign correspondent and designer who hosted a salon
in Manhattan that attracted artists, writers,
and intellectuals. Among her mother's
friends were Theodore Dreiser and Max
Eastman, both of whom Yvette came to
know intimately. The best and fullest record of her life and her long relationship
with Dreiser is her book, *Dearest Wilding: A
Memoir* (1995), which also contains a significant number of Dreiser's letters to her.
She served as Dreiser's editor, typist, and
researcher; occasionally, she drafted reviews of books and introductions that
would go out under the novelist's name.
In this period she attended theater school
and studied ballet with Pavlova's partner,
Michail Mordkin. During the depression
years, she became a social worker and continued in this field until her marriage to
Max Eastman in 1958. She assisted Eastman in his writing, and together they associated with many celebrated figures of the
time, from Charlie Chaplin and Pablo
Casals to Edmund Wilson and James Cag-
ney. A member of the Academy of American Poets, she has translated books from
French to English and has published articles, poetry, and photography. She is pres-
ently at work on a memoir about her life
with Eastman, which will also reflect further on her earlier relationship with
Dreiser.

Thomas P. Riggio

EISENSTEIN, SERGEI M. (1898–1948).
Russian-born film director and theorist,
best known for his classic films *Potemkin*
(1925), *Alexander Nevsky* (1938), and the
incomplete *Ivan the Terrible* (1944, 1958). In
these and other films Eisenstein worked
out the implications of his theory of montage in which the linear arrangement of
the film narrative would be interrupted or,
in some cases, arbitrarily replaced by static
shots or brief running images of other independent actions psychologically allied
to the idea the filmmaker wished to express. In Eisenstein's first film, *Strike*
(1924), for example, narrative scenes of
tsarist soldiers gunning down striking
workers are interspersed with images of
slaughterhouse workers butchering cattle.
Particularly suited to the iconic nature of
silent film and effective in delivering ideological critique, this simplest form of montage was popular among Soviet filmmakers of the era. Pointing to the experimental
poetics of Vladimir Mayakovsky, James
Joyce's radical development of stream of

consciousness, and the linguistic phenomenon of the "portmanteau word," Eisenstein would argue as early as 1924 that the "montage of attractions" offered a cinematic equivalent for representing the natural phenomenon of human perception. However, because montage was so particularly effective in delivering social critique and so much a staple of Soviet film of the immediate post-revolution era, cautious Western filmmakers and critics tend to reject it as a primarily ideological, rather than artistic, tool. Eisenstein was still defending the artistic and psychological value of the device as late as his 1942 text *The Film Sense*: "the juxtaposition of two separate shots by splicing them together resembles not so much a simple sum of one shot plus another shot—as it does a *creation*" (17).

Dreiser first met Eisenstein in 1927 while touring the USSR by invitation of the Soviet government and described him briefly in *Dreiser Looks at Russia*. Paramount Pictures, then known as Famous Players, had purchased silent film rights to *An American Tragedy* in 1926 but shelved the novel for four years. After threat of a lawsuit from Dreiser, Paramount revived the project in 1930, contracting with Eisenstein—then on exchange in Hollywood from Soyuzkino—and with radical British filmmaker Ivor Montagu to prepare an adaptation. While he considered the novel to be "ideologically defective," Eisenstein agreed with Dreiser that American society, not protagonist Clyde Griffiths, was the villain of the piece and produced a script for a fourteen-reel silent film. Montage of attractions is particularly evident in Eisenstein's notes and scenario for the scene in which **Roberta Alden** is drowned.

Later, in an article about the debacle for *Close Up*, Eisenstein reported that Paramount expected a "simple detective story . . . about a love affair between a boy and a girl" (110) and thus rejected the script. The studio may also have been uncomfortable with the film's indictment of American society and bleak tone. Paramount chief David O. Selznick wrote in a memo to partner Bud Schulberg that the proposed script "cannot possibly offer anything but a most miserable two hours to happy-minded young Americans" (qtd. in Leyda and Voynow 58). Paramount paid Dreiser an additional fee to purchase sound film rights to the novel. Eisenstein left Hollywood in disgust the following year.

See also Adaptations, Film.

Further Reading

Eisenstein, Sergei M. "An American Tragedy. *Close Up* 10 (June 1933): 109–24.
———. *The Film Sense*. 1942. Trans. Jay Leyda. London: Faber and Faber, 1948.
Leyda, Jay, and Zina Voynow. *Eisenstein at Work*. New York: Pantheon, 1982.
Murray, Edward. *The Cinematic Imagination: Writers and the Motion Pictures*. New York: Ungar, 1972.

Carol S. Loranger

ELDER, DONALD B. (1913–1965). After graduating from the University of Michigan where he won the Avery Hapgood award in creative writing, Elder was hired as an editor at **Doubleday** & Co. in 1935 at the suggestion of **Sinclair Lewis**, who had taken an interest in his writing. At Doubleday, Elder edited the manuscript of *The Bulwark* for publication. When Dreiser returned to the manuscript of the novel he had begun in 1914, he engaged **Marguerite Tjader** to help him complete it and then paid **Louise Campbell** $500 to edit it. In September 1945 he sent the edited manuscript to Elder and to **James T. Farrell** for comment. Farrell thought Campbell had cut too much and advised both Dreiser and Elder to restore many of the details that Campbell had eliminated. Dreiser then delegated the final editing to Elder, who restored some passages, simplified the narrative, and speeded up the pace. Dreiser was pleased with the result and wrote to Elder on 22 December 1945 that "you have done an excellent job on the final editing. You have been conscientious, sympathetically sensitive and considerate to my work all the way through. . . . Your choice of what should have been restored is very good" (*Letters* 3: 1033). After Dreiser's death, Elder performed a similar, but less extensive, service for *The Stoic*, restoring some passages concerning **Berenice Fleming's** spirituality that Campbell had cut in her editing of the manuscript. In 1947 Elder took a leave of absence to focus on his own writing; his *Ring Lardner, a Biography* appeared in 1956.

Keith Newlin

ELIAS, ROBERT HENRY (1914–), is best known for his pioneering biography of Dreiser, whom he knew personally for the last eight years of the author's life. He was born in New York City on 17 September 1914 to Henry Hart Elias and Edna Barnhard and grew up there and in Larchmont and Scarsdale, New York. He received the A.B. in English from Williams College in 1936, the A.M. in English from Columbia University in 1937, and the Ph.D. in American civilization from the University of Pennsylvania in 1948. During his studies at Columbia Elias first met Dreiser, on whom he was writing his master's thesis. He married Helen Beatrice Larson in 1947, and the couple had four children. He was an instructor in English at the University of Pennsylvania between 1942 and 1945, when he joined the English faculty at Cornell University. There he was one of the editors of the journal *Epoch* between 1947 and 1953 and ultimately became the Ernest I. White Professor of American Studies and later the Goldwin Smith Professor of English Literature and American Studies. Elias served as a Fulbright lecturer in France in 1963–1964 and in the summer of 1968. His books, aside from *Theodore Dreiser: Apostle of Nature* (1948, emended edition 1970), are *"Entangling Alliances with None": An Essay on the Individual in the American Twenties* (1973), editions of *Chapters of Erie* by Charles Francis Adams Jr. and Henry Adams (1956), *Letters of Theodore Dreiser*, 3 vols. (1959), and with Eugene D. Finch, *Letters of Thomas Attwood Digges* (1982).

See also Biographies.

Jerome Loving

"ELLEN ADAMS WRYNN," the third of fifteen semifictionalized sketches in *A Gallery of Women*, is based on the American painter and illustrator **Anne Estelle Rice**. It is central for the entire collection because of its focus on the female artist's struggle to establish her career against inner and outer constraints, a leitmotif in several other sketches, including "Esther Norn," "Olive Brand," and "Emanuela." Ellen is a free-spirited and pagan character, who attends the School of Design in Philadelphia despite her family's resistance. Like a man, she quickly moves beyond her first (conventional) marriage with Walter Wrynn, even leaving her child with her ex-husband in order to be free to pursue her artistic career. In 1907, the drive for artistic expression takes Ellen to Paris, where she plunges into the world of fauvism and cubism. Her style now changes dramatically, transcending earlier inhibitions. "Such colors! Such shouting, yelling contrasts!' I was dumbfounded, really," comments the narrator in genuine admiration. He is equally impressed with her new identity as a successful artist inscribed on the paintings ("And each panel signed: Ellen Adams Wrynn"); the exhibition space in a large Philadelphia department store signifies her increased value.

Then Ellen meets the love of her life, the Scottish painter Keir McKail (John Duncan Fergusson). "They are really living together only not in the same studio," the narrator comments about the couple's unconventional private lives in Paris. Still, McKail, a force in art, was Wrynn's "mental and emotional master," and when he deserts Ellen several years later, she has become so emotionally dependent that she is no longer able to continue her career as an artist. She returns to the United States but is not able to establish herself as an artist during the war years. She marries an insignificant critic, loses all interest in art, leaves her paintings with the narrator, and departs. Fifteen years later, the unclaimed paintings are still with him, as the narrator closes the sketch with a proclamation of her failure: "And no word—nothing—from Ellen Adams Wrynn."

Compared with the real-life model Anne Estelle Rice, Dreiser has stripped the female artist of her artistic powers, as Carol Nathanson argues, perhaps in a gesture of revenge because Rice had scorned his advances and yielded to marriage. Indeed, the sketch also suggests that to become artists, women had to follow the pattern of the selfish male artist/genius that Dreiser had set up in The "Genius." Moreover, there are important gaps in this sketch. Dreiser does not mention the spectacular Armory Show, the International Exhibition of Modern Art at the 69th Regiment Armory on Lexington Avenue in New York City in 1913, which propelled America into visual modernity and may well have prompted an ambitious American artist to return to the New York art scene. Nor does Dreiser consider the **gender** bias rampant in the visual art world in which the works of women were often ignored. Dreiser's theory of a failed love relationship as the poison that kills the artistic drive in Ellen Adams Wrynn ultimately removes the important social field of art production in which women continued to be exposed to a double standard.

Further Reading

Nathanson, Carol A. "Anne Estelle Rice: Theodore Dreiser's 'Ellen Adams Wrynn.' " *Woman's Art Journal* 13.2 (1992/1993): 3–11.
———. "Anne Estelle Rice and 'Ellen Adams Wrynn' ": Dreiser's Perspectives on Gender and Gendered Perspectives on Art." *Dreiser Studies* 32.1 (2001): 3–35.

Irene Gammel

"EMANUELA," the thirteenth of the fifteen semifictional sketches in Dreiser's *A Gallery of Women*, titled "M.J.C." in an earlier version of the manuscript held in the Dreiser Papers, is based on the freelance writer and literary agent **Ann Watkins**, whom Dreiser first met during his early New York years when he was an editor. The narrator (aka Dreiser) is magnetically drawn to Emanuela's beauty, even though he is mockingly critical of her genteel and conservative notions about life (i.e., sex). Thus, he introduces her as "The Iceland Venus" and "Our Lady of Snows," for she does not admit to the new truth: that sex is central in the representation of modern life in art. Despite her "conservatism," however, he notes with resentful jealousy that she is thriving as a writer, publishing in the widely distributed *Saturday Evening Post*, while the narrator and his male friends are having less success with their realist fiction.

Observing Emanuela over a period of one and a half decades, the narrator becomes preoccupied with her sexuality and with breaking down the walls of repression within her to free her for art and life. "There's something wrong with Emanuela," he quotes a male friend as saying. "She's either undersexed or too purely mental, or something. You can't tell me that a girl as beautiful as she is wouldn't have married or had an affair with some one by now. It isn't natural." The narrator proceeds to read her as a classical case of pathological repression, desiring sex but having built up a wall of resistance against it. When Emanuela protests and criticizes his position instead, he reacts with anger: "I could not endure any longer this silly palaver about social inhibitions, especially from a woman of her type." The narrator's sexuality misses the subtler seductive notes and is expressed in a quasi-rapist desire to possess: "I seized her tight and pulled her close to me, sure at last that all her earlier resistance had passed," whereupon she reacts with "an automatic chemic and so vital rejection, which finally resulted in her releasing herself and running, her cape which had come off in the struggle remaining in my hands." What is perhaps most striking about the sketch is the narrator's aggressively masculinist language that imposes a compulsory (hetero)sexuality. There is ample evidence in the text that Emanuela is open to erotic pleasures, and while she likes the narrator as a friend, she leaves no doubt that she does not enjoy his sexuality. Yet he is unable to accept a friendship without intercourse.

By the end, he sees her beautiful body age into a matronly figure. Now he closes the chapter on her and passes a final vindictive judgment: "It was too late. She had never functioned properly as a woman." The naturalist observer inscribes prescriptive norms on the female body, writing a pathological body, when the truth spoken by the female body defies masculinist assumptions. This sketch presents perhaps the most striking example of heterosexism within Dreiser's naturalist logic.

Further Reading

Gammel, Irene. "Female Sexuality and the Naturalist Crisis: 'Emanuela.' " *Sexualizing Power in Naturalism: Theodore Dreiser and Frederick Philip Grove.* Calgary: University of Calgary Press, 1994. 83–99.

———. "Sexualizing the Female Body: Dreiser, Feminism, and Foucault." *Theodore Dreiser: Beyond Naturalism.* Ed. Miriam Gogol. New York: New York University Press, 1995. 31–54.

Irene Gammel

"EQUATION INEVITABLE: A VARIANT IN PHILOSOPHICAL VIEWPOINT."

In this essay from *Hey Rub-a-Dub-Dub*, Dreiser discursively elaborates an idea that had become central to his thinking for some time and that would remain so throughout his life—the idea that there exists a rough balance or "equation" between various opposing forces that is maintained throughout the universe. Originally absorbed during his 1894 reading of **Herbert Spencer's** *First Principles* (1862), this concept influenced works from one of his earliest short stories, "The Shining Slave Makers," to his posthumously published *Notes on Life*.

After offering prima facie evidence for an equilibrium of such forces as light and darkness, heat and cold, and order and disorder, Dreiser repeatedly insists that the existence of this balance or equation of forces is inconsistent with both conventional **religion** and morality. Dreiser specifically finds the notion of a loving and omnipotent God to be painfully at odds with the existence of "criminals, liars, lechers, murderers, self-aggrandizing intellects of all types and sizes, plus accident, disease, cataclysm." In short, if God is all-powerful and all-just, then such evils would not exist, let alone be so prevalent. Likewise, Dreiser writes, dogmatic morals are not consistent with the law of equation, for "our impulses do not always accord with moral or religious law, the so-called will of the Creator here on earth, and yet our impulses are assuredly provided us by a Creator, if no more than the mechanistic one of the chemists and physicists." Since conventional notions of God and ethics cannot be logically reconciled with the rough counterbalancing of extremes, Dreiser argues, they should be dismissed or radically reconceptualized.

In addition to expressing his impatience with conventional religion and morality, Dreiser offers his own reconceptualization of God and ethics based on the scientific view of nature taken by mechanists and monists—"the chemists and physicists"—which he believes is entirely consistent with the law of equation. In place of the view of humans as created in the image of God, Dreiser asserts that a human being is a "chemical and physical impulse in Nature, which acts or reacts as the nature of other chemical and physical stimuli in immediate contact with him suggests or compels." Dreiser asks whether "the fact that we find ourselves . . . confronted by Nature in all Her complexity and with only this necessity for equation to fall back on" should make one unhappy. It should not, replies Dreiser, for "if . . . man is savage he is also tender, inherently so apparently, for by what measure would he measure savageness if not by its contrary?" While it is impossible for a person to achieve permanent peace or happiness, one can nonetheless "seek to hide himself away in some simple peaceful realm . . . and still be secure in one of those minor equilibriums which in the shadow of some of the greater ones are always holding somewhere in part."

Dreiser's advice to isolate one's self from the larger clash of forces is reminiscent of the opening of the second book of Lucretius's *On the Nature of Things*, just as the mechanistic worldview and antireligious sentiment of the essay echo the epic poem generally. Though Dreiser's answer to the problem of the existence of evil may be philosophically naive, it is not obviously less cogent in outline than more venerable and elaborate solutions. Moreover, the essay's greatest weaknesses, namely, its inordinate length and repetitiveness, nonetheless serve to demonstrate the importance of its ideas to Dreiser's thought.

See also Mechanism.

Further Reading

Lundén, Rolf. *The Inevitable Equation: The Antithetic Pattern of Theodore Dreiser's Thought and Art*. Uppsala, Sweden: Studia Anglistica Upsaliensa, no. 16, 1973.

Roberts, Ian F. "Thesis and (Ant)ithesis: Dreiser's 'McEwen of the Shining Slave Makers' and the Game of Life." *Dreiser Studies* 28.2 (1997): 34–43.

Zanine, Louis J. *Mechanism and Mysticism: The Influence of Science on the Thought and Work of Theodore Dreiser*. Philadelphia: University of Pennsylvania Press, 1993.

Ian F. Roberts

"ERNESTINE." First published as "Portrait of a Woman" in the September 1927 *Bookman*, this semifictional sketch of the short, unhappy career and suicide of actress **Florence Deshon** appeared as the tenth portrait in *A Gallery of Women*. The narrator-author first encounters eighteen-year-old Ernestine De Jongh, a "disturbingly beautiful and magnetic" actress, in the company of a theatrical producer, where he is drawn to her beauty and lack of sophistication. Later, at a party, he listens to a "famous critic" describe Ernestine as a type who is "not always so well-equipped mentally" but who uses her beauty to captivate and so dominate men. The narrator is struck by the incongruity of Ernestine providing the inspiration for his companion's comments, for to him "she was not intellectual, in the best sense at least . . . after her fashion she was a personage, not a mere chemical assault upon the sensual hormones of the male." Six months later the narrator sees Ernestine again; she has become the mistress of the liberal poet and intellectual Varn Kinsey (Max Eastman), who has left his wife (Ida Rauh) for Ernestine. The narrator continues his condescending observation, marveling at the contrast the couple present: "That Ernestine understood him I doubt. More likely she was drawn by his virility, looks, charm and public repute—a man connected with the arts and intellectual matters. . . . I doubt she was able to share his finer moods."

In subsequent encounters, the narrator refines his impression of Ernestine as he traces the career of an ambitious woman whose chief asset is her beauty, a woman who wants to be part of the intellectual crowd but lacks the intellectual abilities to gain entrance. Ernestine is "almost abnormally ambitious," the narrators tells us. "A craze for fame was driving her—fame and applause." When she meets an influential movie producer (Samuel Goldwyn), who offers her a contract in exchange for time on the casting couch, Ernestine is willing "to cultivate his friendship," couch and all, because she is drawn to finery and fame. Despite a quarrel with Kinsey that leads to their breakup, she succumbs to the lure of fame and applause and moves to Hollywood.

Three years later Ernestine's star is falling; she no longer is offered leading roles but second- or third-string parts; her tall, dark beauty is out of current fashion. The narrator meets with her frequently and learns how Hollywood works, of the barter of sexual favors for roles. He is "fascinated by the picture she presented of one who keenly realized the defects of the world in which she found herself" but

who cannot relinquish it because of "an ideal implanted in her by Kinsey." She stoops to trading on her acquaintance with the narrator to improve her prospects, and, despite his request that she desist, she persists—and so the narrator avoids her.

A slump occurs in movie industry; roles are fewer—and Ernestine, now in her mid-twenties, is less desirable than younger, less experienced types. In response to the narrator's report of an acquaintance who, before committing suicide, remarked that she "counted the years from sixteen to twenty-eight as the very best of those granted to women" and who killed herself at age twenty-nine, Ernestine comments portentously: "I think she was right. . . . I despise age myself. Any one who had been really beautiful and knows what it means will understand." Shortly thereafter Ernestine returns to New York and turns on the gas. For the narrator, Ernestine's story becomes a parable of mismanaged opportunities and an example that "life itself was a confusing gamble in which the cards were frequently marked and the dice weighted."

Keith Newlin

"ERNITA" is the sixth sketch in the first volume of *A Gallery of Women*. Based on the story of her life that **Ruth Kennell** told Dreiser while he was touring the Soviet Union in 1927, the sketch is about a sexually repressed American woman who finds in communism the means to overcome her repression but who ultimately becomes disillusioned. Of interest in the structure of the narrative is Dreiser's method of paralleling the development of Ernita's sexual and emotional growth with the promise of communism to emancipate women. After a youth marked by privation and fending off the unwanted attentions of men, Ernita trains to become a librarian and so fulfill her "ambition to do something indefinitely wonderful." Through one of her unwelcome beaux, Ernita is introduced to socialism and at a gathering meets Leonard, a divinity student who is her opposite in intelligence and conservative values. She is twenty-one, and despite their differences, she is drawn to him "chemically" and emotionally. Both are virgins, both are deeply troubled by their mutual sexual attraction, and so they elope, but Ernita finds no enjoyment in submission to her husband's desire for sex. Ernita soon becomes disenchanted with marriage and equally disenchanted with domestic duties; she is also becoming disillusioned with socialism and joins the Industrial Workers of the World (IWW), hoping that within that organization she will find the meaning that her domestic life lacks. In the meantime, she has convinced her husband—whose love for her continues unabated—to throw off his political conservatism and join with her in the radicalism that gives her life purpose.

Three years pass, and in her unhappiness with her marital state she is drawn ever deeper into radical causes. She is dismissed from her position as librarian, and her discontent is compounded when she discovers that she is pregnant but too poor in health to obtain an abortion. When she is afforded the opportunity to decamp for Russia and join a group of American radicals in Siberia acting as technical consultants for the new government immediately following the Russian Revolution, she leaves her child with her mother and, with Leonard, journeys to be part of the great experiment. Despite appalling living conditions, she finds her work immensely satisfying and thus fulfilling her early dream of amounting to something; but her marriage to Leonard continues to deteriorate, especially when she meets and falls in love with an American communist, an engineer. When Leonard at last realizes Er-

nita will never be the conventional wife he longs for, he returns to the United States, leaving Ernita to pursue "free love" with her engineer. At this point, Ernita quits the IWW and becomes a communist, expressing her twinned commitment to love and to social activism. But enough of her conventional upbringing remains to trouble her conscience; thoughts of her abandoned child and spouse cause her to drift from her engineer, who was more interested in a casual liaison than a committed relationship. After several failed attempts at reconciliation, Leonard obtains a divorce and remarries; Ernita remains in Russia, still committed to the communist ideal but less sure that it can make humankind better, for she has learned that "life is a dangerous, changeful, beautiful and yet deceiving thing . . . yet always endurable even at its worst."

When *A Gallery of Women* was published, Kennell was deeply offended by Dreiser's betrayal of her confidences as well as by his distortion of her life, which caused her embarrassment among her Russian colleagues. In an unsigned review for the *Chicago Daily News*, she charged Dreiser with being out of step with feminism, of perceiving women as "a commodity for the use of men which loses its value when youth and beauty decline." Of "Ernita" in particular, she noted that, despite his efforts to be progressive, he still attributed conventional motives to his subject: "If 'Ernita' tries to rise above the limitations of her sex in her service to society, he explains (or worse, has her explain) that she does it to escape from a humdrum marriage; when she continues that service under trying conditions he attributes her devotion to the fact that she has fallen in love."

Further Reading

"Airmail Interview: Ruth Kennell." *Dreiser Newsletter* 5.1 (1974): 6–11.

[Kennell, Ruth E.]. "Hell Hath No Fury Like a Woman Scorned." Review of *A Gallery of Women. Chicago Daily News* 11 December 1929: 22.

Keith Newlin

"THE ESSENTIAL TRAGEDY OF LIFE." An essay first published in *Hey Rub-a-Dub-Dub*, this cynical argument attempts to expose as a myth the belief in one's individuality and control over one's fate. Dreiser finds the abilities of people to be pathetically ineffectual, especially in comparison to the natural instincts of animals. The "pathos" of the human condition is that "man is essentially a creation or mechanism . . . of a force or forces" and has very little control over his life. These "forces" are "individual" and "enduring" whereas humans are not. The romantic vision of individual significance is therefore ridiculous, Dreiser insists, because an individual's significance lies only in his or her relationship to a larger unit, such as an army or some other social group. Moreover, Dreiser denounces true individuality as an impossible goal because we are essentially "copies of things"—artists, philosophers, aristocrats, generals, and so forth—which have come innumerable times before. Dreiser rejects the notion that any single person is capable of discovering real knowledge. Any accomplishment one achieves is really a product of **chance**, and that accomplishment helps a person as an "ignorant and yet useful machine, never as a thinker." He also proposes that Nature is actively opposed to our developing intelligence, citing as proof the historical tendency of ignorant masses to suppress the overtures of intelligent people. Dreiser points to organized **religion** as another preventive to intellectual development,

and to escape from religion may be a breakthrough for true intelligence. While Dreiser is unsure of who or what is the ultimate creator, he believes that it actively thwarts the pursuit of self-knowledge in order to maintain its own supremacy. The essential tragedy of life, therefore, is that one blindly acts under an illusion of individuality and control without any knowledge of the very real limitations that Nature has imposed.

Jennifer Marie Raspet

"ESTHER NORN," the penultimate of Dreiser's fifteen semifictionalized sketches of *A Gallery of Women*, paints an idealizing picture of the red-haired and ethereal **Greenwich Village** actress **Mary Pyne**, who paraded the streets of Greenwich Village in her sometimes bizarre dress, including a tam-o'-shanter and a Scotch plaid. The sketch provides insight into her activities in the Little Theater movement, the Provincetown Players in the Village. A "mediaeval Madonna" and woman with an elusive "Mona Lisa smile," she is also the quintessential victim of unjust circumstances. Living in a dingy apartment on Port Street and suffering from pneumonia, she is surrounded by a cast of selfish male figures: her father, an unemployed loafer and womanizer who relies on his daughter for support; her companion Doane, based on the poet Harry Kemp, who falls in love with her but neglects her welfare and later abandons her; and the wealthy J.J., based on the anarchist writer Hutchins Hapgood, who has an affair with Esther but withdraws from her to return to his marriage when his son falls severely ill. "Poor Esther" is the narrator's refrain.

"Esther Norn" presents the male artist figure as fundamentally egotistical, a motif also explored in *The "Genius,"* although the perspective and sympathies differ. The narrator accuses Doane and J.J. of idealizing Esther in their creative writing but in neglecting her when she needs material help. The narrator is keen on highlighting his own charitable impulse in offering help when Esther needs it most. Still, like the two artists he condemns, the narrator, too, idealizes Esther and fails to provide significant help when she is dying in the sanatorium. The narrator resents the sexualizing implications of Doane's wild adoration and of J.J.'s eroticized portraits of Esther Norn, yet the narrator's own portrait of her is equally idealized and emotionally charged.

Within *A Gallery of Women*, "Esther Norn" contrasts with women like "Reina," "Regina C——," and "Olive Brand," women who manipulate men for their own material advantage. Esther, in contrast, is the sacrificial lamb, the incarnation of innocence, a projection that helps Dreiser in his condemnation of selfish and exploitative masculinity, including his own. Ultimately, this figure exposes the male artist ego as parasitically feeding on generously given women. One wonders here to what extent Dreiser was working through his own sense of guilt about his abandonment of his wife Sara (Jug) White, whom he denied significant material support in 1917. Ultimately, Pyne has the sacrificial soul that Dreiser valued and validated in *Jennie Gerhardt*, and the sketch generates a similar sense of pathos at her demise.

Further Reading

Brevda, William. "Love's Brief Immortality: Mary Pyne." *Harry Kemp: The Last Bohemian.* Lewisburg, Pa.: Bucknell University Press, 1986. 97–105.

Hapgood, Hutchins. *A Victorian of the Modern World.* New York: Harcourt, 1939.

Irene Gammel

EV'RY MONTH. For two years in the mid-1890s—between his newspaper jobs and his career as a magazine freelancer—Dreiser edited *Ev'ry Month*, a "ten-cent" magazine sponsored by Howley & Haviland Music Company, which had recently made the charts with its hit "The Sidewalks of New York." *Ev'ry Month* was one of the "cheap" magazines that sprang up late in the century as competition to established journals like *Harper's* and the *Atlantic* that, with their cover price of thirty-five cents, were generally reserved for middle- and upper-class readers. In fact, Dreiser and his brother Paul Dresser, a successful songwriter for Howley & Haviland (after 1900 he became a full partner and the company was renamed Howley, Haviland, and Dresser), were probably responsible for creating and naming the magazine as a scheme for putting Theodore to work after his failure as a reporter for the *New York World*. Details are sketchy since Dreiser said little about this phase of his career once he became an established novelist, but apparently he was given almost complete editorial control over the magazine. He probably designed the layout and appearance (which may have been modeled after the *Ladies' Home Journal*, the best-selling cheap magazine of the era); he certainly created the various columns, and, at least early in the magazine's run, he wrote virtually all the copy himself.

The readers of *Ev'ry Month*, like the audience of most of the other cheap magazines, were women, many of them struggling to find for their families a place in the burgeoning middle class. Dreiser skillfully designed the magazine's features and columns with this readership in mind. He advised women about how to decorate their houses on a budget, how to arrange flowers, and what patterns to buy for their children's clothing and their own. He advertised products like Beecham's Pills, Pears Soap, and Madame Rupert's face bleach, along with pianos, insurance, and dictionaries, to help them behave like full-fledged members of the middle class. He ran photos and posters of the decade's elite: politicians, writers, artists, and, above all, actresses. The irony that he was barely twenty-four, male, and not yet middle-class himself cannot have escaped him, even if it did his readers. The columns sometimes targeted his audience as wives, mothers, and consumers, but more often they treated their readers as intelligent, serious individuals capable of following a political argument, a book review, or a discussion of the current plays on Broadway, of which Dreiser proved himself a real connoisseur. Using a series of pseudonyms, Dreiser created and wrote a number of regular columns. As "Th.D.," he wrote drama criticism under various titles; as "Edward Al," a combination of the names of two of his brothers, he wrote "Literary Notes" and, later, "The Literary Shower"; as "The Prophet," he authored "Review of the Month," the political commentary that became "Reflections"; and as "S. J. White," a tribute to his fiancée, Sara "Jug" White, he wrote articles about people and places. As time passed, he was increasingly able to buy literary pieces from the syndicates (including a short story by Stephen Crane) and to hire freelancers like his old friend **Arthur Henry** to write some features.

According to a letter he wrote later to **Robert Elias**, Dreiser built *Ev'ry Month*'s circulation to 65,000 subscribers, a number that was certainly respectable, though not remarkable. Nevertheless, there were clear signs that he was becoming restless. Issue by issue carried fewer articles that he had written himself, and the tone changed as he exercised less editorial control. By the summer of 1897 he was freelancing for other cheap magazines, probably investigating whether he could make a living without *Ev'ry Month*. There is evidence, too, that the management was becoming unhappy with Dreiser; they wanted to peddle the company's sheet music, while he had completely different aspirations. After the September 1897 issue, almost exactly two years after he created the magazine, he either quit or was fired. *Ev'ry Month* continued for a handful of years without him, absorbing the *J. W. Pepper Piano Music Magazine* in 1902 and then being absorbed in turn by the *Household Ledger* in 1903, when *Ev'ry Month* ceased to exist in its own right.

Because Dreiser adopted a number of literary personae, and because he contemplated what makes good literature work in his literary and dramatic columns (and sometimes in "Reflections" as well), the time he spent editing *Ev'ry Month* was invaluable. He began formulating his own fictional aesthetic and moved closer issue by issue to the author who would write *Sister Carrie* only a few years later. Sometimes he even wrote columns—about the homeless poor watching the carriages of the rich, the wiles of the city, an urban strike, the career of the ambitious youth—that quite literally gave him the opportunity, whether he knew it or not, to try out the material for his first novel. Perhaps most importantly, he learned to write without condescension *to* women, the primary audience of the novel (then and now), and *about* women like Carrie Meeber, **Jennie Gerhardt**, and **Roberta Alden**.

Further Reading

Barrineau, Nancy Warner, ed. *Theodore Dreiser's Ev'ry Month.* Athens: University of Georgia Press, 1996.

Nancy Warner Barrineau

EVOLUTION. In what initiated a rigorous, lifelong process of scientific self-education that helped to nourish his naturalistic philosophy and drive his fiction, Dreiser first encountered evolutionary thought in the writings of such leading contemporary scientists as Thomas Henry Huxley, John Tyndall, **Herbert Spencer**, and Charles Darwin. In 1894, Dreiser, who was intellectually stifled by his Catholic upbringing and education, eagerly ingested Huxley's *Science and the Hebrew Tradition* (1894) and *Science and the Christian Tradition* (1909) and Tyndall's *Fragments of Science* (1897), all of which attacked the legitimacy of traditional religious dogma; perhaps more importantly, though, the writings of Huxley and Tyndall paved the way for Dreiser's exposure to Herbert Spencer, whose evolutionary philosophy had arguably the most profound influence on him.

Spencer's *First Principles* (1896) and *The Data of Ethics* (1879) affirmed Dreiser's bleak, deterministic interpretation of the universe, but he saw for the first time during the course of his scientific self-education the possibility of escaping the fundamental struggle for survival. This escape, according to Spencer, could emerge when an individual sacrificed selfish desires for the sake of society as a whole. This possibility is manifested in Dreiser's 1901 short story "The Shining Slave Makers," in which the protagonist, McEwen, must learn to survive in a jungle after being transformed into a black ant. McEwen realizes quickly that he must find food in order to survive, but the other black ants who selfishly hoard and protect their own food complicate his search. When a belligerent colony of red ants threatens the colony of black ants to which McEwen belongs, the latter experiences an overwhelming innate impulse to aid and assist his black comrades in battle. After

suffering life-threatening wounds in the skirmish, McEwen is metamorphosed back into a human. The Spencerian allegory highlights the tension between individualistic drive and communal sacrifice, but—as seen by McEwen's "awakening" at the end of the story—like Spencer, it ultimately champions cooperation and altruism as the highest levels of human conduct.

While continuing to study the work of Huxley, Tyndall, and Spencer, in 1896 Dreiser began to read Darwin's *The Origin of Species* (1859) and *The Descent of Man* (1874). Introduced for the first time to Darwin's theory of natural selection, best expressed by Spencer's phrase "the survival of the fittest," Dreiser became fascinated by the evolutionary scientist. By applying Darwin's theory of biological evolution to human social evolution, Dreiser made the mistake of many thinkers during the period: he assumed that the former theory entailed the latter. Nonetheless, the influence of social Darwinism was essential to Dreiser's early novels. In *Sister Carrie*, for instance, Dreiser's heroine, motivated principally by "self-interest," manages to "rise" from impoverishment to wealth and fame by the end of the novel largely because of her remarkable capacity to adapt to a variety of different surroundings. Carrie Meeber remains "unpunished" at the close of the novel while her counterpart, the once successful and affluent Hurstwood, ultimately commits suicide because of his inability to adapt. Although the novel alludes to the enduring human conflict between individualistic ambition and communal sacrifice (highlighted especially in conversations between **Ames** and Carrie), *Sister Carrie* resonates most deeply with Darwin's theory of natural selection and its social translation—that struggle and competition inevitably characterize human existence. In other novels such as *Jennie Gerhardt*, *The*

Financier, The Titan, and *The "Genius,"* Dreiser would return to the "survival of the fittest" theme, which played such a significant role in *Sister Carrie.* However, Dreiser would reject social Darwinian ideas toward the end of his life mainly because he believed that they rationalized the privileged, exploitative oligarchies that had come to dominate American **capitalism**.

Further Reading

Martin, Ronald E. "Theodore Dreiser: At Home in the Universe of Force." *American Literature and the Universe of Force.* Durham, N.C.: Duke University Press, 1981. 215–55.

Zanine, Louis J. "The Impact of Evolutionary Thought" and "The Evolutionary Universe in Fiction." *Mechanism and Mysticism: The Influence of Science on the Thought and Work of Theodore Dreiser.* Philadelphia: University of Pennsylvania Press, 1993. 7–35, 36–77.

Marc Johnston

F

FARRELL, JAMES T. (1904–1979). Chicago novelist best known for his Studs Lonigan trilogy: *Young Lonigan* (1932), *The Young Manhood of Studs Lonigan* (1934), and *Judgment Day* (1935). Farrell began to read Dreiser while an evening student attending Chicago's De Paul University in 1924; by 1927 he had read all of the published novels and stories. Without accepting Dreiser's political or general ideas, Farrell admired his literary integrity, his depth of feeling, and his determination in the face of hostile criticism. At the suggestion of H. L. Mencken, Farrell met Dreiser in June 1936 during the Democratic convention in Philadelphia. In Dreiser's hotel room, they talked casually about literature and politics for forty-five minutes. By summer 1944 they had corresponded about Farrell's *Sister Carrie* essay in the *New York Times Book Review* the previous year. Farrell had also been invited by Helen Dreiser to be one of Dreiser's literary executors in the event of her death. Farrell's second and last interview came in Dreiser's New York hotel room in July 1944. For over two hours, they discussed various developments of literature and film in New York and Hollywood. Farrell inquired about completion of the **Cowperwood** trilogy and asked if he might read the still unfinished third volume. Following this visit in

New York, until Dreiser's death, the two writers maintained correspondence, with Dreiser discussing Farrell's published essays on the stories of Ring Lardner, literary Philistinism, Dostoevsky, and *An American Tragedy*.

In May 1945, Dreiser telegraphed a request that Farrell advise him concerning the typescript of *The Bulwark*, scheduled for publication later that year. Dreiser also wrote a letter explaining that an earlier reader (**Louise Campbell**) had negatively criticized the book's style and subject matter. Honored by Dreiser's request, Farrell read the novel and wrote a lengthy, detailed letter, assuring Dreiser that his penchant for dialogue illustrating prior, generalized description or analysis, though unfashionable in the wake of Hemingway's work, need not be generally overhauled. Farrell also supported Dreiser's choice to portray sympathetically the religious character of **Solon Barnes**, despite adverse criticism. Farrell suggested a number of detailed revisions, without venturing to alter substantially the shape of the novel. Subsequently, Dreiser had **Donald Elder**, his editor at **Doubleday**, contact Farrell about these revisions.

On 24 October 1945, Dreiser again wrote Farrell to announce completion of *The Stoic* and to request that Farrell read the typescript prior to publication, "so that as to its merits, as well as its defects, I will hear the truth" (*Letters* 3: 1031). On 10 December, Farrell received the novel by express mail and read it immediately, thirty-three chapters the first night. On 19 December, Farrell sent Dreiser another long letter including a few proposed changes of detail but also important suggestions recasting the conclusion, especially its portrayal of Cowperwood's mistress **Berenice Fleming** and its epilogue, an essay on good and evil, which Farrell thought was "a justification of Cowperwood" that "weakens and reduces the objectivity of the portrait" (Farrell Collection). Dreiser spent his last days implementing Farrell's suggestions. The final chapter of *The Stoic*, completed on 27 December, begins to deepen the character of Berenice in accord with Farrell's call for a more powerful conclusion to the trilogy. The discarded epilogue on good and evil is subsumed among materials Dreiser did not live to complete, culminating in a newly conceived soliloquy in the mind of Berenice, a reflection on Cowperwood's career and her own place in it. After Dreiser's death on 28 December, Farrell received a final letter thanking him for criticism of *The Stoic*, acknowledging that Farrell had been "dead right" about the last chapters, and promising to rewrite them accordingly. "As to the essay on Good and Evil, well, that is something that can be discussed at length, and there is plenty of time for that" (*Letters* 3: 1035).

Further Reading

Correspondence and diary notes in the James T. Farrell Collection, University of Pennsylvania Rare Book and Manuscript Library.

Farrell, James T. "Some Correspondence With Theodore Dreiser." *Reflections at Fifty and Other Essays.* New York: Vanguard, 1954. 124–41.

Dennis Flynn

THE FINANCIER, third of Dreiser's published novels, marks a distinct turning point in his career. It is at once a departure from his characteristic subject matter and the beginning of his use of the larger canvas to which he knew that his fictional works were most ideally suited. Both *Sister Carrie* and *Jennie Gerhardt* had been essentially autobiographical works drawn from Dreiser's family and work experiences, as was *The "Genius,"* which was drafted by 1911 but not yet published. Contrasting strongly with those works, *The Financier* was planned from its inception as an extensive work based (as Émile Zola had advised) upon research. Elements deriving from the writer's personal and professional lives were now held to a mere shadow of their former prominence. The new story itself was huge, involving a multitude of prominent characters interacting with the central figure over a span of years; it was conceived as a cradle-to-grave saga, the *complete* telling of one very significant and individual American life.

As always in Dreiser's realist fiction, *The Financier* is grounded firmly in the socioeconomic context of the author's youth and young manhood: the three decades roughly between 1880 and 1910, known often as a "gilded era" dominated by a "genteel tradition" on its slow path toward obsolescence. That period, the years that the author knew most intimately, were characterized in America by an unbridled faith in the virtues of **capitalism**. The government's laissez-faire attitude toward industry quickly led to the gobbling up of resources by aggressive operators and almost at once to oppressive monopoly. Tolerance for "rugged individualism" became a social manifestation of the "survival of the fittest" doctrine that had emerged with the triumph of Darwinism as the nineteenth century approached its end—hence, the sociological term social Darwinism. From such influences a new American society resulted, not one that was necessarily more benign but one that was extremely urban, dominated by industry, and characterized by drastic imbalances in the distribution of wealth and power. The displacement of our traditional agrarian economy with manufacturing led at once to the rise of the city as factories drew workers off the land with the lure of steady wages. As the cities swelled in size, problems in housing and transportation resulted in the growth of slums where working families were herded together, too often in unsanitary and jerry-built housing. Networks of streetcar systems were built for moving people about the sprawling cities.

From all of this new industrial bustle, with more and more workers—including hordes of immigrants—competing for available jobs, no social paradise resulted. Dreiser, in Chicago and on his own by the time he was sixteen, was a keen observer of conditions, a boy with a phenomenal memory and an innate sensitivity to social balance. Very early on he began to question popular American clichés such as "equality" and "opportunity" and in fact to speculate upon the true meaning, if any, of the easy term "democracy" itself. Chicago, the prime instance of nineteenth-century industrial-urban triumph in the Midwest, was a tremendous social schoolroom. Practical demonstrations providing lessons for the acute observer abounded. The new society that was shaping itself before Dreiser's eyes fascinated him. It served also as a driving force in his determination to write *The Financier*.

By the time that Dreiser had passed through his journalistic apprenticeship, he knew that he must somehow address the problem of wealth and poverty in "the land of the free." In his midwestern wanderings as a newspaperman he had seen much in burgeoning cities like St. Louis, Pittsburgh, and Toledo, all dominated by industrial moguls. He had personally interviewed, among others, steel magnate Andrew Carnegie, meatpacking king Philip D. Armour, and department store prince Marshall Field, and he had decided that his novel-to-be would not concern a drone worker victimized and perhaps crushed by the new economic system but instead would center squarely upon a prominent member of this new breed of millionaires who were at once perpetrators and profiteers. It is a common misapprehension that Dreiser, after researching widely and deeply into the moneyed class, produced for his fictional "hero" a hybrid, a composite figure, a robber baron made up of separate traits borrowed from any number of discrete models. In fact, Dreiser rather early in the game had determined that he would concentrate on a single model, and he had already identified him: the streetcar king **Charles T. Yerkes Jr**.

Dreiser chose Yerkes to represent those who perched atop the pyramidal business society as if enthroned, men who from their lofty positions dominated their communities as well as the nation. His choice was arrived at methodically. It must be a man who could represent every important aspect of what Dreiser was calling "genus financier." Yerkes displayed all of the essential traits of the genre. He was, first of all, intelligent and clever, even cunning—excellent survival traits, as was amorality, an effective weapon in a noncaring world where tooth and fang ruled. Yerkes was a monopolist, and Dreiser had observed that monopoly was the fastest, surest path to wealth in America. A man must obtain control of something that everyone wanted or must have—a resource such as iron or lumber, a utility such as water or fuel—and thereby he would position himself, as it were, the sole seller in a universe of buyers. Yerkes, whom Dreiser had first observed during the 1880s in Chicago, had begun his midwestern career by purchasing Chicago gas franchises and combining them and then had amassed a huge fortune by doing the same with the city's transit lines, pulling all the separate streetcar lines under one ownership. He might then charge what he wished. Yet the man was wise enough not to be an obvious price gouger, for with every commuter paying a modest nickel per ride, the fortune piled up quite steadily, rapidly, in fact, especially if the owner put little back into the streetcars for maintenance or the comfort of passengers. Another trait of the monopolist was to work hand in glove with susceptible politicians in obtaining exclusive civic franchises or to bribe state legislatures in order to assure laws and regulations favorable to his monopoly. The name of Yerkes was notorious in both instances.

The typical gilded-era millionaire felt compelled by a deep need to display his wealth ostentatiously in order that the common citizenry might easily observe that he was very much the prime survivor in the economic struggle. The most common manner of accomplishing this was to erect an impressive and costly mansion, a showplace furnished with the rich loot of the world, and then to use it in entertaining other "survivors" at lavish parties (the daily papers took care of spreading the society news to the people). During the 1890s, the heyday of this new breed, it became the fashion to build one's mansion on "Millionaires Row," Fifth Avenue in New York City. This Yerkes had also done,

making certain that his palace had the finest workmanship and the rarest materials and then stuffing it with French antiques and art masterpieces from all of Europe.

The standard millionaire made his money in ruthless fashion, looking out for number one at all times, and was not weakened by sentiment. Yerkes was probably a tad more ruthless than his compatriots; his personal philosophy, "I satisfy myself," appealed to Dreiser as ideal for the purpose, and he used it in writing the man's story. Finally, after sating his economic greed and sense of egotism, the wealth-laden tycoon was driven by another powerful need: he longed to be accepted, to be loved by the very people he had exploited. Attempts to achieve this form of economic sainthood invariably involved "giving something back" to the society that had been raided. A grand gesture was made, always appropriately publicized—an art gallery, a college, in the case of Carnegie hundreds of public libraries. Such public endowments had as a chief aim the rehabilitation of the donor, seen now as a philanthropist and benefactor of society.

In Charles T. Yerkes Dreiser found a man who had accomplished, or aimed at accomplishing, all of the ends desired by a gilded-age financier. In addition, by the time that Dreiser's plans began to shape up, the man was conveniently dead, which left him fair game, because a writer might proceed to use his life story without fear of recrimination. It amused Dreiser and also established an appropriate touch of irony that Yerkes died not in his splendid palace but in a hotel bedroom hired by the day (never mind that the hotel was the old Waldorf Astoria at Fifth Avenue and Thirty-Fourth Street and the room a luxury suite). With the amount of data concerning Yerkes and his career that were available, in fact, public knowledge, there was little need for Dreiser to supplement from the stories of other millionaires.

The writer's problem, if any, was a superfluity of material, and Dreiser, who had never before attempted a story of this scope, had no method for determining in advance the practical possibility of telling all about Yerkes in a single volume, especially as he intended to tell the whole story, as a means of telling the total truth, and so he began at the beginning, with Yerkes's birth in Philadelphia in 1837, traveling to that city in order to study the urban setting and delve into the financier's early years. For the purpose of maintaining at least a semblance of fiction, the central character's name was altered, to **Frank Algernon Cowperwood Jr**. Aside from such surface alterations and disguises, Dreiser made remarkably few changes in the actual Yerkes record. Frank grows up in comfortable circumstances, the son of a banking vice president. He attends, as Yerkes had, Central High School, then begins in a modest way in business, first working for others as he learns his way in the commission business and soon taking on greater and greater responsibility, until he feels able to establish a business of his own in true entrepreneurial fashion. Along the way Yerkes picked up a wife, **Susanna Gamble**, a few years older than he, and in the novel Cowperwood also marries at age twenty-one an older woman, **Lillian Semple**, and by her fathers two children.

Ever on the alert for a method of bettering himself rapidly, Cowperwood recognizes that a great opportunity has arrived when the Civil War brings him an opportunity to act as agent in selling a part of a massive issue of government bonds intended for financing the federal military campaigns. The success of this venture stamps young Cowperwood as a future financial leader. His honest beginning does not last; within a few years Frank has become involved with the Philadelphia city treasurer in an illegal scheme whereby he is allowed temporary use of city funds for speculation, providing that the original funds are safely back in the treasury by the end of each month, when the accounting must be made. This manipulation of funds, euphemistically called "loans," enriches both the treasurer and Cowperwood. He dreams now of creating a streetcar monopoly in Philadelphia and on Girard Avenue erects the first of his impressive mansions, building another next door for his father. At the lavish party celebrating the opening of his new home, Cowperwood falls in love with the eighteen-year-old daughter of a friend and leading city politician, Edward Malia Butler. The invention of the Butler family is Dreiser's chief addition to the Yerkes record, and old Butler is one of his outstanding fictional characters, as is **Aileen Butler**, his daughter.

The love affair with Aileen marks the apogee of Cowperwood's meteoric rise. In 1871 a business panic triggered by the disastrous burning of Chicago and fueled by the resultant drain on treasury funds causes Cowperwood's "loans" to be called in prior to the end of a month, a time when it is not possible for him to lay his hands on the cash needed. The treasurer's malfeasance uncovered, Cowperwood's role in what now amounts to theft is disclosed, and both men are indicted for embezzlement. At his trial, Cowperwood is convicted and sentenced to Eastern Penitentiary, newly constructed in Philadelphia. His marriage, which had been faltering badly before his arrest, continues to deteriorate while he is incarcerated. He has already decided that Lillian is not quite the mate he will require when he resumes his career after his release, and the clandestine visits made to the penitentiary by Aileen Butler convince him that her beauty, her vitality, and her amorality tally ideally with his own sexual needs and his ruthless personality. When Cowperwood obtains a political pardon after serving only a portion of his term, he understands that there is really no long-term future for him in Philadelphia. Society will not let him forget that he is an ex-convict. Yet it is not possible for him to leave until he has recouped at least enough of his lost fortune to provide a stake for himself when he begins again elsewhere.

Once more, a business panic is influential. This time it is the sudden and catastrophic failure of Jay Cooke and Company, thought to be an impregnable leader in the national financial world. The business crisis unnerves most dealers, but Cowperwood, in a remarkable show of strength, remains cool and level-headed. As one demoralized financial house after another dumps stocks on the market and as prices dive with each successive wave of panic selling, Cowperwood bucks the trend, buying and buying. When the smoke clears, he possesses a huge accumulation of shares whose value is considerably more than the rock-bottom prices he has contracted to pay. He is, in fact, a millionaire. His fortune restored, Cowperwood abandons Lillian for good and, with his adulterous lover Aileen Butler at his side, entrains for the West and a new life in burgeoning Chicago, once again his own man

Dreiser's *Financier* was not scheduled to close at this point but instead was designed to continue through the Chicago, New York, and London careers of Charles Yerkes and to close with the financier's unexpected death from Bright's disease. However, as typically happened with a Dreiser project, the author discovered that, the tap once open, he could write and write, nearly without end. In the case of *The Financier*, Dreiser had contracted for

publication with **Harper & Brothers**, and when he began writing in earnest in 1910, he saw no reason not to assure Harper's that the completed novel—telling the entire life story—would be delivered in time for fall 1912 publication. He had counted on his documentation, which was chiefly Philadelphia histories and daily newspapers, being sufficient for his needs, but as he reached the parts of the story in which his hero amassed his wealth, he found that he knew too little about his man's way of life. Knowing intimately the world of poverty and the world of work, Dreiser felt somewhat at sea imagining daily life in the universe of the wealthy. He also felt an urge to research further into Yerkes's later career, which had been spent in an attempt to wrest control of all the London Underground lines.

Leaving with Harper's the thirty-nine chapters he had drafted, Dreiser late in 1911 sailed for England, there to dog Yerkes's trail. He visited also in Paris, Monte Carlo, and Italy, favorite Yerkes vacation spots and locales where the financier had visited galleries and artists' studios, purchasing additions to his already famous art collection. Returning to America in April 1912, Dreiser found Harper's clamoring for his manuscript. When the publishers learned that the greater share of the story was yet to be drafted, they suggested that the mammoth story be published as a series of novels. Dreiser knew that he could not complete his entire novel in time and came to recognize also that the Philadelphia phase of Yerkes's life itself handily constituted a discrete story. He agreed to Harper's plan. In this manner, *A Trilogy of Desire* had its beginning, Part One: *The Financier*, appearing in October 1912.

The book was issued to a mingling of praise and condemnation. Some reviewers felt it the finest, most powerful, the *truest* piece in the realist manner yet produced by an American, but other, more conservative critics attacked it for its seemingly endless masses of financial detail and even more so for the blatant amorality of its hero, who without any sense of either shame or remorse followed his animal instincts rather than conforming to social mores. Dreiser's candid treatment of sexual passion shocked many and helped raise the call for **censorship**, which was already well on its way to becoming a threat to literary works. Only a handful of reviewers recognized that the novel, beneath its fictional veneer, was true, hewing at almost every point and in nearly every detail to the actual life story of Charles T. Yerkes. Others guessed that he must have had a real-life model, but no one then living could know that Dreiser was setting a literary trend that by the end of the twentieth century would pervade the world of fiction. The current fashion was to insist upon the imaginative powers of the writer, declaring any resemblance of the story and its characters to actual people and events "unintentional and purely coincidental." If it is much in vogue today to announce a new novel (as well as a dramatic work) with the proud disclaimer "Based on a True Story," that trend is one that *The Financier* did much to bring into being. In the twenty-first century the excited furor over Dreiser's alleged salaciousness seems purely academic, and his novel has taken its place as a central monument in American literary efforts devoted to the business theme.

In 1927 a revised edition of the novel was issued by **Boni & Liveright**. Shorter and swifter in narrative pace, the revised version deletes some details of Cowperwood's business dealings and much of Dreiser's philosophical musings; it is the basis for all subsequent reprints.

Further Reading

Brennan, Stephen C. "*The Financier*: Dreiser's Marriage of Heaven and Hell." *Studies in American Fiction* 19.1 (1991): 55–69.

Eby, Clare Virginia. "Business as (Un)usual: The Immaterial Economy in *The Trilogy of Desire*." *Dreiser and Veblen, Saboteurs of the Status Quo*. Columbia: University of Missouri Press, 1998. 65–106.

Gerber, Philip. "Financier, Titan, and Stoic: *A Trilogy of Desire*." *Theodore Dreiser*. New York: Twayne, 1964. 87–110.

Hussman, Lawrence E.. *Dreiser and His Fiction: A Twentieth Century Quest*. Philadelphia: University of Pennsylvania Press, 1983. 70–90.

Hutchisson, James M. "The Creation (and Reduction) of *The Financier*." *Papers on Language and Literature* 27.2 (1991): 243–59.

Jett, Kevin W. "Vision and Revision: Another Look at the 1912 and 1927 Editions of Dreiser's *The Financier*." *Dreiser Studies* 29 (1998): 51–73.

Lehan, Richard. "*The Financier, The Titan*, and *The Stoic*." *Theodore Dreiser: His World and His Novels*. Carbondale: Southern Illinois University Press, 1969. 97–116.

Matthiessen, F. O. "The Business Novel." *Theodore Dreiser*. New York: William Sloane, 1951. 127–58.

O'Neill, John. "The Disproportion of Sadness: Dreiser's *The Financier* and *The Titan*." *Modern Fiction Studies* 23 (1977): 409–22.

Pizer, Donald. "*The Financier*." *The Novels of Theodore Dreiser: A Critical Study*. Minneapolis: University of Minnesota Press, 1976. 160–82.

Shapiro, Charles. "*The Financier, The Titan, The Stoic*." *Theodore Dreiser: Our Bitter Patriot*. Carbondale: Southern Illinois University Press, 1966. 25–44.

Ziff, Larzer. Afterword to *The Financier*. New York: New American Library, 1967. 451–60.

Philip Gerber

FINCHLEY, SONDRA. Dreiser's creation of the character of Sondra Finchley as the "rich girl" who embodies all the hungers for wealth, privileged pleasure, and feminine beauty driving Clyde Griffiths throughout *An American Tragedy* becomes one of the novelist's crucial achievements in telling the tragic tale. In the actual 1906 murder case of **Chester Gillette** which served as a principal source for Dreiser's development of the story, the ambitious youth who drowned a pregnant, poor sweetheart to be free for a presumably more successful future had not fixed upon a specific wealthy girl he desired to wed. Yet the characterization of Sondra and of her powerful, near-mesmerizing impact on Clyde are essential to the novel's effective enactment in fiction of that tragic pattern of poor boys' misguided quests to wed rich girls that Dreiser observed and analyzed at length in his essay "I Find the Real American Tragedy." The depiction of this teenaged socialite and her fateful effect on Clyde is one especially major proof that Dreiser greatly expanded upon his actual sources in shaping the vast story in the *Tragedy*. As the narrative voice says in the first moment of the protagonist's encounter with this beauty of "the leisure class" that all his dreams focus on, "To Clyde's eyes she was the most adorable feminine thing he had seen in all his days. Indeed her effect on him was electric—thrilling—arousing in him a curiously stinging sense of what it was to want and not to have." From that instant forward, Sondra seems to him the unattainable paragon symbolizing everything Clyde lives for and intensely desires. In fact, the ultimately fatal love triangle centrally shaping the plot in Book 2 of the novel is foreshadowed in this immature youth's consciousness of that supreme desire, even at the dawn of his secret romance with the poor factory girl **Roberta Alden**. Just when Clyde first encounters Roberta during a summer outing at a local lake and enthusiastically tells her he has been yearning for chances to spend time with her away from the restrictive realm of the Griffiths fac-

tory, he has actually been consumed with "resentment and disappointment" at being shut out of the world of his rich relatives and of "that beautiful Sondra Finchley, whom he recalled with a keen and biting thrill." This irony of Clyde's conflicting desires—for immediate companionship and sexual release until his longed-for future of union with a wealthy "dream-girl" can somehow be attained—sets the stage for all the subsequent drama of the "American tragedy" pattern. Dreiser originally considered giving this vast novel the title "Mirage." The ominous "mirage" or illusion of possibility for realized dreams of "success" comes into clear perspective in Clyde's fateful thought, ironically encouraged by Sondra's emerging interest in him: "[W]hat harm . . . was there in a poor youth like himself aspiring to such heights? Other youths as poor as himself had married girls as rich as Sondra."

Paul A. Orlov

"FINE FURNITURE." Rejected on nine separate occasions in 1923, Dreiser's "Fine Furniture" was eventually published in two installments in *Household Magazine* (November–December 1929) before being reissued in 1930 in a limited edition of 875 copies in Random House's Prose Quarto series. The controlling premise of the story is announced at the very outset: "That which afflicted Opal was a superiority complex relating to furniture and material surroundings generally." Born and raised in the small logging town of MacCumber, Opal, "ambitious and determined to improve herself" and to find an eligible bachelor suitable to such an enterprise, moves to the larger, more prosperous town of Renton and takes a position as a waitress at the town's most fashionable restaurant, the Calico Cat, where she eventually attracts the interest of Clem Broderson, an oafish, though genial, logger from a nearby camp in Red Ledge. Four months later, she and Clem are married and they move into a logging shack that Opal finds distressingly shabby. To all appearances "a sweet, shrinking violet," Opal is actually driven by ambition, and, anxious to establish her local ascendancy in matters of taste and fashion, she manipulates Clem into spending his life savings on a set of "fine furniture," the likes of which had never been seen in the logging camp. Opal's vain and fastidious attachment to her new furnishings quickly alienates her and Clem from the rest of the camp and incurs the jealousy of the camp superintendent's wife, Mrs. Saxstrom. Not unlike George Amberson in Booth Tarkington's *The Magnificent Ambersons*, Opal "gets her come-uppance" when, following a move to a new camp, the Broderson's shack (transported by rail along with the other shacks) is assigned, largely through the connivance of Mrs. Saxstrom, the worst site in the camp. Rashly quitting his job in protest, Clem suddenly realizes that "fine furniture and Opal's inordinate love of and care for it probably really lay at the bottom of all this trouble," and he thus turns on Opal for the first time in their marriage and chides her for her selfishness and snobbery. Opal thereupon experiences an epiphany of her own and, acknowledging the truth of Clem's criticism, observes they would have been happier without the furniture, which "I wish to God I had never seen." The two are then happily reconciled, and the story concludes with Clem's promise to Opal that one day "we'll have a place where you can have all the swell furniture you want."

Like so many of Dreiser's fictional heroines and not unlike Dreiser himself, Opal aspires to escape the drab and stultifying surroundings of her youth for a more exciting life, though given her social background and unpromising financial circumstances, such a dream can be achieved only through marriage. Though attractive enough, Opal is disadvantaged by the fact that she is "short" and "stocky" and lacks the "swagger and charm" and "svelte" figure of other girls her age. Opal overcomes such handicaps through her undiscouraged ambition, tenacious determination, and resourcefulness, first in manipulating Clem into a proposal of marriage and then in persuading him to purchase the set of "fine furniture" that ensures, if only in her own estimation, her social superiority. That such status is achieved within the shabby environment of a logging community is poignantly lost on Opal. Far from a sympathetic naïf, however, Opal is revealed as a scheming, controlling social climber whose self-serving interests result not only in the loss of Clem's job and their "fine furniture" but in the near loss of her marriage as well.

Michael Wentworth

FLEMING, BERENICE. Appearing midway in *The Titan*, the second novel of Dreiser's *Trilogy of Desire*, Berenice Fleming eventually forms one side of the marital triangle involving **Frank Cowperwood** and **Aileen Butler**. Cowperwood and Aileen are the fictional counterparts to **Charles Tyson Yerkes**, a powerful Chicago traction tycoon of the 1890s, and his wife, **Mary Adelaide Moore** Yerkes. Berenice is a portrait of Yerkes's mistress, **Emilie Grigsby**, and was created almost entirely from Dreiser's collection of newspaper clippings tracing her social activities and her relationship with Yerkes. Cowperwood is first made aware of Berenice when he visits Louisville, Kentucky, on a business trip and meets her mother, Hattie Starr, a woman with a questionable reputation.

Critics consider Berenice to be Cowperwood's most important mistress in that she may well be his ideal woman. In fact, she is the only woman who ever comes close to controlling him. Though she is only a young girl of seventeen when he first meets her, Cowperwood spots great potential, becomes her benefactor, and moves her and her family to New York. Here, she continues to attend the famous Brewster's School for Girls, a school devoted to cultivating aristocratic qualities in young women. Though Cowperwood pays her tuition, he views Berenice as an investment, an object to possess and admire, similar to the expensive paintings that adorn the walls in his office and home. Since socialites have ostracized his wife, Aileen, and since social prestige is important to Cowperwood, he hopes to make Berenice a valuable social companion.

In Berenice, Dreiser provides Cowperwood with a perfect complement to his own artistic temperament, a woman who uses her shrewd and calculating intellect to control her emotions. Her grace, energy, poise, and individualism, which can be juxtaposed to Aileen's unbridled passion, further appeal to Cowperwood, compelling him to think that she "could and would command the utmost reaches of his soul in every direction." Like Cowperwood in the business community, Berenice in social circles commands respect and forces others to view her as superior to them and to accept her on her own terms. Even when her mother's past exploits as a madam are exposed, Berenice maintains her poise and composure, much the same way Cowperwood handles his financial failure in Philadelphia and his ensuing stint in a penitentiary for hypothecating funds from the city treasury. Critics, however, view her increased role in *The Stoic* as oddly romantic and contradictory, especially her interest in the Hindu philosophy of reunification and her desire to sell her home and jewelry to build a hospital in Cowperwood's name for the poor. Essentially, her entire character changes from a materialistic and cunning woman to an altruistic and selfless individual following Cowperwood's death and her brief encounter with Eastern philosophy.

Further Reading

Gerber, Philip L. "The Alabaster Protégé: Dreiser and Berenice Fleming." *American Literature* 43 (1971): 217–30.

Harman, William C. "The Women in Theodore Dreiser's Novels." M.A. thesis, Bowling Green State University, Ohio, 1966.

Kevin Jett

FORT, CHARLES (1874–1932). Over a twenty-seven-year period, from when they met in 1905 until 1932, Theodore Dreiser and Charles Fort maintained a close, dynamic relationship. Both men were born in the 1870s, both became journalists in 1892, both turned to fiction (short stories and novels), and both devoted their final years to writing science and philosophy. In 1905, the two men met when Fort sold stories to Dreiser, who was then an editor at *Smith's Magazine*. Dreiser immediately liked Fort and praised his **realism** and humor.

From 1905 to 1916, Dreiser encouraged Fort to write fiction, buying short stories for magazines he edited and later asking publishers to accept Fort's longer works. In 1907, Dreiser recommended Fort's novel *The Outcast Manufacturers* to **B. W. Dodge and Company,** of which Dreiser was part owner. *The Outcast Manufacturers,* published by Dodge in 1909, is a realistic, ironic, and humorous portrait of poor city dwellers for whom eviction from tenements is a common event. With Dreiser's encouragement, Fort wrote over 3.5 million words of fiction, including two science fiction novels, *X* and *Y*, but Fort destroyed these works when publishers rejected them—only Dreiser's brief descriptions of the novels survive. After Fort failed to interest publishers in his science fiction, he began researching and writing works of nonfiction.

Between 1914 and 1919, Fort estimated that he collected 40,000 notes and newspaper clippings about strange and unexplained phenomena, arranged under 1,300 headings, such as "Harmony," "Equilibrium," "Catalysts," "Saturation," "Supply and Demand," and "Metabolism." This material became worked into Fort's first extended work of nonfiction, *The Book of the Damned* (1919). To support Fort, Dreiser threatened to leave his publisher, **Boni & Liveright**, if they did not accept *The Book of the Damned*. Boni & Liveright acquiesced, and the book was so successful that Fort was able to publish three similar works: *New Lands* (1923), *Lo!* (1931), and *Wild Talents* (1932). Each of these books describes strange phenomena, but Fort's tone is both humorous and ironic, and behind his irony lie three Fortean principles: (1) unexplained events occur daily, but scientists ignore them because the phenomena do not fit into their theories; (2) there exists an underlying oneness to everything, but this oneness or force cannot be known; (3) exploring unexplained phenomena will allow for a better understanding of the oneness behind the apparent chaos. Since 1919, Fort's nonfiction books have never been out of print—the Fortean movement and its publications continue strong.

Dreiser supported Fort, but he also admired and adopted Fort's methods, systematically collecting articles on scientific topics that were eventually included in *Notes on Life*. Dreiser also incorporated Fort's ideas into his creative works. For example, Dreiser claimed that his play *The Dream* is an adaptation of Fort's novel *X*, in which Fort suggests that human beings and the world they inhabit are nothing more than emanations from some cosmic mind. Fort died on 3 May 1932, leaving his papers to Tiffany Thayer, the founder of the Fortean Society, but Fort's widow tried to retrieve the papers so Dreiser could write Fort's biography. Although Dreiser never received the papers and never wrote the biography, he repeatedly acknowledged his admiration of Fort's scientific imagination.

Further Reading

Fort, Charles. *The Complete Books of Charles Fort.* New York: Dover, 1974.

Knight, Damon. *Charles Fort: Prophet of the Unexplained.* London: Victor Gollancz, 1971.

Zanine, Louis J. "Science and the Supernatural." *Mechanism and Mysticism: The Influence of Science on the Thought and Work of Theodore Dreiser.* Philadelphia: University of Pennsylvania Press, 1993. 115–45.

Roark Mulligan

FOSTER, WILLIAM Z. (1881–1959). One of the outstanding labor activists of the Communist Party of the United States, William Z. Foster also had the distinction of being the party's presidential candidate in three consecutive elections, those of 1924, 1928, and 1932, and he was instrumental in the founding and operations of the Trade Union Education League. This was no mean feat, for in its heyday (1920–1929), the league acted as a trade union body opposed to the conservatism of the American Federation of Labor.

Viewed from the perspective of the Dreiser biographer, Foster was a far more transient presence. In the spring of 1931, in Pittsburgh, where Foster was doing organizing work, he had invited Dreiser to witness the Communist Party–affiliated National Miners' Union fight against the more conventional United Mine Workers of John L. Lewis. He also secured Dreiser's reportage on Kentucky's bloody coal protest in 1931 **Harlan County**. Though details are vague, Dreiser supposedly met with Foster there in late 1931 or 1932.

Almost a decade later, in 1941, when Foster was just beginning to criticize **Earl Browder's** policies, the well-known American writer publicly praised the man who had led organizing drives and written so prolifically on syndicalism, the Russian Revolution, and militancy in the American labor movement. Closure to the Dreiser–Foster relationship occurs in 1945, when Foster ousted Browder from the party leadership. Shortly before Dreiser's death the same year, in a now-famous 20 July letter to Foster himself, now the national chairman, the iconoclastic man of letters formally joined the party. (Dreiser's missive was subsequently published in the Communist Party organ *The Daily Worker* on 30 July 1945.)

Some biographers argue for a close social relationship, at least in the early 1930s; others omit Foster almost entirely from their indexes. Thus, as with so much of Dreiser's "leftism," tantalizing questions remain. What was the evolving personal and political relationship between the two men, one accreting fame, the other destined for Cold War notoriety for a career of left-wing mass organizing in the industrial trades? Dreiser's own ambivalence about communism in general and party notables in particular remains underresearched. While he apparently liked Foster, it is not clear why the chief labor organizer of the Communist Party in its early years would appeal to a man whose unionism was as wavering as his interest in joining the Communist Party itself.

Further Reading

Barrett, James R. "Trade Union Educational League." *Encyclopedia of the American Left.* Ed. Mari Jo Buhle, Paul Buhle, and Dan Georgakas. New York: Garland, 1990.

Johanningsmeier, Edward P. *Forging American Communism: The Life of William Z. Foster.* Princeton, N.J.: Princeton University Press, 1994.

Pizer, Donald. " 'The Logic of My Life and Work': Another Look at Dreiser's July 20, 1945, Letter to William Z. Foster." *Dreiser Studies* 30.2 (1999): 24–34.

Laura Hapke

"FREE." If outraging the conventionally minded signifies artistic merit, then "Free" is the best short story Dreiser ever wrote. After publishing it in March 1918, the *Saturday Evening Post* received hundreds of telegrams and letters denouncing Dreiser's sympathetic portrayal of a man who wishes his ailing wife dead. Later that year, however, when reprinted in *Free and Other Stories*, "Free" was praised by a number of reviewers for its honesty and psychological insights. In the years since, it has deservedly been among Dreiser's most anthologized and most critically praised stories.

The protagonist is Rufus Haymaker, a sixty-year-old New York architect who thinks back over his life while doctors fight to save his wife, Ernestine, from kidney disease and heart failure. To all appearances a devoted husband, Haymaker ponders ruefully his failure to make hay while the sun shone, that is, his failure to find true love in his youth. According to his clearly biased memories, he has spent decades of "tremendous and soul-crushing sacrifice" making Ernestine happy while concealing his own misery. His dream of "infinite, inexpressible delight" with some new lover has become "almost an obsession," doubtless a compensation for the "obsession of failure" he attributes to Ernestine's jealous efforts to "poison his own mind in regard to himself and his art."

Rufus pays a tremendous emotional price for the dark desires that increasingly rule his thoughts. When Ernestine's heart weakens, he is awash in sympathy mixed with "an excess of self-condemnation"; when she improves, his death wish reasserts itself along with a sense of "[h]ow queer—how almost evil, sinister—he had become." Once Ernestine succumbs, he fears that his "black thoughts" are to blame and that she will "hate him—haunt him" from beyond the grave. Seeing in the mirror a ridiculous old man no beautiful woman could want, he cries out bitterly, "I am free now, at last! . . . Yes—free . . . to die!" This moment of *anagnorisis*, of gazing into the abyss in what seems to be clear-eyed self-knowledge, gives Rufus tragic stature.

Yet "Free" finally suggests the difficulty, if not the impossibility, of true self knowledge. In an almost Jamesian use of the limited third-person point of view, Dreiser offers numerous clues of Rufus's unreliability. Troubled that no one will ever understand "his own story . . . his life," he unintentionally reveals "her" story, the story of a woman who has sacrificed more in their marriage than he and who, despite her petty flaws, has become his deepest need. When he mourns because "the glorious dream of his youth was gone forever," he does not know the ache is for Ernestine, his first "dream among fair women."

Further Reading

Hussman, Lawrence E., Jr. *Dreiser and His Fiction: A Twentieth-Century Quest*. Philadelphia: University of Pennsylvania Press, 1983. 116–19.

Stephen C. Brennan

FREE AND OTHER STORIES, the first of Dreiser's two collections of short stories, was published in August 1918, "a year of terrible failure and frustration" (Swanberg 227) during which Dreiser received more than 75 rejections. With a $500 advance from the new publishing firm of **Boni & Liveright**, he assembled eleven stories for the volume, nine previously published works and two that had gone the rounds of the magazines with no luck. But Dreiser did not treat the collection as a mere potboiler; despite the heavy cost in extra printer's charges, he so heavily revised the proofs that, **Liveright** complained, he had "practically rewritten the whole book" (qtd. in Swanberg 229). If his intention was to impose unity, the fact has escaped readers, who have for the most part been impressed by the collection's diversity of genres and moods, which range from the whimsical, to the melodramatic, to the tragic. Still, within this variety Dreiser sounds his typical themes—the mystery, wonder, and terror of life, the frustration of desire by circumstances. If there is one dominant theme, though, it is the necessity and danger of illusion, or, as **Jennie Gerhardt** puts it in echoing Hamlet, "There is neither good nor ill, but thinking makes it so."

The four stories written in the summer of 1899, just before Dreiser began *Sister Carrie*, take middle-class readers to a different time or place to reveal the underlying unity of life. "When the Old Century Was New," more sketch than story, follows a wealthy young gentleman, William Walton, as he strolls through old New York on a spring day in 1801. The mood is all "flowers and romance" until the last sentence, when the narrator evokes "the crush and stress and wretchedness" of the modern New York already emerging within the seemingly idyllic setting. In "McEwen of the Shining Slave Makers," Robert McEwen dozes off under a shade tree while watching ants battling in the grass and dreams he becomes one of the black warriors in a world not only of brutal Darwinian struggle but of heroism, loyalty, and compassion. Upon awakening, he understands that there are "worlds within words" and "a vague, sad something" that will endure as long as life endures.

"Old Rogaum and His Theresa" and "Nigger Jeff" explore how the other half lives in an America divided along class and racial lines. When Old Rogaum, an immigrant German butcher obsessed with morality, locks his daughter out of the house for following the lure of love and life out into the night streets, she is nearly despoiled by a cocky street-corner Romeo. But for a cop's chance discovery of the two in the bushes, it is implied, Theresa might well have met the grisly fate of the prostitute found that same evening dying in the gutter from the acid she has swallowed in despair. Such tragedies, the story suggests, are due to the demonizing of normal human desire. "Nigger Jeff" fictionalizes an event from Dreiser's newspaper days in St. Louis. When cub reporter Elmer Davies witnesses the horrible lynching of a black man who has raped a white girl, his belief in poetic justice crumbles, for he cannot fit into any conventional moral scheme the understandable wrath of the raped girl's father, the overpowering lust and equally powerful filial love of the brutalized Jeff Ingalls, and the human grief of Jeff's "weeping mammy." In a moment of epiphany, Davies, with "the cruel instinct of the budding artist," realizes that his function is not to "indict" the world for its injustice but to "interpret" life in all its passion, beauty, and ugliness. "I'll get it all in!" he cries exultantly in the story's last sentence.

Dreiser also fictionalized one of his St. Louis newspaper experiences in "A Story of Stories," which had been rejected by several magazines in 1917. The plot involves the rivalry between two reporters on competing newspapers—"Mr. Augustus Binns," a dreamy, foppish young easterner with artistic pretensions, and the crude, slang-talking "Red" Collins, whose very position on a newspaper is for college-educated Binns "a crime against art and literature." When the two question a notorious bank robber, however, it takes both Collins's fact-finding and Binns's "finer shades of questioning" to bring "a fine tale" of psychological depth into being. Collins gets the story in print first by virtually "hypnotizing" his effete rival with his "gross savage desire . . . to win," but without Binns's artistry there would have been no story worth printing.

"The Cruise of the 'Idlewild,' " originally published in 1909, is based on Dreiser's days as an amateur laborer in 1903, when he worked at a railroad carpentry shop near Spuyten Duyvil in order to recover from his breakdown following the *Sister Carrie* fiasco. Bored with his menial job, the educated narrator first convinces the engineer and then the other workers to pretend their shop is a ship, the *Idlewild*, in which the "men will furnish the idle, and the bosses will furnish the wild." The fantasy collapses when the "bosses" (the engineer and the narrator play at captain and mate) create "rancor and discord" among the crew by abusing their power. When the boredom returns, however, the two decide to invent a new ship, the *Harmony*, and command it with benevolence.

Fantasy, or at least the inability to penetrate to the truth, plays a much more negative role in the previously unpublished "Will You Walk into My Parlor?" a story of political chicanery with a surprise ending in the O. Henry mode. The protagonist, a newspaper reporter named Ed Gregory, is planning an exposé of corruption in the administration of a big-city mayor. Fearing preemptive action by his enemies, he sends his wife and children away and holes up in a seaside resort where a series of ambiguous events suggests that a plot may indeed be afoot. Eventually, his infatuation for the mysterious and beautiful Imogene Carle leads to his being photographed with her in a compromising situation. "Fool! Fool!" he calls himself, knowing that his career is ruined, though even now he cannot decide whether Imogene is part of the plot or merely the unwilling tool he wants to believe she is.

The most effective stories in the collection deal with ambivalence in love relations. "Married" is a chapter lifted from the manuscript of The *"Genius,"* reworked, and published as a short story in 1917. The painter **Eugene Witla** has become Duer Wilde, a talented young pianist who resents the jealousy and insecurity of his conventional midwestern wife, Marjorie. Duer assures Marjorie of her beauty and worth, but all the while he believes the self-abasing image she presents of herself and considers his own consoling words as largely a performance related to his "ability to paint a picture in notes and musical phrases, to extract the last ringing delicacy out of the keys of the piano." Unless Marjorie can change or Duer can willingly suspend his disbelief in her worth, their marriage is doomed.

"The Lost Phoebe," finally published in 1916 after a number of rejections during the previous four years, and the title story "Free," which outraged many *Saturday Evening Post* readers earlier in 1918, are about older men dealing with the loss of their wives. On the surface, Henry and Phoebe Ann Reifsneider in "The Lost Phoebe" are a quaint old couple living in "peace and sympathy" on their ramshackle farm. Still, there are hints of Henry's underlying restlessness, and Phoebe's repeated threats of desertion, a

tactic Dreiser's mother used to terrify and control her children, suggest a deep underlying aggression. When she dies, Henry escapes his loneliness by going mad. Hallucinating that Phoebe has come back only to leave after a quarrel, he begins wandering the countryside in search of her and thus attains a freedom he has never known. When he thinks he sees Phoebe below a cliff "among a silvery bed of apple-trees now blooming in the spring," he plunges gladly to his death believing he has found not the wife of his old age but "a delightful epitome of their quondam youth," the pre-lapsarian Phoebe who was already lost the moment he married her.

While Henry's resentment is unconscious, that of Rufus Haymaker, the protagonist of "Free," is at the very heart of his conscious conflict. Over three days during which doctors fight to save his wife from heart and kidney failure, Rufus thinks back over his life—how he married Ernestine out of a sense of duty, how out of weakness he allowed her to dictate the course of their conventional life, how he has dreamed and dreamed of a free life with a woman who could understand him. As Ernestine's strength waxes and wanes, Rufus alternates between wishing her dead and feeling guilt and sympathy. He is left at her death staring into the mirror at the image of an old man, convinced of life's "innate cruelty, its blazing ironic indifference to him." "I am free now, at last!" he murmurs. "Free! . . . Free! . . . Yes—free . . . to die!" Rufus's effort at honest self-evaluation makes his plight moving and tragic, yet he does not even yet seem to understand that, like Duer Wilde, he suffers because his imagination fails to transform the woman who loves him into the image of his desire.

"The Second Choice," also a magazine piece from early 1918, is the only story in the collection told entirely from a woman's point of view. It opens with a working girl named Shirley reading a rejection letter from Arthur, the footloose stranger who the year before had overwhelmed her with his good looks, egotism, and sexual power. She thinks back over the affair—the delight that transformed her drab life, the torturing fears that Arthur would desert her. Despite her attractiveness, she decides she must settle for Barton, her second choice, the steady, but unexciting, man she had once planned to marry. Beneath her masochistic self-loathing, however, Shirley's choice expresses a will to power. With the devoted Barton, she will be in control and will satisfy her long-held fantasy of standing at the altar "in a pearl satin wedding dress." As for Arthur, she has safely reduced him to a fantasy figure she can summon at will to energize her sexual life.

Free and Other Stories was a moderate financial success, with 2,742 copies being sold within the first three and half months. Sales probably received a boost, however, from the release late in 1918 of an inexpensive edition in Boni & Liveright's Modern Library with a highly appreciative Introduction by **Sherwood Anderson**. The book did not fare so well with reviewers. As usual, many attacked Dreiser's style, and some denied that he had any talent at all for the short story, a form, H. L. Mencken wrote in his *Smart Set* review, "as far outside Dreiser's natural field as the triolet or the mazurka" (rpt. in Salzman 313). This view generally obtains today. Yet in stories such as "Free," "The Lost Phoebe," "Nigger Jeff," "The Second Choice," and "Old Rogaum and His Theresa," the openminded reader will find the "painstaking analysis of psychological processes," as Leonard Cline noted in a review for the *Detroit News* (rpt. in Salzman 305). There are no "cheap tricks" here, Anderson as-

serted in his Introduction, only "sturdy, strong, true and fine" workmanship.

Further Reading

Pizer, Donald. "Introduction: A Summer at Maumee." *The Novels of Theodore Dreiser: A Critical Study*. Minneapolis: University of Minnesota Press, 1976. 3–27.

Stephen C. Brennan

FREUD, SIGMUND (1856–1939), the Viennese neurologist who founded psychoanalysis, was a significant influence on Dreiser in the decade leading up to *An American Tragedy* and beyond. When Dreiser moved to **Greenwich Village** in 1914, Freudianism was all the rage and soon became an undercurrent in his work. In 1918, he began reading Freud seriously, just about the time he struck a friendship with **A. A. Brill**, a prominent psychoanalyst and Freud's American translator. Dreiser thought that Freud had unlocked the secrets of the human mind, and he found the case studies in Brill's *Psychoanalysis* (1913) to be the stuff of high tragedy. Years later, he would remember how *Three Contributions to a Theory of Sex, Totem and Taboo* and *The Interpretation of Dreams* were "a revelation to me—a strong, revealing light thrown on some of the darkest problems that haunted and troubled me and my work" (qtd. in Moers 265).

Among Dreiser's earliest references to the new depth psychology is a passage in *A Hoosier Holiday* attributing the sexual hang-ups of southerners to "the inversion of the psychoanalyst." "Inversion of affect" was Freudian terminology for the expression of a repressed feeling by its opposite. Love, for example, could express itself as hate, even a death wish; aggression toward others, as self-loathing. Without using any specifically Freudian vocabulary, Dreiser began to make such tortured mental states the substance of some of his best stories, most notably, "Free" and "The Second Choice," both initially published in early 1918.

After 1918, Dreiser, like many liberal intellectuals, began to enlist Freud in the battle against conventional morality and prudery. In his essay "Neurotic America and the Sex Impulse," included in *Hey Rub-a-Dub-Dub*, he condemned the country's repressive puritan ethos as a symptom of deep neurosis and in the unpublished "It" depicted the Freudian unconscious as the locus of "horrible lusts and impulses" that, if "thwarted," could erupt "with vast and crushing power" (*Uncollected Prose* 221). This is essentially the thesis of his play *The Hand of the Potter*, which invokes Freud to challenge the moral responsibility of a man driven by overpowering lust to molest and murder a little girl.

While much of Dreiser's work in the 1920s has a Freudian cast, especially those portraits of repressed neurotics in *A Gallery of Women*, *An American Tragedy* represents his most important and effective use of Freud, despite the distracting jargon— "rearranging chemisms," "masochistic yearning," "psychic sex-scar," "repressed or sublimated sex nature." Wishes, Freud and Brill had taught him, not only motivate normal dreams and fantasies but can, with weak egos, lead to psychotic delusions. Clyde's "subconscious need" for a fairy-tale life of beauty, love, and luxury with his dream-girl **Sondra Finchley** is thwarted by the demands of his pregnant lover **Roberta Alden**. Desire becomes his tragic fate, emerging from his unconscious as a genie, or "Efrit," out of the *Arabian Nights*, "the very substance of some leering and diabolic wish or wisdom concealed in his own nature" and whispering of "[t]he way of the Lake." The chapters leading up to Roberta's drowning are among the most

terrifying and pathos-filled in American literature as Clyde struggles against a wish he loathes but finally fulfills willy-nilly.

Further Reading

Brennan, Stephen C. "Sadomasochistic Fantasy in 'The Second Choice." *Dreiser Studies* 31.1 (2000): 43–62.

Clendenning, John. "Desire and Regression in Dreiser's *An American Tragedy*." *Dreiser Studies* 25.2 (1994): 23–35.

Moers, Ellen. "Chemism and Freudianism." *Two Dreisers*. New York: Viking, 1969. 256–70.

Rusch, Frederic E. "Dreiser's Introduction to Freudianism." *Dreiser Studies* 18.2 (1987): 43–46.

Whalen, Terry. "Dreiser's Tragic Sense: The Mind as 'Poor Ego.'" *The Old Northwest* 11 (1985): 61–80.

Zanine, Louis J. *Mechanism and Mysticism: The Influence of Science on the Thought and Work of Theodore Dreiser*. Philadelphia: University of Pennsylvania Press, 1993. 92–95, 108–12.

Stephen C. Brennan

"FULFILMENT." First published in *Holland's Magazine* in February 1924, "Fulfillment" (double "l") was three years later included in *Chains: Lesser Novels and Stories* with the deletion of one "l." Joseph Griffin has compared the various typescripts to the published versions with an eye toward the changes in narrative form, but the motive behind the variant spelling remains unexplained, and Dreiser's reviewers reinserted the "l" in their references.

"Fulfilment" portrays the reflections of Ulrica, who longingly muses over her cherished memories of her beloved Vivan, her second husband, her "ideal," her "spirit-mate." As Richard Lehan points out, Ulrica is likely modeled upon Helen Richardson and Vivian upon Dreiser himself (*Theodore Dreiser* 138). Ulrica is driven from shopping task to shopping task by her personal driver, all the while reviewing her relationships with various men, all of whom, at different points in her young adulthood, offered one form or another of commitment and security. Scarred by the shame of a childhood of poverty, she, at seventeen, ran off with young Byram but experienced more of the same: "unpaid bills . . . ejectment for non-payment of rent, and job after job lost for one reason and another." Leaving that marriage, she takes a job in an office while dreaming of the perfect man who would be "strength, beauty, ideals, power, all the substances of beauty and delight that she could crave." Disillusioned with fending off a bevy of hopeful suitors, she experiences one brief year of "fulfillment" with Vivian, the artist who "touched her." Their connection is pure Dreiserian chemisl: "Yes, it was he indeed, her love, her star, the one by whose mystic light she had been steering her course these many years. She sensed it. Knew it."

Transcendentalist and aesthete, Vivian is the quintessential starving artist, and so Ulrica turns to acting to earn a livable wage. While she is on the road, Vivian contracts the flu; she returns, and he dies under her gaze. She does not recover from an overwhelming sense of loss and mourning but allows Harry Harris to "descen[d] upon her with his millions" and marries him for the convenience of financially assisting her mother and sister. Though she feels no love for Harris, his entrepreneurial ambitions and material successes are highly regarded. He is a Senator Brander–type character: "a man whom the world of commerce respected," though, to Ulrica, he lacks sensitivity and charisma and is, in fact, "a bore." Ulrica's resignation to her marital wasteland evokes intense longing so characteristic of Dreiser's characters. Her lack of emotional fulfillment is ironically juxtaposed to Vivian's posthumous fulfillment—his works are successes, commanding high fees from the elitist collectors—and Harry's fulfillment in the business world is contrasted to his lifelong lack of fulfillment in his personal relationships.

Though Griffin reads Ulrica as distinguished from Dreiser's other short story women characters because of her sense of "idealism" (89), her reminiscences are immobilizing, her depression the primary emotion that frames the story. The "limpness" and "essential drabness" (Griffin 89, 90) of the story reappears in "Chains," an interior monologue about marital alienation from the male point of view. Both stories are structured as paragraphs, memories of the past, alternating with single italicized lines that move the nearly actionless plot forward. While the single lines delimit the present—Ulrica comments to her maid, directs the driver, observes spatial and geographical environs as they recall her time with Vivian—they further anchor the linearity of her day: she returns home to receive Harry and prepare for their evening together, another unfulfilling event in the tedium of their lives.

Kathy Frederickson

FULFILMENT AND OTHER TALES OF WOMEN AND MEN. A collection of Dreiser's sketches and stories drawn from *Twelve Men, A Gallery of Women, Free and Other Stories,* and *Chains: Lesser Novels and Stories,* published in 1992 by Black Sparrow Press and introduced and edited by T. D. Nostwich. Contents: "Rella," "Peter," Reina," " 'Vanity, Vanity,' Saith the Preacher," "Fulfilment," "Mathewson," "The 'Mercy' of God," "Ida Hauchwout," "Chains," "The Second Choice," "Sanctuary," "Bridget Mullanphy," "Muldoon, the Solid Man" (retitled from the original "Culhane, the Solid Man"). The collection is the only book reprinting of "Mathewson" (originally published in *Esquire*, May and June 1934), and the texts of "Chains" and "Mathewson" are supplemented with passages from typescripts in the Dreiser Pa-pers; all stories are annotated with textual notes.

Keith Newlin

G

A GALLERY OF WOMEN. "Will Mr. Dreiser survive? Will he be read in the year 2029? If so the Professor will then take him up. Not before." So wrote Allen W. Porterfield in his 1929 review of *A Gallery of Women* (rpt. in Salman 576), Dreiser's collection of fifteen semifictionalized biographical sketches published in two volumes by **Horace Liveright** in 1929 and reprinted in 1962 by Fawcett Publications with an Introduction by Dreiser's secretary **William C. Lengel**. Indeed, in the twenty-first century, *A Gallery of Women* must count as one of Dreiser's important—and most neglected—texts whose intricate play of biographical fact and fiction allows us to unravel Dreiser's conceptualization of **gender** and sexuality. Despite some naturalist theorizing, essentialist notions of womanhood are deconstructed by an impressive diversity of women's temperaments and careers including acting ("Ernestine," "Esther Norn"), painting ("Ellen Adams Wrynn," "Lucia"), writing ("Emanuela," "Olive Brand"), business ("Rona Murtha"), nursing ("Regina C——"), fortune-telling ("Giff"), farming ("Ida Hauchawout"), domestic work ("Bridget Mullanphy"), and political activism ("Ernita").

What makes *A Gallery of Women* modern for twenty-first-century readers is its focus on the New Woman who claims sexual and professional rights and who disrupts the masculinist assumptions even of realist and naturalist authors. So sensitive and transgressive was *Gallery*'s subject matter that some fictional transformations, including new names, were needed to conceal and protect the identities of the real-life women behind the text. The transgressive topics include shameful domestic violence ("Emanuela," "Bridget Mullanphy"), abortion ("Ernita"), and female adultery and promiscuity ("Olive Brand," "Ellen Adams Wrynn"), as well as women who leave their children to pursue careers ("Ellen Adams Wrynn," "Ernita"). Like Carrie Meeber in Dreiser's first novel, *Sister Carrie,* the women often leave dissatisfying marriages; the New Woman wants more than conventional security as she throws herself into the maelstrom of modern life while also negotiating the dangers of modernity.

Although all the women are admittedly white and of Central or Eastern European extraction, the ethnic, class, and regional diversity of Dreiser's *Gallery* is impressively diverse. An almost Whitmanesque spectrum spans America in the subjects' places of origin; from the East Coast: Philadelphia in "Ellen Adams Wrynn," Jersey City in "Albertine" and "Rona

Murtha"; through the Midwest: "conservative" Illinois in "Emanuela," "a backwoods state such as Arkansas" in "Rella," Utah in "Olive Brand"; to the West: Texas and California in "Ernita," the Northwest in "Ernestine" and in "Reina." Canada is represented in "Giff," who was born there, and in "Lucia," the Russian-born painter who travels to Montreal. Besides a stint in communist Russia ("Ernita"), an excursion to the prewar culture capital of the world, Paris ("Ellen Adams Wrynn" and "Lucia"), and a brief detour into America's rural locale ("Ida Hauchawout"), the primary spatial tension is between two American urban centers, where the narrator meets and observes his subjects from the turn of the century to the late 1920s.

One urban pole is New York City with its pulsating bohemian, activist, and sexually free life of writers, artists, and critics who populate the world of **Greenwich Village**, where Dreiser lived from 1915 to 1918. The second pole is postwar Hollywood, with its growing movie industry, pagan orgies, and luxuries, the city of sex consumption, of "tinsel," "arrogance," and "vainglory" that Dreiser viewed firsthand from 1919 to 1922. For Dreiser the two cities represent the tension between authentic art (New York City's poetry and plays) and consumable art (Hollywood's tinsel), perhaps best played out in the tragic story of Ernestine De Jongh (aka the actress **Florence Deshon**), who leaves New York's stage and her passionate liaison with the poet Varn Kinsey (Max Eastman) to venture into a fast career lane in Hollywood. Here, she commits suicide at age twenty-five, after Hollywood has fallen on hard times in the wake of economic depression.

Dreiser opens *A Gallery of Women* with a signature character: an ordinary woman, "Reina," the uneducated, grammar-bending flapper ("Whoja think me an' Sven seen?"), who is bristling with the in-

tensity and vibrancy of a modern-day spice girl. Hers is a story of risk-taking, mischief, and bravado, as she blithely exploits her husband's labors and trust; Emma Bovary–like, she discards him when their relations become boring and unfulfilling. Reina is based on **Myrtle Patges**, the sister of Dreiser's then common-law spouse Helen Richardson, the Hollywood actress. With the two sisters Dreiser sets up the good-girl/bad-girl dichotomy, highlighting Reina's selfish and egocentric traits by contrasting her with the idealized, yet much less compelling, Rhoda (= Helen), a beautiful, hard-working, and generous woman whose fate as the narrator's companion is relegated into the margins of his text.

The opening sketch creates the paradigm for the collection, for we are drawn to examine the real-life portraits of the women behind the text; these are the women in the inner and outer orbit of Dreiser's private life, for Dreiser was a man with a wicked penchant for womanizing and with a consistent contempt for monogamy and marriage. As we view the photographs of the real Myrtle Patges and Helen Richardson from 1917 to the early 1950s, photographs collected in private albums by Helen Richardson Dreiser and held in the University of Pennsylvania Rare Book and Manuscript Library, we recognize in Myrtle's face and body the mischievous and youthful look that Dreiser described. But the photographs also tell a story not told in Dreiser's sketch: they reveal that Myrtle retained her youthfulness in old age, looking sprite and young beside Helen, who increasingly wears the emotional scars of a hard life with Dreiser on her face and body. Today these archival photograph portraits and snapshots of the real-life women, then, also take us beyond the sketches, drawing attention to the facets omitted in Dreiser's gallery.

In narrating the lives of women, Dreiser assumes the role of the "historiographer," presenting himself as the disinterested naturalist observer-narrator. In each sketch, he presents the biographical facts of the New Woman's life, claiming to write without judgment and **censorship**. A truthful biographer, he recites their personal letters ("Reina"), their poetry ("Olive Brand"), their journalistically recorded and transcribed quotations ("Giff"); by incorporating their voices, he authenticates the truth value of his narration. At the same time, this naturalist narration gains further complexity through the narrator's varying degrees of intimacy or distance vis-à-vis his biographical subjects.

Indeed, the transition from objective historiographer to putative lover of his subjects is a very slippery one in many sketches, as the narrator sexually pursues many of the women portrayed. The narrator's sexual jealousy is palatable in "Esther Norn"; his resentment at female rejection surfaces in "Emanuela" and in "Ellen Adams Wrynn"; he deeply resents that "Ernestine" is careful never to invite him alone. Moreover, there is ample evidence for the narrator's intellectual jealousy, when the women outgrow his guidance and become serious rivals in art. These varying levels of distance and intimacy between the womanizing author-biographer-narrator and his subjects, then, create varying degrees of narrative (un)reliability. Gender-sensitized readers decode the sketches by unraveling the male narrator's biases and blindnesses, as the narrator-biographer is alternately attracted to, and frustrated by, his women-subjects. Through the sketches, then, we read the narrator's male obsessions and fears, ultimately unraveling the limits of the naturalist truth claims of objectivity.

Indeed, the fictional transformations are key in unraveling Dreiser's masculinist assumptions, as well as heterosexist ideology, for Dreiser all but omits references to the richly diverse gay and lesbian communities flourishing in New York City during the teens and 1920s. Many of the sketches are roman-à-clef which allowed Dreiser to take revenge on real-life characters, with an intricate play of the real and the fictional, of revelation and omission.

The endings of the sketches routinely follow the conventions of the naturalist genre with its classical plot of decline in violent and premature death: "Olive Brand" burns up in fever; "Esther Norn" dies prematurely of tuberculosis; "Ernestine" commits suicide; "Giff" dies an accidental death; and "Regina C——" is shown in a self-destructive spiral of drug addiction. Creative or professional stagnation ends the sketches of the painters "Ellen Adams Wrynn" and "Lucia," while empty, circular repetition propels the pragmatic businesswoman "Rona Murtha" back to the beginning of the sketch, echoing the structural circularity of *An American Tragedy*. The real-life biographies, however, were not always as bleak as intimated in Dreiser's *Gallery*. The painter behind Ellen Adams Wrynn (**Anne Estelle Rice**), for instance, was a more successful and dedicated artist than Dreiser allows her alter ego to be. Naturalist conventions, then, allowed Dreiser to contain modern women's threatening powers.

The title, "A Gallery of Women," makes Dreiser the proprietor of an entire museum of beautiful women's portraits, as he invites the reader to view his gallery and appreciate visual art. Dreiser, then, is like the Duke in Robert Browning's "My Last Duchess," controlling the reader and viewer's access to the portrait with whose original he has a special relationship. Dreiser's position can also be likened to the choreographer of erotically charged *tableaux vivants*, a popular performance art, in which women posed in still lives, their bodies often simulating nudity. The author and the reader's relationships with the female subjects are intimately personal, as many women are introduced in the titles by their first names only ("Reina," "Emanuela," "Ernita," "Albertine"), in contrast to *Twelve Men*, the collection of male sketches, where the men are identified through a relationship ("My Brother Paul") or characteristic ("Culhane, the Solid Man"). The courtesy of a last name in the title is reserved for serious women artists ("Ellen Adams Wrynn"), for the strong woman who commands respect ("Rona Murtha," "Olive Brand," "Ida Hauchawout," "Bridget Mullanphy"), and for the idealized woman ("Esther Norn"). The Hollywood actress who relies on "sex appeal" is not given the courtesy of a last name; the title "Ernestine" diminishes Florence Deshon's artist status. Still, Dreiser abstains from assigning the women the mythologized titles that generally accompany the female nude in art history.

A Gallery of Women was written from 1919 to 1929, with some of the sketches having appeared in print before, including "Ernestine," first published as "Portrait of a Woman" in the *Bookman* (September 1927). Several of the sketches conceived for *Gallery* have remained unpublished, including "Gloom," "Dinan," "A Daughter of the Puritans," "Loretta," and "Lolita"; the unpublished manuscripts are held today among the Dreiser Papers in the University of Pennsylvania Rare Book and Manuscript Library. Despite Horace Liveright's energetic 1929 marketing campaign that exploited the book's confessional drive with its putative peek into the sexual lives of real-life modern women, the book brought only modest sales suc-

cess for author and publisher. In Dreiser scholarship, too, the paucity of publications on *A Gallery of Women* has left a cavernous gap that remains to be filled by twenty-first-century scholars of American literature, life writing, art history, and culture. Ultimately, *A Gallery of Women* invites and provokes women into writing back, as **Ruth Kennell** ("Ernita") did in her 1929 review, "Hell Hath No Fury Like a Woman Scorned," her mocking female answer to Dreiser's *A Gallery of Women*. Dreiser's interweaving of biography, autobiography, and fiction has created a text that must be seen as central in unraveling the author's (and his society's) ambivalence about the roles and powers of the New Woman who would come into her own in the course of the twentieth century.

Further Reading

Gammel, Irene. *Sexualizing Power in Naturalism: Theodore Dreiser and Frederick Philip Grove.* Calgary: University of Calgary Press, 1994. 7, 83–99, 174.

Hakutani, Yoshinobu. "The Dream of Success in Dreiser's *A Gallery of Women*." *Zeitschrift für Anglistik und Amerikanistik* 27 (1979): 236–46.

[Kennell, Ruth E.]. "Hell Hath No Fury Like a Woman Scorned." Review of *A Gallery of Women*. *Chicago Daily News* 11 December 1929: 22.

Vinoda. "Don Juans and 'Dancing Dogs': A Note on Dreiser's *A Gallery of Women*." *Indian Journal of American Studies* 13 (July 1983): 147–55.

Irene Gammel

GAMBLE, SUSANNA (1832–?). The first wife of **Charles Tyson Yerkes**, Susanna Guttridge Gamble was the real life counterpart to **Lillian Semple**, the first wife of **Frank Cowperwood** in *The Financier*. Dreiser's characterization of Mrs. Semple, both in her relationship with Cowperwood and in her Victorian mannerisms and placid personality, closely matches Susanna and her relationship with Yerkes, which Dreiser gathered from newspaper clippings and from the Philadelphia publisher Joseph Coates, who knew details about Yerkes's private life. Susanna was the daughter of George Newton Gamble, a native of Leicestershire, England, and Susanna Guttridge. She married Yerkes on 22 December 1859, shortly after the death of her first husband. Like Lillian to Frank, Susanna was five years older than Yerkes when they married, twenty-seven to his twenty-two. Though faithful to his model for the most part, Dreiser did alter the number of offspring his fictional characters produce. Frank and Lillian have two children, Frank Jr. and Lillian, while Mrs. Gamble and Yerkes had six children. Dreiser also reduces the number of years Frank and Lillian stay married. Cowperwood divorces Lillian in 1875 to marry his mistress **Aileen Butler**, while Yerkes divorces Susanna in 1881 and marries his mistress, **Mary Adelaide Moore.**

Kevin Jett

GATES, ELMER (1859–1923). Fascinated by Gates's research in the new field of physiological psychology, Dreiser traveled to his Washington, D.C., laboratory in February 1900 to interview the eccentric, self-educated scientist and inventor for an article for *Pearson's Magazine*. Gates had funded the laboratory with the proceeds he had received from a number of his typically unorthodox inventions. These inventions included an electric loom, a microscope that Gates claimed could increase the power of the human eye by 3 million times, a diamagnetic gold-separator, and an electrical device that, Gates maintained, could remove the perfume from flowers. The prolific, if not always sensible, inventor also dabbled in the fields of color theory, acoustics, and meteorology, but it was

at his laboratory in Washington where Gates conducted his more important research on the mind and its chemical processes. Drawing from his sensory learning experiments with such animals as dogs and guinea pigs, Gates concluded that the mind was a physical, not a spiritual, **mechanism.** He asserted that each conscious mental experience creates distinct structural and chemical changes that are localized in a specific region of the brain. Whereas positive emotions could generate chemicals called "anastates" that nourished and sustained those regions, Gates claimed that certain chemicals called "katastates"—deriving likewise from negative emotions—could poison them. Gates's work had a tremendous impact on Dreiser. Although Dreiser ultimately never published the article, which he had entitled "The Training of the Senses," the meeting with Gates gave Dreiser a chance to observe the practice of science firsthand—quite an opportunity for Dreiser given his rapidly blossoming scientific curiosity. The meeting could not have come at a better time in Dreiser's career. Before meeting Gates, Dreiser had put aside *Sister Carrie* temporarily because he could not figure out how to illustrate Hurstwood's crime and subsequent psychological deterioration in such a way that rendered a moral reading of the novel not only irrelevant but impossible. Gates's research provided him with the scientific basis he sought. After returning to New York that winter, Dreiser hurriedly began working on the second half of the novel. As the descriptions of Hurstwood's state of mind in *Sister Carrie* exhibit, Gates's influence on Dreiser was indeed enormous. For example, shortly after Hurstwood arrives in New York, the narrator says:

As for Hurstwood, he was making a great fight against the difficulties of a changed condition. He was too shrewd not to realize the tremendous mistake he had made, and appreciate that he had done well in getting where he was, and yet he could not help contrasting his present state with his former—hour after hour and day after day. It became a natural method of mentation with him—to think of doing a thing now, and then quickly remembering how he did it formerly.

Hurstwood's endless brooding on the differences between his life in New York and the more comfortable life he had enjoyed in Chicago "poisons" his mind and helps foster his depression—precisely what Gates had claimed such negative emotions would do. His influence also shows up in Dreiser's more psychological novels, such as *An American Tragedy*, where Clyde Griffiths's thought of murdering **Roberta Alden** "causes" the deed to occur. Gates and Dreiser eventually forged a close friendship, corresponding for nearly a decade after their first meeting.

Further Reading

Moers, Ellen. *Two Dreisers*. New York: Viking, 1969. 160–69.

Zanine, Louis Z. *Mechanism and Mysticism: The Influence of Science on the Thought and Work of Theodore Dreiser*. Philadelphia: University of Pennsylvania Press, 1993. 57–61.

Marc Johnston

GENDER. Although in his personal life Dreiser was "hell on women," as **Robert Penn Warren** has said, in his fiction readers find a complex and compelling picture of gender. Through Dreiser, "one can read [his] culture's ambivalences and tensions regarding women," according to Shelley Fisher Fishkin (1), and indeed Dreiser often seems uncertain about whether to embrace or resist the gender stereotypes of his day. Based solely on number of pages, however, Dreiser devotes more time and narrative energy to gender issues than do most of his contemporaries. His novels are

filled with men and women who are struggling to define exactly what it means, in a rapidly changing society, to be men and women.

Most remarkable for an author beginning to write at the turn of the twentieth century, Dreiser populates his novels with determined and complicated female characters. From Carrie Meeber to **Jennie Gerhardt**, from **Aileen Butler** to **Roberta Alden**, Dreiser's women play the roles of victim, inspiration, seductress, mother, successful career woman, and long-suffering wife, sometimes assuming several contradictory roles. Although at times his characters seem mired in contemporary stereotypes, more often than not they manage to escape or transcend those limitations.

Writing about sexuality in Dreiser, Irene Gammel notes that while "every aspect of female life becomes thoroughly sexualized" (44), most of Dreiser's novels offer a critique of this sexualization. Carrie, for example, clearly assumes the role of sex object in *Sister Carrie*, but her desire for increasingly more sophisticated men, as well as for more stylish clothes, drives her toward success in her career. In fact, because she is an actress, her awareness that she is the object of men's sexual attention enhances her performances—and her income. Jennie Gerhardt more directly suffers the consequences of her sexuality (in particular an illegitimate pregnancy), but she nevertheless manages to carve out a peaceful and productive life for herself through meaningful work. As Nancy Warner Barrineau reminds us, Dreiser consistently presents his readers with views of working-class women, a class significantly underrepresented at that time. In *Jennie Gerhardt* in particular, she says, Dreiser "exposes his empathy for women—especially members of the working classes—and his understanding of their plight" (72).

Working women like Carrie and Jennie aren't the only ones Dreiser treats empathically. Although he clearly admires **Frank Cowperwood's** forceful nature in *The Financier*, he also endows Aileen Butler, Cowperwood's second wife, with a will equal to her husband's. By making Aileen such a powerful character in his *Trilogy of Desire*, Dreiser is able to use Cowperwood's repeated betrayals of Aileen as the primary evidence of his inhumanity. Like Aileen's situation, Roberta Alden's plight in *An American Tragedy* highlights her lover Clyde Griffiths's carelessness and self-absorption. Perhaps the saddest of Dreiser's major female characters, Roberta is destroyed in large part because she is female—and pregnant—but also because her pregnancy interferes with Clyde's plans. Also, in giving her letters prominence in Clyde's trial, Dreiser shows a marked sympathy for Roberta's situation and the situation of women in similar straits. Although to be female in Dreiser's novels is to be a "waif amid forces," as Dreiser calls Carrie, it doesn't preclude the possibility of transformation and triumph.

Representations of masculinity in Dreiser are easily as complicated as those of femininity. Often Dreiser's men assume passive roles more traditionally associated with women. The men in *Sister Carrie*, for example—Drouet, Hurstwood, **Ames**—seem to be controlling Carrie's fate and their own, but they fall victim to their own desires and weaknesses. Hurstwood, in particular, loses all of his traditionally masculine identifiers—the respect of his position as manager, his home and fine clothes, and eventually even his will to keep living—when he takes up with Carrie. Like a woman who leaves family and security for an unreliable man, Hurstwood's desire for love finally destroys

him. Clyde Griffiths shares Carrie Meeber's lust for fine clothes and the good life, although his desires lead to murder instead of the footlights. Not surprisingly, neither Hurstwood nor Clyde acts with typically male decisiveness. Hurstwood unintentionally steals the money from the safe, and Clyde inadvertently knocks Roberta out of the boat, although both will suffer for their "accidents." **Lester Kane** in *Jennie Gerhardt* is surprisingly passive as well, except when it comes to sexual desire. Assuming a right to Jennie's body but rejecting her when it looks as if he will lose his inheritance, Lester remains a static figure in his own life.

The more aggressive male characters don't fare so well, either. **Eugene Witla** from *The "Genius,"* perhaps the most autobiographical of Dreiser's male characters, is driven by his compulsive sexuality to destroy his marriage and finally his career. Frank Cowperwood, with his lust for wealth, power, and ever-younger women, appears by the end of the trilogy to be a monster, and *The Stoic* ends with his fortune gone and his legacy destroyed. Thus, while Dreiser's novels celebrate masculine sexuality, they also "simultaneously expose the gender bias, the duplicity, and the arbitrary power politics of its male characters and narrators" (Gammel 50). To be a man in Dreiser's world, then, means being torn between emasculating desire and self-destructive ruthlessness.

Often these tensions between exploiting gender stereotypes and challenging them are most clearly manifested in the novels' narrative structures. Dreiser's narrators seem both drawn to, and uncomfortable with, traditional notions of gender and sexuality, and his characters offer alternative voices that undermine what might remain of the narrators' gender biases. Dreiser does give his readers strong men and weak women, but more importantly, he shows how masculine power can be a dangerous force and feminine passivity a source of strength. Thus, even though they come to us from a distance of 100 years, Dreiser's novels "anticipate much recent theorizing about gender differences" (Brennan 139) and offer contemporary approaches to the politics and complexities of gender.

Further Reading

Brennan, Stephen C. "This Sex Which Is One: Language and the Masculine Self in *Jennie Gerhardt.*" *Theodore Dreiser and American Culture: New Readings.* Ed. Yoshinobu Hakutani. Newark: University of Delaware Press, 2000. 138–157.

Barrineau, Nancy Warner. "Recontextualizing Dreiser: Gender, Class, and Sexuality in *Jennie Gerhardt.*" *Theodore Dreiser: Beyond Naturalism.* Ed. Miriam Gogol. New York: New York University Press, 1995. 55–76.

Fishkin, Shelley Fisher. "Dreiser and the Discourse of Gender." *Theodore Dreiser: Beyond Naturalism.* Ed. Miriam Gogol. New York: New York University Press, 1995. 1–30.

Gammel, Irene. "Sexualizing the Female Body: Dreiser, Feminism, and Foucault." *Theodore Dreiser: Beyond Naturalism.* Ed. Miriam Gogol. New York: New York University Press, 1995. 31–51.

Caren J. Town

THE *"GENIUS."* Originally composed in 1911 with a different ending and various differences in focus, *The "Genius"* was published in 1915 by **John Lane**. Although Dreiser regarded his most autobiographical novel as his favorite work, interestingly, he casts the male protagonist, **Eugene Witla**, as an Ashcan painter (believed to be modeled on the career of **Everett Shinn**) rather than as a writer. Witla's fictional adventures overlap most notably with Dreiser's own life in his troubled marriage, his stint as an advertising executive and publishing house manager

(recalling the novelist's experiences with the **Butterick Publishing Company**), and his work as a manual laborer (bearing marked resemblance to the autobiography *An Amateur Laborer*). Although biographers have periodically used elements of *The "Genius"* as "evidence" for things that happened to Dreiser, the work is in fact a novel, however autobiographical, and should be approached as such.

The novel is divided into three parts. Book 1, "Youth," covers Witla's youth in Alexandria, Illinois, his move to Chicago to study painting at the Art Institute, his early sexual experiences, and his meeting with **Angela Blue**, who eventually becomes his wife. Like *Sister Carrie* and *The Titan*, the Chicago section contains memorable descriptions of the lure of the city. The description of Witla's shocked, yet excited, response to a fleshy nude by the French painter Bouguereau is vintage Dreiser. He portrays Angela as an innately sensual country girl with strong puritanical tendencies. Witla does not so much seduce Angela as secure her consent to deflower her in a scene that is one of the most compelling descriptions of sexual desire in Dreiser's fiction (see Chapters 18, 26–27). Although Witla continues to have sexual relations with other women, including the free-spirited singer Christina Channing, "Youth" ends with his marriage to Angela, in part out of guilt over taking her virginity. Many critics find the novel's best writing in Book 1.

Book 2, "Struggle," concerns Witla's attempt to make a life with Angela and a name for himself in New York. The first is a failure, and the second only partially a success. "Struggle" begins, significantly, with a marriage ceremony in Buffalo, the couple soon moving on to New York City. Angela proves a jealous wife whose moralistic harping on Witla reflects Dreiser's contempt for what he, along with friend and literary champion H. L. Mencken, considered "puritanism." Dreiser casts Angela to represent stifling convention and Eugene, artistic liberation. Witla's early paintings show considerable promise, and he secures an exhibition with a New York gallery, where his realistic paintings "astonish" viewers because their subjects are "commonplace and customary" things, "supposedly beyond the pale of artistic significance." Travels to Paris and London follow, but for a period of several years, "Eugene was not himself." Depression leads to a neurasthenic breakdown that short-circuits his career. Witla and Angela return to the country, visiting Alexandria before settling for a time with her family in Blackwood, Wisconsin, where Witla falls for a local girl.

After further travels, the Witlas return to New York, but his physical and emotional health remains poor. Only after a long stint as a manual laborer working for a railroad company in picturesque Speonk, New York—and a long liaison with his landlady's unhappily married daughter, Carlotta Wilson—does Witla start to become rejuvenated, yet the path to recovery is circuitous, and when Witla returns to Angela, he becomes more a businessman than an artist. After some odd jobs, Witla becomes intrigued with the growing trend of using art in advertising. He lands a job as art director for the irascible Daniel C. Summerfield, who owns an advertising company. Summerfield's decisiveness and sense of purpose make him a good mentor for Eugene, who quickly moves up the ladder of success that most Dreiser characters find so difficult to ascend. But when Witla's and Summerfield's egos clash, the young man moves on to work for the Kalvin Publishing Company of Philadelphia at a large salary. Witla is then stolen away by Hiram C. Colfax, who controls the Swinton-Scudder-Davis publishing

company. The Witlas return to New York City, he now directing the editorial, publication, circulation, art, and advertising departments of United Magazines Corporation from a skyscraper office near Union Square. Although Angela accompanies Witla on his upward climb, Dreiser's focus in this section is more on career than domestic issues. Witla's financial success poses its own problems. As the narrator puts it, "The trouble with this situation was that it involved more power, comfort, ease and luxury than Eugene had ever experienced before, and made him a sort of oriental potentate not only among his large company but in his own home." Witla becomes tainted, if not corrupted, by his worldly success and all but forgets his artistic aspirations. The tension between business and art that runs throughout *The "Genius,"* becoming especially pronounced in "Struggle," can be fruitfully compared with Dreiser's treatment of the theme in *The Trilogy of Desire.*

Witla's love affair with teenager **Suzanne Dale**, strenuously resisted by her mother, Emily, as well as by Angela, forms much of Book 3, "Revolt." Emily Dale works with Witla at the United Magazines Corporation, making the middle-aged man's pursuit of the nymphet all the more inappropriate. Witla's commercial downfall is hastened due to the jealousy of general manager Florence J. White and due to Witla's involvement in some ill-advised speculative real estate dealings with Kenyon C. Winfield. Although Suzanne Dale is modeled on **Thelma Cudlipp**, a young woman Dreiser fell in love with while working for Butterick—a dalliance that cost him his job—this character is among the least believable in Dreiser's work. Witla sees Suzanne both as art object ("his ideal") and as muse: "'My art seems to come back to me through you,'" he tells her. After a series of clandestine meetings,

Angela, who has just become pregnant, catches her husband with Suzanne in his arms. As in *An American Tragedy*, one woman's pregnancy threatens to keep a man from another woman he greatly desires. What Angela had hoped would be her "trump card" to get Witla to behave fails, for he continues his pursuit of Suzanne despite his wife's pregnancy. After Suzanne tells her mother about the affair, Mrs. Dale abducts her daughter, taking her to a Canadian lodge, where Witla eventually finds her. Yet his impractical nature dooms the relationship; once he has Suzanne in his arms again, he doesn't know what else to do. Mrs. Dale tells Colfax of the affair, and so Witla's boss also starts pressuring him to end his affair. The young woman acquiesces to her mother's insistence on taking her away for a year, for she has neither the strength of character nor the conviction to return to the man she supposedly loves. Depressed again, Witla moves out of the house he shared with Angela and toys with **Christian Science**. Even when Angela dies in childbirth, during a scene that ranks as among the grisliest in Dreiser's fiction (Chapters 27–28), Witla does not get his heart's desire. Rather than Suzanne, Witla is left with a baby daughter, whom he names Angela. Witla concludes that no God rules the world but "a devil ruled the world, a Gargantuan Brobdingnagian Mountebank, who plotted tragedy for all ideals." Despite his philosophical despair, after running into his onetime art dealer on the street, Witla returns to painting. He wins the acclaim of critics and other artists, who find his work "strange, eccentric, but great." As a saga of strong desires, some gained but more of them thwarted, *The "Genius"* resonates with many of Dreiser's other works.

The significance of the novel can be divided into several broad categories. As is generally the case with Dreiser's novels, sexual decisions are central not only to characterization but also to plot. Like **Frank Cowperwood** of *The Trilogy of Desire*, Witla is a "varietist" whose promiscuity Dreiser tries to use as a battle cry for artistic liberation. One of the most interesting aspects of the treatment of sexuality is that Dreiser draws an unmistakable causal connection between Witla's sexual excesses with his wife and the breakdown of his artistic talent. Simply put, overindulgence in sex with Angela drains Witla of his art and practically of his sanity. While Witla's sexual exploits form an important aspect of the novel, the sexuality of the female characters, from Christina Channing to Carlotta Wilson to, particularly, Angela Blue, deserves scrutiny as well. Both "New Women" like Christina and Carlotta and more traditional women such as Angela have strong erotic desires and act purposefully to get what they want.

The novel is also of signal importance as an instance of Dreiser's cultural criticism. While he sought to depict the real world objectively and accurately, Dreiser also used fiction (as well as nonfiction) to criticize his culture. His use of Witla as a figure of the artist in *The "Genius,"* beset on one side by the commercialism of the business world and on the other by moralistic strictures, provides one of the best instances of novel merging with cultural criticism. Comparison of the published 1915 text with the holograph (the original manuscript as written in 1911, held in the University of Pennsylvania's Rare Book and Manuscript Library), reveals that as Dreiser prepared the novel for publication, he made some strategic changes that rendered it more decisively a work of cultural criticism. As he had originally conceived of Witla's character in 1911, Dreiser was less decisive in his opposition to conventional morality—particularly regarding sexual matters. Furthermore, in the holograph Dreiser let Witla ultimately get the prize: Suzanne Dale. If we compare these two salient facts with the novel as it was published in 1915, we see that Dreiser consciously transformed his work into a battle cry against a puritanical culture—as well as into more of a naturalistic novel with a bleaker ending.

Another aspect of the novel's significance is literary-historical. While what Dreiser liked to call the "suppression" of *Sister Carrie* is largely a myth he embroidered to advertise his intransigence, *The "Genius"* was in fact attacked by the **New York Society for the Suppression of Vice**, led by **John Sumner** after the 1915 death of **Anthony Comstock**. The antivice organization counted up nearly ninety instances of "lewd," 'profane," and "blasphemous" passages and attempted to have the novel suppressed. Although dozens of notable literary figures from the United States and abroad, from Ezra Pound to Arnold Bennett, signed "A Protest against the Suppression of Theodore Dreiser's *The "Genius,'"* they did so on the grounds of the author's "manifest sincerity," not the novel's literary merits. Although *The "Genius"* has always had its defenders, overall, critical commentary has never been particularly favorable. Even H. L. Mencken, who led the campaign to defend the novel, called it "as shapeless as a Philadelphia pie-woman" (758).

Yet *The "Genius"* continues to have claims on our attention well beyond the fact that Dreiser was so fond of it, beyond the fact that it was the best-selling of his works during his lifetime. Blending autobiography with manifesto, cultural criticism with sexual confession, *The "Genius"* provides a fascinating look at Dreiser's views about the role of the artist in society and about female as well as male sexuality. The novel also provides food for thought concerning the relationship between, on the one hand, literary and visual art, and, on the other hand, propaganda and autobiography.

Further Reading

Bourne, Randolph. "Desire as Hero." *Critical Essays on Theodore Dreiser*. Ed. Donald Pizer. Boston: G. K. Hall, 1981. 243–46.

Bowlby, Rachel. "The Artist as Adman: Dreiser's *The 'Genius.' " Just Looking: Consumer Culture in Dreiser, Gissing, and Zola*. New York: Methuen, 1985. 118–33.

Eby, Clare Virginia. "Cowperwood and Witla, Artists in the Marketplace." *Dreiser Studies* 22.1 (1991): 1–22.

———. "The Rhetoric of Confrontation." *Dreiser and Veblen, Saboteurs of the Status Quo*. Columbia: University of Missouri Press, 1998. 20–64.

Kwiat, Joseph J. "Dreiser's *The 'Genius'* and Everett Shinn, the 'Ash-Can' Painter. *PMLA* 67.2 (1952): 15–31.

Mencken, H. L. "A Literary Behemoth." Rpt. in *D-M Letters* 2: 754–59.

"A Protest against the Suppression of Theodore Dreiser's *The 'Genius.' "* Rpt. in *D-M Letters* 2: 802–4.

Clare Eby

GERHARDT, JENNIE. Jennie Gerhardt, the eponymous heroine of Dreiser's second novel, is one of his most appealing characters. She is psychologically stable and emotionally whole; she is also beautiful, sexually alluring, and maternal. Jennie is based on Dreiser's oldest sister, Mary Frances (Maria Franziska) Dreiser, known within the family as "Mame." Jennie's experiences are patterned after some of Mame's misadventures as a young woman. Mame gave birth to a stillborn child as a teenager; the baby was delivered by her mother in the Dreiser home and buried in their backyard. Mame then formed a long liaison with a likable, hard-drinking businessman named Austin

Brennan, much to the displeasure of Brennan's family.

In *Jennie Gerhardt*, Jennie has a child by Senator William Brander—a girl whom she names Vesta and raises on her own. Jennie then meets **Lester Kane**, the younger of two sons from a wealthy Cincinnati family, and becomes his kept woman, an arrangement that lasts for thirteen years. Lester is powerfully drawn to Jennie, both by her sexuality and her by innate goodness, but he cannot bring himself to go against his family and marry her. Pressure from the Kanes, in fact, eventually brings Lester's arrangement with Jennie to an end, and she lives out her years on a small pension that he provides. Jennie survives many blows in the novel, including the deaths of nearly everyone she loves. Dreiser means to present her as a woman of great spiritual strength who, owing to poverty and necessity, violates many social taboos. Jennie is not a thinking character, but her intuitions about an underlying pattern in Nature, together with her quasi-religious mysticism, function as strong counterweights to Lester's materialism and pessimistic determinism. Editorial cutting at **Harper & Brothers** reduced Jennie's presence and simplified her character in the 1911 edition, but in the 1992 Pennsylvania text she is restored to the role that Dreiser envisioned for her. In the 1992 text she lightens the heavy burden of Lester Kane's nihilism on the novel.

Further Reading

Barrineau, Nancy Warner. "Recontextualizing Dreiser: Gender, Class, and Sexuality in *Jennie Gerhardt.*" *Theodore Dreiser: Beyond Naturalism.* Ed. Miriam Gogol. New York: New York University Press, 1995. 55–76.

Epstein, Joseph. "A Great Good Girl: Dreiser's *Jennie Gerhardt.*" *New Criterion* June 1993: 14–20.

West, James L. W., III. Introduction to *Jennie Gerhardt.* New York: Penguin, 1994. vii–xvii.

James L. W. West III

GERHARDT, MRS. WILLIAM. The fact that **Jennie Gerhardt's** mother is given no first name in Dreiser's second novel is an indication of her low status. She makes her way as a charwoman and a laundress, two of the meanest forms of domestic labor at the time. She plays an important role in *Jennie Gerhardt*, however, by bringing Jennie into initial contact with Senator Brander. Mother and daughter visit the senator to ask if they might wash and iron his shirts, thus setting in motion the events that will dictate the course of Jennie's life. Mrs. Gerhardt is also present in the novel to show readers what Jennie would likely have become, had she not met **Lester Kane.** Dreiser based Mrs. Gerhardt on his own mother, Sarah Schänäb Dreiser, who was a source of love within his family and who, like Mrs. Gerhardt, interceded between the children and their stern, inflexible father. Mrs. Gerhardt dies early, worn out by childbearing, hard work, and poverty.

Further Reading

Hapke, Laura. "Dreiser and the Tradition of the American Working Girl." *Dreiser Studies* 22.2 (1991): 2–19.

James L. W. West III

GERHARDT, WILLIAM. Jennie Gerhardt's father, a sternly religious and emotionally austere man, is based on the author's own father, John Paul Dreiser. Old Gerhardt is an immigrant worker, a glassblower who loses his means of earning a living when he burns his hands in an accident. Thereafter he becomes a pitiful figure, earning a little money by sawing firewood and serving as a night watchman at a factory. He is taciturn and inflexible, interested mainly in the Lutheran Church and in his German-language newspaper. He bars Jennie from the Gerhardt home when he learns that she is pregnant but later relents and allows her to return. Father and daughter are eventually reconciled: Old Gerhardt lives out his last years with Jennie and **Lester Kane**, tending their furnace and performing yard work. He forgives his daughter in the end: "You're a good girl, Jennie," he tells her on his deathbed. "You've been good to me." William Gerhardt is paired with Lester's father, Archibald Kane, in the moral framework of *Jennie Gerhardt*. Though from opposite ends of the social scale, both are rigid and judgmental, and both put heavy pressure on their children to conform. Dreiser's portrayal of William Gerhardt mixes affection with fear—a reflection of his ambiguous feelings about his own father.

Further Reading

Wilson, Christopher P. "Labor and Capital in *Jennie Gerhardt*." *Dreiser's* Jennie Gerhardt: *New Essays on the Restored Text*. Ed. James L. W. West III. Philadelphia: University of Pennsylvania Press, 1995. 103–14.

James L. W. West III

"GIFF." Dreiser based this sketch, which appears as the fifth piece in the first volume of *A Gallery of Women*, on New York fortune-teller **Jessie Spafford**. Dreiser intermittently went to Spafford for predictions about his future, and a number of the details of her life, recorded in a 7 November 1917 diary entry, appear in the story (see *American Diaries* 200).

The narrator of this sketch describes Honoria Gifford, known as "Giff," as a "soothsayer, interpreter of tea leaves, coffee grounds, dreams." She is a kind soul of "buoyant optimism" and "exalted faith" who refuses to take advantage of anyone,

believing that God will enable her to make a living as a fortune-teller as long as her predictions are truthful and helpful. In her earlier years, during an illness, Giff's Canadian relatives committed her to an insane asylum, where she remained for three years, in order to enable them to take possession of her inheritance, which she intended to share with the less fortunate. An attendant in the hospital aided her escape, and afterward she worked in resorts as a dishwasher, waitress, chambermaid, fortune-teller, and harpist. At fifty-five years of age, she buys a small property in St. Petersburg, Florida, where she intends to establish a home and means of support so that she may adopt a baby boy. She decides to open a teahouse for tourists, saves money, and works hard to see her dream realized.

During a visit to New York, she takes a room heated by an oil stove, where she dies from the fumes emitted by the poorly vented stove. "Weep not. She rests well," the narrator notes, struck by the irony of a soothsayer who cannot predict her own future. In a postscript, the narrator reveals further irony by discussing his friend Nan (based on Dreiser's mistress **Estelle Kubitz**), who so devoutly believed in the veracity of Giff's predictions that she prepared a 100-page sketch of Giff, upon which he has drawn for his own, but who came to doubt Giff's power. Three years after Giff's death, her final prediction, that Nan would meet a wealthy lover, comes true, and Nan marries a millionaire on New Year's Day, thereby beginning her prophesied life.

Dreiser's sketch of Giff illustrates how a seemingly powerless, poor, and outwardly downtrodden woman affects the lives of many people. Ironically, Giff, a woman who had dreams, continued to strive to make those dreams come true and succeeded in making progress toward realizing those dreams while overcoming adversity, yet she could not predict her own demise. In this sketch Dreiser thereby emphasizes the powerlessness of the individual to determine one's fate.

Amy E. Ujvari

GILLETTE, CHESTER (1883–1908). The plot of *An American Tragedy* is based in large part on Chester Gillette's murder of **Grace Brown** in 1906. Many details in the story of Clyde Griffiths are similar to those in Chester Gillette's life. For example, Gillette's parents, while not destitute street preachers, were members of the Salvation Army. Gillette eventually went to Cortland, New York (the Lycurgus of the novel), to work in his uncle's skirt factory. There he had an affair with Grace Brown, who also worked in the factory, and she became pregnant. Then, using an assumed name, he took her on a trip to the Adirondacks, letting her think they were going to get married. They went out in a boat on Big Moose Lake, and he killed her. After a sensational trial, Gillette was arrested, convicted, and executed for the crime on 8 March 1908.

In the novel, Dreiser quotes extensively from newspaper accounts of the trial and even incorporates verbatim Gillette's final written statement. Many of the details of the murder and court proceedings in the book come directly from the real crime, leading some to claim that *An American Tragedy* was little more than a fictionalized version of the Gillette case. In fact, when Dreiser sued Paramount Pictures in 1931 because their film version of the book did not reflect his themes, the New York Supreme Court ruled against him, saying that *An American Tragedy* was the story of Chester Gillette and therefore was in public domain.

An American Tragedy differs from the Gillette case significantly. Most noticeably,

Dreiser added the social and economic motivation for the crime. Chester was not as poor as Clyde, nor was his uncle as rich as is depicted in the novel. Furthermore, there was no rich young woman like the character of **Sondra Finchley** whom Gillette wanted to marry. Dreiser borrowed the details of the Gillette murder to provide **realism** for his story, but he created the whole apparatus of motivation that makes Clyde a victim of society. As Dreiser argued in his deposition in the Paramount case, this indictment of society was more than just the case of one young man and his pregnant girlfriend.

Further Reading

Brandon, Craig. *Murder in the Adirondacks:* An American Tragedy *Revisited.* Utica, N.Y.: North Country Books, 1986.
Castle, John F. "The Making of *An American Tragedy.*" Diss., University of Michigan, 1952.

Kathryn M. Plank

THE GIRL IN THE COFFIN. Written in 1913 while Dreiser was working on *The Titan, The Girl in the Coffin* was first published in *Smart Set* in October 1913 before being collected in *Plays of the Natural and Supernatural.* Dreiser's first published one-act play enacts the success of labor leaders' collaborative efforts to sustain fellow workers in the face of a waning interest to strike. A parallel plot involves the denouement's disclosure of the identity of the man responsible for the botched abortion and consequent death of the protagonist's daughter Mary, the girl in the coffin. Labor politics and sexual politics merge the "personal" as "political" in this drama of working-class relationships, a "study of the conflict between duty and desire" (Newlin 31). Protagonist William Magnet mourns his deceased daughter, while workers from the Tabitha Mill are scheduled to meet and discuss the consequences and goals of striking. Only Magnet can rouse the workers' sense of solidarity since he speaks Italian and strike leader John Ferguson does not. The play centers on Ferguson's appeals to Magnet to address the strikers, but the bereaved Magnet resists as daughter Mary lies foregrounded in a coffin in center stage. Estranged from his wife, Ferguson is also Mary's secret lover. By the drama's conclusion, Ferguson convinces Magnet to "prove [his] sorrow [and] meet it the way a man ought" by rising to the call of duty, embracing alliance for the good of others.

Like working-class **Roberta Alden**, whose inability to arrange for an abortion dooms her, Mary Magnet cannot successfully "cover her tracks." Unlike Carrie Meeber, who is not punished for sexual transgressions, Mary is doubly so since her lover is a legally married man. Literally a "fallen woman" narrative, *The Girl in the Coffin* presents tensions that seem to fascinate Dreiser. Mary is not simply seduced by Ferguson but has willingly engaged in sexual relations—suggesting both her personal decision to give away her virtue and Dreiser's allusion to the suspect moral values of the working class. Illicit sexual behaviors are alluded to in *The Girl in the Coffin*, but the uncertainty of whether Dreiser is critiquing those behaviors or the censure from judgmental observers (or both) suggests his ambivalence about female sexuality and, more generally, about wage-earning women. As noted by Laura Hapke, Dreiser both "locate[s] his heroines in the workplace and rescu[es] them from their coarsening influence" (4).

Yet Dreiser is reluctant to portray Ferguson as the "coward" Magnet thinks the (unknown) lover is. Magnet tries to piece together clues that will reveal the identity of the man who "ruined" his daughter. Like old **Gerhardt** who labels daughter

Jennie as a "street-walker" "ruined" by the "fine" Senator Brander, Magnet struggles with feeling dishonored, but in a final gesture of triumphant altruism, Magnet and Ferguson exit the stage to work for the cause. Dreiser's sympathy with labor is, as R. N. Mookerjee notes, portrayed during the same year of profiling the "superman and survival of the fittest" (61) in **Frank Cowperwood**. Thus, Dreiser's writing during 1913 marks his range of themes as well as his belief that male–female relationships constitute a primary vein for fiction.

See also Plays, Productions of.

Further Reading

Frederickson, Kathy. "Dreiser's 'The Girl in the Coffin,' or, What's Death Got to do With it?" *Dreiser Studies* 27.1 (1996): 3–19.

Hapke, Laura. "Dreiser and the Tradition of the American Working Girl Novel." *Dreiser Studies* 22.2 (1991): 2–19.

Mookerjee R. N. *Theodore Dreiser: His Thought and Social Criticism.* Delhi: National Publishing House, 1974.

Newlin, Keith. "Dreiser's 'The Girl in the Coffin' in the Little Theater." *Dreiser Studies* 25.1 (1994): 31–50.

Kathy Frederickson

"GOLD TEETH." First published in *Dreiser Studies* 27.2 (1996), fifty-one years after the author's death, "Gold Teeth" focuses on the personal tragedy of John Hillman, a poor West Virginia mountaineer whose primary source of income for his family of nine is the manufacture of corn whiskey. To circumvent the predatory extortion of the local marshal, Crawhide, Hillman builds a new still, which he is confident will elude Crawhide's detection. When Crawhide, in fact, does discover the still and doubles the previous extortion fee, Hillman, infuriated as much by the marshal's gold teeth (an undeserved extravagance in Hillman's estimation) as the outrageousness of his demand, bludgeons Crawhide to death with a sledgehammer and buries the body in a nearby sandpit. Shortly thereafter, Hillman is questioned by the local sheriff, and, though released due to a lack of evidence, he is still viewed as a primary suspect in Crawhide's disappearance, as a result of which his wife and oldest son evict him from his home. Over the following year, Hillman manages a makeshift existence, first as a cook in a logging camp, then as a seasonal harvester, and ultimately as a handyman for an elderly farm couple. Throughout this period, Hillman is tormented by the fear of discovery and is nagged by the perceived injustice of his situation. At the same time, he is beset by a series of nervous breakdowns and recurring nightmares in which he is relentlessly persecuted by Crawhide, who "invariably . . . glowered and overpowered him as a giant or demon." Acting upon rumors of gold, several boys upon digging in the potentially incriminating sandpit discover Crawhide's skeleton. Shortly thereafter, the sheriff confronts Hillman with Crawhide's skull, at which point Hillman confesses to the murder and, noticing the gold teeth, seizes the skull and repeatedly smashes it in a fit of rage.

The idea for "Gold Teeth" originated in Dreiser's discovery of a newspaper account in the *New York World* dated 14 July 1922 of Alabama moonshiner Monroe Hill, who kills a deputy sheriff when he reneges on an agreement to conceal Hill's moonshining activities from the law. Though he changes the setting, the details in Dreiser's story, including the murder victim's gold teeth, closely parallel those of the actual murder. Influenced no doubt by Frank Norris's *McTeague* (1899), Dreiser makes masterful use of gold as a unifying motif, most notably, with Crawhide's gold teeth, which serve as a symbol of Crawhide's avarice and scavenging materialism and,

even more interesting, as the synecdochic focus, reminiscent of the pathological fixation in Poe's "The Tell-Tale Heart," of Hillman's rage, madness, and eventual self-indictment. The story further reveals an artful use of interior monologue and nightmarish dream sequences in dramatizing Hillman's fear, paranoia, and persecution complex. Equally innovative is the fact that Hillman's neurosis is manifested in a compulsive eating disorder, though paradoxically he becomes progressively more emaciated. Hillman never acknowledges a sense of culpability but rather perceives himself as an undeserving victim of circumstance and Crawhide's merciless exploitation. In this regard, Hillman, like so many of Dreiser's protagonists, is an unwitting pawn in a mechanistic universe, the governing forces of which he can neither counteract nor even remotely understand.

Further Reading

Riggio, Thomas P. "'Gold Teeth': A Minor American Tragedy." *Dreiser Studies* 27.2 (1996): 3–21.

Michael Wentworth

GREENWICH VILLAGE. In 1914, after leaving his first wife permanently, Dreiser moved to Greenwich Village, taking an apartment at 165 West 10th Street. Lured by the inexpensive rents and the unconventional residents, Dreiser thrived, meeting American atheists, socialists, cubists, anarchists, birth control advocates, and women with bobbed hair. Greenwich Village's community of artists and intellectuals encouraged experimentation, and this community—whose luminaries included **Floyd Dell**, Max Eastman, Margaret Sanger, John Reed, **Sinclair Lewis**, and Eugene O'Neill—nurtured Dreiser and encouraged his exploration of the unconventional, in both his living arrangements and his writing.

While living in Greenwich Village, Dreiser attended and held social evenings during which he discussed art, literature, philosophy, and psychology with New York's intelligentsia. One of these evenings is described in a letter from Kenneth Burke to Malcolm Cowley: "Last night I had the fullest hours of my life; I was at Dreiser's. I am not going to write you about all I experienced. It would seem almost like sacrilege to me. You see, to me the evening was an epoch" (*The Selected Correspondence of Kenneth Burke and Malcolm Cowley: 1915–1981*, ed. Paul Jay [Berkeley: University of California Press, 1990], 7). Burke did not praise Dreiser's intellectual prowess or his novels, but Burke greatly admired Dreiser's stature as a literary giant—who might, incidentally, further Burke's own literary aspirations.

Dreiser thrived among the Greenwich Village iconoclasts and embraced the community's artistic assumptions, which came to influence his writing. Dreiser's experimental plays were written during his five years in Greenwich Village, and Dreiser was both personally and professionally connected to New York avant-garde theater. During his first two years as a resident, Dreiser lived with **Kirah Markham**, an actress who performed with the Provincetown Players. Dreiser's one-act play *The Girl in the Coffin* was produced by the Washington Square Players in 1915, and his four-act tragedy *The Hand of the Potter* was staged by the Provincetown Players in 1921. In addition, Dreiser's autobiographical novel *The "Genius"* was published while he lived in Greenwich Village, and his decision to depict **Eugene Witla** as a painter, not a writer, occurred after Dreiser moved to Greenwich Village and after he attended the Armory art show where he saw paintings by expressionists and cubists. Just as Dreiser's taste in painting shifted from the "Ashcan" school to impressionism, so Dreiser's approach to writing shifted. Although Greenwich Village did not alter Dreiser's essential belief in **realism**, the avant-garde environment did influence the means by which Dreiser depicted his characters and their lives. For example, during this period, Dreiser befriended **A. A. Brill**, a student of Carl Jung and the first to translate **Freud** for American readers. Psychoanalysis was the rage in Greenwich Village, and Dreiser knew writers, such as Floyd Dell, who had been psychoanalyzed. As a man who suffered depression and anxiety, Dreiser embraced the new field of psychology, and this interest affected his writing, especially his characterization of Clyde Griffiths in *An American Tragedy*.

For five years, during the formation of American modernism, Dreiser lived in Greenwich Village, where the leaders of the avant-garde art movement flourished. If Dreiser had not entered Greenwich Village as an established writer who was already labeled as America's great realist, he may have emerged from this environment with a different epithet: an American modern, a writer of experimental plays, fiction, and nonfiction.

Further Reading

Heller, Adele, and Lois Rudnick, eds. *1915, The Cultural Moment: The New Politics, the New Woman, the New Psychology, the New Art & the New Theatre in America*. New Brunswick, N.J.: Rutgers University Press, 1991.

Humphrey, Robert. E. *Children of Fantasy: The First Rebels of Greenwich Village*. New York: Wiley, 1978.

Roark Mulligan

GRIDLEY, DR. This is the fictitious name given by Dreiser to his "Country Doctor" in *Twelve Men*. Dr. Gridley was a composite of two physicians: Dr. **Amos Woolley** of Warsaw, Indiana, and Dr. **William B. Adams** of Montgomery City, Missouri.

Robert Coltrane

GRIFFITHS, CLYDE, is the protagonist in Dreiser's *An American Tragedy*. In this vast novel, Dreiser portrays in a massively detailed manner typical of naturalistic fiction the tragically misguided story of this representative seeker after materialistic "success" in America, from Clyde's childhood to his death, at about age twenty-two, through execution for the murder of **Roberta Alden**, that lower-class secret sweetheart he had made pregnant but then wished to eliminate from his life. In his pursuit of wealth, privilege, and pleasure to be made possible through marriage to beautiful, rich **Sondra Finchley**, Clyde illustrates hauntingly what the novelist saw as an all-too-common kind of destructive pattern in American society. In fact, as scholars long ago established, Dreiser's ultimate shaping of the character of Clyde came as the artistic culmination of several abandoned starts at a fictional study of a young man victimized by belief in that dream of fulfillment and "success." As his 1935 essay "I Find the Real American Tragedy" points out, Dreiser discovered in American life—between about 1895 and the 1920s—a great many recurring cases of young men moved to acts of murder in their quests for fortune-hunting through marriage to wealthy girls when such a pursuit was prevented by the "trap" of poor girls previously made pregnant. But the basis for the novelist's characterization of Clyde Griffiths came not just from details of real enactors of that "American tragedy pattern" Dreiser perceived in diverse news stories (most notably, the case of **Chester Gillette**, convicted in 1906 for the murder of **Grace Brown** in upstate New York) but also from Dreiser's own

intensely sympathetic identification with the plight of poor boys dreaming of lives with beautiful, rich girls.

Despite Dreiser's reliance on the Gillette case for many of the details of his portrayal of Clyde, both Clyde's individual nature and some crucial elements of his story, essential to his unfolding, terrible fate, derived instead from Dreiser's imagination. Of particular note is the novelist's not merely investing the character of Clyde with the quality of "life" but also succeeding artistically—through the powerful device of indirect discourse in much of the work's second and third books—in causing readers to feel this protagonist's predicament and desires, seeing through his eyes the events leading tragically toward death.

Clyde early feels both a sense of humiliation at his family's life and a growing hunger for the very worldly ways of living that his parents, in their obsession with God and heaven, see as sin and modern decadence. Indeed, Clyde rebels emphatically against his parents' spiritual focus, replacing their actual evangelist **religion** with the modern American "religion" of impassioned yearning for money, status, and physical pleasures, yet it is a sad, fateful irony that Clyde has little in the way of education, intelligence, or even readiness for hard work to recommend him or to favor his feverish dreams' fulfillment. He has only his good looks, an eagerness to please those with power to help him, a total desire to "be somebody" in his society's materialistic terms, and an intense belief in the credo that a meaningful, happy life depends utterly on attainment of wealth and privileged social position.

With this unpromising combination of character traits—the often-indecisive dreamer driven by determination, somehow, to enjoy fairy-tale-like magical fulfillments—a teenaged Clyde quits school and parlays a position as bellhop in a luxurious Kansas City hotel into his initial grasping of money, nice clothes, and hedonistic pursuits. Both this first phase of Clyde's worldly initiation as a whole and his hungry drive toward sexual satisfaction (focused on the figure of Hortense Briggs, a formative first lust-object) come to an abrupt, awful end in the car crash episode that concludes *An American Tragedy*'s opening book. Dreiser uses this scene of disaster (leading to a little girl's death) as well as Clyde's flight from the area as ominous foreshadowing of the story's tragic climax closing Book 2—when a different sort of "accident" more fully of Clyde's creation leads to death, first for Roberta Alden and then, after the criminal trial in which society condemns him without truly understanding him or his history, for Clyde.

The flight from Kansas City to Chicago leads to Clyde's chance encounter with his rich uncle, **Samuel Griffiths**, the industrialist from the East whose invitation to his nephew to move to Lycurgus, New York, typifies the way events seeming to favor magically fulfilling the youth's dreams instead ultimately move him toward the tragic outcome of an ill-fated, overreaching quest. In moving to Lycurgus and starting to experience its class-bound life, Clyde soon becomes involved in a love triangle that places him between a poor girl he makes pregnant and the rich one who embodies his ultimate dreams. Thus caught in a nightmarish reality blocking his path toward the paradise of pleasures apparently beckoning to him in the promises of Sondra to wed him, Clyde moves toward the lonely lake where the novel's famous, defining moment occurs—in a sense doomed, Dreiser shows, to enact the cruel "American tragedy" pattern betraying and ruining such a youth.

Paul A. Orlov

GRIFFITHS, GILBERT, in *An American Tragedy*, plays a critical part in the tragic quest for "success" of the novel's protagonist, Clyde Griffiths. Looking remarkably like Clyde, Gilbert becomes Clyde's doppelganger or double: a figure reflecting the increasing psychological insight informing fiction in response to new socioeconomic forces. Dreiser's use of Gilbert as a "double" for Clyde is apt, since *An American Tragedy* dramatizes the dire effects for individual integrity of the pursuit of wealth and worldly prestige. Moreover, in keeping with the way a double's appearance in fiction usually signals an antithetical nature spelling trouble for a protagonist, Gilbert's hostility toward Clyde, as well as the prestigious fame of the rich youth's name and face in and near Lycurgus, become key causes for increasingly tragic complications in Clyde's life story. Ironically, Clyde's great resemblance to Gilbert—the enviable cousin who is a symbol of all that Clyde, as a "success"-seeker, wishes to *be* and *have*—makes possible the fulfillment of several major dreams and desires for Clyde. Despite Clyde's typical ineptness and lack of assertiveness, the intertwined facts of his being "good-looking" and looking so much like **Samuel Griffiths's** powerful, respected son help influence the rich uncle first to hire and then to promote Clyde; lead **Roberta Alden** to yearn for Clyde as her supposed superior and thus to yield to his sexual demands lest she lose him; and, most amazingly, prompt **Sondra Finchley** (the epitome of all the wealth and beauty for which Clyde hungers) to find him intriguing and then, with her conceit fed gratifyingly by Clyde's reverence for her, to decide she reciprocates his "love"— apparently promising to make possible the realization of the poor boy's ultimate dream of marriage to the enchanting rich girl.

Clearly, then, Gilbert proves indispensably important to the plot in essential ways as the novel portrays Clyde's representative "American tragedy" of a dangerous quest for the "dream of success." Dreiser's creation of the character of Gilbert—who simultaneously symbolizes a fulfillment of Clyde's fantasies of a new, grandly enhanced identity and, through his mere outward likeness to Clyde, unwittingly empowers so many of Clyde's fantasies to come true—is an ingeniously apt fictive device in a novel portraying a society excessively valuing appearances and purchasable externals. Despite misconceptions about Dreiser's dependence on real-life news stories (of "murder-for-wealth"), the complex characterization of Gilbert is one of various essential ways in which the novelist improved upon the 1906 Gillette case to shape artistically the hauntingly terrible tale that is *An American Tragedy*.

Paul A. Orlov

GRIFFITHS, SAMUEL, in *An American Tragedy*, is the "self-made man" and wealthy uncle who plays a critically important part in the life history of the novel's protagonist, Clyde Griffiths. As Clyde yearns secretly for a world away from his religious family's, with a growing sense of devotion to the "religion" of Mammon, he concludes (notes the narrative early in Book 1) that "[t]he one thing that really interested him in connection with his parents was the existence somewhere in the east—in a small city called Lycurgus, near Utica he understood—of an uncle, a brother of his father's, who was plainly different from" his parents and their impoverished realm of experience. "That uncle—Samuel Griffiths by name—was rich." This passage identifies a major motif—Clyde's fascination with, and desire to achieve, the materialistic goals of

comfort, pleasure, and displays of "conspicuous consumption" (in Thorstein Veblen's famous phrase) that he associates with the rich.

Clyde's uncle Samuel crucially affects the fortunes of the youth in Lycurgus in several ways. Once Clyde has labored in a menial position at the Griffiths factory (aptly called "the shrinking-room" as it deflates the young man's hopes and ambitions) for months, he gains a promotion to a superficial foreman's position not because he has actually merited it but because the very class-conscious owner of the business is appalled to see his nephew (bearing the family's proud name and looking so much like his own son, **Gilbert**) working as a poorly dressed, apparently primitive, and lower-class drone.

Unfortunately for Clyde, stubborn class-consciousness, belief in the virtues of social stratification, and insistence that others work hard to rise in society just as the proud business-owning uncle had—central aspects of Samuel's nature—determine, along with Gilbert's enmity and contempt toward Clyde, that once this ambitious newcomer to Lycurgus is settled into his factory work, he will be left dangerously alone and unsupervised, as well as "unsponsored," in his shadowy private hours. In this way, the rich uncle helps sow the seeds of Clyde's secret liaison, despite company rules against it and this deluded youth's supposed social superiority, with **Roberta Alden** and helps prompt **Sondra Finchley's** sense of intrigue and pride in "taking up" the handsome aspirant to success in defiance of his relatives' cold attitudes toward him. Yet after largely ignoring Clyde for the many months that lead to the catastrophic complexities of the love triangle and the desire-driven boy's tragic overreaching, Samuel responds to the grotesque ironies of his nephew's notoriety as a murderer with little understanding of the way terrible events might have been averted, minimal readiness to use money or status to aid Clyde's legal defense, and proudly self-protective apathy toward the young man's confusions of socioeconomic status or possibility. In sum, amid Dreiser's haunting depiction of the grim realities of a world in which fairy tales such as "dreams of success" seldom come true for youths like this novel's antihero, Clyde experiences failure and then a sentence of death, rather than the wonders of ascent to wealth and privileged life, through the impact of the same Samuel who first seemed a magically favoring force.

Paul A. Orlov

GRIGSBY, EMILIE (1879–1964). Emilie Grigsby, the long-term mistress of Chicago traction tycoon **Charles Tyson Yerkes** (**Frank Cowperwood's** real-life counterpart), is the basis for Dreiser's character **Berenice Fleming** in the novels *The Titan* and *The Stoic*. Born in Kentucky, Emilie was the convent-educated daughter of Mrs. Louis "Sue" Grigsby, known for her exploits as a madam. Around 1897, Yerkes, at the age of fifty-seven, met her and became her benefactor, moving the entire Grigsby family to the posh Hotel Grenoble in New York. Here, Yerkes paid for Emilie's education at a prestigious school for girls. At first, the socially ambitious Emilie enjoyed acceptance into New York society, but her mother's past eventually spoiled this opportunity and frightened potential suitors. In particular, Dreiser makes use of

an incident involving a drunken racehorse owner at the Waldorf-Astoria, where the exposure of Sue Grigsby's past causes Emilie some embarrassment. With her social prospects dissipating, Emilie decided to become Yerkes's mistress. Yerkes, infatuated with her beauty and grace, built an elegant, four-story home for her at the corner of 67th Street and Park Avenue and included her in his will. Though their relationship was not a secret, they often traveled to Europe separately but met in London or Paris. Dreiser employs all of these biographical details in his novels, including a modified version of the infamous confrontation between Emilie and **Mary Adelaide Moore** Yerkes just before her husband dies. Dreiser also includes her trips to India and subsequent interest in yoga. Rumor has it that just before *The Titan* was to be printed in the spring of 1914, friends of Emilie, unhappy about the obvious parallels to Berenice, influenced **Harper & Brothers** not to publish the novel, thus forcing Dreiser to call upon **John Lane**.

Further Reading

Forrey, Robert. "Charles Tyson Yerkes: Philadelphia-born Robber Baron." *Pennsylvania Magazine of History and Biography* 99.2 (1975): 226–41.

Gerber, Philip L. "The Alabaster Protégé: Dreiser and Berenice Fleming." *American Literature* 43 (1971): 217–30.

Kevin Jett

H

HAECKEL, ERNST (1834–1919), was a German professor of zoology and comparative anatomy most noted for his theory that "ontogeny recapitulates phylogeny," that is, that the development of the embryo recapitulates that of the species. He wrote prolifically in support of **evolution** but was known by Dreiser primarily for *The Riddle of the Universe at the Close of the Nineteenth Century* (1900). "I read Haeckel," Dreiser wrote **Edward H. Smith** in 1921, "and have for years, (re-read) with unwearied interest" (*Letters* 1: 337).

Haeckel's appeal lay in a thoroughgoing materialism that could yet stir the will to believe. Ridiculing Christianity's immaterial, anthropomorphic God as a "gaseous vertebrate" (*Riddle* 12), Haeckel maintained that science was a new monistic, pantheistic **religion** whose central tenet was the "law of substance," a variation of the theory of the persistence of matter and force that Dreiser had found so compelling in **Herbert Spencer**. The old dualities of matter and energy, body and soul, and body and mind, Haeckel affirmed, are merely passing states of the one underlying "substance," which is "everywhere and always in . . . transformation" (242). The nature of substance, however, like the "Unknowable" of Spencer and the "thing-in-itself" of Kant and **Schopenhauer**, is a

"riddle." To give this monism emotional appeal, Haeckel contended, it was necessary to incarnate the "real trinity" (336) of the true, the good, and the beautiful in a new mythology employing the now empty forms of Christianity. Dreiser echoed this idea in Chapters 34 and 35 of *A Traveler at Forty*. Modern materialism, he concluded, has destroyed "religious legend" without solving "the riddle of the universe," and so it was necessary to emphasize the "thought of divinity *in the individual*." When he wrote this, he was emphasizing that very thought in *The Financier* by making his Nietzschean hero **Frank Cowperwood** a quasi-satanic, quasi-messianic embodiment of cosmic forces.

The word "substance" became part of Dreiser's working vocabulary for any union of seeming opposites, as when in Chapter 37 of *Dawn* he defined **realism** as the "very substance" of "true life" and "romance." More importantly, Haeckel offered a solution to the problem of consciousness by positing an elemental "psychoplasm" (*Riddle* 91) in substance that makes mind an immanent quality of the universe. In the late 1910s and early 1920s, however, when he was exploring the deterministic theories of **Jacques Loeb** and **Sigmund Freud**, Dreiser bridled at what he took to be Haeckel's tacit acceptance of free will. He could, with Haeckel, dismiss the soul as "a sum of plasma movements" (*Uncollected Prose* 216), the mind as an effect of brain chemistry, and personal immortality as an absurdity, but if individuals were part of a larger organism, that organism could not be free, and if not free, not good. Haeckel's modern trinity needed correction. Nature, Dreiser wrote, must be "*compelled* to accept, admire, desire itself as beautiful, *accurate*, true" (216–17, emphasis added).

At this point Dreiser placed his hopes for humankind in the mechanistic "equation inevitable," but Haeckel's monism certainly figured into his later acceptance of a benevolent, conscious Creative Force, "the ultimate substance" that generates the world in an act of "self-expression" (*Notes on Life* 283).

See also "Equation Inevitable."

Further Reading

Brennan, Stephen C. *The Financier*: Dreiser's Marriage of Heaven and Hell." *Studies in American Fiction* 19.1 (1991): 55–69.

Dreiser, Theodore. "Some Additional Comments on the Life Force, or God." *Theodore Dreiser: A Selection of Uncollected Prose.* Ed. Donald Pizer. Detroit: Wayne State University Press, 1977. 212–20.

Haeckel, Ernst. *The Riddle of the Universe at the Close of the Nineteenth Century.* Trans. Joseph McCabe. New York: Harper & Brothers, 1900.

Zanine, Louis J. *Mechanism and Mysticism: The Influence of Science on the Thought and Work of Theodore Dreiser.* Philadelphia: University of Pennsylvania Press, 1993. 90–92, 181–85.

Stephen C. Brennan

"THE HAND." First published by *Munsey's* in May 1919 after being rejected by at least eight other magazines, "The Hand" was reprinted in *Chains: Lesser Novels and Stories* and illustrates Dreiser's experiments with form and point of view. In 1942 Dreiser sent it to Whit Burnett for inclusion in *This Is My Best*, with the note, "I look upon 'The Hand' as illustrative as well as representative of the diversity of my subject matter and my psychological interests" (qtd. in Griffin 181).

"The Hand" tells the story of the prospector Davidson, who kills his former partner Mersereau, who has threatened to expose their previous shady dealings and so drive Davidson out of the public and financial life he covets. The dying Mersereau extends his hand toward Davidson in a gesture of revenge, and the rest of the story describes Davidson's experience with threatening psychic phenomena involving the hand over the next few years. The story is divided into thirteen sections, all but the first titled with a month and year. The times range from June 1905 to 17 February 1909.

In sections 2 through 9, Davidson experiences a variety of inexplicable events: he sees a hand like Mersereau's painted on his ceiling by dripping water; he hears tapping sounds in his room and hears or imagines a message from Mersereau, telling Davidson that he will be with him from now on; and he seems to be followed by loud crashes. In section 6 he feels the hand on his throat for the first time. He visits a doctor, who tells him that his experiences are delusions. In section 9 Mersereau's ghost tells him, "I'll choke you yet! You can't escape!" Davidson wakes at night feeling a clutch at his throat and decides to commit himself to an asylum.

In section 10, for the first time, we leave Davidson's consciousness and hear a nurse's report, which attributes the calluses on his throat to incipient tuberculosis. In the final two sections, we see a play-like dramatization of, first, the voices of Mersereau and the other spirits as Mersereau chokes Davidson to death and his soul leaves his body and, last, a discussion between the nurse and doctor concerning Davidson's death.

The modern reader might assume that "The Hand" is the story of a guilt-ridden murderer's psychological disintegration. Several events occur after they have been suggested by others (tapping, crashes, seeing spirits). On the other hand, Dreiser makes a point of having other witnesses confirm some of the happenings. Dreiser appears to be describing psychic phenomena, in which he was interested, and contrasting their mystery with the relative comfort of science. Davidson bemoans the inability of the doctors to see beyond their usual diagnoses, and the doctors do dismiss the psychic explanations automatically. Their unwillingness to consider the possibility that the events are real, coupled with Davidson's conviction and descriptions, suggest that we should be open to the possibility that the hand that chokes him is Mersereau's rather than his own and in general that we should not rush to accept safe, scientific explanations of things we don't understand.

Further Reading

Griffin, Joseph. "Dreiser Experiments with Form: Five Short Stories from *Chains*." *English Studies in Canada* 8 (1982): 174–86.

James F. Collins

THE HAND OF THE POTTER, Dreiser's only four-act play, is the story of a sex crime and its aftermath. Dreiser began the play in late October or early November 1916 and finished it in early December. After his editor/typist **Estelle Kubitz** completed a typescript of his manuscript, he sent a copy to H. L. Mencken for his opinion. Mencken was furious. In a series of letters, the critic found fault with the subject matter, the structure, and, above all, the timing, as he had just finished convincing members of the **Authors' League of America** to sign a protest over the suppression of *The "Genius."* Not surprisingly, in his responses Dreiser defended the work, noting that the play was "not a defense of perversion" but, rather, a tragedy illuminating "the inscrutability of life and its forces and its accidents" (*D-M Letters* 1: 284), and asked repeatedly to set the disagreement aside. In the meantime, he sought the reactions of others and by May 1917 sold an option for a production of the play to Arthur Hopkins, one of the foremost producers of serious drama on Broadway at the time. At the same time he sought a publisher for the work, finally offering it to **Boni & Liveright** in January 1918 to test the sincerity of the firm's offer to become his publisher. After some hesitation, the publishing house finally agreed to Dreiser's terms, and when it became clear that Hopkins had failed in his efforts to launch a production, it began the process of printing the play in the spring of 1918. Because of the numerous corrections and revisions Dreiser made in the various stages of proofs, the final text was not finished until August, and by then Dreiser had found another company willing to sign a contract for a production provided that Dreiser agreed to delay publication. These plans also fell through, as did the interest of yet another production company in the spring of 1919, but as a result of these delays and the publication of *Twelve Men* in the spring, the book version was not issued to the public until September 1919.

Dreiser based much of the action and many of the characters in *The Hand of the Potter* on newspaper accounts of the murder of twelve-year-old Julia Connors by twenty-four-year-old Nathan Swartz in the Bronx in 1912, the behavior of Swartz's family before the Grand Jury called to bring an indictment against him, and the circumstances surrounding Swartz's suicide while police were searching for him. Unlike the newspapers, however, which sensationalized the gruesome events of the murder and suicide, Dreiser structured his play to emphasize the forces that led the central character Isadore Berchansky to commit a sex crime and the effects of his act on his family. Set in a top-floor flat of Isadore's parents, the first act of the play focuses on Isadore's inability to control an "unnatural sex interest" in young girls and concludes with Isadore, while left alone in the apartment, forcing his attentions on eleven-year-old Kitty Neafie, an Irish neighbor's daughter who has come to see his niece, dragging her offstage where sounds of assault are heard, and then returning onstage carrying her body out of the apartment.

In act 2, also set in the Berchansky apartment, Dreiser focuses on Isadore's family. In the first scene the character of Aaron Berchansky, Isadore's father, is depicted as an old-fashioned, but good, man who cares for the well-being of his children in conversations with a daughter and granddaughter while his wife and another daughter are discovering a girl's shoe and noticing that a box and some oilcloth are missing. Shortly thereafter, the family learns of Kitty's disappearance, and then Isadore returns with his face scratched and his clothes torn. When Mr. Berchansky questions Isadore about the things the family has discovered, Isadore refuses to answer and, following a brief struggle with his father, runs out of the flat. The second scene develops the family's growing concern that Isadore may be responsible for Kitty's disappearance and concludes when they learn that her body has been found in a box covered with oilcloth.

Set in the Criminal Courts Building in New York City about two weeks later, the third act comprises testimony by members of the Berchansky family and other witnesses regarding the discovery of Kitty's body and the family's behavior after they learned of the discovery. It concludes with Mr. Berchansky's breaking down and admitting Isadore committed the crime when he is shown Kitty's clothing and hair. Dreiser returns to Isadore in the first scene of act 4, set in a hall bedroom of a tenement building. It opens with a long soliloquy by Isadore, in which he expresses remorse for the shame he has brought upon his parents and laments that he cannot control his sexual desires. Shortly afterward, when he almost loses control again during a visit by the daughter of his landlord, he commits suicide by putting one end of a tube in a gas jet and the other end in his mouth. The final scene is also set in the hall bedroom after the body of Isadore is discovered. While a policeman waits for the arrival of Mr. Berchansky to identify his son's body, three reporters stand around reading notes left by Isadore and arguing over whether Isadore was "a vile, horrible, creature" or a victim of forces he could not control. It ends with the arrival of Berchansky, who, when accused of failing to bring up his children right, cries out, "Vy pull at de walls of my house? Dey are already down."

Thematically, *The Hand of the Potter* focuses on a number of ideas that interested Dreiser at the time he wrote the play and was exploring in other writings as well. One was his belief that one's chemical make-up was the cause of human behavior and not free will. To Dreiser, Nature was constantly working toward an "equation" or balance in the world, particularly as it relates to one's moral behavior. Thus, as noted by one of the reporters in the play, the hormones or sex instinct that led to Isadore's unnatural interest in girls was something he neither created or controlled. It was, rather, brought about by Nature as

Nature sought to provide a balance or some kind of equation in the world.

The other idea that attracted Dreiser was how often a good, upright man would suffer because of the actions of his children. He had begun to explore this idea in 1914, when he began work on *The Bulwark*, a novel in which the protagonist, **Solon Barnes**, falls into deep despair and almost loses his faith because of the sex crime and subsequent suicide of his son. Like Solon, Aaron Berchansky is also a kind and religious man whose suffering over the actions of Isadore is dramatized at the conclusions of the third and fourth acts of *The Hand of the Potter*.

The book version of Dreiser's play received mixed reviews when it finally was issued to the public. Predictably, some reviewers condemned it on moral grounds, but others praised Dreiser for his courage and sincerity in dealing with a controversial subject. Almost universally, however, the reviewers agreed that the scene with the reporters arguing over Isadore's responsibility for his actions in the fourth act was undramatic and unnecessary. As a consequence, Dreiser made extensive cuts in this scene when he revised the play for a new edition of it issued in 1927.

See also "Equation Inevitable"; Plays, Productions of.

Further Reading

Rusch, Frederic E. "Dreiser's Other Tragedy." *Modern Fiction Studies* 23 (1977): 449–56.

Frederic E. Rusch

HANSON, MINNIE, is Carrie Meeber's "lean-faced, rather commonplace" sister in *Sister Carrie*. Her name suggests the *mini*mal gratification of emotional and physical needs Carrie will experience while boarding with the Hansons during her early days in Chicago. Minnie first appears at the end of Chapter 1, when she greets her sister at the Chicago train station and brings with her "most of the grimness of shift and toil." Carrie is still "feeling the goodness" of Charlie Drouet, the warmhearted "masher" who has tried to pick her up on the journey, but "the change of affectional atmosphere" produced by Minnie leaves her feeling "much alone, a lone figure in a tossing, thoughtless sea." Minnie has come to the city some years before seeking freedom but finding only "a lean and narrow life" as household drudge. Despite the novel's faintly Darwinian cast, Minnie illustrates that mere survival of the fittest hardly suffices for human happiness. If she has become "solemnly adapted to a condition," life with her husband **Sven**, a penurious, second-generation Swede who cleans refrigerator cars in the stockyards, is not fortunate: "She was now a thin, though rugged, woman of twenty-seven, with ideas of life coloured by her husband's, and fast hardening into narrower conceptions of pleasure and duty than had ever been hers in a thoroughly circumscribed youth." As an image of what conventional life holds for the average working-class woman, Minnie helps propel Carrie into the arms of Drouet.

Still, even though she is too old to be a good companion for eighteen-year-old Carrie, Minnie retains something of her sister's youthful vitality. Under "the warming influence of Carrie's good spirits," she begins to describe "the well-known things to see" in Chicago, though only "things the enjoyment of which cost nothing" and only until Sven's "unspoken shade of disapproval" silences her. Her complexity is most evident when Carrie unexpectedly disappears into the city, leaving only a terse note of farewell. While Sven responds to Carrie's seemingly inevitable seduction with a cynical "Now she has gone and done it," Minnie's "womanly nature," which is "higher" than his, requires empathy: "Oh, . . . poor Sister Carrie!" This feminine "higher" nature also embodies the "first principles of morals," a universal desire for love and beauty that the narrator opposes to the "arbitrary scale" conventionally applied to fallen women. There is certainly a veneer of Victorian prudery when, on the night Carrie first sleeps with Drouet, Minnie dreams of Carrie's being "swallowed" by a "deep pit," "sinking" into "strange waters," and "slipping away" over a cliff. Given Minnie's own disappointments in love, however, unconscious wish-fulfillment is likely at work. Minnie awakes "suffering as though she had lost something," and what she has lost besides her sister is the chance to follow the dream-Carrie's invitation ("Yes, come on") to descend with her into those "waters she had never seen." If this interpretation is valid, the appearance of *Sister Carrie* in the same year as **Freud's** *Interpretation of Dreams* indicates Dreiser's prescience as a psychologist of desire.

Further Reading

Gammel, Irene. "Sexualizing the Female Body: Dreiser, Feminism, and Foucault." *Theodore Dreiser: Beyond Naturalism*. Ed. Miriam Gogol. New York: New York University Press, 1995. 31–54.

Stephen C. Brennan

HANSON, SVEN, is Carrie Meeber's brother-in-law in *Sister Carrie*. When Carrie arrives in Chicago to board with the Hansons in a working-class neighborhood of Chicago's near West Side, she finds in Sven's "morbid turn of character" and "cold" attitude a sharp contrast to the volubility, generosity, and hedonism of her eventual seducer, the "radiant" Charlie Drouet, whom she has just met on the train from Columbia City, Wisconsin. A second-generation Swedish American who

still speaks with an accent, Sven has fully embraced the Protestant work ethic. With his "clean, saving disposition," he supports his wife, **Minnie**, and their infant son by cleaning refrigerator cars in the Chicago stockyards, and he dreams of one day building a home in the western suburbs on property he is buying on the installment plan. He is dour and tight-fisted. He rises before dawn, spends his evenings dressed in old clothes and buried in his newspapers, and goes to bed at nine. When Carrie suggests a pleasure outing at the theater, Sven disapproves, seeing in her simple request the promise of a dissolute future, "a full career of vanity and wastefulness" that would subtract from the profit he hopes to make from her. His "settled opposition to anything save a conservative round of toil" permeates the flat's atmosphere and eventually arouses "all the antagonism of her nature." The flat becomes a force (her shoe factory is another) that repels Carrie into the charged field of Chicago, that "giant magnet, drawing to itself, from all quarters, the hopeful and the hopeless." Even Sven's "pleasant side," his devotion to his infant son, helps drive her into the arms of her first lover. "[W]rapped up in his offspring," he reveals parenthood as a biological trap and makes life as Drouet's kept woman seem, at least for a time, "the welcome breath of an open door." Carrie will always yearn for the respectability of the middle-class wife, but perhaps because family life at the Hansons' is so dreary, she never feels the maternal impulse. Sven is also the shadow of **Robert Ames**, Carrie's bright "ideal" of the later chapters. While the handsome, intellectual, and altruistic Ames makes life with Hurstwood seem "disagreeable" by contrast, Carrie's "heart revolted" only when Hurstwood's business failure threatens a return to the "commonplace struggle and privation" of her days in the Hanson flat. She will be disgusted enough to leave the ex-manager when his tight-fistedness, slovenly appearance, and habitual silent reading of his newspapers make him the image of an aging, apathetic Sven Hanson.

Stephen C. Brennan

HARLAN COUNTY. A series of turbulent strikes during 1931–1932 in the eastern coalfields of Kentucky inspired Dreiser's political humanitarianism at a time when he was renewing his interest in the Communist Party of the United States. He was among the many public intellectuals outraged by the use of National Guardsmen to support unorthodox strikebreaking tactics, blacklisting of unionist leaders, and the general violation of strikers' civil rights. Dreiser thus agreed, at the urging of **William Z. Foster**, a party labor tribune, to visit the warring region, where the Communist-led National Miners' Union, breaking from the United Mine Workers, was spearheading a radical unionization drive. Dreiser did not officially represent the party, but he was the power behind a "red-left" writers' group, including John Dos Passos and Samuel Ornitz, which he had assembled to conduct on-site investigations. With Dreiser as its luminary, the group spent five days in Harlan and nearby Pineville, spied on by authorities, conducting grassroots fact-finding, and interviewing militant miners. The resultant book, *Harlan Miners Speak* (1932), indebted to Dos Passos' organizing intelligence, appeared under the Dreiser aegis.

Dreiser's fame as a late-middle-aged statesman of American letters smoothed the way for this well-publicized trip to the oppressed coal-mining area. Not only did he hold the local authorities publicly accountable for the safety of his ad hoc commission, but on 6 November 1931 he began hearings of sorts in a local hotel, the Lewallen, in which he gathered an

unlikely mix of aggrieved, impoverished strikers and their families and local pro-business newsmen.

Dreiser's Harlan legacy remains as unclear as it is underresearched. With his usual sense of entitlement in romantic relations, the married Dreiser chose to travel with a young woman, pseudonymously named Marie Pergain, with whom he shared living arrangements during that politically volatile week. The conservative local forces used this liaison to discredit Dreiser's moral fervor. A week after the author of *An American Tragedy* and his party rather hurriedly left the vigilante locale, a Bell County Circuit Court indicted the whole Dreiser committee for "criminal syndicalism," a charge later dismissed.

The damage, however, had been done: the spotlight soon shifted to Dreiser's amatory encounter from the great novelist's earnest efforts to humanize the political climate of "bloody Harlan." By late 1932, the National Miners' Union was also backgrounded, ending what had briefly seemed a two-pronged initiative to bring left-of-center industrial democracy to a union-busting state.

Further Reading

Bubka, Tony. "The Harlan County Coal Strike of 1931." *Labor History* 11 (1970): 43–57.

Dreiser, Theodore, comp., for the National Committee for the Defense of Political Prisoners. *Harlan Miners Speak: Report on Terrorism in the Kentucky Coal Fields*. New York: Harcourt, Brace, 1932.

Laura Hapke

HARPER & BROTHERS. Established in 1817 by James and John Harper, Harper & Brothers was soon the largest and most active publishing firm in nineteenth-century America, publishing such venerable authors as Edgar Allan Poe, Herman Melville, **William Dean Howells**, Mark

Twain, and Henry James. By the 1890s the firm met with increasing financial difficulties and borrowed heavily from the J. P. Morgan bank; faced with bankruptcy proceedings and under pressure from Morgan, George B. Harvey became president in an effort to make the firm more efficient. Dreiser's first encounter with Harper's occurred in April 1900, after he completed the manuscript of *Sister Carrie* and sent it to Henry Mills Alden, the editor of *Harper's Monthly*, who liked the story but thought the subject matter was too frank. Nevertheless, he forwarded it to the parent company, which declined to publish the novel. Dreiser made extensive cuts and revisions to the manuscript and later arranged to publish the novel with the new firm of **Doubleday, Page & Co.**

By 1910, Dreiser had returned to working on *Jennie Gerhardt* and wanted to find a publisher interested in his novel and in a republication of *Sister Carrie*. Dreiser's agent, Flora Mai Holly, sent a copy of *Jennie* to Macmillan, but they were uninterested. Holly next sent the manuscript to **Ripley Hitchcock** at Harper's. Apprehensive at first because of the questionable morality of the novel, Harper's eventually offered Dreiser a conditional contract that would allow the firm to revise the manuscript and cut material it deemed offensive. Dreiser would retain an escape clause; if he disapproved of the revision, he could withdraw the manuscript without obligation to pay for Harper's revisions. Despite his reluctance to accede to Harper's terms, Dreiser accepted the offer because Harper's was a large and prestigious publishing house and, as James L. W. West III mentions, the firm "would validate his work publicly and professionally" (435). The editorial work began in late April 1911 with some 25,000 words being removed and with major alterations to the plot, characterization, and style of the novel. Dreiser was unhappy with much of the revision but arrived at a compromise with Hitchcock, who restored some of the original material. *Jennie Gerhardt* was published on 19 October 1911; the firm reissued *Sister Carrie* in 1912.

In the beginning of his relationship with Harper's, Dreiser was satisfied with what he might gain from working with such a well-known firm, and Harper's believed in Dreiser's potential, but the relationship soon became strained because Dreiser feared the firm would not promote the novel. One such instance occurred when Dreiser flooded Harper's with suggestions about how to publicize *Jennie* and complained about their lack of advertising to Frederick T. Leigh, the treasurer of the company. Leigh reassured Dreiser that Harper's stood behind the novel and that they "had spent more than $1500 on advertising in the book's first month" (Lingeman 2: 49).

Dreiser contemplated leaving Harper's, but his contract gave Harper's the rights to his next novel, *The Financier*. Dreiser made rapid progress with the novel but found that his subject had ballooned—so much so that, eager to get another of Dreiser's novels into print and begin recouping their advances, the firm decided to publish the story of financier **Frank Cowperwood** in three volumes, with the first volume, *The Financier*, appearing on 24 October 1912. When Dreiser completed the manuscript of the second installment, *The Titan*, Hitchcock and W. G. van Tassel Sutphen, another editor at Harper's, made cuts and revisions. After receiving advance orders for 4,000 copies and printing sheets for 8,000, Harper's abruptly decided to withdraw from publishing the novel. Dreiser's biographers suggest a number of reasons for Harper's decision: the firm might have feared antagonizing and thus being sued by the persons upon whom the novel's characters were based; it may have worried that a novel about an unscrupulous tycoon might antagonize its leading creditor, J. P. Morgan; and Dreiser himself wrote Mencken on 6 March 1914 that the novel was rejected because "the realism is too hard and uncompromising and their policy cannot stand it" (*D-M Letters* 1: 132). Moreover, Dreiser was a troublesome author whose works weren't selling well and who resisted the revisions Harper's wanted to make, all the while complaining about the advertising and poor sales of his novels. The novel would be published on 22 May 1914 by the **John Lane Company**, and Dreiser thereby severed his relationship with Harper & Brothers.

Further Reading

Lingeman, Richard. "The Biographical Significance of *Jennie Gerhardt*." *Dreiser's* Jennie Gerhardt: *New Essays on the Restored Text*. Ed. James L. W. West III. Philadelphia: University of Pennsylvania Press, 1995. 9–16.

West, James L. W., III. "The Composition and Publication of *Jennie Gerhardt*." *Jennie Gerhardt*. Ed. James L. W. West III. Philadelphia: University of Pennsylvania Press, 1992. 420–60.

Dana Stolte Koller

HARRIS, MARGUERITE TJADER. *See* Tjader, Marguerite.

HENRY, ANNA MALLON (1862–1921).

Anna Mallon was born in 1862, the only child of an affluent Brooklyn family. Her father, James, was a brevetted general in the Civil War. She was three when he was killed in the Virginia campaigns. Upon graduating from Brooklyn's Academy of the Visitation, a convent preparatory school, she founded Anna T. Mallon & Co., Stenographers and Typewriters, a secretarial service located at the edge of New York's newspaper district. Her clients included journalists and authors, among them Theodore Dreiser; her "typewriters" produced his *Sister Carrie* manuscript. She met **Arthur Henry** in 1896, when he was in New York as publicity agent for magician Herrmann the Great.

In 1899, following the Dreisers' summer-long visit with the Henrys in Maumee, Ohio, Arthur Henry informed his wife, **Maude**, that he wanted a divorce, sold Dreiser half interest in their house for $200, and departed for New York, settling in with the Dreisers. During this period Arthur's friendship with Dreiser was nurtured most fully. Arthur was seeing Anna with a consuming frequency, so much so that he moved into the Mallon household as a boarder—to the dismay of both Anna's mother and Dreiser. Henry's *A Princess of Arcady* was published in 1900 and dedicated to Anna Mallon, his "tutor in convent education."

In 1901, Anna and Arthur vacationed in the Catskill Mountains, where they bought a piece of land, built a chimney, and started the shell of a house, all underwritten by Anna, and then left the Catskills for a three-year absence. That summer, Henry spent a few months on an island off the coast of Noank, Connecticut, writing another back-to-nature book; Anna was a frequent visitor. Toward the end of his stay, Dreiser and his wife, Jug, and later Henry's wife, Maude, joined them. Arthur announced again that he wanted a divorce and that he intended to marry Anna. Arthur and Maude were divorced in 1902. Anna and Arthur were married on 9 March 1903. She was forty-one years old; he claimed thirty-five. Upon her daughter's marriage, Anna's mother disinherited her.

When *An Island Cabin* was published in 1902, Dreiser recognized himself as the foil for Henry's liberal idealism, and his anger shattered their friendship; he also switched secretarial services. Dreiser's belated revenge came in the unflattering portrait of Arthur and Anna's courtship in "Rona Murtha," published in 1929 in *A Gallery of Women*.

Arthur and Anna returned to the Catskills in 1902, built their "House in the Woods," and lived a rural existence that Henry idealized in *The House in the Woods*, published in 1904. Hardly a year later, the house burned to the ground. Anna sold her copying office to underwrite the building of a new house, which still required chattel mortgages to complete. Without her mother's support, their financial plight became desperate. Facing insolvency, they accepted an offer from Arthur's brother, Alfred, to join him in Henry Bros. Realty and Investment Company in Yakima, Washington. Anna would lend her business acumen to the venture, and Arthur would be the on-the-road partner and salesman. Arthur had some success recruiting investors, but word reached Anna in Yakima that he was seen frequently with Clare Kummer, a successful playwright. Anna went east to retrieve her husband, but to no avail. They were divorced in 1910, and Arthur Henry married Clare Kummer, twenty-one years his junior, later that year.

Following her divorce from Arthur, Anna, suffering from a number of ailments, worked variously as a chicken farmer, teahouse entrepreneur, and housekeeper, marrying and then divorcing a man who abused her, at times receiving sympathetic support from Maude Wood Henry. On 7 May 1921, Anna Mallon fell into the Naches River and drowned. Her obituary notice read: "Authoress . . . Writer of Some Note . . . With her husband, Arthur Henry, she wrote *The House in the Woods* and other popular works of fiction." She was fifty-nine.

Further Reading

Oakes, Donald T. Afterword to *The House in the Woods*, by Arthur Henry. Hensonville, N.Y.: Black Dome, 2000. 155–96.

                                    Donald T. Oakes

HENRY, ARTHUR (1867–1934). Born on a farm in East Homer, New York, Arthur Henry was raised by his mother, Serepta, a temperance crusader, his father, James, having died from wounds sustained in the Civil War. From 1882 to 1883 Henry attended Northwestern University Preparatory School before going to Chicago, at age sixteen, to make a career in writing. From 1884 through 1892, Henry was a political reporter for the *Chicago Globe*. In 1890, his first novel was published: *Nicholas Blood, Candidate*, and he became a member of the Whitechapel Club, a mix of journalists and public figures, among them Brand Whitlock, who, in 1892, recommended him as city editor of the *Toledo Blade*.

By the time Dreiser met Henry in Toledo in 1894, Henry had married Maude Wood, a reporter for the *Blade*, had a daughter, and had purchased the House of Four Pillars, a historical home in Maumee, Ohio. Dreiser, making his rounds of midwestern papers, paused in Toledo long enough to be assigned, with Maude, to cover the city's streetcar strike. According to Dreiser, he and Henry became instant and fast friends.

Both Henry and Maude left the *Blade* in 1894. Together they wrote *The Flight of a Pigeon* (1894), published a local newspaper, and shared some business interests in Toledo. In 1896, Henry became publicity agent for Herrmann the Great, a magician friend from Whitechapel Club days, a job that required frequent trips to New York City. There he found time to run story ideas past publishers and, at Dreiser's urging, even contributed a few pieces to *Ev'ry Month*, the magazine Dreiser was editing. The friendship with Dreiser gradually intensified, with Henry encouraging Dreiser to start work on a novel. During the 1896 visits, Henry met **Anna Mallon**, the head of Anna T. Mallon & Co., Stenographers and Typewriters, a successful typing and secretarial service that counted a number of writers as clients, including Dreiser. The Mallon Company typed the *Sister Carrie* manuscript.

In the summer of 1899, Dreiser visited the Henrys with his wife, Sara, for a two-week stay that encompassed nearly the entire summer, putting a heavy drain on the Henrys' resources. At Henry's urging, Dreiser produced five short stories—"finger exercises," Henry called them—as warm-ups for the writing of a novel. Before the Dreisers left, Henry—unbeknownst to Maude—sold Dreiser a half interest in the House of Four Pillars for $200, not to pay creditors but to provide cash for his impending return to New York City in the fall.

Henry lived with the Dreisers that fall, and a literary partnership was formed. They shared freelance assignments before turning to writing fiction, with Henry working on his *A Princess of Arcady* and Dreiser on *Sister Carrie*. It is certainly Henry's greatest contribution to American literature that he badgered and repeatedly threatened to leave the often-discouraged Dreiser until *Sister Carrie* was finished. The closeness of their relationship is evident in notes and revisions in Henry's handwriting in the final *Carrie* manuscript; and, when **Doubleday, Page** wanted to renege on publishing *Sister Carrie*, Henry advised Dreiser to threaten legal action to force fulfillment of the contract. When Doubleday published the novel in 1900, it was dedicated "To My Friend ARTHUR

HENRY whose steadfast ideals and serene devotion to truth and beauty have served to lighten the method and strengthen the purpose of this volume." The contractual minimum of 1,000 copies was printed.

Henry's return to New York City made possible the renewal of his relationship with Anna. He began to disappear from the Dreiser household with increasing frequency, finally moving in with the Mallon family as a boarder. These often lengthy absences distracted Henry from the task of writing, so much so—claimed Dreiser—that Dreiser had to write the concluding chapter of Henry's novel to meet its publication deadline.

In 1901, Arthur Henry and Anna Mallon, with a chaperone, visited the Catskill Mountains and were enchanted by the Valley of the Plattekill. They purchased land, built a chimney, and started the shell of a house, all underwritten by Anna. That summer Henry spent a few months on an island off the coast of Noank, Connecticut, writing *An Island Cabin*. The unequal sharing of time and attention, now weighted toward Anna, engendered in Dreiser a petulant jealousy of Anna, which reached its zenith during his visit with her and Arthur in the cabin on Dumpling Island.

Published in 1902, *An Island Cabin* contained long philosophical conversations with a visiting friend whom Henry had always assumed to be a like-minded liberal idealist but, when confronted by Nature-in-the-raw, proved to be the possessor of conventional values and attitudes. Dreiser recognized himself as the target of Henry's unflattering depiction, and his anger shattered their friendship. It would never again be the same. The 1907 **Dodge** edition of *Sister Carrie* appeared with the Arthur Henry dedication removed. Dreiser's belated revenge came in his unflattering portrait of Arthur and Anna's courtship in "Rona Murtha," published in *A Gallery of Women* in 1929.

Quite apart from the portrait of Dreiser in *An Island* Cabin, other events transpired to keep them apart. For Dreiser, it was a long period of nervous depression; for Henry, he divorced Maude in 1902 and married Anna Mallon in March 1903. Over the next two years, they lived a rural existence in the Catskills, which Henry idealized in *The House in the Woods*, published in 1904. Hardly a year later, the Catskill house burned, and Anna sold her copying office to underwrite the building of a new house, which even then required chattel mortgages to complete. Further accentuating their financial problems, Anna was disinherited by her mother.

Facing insolvency, in 1905 they moved back to New York. Henry was invited to become general manager of A. S. Barnes, Co., publisher of his *Lodgings in Town* and *The Unwritten Law* (both 1905). Before Henry could accept, his brother, Alfred, offered him a partnership in Henry Bros. Realty and Investment Company in Yakima, Washington, which he hastened to accept. He and Anna moved west, she to provide business acumen, and he to be the company's salesman on the road.

Henry had some success soliciting his literary and publishing contacts back east, even including Dreiser, with whom there had been little contact since *An Island Cabin*. Dreiser's willingness to invest in the company was possibly the result of a recent visit to the House in the Woods with Henry but was perhaps because he still was "inclined to let him have his way in everything," as he remarked in his fictional portrayal of their relationship in "Rona Murtha."

During this time, Henry was seen frequently with Clare Kummer, a successful playwright, whom he met through Dreiser. In 1910, he divorced Anna and married Clare; he was forty-three and she twenty-one years his junior. News of the marriage set Anna on a tragic course of emotional instability that ended with her death in 1921, by drowning.

The marriage to Clare Kummer marked the decline of Henry's writing career. From 1912 to 1927, just eleven magazine articles were published. Four one-act plays for children were written, and a Broadway-bound play, *The Night Before,* was produced in 1928, all coauthored with his daughter, Dorothy. The latter was closed by the police after four performances as an offense to public sensibilities, and Henry and his cast were jailed overnight. *The Life of Roger Allen*, an autobiographical novel, lay unfinished at the time of his death.

Arthur Henry died on 2 June 1934 in the home he shared with Clare Kummer at Narragansett Pier, Rhode Island. Dreiser wrote to the widow: "Dear Claire [*sic*]: The first news I had [of Arthur's death] was from **Will Lengel** . . . who knew of our friendship and called to say that Arthur was dead. . . . I assumed you were in Hollywood or elsewhere and in my hurry to say something, I addressed my telegram [to Dorothy]. . . . I don't think I need to explain or say anything more to you. As I said, Hen's death struck close to me" (qtd. in Oakes 176).

Further Reading

Oakes, Donald T. Afterword to *The House in the Woods*, by Arthur Henry. Hensonville, N.Y.: Black Dome, 2000. 155–96.

Donald T. Oakes

HENRY, MAUDE WOOD (1873–1957). In 1891, eighteen-year-old Maude Wood noticed that her male coworkers in the accounting office earned more for identical work than did female workers. She wrote an angry letter to the editor of the *Toledo Blade* that concluded, "All I want is

JUSTICE." She was hired as the paper's first woman reporter. When Dreiser arrived on the scene in 1894, she was assigned with him to cover the Toledo streetcar strike. Maude claimed it was she who wrote the story, although Dreiser was accorded the byline.

In 1893, she married **Arthur Henry**, city editor of the *Blade*. They made a down payment on the House of Four Pillars, a historic residence in nearby Maumee. There the couple lived what neighbors characterized as a "bohemian life." Their only child, Dorothy, was born the following year. Henry and Maude resigned from the *Blade* in 1894. They collaborated as writers, produced a book (*The Flight of a Pigeon*, 1894), published a newspaper (the *Maumee Liar*), and developed business interests in Toledo. Henry joined a magician friend, Alexander Herrmann, as his publicity agent. Maude became assistant manager of the Theodore Thomas Orchestra, soon to be reborn as the Chicago Symphony.

Henry's stint with Herrmann took him on the road, primarily to New York City, where his friendship with Dreiser was renewed and where his first meeting with **Anna Mallon** occurred. In 1899, the Dreisers came to Maumee on Henry's invitation, a visit that extended into September. Encouraged by Henry, Dreiser wrote for hours at a time in the basement den, concentrating on "finger exercises" as prelude to a novel. Maude's recollection is that *Sister Carrie* had its start there that summer.

Henry told Maude of his interest in Anna Mallon and that he wished to end their marriage; Maude seemed to agree to an amicable divorce. Without Maude's knowledge or consent, Henry sold a one-half interest in their house to Dreiser for $200 to underwrite a move to New York to stay with the Dreisers at summer's end. That closed the door on Maumee, the House of Four Pillars, and on Maude and Dorothy. For Maude, now alone, the burden of debt grew. The House of Four Pillars was lost by foreclosure, and she and Dorothy moved back to Toledo to live with her mother and two sisters. Arthur Henry and Maude Wood were divorced in 1902.

In 1903, Arthur Henry and Anna Mallon put the construction of the Catskill House in the Woods on hold to vacation on an island off the coast of Noank, Connecticut. The Dreisers joined them; Anna had invited Maude and Dorothy as well. Dreiser made clear his disapproval of Henry's abandonment of Maude for Anna; Maude, while warning Anna about Henry's casualness about both money and women, still served as a peacemaker between them; and Henry cast Dreiser as his reactionary adversary in *An Island Cabin*, which was published in 1902 and dedicated to Maude.

When Dreiser's depiction of the triangle appeared in "Rona Murtha," Maude was outraged. "I am boiling with rage . . . for that traitorous treatment of his dear friend Arthur," Maude wrote in a 13 May 1945 letter to Dreiser biographer **Robert Elias**. "[It is] written in a vengeful spirit . . . a rotten over-rating of Arthur's weak points" (qtd. in Oakes 170).

Maude's life following her divorce from Arthur Henry was varied: she became a real estate agent, an editor of a railroad magazine, the field secretary for the National Rivers and Harbors Congress, and the executive of her own advertising/public relations agency, but first and foremost, she was a prolific writer of verse, nature articles, and children's stories, publishing in teachers' journals and in home and garden, children's, and nature magazines. At the time of her death in April 1957, she had been legally blind and an invalid for a decade. Yet, until the very last, she continued writing and, with the vigor and the vision of the young woman who cried for "JUSTICE," still protested that *Sister Carrie* had its beginning in the basement den of her Maumee home—and that she, not Dreiser, wrote the strike story.

Further Reading

Oakes, Donald T. Afterword to *The House in the Woods*, by Arthur Henry. Hensonville, N.Y.: Black Dome, 2000. 155–96.

Donald T. Oakes

"HEY RUB-A-DUB-DUB." This essay first appeared in the *Nation* in August 1919 and was reprinted as the first item of Dreiser's collection of philosophical essays under the same title. In it, Dreiser assumes the persona of forty-year-old John Paradiso, a name taken from his first employer in Chicago, who is living in New Jersey in an impoverished neighborhood. Paradiso describes himself as a "scrivener by trade" who does not have much luck with women. He confesses to spending much of his free time reading anything he can get his hands on, usually leaving him amazed, confused, and intrigued among the essayists and philosophers who attempt to make sense of life. Early in the essay, he states he is a man who is curious about life and its obscure details and cannot make up his mind regarding what is right or wrong. Paradiso does not buy into the myth of success and fails to discern much evidence of the divine, truth, or justice in anything. He believes the average person does not know the true meanings of duty, truth, and justice and cites dozens of specific cases from newspaper articles where wrongs and injustices have occurred. Where he asks, does God or Spirit, morality, or truth reside in each one?

Paradiso does not attempt to resolve the paradoxes in life discovered through his reading and admits to ignorance about the meaning of life. However, he does enjoy life and all the "spectacles" it produces for him to ponder. Paradiso admits his own confusion about the world, knowing that nothing can be done about existing conditions. However, he believes we can refuse to accept belief systems that do not take into account the cruelties and injustices life and nature throw at us. Clearly, Paradiso's skepticism is Dreiser's, and Dreiser himself was skeptical of believing in any one solution to life's many mysteries.

Further Reading

Lundquist, James. *Theodore Dreiser*. New York: Ungar, 1974. 105–21.

Reneé D. McElheney

HEY RUB-A-DUB-DUB: A BOOK OF THE MYSTERY AND WONDER AND TERROR OF LIFE. Published on 15 January 1920 by **Boni & Liveright**, this collection of twenty philosophical essays (three in dramatic form) represents Dreiser's attempt to articulate in more explicit fashion the issues and themes he had been working out in his fiction. Dreiser had long been fascinated with a mechanistic explanation for human behavior, and he had found an outlet for his philosophical musings in his "Reflections" column in **Ev'ry Month** as well as in contemplative passages in his novels. Around 1915 he began to pursue his interest more directly by embarking on an ambitious program of reading in science and scientific philosophy, even applying for a study room in the New York Public Library. His 1916 book *Plays of the Natural and Supernatural* was his first attempt to articulate in dramatic form his conception of the ultimate inscrutability of life, its fascination and terror; *Hey Rub-a-Dub-Dub* extends that effort by gathering together six essays and one play that had previously appeared in periodicals, with the remaining eleven essays and two plays representing pieces that either had been rejected by magazines or were written expressly for the volume.

Reviewers panned the book. While an individual essay might receive praise, reviewers condemned the collection's repetition, clumsy expression, the commonplaceness of its ideas, and its author's egotism. The *New York Evening Post*, for example, described it as "written wretchedly and full of vain iterations like an old man's gossip before the fire" (rpt. in Salzman 371); the *Chicago News* ridiculed Dreiser's thinking: "[O]n many subjects he is as ill informed and illogical as many of his countrymen whom he ponders about" (rpt. in Salzman 378); and in a lengthy but balanced review, Francis Hackett, writing for the *New Republic*, concluded that "our leading novelist is intellectually in serious confusion, and needs a deeper philosophy than—hey rub-a-dub-dub" (rpt. in Salzman 390).

While H. L. Mencken thought the book appealed to "the defectively educated" (*D-M Letters* 2: 416), the volume remained close to Dreiser's heart. As he wrote to **Edward Smith**, "*Hey, Rub* contains the sub-stone of a new and better philosophy, something on which can be reared a sounder approach to life than is now voiced. Some one is going to come along who will get it and make it very clear" (*Letters* 1: 346). Twenty years later Dreiser himself attempted to be that "some one" as he extended and revised his philosophical thinking in what would posthumously appear as *Notes on Life*.

Contents: "Hey Rub-a-Dub-Dub," "Change," "Some Aspects of Our National Character," *The Dream*, "The American Financier," "The Toil of the Laborer," "Personality," "A Counsel to Perfection," "Neurotic America and the Sex Impulse," "Secrecy—

Its Value," "Ideals, Morals, and the Daily Newspaper," "Equation Inevitable," *Phantasmagoria*, "Ashtoreth," "The Reformer," "Marriage and Divorce," "More Democracy or Less? An Inquiry," "The Essential Tragedy of Life," "Life, Art, and America," *The Court of Progress*.

Further Reading

Martin, Ronald E. "Theodore Dreiser: At Home in the Universe of Force." *American Literature and the Universe of Force*. Durham, N.C.: Duke University Press, 1981. 215–55

Keith Newlin

HITCHCOCK, RIPLEY (1857–1918). Born in Fitchburg, Massachusetts, Hitchcock graduated from Harvard University in 1877. After flirting with a career in medicine he went into journalism, writing freelance for newspapers and magazines. In 1882 he became the art critic for the *New York Tribune* but left the paper in June 1890 for an editorial position with D. Appleton and Company. Twelve years later he moved to A. S. Barnes and then to **Harper & Brothers** in 1906, remaining with the firm until his death from heart failure on 4 May 1918. A talented, powerful, and well-respected editor, Hitchcock worked with such authors as Rudyard Kipling, Stephen Crane, Gilbert Parker, Zane Gray, Hamilton Wright Mabie, Woodrow Wilson, and John Jacob Astor. He was also an avid writer of American history, publishing four books on the subject between 1899 and 1909. However, he is best known and perhaps most proud of his work on Edward Noyes Westcott's *David Harum* (1898), which came to D. Appleton after having been rejected by numerous publishers. Hitchcock completely revised the novel, and it became an immediate bestseller. In the same vein he heavily edited Stephen Crane's *Maggie: A Girl of the Streets* and *The Red Badge of Courage*. Recently, he has come under some scrutiny for being too heavy-handed with *Red Badge*, having cut some 37,000 words. A restored edition has been published as a result.

On 24 February 1903 Hitchcock wrote to Dreiser, noting that he had been impressed with *Sister Carrie* and would like to consider his next novel for publication (*Letters* 1: 70). In 1911, Dreiser sent him a copy of his second novel, *Jennie Gerhardt*. Harper picked up the contract, and Hitchcock was put in charge of the editorial process. Hitchcock and his editorial team cut some 25,000 words from the manuscript. The correspondence between Dreiser and Hitchcock indicates that Dreiser was not happy with the changes. In an unpublished letter dated 24 July 1911, Hitchcock assures Dreiser that "your judgements and preferences have been given full consideration. . . . I have put back pages and pages of MS. in accordance with your request" (Dreiser Papers). In the end, 9,000 words were restored to the manuscript, and the novel was published on 24 October 1911. Although a number of Dreiser scholars believe that Hitchcock's editing did not hurt the novel, equally as many believe it did. James L. W. West III and even Dreiser's friend H. L. Mencken argue that the changes are so drastic that they render the novel virtually unrecognizable. In a 25 October 1911 letter to Harry Leon Wilson, for example, Mencken wrote that "[s]uch ruthless slashing is alarming . . . . The story [Dreiser] tells, reduced to a mere story is nothing" (*Letters of H. L. Mencken*, ed. Guy J. Forgue [New York: Knopf, 1961], 18–19). Hitchcock was probably most concerned about making the novel palatable to the largest possible audience, which would have been the religiously traditional and socially conservative middle class. In addition to removing profanity and references to alcohol, he cut

much of Dreiser's social commentary and made the story of the two protagonists, **Jennie Gerhardt** and **Lester Kane**, more sentimental. A restored edition was published by the University of Pennsylvania Press in 1992.

Further Reading

Malone, Dumas, ed. *Dictionary of American Biography*. Vol. 5. New York: Scribner, 1961.

West, James L. W. III. *American Authors and the Literary Market Place since 1900*. Philadelphia: University of Pennsylvania Press, 1988. 51–55.

———. "The Composition and Publication of *Jennie Gerhardt*." *Jennie Gerhardt*. Ed. James L. W. West III. Philadelphia: University of Pennsylvania Press, 1992. 420–60.

Annemarie Whaley

A HOOSIER HOLIDAY. The occasion for *A Hoosier Holiday* originated quite by chance in early August 1915 at "a modest evening reception" hosted by Dreiser in honor of **Edgar Lee Masters**, whose *Spoon River Anthology* had been published the previous April and had since attracted both critical and popular acclaim. At one point in the evening, **Franklin Booth**, a well-known illustrator and fellow Hoosier whom Dreiser had first met in 1904, when both worked on the *New York Daily News*, invited Dreiser on a road trip to their native state in his new touring auto, a sixty-horsepower Pathfinder. Largely motivated by a sentimental recollection of the romantic illusions and "delicious years" of his boyhood, as he remarks in his account of the trip, Dreiser had previously toyed with the notion of making a return journey to Indiana, which he had left twenty-eight years before at the age of sixteen, and "writing a book about it." Dreiser immediately accepted Booth's offer on condition that they tour various Indiana towns where Dreiser had grown up, and he proposed that Booth "sign on" as illustrator of Dreiser's intended travelogue. Booth readily agreed, and on 11 August, Dreiser, Booth, and a driver and all-purpose mechanic named "Speed" set out on a two-week, 2,000-mile journey from New York City to Indiana in which Dreiser revisited such towns as Warsaw, Terre Haute, Sullivan, Vermillion, Evansville, and Bloomington as well as Booth's own family home in Carmel, just outside Indianapolis.

Upon returning to New York, Dreiser immediately began drafting *A Hoosier Holiday*, eventually completing the first draft in Savannah, Georgia, in February 1916. Shortly thereafter, Dreiser sent the manuscript to his friend and avid supporter H. L. Mencken with the request that he edit a manuscript, which, compared to Dreiser's original projection of 50,000 words, now ran to approximately 250,000 words in length. Mencken, as cognizant of Dreiser's technical flaws as a writer as he was admiring of his outspoken radical views, was more than happy to comply, and *A Hoosier Holiday*, including thirty-one scenic sketches by Booth, was published in November 1916 in a handsomely executed volume by **John Lane** at a cost of three dollars a copy. Unfortunately, in view of Dreiser's nagging financial concerns at the time, sales were disappointing and totaled roughly 1,600 copies over the six months following its release, one-half the royalties from which went to Booth as illustrator.

Following its publication, *A Hoosier Holiday* was faulted in the critical press on several familiar and by now predictable charges: prolixity, tediousness of detail, and a frequent lack of technical control. Aside from style, other reviews condemned Dreiser's shameless egotism; his arrogant disavowal of all respectable social conventions; his indecorous airing of soiled family linen; his philosophical nihilism; his unorthodox views on monogamy,

religion, and morality; and, of course, the persistent critical bugaboo, his overwrought preoccupation with sex. On the other hand, more favorable reviews admired Dreiser's vivid, lyrical, even "poetic" descriptive passages; his moving and poignant recollection of his boyhood, especially his ardent devotion to his mother; his faithful representation of the American Midwest; his outspoken and fearless condemnation of sham and pretension; his alternately critical and affectionate estimate of America; and Dreiser's own engaging self-presentation. Particularly noteworthy is H. L. Mencken's substantial review "The Creed of a Novelist" in which the Baltimorean sage regards the volume, whatever the usual stylistic and technical flaws, as "the high tide of Dreiser's writing—that is, as sheer writing." Further, Mencken assigns special value to the book since "much more than a mere travel book, . . . it offers, and for the first time, a clear understanding of the fundamental faiths and ideas, and of the intellectual and spiritual background no less, of a man with whom the future historian of American literature will have to deal at no little length" (rpt. in *D-M Letters* 2: 765, 766).

A Hoosier Holiday faithfully records Dreiser's descriptive impressions and reflective reading of the American landscape from the novel vantage point of the early-twentieth-century auto tourist. Prior to Booth's invitation, Dreiser had intended at some point to return to Indiana by train, the more usual means of cross-country travel at the time. As it turns out, he hardly regrets his decision since one of the greatest "charms" of touring by auto is "the pleasure of stopping anywhere and proceeding at our leisure," compared to rail travel and "the necessity of riding over a fixed route, which once or twice seen, or ten times, as in my case, had already become an old story." Indeed, early on

Dreiser discovers that "I can think of nothing more suited to my temperament than automobiling." In fact, the "ever-changing panorama," "the anticipation of new fields and strange scenes," the leisurely, unrushed pace and hypnotic "tr-r-r-r-r" of the motor, and the sheer physical exhilaration of "spinning along the bank of some winding stream" largely explain Dreiser's rhapsodic enthusiasm for auto travel and, like so many vagabond adventurers before and after, "the magic" of the open road. Not unlike William Least Heat-Moon in *Blue Highways*, Dreiser's freelanced agenda and his preference for "the poor undernourished routes which the dull, imitative rabble shun" over the "so-called good roads" figure decisively in his choice of routes. Dreiser's predisposition to scenic distraction is frequently rewarded whether picnicking in a Watteau-like setting along the Passaic River, bathing in a swift-running roadside stream, walking the streets of small-town America, observing such architectural marvels as a massive railroad bridge outside Nicholsen, Pennsylvania (a "new wonder of the world"), or crossing "the border of boyland" from Ohio into Indiana.

On the other hand, Dreiser is often appalled by America's lack of taste and imagination in matters of cuisine, urban planning, and small-town architecture, leading to the despairing conclusion that "a land with such tendencies can scarcely be saved, unless it be by disaster. . . . We do not grasp the first principles of intellectual progress." Dreiser is equally discouraged by the stifling "ethical and social conventions" of the American middle class, the suggestibility of the mob, small-town provincialism, urban blight, political and financial scandals, the vulgarity of the nouveau riche, the staid routine and conformity of the typical American family, the tyranny of organized religion, and puritanical attitudes toward sex. Such criticism is frequently offset, however, by Dreiser's yea-saying affection for the American people, the magnitude and inclusiveness of which at times rival Whitman's and Sandburg's. Whatever its faults, America, in Dreiser's estimation, is "actually better than Europe" and the "average" American "a better or at least a more dynamic person than the average European at home." Dreiser is equally struck by America's naive belief in "impossible ideals," most notably, the assumption that man "is endowed by his creator with certain inalienable rights," including freedom and equality. Given his deterministic bent, Dreiser rejects such a belief since "freedom, equality . . . is certainly not an inalienable right" but, rather, "a stroke, almost, of unparalleled fortune." Yet with a characteristic shift from cynicism to apostrophic sentiment, Dreiser concludes, in addressing his "native land," "Dream on. Believe. Perhaps it is unwise, foolish, childlike, but dream anyhow. Disillusionment is destined to appear. You may vanish as have other great dreams, but even so, what a glorious, an imperishable memory!"

Aside from its value as a travelogue of America "off the beaten path" and Dreiser's euphoric endorsement of auto travel, *A Hoosier Holiday* provides any number of fascinating insights into American automotive history and American road travel through the early decades of the twentieth century. At one point, for example, Dreiser fondly comments upon the "modern" automotive service center as a social forum for "the transmission of information and a certain kind of railroad station gossip." Other personal observations, from a modern vantage point, assume a nostalgic charm, as when Dreiser notes the cost of fuel, which might range anywhere from $1.25 to $1.75 for a quart of oil and seven gallons of gasoline, or when

Speed ignores the 25 m.p.h. speed limit on the open road, accelerating, much to Dreiser's delight, to 45 m.p.h.

Throughout the course of his journey, Dreiser consults with various local chapters of the Automobile Club of America for maps, routes, and information about road conditions (a recurring preoccupation throughout the trip). Seven hundred miles into his journey, Dreiser reflects that "we could scarcely say that we had seen any bad roads." Shortly thereafter, he comments on the quality of a newly constructed red brick boulevard leading into Buffalo and projects, "If many such roads are to be built, and they stand the wear, America will have a road system unrivaled." Whatever such a sanguine view of the future, auto travel in 1916 was still fraught with a good deal of inconvenience and aggravation. Detours ("the invention of the devil himself") were an especially irritating nuisance and were necessitated, as Dreiser explains, by road repairs encumbered by an increase in auto traffic or the conversion of clay roads into macadam or vitrified brick. Blowouts were also a frequent inconvenience. A number of Dreiser's quibbles have proven more timely than he might have suspected. In addition to crazed motorcyclists and "road hogs," Dreiser regrets an increasing "passion for regulating street traffic" as well as occasional instances of traffic congestion, which at one point leads to his recognition of "the magnitude of the revolution which the automobile had effected." Such inconveniences, however, are finally far outweighed by the sheer pleasure of "cruising" (a term often employed by Speed) at one's own pace and taking note of the various roadside attractions en route, leading Dreiser to reflect at one point, "I could think of nothing better than motoring on and on."

Though directly accessible as a travelogue, *A Hoosier Holiday*, given Dreiser's discursive and digressive proclivities, is interlarded with a good deal of topical commentary, including his frequent philosophical reflections on the nature of the universe and one's place in it—what, according to the publisher's flyleaf, amounts to a "confession of faith" or, more aptly in Dreiser's case, the lack thereof. Such reflections, decidedly bleak and verging at times on nihilism, often qualify the high spirits and "holiday mood" induced by "automobiling" and the romance of the open road.

Perhaps the most memorable and certainly the most haunting feature of *A Hoosier Holiday* is the ultimate failure of Dreiser's return visit to Indiana as measured against his original expectations. Outside Paterson, New Jersey, Dreiser and his companions are eager to find "an ideal spot" to picnic, though such a prospect proves difficult, "for we were in a holiday mood and content with nothing less than perfection." The mood is dissipated upon actually entering Indiana. In contrast to his hopelessly naive and romantic expectations, he experiences a sense of disappointment in the "mighty alteration" of once-familiar settings and thus reflects that "it is all very well to dream of revisiting your native soil and finding at least traces, if no more, of your early world, but I tell you it is a painful and dismal business." Dreiser's initial disappointment soon gives way to "a sudden, overpowering, almost sickening depression at the lapse of time and all that had gone with it." Often, such depression leads to a profound melancholy as Dreiser realizes that "at least four sevenths of my allotted three score years and ten had gone," and he eventually concludes, "Drop you the curtain then on me. I do not care—I am very tired. Drop it and let me dream no more the endless wonders and delights that never, never, can be."

Dreiser's return is not entirely an occasion of unmitigated gloom. His stay in Carmel, for example, is enlivened by his interest in Franklin Booth's niece and various neighborhood girls, his conversation with Booth's father regarding local politics, the "lush, Egyptian land" of the Indiana countryside, and the charm of small Indiana towns such as Huntingberg and Jasper. Such instances, however, are merely fleeting distractions, and Dreiser's anticipated "hoosier holiday" proves in reality to be a thoroughly dispiriting experience.

Prior to his first trip out west, Sal Paradise, the narrator in Jack Kerouac's *On the Road* and an alias for Kerouac himself, imagines that "somewhere along the line the pearl would be handed to me." For Sal, the "pearl" is romantically, if vaguely, associated with the future and the mythical American West. For Dreiser, on the other hand, "the pearl" is situated in the past of his midwestern boyhood, and his return is motivated by a Wordsworthian attempt to recover the innocence and visionary imagination of youth, though eventually, like Wordsworth, he sadly discovers the daunting improbability of such a venture. Finally, then, for Dreiser, like so many other vagabond-adventurers, the process of the journey itself and a sense of imminent arrival rather than the achievement of some overidealized destination more accurately, if poignantly, provide the "stuff our dreams are made of." As such, the title of Dreiser's travelogue is ironically misleading since his "hoosier holiday" is essentially a "done deal" the moment he crosses the Ohio-Indiana state line and is eventually led to a painful recognition of his failed imagination and, far from the expected recovery of his youth, a sense of his own impending mortality.

Dreiser's biographer Richard Lingeman regards *A Hoosier Holiday* as "perhaps Dreiser's most accessible book, philosophical in parts and pessimistic in outlook, yet steeped in the sights, sounds, and talk of the Middle West and leavened by his rather ponderous humor" (Lingeman 1: 140). Surprisingly, in view of Lingeman's estimate, *A Hoosier Holiday* has attracted very little critical attention. Douglas Brinkley's Introduction to the reissue of *A Hoosier Holiday* by Indiana University Press (1998) is a notable exception. Describing Dreiser as "a modern-day Alexis de Toqueville careening through the Heartland at 40 m.p.h." (8), Brinkley credits Dreiser with "creating a "new genre"—the American "road book"—nearly forty years before the term became fashionable with the publication of Jack Kerouac's *On the Road*.

Aside from its distinction as the first "automobile road book" and its considerable charm as an American roadside travelogue, *A Hoosier Holiday* is no less noteworthy as a social and cultural critique of the American scene in the early twentieth century, as a manifesto of Dreiser's personal philosophy, as an illuminating foil to the beliefs and values that inform both Dreiser's previous and later works, as a revealing record of Dreiser's early history, as a running inventory of the author's aversions, passions, and myriad topical interests, and, not least, as a confessional register of Dreiser's fears, anxieties, and severe mood swings. As such, *A Hoosier Holiday*, which Douglas Brinkley pronounces "a classic literary contribution to our national canon" (10), clearly invites and warrants further study.

Further Reading

Brinkley, Douglas. Introduction to *A Hoosier Holiday*. Bloomington: Indiana University Press, 1997. 3–11.

Michael Wentworth

HOPKINS, L. A. (?–?), the husband of Dreiser's sister Emma. Hopkins and Emma were nearly seventeen years apart when they met in Chicago in 1886 while he was working as a clerk for a tavern named Chapin and Gore. At this time, the forty-year-old Hopkins was married and had an eighteen-year-old daughter. He stole $3,500 in cash and $200 worth of jewelry, which consisted of a gold watch and chain and a diamond ring and stud, from his employer's safe and fled to Montreal with Emma. When he realized the authorities were after him, he returned all but $800. He and Emma moved to New York, where they rented rooms to prostitutes. When Dreiser visited them in 1894, he learned many of the details about Hopkins that he would later use to develop the character of Hurstwood in *Sister Carrie*.

Dreiser exaggerated some of the details of Hopkins's life when he created Hurstwood because he was not then aware of all the events of Emma and Hopkins's relationship. In the novel, Hurstwood steals $10,000 and has two children, which resembles Hopkins's situation with the notable exception that, unlike Hurstwood, Hopkins and Emma together planned the theft. Like Hopkins, Hurstwood is competent in the affairs of the world, except that as a manager of a saloon, he holds a higher position than Hopkins did, and this is another contributing factor to Carrie's attraction. When Hopkins and Emma moved to New York, Hopkins became involved in politics, at one time holding an inspectorship in the Tammany administration until it ended when there was an investigation of police corruption by the Lexow Committee. Hurstwood follows a similar downward spiral when he becomes the co-owner of a local restaurant until it closes. Both then fall to a long span of unemployment. Like Hurstwood, Hopkins worked odd jobs here and there but was unable to find a career or permanent place. Eventually, with Dreiser's help, Emma left him, as Carrie does Hurstwood, and the two never communicated again.

Further Reading

Lingeman, Richard. *Theodore Dreiser: At the Gates of the City, 1871–1907*. New York: Putnam, 1986. 66–68, 138, 153–55.

Moers, Ellen. *Two Dreisers*. New York: Viking, 1969. 28–31.

Dana Stolte Koller

HOWELLS, WILLIAM DEAN (1837–1920). Novelist, poet, dramatist, influential critic, and editor of *Harper's Monthly*, Howells used his "Editor's Easy Chair" feature in that magazine to promote the work of the younger generation of realist writers, including Hamlin Garland, Stephen Crane, **Frank Norris**, Harold Frederic, Charles Chesnutt, and Charlotte Perkins Gilman. In his own fiction, Howells's **realism** harked to the more genteel tradition of the latter half of the nineteenth century, one in which careful observations of life, preferably, in Howells's view, drawing on the artist's own experience, were combined with political liberalism in a narrative suitable to perusal by young ladies. He admired the Russian realists Ivan Turgenev and Leo Tolstoy, rather than the grittier **naturalism** of his French contemporary Émile Zola. Despite this, his review of Frank Norris's Zola-influenced *McTeague* in 1899, besides being one of very few laudatory reviews, formulated a call for the American novel to break away from "provincial proprieties" the better to depict "the passions and motives of the savage world which underlies as well as environs civilization" (qtd. in Lingeman 1: 231).

In 1899, shortly after commencing to write *Sister Carrie*, Dreiser interviewed Howells for *Ainslee's*. "The Real Howells" appeared in March 1900 (rpt. in *SMA* 1). In it Dreiser lionizes Howells, lauding him pointedly for his efforts on behalf of unknown young writers. According to John W. Crowley, Dreiser first gave Howells, in this article, the lasting sobriquet "the Dean of American Letters" (72). If Dreiser was hoping that "the great literary philanthropist"—as he also named him—would do for *Sister Carrie* in 1900 what he had done for Crane's *Maggie: A Girl of the Streets* in 1893 and Norris's *McTeague* in 1899, Dreiser was mistaken. Poorly presented and underpublicized by **Doubleday**— *Sister Carrie* was not even listed in the publisher's catalog—the novel received few and mixed reviews, despite Frank Norris's generous efforts to place copies of the novel in the hands of over 100 reviewers. Howells's *Harper's* merely listed *Sister Carrie* among its "Books Received"; Howells himself wrote nothing. According to Dreiser, Howells later told him, simply, "I don't like *Sister Carrie*" (qtd. in Crowley 78). Later, in 1916, when the **New York Society for the Suppression of Vice** and allied organizations in various midwestern states worked to suppress *The "Genius"* and the Post Office was investigating charges of the novel's obscenity, Howells and his "Easy Chair" were conspicuously silent. Howells did not once mention Dreiser in any of his magazine writing between 1900 and 1920, nor did he review any of Dreiser's work. After 1902 Dreiser appears to have revised his views of Howells reciprocally.

Why Howells seems to have singled out Dreiser alone of his generation of writers to ignore is an open question. The simplest answer would be that *Sister Carrie* broke provincial proprieties to an extent greater than did *Maggie, McTeague,* or, for that matter, Zola's *Nana*—whose title characters had the grace to die, thus preserving a final taboo Howells was unwilling to see broken. Others have speculated that Dreiser himself alienated Howells, some arguing that Dreiser fabricated the interview for *Ainslee's* as well as an earlier interview in *Success*, "How He Climbed Fame's Ladder" (rpt. in *Art, Music, and Literature, 1897–1902*), earning Howells's lasting scorn. Whatever the cause, insofar as *Harper's Monthly* was a major arbiter of novelists' success during the Howells years, Howells's twenty-year silence concerning Dreiser had a significant impact on Dreiser's fortunes.

Further Reading

Crowley, John W. *The Dean of American Letters: The Late Career of William Dean Howells.* Amherst: University of Massachusetts Press, 1999.

Carol S. Loranger

HURSTWOOD, GEORGE W., is the suave and socially prominent saloon manager who becomes Carrie Meeber's second lover in *Sister Carrie*. In his late thirties at the novel's beginning, Hurstwood is ripe for a midlife crisis, for he finds only "selfish indifference" at home with his social-climbing wife and children and little real satisfaction at work. Seemingly a self-made man who has worked his way up from the lowly position of bartender to manager of Fitzgerald and Moy's, "a truly swell saloon," he is really only a front man whose job is to create "a good impression" by glad-handing the customers and projecting himself as "the picture of fastidious comfort" and moral probity. Considerable experience with "that under-world where grovel the beast-men of society" has made him cynical about love, yet he remains "something of a romanticist" who, "under a stress of desire," expresses himself with considerable "poetic" force. He is always onstage, and, often "seeing what he wanted to see," he deludes both Carrie and himself about the depth of his love. Fittingly, he casts off from his secure, "respectable home anchorage" only under the "fascinating make-believe" of the theater, when he confuses Carrie with the virtuous heroine she portrays in a popular melodrama put on by Drouet's Elks lodge.

The tendency for self-delusion is an aspect of Hurstwood's essentially escapist personality. Even in his home life, he has tended "to walk away from the impossible thing," simply to "ignore" problems. By the time his wife, **Julia**, discovers the affair and sics her lawyers on him, what started as an ego-pleasing dalliance has become the source of an intense conflict he cannot ignore. Torn by powerful attracting and repelling forces—the radiant, ingenuous Carrie and the cold, calculating Julia—Hurstwood is incapable of considering the "true ethics of the situation" when chance confronts him with his employers' unlocked safe. Trembling "in the balance between duty and desire," he springs into action only when the lock springs shut, perhaps by force of his own unconscious willing. "I must get out of this," he thinks instinctively as he walks or runs away from the impossible thing his life has become.

In the New York half of the novel, Hurstwood is the central figure in a naturalistic plot of decline, the victim of external and internal forces whose "sagging to the grave side," when juxtaposed against Carrie's rise to Broadway stardom, constitutes the novel's chiasmic structure. His adopted name "Wheeler" is significant, for he is trapped in a cycle of regressive return to the past. In Chicago, he has fantasized

himself the "old Hurstwood, who was neither married nor fixed in a solid position for life." Brooding over lost glory, as well as natural aging, freezes his will and weakens his body. As the day approaches for the dissolution of his partnership in the Warren Street saloon, he immerses himself in a different past, the "Lethean waters" of events reported in the daily newspapers, which he reads in his rocking chair at home or in the womblike comfort of warm hotel lobbies.

The name Wheeler also suggests that he is bound to fortune's wheel. Like Melville's crazy captain and Miller's dreaming salesman, he is among the more notable efforts by American writers to give a common person tragic stature. Strutting and posturing among his cronies on the night of Carrie's acting debut, Hurstwood has achieved "greatness in a way, small as it was"; once her performance makes her seem all-desirable, his commonplace philandering becomes a "tragedy of affection," his hazy plan for running off with her a quest for the transcendent: "He would promise anything, everything, and trust to fortune to disentangle him. He would make a try for Paradise, whatever might be the result." His passion is more than a foolish delusion; it is "deeper than mere desire . . . a flowering out of feelings which had been withering in dry and almost barren soil for many years." His theft and flight are thus motivated by what is good in him; in Aristotelian terms, they are a "great mistake" and a sign of his flawed humanity, not an expression of depravity.

As his loss of vitality repels Carrie first out of his bed and then out of his life, shame accelerates his fatal slide toward beggary and suicide; he blows money he cannot spare on dinners, booze, and poker "to hide his own shame from himself" by acting the role once more as "the old Hurstwood." Yet shame also saves him from finally degenerating into a "brute," the image of which haunted the middle-class imagination at the turn of the nineteenth century. Even in his most humiliating moment, when the doorman at Carrie's theater pushes him down in the snow, his "vague sense of shame" and angry assertion that Carrie "owes me something to eat" signify his resistance to a dehumanizing and unjust doom. On his last night, he takes his place among the "dumb brutes" waiting in the snow outside the flophouse; nevertheless, his suicide, unlike the theft that has turned his fortunes around, follows from the "one distinct mental decision" that makes him one of us. While the act itself involves no tragic recognition, its ritual quality gives it an element of human significance. "I'm not anything," he has told the clerk when signing up as a scab during the Brooklyn streetcar strike. Yet we never quite lose our sense that he is something, one like ourselves whose surrender to "the kindness which is night" purges us of pity and fear.

Further Reading

Howard, June. *Form and History in American Literary Naturalism*. Chapel Hill: University of North Carolina Press, 1985. 99–103.

Morelli-White, Nan. " 'When Waters Engulf Us We Reach for a Star': Psychomachic Struggle in Dreiser's *Sister Carrie*." *Dreiser Studies* 23.2 (1992): 13–27.

Pizer, Donald. "Dreiser and the Naturalistic Drama of Consciousness." *Journal of Narrative Technique* 21.2 (1991): 202–11.

———. *The Novels of Theodore Dreiser: A Critical Study*. Minneapolis: University of Minnesota Press, 1976. 72–81.

Tavernier-Courbin, Jacqueline. "Hurstwood Achieved: A Study of Dreiser's Reluctant Art." *Dreiser Newsletter* 9.2 (1978): 1–16.

Zaluda, Scott. "Hurstwood and Tammany, 'an all-controlling power.' " *Dreiser Studies* 23.2 (1992): 3–12.

Zender, Karl F. "Walking Away from the Impossible Thing: Identity and Denial in *Sister Carrie*." *Studies in the Novel* 30.1 (1998): 63–76.

Stephen C. Brennan

HURSTWOOD, JULIA, is the "cold, self-centered" wife of George Hurstwood in *Sister Carrie*. Ironically, before his own "tragedy of affection," George fears that Julia's good looks and vanity might bring a tragic scandal. However, just as he finds his own "life" in his saloon, she lives vicariously through her children. She believes her own chance to "shine" is over and so hopes "to rise a little" through the social successes of her seventeen-year-old daughter Jessica and twenty-year-old son George Jr., the one a high school girl bent on joining the clique of wealthy schoolmates, the other a bon vivant making his way up in the real estate business. If there is "no love lost" between husband and wife, there has been for some years "no great feeling of dissatisfaction" either, but a marriage that "ran along by force of habit, by force of conventional opinion" must eventually become dry "tinder, easily lighted and destroyed." When Carrie becomes "a new light" shining on George's "horizon" and Julia merely an "older luminary" fading in the west, the conflagration soon follows.

Julia's vindictiveness and legalistic cast of mind make her function as Nemesis, the Greek goddess of retributive justice, in George's tragic fall. Even before the advent of Carrie, she has begun to keep score. At some time in the past, George has gone off to Philadelphia for "a good time" with his male friends—"on business" he has told her—and she in retaliation has started spending more on clothes and entertainment for herself. Deeply jealous of the husband she no longer loves, she is "too calculating" to "fly into a passion." Her modus operandi is to study the situation and gather the evidence "until her power might be commensurate with her desire for revenge." Reminiscent of the sentimental melodramas the novel usually mocks, Julia has had her husband put all his property in her name. Once she drives him out of the house, she vows to "make her word *law* in the future," not caring whether he returns home or not since "[t]he household would move along much more pleasantly without him." From this point on, she becomes an invisible force, the law of her word communicating itself to Hurstwood in letters from her and her lawyers demanding money and threatening a suit for divorce and alimony, letters that drive Hurstwood to his desperate theft and flight.

In some of the novel's most melodramatic scenes, Julia proves herself victor in a conflict that is at once a Darwinian struggle, an act of divine retribution, and a military battle. Her increasing "indifference and independence" and her demands for money to "exhibit" her daughter and "parade among her acquaintances and the common throng " begin to irritate George and make Carrie seem even more attractive. When an unusually unreasonable demand for money raises George's hackles, she decides he is a "brute" and determines to get "more lady-like treatment or she would know why." But as the catastrophe approaches, Julia becomes less and less ladylike. Hurstwood's general "airy grace" and attention to his clothes leave her "sniffing change, as animals do danger, afar off." Reports of George's riding with another woman or attending a play with an unknown couple start forming a pattern. "The clear proof of one overt deed," the narrator announces ominously, "was the cold breath needed to convert the lowering clouds of suspicion into a rain of wrath." When such proof comes, she waits

to unleash the fury of a woman scorned, "the rudimentary muscles of savagery fixing the hard lines of her mouth" and "the shining sword of her wrath" hanging "weakly suspended by a thread of thought." When she finally springs, openly accusing him of philandering, this "pythoness in humour" proves herself the fittest, overwhelming his defenses and becoming the "master" of the household. Despite George's impulse to "strangle her," the threat of legal action is the "magnificent play" that wins the day: "Hurstwood fell back beaten."

Julia appears again briefly at novel's end in one of the vignettes that intensify the pathos of Hurstwood's last moments. While George waits in line with other derelicts outside the Bowery flophouse where he will die, she is speeding toward New York in a comfortable Pullman and smiling at the sight of Jessica, "a supercilious beauty," and Jessica's new husband, "a rich young man—one whose financial state had borne her personal inspection." This scene is part of Dreiser's savage satire of American **gender** ideology, which proclaimed the wife to be the family's primary spiritual and cultural influence. Earlier, the narrator has bemoaned the fact that Hurstwood's North Side residence lacks the "beneficent influence" of a "lovely home atmosphere," one "calculated to make strong and just the natures cradled and nourished within it." Julia's calculated, selfish behavior brings far different consequences. As Hurstwood utters "weakly" his final "What's the use?" we recognize the irony of the American myth of womanhood, as well as the tragic injustice of things.

Stephen C. Brennan

HYMAN, ELAINE. *See* Markham, Kirah.

I

"I FIND THE REAL AMERICAN TRAG-EDY." Published serially in *Mystery Magazine* from February to June 1935, "I Find the Real American Tragedy" describes some of the philosophical and historical sources of *An American Tragedy*. Dreiser originally wrote this essay, as well as a number of newspaper articles, in response to the trial of Robert Allen Edwards in Wilkes-Barre, Pennsylvania. Edwards was accused of killing his pregnant girlfriend, Freda McKechnie, in order to marry another woman. The parallels with *An American Tragedy* were immediately noted by the press, and Dreiser was invited to comment on the crime. He went to Wilkes-Barre, interviewed some of the people involved, and observed the trial. In "I Find the Real American Tragedy," Dreiser offers his psychological interpretation of the crime, arguing that Edwards was not *anti*-social but rather *pro*-social because he was doing only what society forced him to do. Like Clyde Griffiths, Edwards was driven to succeed, but not given the means to do so.

In the introductory section of the article, Dreiser establishes the basis for his argument by describing a larger pattern of similar crimes caused by America's obsession with wealth. Although he claims that *An American Tragedy* grew out of this ob-served pattern, in reality most of the actual murders he cites bear little resemblance to the crime in the novel. Whereas Dreiser refers to them to add a sense of historical verifiability to his theory of social and economic motivation for murder, this very motivation is lacking from the real crimes he lists. The crime in *An American Tragedy* is truly the creative product of the author's philosophy and experience, not simply a reflection of historical cases. In fact, "I Find the Real American Tragedy" reveals that Dreiser depended less on historical events and factual details than many people have argued. Although perhaps not in the way Dreiser had intended, this article helps us better understand the composition of *An American Tragedy*. It also offers one of the clearest statements of Dreiser's ideas about society, marriage, ambition, and murder.

See also Molineux, Roland B.; Gillette, Chester; "The Rake."

Further Reading

Plank, Kathryn M. "Dreiser's Real American Tragedy." *Papers on Language and Literature* 27 (1991): 268–87.

Salzman, Jack, ed. " 'I Find the Real American Tragedy' by Theodore Dreiser." *Resources for American Literary Study* 2 (1972): 3–74.

Kathryn M. Plank

"IDA HAUCHAWOUT." First appearing in *Century Magazine* in July 1923, "Ida Hauchawout" is believed to have originated as Dreiser's response to visiting a friend's farm in Westminster, Maryland, during the summer of 1917 (Nostwich 403). The sketch later appeared as one of fifteen semifictional portraits of women in *A Gallery of Women*. Some reviewers called the work honest, sympathetic, and authoritative; but others, including H. L. Mencken, equated the portraits with "pathetic silliness" (rpt. in Salzman 579), and "Ida Hauchawout" was summarily viewed as a profile of a **Jennie Gerhardt**-type of obedient, sacrificing, pure, selfless nurturer. Diametrically opposed to several of the career-aspiring, cosmopolitan women highlighted in *Gallery*—"Ellen Adams Wrynn," "Olive Brand," "Esther Norn," "Emanuela"—Ida assumes no agency save for her ability to physically provide and labor for others. She is virtually asexual, though she becomes pregnant in her brief marriage, and her passive acceptance of her lot in life—she works as laundress, canner, and housekeeper before marrying unfavorably—underscores the futility and waste the narrator sees as her life.

The narrator-author opens his reminiscence of Ida with a connection to Nature, abundance, and fertility, a land of "milk and honey." Ida is introduced as a twenty-eight-year-old single woman whose chances for marriage have all but passed her by. Caring for her laborer-farmer father, Ida devotes herself entirely to his well-being, but when he dies, she marries an ignorant "ne'er-do-well," Henry Widdle, who offers no assistance to the maintenance of their farm and household. Ida works "just as she did for her father," having "secured" a man and "mad[e] a god of him." She dutifully performs all tasks until, during her final trimester of pregnancy, she totally collapses under the strain of intensive labor and both she and the infant die. As Yoshinobu Hakutani notes, the "ever-present parasitic way of life led by her father" is carried over to the husband's and obliterates this woman whose "function in life is to be a wife and mother, [whose] dream of success is survival" (16). Survival is not possible; she is literally worked to death. The sketch does not conclude with her death, however; Widdle approaches the narrator for guidance with the legalities of his assuming sole ownership of Ida's "capital" and seeks a response to a poem he composed to honor Ida. The narrator listens patiently, but Widdle's doggerel stuns: "Could a mind be so obtuse as to believe that this was not ridiculous?" The poem evokes a meditation on the ironies and complexities of life, with all its attendant "mystery, and the suffering and the bitterness" that yet transpire in a "golden day, an enormous treasure in itself."

The reviewer who writes, "[F]ancy what a professor of sociology could make out of 'Ida Hauchawout!' " (rpt. in Salzman 577), directs our attention to several key themes that emerge in Dreiser's oeuvre: father–daughter relationships; marriage and sex; women and labor; the domestic realm; the power of language and silence; **naturalism** and determinism; the restorative power of nature; death and sacrifice. A sociological reading of "Ida Hauchawout" might inquire what "free victim," the oxymoron that seems to capture Ida's essence, means in Dreiser's contemporary cultural context with a focus on the ideology of **gender** and class.

Further Reading

Hakutani, Yoshinobu. "The Dream of Success in Dreiser's *A Gallery of Women*." *Zeitschrift für Anglistik und Amerikanistik* 27 (1979): 236–46.

Nostwich, T. D. Notes to "Ida Hauchawout." *Fulfilment and Other Tales of Women and Men.* Santa Rosa, Calif.: Black Sparrow, 1992. 403.

Kathy Frederickson

"IDEALS, MORALS, AND THE DAILY NEWSPAPER." This "slight diatribe" on the hypocrisy of the American press appears in *Hey Rub-a-Dub-Dub.* As with other essays written for, or reprinted in, this volume, Dreiser's scathing critique of an aspect of American culture seems at times more prescient than dated. Dreiser finds a complementary balance between the political and financial self-interest of newspapers and their publishers and the "moderate" intellects of Americans who "slavishly" follow them. Mendacity and pandering to powerful and moneyed interests, Dreiser argues, have been the hallmark of newspapers since their first appearance in the eighteenth century. In the United States, he continues, they have "successfully clouded issue after issue since America began"—from currency, slavery, trusts and tariffs, to the just-ended world war. Driven solely by circulation, yet promising to report news accurately and to offer readers both moral and social leadership, newspapers cravenly do neither. Dreiser concludes by calling for stricter judicial supervision of the press and advising that readers not give newspapers "even a moment's serious consideration."

Carol S. Loranger

IN THE DARK. First published in *Smart Set* in January 1915, this one-act dramatic objectification of a guilty conscience was included in *Plays of the Natural and Supernatural.* During a quarrel, John Repiso, an Italian fruit peddler, murders his brother. As he seeks to conceal the dismembered body, he is pursued by various spirits, who function as Greek furies publicizing his guilt. A chorus of howling dogs rouse the nodding police to action, who begin to investigate while being guided to the murderer by a cloud of spirits who call out, "A murder! A murder! Awake! Awake!"

Dreiser's chief interest in this murder melodrama is the disembodied wraith of the dead man who lingers near the corpse, repeating at intervals, "Am I alive? Am I dead? I must stay near. I do not want to die!" While the wraith resists death, Repiso is pursued by the incarnation of his guilty conscience, a "ghost with vile red eyes" who trails behind calling for "Blood! More blood!" While *Laughing Gas* and *The Blue Sphere* (written at the same time as *In the Dark*) suggest that life lacks purpose and that morality is an arbitrarily imposed construct, *In the Dark* reveals Dreiser wavering between that position, to which his philosophy commits him, and his own desire that life have purpose. Repiso is eventually caught and punished, and conventional justice prevails. In the terminology of "equation inevitable," Dreiser's adaptation of **Spencer's** notion that opposing forces tend to attain a balance, the spirits guiding the police to Repiso's victim have restored the disrupted moral order to equilibrium. The two conflicting forces—the desire to escape and the need for justice—have been balanced. The spirits disappear, the wraith accepts his mortality, and the ghost with red eyes remains, his call for "Blood! More blood!" having reestablished universal harmony.

See also "Equation Inevitable."

Keith Newlin

INDIANA was Theodore Dreiser's state of birth and his residence for almost sixteen years. On 27 August 1871, he was born in Terre Haute at a site that was probably 525 South Ninth Street, though that birthplace has been neither commemorated nor officially identified by the city. The following month, on the day after Theodore was christened at St. Benedict's Catholic Church, the Dreisers finalized the purchase of a home on the southwest corner of Twelfth and Walnut, where for over six years the family of ultimately twelve lived a meager and somewhat chaotic existence. In the summer of 1878, they were forced to sell that home and move into a succession of cheaper rentals. Increasingly over those years, John Paul Dreiser's religious zealotry clashed with his children's lust for life and his wife Sarah's permissive nature, until this tension, coupled with the mounting financial pressures, tore the family unit apart.

During the summer of 1879, Sarah took the three youngest children, Claire, Theodore, and Edward, thirty miles south to Vincennes, where they were taken in by a former Terre Haute acquaintance and were allowed to live in an apartment over the local firehouse. To appease their father, the children were enrolled in a parochial school. The firehouse proved to be an exciting environment, but its moral tone so distressed Sarah that their Vincennes residence lasted little more than five weeks. Then they were again on the move, beginning a questing lifestyle that would set the tone for Dreiser's entire life. As he later wrote to **Richard Duffy**, "[I]t would be more truthful if my early life were ascribed not so much to one place as to the whole state [of Indiana]. All my life I have been a traveler" (qtd. in Lingeman 1: 61).

Not wishing to return to Terre Haute, Sarah moved her small brood to Sullivan, where John Paul had ten years earlier prospered as the manager of a woolen mill. This time, however, Sarah was dependent on the generosity of former friends and the contributions of working family members. She herself washed clothes for affluent families and took in boarders employed at the local mine. Theodore responded positively to the rural

setting but felt the shame of delivering laundry and being suspended from the parochial school for having no shoes during the colder months. By the winter of 1881, the mine had closed, plunging Sarah and her children once again to the subsistence level.

At this point, they were rescued by Theodore's oldest brother, John Paul Jr., a blackface comedian and burgeoning songwriter known professionally as Paul Dresser. He was at that time the headliner at the Evansville Opera House and the paramour of local madam Annie Brace (alias Sallie Walker, later immortalized as "My Gal Sal"). In the spring of 1882, Paul moved Sarah with her three youngest to Evansville, where they occupied a new half-story brick cottage on the edge of the city, 1415 East Franklin. For two years, they lived comfortably through the largesse of Paul and Sallie. The Catholic school remained the bane of Theodore's existence, and he sensed the gossip generated by Paul's relationship with Sallie Walker, yet the Evansville stay was pleasurable. He enjoyed the ease of living, particularly after the Sullivan privations, and basked in the reflected glory of Paul's celebrity. The end of this halcyon period came in 1884, when Paul and Sallie separated. Paul left town with a minstrel troupe, and Sarah, bereft of financial support, moved the children to Chicago, where her oldest daughters Mame, Emma, and Theresa were living.

When the Chicago venture failed quickly, Sarah returned to Indiana, this time to Warsaw, near which she owned a five-acre plot of land left to her by her father. She hoped someday to live on it but in the meantime settled with the children into a run-down, twelve-room home known locally as "Thralls mansion." Theodore later identified Warsaw as the city in which he was "raised." There he first attended public school and was intellectually stimulated by teachers May Calvert and Mildred Fielding. There also that he endured the throes of puberty. In Warsaw his sister Sylvia gave birth to an illegitimate child, eroding the family's already tenuous social standing. In the summer of 1887, depressed by the family's fall from grace and desirous of making his way in the world, Theodore, not yet sixteen and just through his freshman year, departed again for Chicago.

After two years in Chicago, Dreiser had made little progress toward making his fortune. He was working at a dead-end job with a hardware firm and was wracked by a lung disease. Finding him in this situation, Mildred Fielding, his former Warsaw teacher, offered to underwrite a year at **Indiana University** in Bloomington, where he was admitted as a special student. So he returned to the state of his birth for the academic year 1889–1890. By scholarly standards, it was an undistinguished year, for his grades were average at best, but according to his later assessments, he left Bloomington in the spring of 1890 with greater confidence and determination. His life as a Hoosier had ended. Except for a visit in 1915 to collect material for *A Hoosier Holiday* and occasional stops later in life, mostly on speaking tours, he never returned.

The experiences of childhood—the poverty, the nomadic existence, the social exclusion, the dysfunctional family— clearly left their marks on Dreiser's writing, but apart from autobiographical works like *Dawn* and *A Hoosier Holiday*, Indiana settings and themes had a minimal role. The possible exception would be *Jennie Gerhardt*, in which, though set in Columbus, Ohio, the Dreisers' hand-to-mouth struggles in Terre Haute were visited upon the Gerhardt family. Dreiser was never a "Hoosier author" in the sense that

contemporaries such as Booth Tarkington, Jean Stratton Porter, and James Whitcomb Riley were. Nor was he embraced by his home state as they were. His naturalistic emphases, his liberal politics, and his final flirtation with communism alienated many Indiana readers and robbed him of an honored place among the state's writers. As W. A. Swanberg wrote, regarding Paul Dresser's love affair with Indiana, specifically Terre Haute, "The far greater brother is forgotten" (330–31).

Richard W. Dowell

INDIANA UNIVERSITY. Dreiser's alma mater for the academic year 1889–1890, located in Bloomington, Indiana. In 1887, he had left Warsaw High School at the end of his freshman year and set out for Chicago, where he hoped to prosper. Two years later, however, his health, both physical and emotional, was precarious, and he was working in a hardware store at a job he detested for five dollars a week. At that point, one of his Warsaw teachers, Mildred Fielding, by then principal of a Chicago school, came to his rescue. As his teacher, she had recognized his ability and lamented his lack of opportunity; now that she had the wherewithal, she offered to underwrite at least one year at Indiana University, paying his tuition and providing him fifty dollars a month for expenses. She also called upon her friendship with President David Starr Jordan to get him admitted as a "special student."

After his struggles in Chicago, Dreiser found the vigor of the university stimulating and its rural setting appealing, offering him, as he noted in *Dawn*, a "surcease from all my recent woes." He also made numerous friends, joined a spelunking club, and was elected secretary of Philomatheon, a literary society. Yet he felt humiliated by his poverty, his homelessness, and his almost pathological shyness. He received no fraternity bids and proved himself unequal to the potentially amorous trysts occasionally set up by his more worldly acquaintances. As a result, his stay at Indiana was largely a time of social and sexual frustration.

Academically, he fared little better. As a "Special Student," he could have had considerable flexibility in his course selections, but instead he enrolled in courses prescribed for degree students, suggesting that his plans at the outset may have been more long-range than he later implied. He took three trimesters of Latin, two of geometry, and one each of Anglo-Saxon, philology, algebra, and "the Study of Words." Unfortunately, his lack of preparation and a confessed sense of boredom in the classroom compromised his achievement and resulted in grades that were fair to poor. Only in "the Study of Words" did he receive a "Good."

Though Mildred Fielding was apparently willing to continue his study at the university, Dreiser decided to leave at the end of his freshman year and return to Chicago to find work in a real estate office. He was impatient to succeed in life and feared that his stay at Indiana University was too directionless and time-consuming. In retrospect, however, he changed his mind, realizing that he had left with more confidence, more courage, and a greater sense of purpose. His time at the university, he later wrote in *A Hoosier Holiday*, was "one of the most vitalizing years of my life."

Further Reading

Katz, Joseph. "Theodore Dreiser at Indiana University." *Notes and Queries* 13 (March 1966): 100–101.

Richard W. Dowell

INTERNATIONAL THEODORE DREISER SOCIETY. *See* Dreiser Society, International Theodore.

IROKI, Dreiser's estate near Mt. Kisco, New York, was named for the Japanese word for "spirit of beauty." In May 1927 Dreiser invested part of the proceeds from *An American Tragedy* in a thirty-seven-acre parcel of land, which included a hunting lodge constructed of white birch logs, on top of a hill overlooking Croton Lake. Since the original cabin was small, Dreiser relegated it to a guesthouse and embarked on an ambitious program of expansion. He began by building a garage out of fieldstone, then had the roof torn off and the building enlarged to two stories, topped by a steep-pitched roof of heavy, barkencrusted shingles, surrounded by verandas on three sides. He enlarged a small pond into a rock-lined swimming pond, with two sets of stone steps descending into it. Nearby he added two smaller log cabins with thatched roofs. Assisted in the planning and construction by several of his artist friends, among them Ralph Fabri, Wharton Esherick, Hubert Davis, Jerome Blum, and Henry Varnum Poor, the resulting buildings were a hodgepodge of whimsical designs and shapes. Esherick, one of the leaders of the American arts and crafts movement, designed two Prussian blue gates decorated with the word "Iroki." Beginning in 1936, Dreiser began to seek a buyer for the estate since his expenses were mounting; he leased the main house and settled into one of the cabins, which did not have plumbing or a telephone. On 13 May 1938 the roof of the main building caught fire from a chimney spark, and Dreiser rebuilt the main cabin. In 1944 his attorney found a buyer willing to pay $15,000 for the house and half of the land.

Further Reading

Swanberg, W. A. *Dreiser*. New York: Scribner, 1965. 357–58, 377–78.

Tjader, Marguerite. *Theodore Dreiser, A New Dimension*. Norwalk, Conn: Silvermine, 1965. 26–30, 68–70.

Keith Newlin

J

JAEGER, CLARA. *See* Clark, Clara.

JARMUTH, EDITH DELONG (?–1919). The model for "Olive Brand" in *A Gallery of Women*, Jarmuth became a friend of Dreiser's after she left her husband in Colorado and moved to New York City, where she adopted a bohemian lifestyle. The two met in 1912 at one of the gatherings she often held for the artists and political radicals of **Greenwich Village** and acquaintances at Columbia University. Her letters to Dreiser plus his comments about her in his diary support his statement in "Olive Brand" that "she introduced me, and no doubt others, to interesting people and thoughts, events and books." Among these introductions, the most important were to **Freud's** *Three Contributions to the Theory of Sex* and to **A. A. Brill**, a psychiatrist and translator of Freud's works into English, for they led to the significant influence of Freud's theories on Dreiser's work beginning in 1918.

At one of her social events, Dreiser also met **Edward H. Smith**, who became one of his close friends and supporters. Identified as Jethro in "Olive Brand," Smith fell in love with Edith and helped her get a divorce. When the two were married in the fall of 1918, Dreiser served as best man at the wedding. Tragically, Edith died unexpectedly nine months later, a victim of the influenza epidemic of 1919.

Further Reading

Rusch, Frederic E. "Dreiser's Introduction to Freudianism." *Dreiser Studies* 18.1 (1987): 34–38.

Frederic E. Rusch

JENNIE GERHARDT. Dreiser began composing his second novel on 6 January 1901, only two months after the publication of *Sister Carrie*. He was still very much in motion, sure that he could produce another novel quickly and anxious to get on with his literary career. After his difficulties with **Frank Doubleday**, Dreiser knew that he would have to change publishers, so with approximately half of his new novel composed, he approached George P. Brett, head of the American branch of Macmillan. Dreiser wanted a contract that would offer publication of his second novel, to be followed by a reissue of *Sister Carrie*. Brett was not prepared to meet that offer, so Dreiser contacted **Ripley Hitchcock**, an editor at D. Appleton & Co. Though Hitchcock had admired *Sister Carrie*, he shied away from Dreiser's proposed second novel, probably because Appleton's was in financial straits, and Hitchcock thought Dreiser might produce another "immoral" and unpublishable book. Dreiser therefore signed a contract with a smaller house, an up-and-coming firm called J. F. Taylor & Co., which agreed to publish the work in progress (which Dreiser was calling "The Transgressor") and to reissue *Sister Carrie* after the new novel had finished its run.

While under contract to J. F. Taylor, Dreiser revised much of the material that he had already written. He had come to believe that his depiction of the heroine, whose name was **Jennie Gerhardt**, was not sympathetic enough and that her liaison with **Lester Kane** was drawn with strokes that were too blunt. This early version of the novel, never published, survives in two forms in Dreiser's papers at the University of Pennsylvania. It is indeed straightforward about Jennie's attitude toward her sexual charms: she sees them (as girls of the working classes had to do) as assets for barter. Certainly, she is not romantic about Lester Kane's attraction to her. Lester, for his part, is more of a sensualist and a rake in the unrevised text, with little of the philosophical skepticism and independence of mind that make him attractive in the revised version. Dreiser managed to alter these characterizations while under contract to J. F. Taylor, but he was unable to push his manuscript beyond the midway point.

By the summer of 1902, Dreiser was beginning to suffer from the **neurasthenia**, or "nerve sickness," that would afflict him for the next several years. His illness, quite severe, brought all work on "The Transgressor" to a halt and landed him in the Olympia Sanitarium near White Plains, New York, a rehabilitation center for alcoholics and depressives. Dreiser recovered his mental health, reentered the world of **journalism**, and, in the years that followed, rose to the editorship of several

magazines in the **Butterick** empire. He did not, however, again take up the novel in progress until the fall of 1910. At that point he made two deliberate changes in his life, resigning from his Butterick position and separating from his wife, Sara. He set himself to finishing his novel, and by early January 1911 he had completed a full draft of the narrative, now entitled *Jennie Gerhardt*. Its heroine was based on his sister Mary Frances Dreiser, called "Mame" within the family. Mame's youthful misadventures, which included giving birth to a stillborn child, and her long liaison with Austin Brennan, a high-living businessman, provide the patterns for much of what happens to Jennie in Dreiser's narrative.

In the novel, Jennie becomes the kept woman of Lester Kane, a wealthy Cleveland businessman, and lives with him off and on for some thirteen years, during most of which time she keeps secret the existence of Vesta, her out-of-wedlock child by another man—Senator Brander, for whom Jennie and her mother did laundry when Jennie was a teenager. Eventually, Lester learns of Vesta; at first he is angry, but he quickly forgives Jennie. He and she form a household with Vesta and with Jennie's aging father in the Hyde Park section of Chicago. This unconventional arrangement is carried on much against the wishes of Lester's family, however, and he is eventually compelled by the provisions of his father's will to give up his living arrangements with Jennie. She goes into retirement, supported by money from Lester, and he marries Letty Gerald, a wealthy socialite. Lester reenters the business world and cuts a large figure for a time, but he is no happier as a member of the class to which he was born and dies at the age of fifty-nine, with Jennie at his bedside.

The central tension in *Jennie Gerhardt* is between Lester's pessimistic, skeptical determinism and Jennie's mystical faith in the wholeness of nature. The two characters mirror two facets of Dreiser's own nature, and the friction between their approaches to the living of life generates much of the interest in the story. *Jennie Gerhardt* can also be seen as a powerful novel of manners, with Lester attempting to rebel against the expectations of his class but finally being brought back into line by social pressures. There is no good choice for Lester; marrying Jennie will not solve his problems, and leaving her only increases his melancholia. He and Jennie represent the opposite sides of a dialectic that is being posed, but not resolved, in Dreiser's novel.

Dreiser sent his finished typescript to Ripley Hitchcock, who was now an editor at **Harper & Brothers**. Hitchcock wanted to publish *Jennie Gerhardt*, but he and the other Harper's executives were nervous about issuing a novel in which the heroine gave birth to an illegitimate child by one man and then lived openly, without benefit of matrimony, with another. Harper's offered Dreiser a contract, but its provisions reflect their misgivings: the agreement stipulates that Hitchcock and his subeditors will revise the novel before typesetting and that if Dreiser is dissatisfied with the results, he is free to take his book elsewhere. Hitchcock and his staff did indeed revise the typescript—so thoroughly, in fact, that the entire text had to be retyped. This revision changed the book radically, taking away its sexual charge and muting its criticisms of organized **religion** and of wealthy socialites. Harper's editors also removed much of the material that presented Jennie's point of view, thus throwing the novel out of balance. Lester's pessimism and inertia now dominate the narrative; he seems to be little more than a

textbook naturalist, convinced that all human effort is futile and ultimately absurd. Without Jennie's quasi-religious mysticism to balance his outlook, the novel seems philosophically to be his territory alone. Dreiser was alarmed by Hitchcock's alterations, though not enough to seek another publisher. He did protest and was able to have some of the cut material restored. The book published by Harper's in the fall of 1911, however, was very different from the one originally submitted to the firm.

Jennie Gerhardt drew generally good reviews and sold a little under 14,000 copies, earning Dreiser something over $2,500 in royalties. He was confident enough now to proceed with his *Trilogy of Desire* and to publish the first volume, entitled *The Financier*, with Harper's in 1912. Eventually his balkiness as an author and Hitchcock's wariness of the subject matter of his novels brought the connection with Harper's to an end.

The text of *Jennie* that Hitchcock published in 1911 is a good example of a negotiated or domesticated text, one that reflects the cultural forces of its time. It is a collaborative work of art, composed originally by Dreiser but "socialized" by the Harper's editors into a narrative acceptable to the notions of conventional morality then dominant in American publishing. The 1992 **Pennsylvania Dreiser Edition** of *Jennie Gerhardt* is an effort to undo this damage and to present the novel that Dreiser would have published in 1911, had he not come under pressure from Harper's to change his narrative. The Pennsylvania version is an eclectic text, constructed from extant manuscripts and typescripts that preserve the novel as Dreiser submitted it to Harper's. Both editions merit study: the Harper's edition presents the novel that brought Dreiser back into the public eye in 1911, and the Pennsylvania Dreiser Edition provides the text that he meant originally to publish. The two versions should be read against each other for what they show about Dreiser's original intentions and about what the publishing climate of 1911 would allow.

See also Adaptations, Film.

Further Reading

Epstein, Joseph. "A Great Good Girl: Dreiser's *Jennie Gerhardt.*" *New Criterion* (June 1993): 14–20.

Marcus, Mordecai. "Loneliness, Death, and Fulfillment in *Jennie Gerhardt.*" *Studies in American Fiction* 7 (1979): 61–73.

Schwartz, Carol A. "*Jennie Gerhardt*: Fairy Tale as Social Criticism." *American Literary Realism* 19.2 (1987): 16–29.

West, James L. W., III, ed. *Dreiser's* Jennie Gerhardt: *New Essays on the Restored Text.* Philadelphia: University of Pennsylvania Press, 1995.

———. Introduction to *Jennie Gerhardt.* New York: Penguin, 1994. vii–xvii.

Whaley, Annemarie Koning. "Obscuring the Home: Textual Editing and Dreiser's *Jennie Gerhardt.*" *Theodore Dreiser and American Culture: New Readings.* Ed. Yoshinobu Hakutani. Newark: University of Delaware Press, 2000. 161–76.

James L. W. West III

JOHN LANE COMPANY. After **Harper & Brothers**, which had already printed 8,500 sets of sheets of *The Titan*, refused to publish the novel because its sexual content was too explicit and because Dreiser's depiction of **Berenice Fleming** was potentially libelous, Dreiser's friend and sometime agent **William Lengel** offered a copy of the *Titan* manuscript to **J. Jefferson Jones**, manager of the New York branch of the English publisher John Lane. After Jones received a favorable opinion from **Frederic Chapman**, an English reader for Lane, Jones offered to publish *The Titan* and thereby became Dreiser's publisher.

In October 1915 Lane published *The "Genius,"* Dreiser's most autobiographical novel, to considerable controversy. Upon learning from Lane that, despite the controversy, only 6,577 copies had sold to the end of 1915, Dreiser's suspicions were aroused. Ever distrustful of publishers since the *Sister Carrie* debacle, Dreiser suspected that his publisher was cheating him and quickly canvassed local bookstores, even enlisting a reluctant H. L. Mencken to check on sales in Baltimore. He was relieved to learn that Jones was reputed to be an honest man, since he was reluctant to change publishers yet again. However, trouble descended on 25 July 1916, when **John Sumner**, of the **New York Society for the Prevention of Vice**, went to the offices of John Lane and threatened to sue the company for distributing lewd and profane material unless it ceased distributing *The "Genius"* and recalled all copies from bookstores. Rather than face prosecution, Jones acceded to Sumner's request, pending a court decision. Jones did not wish to jeopardize the firm's profit line with a court battle, which inflamed Dreiser and exacerbated the tensions between author and publisher. To resolve the issue, in February 1917, Dreiser and his attorneys, with the cooperation of Jones, brought a "friendly suit" against the John Lane Company, alleging breach of contract. In July 1918 the New York Appellate Court dismissed the case on the grounds that "since no prosecution had been brought, the question of obscenity was not before them" (Lingeman 2: 170).

In 1917, Dreiser met **Horace Liveright**, who impressed Dreiser with his vision of a more muscular promotion of books. He therefore decided to relinquish his ties to Lane and sign on with **Boni & Liveright**, the firm Liveright had formed with Albert Boni in 1916. In many ways the antithesis of the cautious Jones, Liveright was eager to take over all of Dreiser's books, promising to double sales, publish anything Dreiser submitted, vigorously promote his works, and fight any attacks by the censors (Lingeman 2: 163). Dreiser would squabble for years with the John Lane Company over repayment for advances against *The Bulwark*, which Lane had announced for publication in 1917. In 1922, Lane closed its New York branch and was taken over by Dodd, Mead & Company, which now owned the rights to Dreiser's work under Lane. In December 1922 Liveright arranged to pay off Dreiser's Lane debts and buy the rights, plates, and stock of his Lane and Harper's books, thus becoming Dreiser's sole publisher.

From 1914 to 1916, John Lane published Dreiser's *The Titan* (22 May 1914), *The "Genius"* (1 October 1915), *Plays of the Natural and Supernatural* (18 February 1916), and *A Hoosier Holiday* (17 November 1916).

Dana Stolte Koller

JONES, J. JEFFERSON (1880–1941), vice-president and managing director of the New York branch of the British **John Lane Company**, Dreiser's fifth publisher. The most remarkable phase of the Jones–Dreiser relationship centers on publication and suppression of the novel *The "Genius."* The relationship began when Jones took over the publication of *The Titan* after Harper's, which had already printed 8,500 sets of sheets, refused to publish the novel on grounds that the hero's seductions were made too explicit and **Berenice Fleming's** similarity to **Emilie Grigsby** was potentially libelous. An admirer of Dreiser's brand of naturalism, Jones wired Dreiser in 1914, "PROUD TO PUBLISH TITAN."

On 25 July 1916, **John S. Sumner**, **Anthony Comstock's** successor as executive secretary of the **New York Society for the Suppression of Vice**, threatened Lane with

criminal proceedings, alleging that *The "Genius"* violated Section 1141 of Article 106 of the New York Penal Laws of 1909. When he delivered to Jones the list of allegations—seventeen profane and seventy-five lewd passages—Sumner demanded that Jones delete the passages or discontinue publication and destroy the plates. Unwilling to risk adverse publicity, a fine, or jail time by resisting the society, Jones withdrew the novel from sale. After a subsequent visit from postal inspectors who cited the penalties for sending obscene material through the mail, Jones asked bookstores across the country to return unsold copies and refused sale even to Dreiser. Thus, Sumner's intimidation of Jones constituted suppression of *The "Genius"* without due process. However, the novel remained available in many public and academic libraries across the nation.

To secure support of the **Authors' League of America**, Jones arranged a meeting for Dreiser and himself with the league's executive committee on 24 August 1916. Jones sought their help to resume publication, explaining that the narrowness of Sumner's test for obscenity could prevent sale of both contemporary literature and classics. In October, the league sought signatures to a leaflet titled "A Protest against the Suppression of Theodore Dreiser's *The 'Genius,'* " a collaboration among Jones, Dreiser, H. L. Mencken, and **John Cowper Powys**. By the end of 1916, Mencken, Harold Hersey, Jones, and others had elicited more than 500 signatures and nearly 800 when the venture ended in 1917, including those of **Sherwood Anderson**, Arnold Bennett, Willa Cather, Robert Frost, **Sinclair Lewis**, Harriet Monroe, Edwin Arlington Robinson, and H. G. Wells.

Dreiser asked Lane to fund a legal defense of his novel, but Jones's strategy was controlled by the firm's cautious London directors. Dreiser himself engaged John B. Stanchfield, a trial attorney, who took the case pro bono. U.S. attorney H. Snowden Marshall informed Stanchfield that *The "Genius"* did not violate the law. The Solicitor of the Post Office Department concurred. In January 1917, Jones and Stanchfield attorneys agreed that, to save Lane from breaking its publishing contract, Dreiser would seek a "friendly suit" in the Appellate Division of the New York Supreme Court on the ground that *The "Genius"* violated no law. The case finally came to court in May 1918. Ten weeks later, the five judges threw out the case on a technicality: no criminal charge had been brought against either Dreiser or Lane since the publisher voluntarily withdrew the novel from publication, with no subsequent sale by either author or publisher. Moreover, the court declared that it lacked jurisdiction to render advisory opinions regarding a book's propriety. In August 1918, **Boni & Liveright** became Dreiser's publishers, negotiating with Jones for Lane's four Dreiser books.

Lane doubled its original price for *The "Genius"* to $5,000, a sum too large for the new firm to spend to reissue a three-year-old novel. By 1923, the Jones chapter of Dreiser's publishing history closed when Boni & Liveright gained rights to *The Titan, The "Genius,"* and *A Hoosier Holiday*.

Further Reading

Lingeman, Richard. *Theodore Dreiser: An American Journey, 1908–1945.* New York: Putnam, 1990. 95–118, 130–53, 170–81.

Louis J. Oldani

JOURNALISM, MAGAZINE, 1897–1902.

Between his resignation from the editorship of *Ev'ry Month* in 1897 and his essay "Christmas in the Tenements" in *Harper's Weekly* in December 1902, Dreiser wrote well over 125 pieces, mostly freelance articles, that appeared in various popular magazines, some 78 of which have been reprinted in three volumes edited by Yoshinobu Hakutani. This massive body of writing, unparalleled by that of any other writer, casts significant light not only upon Dreiser the novelist but more importantly upon the turn of the century, an exciting era in the development of American civilization. As a young individual who was to become a major American writer of the new century, Dreiser made original, innovative judgments about the status of art, music, and literature, as well as about American life in general.

The largest part of this writing—about thirty essays—concerned art and artists. By the end of the nineteenth century the battle against prudery in American art had gained momentum. As Dreiser's essay on this issue shows ("The Art of MacMonnies and Morgan," *Metropolitan*, February 1898: 143–51), a genuinely original work like Frederick MacMonnies's *Bacchante and Child*, often rejected for public display, was seriously considered for the chief monument at the Boston Public Library. As the nation became a more open society with urbanized and formally educated people, art came to reflect more of the society's diversity and freedom. As Dreiser's magazine articles strongly indicate, influences from society cannot create art but they can change it, help it grow—or stifle it. This interplay between personality, society, and history characterized a principal development of American visual art of this period.

As Dreiser noted, foreign influences were often strong and the borrowing great, yet characteristics of its native culture and society proved to be the major determinants in forming American art. At the end of the nineteenth century and well into the new one, America was building skyscrapers in earnest while modernists like Alfred Mauer and Max Weber had yet to struggle against academic domination, but the direction in art was clearly signaled: the modernist movement in America was helped by the radical Robert Henri school and the pioneer leadership of Alfred Stieglitz. Dreiser was inspired by Stieglitz and **William Louis Sonntag**: both advocated a closer and more harmonious relationship between art and technology than did their predecessors.

In this period Dreiser was also fascinated by American music. The traditional choral singing of the East was presented in music festivals in the West, and a rich opera tradition in Boston and New York was accompanied by fine orchestras. Eventually any top performer, as Dreiser noted in "The Story of a Song-Queen's Triumph," could compete with any artist in the world. In New York, where the era of gaudy concerts was coming to an end, the fine arts were brought to everyone. In "His Life Given Up to Music" (*Success*, 4 February 1899: 167–68), Dreiser recounts how Theodore Thomas—"the greatest living American leader"—struggled to build a broad base of support for classical music but finally succeeded.

Despite a severe economic depression, the music of the 1890s reflected the joyful sentiments of the nation. The Spanish-American War of 1898, short though it was, left in its wake many popular songs. The legendary "A Hot Time in the Old Town" was said to be sung by Theodore Roosevelt's Rough Riders during their attack on San Juan Hill. The Civil War song "When Johnny Comes Marching Home" resurfaced during this war and became popular again during World War I. Other songs of the decade are still remembered, including "Good-bye Dolly Gray" and "Just Break the News to Mother." **"On the Banks of the Wabash,"** the official state

song of Indiana, was originally composed by Dreiser's brother Paul Dresser with part of its lyrics written by Dreiser when he was editor of *Ev'ry Month*. The continued popularity of such songs indicates how widely music, regardless of its type, came to be shared by the masses at the end of the century.

Dreiser may not have had an ear or a taste for serious music, but no other writer so vividly captured the exuberant spirits of the people involved in the music world of the 1890s as did Dreiser in "Whence the Song." From the perspective of a novelist-to-be, Dreiser envisioned in this piece the age of democracy that was beginning to manifest itself. In music this new way of thinking was reflected in the serious attention the public and critics were paying to women. Further, composers and performers should not be viewed as types and patterns considered embodiments of tradition and convention. As Dreiser emphasized, they should be viewed as individual artists deserving of recognition. The acknowledgment of the rich music native to the country continued this focus on unique compositions and profoundly affected the development of American music in the twentieth century.

While Dreiser vigorously pursued art and music criticism in these years, he did not present literary criticism with equal enthusiasm. Some of his essays on literary figures suggest that Dreiser was more impressed by a nostalgic writer like Robert Louis Stevenson and a mystic poet of the older generation like Bayard Taylor than he was by a contemporary analytical critic like Israel Zangwill, who, Dreiser felt, often smacked of egotism. Another eminent writer and critic Dreiser interviewed was **William Dean Howells**, whom he described in "The Real Howells" (*Ainslee's*, March 1900: 137–42) as "one of the noblemen of literature"—honest, sincere, and generous. Such laudatory remarks sound incongruous today since it has become legend that the two men never liked each other. Dreiser later confided to **Dorothy Dudley** that Howells's novels failed to give him a sense of American life. Dreiser, however, called Howells a "literary Columbus" for discovering Stephen Crane and Abraham Cahan. Howells's support for Hamlin Garland and **Frank Norris** is well known, but Howells was blind to *Sister Carrie* and never tried to appreciate Dreiser's work.

In his articles about literary figures, Dreiser typically commented upon two related themes in his own fiction: disillusionment with city life and longing for the beauty of Nature. When he turned to contemporary authors, he searched for some transcendental reality beyond material appearances. He was surprised and at the same time gratified to discover that the commercial environment of Wall Street had left no mark on Edmund Clarence Stedman's creative work. The work and career of the travel writer Bayard Taylor, who is forgotten today, provided Dreiser with quiet reflections and warm sentiments. The most significant point of Dreiser's tribute, published as "The Haunts of Bayard Taylor" (*Munsey's*, January 1898: 594–601), comes toward the end of the essay, where Dreiser infuses the scene with an Emersonian, mystic quality that one finds from time to time in his own fiction: "The pale moonlight flooded all the ground, the leaves gained voices from the wind, and over them all brooded the poetic mind, wondering, awed, and yearning." His expression of sympathy was extended not only to humans and animals but also to plants. Discussing the importance of studying plant roots scientifically, Dreiser explains how a microscope could trace down their "infinitesimal . . . threads as light as gossamer, almost—they did not

naturally end." "In that unseen part," he envisioned, "there was a friendly union between the life of the plant and the life of the earth, and the latter had given some of itself to course up the hair-like root and become a part of the plant." Based on new research on the relationship of weeds to the soil, Dreiser even pleaded for the preservation of some weeds.

Such sensitive treatments of plant and animal life in the light of human progress were characteristic of Dreiser the transcendentalist. In the late 1890s his interest in this philosophy led to his reading of Emerson's and Thoreau's writings and to his interview with John Burroughs. In one of his two magazine articles about this contemporary philosopher, "John Burroughs in His Mountain Hut" (*New Voice*, 19 August 1899: 7, 13), Dreiser asked him to define success in life and to compare his own success with that of Jay Gould, Burroughs's boyhood friend. Burroughs remarked, "I always looked upon achievement in life as being more of a mental than a material matter." About writing, Burroughs told Dreiser that the most important element is not one's desire to describe objects like birds and trees but the "sympathy and love" one feels toward them. "Whenever the subject recurs to me," Burroughs stressed, "it must awaken a warm, personal response. My confidence that I ought to write comes from the attraction which some subjects exercise over me. The work is pleasure and the result gives pleasure."

Impressed by Dreiser's abilities to brighten up the contemporary scene, **Orison Swett Marden**, the editor of *Success*, asked Dreiser to interview successful men in business, industry, science, art, music, and literature, including such legendary figures as Thomas Edison, Andrew Carnegie, and Marshall Field. Thirty of these interviews appeared in the pages of *Suc-*

cess, from January 1898 to June 1900, and they can be grouped into two categories: one based on the traditional success story and the other modified, or perhaps reversed, by the principle of humanitarianism. Dreiser believed that the type of material success advocated by the celebrated public figures in the 1890s gave rise to beauty, which money and leisure could buy and enjoy in America. For him this ideal cannot and should not be sneered at, much less denied, because material success is only a resilient springboard to the composite goal of an individual's happiness on earth and in American life in particular.

Dreiser swiftly conducted these interviews, and the monotonous similarity of these articles stemmed from the identical questions he asked of the men he interviewed: "What quality in you was most essential to your success?" "Were you rich or poor before starting a career?" "Were reading and schooling necessary for your success?" "What is your philosophy of happiness?" To stock questions there were stock answers. All the men, of course, said that hard work led to their success. To this they added such traits as "perseverance" and "consistency" in their work; they all stressed "honesty" and "integrity" as the moral principles rewarded by success. Except for Edison, they did not believe in "overwork." All were convinced that the fewer advantages one had in his youth, the greater chances for success one could hope for. Even a man from a relatively distinguished family such as Joseph H. Choate, a leading lawyer and later an ambassador, said: "I never met a great man who was born rich" ("The Real Choate," *Ainslee's,* April 1899: 324–33). They all advocated thrift, saving, and investment as necessary means to accumulate wealth. They also stated that education and book learning had little influence on their careers. Given

his own experience, Dreiser dared not dispute their point.

During his years as a journalist, Dreiser was genuinely concerned about contemporary social issues. The "Gay" Nineties derived its term from the flourishing lifestyles of the city, but the spirit of the decade suffered from the worst economic depression of the century. Although the problem first started with the dropping of prices in agricultural products and the wayward railroad expansion in the West, the depression dealt city residents the hardest blow. Strikers were everywhere— and sometimes became violent, as demonstrated by the riot at Carnegie Steel's Homestead plant in Pittsburgh in 1892, which Dreiser witnessed as a newspaper reporter. The strikers at the Brooklyn streetcar lines in 1896 also hit the newspaper headlines: using this scene, Dreiser describes Hurstwood's ordeal as a scab in *Sister Carrie.* Between 1894 and 1898 the number of the unemployed tripled. At the worst stage of the depression in the mid-1890s, 20 percent of labor force in the entire nation was out of work. The wide gulf dividing the rich and the poor became a literary theme—so vividly depicted in Stephen Crane's "An Experiment in Misery" with the soaring commercial buildings and the tattered tramps roaming the Bowery, or in Dreiser's "Curious Shifts of the Poor," in cold winter with the life of gaiety on Broadway and the long bread lines a few blocks away.

In his magazine pieces Dreiser referred occasionally to such a political site as Tammany Hall, but he was more seriously concerned with the stories of human interest than with those of economic, social, and political events. Dreiser's articles on tenement living in New York, such as "The Transmigration of the Sweat Shop" (*Puritan,* July 1900: 498–502) and "The Tenement Toilers," present less ferocity and more hope than those of Jacob Riis a decade earlier. Dreiser's interest in human stories is also shown by his article on a boys' reformatory, "Little Clubmen of the Tenements" (*Puritan*, February 1900: 665–72), in which he proudly reported that there were among the public at the end of the century a wide acceptance of, and appreciation for, such movements.

Such an article as "Little Clubmen of the Tenements" demonstrates Dreiser's acumen and insight, unsurpassed by those of any other journalist of the period, in analyzing human conditions. This article served Dreiser as a counterargument to Stephen Crane's "An Experiment in Misery." Dreiser's experiment shows that, however poorly such children were brought up in the tenements, they could still acquire good manners and attitudes once they were placed in the club. In the past, some of the boys had lived with alcoholic parents; others had been orphans, motherless and fatherless, and had been turned out to roam the streets at night. Scars of environment on the children were deep, yet Dreiser learned they could be healed. "Delaware's Blue Laws" (*Ainslee's*, February 1901: 53–57) was also a penetrating study of reform. Interviewing those familiar with the public exhibition of corporal punishment, Dreiser reached a consensus that such punishment failed to deter crime. He asked an African American waiter, "Don't you think it stops these people from doing the same thing over again?" The man replied, "No, suh, not any mo' than jail would. They is men here that has been whipped an' whipped until they is so hard they don't care no more foh it than foh a flea. It juss makes 'm wuss, I think." Even a jailer who does the whipping told Dreiser: "It is all wrong. . . . Because it degrades the man that does the whipping, and if it degrades him, I know it must have much the same effect upon

those who see it." Dreiser was appalled that while black offenders had no chance to lessen their punishment, the white offenders who had a high standing in their community and could afford to offer their possessions could leave the state to escape this public punishment. He concluded his study: "It is the man with conscience and feeling upon whom this relic of an older order of civilization weighs unjustly. The hardened criminal whom it is supposed to reach does not suffer at all, and is not corrected thereby."

In short, Dreiser's early magazine journalism shows that whether he was commenting on artists, musicians, writers, or topical events, his attitude resulted from his lifelong conviction, stated in *Ev'ry Month* in 1896, that "the surest guide is a true and responsive heart." Many of his magazine articles addressing human problems reveal Dreiser's conviction that a human being was not necessarily a victim of his or her conditions; it should therefore always be possible for the individual as well as for society to ameliorate those conditions. Sympathy and compassion indisputably color his fiction, but his magazine work bears witness to the fact that Dreiser was not the simple commiserator that Edward D. McDonald portrayed him to be in a June 1928 *Bookman* caricature entitled "Dreiser before *Sister Carrie*": in tears, devouring a tragic story in the newspaper. His compassionate appreciation of all stories of human interest cannot be doubted, but Dreiser before *Sister Carrie* also acquired a capacity for detachment and objectivity. Rarely do his magazine essays display passionate outbursts. In effect, Dreiser was a literary realist and modernist in the best sense of the words. These magazine pieces suggest that, although he was eager to learn from literary and philosophical sources, he trusted his own vision and portrayed life based on his own experience.

Further Reading

Hakutani, Yoshinobu, ed. *Art, Music, and Literature, 1897–1902.* Urbana: University of Illinois Press, 2001.

———. *Selected Magazine Articles of Theodore Dreiser: Life and Art in the American 1890s.* 2 vols. Rutherford, N.J.: Fairleigh Dickinson University Press, 1985, 1987.

Moers, Ellen. "Magazines and Pictures." *Two Dreisers.* New York: Viking, 1969. 32–42.

Yoshinobu Hakutani

JOURNALISM, NEWSPAPER, 1892–1895. From June 1892 until March 1895 Theodore Dreiser was a full-time newspaper reporter, at the time a demanding and formative apprenticeship for a professional writer. As the whaling ship was for Melville's Ishmael, so the newspaper was for Dreiser his Harvard College and his Yale.

In form and content, the newspaper of today is much the same as it was in the 1890s. The two kinds of newspaper writing are straight news and features. Intended to inform and give an account of news as it occurs, straight news is either "hard" or "soft," terms describing not the kind of news but rather the form and style. Primarily news of timely significance, hard news is an objective and concise account of the who, where, when, what, and how of a current event. Soft news, on the other hand, is news strong in "human interest," a term for what in *Newspaper Days* Dreiser calls "romance." Usually neither concise nor objective, human interest establishes emotional contact with the reader. Both hard news and soft news are accounts of events as they occur, that is, current events. All straight news is timely.

Although it, too, may refer to current events, a feature story is intended to entertain or to supplement straight news. For his newspapers except the *New York World*, Dreiser was a valued and successful writer of soft news and features; as he wrote in *Newspaper Days*, he "could write reams on any topic." Although Dreiser's editors distinguished between feature stories and the "soft" version of straight news, for today's reader of Dreiser's journalism the essential distinction, timeliness, dissolves when the news is over.

In the late nineteenth century, the United States grew explosively; between 1870 and 1890 the population increased 63 percent, industrial production from $3.3 million to $11.4 million, and newspaper circulation 222 percent. By 1893 the two newspapers Dreiser worked for in St. Louis had tripled their circulation in five years, the *Globe-Democrat* from 32,000 to 90,000 and the *Republic* from 27,000 to 100,000. In Chicago in 1892 Dreiser sensed this energy and wanted to write about its scenes and join a newspaper, expecting to win fame and fortune, a naive, but not impossible, goal; Chicago newspaper writers Finley Peter Dunne, George Ade, and Eugene Field were media celebrities. The newspaper was the only mass medium for information and entertainment; very few could afford to attend the theater regularly; and movies, radio, and television did not exist. In *Sister Carrie* **Sven Hanson**, Carrie's brother-in-law, a cleaner of railroad refrigerator cars, silently reads the newspaper between supper and bedtime; today he would watch television. Like the other industries, the big-city newspaper was not limited to urban consumers and had something for everyone; Sunday editions of the *Globe-Democrat* and the *Republic* had agriculture sections; puzzles, jokes, and juvenile stories for children; fashion and cooking sections; and serialized fiction by H. Rider Haggard, Émile Zola, Robert Louis Stevenson, and others.

To satisfy this mass audience, the newspapers needed people who could write competently, continuously, and, if necessary, voluminously on a variety of topics. They attracted to their staffs men (and a few women) with literary ambitions and interests; even Wallace Stevens worked briefly in his youth for a New York newspaper. Several of Dreiser's colleagues in Chicago and St. Louis had written unpublished fiction, and Dreiser hoped to write for the theater, but with few exceptions, literary ambition was burned out rather than nurtured by reporting. When Dreiser was at the *Globe-Democrat* in 1893, the reporters' workweek was seventy-seven hours, 12:30 P.M. to 11:30 P.M., seven days a week. In addition, many of these mostly young men were possessed by a ferocious cynicism. Dreiser's copy editor at the *Chicago Daily Globe*, John Maxwell, told him (as recounted in *Newspaper Days*), "Life is a God-damned, stinking, treacherous game, and nine hundred and ninety-nine men out of a thousand are bastards." Writing on daily assignments, reporters could not attempt in print an intelligible explanation of what they witnessed and described day after day. In competition with each other, the newspapers demanded daily and exciting news that would be forgotten the next day. Dreiser, for example, was so involved in daily reporting in St. Louis that he was unaware of a serious economic depression, the Panic of 1893. Bored by the editorials about the depression and ignoring the visible facts of unemployment and business failures, he urged two of his brothers to quit their Chicago jobs and to join him in St. Louis to find better ones. Ironically, it did not matter that he had ignored the editorials, for they repeatedly insisted that the economy was improving, or soon would be.

The cynicism of the newspaper business was frequently accompanied by physical self-destructiveness. Joseph B. McCullagh, the highly regarded *Globe-Democrat* managing editor who in five years had helped triple his paper's circulation, in 1897 jumped to his death from his bedroom window. One of Dreiser's *Globe-Democrat* colleagues, Bob Hazard, after marrying and becoming a successful Washington correspondent, shot himself in the head. Another *Globe-Democrat* friend, thoroughly drunk, swallowed a dozen morphine pills before Dreiser and others could get him to the hospital. Alcoholism seems to have been the newspaperman's occupational disease. In his own *Newspaper Days*, Dreiser's friend H. L. Mencken sardonically observed that when he was a newspaperman in the 1900s, "there was only one reporter south of the Mason & Dixon line who did not drink at all, and he was considered insane. In New York, so far as I could make out, there was not even one" (New York: Knopf, 1941, 181).

Other than a few days reporting in March and April 1894 for the *Toledo Blade* and then the *Cleveland Leader*, Dreiser reported for five newspapers: the *Chicago Daily Globe* (June–November 1892), the *St. Louis Globe-Democrat* (November 1892–April 1893), the *St. Louis Republic* (May 1893–March 1894), the *Pittsburg Dispatch* (April–November 1894), and the *New York World* (December 1894–March 1895). The *Chicago Daily Globe* was owned and published by one Michael Cassius McDonald, an out-of-office Democratic politician hostile to the city's Republican administration; it went into receivership and out of business in September 1893. The copy editor, John Maxwell, was the first to recognize Dreiser's literary gifts and was the first of his acquaintances to articulate total contempt toward any idealistic view of human behavior. The city editor, John T. McEnnis, also recognized Dreiser's talent and helped advance his career by recommending him to Joseph B. McCullagh, the well-known and highly regarded managing editor of the *St. Louis Globe-Democrat* where McEnnis had once worked before alcoholism wrecked his career. Once at the *Globe-Democrat*, St. Louis's best-capitalized, best-equipped, and Republican-allied newspaper, Dreiser was assigned several substantial feature stories as well as regular news stories. As a reward for his lengthy and detailed stories of a horrific train wreck and subsequent oil car explosion that killed and maimed many spectators, McCullagh gave Dreiser his request for the job of drama critic, which allowed him to attend the theaters for free. Because of conflicting reporting assignments, one evening Dreiser skipped attendance and wrote reviews based on advance press releases of plays that had not appeared; railroad washouts had kept the theater companies from reaching St. Louis. Humiliated and convinced he would be fired, he quit the *Globe-Democrat* and then in need of work was hired at a lower salary by a *Globe-Democrat* rival, the *St. Louis Republic*.

Even without a famous managing editor like McCullagh and without the money and equipment of the *Globe-Democrat*, the Democrat-allied *Republic* was Dreiser's most important (and longest) newspaper experience. The city editor, H. B. Wandell, another fan of Dreiser's talents, piled on long assignment after assignment, advising the young man to imitate Dickens, Hugo, Balzac, and Zola. Dreiser had done some substantial feature stories for the *Globe-Democrat*; under Wandell his work increased in amount and scope. For the *Chicago Daily Globe* he had done a series exposing a petty street-corner confidence game supposedly protected by the city administration; Wandell assigned him a more demanding crusade exposing a fake and successful spiritualist, Jules Wallace,

who was conducting large public meetings and private séances; Dreiser's series drove Wallace out of St. Louis. In light of his somber fiction about human defeat, his most un-Dreiserian assignment was a series of broadly facetious comic stories intended to build up interest in a *Republic*-sponsored baseball game between two local fraternal organizations, the Owls and the Elks, benefiting the newspaper's annual charity, free riverboat excursions for slum children. (Among themselves, newspapermen referred to such charities as "publicity stunts.") Judged the only reporter able to do these, Dreiser, in the summer of 1893, spent an hour or two each day dashing them off.

Besides these, he did an 8,000-word portrait of the St. Louis poorhouse superintendent Joseph Gallagher, a stalwart opponent of the dirty politics trying to oust him; and, most important, a 10,000-word description of the camp of unskilled laborers preparing material in the winter for the construction in the coming spring of the St. Louis water supply extension, "A Cosmopolitan Camp" (*St. Louis Republic*, 17 December 1893: 30–31). A year before for the *Globe-Democrat* he had done a 7,500-word description of the project itself, "Water Works Extension" (15 January 1893: 31). This article portrays three separate and distinct communities, native-born white, African American, and Italian immigrant, bound by the human imperatives of law and work within a single society, the construction camp. The vivid portraiture omits much of the lengthy and somewhat empty, space-filling dialogue between interviewer and subject characteristic of some of his earlier feature stories. Here, too, there is an un-Dreiserian comedy, in this case not the broad (and dated) farce of the baseball series but rather the sophisticated irony of the narrative voice, its elaborate fancifulness incongruous with the lowly and clownish characters described. In an attempted wife-stealing in the African American community, the jealous husband is "that African," and the camp policeman, going to the wife-stealer's shanty, "repaired to the Washington domicile."

For the *Toledo Blade* in March 1894 Dreiser did four stories on a strike against a local, privately owned streetcar company, the source of Chapter 41, "The Strike," in *Sister Carrie*, Hurstwood's experience as a scab driver in Brooklyn. Dreiser jokes that when a company superintendent tried to drive a streetcar and break the strike, "an artful and sagacious citizen greeted him with the first missile of the day. It was an egg, and lingered in large gobs about the brim of his black slouch hat." The parallels and contrasts between newspaper story and novel are striking. Both the *Blade* scab driver and *Carrie*'s Hurstwood abandon their cars and flee. The *Blade* scab, "dripping with rotten eggs," is the butt of slapstick comedy; the terrified Hurstwood, on the other hand, disintegrates under the violent hostility—he flees when grazed by a bullet, not an egg—which becomes, he confesses to himself, "too much for me," and completely defeated, trudges home "in a blinding snowstorm."

Quitting the *Republic* in late winter 1894, restless and convinced his hard work there was a dead end, and despite the paper's offer of an editorial position to a twenty-two-year-old with only eighteen months' newspaper experience, Dreiser pooled his small resources with another reporter to buy and run an Ohio country newspaper, only to find that what they could afford would not support them. Wandering then to Toledo, he was hired for a few days' work by **Arthur Henry**, the city editor of the *Toledo Blade*. (Immediately becoming friends and staying in

touch, Dreiser—now married—and Henry spent the summer of 1899 at Henry's home writing and admiring each other's short stories. Urged by Henry to do a novel, Dreiser started *Sister Carrie*, published the next year by Doubleday.) Then after a few days reporting for the *Cleveland Leader*, Dreiser was hired by the *Pittsburg Dispatch*.

Conservative, Republican, supported by the local steel industry, and not interested in the kind of substantial work Dreiser had done in St. Louis, the *Dispatch* assigned him almost daily what in *Newspaper Days* he scornfully calls "idle feature stuff." The importance of the *Dispatch* to Dreiser was his assignment to the Allegheny city hall and police station; he spent many afternoons across the street in the Carnegie Public Library reading Balzac, one of the literary idols of his *Republic* city editor, H. B. Wandell. Once again restless and dissatisfied with the demands and limitations of daily reporting and strongly attracted to New York City by his summer 1894 visit to see his brother Paul, Dreiser quit the *Dispatch* and moved to New York in November 1894. This was the beginning of the end of his newspaper career. Although managing with difficulty to be hired by Joseph Pulitzer's *New York World*, he never had a chance there to show the skills that had made him a valued and successful reporter for his Chicago and St. Louis newspapers. (Even if he had had a chance, his skills probably would not have been appreciated: the *World* was not interested in imitation Dickens and Balzac.) The *World*'s reporters, with few exceptions, had to dig up news and then give it to a "rewrite man" to write. As a legman, Dreiser was paid by the space his news was given, and he could not support himself without drawing on his savings. Going broke, not allowed to write his own stories, and convinced he would be fired for incompetence, Dreiser quit in March 1895 and never worked again as a full-time newspaper reporter.

Further Reading

Bigelow, Blair F. "The Collected Newspaper Articles, 1892–1894, of Theodore Dreiser." 2 vols. Diss., Brandeis University, 1973.

Fishkin, Shelley Fisher. "Theodore Dreiser." *From Fact to Fiction: Journalism and Imaginative Writing in America.* Baltimore: Johns Hopkins University Press, 1985. 85–134.

Kwiat, Joseph J. "The Newspaper Experience: Crane, Norris, and Dreiser." *Nineteenth Century Fiction* 8 (1953): 99–117.

Moers, Ellen. "Newspapers and the Bowery." *Two Dreisers.* New York: Viking, 1969. 15–31.

Mott, Frank Luther. *American Journalism: A History of Newspapers in the United States through 250 Years, 1690–1940.* New York: Macmillan, 1941.

Nostwich, T. D., ed. *Theodore Dreiser Journalism,* Vol. 1. *Newspaper Writings, 1892–1895.* Philadelphia: University of Pennsylvania Press, 1988.

———. *Theodore Dreiser's "Heard in the Corridors" Articles and Related Writings.* Ames: Iowa State University Press, 1988.

Ziff, Larzer. "The School of the Cemetery: Newspapers." *The American 1890s: Life and Times of a Lost Generation.* New York: Viking, 1966. 146–65.

Blair F. Bigelow

K

KANE, LESTER. Lester Kane, the protagonist of *Jennie Gerhardt*, may be Dreiser's most consistently "naturalistic" character. He is a thoroughgoing skeptic, a pessimist who sees no order in Nature or society. For him, the affairs of people are determined by **chance**, and all human activity is ultimately pointless. Lester's bleak conception of life is counterpoised in the novel against Jennie's more hopeful view: she is a quasi-religious mystic who senses some deep order in nature, though she cannot put into words what she intuits. Lester, the younger of two sons in the wealthy Kane family, is accustomed to wealth and power. He is a bon vivant and a sensualist; before he meets Jennie, he is cynical about women and marriage. He is touched by Jennie's plight, however, and is powerfully attracted by her wholesomeness and her need. He is also drawn to her, and she to him, by strong sexual desire. Jennie becomes his kept woman for thirteen years; he travels with her, and they live together for a period as husband and wife. Provisions in his father's will, however, compel Lester to leave Jennie and to resume his life as a member of the privileged classes. He marries Letty Gerald, a wealthy widow, and takes up his old social and business responsibilities; but he is not happy in the arrangement.

His overindulgence in food and drink damages his health, and he dies in 1906, at the age of fifty-nine, with Jennie at his bedside. Lester is based in part on Austin Brennan, the good-natured businessman who maintained a long liaison with Dreiser's sister Mame. In early drafts of *Jennie Gerhardt*, Dreiser allowed Lester and Jennie to marry, but, acting on the advice of friends who read the manuscript, he revised the final chapters and kept the two characters apart. Lester does tell Jennie, on his deathbed, that he has always loved her, but Dreiser added this confession at a late stage of composition, probably in galley proofs. His initial instinct was to have Lester remain silent, perhaps because he realized that deathbed protestations of love are easy to make.

Further Reading

West, James L. W., III. "Double Quotes and Double Meanings in *Jennie Gerhardt*." *Dreiser Studies* 18.1 (1987): 1–11.

James L. W. West III

KENNELL, RUTH (1893–1977). Dreiser met Ruth Epperson Kennell in November 1927 while he was on a trip to the Soviet Union. She was a thirty-four-year-old American expatriate who had been living in Russia for more than five years. She supported herself by translating and editing so-called anniversary editions of American writers, including Dreiser, for the government publishing house. Dreiser had been invited, along with other international celebrities, for a weeklong observation of the tenth anniversary of the October Revolution. When he requested that the government extend the invitation and finance him to a longer tour of the country, he was obliged. He also requested that Ruth Kennell be his secretary, translator, and guide for what turned out to be a three-month stay. Kennell, who had become Dreiser's lover, accompanied him during his travels, making shorthand notes of his reactions and conversations, taking dictation, and each evening organizing her notes in the form of a typed diary. She was instructed to use "I" in the manuscript and then to hand it to Dreiser for emendation and expansion. This became the basis of his diary, which was published in 1996 as *Dreiser's Russian Diary*. He also used the diary notes in a limited way in the writing of his *Dreiser Looks at Russia*. The composition of a second, secret diary of her own added to Kennell's workload. In it she recorded conversations and events not included in the text she had presented to the novelist. When she came to write a book about Dreiser's trip and later ideas about Russia, *Theodore Dreiser and the Soviet Union* (1969), she turned to these pages for scenes that are based on her own, not Dreiser's, diary. Kennell returned to America in 1928; she and Dreiser rarely met, but she worked on the proofs of Dreiser's book on Russia and maintained a spirited correspondence on public issues with him until his death in 1945. Dreiser's portrait of Kennell appears as the sketch "Ernita," which he published in *A Gallery of Women*. Kennell herself became a writer of fiction, mainly children's books set in Russia such as *That Boy Nikolka, and*

Other Tales of Soviet Children (1945) and *Adventures in Russia and Other Stories about Soviet Children* (1947).

Further Reading

Kennell, Ruth Epperson. *Theodore Dreiser and the Soviet Union, 1927–1945: A First-Hand Chronicle*. New York: International, 1969.

Thomas P. Riggio

"KHAT." Repeatedly rejected by magazine editors, the story was first published in *Chains: Lesser Novels and Stories*. One of two stories he set in Arabia (the other is "The Prince Who Was a Thief"), "Khat" represents a departure for Dreiser from his usual method of writing fiction based on personal observation or extensive research. As a result, the story lacks the depth of detail, especially in regard to setting, typical of his other stories. Thematically, however, "Khat" exhibits several of Dreiser's principal fictional concerns.

A dramatization of always unsatisfied appetite, the story depicts Ibn Abdullah's hunger for khat (*catha edulis*), a much-used stimulant in the Yemen that Dreiser portrays. This "life-giving weed" functions in the story as an object of desire and as a metaphor for the transcendence of earthly hardship. It also becomes the basis for class differences because Abdullah's caste status erodes in conjunction with his increasing inability to purchase khat. Reduced to begging when the story opens, Abdullah was raised as the son of a prosperous khat farmer. His social, material, and physical degeneration is reminiscent of Hurstwood's plight in *Sister Carrie*, and its depiction here provides another example of Dreiser's sympathy for characters caught in an inevitable decline caused by age and relentless competition with the young and strong. While the distant setting of "Khat" underscores Dreiser's adherence to a philosophy of universal economic and physical determinism, Abdullah's position as a failed storyteller suggests a more personal meaning. Having lost his voice and his audience, Abdullah may reflect Dreiser's own fear of professional failure, an understandable fear given the difficulty he had publishing this and other stories ten years before *Chains*.

Scott Emmert

KUBITZ, ESTELLE BLOOM (1886–1954).

Estelle Kubitz was introduced to Dreiser in August 1916 by H. L. Mencken, who was the lover of her younger sister, Marion Bloom. At the time of their meeting, Kubitz was separated from her husband, Hans Kubitz, and living in Washington, D.C., with Miriam Taylor, the nurse who is the subject of Dreiser's sketch "Regina C——" in *A Gallery of Women* (Estelle and Marion are identified as the Redmond sisters in the sketch). Nicknamed Gloom by Marion because of her love of Russian novels, she impressed Dreiser with her intellect and knowledge of literature, and shortly after Mencken's introduction, she moved to New York to assist him as an editor/typist in addition to becoming his lover. Her affair with Dreiser ended in the fall of 1919, when he met Helen Richardson and moved to California, but she continued to do secretarial work for him until her marriage to Arthur Williams in 1923.

As Dreiser's secretary, Kubitz worked on a variety of literary projects, including preparing typescripts of *The Hand of the Potter*, Dreiser's revisions of the short stories that appeared in *Free and Other Stories* and the sketches that appeared in *Twelve Men*, and the manuscript and various revisions of *A Book about Myself* (*Newspaper Days*). Also at some point either during or after her affair with Dreiser and probably without Dreiser's knowledge, she made a typescript of his diary for 1917–1918, which provides a detailed picture of his daily routine and writing habits during his years in **Greenwich Village** along with his relationship with her and his liaisons with **Louise Campbell** and other women. In the diary, he refers to Kubitz as Little Bill, Bert, and Rosie Bo, pet names he appears to have used for her privately, since he refers to her by her nickname Gloom in his correspondence.

In addition to being chronicled in the diary, Kubitz's relationship with Dreiser is captured in published correspondence between her and her sister and between her and Mencken, who became her close friend and confidant from the time he met her to the end of her life. Largely because of her relationship with Mencken a number of the manuscripts and documents of Dreiser's years in Greenwich Village survive. According to Mencken on a note attached to the diary, Kubitz sent it to him "in 1920 or thereabout." In 1934 she sent him the manuscript of *The Hand of the Potter*, and following her death, her executor sent him the Dreiser materials he found among her papers, including correspondence with him plus transcripts of *A Hoosier Holiday* and *A Gallery of Women*. Mencken, in turn, deposited these materials in the New York Public Library, where some of them, principally the diary, the manuscript of *The Hand of the Potter*, and Estelle's papers, are located. Others were at some time turned over to the University of Pennsylvania.

As noted earlier, Kubitz's relationship with Dreiser came to an end with her marriage to Arthur Williams in 1923. In 1937, she left Williams and moved to her family home in New Windsor, Maryland, where she remained for the rest of her life. She had a double mastectomy in 1940 and died in 1954, a virtual recluse and alcoholic living with cats and a radio.

Further Reading

Dreiser, Theodore. "Greenwich Village, 1917–18." *American Diaries: 1902–1926*. Ed. Thomas P. Riggio. Philadelphia: University of Pennsylvania Press, 1983. 147–256.

Martin, Edward A., ed. *In Defense of Marion: The Love of Marion Bloom & H. L. Mencken*. Athens: University of Georgia Press, 1996.

Frederic E. Rusch

KUSELL, SALLIE (1892–1982). Born in Aurora, Illinois, Kusell was the daughter of a successful clothing manufacturer, Samuel H. Kusell. During the spring of 1923 Kusell was working for her brother Daniel, a theatrical writer and producer, who was staging the successful musical comedy *The Gingham Girl* at the Earl Carroll Theatre. One evening while at the theater a poet friend mentioned to Kusell that Theodore Dreiser was looking for a secretary. Kusell, who had written several short stories and had hopes of becoming a professional writer, perhaps saw this secretarial position as an opportunity to advance her career. At her interview, Kusell was intimidated by Dreiser's formidable presence, yet she impressed Dreiser, who put her to work on several of the sketches that would later become part of *A Gallery of Women*. This initial meeting and preliminary editorial work were the beginning of an intense relationship that would have direct consequence on Dreiser's and Helen's relationship and, moreover, on the making of *An American Tragedy*. When Dreiser began writing *An American Tragedy* in earnest during the summer of 1923, he relied primarily on Kusell as his typist, editor, and sounding board. Later, Dreiser would also employ **Louise Campbell** to help with the ever-growing work on the novel. Dreiser and Kusell worked closely on the composition of Books 1 and 2. Kusell had also entered into a sexual relationship with Dreiser, and after they had a falling-out in the late summer of 1925, she did not take part in the completion of Book 3. In early 1926, Kusell and Dreiser reconciled, but Dreiser gave Kusell only some minor secretarial work. For Dreiser, their relationship was clearly at an end. In 1927, perhaps to show his appreciation for her work on *An American Tragedy*, Dreiser provided Kusell with a trip to Europe. While visiting London, she met her future husband, a British pilot. They were married in August 1927, but the marriage was ill-fated. In February 1929, Kusell, very ill and broke in a London nursing home, wired Dreiser for financial assistance. He generously sent her $500 to pay her medical bills. By 1930, Kusell had returned to America, with her marriage ended and her relationship with Dreiser severely strained. There is little evidence to suggest that they had much contact on her return to America or that she continued to pursue her ambition of a literary career.

John W. Reynolds

L

LAUGHING GAS. A one-act play composed during the summer of 1914, *Laughing Gas* was first published in the February 1915 *Smart Set* and then collected in *Plays of the Natural and Supernatural*. Prompted by Dreiser's own surgical experience in March 1914, the play suggests that life is nothing more than senseless, cyclical repetition, with people its helpless victims struggling to live amid its mechanistic forces. The play operates on two levels: the physical plane, in which Dr. Jason James Vatabeel undergoes an operation to remove a neck tumor; and the spiritual plane, in which Vatabeel, anesthetized with nitrous oxide, participates in a colloquy with personifications of the forces that determine life, among them the Rhythm of the Universe, Demyaphon (nitrous oxide), Alcephoran ("an element of physics"), and various shadows. While Vatabeel breathes the gas, he remembers a former dream experience while under its influence and wonders whether it will repeat itself. These thoughts both prompt him to dream and dramatically enact the play's thesis that all events in life are endless repetitions, without meaning or purpose. The cosmic joke is upon Vatabeel, who has deluded himself into believing that life has meaning, and upon awaking he is convulsed by laughter, the twin effect of the gas and his realization of life's purposelessness.

Despite its apparently slight form, *Laughing Gas* was an important experiment for Dreiser. He once wrote Mencken that he thought the play was "the best thing I ever did" (*D-M Letters* 1: 233), and while Mencken was aghast at Dreiser's judgment, the play is Dreiser's clearest, most concise expression of the cosmic balance of conflicting forces that Dreiser believed determine life. Vatabeel is the archetypal Dreiser victim, helplessly buffeted about by chemical and physical forces that guide his every thought and action. As Demyaphon tells him, "You are a mere machine run by forces which you cannot understand." The play was one of the earliest explorations of Dreiser's concept of "equation inevitable," the notion that all life was composed of conflicting forces that tended toward balance, what he called "equation," adapted from **Herbert Spencer's** notion of equilibration.

See also "Equation Inevitable"; Plays, Productions of.

Further Reading

Boren, Lynda S. "William James, Theodore Roosevelt, and the 'Anaesthetic Revelation.'" *American Studies* 24 (Spring 1983): 5–18.

Newlin, Keith. "Expressionism Takes the Stage: Dreiser's 'Laughing Gas.' " *Journal of American Drama and Theatre* 4.1 (1992): 5–22.

Keith Newlin

LENGEL, WILLIAM CHARLES (1888–1965). His literary and theatrical career had already begun when in 1910 Lengel went to work for Dreiser, then editor of *The Delineator*, and it was not to conclude until the mid-1960s, when he held the post of senior editor at Fawcett Publications. In the intervening years Lengel—originally a lawyer—served under Ray Long, editor of *Cosmopolitan*, as his chief editorial associate; was a motion picture story editor, as well as the operator of a successful literary agency; and filled various senior editorial posts in the Hearst, Macfadden, and Fawcett organizations. As an author in his own right, Lengel published five novels and numerous short stories and articles and had several plays produced. Although initially Dreiser's private secretary at **Butterick**, Lengel served as jack-of-all-trades to Dreiser over the course of their thirty-five-year personal and professional relationship. Among the tasks that Lengel assumed were literary agent, editor, adviser, host, and admirer. Lengel, for example, put Dreiser up when he visited Chicago in 1912–1913, found a publisher for *The Titan*, and witnessed the slaps Dreiser handed **Sinclair Lewis** in 1931, when the latter accused the former of plagiarizing from **Dorothy Thompson's** book on Russia (Thompson was Lewis's wife). Lengel negotiated Dreiser's contract for *America Is Worth Saving* and effectively encouraged Dreiser to finish *The Bulwark*. Dreiser did not always treat Lengel well; for example, although Lengel was Dreiser's agent and had worked diligently to sell the motion picture rights to *Sister Carrie*, Dreiser engaged another representative who eventually negotiated the rights and received the commission. No published biography or autobiography exists for Lengel; his contribution to American letters and to Dreiser's life and work, specifically, can best be discovered through his unpublished papers and those of Dreiser, both held by the Rare Book and Manuscript Library of the University of Pennsylvania.

Further Reading

Lengel, William C. "The 'Genius' Himself." *Esquire* 10 (September 1938): 55, 120, 124, 126.

Nancy M. Shawcross

LEWIS, SINCLAIR (1885–1951). Sinclair Lewis was the author of *Main Street* (1920), *Babbitt* (1922), and a string of other best-selling satires that debunked American institutions and gibbeted the frauds and opportunists that emerged in the powerful postwar economy. He had much in common with Dreiser. Both were products of a midwestern upbringing, both served apprenticeships in newspaper and periodical work, and both were trailblazers in clearing American literature of its genteel ethos and in drawing strong, independent-minded female characters. Lewis's characterizations of Carol Kennicott of *Main Street* and Una Golden of *The Job* (1917) seem to have been influenced by Dreiser's portrait of Carrie Meeber. Both writers also snubbed the prevailing stylistic standards of high modernism, and thus both were unwelcome in the expatriate circle of the 1920s.

Lewis first met Dreiser in 1907, when he profiled him for *Life* magazine. Their paths intersected occasionally at parties and other gatherings within the bohemian circle of **Greenwich Village**, where both lived in the 1910s. Lewis admired Dreiser greatly and in some ways became his unofficial champion. Three years later, as an editor for Frederick A. Stokes, Lewis unsuccessfully lobbied his boss to publish

Jennie Gerhardt. The following year, Lewis again hailed Dreiser in a review of *A Traveler at Forty* for the *St. Louis Republic.*

By the 1920s, when Lewis's star was rising at a meteoric rate and it looked as if Dreiser's was in eclipse, a stiff professional rivalry developed. Dreiser held Lewis's somewhat flashy satires in low regard, reputedly deriding *Main Street* as merely a "catch novel." With their publishers as go-betweens, each unsuccessfully petitioned the other for a blurb—Dreiser on Lewis's *Arrowsmith* (1925) and Lewis on Dreiser's *An American Tragedy.* Lewis seems to have genuinely admired Dreiser's work (the reasons for his not commenting on *An American Tragedy* remain in dispute), yet Dreiser openly spoke disparagingly of Lewis and described him in his *Russian Diary* as "noisy, ostentatious, and shallow company."

Hostilities reached a flash point in 1927, when Dreiser was accused of plagiarizing material on the new Soviet regime from newspaper articles written by Lewis's second wife, Dorothy Thompson. Then in 1930 the two writers became competitors in the race to become the first American to win the **Nobel Prize** in literature. Lewis edged out Dreiser for the honor, leading in part to an infamous row at a club in New York the following year when the two men got into a slapping match after Lewis loudly reiterated that Dreiser had stolen Thompson's material. Relations between Dreiser and Lewis remained cool from that point on.

Further Reading

Hakutani, Yoshinobu. "Sinclair Lewis and Theodore Dreiser: A Study in Continuity and Development." *Discourse* 7 (1963): 254–76.

Hutchisson, James M. *The Rise of Sinclair Lewis, 1920–1930.* University Park: Pennsylvania State University Press, 1996.

James M. Hutchisson

LIBERAL CLUB. A loose social, political, and artistic organization with a diverse membership of feminist, socialist, anarchist, and bohemian habitués of New York City's **Greenwich Village**, the Liberal Club was founded as a lecture society in 1912 but rapidly evolved into a haven for artists and free thinkers, a trying-ground for experimental theater and vers libre poets, and a rallying point for political demonstrations until its dissolution in 1918. In 1913 the club found permanent headquarters at 137 MacDougal Street next to the popular café Polly's, run by anarchist Polly Holladay. The club's diverse membership offers a who's who of American intellectuals of the immediate pre-war years; besides Dreiser, members included John Reed, Henrietta Rodman, Louise Bryant, Charles Demuth, Edna St. Vincent Millay, **Floyd Dell**, and Lincoln Steffens.

Dreiser and then mistress **Kirah Markham** were regulars throughout Dreiser's Village years, with Markham acting in amateur productions of plays by such Village luminaries as John Reed and **Sherwood Anderson.** Liberal Club theatricals helped give rise to such pioneer theater groups as the Provincetown Players and the Washington Square Players. When *The "Genius"* was suppressed by the **New York Society for the Suppression of Vice** in 1916, Dreiser spoke on **censorship** at the club's request and relied on the club's membership to circulate petitions and write letters and testimonials in defense of that novel's artistic merit, much to the dismay of H. L. Mencken, who regarded the Liberal Club as a collection of "tinpot revolutionaries and sophomoric advanced thinkers" (*D-M Letters* 1: 261).

Although the Liberal Club is fondly and often expansively recollected in the published memoirs of many of its membership, none devoted any extensive writing to it, and club records were not kept. The most exhaustive source of information about the club, culled from memoirs, correspondence, and contemporary newspaper coverage, remains Richwine's unpublished 1968 dissertation.

Further Reading

Richwine, Keith Norton. "The Liberal Club: Bohemia and the Resurgence in Greenwich Village, 1912–1918." Diss., University of Pennsylvania, 1968.

Carol S. Loranger

"LIFE, ART AND AMERICA" was first published in *Seven Arts* (February 1917) and was reprinted in *Hey Rub-a-Dub-Dub*. Written and published within six months of the **New York Society for the Suppression of Vice's** action against *The "Genius,"* "Life, Art and America" amounts to a denunciation of the puritanism bred into Americans from birth that Dreiser felt underlay **censorship** of works like his. Dreiser begins the article by describing the intellectual privations and moral dogmatism of his own midwestern childhood and education as both perverted and typical of all Americans' upbringing. School history texts commonly sacrificed accuracy for moral and ideological lessons, so that Socrates's death, for example, was ascribed to the philosopher's unchristian private life rather than a state that feared his intellectual integrity. Newspapers, compulsive weekly church sermons, and good books— "which meant, of course books from which any reference to sex had been eliminated [and] intelligent interpretation of character and human nature was immediately discounted"—hypocritically conspired to promote a sanitized view of business, community, and family life totally at odds with the individual's immediate experience and the hard lessons real life taught. Even universities, writes Dreiser, are in the business of suiting Americans to rote acceptance of convention and passive performance of their commercial function. Intellectual freedom, he adds, has not been permitted since the puritans arrived. As a result, the arts, which should supply thought and nourish the national and individual intellect after material wants are satisfied, are enfeebled, and American artists—Dreiser names Poe, Hawthorne, Whitman, and Thoreau—become "the butt and jibe of unintelligent Americans" and Americans "the laughing stock of the world."

Nowhere in the essay does Dreiser mention his own immediate problems with the New York Society for the Prevention of Vice. But his direct reference to **Comstock** and Comstockery and his assertion that "wasp-like censors" are delivering the coup de grâce to American literature "now" in 1917 would have made the referent clear both to his readers in *Seven Arts* and in *Hey Rub-a-Dub-Dub* three years later. Recalling the essay in *My Life as Author and Editor* (New York: Knopf, 1993), an unsympathetic Mencken dismissed the "pronunciamento" as consisting mostly of ideas borrowed from him but enfeebled by Dreiser's "whooping up" of *The "Genius"* case (218).

The "Genius" case aside, "Life, Art and America" is notable for Dreiser's amusing extended closing conceit depicting America as the donkey-eared Bottom the Weaver to the world and in its crudely personal, but prescient, opening critique of commonplace social arrangements—from the family home to the university campus—as ideological state apparatuses, some a half century before French neo-

Marxists would formalize the concept.

Carol S. Loranger

LIGHT, EVELYN (1904–1958). Evelyn Light was Dreiser's full-time secretary from February 1931 to June 1934, and they became intimate at some point during their relationship. Light was most likely drawn to Dreiser because of his leftist politics, for she had been an associate editor for *Plain Talk*, a leftist weekly, from 1928 to 1930. In the 1930s Dreiser turned his attention to the social ills of America, becoming involved, for example, with the **National Committee for the Defense of Political Prisoners** (NCDPP) and accepting its chairmanship in April 1931. Light assisted Dreiser with his work for the NCDPP, and, along with Kathryn Sayre, she helped to research *Tragic America*, Dreiser's critique of capitalist America. During the first six months of 1931, Light also assisted Dreiser in his suit against Paramount Pictures, which sought to prevent the studio from releasing what he regarded as an unfaithful adaptation of *An American Tragedy*, directed by Josef von Sternberg. In addition, Light worked on some of Dreiser's other literary enterprises, typing, for example, chapters of *The Stoic* during his intermittent work on the novel. In June 1934, Light, much to Dreiser's dismay, left his employment to work at the American Book Company, and she thereafter worked in a number of editing and publishing positions while occasionally assisting him with various projects throughout the remainder of his life. She became an editor at Richard R. Smith Publishing in 1945, married Smith in 1946, and served as president of the company from 1948 until her death. In 1952 she published *Ways and Means to a Successful Retirement* under the pen name of Evelyn Colby.

John W. Reynolds

THE LIGHT IN THE WINDOW, a one-act play completed in late August 1914, is of interest for two reasons. Its technique of intercutting scenes, which abruptly switch from conversation in the house to comments from passersby, reveals the influence of cinematic splicing. (Shortly after he completed this play Dreiser wrote H. L. Mencken that he was negotiating with Pathé Freres, a film company, for a scenario that was eventually published as the short story "The Prince Who Was a Thief" [*D-M Letters* 1: 153].) More important, the play anticipates *An American Tragedy* in its theme and tone. Truro Kindelling is torn between his wife Laura, a former actress, and a more socially prosperous match with Althea Cameron, whom his mother favors. Truro has become weary of Laura's jealousy and is being pressured by his mother, who controls his inheritance, to divorce her and marry Althea. The action of the play consists of Laura and Truro's bickering about Althea and about his mother's influence. Intercutting their argument are the ironic comments of passersby, which dramatically underscore the pettiness of the Kindellings' squabble. Dreiser is perhaps too obvious in his irony; the comments range from the banal ("Oh, to be rich! And happy!") to the clichéd ("Ah, the rich have the easy time! No worries.") to the didactic ("Now, that is what I call a lovely home. All peace and quiet and family affection. Hard-earned, no doubt. After all, prosperity depends on moral order and honesty. People get rich and stay rich because they deserve to.").

When Dreiser sent the play to Mencken on 22 August 1914, he called it "a disguised melodrama" (*D-M Letters* 1: 152), but the disguise is inept. Truro, the villain of the piece, enters with "*One carefully poised hand . . . twirling first one and then the other of a handsome pair of mustaches.*" Laura, the innocent heroine wronged by an unfaithful husband, wails in an aside, "Oh, God! Oh, God! He forsakes his own wife for his mother, and another woman, and after only two years! To think that I should come to this. To think that that cold, scheming cat should be able to separate us—and after all that has been between us! Oh, oh, oh!!!"

Mencken rejected the play for *Smart Set*, and it was published in the January 1916 issue of *International* before being collected in *Plays of the Natural and Supernatural*.

Keith Newlin

LIVERIGHT, HORACE (1886–1933). Horace Brisbin Liveright was one of the most visible and flamboyant book publishers of the American 1920s. He had an instinct for talent; he published Ernest Hemingway's first book and William Faulkner's first two novels, and his stable of authors included Eugene O'Neill, Ezra Pound, **Sherwood Anderson**, Hart Crane, and e. e. cummings. Liveright was nervy and bold, fighting several vigorous court battles against the suppression of literary works by the **New York Society for the Suppression of Vice** and thereby earning praise from Dreiser, H. L. Mencken, and members of Mencken's circle. Liveright had a weakness, however: he liked to gamble on the stock market and on Broadway productions. His speculations frequently brought his publishing house into financial peril; fortunately, he was able to keep the firm afloat with a string of improbable best-sellers, including Hendrik Willem Van Loon's *The Story of Mankind* (1921) and Anita Loos's *Gentlemen Prefer Blondes* (1925). Dreiser came to Liveright in 1917 and published some of his best writing under the various Liveright imprints, including *Free and Other Stories, Twelve Men, Hey Rub-a-Dub-Dub, A Book about Myself, An American Tragedy, Chains,* and *Dawn*. Relations between publisher and author were never particularly good, though; Dreiser distrusted all publishers, probably because of his misadventures with **Doubleday** and **Harper & Brothers**. Dreiser regularly inspected Liveright's financial and sales records, searching for errors that would diminish his royalties, but there is no evidence that Liveright was other than fair with Dreiser.

Liveright and Dreiser were the principals in one of the most infamous scenes in American publishing history, played out on 19 March 1926 in the dining room of the Ritz-Carlton Hotel in New York. At a luncheon with Liveright and two Hollywood moguls, Dreiser refused to grant Liveright a percentage of the movie money for *An American Tragedy*—a percentage to which Liveright was probably entitled. Dreiser became so enraged at Liveright that he threw a cupful of hot coffee in the publisher's face. Dreiser is usually cast as the villain of this episode (and indeed his behavior was boorish), but one can understand his fears about Liveright, who was known to be feckless with money and who had not made his negotiating position clear to Dreiser ahead of time. The author's apprehensions were borne out in 1930, when Liveright was forced out of his own firm by a majority of its stockholders. Three years later the house became insolvent and filed for bankruptcy. Dreiser's copyrights were tied up in the ensuing legalities; the imprint was eventually reorganized, and most of Dreiser's writings were kept in print, but promotion of backlist titles was minimal, and continuing royalties from the large body of work that Dreiser had published with Liveright were slim.

Further Reading

Dardis, Tom. *Firebrand: The Life of Horace Liveright*. New York: Random House, 1995.

Gilmer, Walker. *Horace Liveright: Publisher of the Twenties*. New York: David Lewis, 1970.

James L. W. West III

THE LIVING THOUGHTS OF THOREAU.

Shortly before Dreiser went to Spain in support of the Loyalists in 1938, he was offered $500 to introduce a selection of quotations culled from Henry David Thoreau's complete works at the time, which was published in 1939 by Longmans, Green, and Co. as *The Living Thoughts of Thoreau*. His secretary **Harriet Bissell** made the selections that were the basis for Dreiser's thirty-two-page Introduction. He had read Thoreau's *Walden* in his youth, and its ant scene may have been the basis for one of his earliest short stories, "The Shining Slave Makers" (later called "McEwen of the Shining Slave Makers"). As recorded in *Dawn*, he was strongly drawn to Nature as a child growing up in Indiana. Some of the notable figures who introduced famous writers in the series were André Gide (Montaigne), Julian Huxley (Darwin), John Dewey (Jefferson), and **Edgar Lee Masters** (Emerson).

At the time of the composition, following his return from Spain, Dreiser was, in the words of **Marguerite Tjader**, "eating and sleeping *science*" (Swanberg interview, Dreiser Papers), and the first four pages of his Introduction show how steeped and perhaps lost Dreiser was in his fanatical inquiries into natural science to solve the riddle of the universe. Dreiser knew, of course, that such a quest was futile, and later on he quotes Thoreau: "All science is only a make-shift, a means to an end which is never attained." Still, he appears to fault current-day scientists for ruling out the actions of God: "All talk of any supreme regulating and hence, legal [*sic*]

and directing force or spirit is *out*. There is no known God or Spirit." When he finally mentions Thoreau by name, however, he describes Thoreau's sojourns through the woods around Concord as an exercise in "forever knocking at the door of the mystery." Dreiser sees Thoreau as a mystic who as a youth was "practically imbedded" in transcendental New England. His subsequent confusion, Dreiser insists, is what makes Thoreau "the best of New England" because he developed a healthy skepticism in the face of transcendentalist optimism and belief that nature was the "last word of God." Apparently, Dreiser was not familiar with Thoreau's pessimism in *The Maine Woods*, even though he senses the faint depression in *Walden*. Claiming to have read 2,400,000 words of Thoreau, he argues that Thoreau's "inconsistencies count for nothing, because, as I see it, his *source* [Nature] is inconsistent," or, Dreiser adds significantly, "in another sense, pure relativity." On the other hand, he feels as if Thoreau "were tapping some marvelous, musical, lyrical source which *was* life, *is* a dream."

The Introduction tells us as much about Dreiser in 1938 as it does Thoreau in the nineteenth century, before Darwin. His statement that Thoreau would have disapproved of the approaching World War II "as a commercial enterprise" reflects his own "America First" isolationist policies as well as his conversion to Communism after his visit to the Soviet Union in 1927. It also reveals Dreiser's lifelong ambivalence or inability to reconcile the beauty and terror of life.

Jerome Loving

LOEB, JACQUES (1859–1924).

In a letter to **George Douglas** written in 1935, Dreiser wrote: "The more I examine the various scientific attempts at an interpretation of life the more I respect and admire

Loeb. He has not been superseded—he has not even as yet been approximated" (*Letters* 2: 742). Not surprisingly, biologist and champion of philosophical **mechanism** Jacques Loeb had a most profound influence on Dreiser's thought. Dreiser's first exposure to Loeb's writings probably came in 1915, and Dreiser would read and re-read his works from then on, including such works as *The Dynamics of Living Matter* (1906), *The Mechanistic Conception of Life* (1912), *The Organism as a Whole* (1916), and *Forced Movements, Tropisms, and Animal Conduct* (1918). Moreover, Dreiser began a correspondence with Loeb in 1919 and began visiting him in his laboratory in 1923. The many ideas Dreiser absorbed from Loeb are apparent in his play *The Hand of the Potter* and in his characterization of Clyde Griffiths in *An American Tragedy*.

Loeb emigrated to the United States from Germany in 1891, gaining fame for his examination of artificial parthenogenesis (artificial fertilization) and animal tropisms (reflex reactions to various stimuli). For his work on tropisms, Loeb was repeatedly nominated for the **Nobel Prize**. His research on both subjects lent support to the view that life was purely biochemical in nature and that much, if not all, behavior could be explained mechanistically rather than by reference to vitalism or free will. In an article suggestively entitled "Mechanistic Science and Metaphysical Romance" (1915), Loeb wrote, "Since no discontinuity exists between the matter constituting living and non-living bodies, biology must also be mechanistic" (771), and went on to conclude that "what progress humanity has made, not only in physical welfare but also in the conquest of superstition and hatred, and in the formation of a correct view of life, it owes directly or indirectly to mechanistic science" (785).

Though Dreiser's enthusiasm for Loeb's writings coexisted in his mind with much that Loeb himself would have considered the worst kind of metaphysical romance, Dreiser's respect and admiration for Loeb never waned; Dreiser repeatedly referred to Loeb as representative of the scientific worldview, as in the essay "Equation Inevitable." In "Mark the Double Twain" (*English Journal* 24 [October 1935]: 615–27), Dreiser lamented that Mark Twain, whose thought he also considered to be mechanistic, had not known of Loeb—unaware that Twain not only knew of Loeb but had even defended him in 1905 ("Dr. Loeb's Incredible Discovery") after a newspaper expressed skepticism regarding the results of his experiments. Loeb was also indirectly immortalized by **Sinclair Lewis** in *Arrowsmith* (1925), serving as a model for the character of Max Gottlieb. The idea for this novel was originally presented to Dreiser, who later regretted his decision to decline the offer.

Further Reading

Land, Mary G. "Three Max Gottliebs: Lewis's, Dreiser's, and Walker Percy's View of the Mechanist-Vitalist Controversy." *Studies in the Novel* 15.4 (1983): 314–31.

Loeb, Jacques. "Mechanistic Science and Metaphysical Romance." *Yale Review* 4 (1915): 766–85.

Moers, Ellen. *Two Dreisers*. New York: Viking, 1969. 240–60.

Pauly, Philip J. *Controlling Life: Jacques Loeb and the Engineering Ideal in Biology*. Berkeley: University of California Press, 1987.

Zanine, Louis J. *Mechanism and Mysticism: The Influence of Science on the Thought and Work of Theodore Dreiser*. Philadelphia: University of Pennsylvania Press, 1993. 78–90.

Ian F. Roberts

"THE LOG OF AN OCEAN PILOT." This article about the work and life of the ocean pilot first appeared in *Ainslee's* in July 1899 before being reprinted, with numerous minor changes, as "The Log of a Harbor Pilot" in *The Color of a Great City*. The *Ainslee's* version was reprinted in *SMA 2*.

Stephen Crane's "The Open Boat" (1897), based on his shipwreck experience, dramatizes the dangers of the sea and Nature's indifference to human beings. By contrast, "The Log of an Ocean Pilot" portrays the friendly interaction between people and the sea. Yet for all the harmonious sustenance, the seafarer's life is a lonely one, and the crews of the pilot boats long for stimulation of a large urban community like New York, for the city was the generating center for intellectual, scientific, and artistic progress. In response to Dreiser's observation that an ocean pilot's life is a pleasant one, the pilot answers: "Yes, it's not a bad life. Rather cold in winter, but summer makes up for it. Then we're in port every fourth or fifth day. Sometimes we get a night off." Dreiser learned about pilots' enjoyment of card games and other diversions while idling about, waiting for the next steamer to arrive. He was struck, in particular, by "the friendly feeling among the men. One might fancy oneself anywhere but at sea, save for the rocking of the boat." Ocean pilots all yearned for "nights off" and holidays. City life, for an ocean pilot's vision, was "a kind of earthly heaven. To be there of an evening when people were passing, to loaf on the corner and see the bright-eyed girls go by, to be in the village hubbub was to him the epitome of living. The great, silent, suggestive sea"—another pastoral of which Melville had earlier made a myth of life—"meant nothing." Despite occasional dangers of the sea, an ocean pilot's work was safe and pleasant. "The harbor," Dreiser concludes the essay, "looked like a city of masts. After the lonely sea, it was alive with a multitude of people. Tugs went puffing by. Scows and steamers mingled. Amid so much life, the sea seemed safe."

Yoshinobu Hakutani

"THE LOST PHOEBE" was completed in 1912 but was not published until the April 1916 issue of *Century*. Revised for *Free and Other Stories*, it has often been reprinted, though its mixture of local color and Gothic horror is unusual for Dreiser, as is the sentimental ending in which old Henry Reifsneider joins his long-lost Phoebe Ann in death. More typical of the author is the suggestion of complex, even dark motives within this simple-minded and devoted old couple.

Henry and Phoebe have "lived in peace and sympathy" on their isolated, decaying farm for almost half a century, so Henry's becoming at times "unduly cranky" may be just a humorous peculiarity, yet, the narrator explains, people often become "peculiar" by an "involute and pathetic" process. The Reifsneiders are a "loving couple" largely because they "have nothing else in this life to be fond of." Whenever Henry becomes restless, Phoebe threatens to walk out, just as Dreiser's mother did to terrify her children into submission. In response, Henry wonders "what he would do if she were to die," an indication that, like Rufus Haymaker in "Free," though less consciously, he wants his wife dead.

Once Phoebe dies, Henry resembles the deranged girl in "The 'Mercy' of God" more than the despairing Rufus, for his hallucinations both satisfy his long-repressed desire for freedom and punish him for his guilty thoughts. At first he thinks he sees Phoebe's ghost in the shadows and mist. Then, perhaps because he does not really want her back, he creates the "fixed illusion" that to repay him for starting "a senseless quarrel," she has merely carried out "her old jesting threat that if he did not behave himself she would leave him." When he sets out to find her, he is a "patriarchal" old man, but during the six years of his quest he regresses into an irresponsible vagabond free of the "terror" of farm work and living off the generosity of neighbors and strangers. The "circle of his inquiry ever widening," he continually calls his wife's name but always takes "ample time to search before he called again," as though he really just wants to see the world.

Finally, Henry hallucinates "a strangely younger Phoebe" who beckons him onward until, with "a gay cry," he leaps from a cliff to join her. But the "vision" he chases is only an idea, not even the young Phoebe but a "delightful epitome of their quondam youth" who was lost the moment they settled into harness. When he plunges into "a silvery bed of apple-trees now blooming in the spring," he inverts the traditional *felix culpa*, the fortunate fall that brings sin and death—and farm work—into the world, for only in his dying does he achieve prelapsarian innocence. The question is whether his short happy life is enough.

Further Reading

Graham, Don. "Psychological Veracity in 'The Lost Phoebe': Dreiser's Revisions." *Studies in American Fiction* 6 (1978): 100–105.

West, Ray B., Jr. *The Short Story in America, 1900–1950*. Chicago: Henry Regnery, 1952. 33–42.

Stephen C. Brennan

"LUCIA," the fourth sketch in the first volume of *A Gallery of Women*, is a study of the emotional and sexual frustrations of the New Woman. Lucia is the Russian-born daughter of a cold and remote mother and a more permissive father whom she idolizes. When her father dies, she is sent to a convent school where her "exotic, sensuous and serious nature already boiling with its own pent up fires" leads her to develop a girlish crush on the remote and ascetic Sister Agatha. She learns to paint, and, given her background, it's no surprise that all of her sketches are of "scenes of lovers, parting or killing each other"; all the faces resemble Sister Agatha's. When she is eighteen, Lucia goes to Paris to study art, and the repressions of her girlhood offer little protection from the sensual temptations of the Parisian bohemian scene. She is both perplexed and curious about sex but is also confused about its relation to love. After two years of half-hearted flirtation that includes some distant kissing, Lucia, at age twenty, deliberately sets out to experience sex. After rejecting a number of potential partners who would expect a serious commitment, she settles on Daniel Sarvasti, a fifty-year-old world-famous inventor whose considerable experience as a womanizer seemingly offers the uncomplicated experience she desires.

At the midpoint of his life, however, Daniel has "worn himself out physically" and is no longer able to offer the physical pleasure Lucia craves; worse, he becomes dependent on her. When temptation appears in the form of Frank Stafford, the manager of a Montreal bank, Lucia leaves Daniel to experience the love and sexual pleasure she seeks. Frank proves to have a rigidly conventional temperament; insisting upon marriage, worried what his conservative family might think, he disapproves of Lucia's desire to pursue her art, and so Lucia breaks off the engagement and returns to Paris, determined to take a series of lovers who will present no complications. There she drifts—and in London befriends the narrator-author, whom she rejects as a potential lover but to whom she confesses that she feels doomed to drift and dream of a fulfilling love that she knows she will never experience. "I need a strong compelling force whom I could love," she tells the narrator, "before whose strength and temperament I could be humble—maybe." Lucia may be Dreiser's portrait of a sexually liberated New Woman, but, ironically, she is as conventional as Frank in her need for a man to complete her.

Keith Newlin

LYON, HARRIS MERTON (1882–1916). When Dreiser became editor of *Broadway Magazine* in April 1906, he assembled an editorial staff of bright young people to assist him in transforming the magazine into a sophisticated journal catering to the lifestyle of cultivated urbanites. One of the most promising members on this staff was a writer named Harris Merton Lyon, a young man whose enthusiasm, brashness, and ultimate failure are depicted in the *Twelve Men* sketch "De Maupassant, Jr."

Lyon was born in Santa Fe, New Mexico, in 1882 and had, according to Dreiser, put himself through the University of Missouri by working in the school restaurant and laundry. Lyon came to New York City in the early 1900s to advance his career as a writer of serious short stories. In the meantime, he earned his living as a journalist. Lyon was able to produce the kind of material Dreiser wanted—sophisticated sketches of urban life and ironic short stories. So he soon became a permanent member of the *Broadway Magazine* staff.

When Dreiser became editor of the more prestigious **Butterick Publishing Company** in July 1907, Lyon remained at *Broadway* with owner Ben Hampton and reportedly assumed the pose of an Englishman in dress and attitude. By this time, his stories were appearing in other magazines, such as *McClure's*, *Collier's*, and *Smart Set*. He also published two collections of stories, *Sardonics* in 1908 and *Graphics* in 1913.

By August 1913, Lyon was writing mainly for *Reedy's Mirror*, a St. Louis periodical, contributing essays and some fiction under the heading "From an Old Farmhouse." He was now spending much of his time on a farm in Connecticut. Lyon had published a few more stories in other journals and was trying to write a novel at the time of his death from Bright's disease at age thirty-four on 2 June 1916. In August, Dreiser began to examine Lyon's unpublished and uncollected stories with the intention of publishing them as a book. After conferring with William Marion Reedy (1862–1920), who had served as Lyon's mentor, Dreiser conceded that the quality was not good enough to justify publication as a collection. He abandoned the project and instead provided what little immortality Lyon was destined to achieve by creating the portrait that appeared in *Twelve Men*.

Robert Coltrane

M

MALLON, ANNA. *See* Henry, Anna Mallon.

MARDEN, ORISON SWETT (1848–1924) was a self-help guru who founded and edited *Success*, an inspirational monthly journal in which Dreiser published thirty-three articles and one poem from January 1898 through April 1902. *Success*, as well as the many books Marden produced, was dedicated to the principle that " 'No surrender' must ever be the slogan of the man or woman who would overcome the obstacles that block the road to success" (Connolly 128).

Marden's own life had indeed been fraught with obstacles. An orphan at seven years of age, he spent the next ten years as a "hired boy" in a series of austere and often abusive foster homes. Then came years of struggle to support himself while gaining a long-neglected formal education. At twenty-three, he entered Boston University and within nine years had attained five degrees, including one from that university's law school and another from the Harvard School of Medicine. After an up-and-down entrepreneurial career in hotel management, Dr. Marden, as he was typically addressed, set out to emulate British gospeler of success Samuel Smiles, whose *Self-Help* (1859) had had such a salutary influence on Marden's own early life. To this end, he published *Pushing to the Front* in 1894. It was Marden's contention that "[n]othing is more fascinating than the romance of reality in worthy achievement under difficulty, than contrasting pictures of obscure beginnings and triumphant endings, than stirring stories of strenuous endeavor and final victory" (qtd. in Lingeman 1: 184). Apparently, the reading public agreed with this assessment, for *Pushing to the Front* eventually went through 250 editions and was translated into twenty-five languages. During the next twenty-seven years, Marden published over fifty similar success manuals.

During the fall of 1897, Marden met Dreiser, who had also been a childhood reader of Samuel Smiles's *Self-Help*. Marden, at the time, was in the process of launching *Success* magazine, which would feature interviews with prominent Americans who had overcome adversity through such virtues as hard work, perseverance, honesty, thrift, and self-reliance.

The previous August, Dreiser had left the editorship of *Ev'ry Month* and was striving to establish himself as a freelance journalist. Six months earlier, in his "Reflections" column for *Ev'ry Month* (April 1897), Dreiser had written the following tribute to success: "Great men . . . are not so generously extant, and it is for the company of these that one should strive. Nothing can be more elevating, and no more rapid way of gaining knowledge could possibly be conceived of. There is an atmosphere surrounding the great in which it is elevating to live."

Thus, the opportunity to interview these "great men" must have appealed to Dreiser, as did the $100 Marden offered for each contribution. Together, they drew up a list of potential interviewees that included Thomas Edison, Philip Armour, Marshall Field, Chauncey Depew, Andrew Carnegie, and **William Dean Howells**. Over the next two and a half years, Dreiser was one of *Success*'s most prolific contributors. To mask the frequency of these contributions, several were published under the pseudonyms "Edward Al" and "S. J. White." Marden reprinted sixteen of the interviews, unacknowledged, spreading them among *How They Succeeded* (1901), *Talks with Great Workers* (1901), and *Little Visits with Great Americans* (1904).

Further Reading

Connolly, Margaret. *The Life Story of Orison Swett Marden: The Man Who Benefited Men.* New York: Crowell, 1925.

Richard W. Dowell

MARKHAM, KIRAH (1891–1967). Born Elaine Hyman in Chicago, she was an artist, poet, and actress. When Dreiser first met her in 1913, she was performing the part of Andromache in Euripides's *The Trojan Women* at the Chicago Little Theater. She soon moved to New York, where she and Dreiser lived together at 165 West 10th Street and where she took the name of Kirah (or Kyra) Markham. There they often held weekly open house for artists and intellectuals. Their invitation card read: "Friends can always find Kirah Markham and Theodore Dreiser at home on Sunday evenings, November–March" along with their address and telephone number. She helped Dreiser edit the manuscript of *The "Genius,"* wrote the songs for his play *The Spring Recital*, and did the design for *The Plays of the Natural and the Supernatural*. Their intimacy ended in 1916, when she left Dreiser and moved on to become part of the Provincetown Players, the theater group led by George Cram Cook whose most important playwrights were Eugene O'Neill and Susan Glaspell. Dreiser used Markham as the model for Stephanie Platow in *The Titan*, in which he also portrayed other associates of the Chicago Little Theater—including its director, Maurice Browne, and the drama critic and author **Floyd Dell**. Markham would also appear as Sidonie Platow in "This Madness: The Book of Sidonie," part of the "This Madness" series of sketches Dreiser wrote for *Hearst's International-Cosmopolitan* in 1929. In the 1930s she worked with the Works Progress Administration (WPA) as an artist and was a stage decorator for the Fox Film Corporation. In later years, Markham moved to Vermont with her husband, and there she resumed her career as a painter. She maintained a friendly, but distant, relationship with Dreiser. She spent the final seven years of her life in Haiti, where she painted, taught drawing, and established a local theater group and a workshop that trained acting students.

Thomas P. Riggio

"MARRIAGE AND DIVORCE." First published in *Hey Rub-a-Dub-Dub*, this short essay sets forth concisely and characteristically Dreiser's rejection of monogamy as a practice and marriage as an institution. Dreiser's personal aversion to both is well known. The intellectual justification for that aversion given here is interesting for its broad and unfounded assertions about animal behavior and biology and human social history. Interesting, too, are an implicit theory of sexual Darwinism and a vision of the role the socialist state might take in child raising. The essay is structured as Dreiser's answers to six philosophical questions about the sanctity of marriage and morality of divorce.

Dreiser begins by pointing out somewhat disingenuously that among all other animals procreative unions are limited to the duration of the helplessness of the young, if indeed they endure at all beyond the initial sexual contact. For humans, too, marriage arises out of the biological necessity of raising offspring—the unavoidable side effects of our innate sex drive. The unnecessary and unnatural prolongation of this union among humans Dreiser blames on the human female who, far from relinquishing her young at maturity, has persisted in extending maternal control beyond all necessity. This unfettered maternalism, according to Dreiser, has resulted in multiple social ills, including materialism, war, tribalism, narrow religiosity, and, feminists will be surprised to note, patriarchy.

Dreiser's second justification invokes a quasi-Darwinian analysis of human types in relation to marriage. The "weak," "sniveling," "rat-like," "charmless," "masochistic," and "inert" among us are drawn or driven to marriage in order to compensate for a biological, sexual, and evolutionary weakness that might otherwise lead to their extinction. On the other hand, by confining them to single partners, marriage is an impediment to the "strong successful man" and "beautiful and dynamic woman" whose evolutionary dominance requires multiple and varied sexual partners. Freed of the narrow confines of marriage, these individuals will, Dreiser speculates, adapting freely from Plato's *Symposium*, achieve an ultimate evolutionary stage: the reunion of humankind's divided self into an ultimate hermaphrodite soul in responsive intercourse with the universe.

Whether individual men and women choose to embark upon this evolutionary path or not, the state, Dreiser says, should take on the responsibility of raising children. Modern children are already essentially raised by the state via public schools and courts of law, he points out, adding that only the most extreme sentimentalism regards the home as in every case the best place for children and then only by ignoring the well-documented effects of poverty and strife in the American home. These ills, Dreiser implies, moving full circle, arise from the institution of marriage itself, which gathers together the weakest of humans and charges them with performing a job for which few are fit. When the state fully takes over the raising of children, "the extremes of misery in childhood are going to be done away with."

Carol S. Loranger

"MARRIAGE—FOR ONE." After being syndicated by the United Features Syndicate on 14 and 15 October 1922, this story was reprinted in *Marriage: Short Stories of Married Life by American Writers* (1923), a collection of twenty short stories that had been published in newspapers as part of the All-State Programme of American Fiction series. In 1927 it was included in *Chains: Lesser Novels and Stories*.

The story begins with Wray, an up-and-coming businessman, who meets Bessie, a conservative stenographer, with whom he falls in love. With aspirations to "make her more liberal," Wray introduces Bessie to "books, especially bits of history and philosophy that he thought very liberal and which no doubt generated some thin wisps of doubt in her mind," and to the theater. When Bessie evolves into the liberated woman he desires, he marries her. Wray is mortified, however, when Bessie takes control of her liberation. She joins literary groups and befriends liberal-minded women; it becomes clear that Bessie "might yet outstrip him in the very realm in which he had hoped to be her permanent guide." Eventually, Bessie leaves, accusing Wray of being "narrow and stubborn" and "trying to hold her back intellectually." Wray does persuade her to return home, and within a year she gives birth to a daughter, Janet, but because of a proclivity for independence and a desire for sexual freedom, Bessie cannot conform to the demands of marriage and motherhood. Bessie takes Janet and leaves her husband behind for a second and final time. In the end, Wray is weakened and defeated but still very much in love with his cuckolding wife. Although she clearly has lost all feeling for him, Wray's devotion continues, proving that their marriage is, indeed, a "marriage, for one."

Although Joseph Griffin concludes that "Marriage—for One" "seems more a veiled promulgation of ideas rather than a successful piece of fiction" (88), this story does offer interesting commentary on the changing roles of women during the 1920s. Contrary to convention, Dreiser suggests that women do not have to settle for a life of imposed domesticity but that they can be autonomous individuals, both intellectually and sexually. In his refusal to criticize Bessie for her eccentric behavior, Dreiser also challenges the conventions of marriage and asserts his own philosophies about the conflicts between marriage and individual sexual freedom. The reader, as Griffin observes, "catches Dreiser's own voice" in this story, and Dreiser's "philosophy and style of life are reflected in . . . his tacit sanctioning of Bessie's conduct" (88). Though typically regarded as unsuccessful, "Marriage—for One" promotes early feminist ideals and challenges an

ideology of conservatism. Consequently, this overlooked story emerges as a text that participates in a social dialogue and seeks to transform the ways in which women, marriage, and monogamy were viewed in Dreiser's day.

Further Reading

Packer-Kinlaw, Donna. "Life on the Margins: The Silent Feminist in Theodore Dreiser's 'Marriage—for One.' " *Dreiser Studies* 32.2 (2001): 3–18.

Donna Packer-Kinlaw

"MARRIED" began as a chapter in Dreiser's autobiographical novel *The "Genius."* Sometime before the novel's publication in 1915, Dreiser removed the chapter from the manuscript, changed the names and other details of his characters, and shaped the piece for separate publication. The story appeared first in the September 1917 issue of *Cosmopolitan* and then in *Free and Other Stories* the next year. The central conflict is between an artist's desire for intellectual and sexual freedom and the demands of his jealous, insecure wife, who, like Sara White Dreiser, is a conventional ex-schoolteacher from sturdy midwestern farmer stock. But the story is hardly a defense of bohemianism. Offering access to both characters' inner lives, it portrays a marriage tragically doomed by a mutual failure of mind and heart.

Duer Wilde, a rising young pianist, confronts the "problematic relationship" with his wife, Marjorie, who would turn him into "a quiet, reserved, forceful man" who is "truly great" and cure him of the "raging disease" of desire for the "nasty women" in his studio crowd. Treating him like a misbehaving schoolboy and exploiting his "sympathy for her obvious weakness and apparent helplessness," she cuddles him, strokes him, and baby-talks him in "a curious effort to combine affection and punishment," often reducing him to helpless anger and ineffectuality. Still, Marjorie is no monster. When a "sumptuous dinner at the Plaza" becomes a phantasmagoria of "vampirish-looking maidens" surrounding her husband and a frightening "artistic storm" of incomprehensible babble, she responds with a welter of fully human emotions—envy, fear, rage, self-contempt—and finally comes to Duer with a heart-wrenching plea: "What's the matter with me, Duer? Why am I so dull—so uninteresting—so worthless?" Her petite body, usually an instrument of covert manipulation, is now an open signifier of her pain: "[A] torrent of heart-breaking sobs . . . shook her frame from head to toe."

For a moment, Duer feels in Marjorie the sincerity and expressive power that only a few "masters of the stage" and "great composers" have, what in *Sister Carrie* Dreiser had called Carrie's "emotional greatness." "You're better than you say you are," he tells her—and for once means it. Ironically, Duer the aspiring artist lacks this very quality. The chance for real intimacy passes as both regress to their usual infantile posturing. Marjorie grasps at half-lies about his devotion; Duer dismisses his own heartfelt words as mere artifice and accepts as true her overwrought self-condemnation. In the story's concluding sentences, he thinks that "[s]he did not understand" the people in his world and "she never would," that "[h]e would always be soothing and coaxing," she "crying and worrying." But things might well be different if he understood less and felt more.

Further Reading

Hussman, Lawrence E., Jr. *Dreiser and His Fiction: A Twentieth-Century Quest.* Philadelphia: University of Pennsylvania Press, 1983. 113–15.

Stephen C. Brennan

"A MASTER OF PHOTOGRAPHY." Dreiser was an early enthusiast of Alfred Stieglitz (1864–1946), and in this essay, published in *Success* on 10 June 1899, the first on the photographer's work, Dreiser argues that Stieglitz's photography should be regarded as an art, not as mere photography, and that creating art requires an artistic sensibility and imagination. At the time, Stieglitz was experimenting with the potential of the new Kodak "detective" camera to capture city scenes. The realism of his widely reproduced *Fifth Avenue in Winter* (1893) exemplifies the camera's potential and influenced Dreiser's depiction of the winter snow scenes in "Curious Shifts of the Poor." An artistic photographer like Stieglitz, Dreiser explains, "did not snap his camera right and left. In the end, patience prevailed." His photograph "looks more like a painting," just as good writing should not be merely descriptive. Good photographs, as does good writing, capture "that delicacy of treatment, and that charm of situation and sentiment which all rare paintings have." Commenting on the success of Stieglitz's *The L in a Storm*, Dreiser analyzes its creation. Stieglitz initially photographed a blinding snowstorm and made a print of a striking scene. Most photographers, Dreiser notes, would have been satisfied with the work at that point, but Stieglitz realized that the initial print "contained much that was unessential and weakened the composition." As a result, "all this was cut out and an enlarged transparency made of the part which was to be kept. . . . The contrast had to be reduced, parts held back, and others brought forward. In fact, everything had to be done which could, by purely photographic methods, tend to convey the impression produced by the original scene." In short, by modifying the range of tone and removing a couple of girders in the foreground, Stieglitz succeeded in making the falling snow more prominent. In creating such a photograph, there should be no retouching, "for that is something which no pictorial worker will countenance."

Dreiser later reworked this material, supplemented by an interview with Stieglitz about the nature of his art, as "A Remarkable Art: Alfred Stieglitz," published in *Great Round World* on 3 May 1902. Dreiser interviewed Stieglitz in the spacious quarters of the New York Camera Club on a late April afternoon in 1902. "Our idea," Stieglitz told Dreiser, "was to do the work and force recognition. We are 'photo secessionists'—seceding from that which is conventional. It is a revolution to put photography among the fine arts." In response to Dreiser's question about the secret of serious photographic art, Stieglitz replied, "Individualism . . . working out the beauty of a picture as you see it, unhampered by conventionality—unhampered by anything—not even the negative." When Dreiser hesitantly objected, "But strictly speaking, that is not photography," Stieglitz retorted: "You admit it is beautiful. Well, then call it by any new name you please." On that afternoon both saw a remarkable scene of the city: "Dark clouds had clustered around the sun; gray tones were creeping over the plateau of roofs; the roar of the city surged up tense, somber and pitiless. 'If we could but picture that mood!' said Mr. Stieglitz, waving his hand over the city. Then he led the way back to earth."

"A Master of Photography" was reprinted in *SMA* 1; "A Remarkable Art: Alfred Stieglitz" is included in Dreiser, *Art, Music, and Literature, 1897–1902*.

Further Reading

Dreiser, Theodore. "The Camera Club of New York." *Ainslee's* 4 (October 1899): 324–35. Rpt. Dreiser, *Art, Music, and Literature, 1897–1902*. Ed. Yoshinobu Hakutani. Urbana: University of Illinois Press, 2001.
    Yoshinobu Hakutani

MASTERS, EDGAR LEE (1868–1950). A partner in Clarence Darrow's Chicago law firm, Masters was composing and privately publishing his own poetry when he first corresponded with Dreiser in 1912 to praise *The Financier*. According to this letter, Masters had followed Dreiser's novels from the beginning: "You have such a capacity for detail and for the pure fact from which truth is secreted that you pile up in tireless fashion the evidence for your argument" (3 December 1912, Dreiser Papers). The two first met in December 1912, while Dreiser was in Chicago to interview people, including Masters, who had known **Charles Tyson Yerkes** as part of his research for *The Titan*, the second volume of the **Cowperwood** trilogy. Not only was Masters useful at that time by providing additional people for Dreiser to interview, but he was also responsible in 1914 for arranging a meeting between Dreiser and Jack Armstrong, son of the man whom Abraham Lincoln had defended in a murder trial. Dreiser was tireless in his pursuit of a publisher for Masters's *Spoon River Anthology* and was eventually persuasive with Macmillan, whose 1916 edition was enormously successful; Dreiser's copy of the anthology is inscribed: "For Theodore Dreiser / artist and master / Edgar Lee Masters." For the initial years after their first meeting, the two were encouraging of each other's work and saw each other regularly, but by 1920 their correspondence and meetings had dropped off. By the 1930s both were living in New York, but not until December 1937 did the two resurrect their supportive exchange, after Dreiser sent Masters a Christmas card. Masters responded: "I have a certain proposition to make to you, which is that some afternoon we get in the backroom of a comfortable doggery and there talk and partake carefully of intoxicating likker. I don't want anyone else to be present. I am not going to harm you, w[ith] anything" (20 December 1937, Dreiser Papers). In their later friendship Dreiser attempted to interest the motion picture industry in a film based on *Spoon River Anthology* and was responsible for securing Longmans, Green and Co. as publisher for Masters's 1940 edition of *The Living Thoughts of Emerson*. For the presentation to Dreiser of the Award of Merit Medal by the American Academy of Arts and Letters in 1944, it was Masters who accompanied his aged friend to the ceremony (H. L. Mencken having steadfastly refused). Ill health, distance, and Masters's marriage eventually contrived to create a final separation between the two, although they each managed to exchange a few letters between the time that Dreiser had relocated to California in late 1938 and his death on 28 December 1945.

Further Reading:

Powys, John Cowper. *Autobiography*. Hamilton, N.Y.: Colgate University Press, 1968. 551–56.
Russell, Herbert K. *Edgar Lee Masters: A Biography*. Urbana: University of Illinois Press, 2001.

Nancy M. Shawcross

"MATHEWSON." First published in two installments in *Esquire* (May and June 1934) and later reprinted, with supplemental passages from typescripts in the Dreiser Papers, in *Fulfillment and Other Tales of Women and Men*, "Mathewson" provides a profile of, and homage to, the titular character from the vantage point of an unnamed first-person narrator. The son of a prominent printer in St. Joseph, Missouri, Mathewson spurns his family's wealth and social position and moves to St. Louis, where he freelances as a reporter and editor for a number of St. Louis dailies. Though exceptionally gifted and much respected by his fellow journalists, Mathewson is disinclined toward newspaper work. The prospect of a successful career is further undermined by Mathewson's fatalism, verging at times on nihilism, and his self-perceived unsuitability for the real world. As a result, he engages in a course of willful self-dissipation, including alcohol, drugs, and women of questionable reputation. Originally attracted by Mathewson's reticence, otherworldliness, and sensitivity and curiously intrigued by rumors of his dissolute lifestyle, the narrator befriends him. Due to Mathewson's declining health and frequent debauches, their meetings are infrequent, but they have a profound influence on the narrator, who is struck by the contrast between his own fascination with, and immersion in, the material world and Mathewson's "esthetic asceticism" and self-destructive compulsions. The narrator is perhaps even more profoundly impressed by Mathewson's cynical personal philosophy, which leads him to question his own material ambition and interests. Eventually, the narrator leaves St. Louis to take a position as a reporter on a Pittsburgh newspaper and discovers shortly afterward that Mathewson has committed suicide, the result of an apparent drug overdose.

Though unnamed, Dreiser's narrator is clearly a surrogate for Dreiser himself who, in fact, did work as a reporter, first, for the *St. Louis Globe Democrat* and, then, the *St. Louis Republic* from November 1892 through March 1894. Moreover, several incidents and journalistic assignments as well as the identity of various newspapermen in Dreiser's sketch are drawn directly from his stint in St. Louis. Regrettably, aside from Dreiser's *Esquire* sketch, the only other reference to a "Mathewson" in his work occurs in *Newspaper Days*, where he is mentioned, in passing, as a onetime drama critic for the *St. Louis Globe Democrat*. Most accurately regarded, then, as a semi-fictional story, "Mathewson" is an eloquent and sympathetic treatment of what the narrator describes as a "priest-and-neophyte" or "teacher-and-student" relationship. Dreiser's sketch is further notable both as a chronicle of Dreiser's experiences, attitudes, and aspirations at the onset of his journalistic career and as an account of Dreiser's initial contact with those unorthodox social, philosophical, moral, sexual, and artistic views that would inform his mature work. Finally, however, "Mathewson" is most memorable as a compelling study in self-destruction and failed genius, a recurring preoccupation throughout Dreiser's work.

See also Journalism, Newspaper, 1892–1895.

Michael Wentworth

"A MAYOR AND HIS PEOPLE." This sketch about a nameless mayor of a "dreary New England mill town in northern Massachusetts" was based on the life of **Thomas P. Taylor**, the controversial mayor of Bridgeport, Connecticut, from 1897 to 1899. Dreiser likely interviewed Taylor in March 1898 while in Bridgeport to gather material for articles about munitions and weapons for the impending war with Spain. The interview that became the basis for "A Mayor and His People," however, was conducted in the summer of 1901, after Taylor was out of office. This sketch was published by *Era* in June 1903 and then extensively revised by Dreiser for *Twelve Men*. Because this was a composite sketch, based on the political life of Taylor but fleshed out with borrowed or fabricated material, Dreiser deliberately concealed his Mayor's identity and changed several facts, including the location of the town.

Like Taylor, Dreiser's Mayor rose to political prominence when his political club made a serious effort to have its candidate elected. Unlike Taylor, Dreiser's Mayor is successful in giving the taxpayers their money's worth: "Streets were clean; contracts fairly executed"; so he is re-elected to a second one-year term. The forces of corruption, however, succeed in overthrowing him in the next election. Some time after the Mayor has retired from public life, the narrator interviews him, seeking to discover how he has been able to deal with defeat. The Mayor concludes that he has not been defeated but will return to the political arena when the time is appropriate. The original 1901 version concludes on a note of hope. When Dreiser later rewrote the sketch for *Twelve Men*, he made changes that eliminated the positive tone of the original and created a pessimistic attitude that permeates the revised version. The temporary defeat of the Mayor is changed to a permanent one in which the Mayor failed to return to public life, accepting instead "a fairly comfortable managerial position in New York." Through the revised version, Dreiser suggests that no matter how hard one tries to improve the lot of one's fellows, that effort will be in vain. Dreiser placed this sketch among the second six in *Twelve Men*: a Good Samaritan who tried but failed.

Robert Coltrane

McCORD, PETER B. (1870–1908). Born in Lynn, Missouri, Peter B. McCord was one of Dreiser's close friends from the time they met in 1892, while both worked for the *St. Louis Globe-Democrat*, until McCord's death from pneumonia at age thirty-eight in Newark, New Jersey, on 10 November 1908. McCord was a newspaper artist who was gaining a reputation as an accomplished watercolorist when he died. Dreiser used their earlier relationship in St. Louis as the basis for the story "Convention," and he placed "Peter," his sketch about McCord written especially for *Twelve Men*, at the beginning of the collection to pair with the concluding sketch about **William Louis Sonntag**, "W. L. S.," another close friend and artist who also died young just as his talent was beginning to be recognized.

McCord worked as an artist for the *Globe-Democrat* from 1891 until 1898, when he moved east to work as an artist and cartoonist for the *North American* in Philadelphia for two years. From 1900 until his death in 1908, he worked as a staff artist for the *Newark Evening News*. He authored and illustrated a fictionalized account of a prehistoric man, called *Wolf: The Memoirs of a Cave-Dweller*, published in 1908 by **B. W. Dodge**, the house with which Dreiser was then associated. McCord's reputation as a watercolor artist had grown by 1907 to the extent that he was one of the featured artists whose works were on display that April at the Newark Public Library. This library still owns an extensive collection of McCord's watercolors, rendered in a Japanese style. McCord's caricature of Dreiser in Japanese style, wearing a kimono, was published in the 2 December 1916 review section of the *New York Evening Post* and in a pamphlet issued by the **John Lane Company**, entitled "Theodore Dreiser, America's Foremost Novelist." McCord's obitu-ary appeared in the *American Art Annual, 1909–1910*.

Robert Coltrane

McCOY, ESTHER (1904–1989), author and architectural historian. Born in Arkansas in 1904, she grew up in Kansas and attended the University of Michigan. She first wrote to Dreiser in 1924, and they met in Michigan in that year. In 1926 she moved to New York to begin a writing career. In addition to her own writing, she began doing research for Dreiser on the side. She wrote novels, short stories, and screenplays between 1929 and 1962. In 1932 she moved to Los Angeles, and there she contributed essays to many leftist political publications. During World War II, she trained to be an architectural draftsman. She wrote her first article on architecture in 1945 and thereafter made a solid reputation for her pioneering work as an architectural historian. She became one of the leading authorities on Southern California's architects and their work. Of her many books, *Five California Architects* (1960) is a classic in the field. She also wrote about Italian architecture and the folk culture of Mexico. Her relationship with Dreiser continued after he moved to California in 1938, close to where she was then living with her husband, Berkeley Greene Tobey. In the 1940s, she worked for the noted architect R. M. Schindler, whose office was within walking distance of Dreiser's home at 833 Kings Road. She and her husband socialized with Dreiser and Helen Richardson Dreiser, occasionally taking vacations in Mexico together. During Dreiser's final illness, she assisted Helen in caring for him, and afterward wrote a vivid and moving account of events before and immediately after his death ("The Death of Dreiser," *Grand Street* 7 [Winter 1988]: 73–85).

Thomas P. Riggio

"McEWEN OF THE SHINING SLAVE MAKERS."

Dreiser began what was his first serious attempt at a short story in 1899. This was published by *Ainslee's* in June 1901 as "The Shining Slave Makers," after having been refused by at least two other magazines. The story was then revised for republication in *Free and Other Stories* under its longer title. Because of both the date of its initial composition and its revisions, the story is of particular importance to understanding Dreiser's early thought. Much criticism of the story has focused on whether it should be viewed as an expression of harsh and egotistical Darwinism, as a celebration of self-sacrifice and cooperation, or as an interlinking of the two. While the place of egoism and altruism in the story is important, perhaps the most significant concept in the work is that of life as a struggle or game between antithetical forces, a theme that would remain central to Dreiser's thought throughout his life.

After falling asleep on a park bench, McEwen—the story's protagonist—dreams that he has become a black ant. He then joins forces with other black ants against a species of red ants, the coloring and territorial disputes of the antagonists being suggestive of a game of chess or checkers. McEwen eventually suffers a fatal wound in battle and awakens to his workaday existence. As a result of his individual struggles against other ants and his cooperation as a member of a larger community, however, he learns both the fiercely competitive nature of life and the importance of self-sacrifice, each of which is opposed to the other, yet interdependent and necessary for survival.

The story's themes and images are influenced by Dreiser's reading of works by **Herbert Spencer**, Charles Darwin, and the entomologist John Lubbock, and Dreiser pointedly defended the scientific accuracy of the work's details in response to a skeptical editor. Only two years after the publication of "McEwen of the Shining Slave Makers" in *Free*, Dreiser again developed the idea of life as a game between opposing elements, this time in the essay "Equation Inevitable," which serves as a discursive counterpart to his ant parable. Interestingly, in both "Equation Inevitable" and his posthumously published *Notes on Life*, Dreiser again made explicit reference to ants in describing his view of life as a game played by antagonistic forces.

Further Reading

Graham, Don B. "Dreiser's Ant Tragedy: The Revision of 'The Shining Slave Makers.'" *Studies in Short Fiction* 14 (1977): 41–48.

Pizer, Donald. "Introduction: A Summer at Maumee." *The Novels of Theodore Dreiser: A Critical Study.* Minneapolis: University of Minnesota Press, 1976. 3–27.

Roberts, Ian F. "Thesis and (Ant)ithesis: Dreiser's 'McEwen of the Shining Slave Makers' and the Game of Life." *Dreiser Studies* 28.2 (1997): 34–43.

Ian F. Roberts

MECHANISM. The philosophy known as mechanism is itself a confluence of two other philosophical concepts: materialism and determinism. Materialism is the view that all that exists is matter in motion. Materialism therefore denies any spiritual or vitalistic existence that cannot be reduced to some variety of physical being. Determinism is the view that every event is caused and that for any given set of causes only one consequence can follow. Hence, determinism denies the existence of any random or miraculous occurrences that could not, in theory, be predicted on the basis of a complete knowledge of any one point in history. Determinism must be distinguished from fatalism, or the view that certain events will occur regardless of any attempts to influence them, for determinism simply asserts that such attempts, while they may or may not be successful, are themselves always part of a causal chain. While fatalism is pessimistic in nature, determinism need not be. Mechanism, then, is the view that everything can ultimately be explained by reference to matter and the physical laws that govern it. Mechanism is typically scientifically inspired and rejects any appeals to teleology or final causes.

Dreiser absorbed his knowledge of mechanism from the writings of such scientific thinkers as **Herbert Spencer**, T. H. Huxley, Charles Darwin, **Ernst Haeckel**, **Jacques Loeb**, **Elmer Gates**, and George Crile. While Dreiser apparently never completely relinquished a belief in a spiritual or **supernatural** force in the universe, he nonetheless repeatedly expressed his acceptance of, and enthusiasm for, mechanistic philosophy. Dreiser's essay "Equation Inevitable," for example, defends mechanistic philosophy as providing a more reasonable explanation of life and a more sound basis for understanding ethics than conventional **religion**. Indeed, the ethical implications of mechanism were of particular interest to Dreiser.

Unfortunately, the ethical implications of Dreiser's mechanistic beliefs have been most frequently and most seriously misunderstood, as humanistic critics have often reacted in an exaggerated way to the threat posed by Dreiser's mechanism to the belief in free will and moral responsibility. This has resulted in a tendency by some either to denigrate Dreiser's interest in mechanism, and mechanism itself, as sophomoric and illogical or simply to ignore or apologize for what is seen as Dreiser's embarrassing attachment to a seemingly bleak and amoral outlook. However, a study of the philosophical debate surrounding the issue of free will and determinism serves to show that mecha-

nistic thought need not be logically incompatible with a belief in moral responsibility, as Dreiser himself seemed to recognize. Moreover, certain interpretations of quantum theory notwithstanding, a broadly mechanistic worldview remains consistent with contemporary scientific knowledge.

In practice, the term "mechanism" has become essentially synonymous with **naturalism**, and Dreiser's mechanistic beliefs are precisely those offered as evidence for his categorization as a naturalistic author.

Further Reading

Land, Mary G. "Three Max Gottliebs: Lewis's, Dreiser's, and Walker Percy's View of the Mechanist-Vitalist Controversy." *Studies in the Novel* 15.4 (1983): 314–31.

Pizer, Donald. "American Literary Naturalism: The Example of Dreiser." *Studies in American Fiction* 5 (1977): 51–63.

Vivas, Eliseo. "Dreiser, An Inconsistent Mechanist." *Ethics* 48.4 (1938): 498–508.

Zanine, Louis J. "The Lure of Mechanistic Science." *Mechanism and Mysticism: The Influence of Science on the Thought and Writing of Theodore Dreiser.* Philadelphia: University of Pennsylvania Press, 1993. 78–114.

Ian F. Roberts

MEEBER, CARRIE, the protagonist of *Sister Carrie*, is a naive, innocent country girl who enters Chicago in the first chapter as a "waif amid forces," a "half-equipped little knight" dreaming of conquest. Her name is appropriate. Being "of a passive and receptive rather than an active and aggressive nature," she is much of the time *carried* by the shifting currents of the "thoughtless, tossing sea" that is the new urban environment. She is not only her author's alter ego, his other *me*, but a woman whose "guiding characteristic" is "[s]elf interest." When life with her sister's family and her job in a shoe factory bring only "a conservative round of toil," she is seduced by the city and its "personal representatives," Charlie Drouet and George Hurstwood. Influenced by these men and the modish women she meets along the way, she seemingly adopts the "cosmopolitan standard of virtue," as well as of dress and manners, and, with good fortune and determination to escape poverty, finds herself living her dream. In a theatricalized environment in which everyone is playing a role, Carrie's "innate taste for imitation" makes her the consummate actress, slipping in and out of one identity after another as circumstances demand. By the end of the novel, she is a celebrated Broadway star who knows the way of the world, exerting a powerful attraction on men while yet retaining her independence as breadwinner for herself and the young chorus girl Lola Osborne. Inspired by her "ideal," the "genius" **Robert Ames**, she reads serious literature, questions the materialism and conspicuous consumption of American life, and considers using her talent to better the lot of humankind.

Dreiser's problem was to convince readers that the "arbitrary scale" of conventional morality does not apply to his fallen heroine. Perhaps with Thomas Hardy's "pure woman," Tess Durbeyfield, in mind, he portrays Carrie as a child of nature still "aligned" with "the forces of life." " 'He keepeth His creatures whole,' was not written of beasts alone," the narrator intones to invoke the protection of a benign power in Nature. Unlike Tess, however, Carrie lacks the capacity for enduring love that would guarantee readers' sympathy. When she boards the train for Chicago in the first chapter, "the threads which bound her so lightly to girlhood and home were irretrievably broken," as are most of her succeeding ties. In fairness, it should be pointed out that Carrie works up the courage to leave for greener pastures only after her onetime intimates have abandoned her emotionally. Though her eyes are usually cast toward the future rather than the past, she is hardly immoral, or even amoral. Every new desire brings unhappiness and indecision—signified by her repeated rocking back and forth in her famous rocking chair—and every step toward the new is accompanied by shame. But Dreiser insists that an "average little conscience" like hers is irrelevant when survival is at stake. It tells her to "[l]ook at the good girls" and feel guilty, but the "voice of want" has the last word.

Dreiser also emphasizes in Carrie the essential morality of beauty and growth. Shortly after becoming Drouet's mistress, Carrie looks into her mirror expecting to see a "worse" self but finds instead a "prettier Carrie than she had ever seen before," suggesting her intuitive recognition that the "first principles of morals" lie in the opposition beautiful/ugly, not the conventional good/bad. Carrie's continual "depression and loneliness" are the necessary consequences of her "finer mental strain." Though her mind is "rudimentary in its power of observation and analysis," it is extremely sensitive to contrasts in her environment; in the gap between what she is and what she might become is engendered "the drag of desire for all which was new and pleasing." She is, above all, responsive to "the change of affectional atmosphere." This "daisy" wilts in the cold atmosphere of the Hansons' dreary flat and blossoms in "the warmth" of Drouet's "spirit" and Hurtswood's "flood of feeling." True, in the early stages of her growth, the things that please her are often trivial and meretricious—"the remarkable displays of trinkets" and other goods in the department stores, the "[f]ine clothes," which "spoke tenderly and Jesuitically for themselves." In the "friendly" atmosphere of Chicago's Avery Theater, where she has her acting debut in an amateur melodrama, her childlike imagination transforms the tawdry setting into a "chamber of diamonds and delight" out of the *Arabian Nights*, a place, she thinks, where there is "no illusion." With experience, however, come disillusionment and higher wants. Whether or not, as some critics have suggested, Carrie's insatiable desires represent an implicit endorsement of the emerging consumer **capitalism** the novel ostensibly attacks, her unhappiness is a *"helpful,* urging melancholy" (emphasis added) that drives her spiritual development. Although she feels "somewhat justified in the eyes of society" when "settled" in her cozy New York flat as Hurstwood's wife, justification does not bring the "delight" she seeks, a rapturous, ecstatic, quasi-religious experience she identifies with the stage. "Blessed be its wondrous reality," she thinks of the Broadway theater where she gets her first job in a chorus line. "How hard she would try to be worthy of it." In this "shadowy play-house," a version of Plato's cave, Carrie continues her quest for the good, the true, and the beautiful.

By the time she has made it to the top, money and men have revealed their "impotence"; to do "anything better or move higher she must have more—a great deal more." Yet in her "emotional greatness" she already has this "more," as Ames reveals to her in the penultimate chapter. A melancholy romantic artist chasing the will-o'-the-wisp happiness, she possesses both a deep responsiveness to beauty and an extraordinary expressive power. She is a "genius," Ames tells her, because Nature has made her face "representative of all desire." She therefore has "a burden of duty" to become a serious actress, to make her "sympathy" "valuable to others" as well as to herself. As the original ending presented in the **Pennsylvania Dreiser**

Edition suggests, Dreiser first thought of a final love match between "the perfect Carrie" and Ames but decided it was truer to her character if she kept rocking and dreaming of some far-off divine event. Her heart, the narrator forecasts in the Coda, will continue to urge her "Onward, onward" in pursuit of the distant "glimmer of beauty." Though, as the narrator has said earlier, she is "saved in that she was hopeful," she will never find in the play of shadows the "state most blessed" she seeks. Sadder yet, she will never know she has always been one of the good girls.

Further Reading

Brennan, Stephen C. "*Sister Carrie* and the Tolstoyan Artist." *Research Studies* 47 (1979): 1–16.

Fisher, Philip. "Acting, Reading, Fortune's Wheel: *Sister Carrie* and the Life History of Objects." *American Realism: New Essays*. Ed. Eric J. Sundquist. Baltimore: Johns Hopkins University Press, 1982. 259–77.

Gelfant, Blanche H. "What More Can Carrie Want? Naturalistic Ways of Consuming Women." *The Cambridge Companion to American Realism and Naturalism: Howells to London*. Ed. Donald Pizer. Cambridge: Cambridge University Press, 1995. 178–210.

Markels, Julian. "Dreiser and the Plotting of Inarticulate Experience." *Massachusetts Review* 2 (1961): 431–48.

Michaels, Walter Benn. "*Sister Carrie*'s Popular Economy." *The Gold Standard and the Logic of Naturalism*. Berkeley: University of California Press, 1987. 29–58.

Orlov, Paul. "An Emersonian Perspective on Dreiser's Characterization of Carrie." *Dreiser Studies* 32.2 (2001): 19–37.

Pizer, Donald. *The Novels of Theodore Dreiser: A Critical Study*. Minneapolis: University of Minnesota Press, 1976. 53–72.

Riggio, Thomas P. "Carrie's Blues." *New Essays on* Sister Carrie. Ed. Donald Pizer. Cambridge and New York: Cambridge University Press, 1991. 23–41.

Witemeyer, Hugh. "Gaslight and Magic Lamp in *Sister Carrie*." *PMLA* 86 (1971): 236–40.

Stephen C. Brennan

MENCKEN, H. L. (HENRY LOUIS)

(1880–1956). Although Theodore Dreiser once dedicated a book "To H. L. Mencken, my oldest living enemy," their friendship was one of the longest and most productive in American letters. Aside from the quarrels and the times they weren't speaking, it endured from 1908, when they first met, until Dreiser's death in December 1945.

The two hit it off from the start; they had many affinities, temperamental, philosophical, ethnic. Both were of German descent—Dreiser, second-generation. Both were passionately committed to the cause of literary **realism**, which was entering a bolder, franker stage than that championed and practiced by **William Dean Howells** in the late nineteenth century. Temperamentally, they were different, yet in ways that proved complementary. Dreiser had his gloomy spells and was more introspective and emotional than Mencken, but he seemed to enjoy all the more the latter's wit, practical bent, and newspaperman's cynicism. Mencken respected Dreiser's deep pessimism and shared it, without its externally manifested gloom. Philosophically, they both inhabited a bleak, mechanistic universe. Both had been impressed by Darwinism, as popularized and interpreted in the writings of **Ernst Haeckel**, T. H. Huxley, and **Herbert Spencer**.

Along with these similarities there were differences. Dreiser was thirty-seven, and Mencken ten years younger when they met. Dreiser was born poor in Terre Haute, Indiana, while Mencken was brought up in bourgeois comfort as the son of a Baltimore cigar manufacturer. Dreiser's family had been smudged with scandal, while Mencken's was white-marble-step Baltimore respectable and boasted Prussian aristocrats in the ancestral tree. Mencken's father was a free-thinker; Dreiser's a fanatical Catholic.

When they met, Dreiser was an established figure in the New York magazine world, editor in chief of **The Delineator**, the flagship of the three ladies' magazines published by the **Butterick Publishing Company**. He had the mystique of having written a seminal work of twentieth-century realism, *Sister Carrie*, which had made an "enormous impression" on Mencken when he read it in 1900.

Mencken at this time was enjoying the show as a rising reporter and editor with the *Baltimore Sun*. He loved the raffish underworld to which the reporter had a season ticket but harbored ambitions to do serious literary work. He had written books on Shaw and Nietzsche and was yearning to write a play. Dreiser had initially proposed to him that he ready a book for the **B. W. Dodge Company**, a publisher of which Dreiser was an active director, but Mencken ended up as a contributor to *The Delineator*, impelled by a desire to augment his managing editor's salary while expanding his literary contacts in New York under his literary hero's wing. Dreiser appreciated Mencken's style, which, he recalled in "Henry L. Mencken and Myself," "bristled with gay phraseology and a largely suppressed though still peeping mirth" (rpt. in *D-M Letters* 2: 738).

In March 1908 Mencken called on Dreiser in New York. The editor was charmed by this jaunty, brash young man, who reminded him of an "over-financed brewer's or wholesale grocer's son who was out for a lark" (*D-M Letters* 2: 739). In one of the noteworthy comic episodes of American literary history, he recruited Mencken, already a dedicated bachelor, into ghostwriting a series of articles about child care. Dreiser came to depend on

Mencken for other editorial services such as advising on articles he was debating about publishing.

In this phase of their relationship Dreiser was the mentor figure; Mencken, the bright protégé. They shared a thirst for German beer and philosophical disputation, and Dreiser took Mencken to his favorite *Brauhäuser*. Most significantly, Dreiser recommended him for the job of book reviewer at the *Smart Set*, a magazine of social and intellectual pretensions. As Mencken remarked, "Dreiser got me my job . . . and so made a literary critic of me" (qtd. in *D-M Letters* 1: 5), and it was as a literary critic that he made his name.

While in New York Mencken would stay with the Dreisers, often left to keep company with Dreiser's neglected wife, Sara (known as "Jug"), whom Dreiser abandoned in 1910 for the eighteen-year-old daughter of a *Delineator* employee. This infatuation ignited a scandal that forced his resignation, but now he was free to return to full-time writing and complete his second novel, *Jennie Gerhardt*. "Bully news!" Mencken cried when he heard of Dreiser's resignation: "[G]ive the game a fair trial—you have got the goods" (*D-M Letters* 1: 64).

Mencken now had a microphone at *Smart Set*, and he was itching to hold forth on behalf of Dreiser, whom he regarded as the flag-bearer in the fight for a more mature, European-style American fiction. "Dreiser simply gave me a good chance to unload my own ideas, which were identical with his," as he later put it in a 20 August 1925 letter to Ernest Boyd (*Letters of H. L. Mencken*, ed. Guy J. Forgue [New York: Knopf, 1961], 281).

The publication of *Jennie Gerhardt* in 1911 provided him with his first opportunity to blaze out with an opening salvo. As soon as he read the manuscript, he wrote Dreiser a tribute that was a checklist of his own critical standards: "The story comes upon me with great force; it touches my own experience of life in a hundred places; it preaches (or perhaps I had better say exhibits) a philosophy of life that seems to me to be sound; altogether I get a powerful effect of reality, stark and unashamed. It is drab and gloomy, but so is the struggle for existence. It is without humor, but so are the jests of that great comedian who shoots at our heels and makes us do our grotesque dancing" (*D-M Letters* 1: 68). Mencken's enthusiasm for *Jennie Gerhardt* was tied to his ambitions, but it was not opportunistic. He regarded the novel as an advance over *Sister Carrie* and would for the rest of his days rank it among the best novels in American literature, "with the lonesome but Himalayan exception of 'Huckleberry Finn,' " as he noted in his *Smart Set* review of the novel (rpt. in *D-M Letters* 2: 740). (He would later elevate *The Titan* above it in his personal Dreiser canon—in part because its amoral masculine hero was more congenial to his anti-feminist views.)

Mencken led the critical pack with laudatory reviews in *Smart Set*; in his *Baltimore Sun* column, "The Free Lance"; and in the *Los Angeles Times*. Though his praise was echoed by others of the younger generation, Mencken was launched as Dreiser's most effective publicist. Dreiser warned him about becoming implicated in his literary rebellion: "It looks to me as though your stand on Jennie would either make or break you" (*D-M Letters* 1: 80), but Mencken enjoyed the fray and loved baiting the moralists and the literary conservatives who were the novel's main critics.

On Dreiser's next two novels, *The Financier* and *The Titan*, Mencken served as first reader, adviser, and editor. Dreiser's publisher, on whom he was financially dependent, was **Harper & Brothers**, a conservative house, so he craved independent advice from someone who was sympathetic to what he was trying to do. Mencken stood ready to oblige with honest judgments. He criticized prolix sections of *The Financier*, for example, causing Dreiser to prune some of the excess verbiage. Dreiser worried about the lengthiness of his manuscripts and trusted Mencken to steer him straight on cutting them. Sensitive to criticism of his style, he welcomed grammatical help—though with the instinct of genius clung to the style that was truest to his inner voice. Mencken respected the clumsy power of Dreiser's style (he was appalled by the way Harper's editors smoothed out the rough edges of *Jennie Gerhardt*), but when Dreiser sent him the manuscript of his 1916 travelogue *A Hoosier Holiday*, Mencken complained about repetitions and banalities. Dreiser told him to have at them.

The onset of the Great War in 1914 threw the two men closer together, as they both were sympathetic to the Kaiser and violently anti-British, mirroring their rebellion against the "Anglo-Saxon" dominance of American letters. As the war dragged on and pro-British propaganda saturated the U.S. media, they became more alienated from American society. Some of the academics who cherished British letters began sniping at their writings, implying they bore the mark of the beastly Hun. After the U.S. entry to the war, Mencken came close to being prosecuted under the Espionage and Sedition Act (he was improbably suspected of being a German spy), while Dreiser found his German name and sympathies made it more difficult for him to sell his stories to mainstream publications like the *Saturday Evening Post*.

Dreiser's reputation as a novelist had received a setback when Harper & Brothers canceled *The Titan* just before its publication on grounds of immorality. He found another publisher, but the puritans (as Mencken dubbed the moralistic critics) were clearly on his case.

In 1915, his fifth novel, *The "Genius,"* was threatened with prosecution for obscenity by **John Sumner**, head of the **New York Society for the Suppression of Vice**, a quasi-official **censorship** body, and the publisher withdrew it. Mencken, who might have said, "I told you so"—he had read the novel in manuscript, hated it, and complained there was too much sex in it—rallied to Dreiser's defense. He commanded a campaign to get the signature of every prominent American writer on a petition condemning the book's suppression.

The quarrel over the novel marked a kind of turning point in the latter's attitude toward his friend's work, heretofore entirely supportive. He damned *The "Genius"* as sloppy and reflective of what he saw as Dreiser's credulousness, his weakness for quasi-religious mysticism (the hero of the novel is sympathetic to **Christian Science** and spiritualism). He also disdained Dreiser's lifestyle in **Greenwich Village**, surrounded by promiscuous feminists, who were turning Dreiser into a Village aesthete, one of the "red-ink boys." Mencken admonished his quondam mentor to "Take the advice of men with hair on their chests" (*D-M Letters* 1: 285).

During the *"Genius"* campaign, Dreiser had ticked off Mencken by asking Village radicals like Max Eastman to sign the petition; Mencken regarded the use of such names as dragging Dreiser's banner in the muck of free love, birth control, socialism and other outré bohemian causes. Dreiser complained about Mencken's "dictatorial" tone. By then Mencken regarded the petition campaign as his own rather than Dreiser's. Dreiser also resented Mencken's sarcastic allusions to his alleged Village harem.

Exacerbating the friction was the fact that Dreiser's current mistress in 1917–1918 was **Estelle Bloom Kubitz**, sister of Mencken's girlfriend Marion Bloom. Estelle confided in Mencken her complaints about Dreiser's cruel treatment of her. Later she typed up a copy of Dreiser's intimate diary, which described his various boudoir encounters with other women, which she passed on to Mencken. The younger man's attitude toward sexual morality was more conventional than Dreiser's. It was all right for a man to patronize a sporting house or disport himself with an amateur, so long as he did so discreetly and in a way that did not threaten his or another man's home.

Dreiser's final betrayal from Mencken's point of view came during the *"Genius"* campaign. He wrote a play called *The Hand of the Potter* and innocently asked Mencken's opinion. When the latter discovered that the play concerned a pervert—a child molester—he hit the ceiling. If someone produced this pornography, he wrote Dreiser, it would undermine the anticensorship battle. Dreiser did not budge an inch, and the play was not produced at this time, but the friendship grew more shaky and almost collapsed after Mencken published a long critical essay in *A Book of Prefaces* (1917), in which his praise for Dreiser's greatness and uncompromising truth-telling was peppered with unflattering allusions, for example, "the Indiana peasant, snuffling absurdly over imbecile sentimentalities" (rpt. in *D-M Letters* 2: 786). Dreiser was deeply depressed, fearing that the negative notes in his former champion's appraisal would sink his reputation for good.

At this phase in his career, Mencken seems to have felt he had become too closely identified with Dreiser. He cared only for the novels he had championed, from *Jennie Gerhardt* to *The Titan*, and

sought to distance himself from the later novels, stories, and avant-garde plays, which he rejected as Greenwich Village exotica. A deep freeze set in between them, but by the time Dreiser departed for Hollywood in 1919 with his new mistress, Helen Richardson, an aspiring actress, they were exchanging the usual jokes. During Dreiser's three years in Los Angeles, they communicated amiably enough in letters, and Mencken continued to perform literary services, such as parleying with John Sumner over cuts in *The "Genius"* that would make it publishable (Dreiser ultimately backed out, and the novel was republished without incident in 1923). At one point Mencken sought to set ground rules that would prevent future blowups between them: "When I write about you as an author I put aside all friendship and try to consider you objectively," he wrote in 1921. "When as an author, you discuss me as a critic, you are free to do the same thing, and ought to do it. In this department I am a maniacal advocate of free speech" (*D-M Letters* 2: 437). Fine rules, but neither man could follow them.

In 1923 Dreiser and Helen returned to New York. He had a new publisher, **Horace Liveright**, who was backing him financially and eager to challenge the censors, and a new novel in the works, *An American Tragedy*. When this novel, Dreiser's masterpiece, was published in December 1925, it opened a new rift between the old literary comrades. Mencken was then smoldering at the seemingly callous way Dreiser failed to express sympathy at his beloved mother's fatal illness during a brief stopover in Baltimore. Also there had been a misunderstanding over access Mencken secured for Dreiser to death row in connection with the *Tragedy*. Whether influenced by this lingering ill will or not, Mencken composed a damning review of *An American Tragedy*. He dismissed Dreiser's greatest novel as "a shapeless and forbidding monster . . . a vast, sloppy, chaotic thing of 385,000 words—at least 250,000 of them unnecessary!" (rpt. in *D-M Letters* 2: 797). He did offer some compensatory praise for the 135,000 presumably *necessary* words, but it was lost in the roar of his critical fusillade. Dreiser lashed back in spluttering fury, telling Mencken that no one read him any more, that he wrote "for bums and loafers" (*D-M Letters* 2: 554).

They did not speak for seven years. Then in 1933, Dreiser's correction of inaccuracies in a history of the *Smart Set* drew a. thank-you letter from Mencken, and Dreiser proposed a meeting, "white flags in hand." Although permanently disillusioned with Dreiser, Mencken wrote in his diary: "It was impossible to say no" (*The Diary of H. L. Mencken*, ed. Charles A Fecher [New York: Knopf, 1989], 140). They had a tense reunion over two bottles of vodka, but the ice was broken.

Not long after their latest reconciliation, Dreiser moved to California. They would never meet again, but they stayed in touch through letters, livened by some political disputation. Mencken, who deplored Dreiser's alliance with communist causes as still another case of the credulous peasant seeking a new **religion**, held back his obvious disagreement.

Dreiser was struggling to finish a long book of philosophy, and his novel-writing career was in the doldrums. Mencken was a forgotten figure, a Tory and Roosevelt-hater who was scorned by the politically radical generation of younger novelists.

There was one last flurry between them when Dreiser accepted a medal from the American Academy of Arts and Letters, an institution Mencken had spent his adult life excoriating as a bastion of literary conservatism. He protested Dreiser's cave-in and found other business to detain him when Dreiser begged for a reunion in New York in conjunction with the award ceremony.

When Dreiser died in December 1945, Mencken summed up their friendship to Helen Richardson: "[H]e was my captain in a war that will never end, and we had a swell time together. No other man had a greater influence upon my youth" (*D-M Letters* 2: 725), but he wrote in his diary: "We were never really close friends, for I was a congenial skeptic and he was of a believing type of mind" (Fecher 401). Dreiser's anger had been distilled over time into mellow gratitude. A few years before he died he told Mencken: "[Y]ou arrived in my life when, from a literary point of view, I was down and out, and you proceeded to fight for me. Night and day apparently. Swack! Smack! Crack!" (*D-M Letters* 2: 690).

Further Reading

Bode, Carl. *Mencken*. Carbondale: Southern Illinois University Press, 1969.

Hobson, Fred. *Mencken: A Life*. New York: Random, 1994.

Mencken, H. L. *My Life as Author and Editor*. Ed. Jonathan Yardley. New York: Knopf, 1993.

Richard Lingeman

"THE 'MERCY' OF GOD" first appeared in the August 1924 issue of *American Mercury* and was later collected in *Chains: Lesser Novels and Stories*. The story of Marguerite Ryan, a homely girl rejected by a world that celebrates beauty, is framed by a philosophical debate over the validity of **mechanism**, a belief that all events in the world can be attributed to physical causes. The story opens with the narrator, who is inclined to stoical indifference to action, conversing with his friend, a celebrated Freudian neurologist who believes that only by taking action can one make life endurable. They fall to discussing the theories of a mutual friend, Z——, a thoroughgoing mechanist who believes life is a cosmic accident, a series of unplanned and unforeseeable events. The neurologist takes issue with the mechanist viewpoint, believing that "nature isn't altogether hard or cruel or careless, even though accidents appear to happen," and instead tends toward a harmonic equilibrium.

To convince the narrator that Nature adjusts itself to "make life easier for man," he offers the story of one of his patients, Marguerite Ryan, who grows up exceedingly burdened by her lack of beauty and its consequent social ostracism. After the death of her mother, Marguerite's father, a staunch Catholic, becomes even more "narrowly religious," and Marguerite, who has been reading de Maupassant and Dostoyevsky, maintains that **religion** is "worthless, or at the very least not very important as a relief from pain." Then, without warning, Marguerite manifests "a most exaggerated and extraordinary interest in her facial appearance and physical well-being." Her style of dress becomes garish, and she fancies herself a raving beauty. Eventually, she claims that her beauty is such that men cannot resist her; with just one look, men become "enslaved" and even follow her home. When the neurologist is called in, Marguerite is hesitant to look him in the eye for fear of jeopardizing his morality. Here, the story returns to the original debate between the narrator and the neurologist, who concludes that "via insanity, Marguerite attained to all the lovely things she had ever longed for"; Nature had a "change of heart, a wish . . . to make amends to her for all that she suffered." The narrator, who has been leaning toward mechanism, wavers in his conviction as the story closes: "Truly, truly, I thought, I wish I might believe."

Though the neurologist claims that Nature has corrected its mistake, it is, finally, difficult to "believe," as the narrator puts it. Dreiser's use of quotation marks around "Mercy" suggests that even he remains unconvinced of the neurologist's optimism. In the end, a mentally unstable Marguerite sees herself as beautiful and desirable; but, in reality, not only does she remain unattractive and, thus, unlovable to others, but her desire to be beautiful also has driven her beyond the edge of sanity to a place where no one is likely to see beyond her madness.

Donna Packer-Kinlaw

"THE MIGHTY BURKE." *See* "The Mighty Rourke."

"THE MIGHTY ROURKE." A revised version of "The Mighty Burke" (*McClure's*, May 1911: 40–50) and first published in *Twelve Men* in 1919, this character sketch was based on Dreiser's stint as a clerical assistant to Mike Burke, a masonry foreman for the New York Central Railroad. For much of 1903, Dreiser had been employed by that company as "an amateur laborer" while recovering from an onset of **neurasthenia**, serving the last four months with Burke's crew. Assisting out-of-doors in the construction of culverts, coal bins, sidewalks, and other concrete structures strengthened Dreiser physically and helped lift his depression. Burke was later given considerable credit for that recovery. Yet, despite this seeming debt of gratitude, Dreiser, upon his return to the literary world in 1904, initially cast the unnamed Burke as a tyrannical pawn of the capitalistic system in an essay titled "The Toil of the Laborer."

In "The Mighty Burke," also written in 1904, Burke was introduced in much the same manner. The narrator, identified as Dreiser himself, hears the foreman excitedly berating his twelve-man Italian crew (termed by him "nagurs") for their sloth and stupidity. The narrator's first response is sympathy for these victims of such an "Irish brute," but then he notes their imperviousness to the nearly-hysterical Burke, who, on closer inspection, proves to be the paternal leader of this close-knit, if contentious, band. Pleased by this rough-hewn amiability, the narrator asks to join the crew and is taken on to deal with the "O.K. blanks," thereby freeing Burke to do the manual labor he loves and eliminating the "nonsinse" that keeps him constantly embroiled in disputes with his nemesis, the chief clerk.

The sketch was then fleshed out with episodes demonstrating Burke's expert workmanship, his blustery affection for his men, and his complete contentment with what life brings. "A wonderful lamp of health," the foreman creates an atmosphere the narrator finds therapeutic. To conclude this portrait of the laborer at his best, Dreiser resorted to some obvious fiction. Though Burke was alive and well when Dreiser left the New York Central, "The Mighty Burke" concludes with a construction accident. Burke, along with several of his men, is injured and, after lingering, dies, a tragedy that brings into final focus his nobility and reciprocated devotion to his men.

When Dreiser revised the sketch for *Twelve Men*, Burke, of course, became Rourke, and the dialogue was reworked for greater consistency and authenticity. Dreiser also added considerable detail to vivify scenes and sharpen the contrast between Rourke's strength and his own weakness. Also added was a lengthy scene in which Rourke is confronted by a drunken ex-employee demanding back pay. During the melee, the Prince Albert coat Rourke has worn from mass that Sunday morning is ripped up the back. In

all, Dreiser increased the length of the sketch by over a third but did little to alter the narrative line or the sentimental tone of what F. O. Matthiessen has called "probably the best of Dreiser's short portraits" (101).

Further Reading

Dowell, Richard W. "Will the Real Mike Burke Stand Up, Please!" *Dreiser Newsletter* 14.1 (1983): 1–9.

Richard W. Dowell

MOLINEUX, ROLAND B. (1866–1917). Dreiser based his unfinished manuscript "The Rake" on the New York murder trial of Roland B. Molineux. The case centers around the Knickerbocker Athletic Club, where Molineux was a member and an officer. The victim was Kate Adams, the aunt of Harry Cornish, physical director of the club. In December 1898, Adams swallowed cyanide disguised as a sample of Bromo-Seltzer sent to Cornish. Cornish blamed Roland Molineux, a chemist and color-maker in a paint factory. Two years earlier, Molineux had complained about Cornish's management of the club, and Cornish allegedly retaliated by spreading rumors that Molineux owned a brothel. A month before Adams's death, another club member, Henry C. Barnet, had died suddenly after he, too, had received a sample of a patent medicine in the mail. The prosecution, alleging that Barnet had had an affair with Molineux's wife, attempted to prove that Molineux had killed Barnet as well as Adams.

The Molineux case attracted much public interest, and newspapers carried long daily reports for over four years of hearings and trials. Molineux was originally convicted in 1899 of the Adams murder, served twenty months in Sing Sing, and was then acquitted in 1902. By that time, he had become a popular figure in New

York whose acquittal was greeted with an ovation and a triumphal procession home.

Many aspects of this famous case made it promising material for a best-seller. Not only would the case have been well known by readers, but it also featured a charismatic central figure, hints of an illicit affair, an inside view of New York society, and a dramatic plot twist in which the wrong person is poisoned. It is easy to understand the appeal of the case to Dreiser but more difficult to see how the suave, self-assured Molineux could be a model for a character like Clyde Griffiths or how a story of infighting among clubmen would have given Dreiser an opportunity for expressing his political views. In the end, Dreiser abandoned the Molineux case and his unfinished manuscript of "The Rake."

Kathryn M. Plank

MOODS: CADENCED AND DECLAIMED. The first edition of *Moods* was published by **Boni & Liveright** in 1926 as a limited edition of 550 signed copies, containing 177 poems. Of these poems, 25 had appeared previously in magazines from 1916 onward. The book was then reprinted in 1928 as a regular trade edition and expanded with 29 additional poems (for a total of 206) and 15 "symbols" (drawings) by Hugh Gray Lieber. In 1935, Dreiser revised *Moods* by omitting 37 poems and adding 77 new ones to the remaining 173 for a total of 250, with Simon and Schuster publishing the result as *Moods: Philosophical and Emotional (Cadenced and Declaimed)*, with an Introduction by Sulamith Ish-Kishor.

As Robert Palmer Saalbach points out, Dreiser began writing poetry in 1895, and his earliest, unpublished poems are conventional lyrics written in iambic pentameter and follow conventional rhyme schemes, giving the poems a youthful, na-

ive quality (11). Between 1907 and 1910, influenced by Walt Whitman, he changed from rhymed to free verse, and the poems in *Moods* were written between 1916 and 1926. In letter to Richard L. Simon, the publisher of the third edition, he explained that his poetry "is not an attempt at lyrical poetry in a non-lyrical form but an attempt to achieve lyrical philosophy" (*Letters* 2: 729–30). Very personal in expression, Dreiser's poems are about people's search for their place in the universe and their struggles with the forces that often control their destiny.

The dream is a major motif in *Moods* and enables Dreiser, as it did Whitman in "Song of Myself," to adopt a speculative, musing perspective as he ponders the meaning of life. For example, in "Proteus," the speaker merges his identity into the elements of his world. After noting the "Birds flying in the air over a river. / And children playing in a meadow beside it," the speaker shifts to awareness of his self—"And myself / And not myself / Dreaming in the grass"—and then merges his identity with the objects he perceives: "And I am the birds flying in the air over the river. / And the children playing in the meadow." Writing at a time of obsessive preoccupation with forming a philosophy adequate to account for the "mystery and wonder and terror of life," as he subtitled his 1920 collection of essays, *Hey Rub-a-Dub-Dub*, Dreiser was fascinated with attempting to demonstrate the interconnection of people, the natural world, and the cosmos. In "Proteus," he is connected and hopeful: "For it is spring / And youth is in my heart." Yet this optimism is difficult to sustain. In "Amid the Ruins of My Dreams," the images are of "crumbled pillars" and "Disordered / Fallen / Girders / . . . of my temple of desire / Cracked and fallen." It is a darker, more nightmarish dream, where he is "Alone and silent."

All of the poems in *Moods* reflect Dreiser's quest for truth, both intellectual and spiritual, and illustrate at times a pessimistic determinism and at other times an optimistic mysticism. In poems like "For I Have Made Me a Garden," his is a brighter garden, even "under swords": "A rising sun / And a setting sun / . . . Make colour / And bloom / And beauty, / Lighting it always." In contrast, the poem "Little Flowers of Love and Wonder" reveals a more sinister and less hopeful view of one's salvation. The "flowers of love and wonder" grow in "dark places / And between the giant rocks of chance / And the coarse winds of space." They have no chance of surviving "dread rains" and "chill forests" and "quickly die." For all the beauty of Nature, Dreiser sees it as a cold and indifferent place: love and wonder, once born, live briefly and then die. Within the beautiful images is the banality of existence. Dreiser tends to link the specific objects of the natural world to a symbolic exploration of the **supernatural**, reflecting his quest to understand how one is connected to the universe. As we become more connected with the mundane, materialistic world, we become more disconnected from the spiritual. "The 'Bad' House," with its harsh look at sexual hunger, reflects Dreiser's social awareness as he sets up the scene of the lost souls of the "Babbling houses of bawds." With suggestively florid images of debauchery he offers a rough, realistic portrait of the "bawds and roysterers / . . . With their screaming orgies / And pulsing sweating hungers." Dreiser seems to be an objective observer, deeply remorseful over human stupidity. Perhaps referring to himself as he watches the decadence around him, he observes that "chiller passioned souls / Elsewhere dream pale dreams / Of better worlds and ways." With the bitter experience of age comes, perhaps, remorse.

As Dreiser used listing and repetition in "Proteus" to convey the rhythm of dreams, in " ' Material' Possessions" he catalogs seemingly unrelated objects to compare his soul to the inanimate world, drawing comfort from his connection to Nature. "A tree that I have planted / A bed of flowers set out by me / . . . What is there / Between them and myself / That calls from them to me?" The poet broodingly asks, "Animate / Inanimate? / . . . But why? / Why?" He fervently searches for his place in Nature as he fights the machinations of Life. This questing is repeated throughout the poems and, as one critic noted, may have proved more powerful had there been less.

The reviews of *Moods* were reserved. Mainstream America really didn't know how to respond to Dreiser's poetry, with its blend of mysticism and pessimism. The more conservative papers were, as to be expected, lukewarm in their response. The critic for the *Salt Lake City Telegram* stated, "It reads like Cubist painting looks, and like that bastard art, is devoid of beauty. It is monotonous, unoriginal, at times humdrum" (rpt. in Salzman 531). The critic did not deny Dreiser's "power and magnitude," but he did question whether *Moods* deserved to be classified as poetry. The reviewer for the *San Francisco Bulletin* wrote, "Dreiser is not a poet, but he has the poet's gift of values; of elaboration and elimination" (rpt. in Salzman 527). The *Denver News* described *Moods* as "A strange book . . . and at times an interesting one. It can hardly be classified as poetry, tho it is sometimes rhythmic" (rpt. in Salzman 525). Only a few were socially aware enough to see the tides of change reflected in Dreiser's work. Most saw it as an autobiographical, poetic confessional, not poetry. Only a very few saw the bravery and boldness of the work and its challenge to the forces of intellectual authority.

As the reviewer for the *Cincinnati Times Star* observed, "It marks not only a new development in the genius of America's foremost novelist, but a memorable date in the history of American poetry" (rpt. in Salzman 529). Their honesty and directness, their vulnerability, are what is most compelling about these poems. One sees the man behind his work, the original impulses out of which grew the great characters in his novels. As the critic for the *San Francisco Bulletin* remarked, "It is the scenario of the soul of Theodore Dreiser" (rpt. in Salzman 527).

See also Transcendentalism.

Further Reading

Saalbach, Robert Palmer. Introduction to *Selected Poems (from Moods) by Theodore Dreiser*. Jericho, N.Y.: Exposition Press, 1963. 9–22.

D. L. Anderson

MOONEY, TOM (1882–1942). American-born socialist, union organizer, activist, and publisher. Born Thomas Joseph Mooney to an impoverished Indiana coal-mining family, Mooney became an apprentice ironworker at age fourteen to help support his family. He joined the International Molders Union upon becoming a journeyman in 1902 and remained a life-long member of that union and the Industrial Workers of the World, which he joined in 1910. Mooney's interest in socialism was sparked in 1906 during a trip to Europe and was confirmed the following year in the United States during the panic of 1907. He joined the Socialist Party that year and began his career as soapbox speaker and labor organizer.

Mooney and other activists were arrested following an explosion at the San Francisco Preparedness Day Parade on 22 July 1916. Corporate-organized Preparedness Day demonstrations in support of increasing the size and armament of the U.S. military were being staged in cities across the United States that year, sponsored in San Francisco by the likes of California magnates William Randolph Hearst, William Sproule, Jesse W. Lilienthal, and William H. Crocker. Labor organizations, opposed to rampant militarism and concerned that such demonstrations merely filled the pockets of capitalists at the expense of workers, urged and in some cases forbade union workers to participate in the parades and promised to protect from firing those workers who refused employers' demands that they march. Antipreparedness demonstrations were organized for the days previous to the parade. There is little indication that labor planned on disrupting the parade itself with a bombing, but an explosion did occur at the Ferry Building on Market Steet as companies of veterans waited to join the parade. Forty people were injured, and ten killed. Mooney, his wife, and several others were arrested, indicted, and convicted of murder in 1917. Mooney was sentenced to death, though the sentence was later commuted to life. In 1939, given the dubious nature of the evidence offered at his trial, Mooney was pardoned by California governor Culbert Olson—his first act upon election to office.

Mooney's case became a cause célèbre among intellectuals of the American Left almost immediately. Dreiser's active interest in Mooney appears not to have begun until 1929, when he joined with Ella Winter, Eugene Debs, Lincoln Steffens, Upton Sinclair, and **Sinclair Lewis**, among others, in calling for Mooney's release. Continuing to steer his complicated path between his capitalist yearnings and socialist leanings, Dreiser also dined with William Randolph Hearst that year. Dreiser began a correspondence with Mooney, incarcerated in San Quentin prison, in 1929 and contributed to the American Civil Liberties

Union (ACLU), the *New Masses,* and other leftist organizations on Mooney's behalf. Dreiser visited with Mooney in San Quentin in 1930, 1931, and 1932, discussing, among other things, *An American Tragedy,* which Mooney had read in prison. In November 1932 Dreiser spoke, with Steffens, Winter, and others, at a "Free Tom Mooney" rally before 15,000 people, including an amused San Francisco press, which translated its hostility toward Mooney into ridicule of Dreiser's personal appearance. Despite his interest in Mooney and the example of Upton Sinclair, who wrote *100%: The Story of a Patriot* about Mooney in 1920, Dreiser did little extended writing specifically about the Mooney case other than contributions to two pamphlets, several newspaper interviews, and a short magazine article.

Further Reading

Dreiser, Theodore. "Mooney and America." *Hesperian* 1 (1930): 2–4.

Frost, Richard H. *The Mooney Case.* Stanford, Calif.: Stanford University Press, 1968.

Carol S. Loranger

MOORE, MARY ADELAIDE (1858–1911). Known for her headstrong, passionate, and often rebellious demeanor, Mollie, as she was often called, became Dreiser's model for **Aileen Butler,** the first mistress and second wife of **Frank Cowperwood** in the *Trilogy of Desire.* Mary Moore was one of nine children of a chemist employed by a drug firm and met her future husband, **Charles Tyson Yerkes,** the man Dreiser used as a basis for Cowperwood, as a young teenager in the early 1870s. She soon became Yerkes's mistress, even visiting him in prison after his conviction for hypothecating funds from the city treasury. Prison officials dubbed her the "prison angel." After Yerkes's release in 1872, they attempted to rebuild their repu-

tations together in Philadelphia society, but after years of battling the public's perception of Mollie as a home wrecker, they moved to Chicago in 1880 and married in 1881. In the fictional account, Dreiser cut the time that Cowperwood and Aileen remain in Philadelphia to only six months, an alteration that scholars believe was intended to seal their fate together. Critics also note that the lack of a prominent figure in Mollie's family life, combined with her rebellious nature, good looks, and unbridled passion, led Dreiser to create the Butler family, namely, the patriarch of the family, Edward Butler, who, despite a corrupt public life, maintains a rather conservative, virtuous family life. The clash between father and daughter over her affair with Cowperwood provided Dreiser with excellent plot material for *The Financier.*

Chicago did little to improve the couple's social ambitions. In fact, Mollie's failure as a socialite, partly resulting from her husband's cutthroat business tactics, encouraged Yerkes to form relations with several younger women. In 1894, they moved to New York, where Yerkes attempted to establish his wife in society by dressing her up in expensive gowns and jewelry. However, her poor reputation and obvious social climbing again caused her to fail as a social host. This failure and fits of jealous rage at Yerkes's many affairs, especially with his long-term mistress **Emilie Grigsby,** became material for Dreiser's portrayal of Aileen Butler in *The Titan* and *The Stoic.*

During the summer of 1905, Yerkes pressured Mollie for a divorce, even asking her to leave their mansion at 864 Fifth Avenue. When she refused, he threatened to write her out of the will. After his death in December 1905, Yerkes's son, Charles E. Tyson, attempted to force her out of the mansion and prevent her from profiting from the will. She successfully sued for possession of everything in the mansion, but despite this victory, everything had to be sold to meet debts, thereby forcing Mollie to move to a lesser house on Madison Avenue. The entire contents of the mansion went to auction in 1910. After Yerkes's creditors were paid, Mollie was left with less than $200,000. Bitterly disappointed, suffering from ill health, and lonely, she died in April 1911. Dreiser passes on the same fate to Aileen in *The Stoic*.

Further Reading

Gerber, Philip. "Jolly Mrs. Yerkes Is Home from Abroad: Dreiser and the Celebrity Culture." *Theodore Dreiser and American Culture: New Readings*. Ed. Yoshinobu Hakutani. Newark: University of Delaware Press, 2000. 79–103.
Kevin Jett

"MORE DEMOCRACY OR LESS? AN INQUIRY." First published in the journal *Reconstruction* in December 1919, this essay was included in *Hey Rub-a-Dub-Dub*. Like the longer "Life, Art and America," also reprinted in *Hey Rub-a-Dub-Dub*, "More Democracy or Less?" begins with a Menckenesque skewering of American philistinism. Americans have sacrificed intellectual accomplishment to the crassest forms of materialism. As a result, American arts are commercial and derivative, American science and philosophy rudimentary, and American influence on world affairs paltry compared with that of the similarly situated ancient Greeks. Internal American politics are a shambles due to the combined influence of puritanism and Americans' unexamined faith in the success of the democratic experiment. The only areas of endeavor in which Dreiser finds Americans equivocally accomplished are commercial: in finance and trade. Even there, Dreiser points out, other nations have their Royal Dutch Shells and Cecil Rhodeses.

Where "Life, Art and America" focuses on Americans' need for spiritual sustenance through art, here Dreiser concerns himself with politics, specifically with outlining a critique of democracy, American-style. Thanks to ideologically driven education and the resulting ignorance of the mass of Americans, Dreiser says, Americans persist in believing they are the freest and happiest people on earth despite trusts and monopolies, the 1917 Espionage Act, wage-slavery, legislative corruption, machine politics, "five per cent . . . of the population controlling ninety-five per cent of the wealth," and an illiteracy rate of 13 percent. In all, Dreiser's assessment of American social ills of the first decades of the twentieth century accords with that of the era's socialist movement, in which he maintained an erratic interest himself. But Dreiser's proposed solution departs radically from socialism, which requires an optimism about human nature, its altruism and intelligence, that Dreiser did not share. Instead, Dreiser points to Standard Oil Company, a "great business corporation . . . built about the personality, the leadership, the autocracy, of one man" as the best model for American political organization. Under a businesslike autocracy and freely admitting, to and directing, humans' innate selfishness, America could, like Standard Oil, increase its prosperity and stability. Strong laws and leadership unhindered by checks and balances and regular elections would permit strong and ambitious men with "something to offer which makes . . . dictatorship bearable" until they fail to satisfy the wants of the people. Dreiser points to Caesar, Napoleon, and Kaiser Wilhelm, along with John D. Rockefeller, as model autocrats. The Roman Empire and Catholic Church ("the most impressive organization in human history") thrived when they ceased to be democratic. Dreiser does not indicate how government along the lines of Standard Oil would alleviate the social inequities he has listed. Indeed, elsewhere in the article he includes Standard Oil among those money interests that he believes have suborned American democracy, but he admires their efficiency. Rule by the masses, Dreiser adds, is always inefficient, both in meeting crises such as the recent world war and in managing the competing wants of ordinary citizens and moneyed interests.

In all, Dreiser's vision of strongman leadership as a solution to modern ills accords with his naturalist philosophy and his lifelong fascination with tycoons, inventors, celebrities, and other successful men, against which his mild socialist leanings seldom, if ever, would prevail. However, historical context cautions against dismissing this essay as arising solely from Dreiser's personal quirks. The multiplication of states governed by personality-laden dictators worldwide during the ensuing two decades suggests that autocracy, with its promises of efficiency, organization, and prosperity, was considered sufficiently attractive by many of Dreiser's contemporaries.

Carol S. Loranger

MULDOON, WILLIAM (1845–1933). Muldoon was one of the more colorful and imposing figures of his era, "a kind of tiger in collar and boots," as Dreiser termed him. After serving with the Union forces during the Civil War, Muldoon first performed as a boxer and then as a wrestler, achieving championship status in the latter profession. Later he managed such notable boxers as heavyweight champion John L. Sullivan and middleweight champion Kid McCoy. He was also at various stages of his career a patrolman for the New York

City Police Department, a saloon keeper, and a single-role actor, appearing as Charles the Wrestler in the Helena Modjeska and Maurice Barrymore production of *As You Like It*. At the age of seventy-six, Muldoon became the first chairman of the New York State Boxing Commission.

In 1900, still a magnificent physical specimen, Muldoon opened Olympia, a sanitarium near White Plains, New York, which catered to a white-collar clientele and featured a strict regimen of regular hours, balanced meals, abstinence from tobacco and liquor, vigorous exercise, and withering attacks by Muldoon himself on lethargy, self-pity, and slovenly habits. From 21 April through 2 June 1903, during rehabilitation from a debilitating period of **neurasthenia**, Dreiser was one of Muldoon's clients, an arrangement made and financed by Dreiser's oldest brother, Paul Dresser, one of Muldoon's friends and admirers. By all accounts, Dreiser found the physical demands exhausting and Muldoon's verbal abuse frightening and humiliating, but the results were positive. He gained some much-needed weight, and his interest in life and literature was rekindled. By the time he left Olympia, he had reopened negotiations with a publisher to reissue *Sister Carrie* and had written "Scared Back to Nature," an article on his experiences at the sanitarium, published by *Harper's Weekly* (16 May 1903: 816), while he was still in residence.

In "Scared Back to Nature," Dreiser's sympathies seem largely with Olympia's patients, men of significant achievement whose physical deterioration had left them vulnerable to the unnamed Muldoon's mockery and intimidation. Describing his association with this group, Dreiser wrote, "There . . . was an all-pervading atmosphere of good-fellowship, except for a marked strain of autocracy on the part of the host and a certain helpless servility on that of the guests." The essay was then fleshed out by a series of examples of "rough treatment" defended by Muldoon as "a method of wrestling a man's mental control from him in order to increase his mental energy."

When Dreiser returned to the Olympia experience a year later in the manuscript of *An Amateur Laborer*, his memories had darkened considerably. "In those days," he recalled, "I think I took about the bitterest view of humanity that I have ever had." His fellow patients he now described as men whose urbanity was a thinly veiled attempt to mask their materialism, arrogance, vacuity, and self-indulgence. Muldoon's harassment of these otherwise pampered individuals seemed justified and often efficacious. The attacks on his own weaknesses Dreiser deeply resented and found capricious. Muldoon, he felt, was a "brute" and a "scourge." In retrospect, however, Dreiser had to admit that such scathing assessments were perhaps accurate. He was "selfish" and about many things an "ignoramus." Also, the Spartan regimen had had therapeutic results. Thus, he took leave of Muldoon with a grudging compliment: "[Y[ou are an able man. You may not think you do good, but some of us cannot help but be better for having known you. I know I shall be."

Dreiser's final portrait of Muldoon was titled "Culhane, the Solid Man," published in *Twelve Men*. Though several new episodes were recalled or invented to demonstrate Culhane's contempt for weakness, deception, and slovenliness, "Culhane, the Solid Man" is largely an amalgam of "Scared Back to Nature" and the Olympia section of *An Amateur Laborer*. Virtually eliminated, however, were Dreiser's own feelings of bitterness and intimidation. The castigation of the wealthy patients for their shortcomings was presented largely through Culhane's diatribes, and though

Dreiser often included himself among those feeling the sting of Culhane's sarcasm, the one-on-one confrontations described in *An Amateur Laborer* were minimized or another patient was substituted as the victim. In general, Dreiser cast himself in the role of observer, praising Culhane for his marvelous physical and mental strength, his magnetic personality, and the efficacy of his tough humanitarianism. Culhane, he concluded, "was really one of the most remarkable men I had ever known—because he dealt so successfully with the most difficult of men." In the final analysis, "Culhane, the Solid Man" is a tribute to strength and the belief that human dignity grows out of discipline and cleanliness.

Muldoon did not return the compliment. Instead, in his biography *Muldoon, the Solid Man of Sport,* he reported that he had never read the sketch because of his annoyance with Dreiser for depicting Paul Dresser as a wastrel and philanderer in "My Brother Paul." Muldoon also pronounced "Culhane, the Solid Man" fraudulent, as Dreiser, unable to endure the rigors of the sanitarium, had departed after only one day. Existing correspondence and bills paid by Dresser show this accusation to be in error.

Further Reading

Van Every, Edward. *Muldoon, The Solid Man of Sport: His Amazing Story as Related for the First Time by Him to His Friend, Edward Van Every.* New York: Frederick A. Stokes, 1929.
                                    Richard W. Dowell

"MY BROTHER PAUL" is Dreiser's anecdotal tribute to his oldest brother, John Paul Jr., comedic actor and popular songwriter known professionally as Paul Dresser. The sketch was first published in *Twelve Men* thirteen years after Paul's death in 1906. During Paul's final days, he had reminisced, and Theodore had taken notes, promising "to write a story some time, tell something about [Paul]." With "My Brother Paul," Dreiser honored that pledge: "Best of brothers, here it is, a thin little flower to lay at your feet!"

As a child thirteen years Paul's junior, Theodore idolized his oldest brother, whose ostentatious lifestyle, local celebrity, and generous support of the family during financial crises made him a flamboyant guardian angel. Their adult lives, however, were less harmonious, particularly after 1894, when Theodore arrived in New York and failed almost immediately as a newspaper reporter. Paul, then at the height of his fame and financial success as a partner in a song-publishing firm, rescued his younger brother by allowing him to edit *Ev'ry Month*, a promotional journal. But soon their relationship became contentious. The serious, success-starved Theodore grew increasingly critical of Paul's pedestrian tastes, vulgar humor, intellectual barrenness, naiveté, and indiscriminate womanizing, the latter seeming at odds with the high ideals expressed in his songs, songs described by Theodore as "pale little things . . . mere bits and scraps of sentiment and melodrama . . . most asinine sighings over home and mother." Eventually, they quarreled over Theodore's ambitions for the magazine, and he left the firm, initiating a period of estrangement that lasted until 1903, when Paul provided Theodore steadfast support during the latter's struggle with depression. This support was returned by Theodore during the months prior to Paul's untimely death. Paul died a failed and broken man at forty-seven, his childlike nature being unable to cope with the reversals of his fortune.

"My Brother Paul" does not ignore Theodore's annoyances with his oldest brother. They are, however, tolerantly presented in passing as all-too-human weaknesses or given a disarming overlay of humor. The emphasis of the sketch is on Paul's exuberance, his generosity, and his tenderness, both as a songwriter and as a boon companion. "This tenderness or sympathy," Dreiser wrote, was "by far [Paul's] outstanding and most engaging quality." The sketch places Paul at the apex of his celebrity, during the 1890s, when he was an omnipresent figure along Broadway. Surrounded by the political, theatrical, and sporting greats of the day, Paul "shone like a star when only one is in the sky." The majority of the anecdotes reveal Paul's acts of kindness, usually in a monetary form—kindness to his mother, other members of the family, including Theodore himself, friends from the past, indigent actors, beggars on the street. "Some people," Dreiser noted, "are so successful, and yet you know their success is purely selfish—exclusive, not inclusive; they never permit you to share in their lives. Not so my good brother. He was generous to the point of self-destruction, and that is literally true."

As biography, "My Brother Paul" should be read with caution, for Dreiser often manipulated the facts to achieve narrative ends. On the other hand, as an overdue attempt at closure to an ambivalent and often strained relationship, it is one of Dreiser's most compelling pieces.

See also Adaptations, Film.

Further Reading

O'Neill, John P. " 'My Brother Paul' and *Sister Carrie*." *Canadian Review of American Studies* 16 (1985): 411–24.

Richard W. Dowell

N

NATHAN, GEORGE JEAN (1882–1958). Born in Fort Wayne, Indiana, and raised in Cleveland, Ohio, Nathan soon became America's foremost dramatic critic and an influential editor. Nathan's family wealth and cosmopolitan background imbued him with sophistication and nonchalance from childhood. He summered in Europe throughout his youth, and after being graduated from Cornell in 1904, Nathan took a cub reporter's job at the *New York Herald.* Two years later Nathan managed to secure himself a third-string reviewer's post, and with his review of Lincoln J. Carter's play *Bedford's Hope* (29 January 1906), the most important career in twentieth-century American dramatic criticism was launched. His greatest achievement was championing Eugene O'Neill.

Nathan settled into a bachelor's apartment at New York's Royalton Hotel. He remained there for forty-five years, the rooms gradually filling with books and manuscripts. Romantically linked with numerous actresses throughout his career (including a long relationship with Lillian Gish), Nathan finally married Julie Haydon, after a fourteen-year courtship, in 1956. More than the most feared first-nighter in New York, Nathan was a renowned man-about-town (and the model for the acerbic critic Addison De Witt in the film *All about Eve*). Oddly, in Nathan's published reminiscences of his friendship with Dreiser he chides him for his amorous adventures.

Dissatisfied with the daily grind at the *Herald,* Nathan left the newspaper and began writing for magazines, where he began to make his mark as a critic. In 1908 he joined the *Smart Set* as its dramatic critic and met H. L. Mencken, its book reviewer; the two became friends and in 1914 assumed joint editorship of the magazine. Here was one of the great partnerships in American letters, for Mencken and Nathan were the arbiters, if not dictators, for what the "flaming youth" of 1920s America deemed worthwhile reading. Nathan and Mencken were much more than trend selectors, for in the pages of their magazine appeared the most influential and artistically promising writing of the era. Dreiser was, of course, one of the favored few. A satirical poem of the day, "Mencken, Nathan and God," summed up their particular hold on the literate public of the 1920s. The poem referred to Dreiser's frequent *Smart Set* contributions: "And they quite agreed from the very start / That nothing was any good / Except some novels that Dreiser wrote." In 1924, when Mencken and Nathan moved on to cofound and edit *The American Mercury*, they published four of Dreiser's poems in the first issue.

Nathan claimed that he first got to know Dreiser in 1916, when he and Mencken attempted to alleviate the novelist's penury by arranging a cameo appearance in a motion picture. Dreiser would be filmed working at his writing desk to lend authenticity to a film about a novelist and would be paid $2,000. Dreiser was offended, believing the whole scheme to be a joke at his expense. Nonetheless, Nathan and Dreiser became friends and colleagues. Though Nathan encouraged Dreiser's playwriting and published his plays, overall he had mixed feelings about Dreiser's dramas. Nathan did summon enthusiasm for the published version of *The Hand of the Potter*, opining in a review for *Smart Set* that in spite of its excessively sensational theme the play possessed "extremely effective theatrical scenes" (rpt. in Salzman 352).

The closest collaboration between the two occurred from 1932 to 1934, when Nathan invited Dreiser to join the editorial board of a new monthly, **The American Spectator**. Dreiser was most enthusiastic about the venture and took his duties quite seriously. According to Nathan, Dreiser barraged his coeditors with so many suggestions about everything from story ideas to plans for reforming American literature as a whole that he exasperated them. For his part, Dreiser was frustrated by Nathan's unwillingness to print any articles satirizing the Catholic Church. Dreiser found this to be hypocritical since Nathan had always happily mocked every other **religion**. In spite of its ability to attract leading writers, *The American Spectator* foundered not so much because of the Great Depression per se but because its finances were unsound from the start. Its two chief financial backers fled the

country just after the first issue went on sale. After struggling for two years, Dreiser and Nathan were daunted in their attempt at a publication that would be a complete journal of American arts and culture.

Until his death, Nathan continued to wield influence by explaining the differences between the theater that he saw and the theater that he wanted to see. He did so with a singular, if sometimes antic style that reached a tremendous audience. Nathan's erudition, combined with his zany and breathtaking wit, made him the most famous, the highest paid, and the most widely read and translated theater critic in the world. He created modern American drama criticism and was crucial to the development of the modern American theater and its drama.

Further Reading

Connolly, Thomas F. *George Jean Nathan and the Making of Modern American Drama Criticism*. Cranbury, N.J.: Fairleigh Dickinson University Press, 2000.

Nathan, George Jean. *The Intimate Notebooks of George Jean Nathan*. New York: Knopf, 1931.

——. *The Theatre, the Drama, the Girls*. New York: Knopf, 1921.

Nathan, George Jean, et al. *The American Spectator Year Book*. New York: Frederick A. Stokes, 1934.

Thomas F. Connolly

NATIONAL COMMITTEE FOR THE DEFENSE OF POLITICAL PRISONERS (NCDPP). Sponsored by the American Communist Party (CPUSA) and particularly attractive to American intellectuals committed to social justice, the NCDPP offered legal and humanitarian aid to workers organizing for improved conditions and basic civil rights. Because its work focused largely on stimulating public interest in the plight of workers through holding public hearings, publishing investigative reports, and personally lobbying government officials, the NCDPP offered Dreiser and other leading figures in literature and the arts a means to employ their skills and eminence on behalf of oppressed individuals and groups in depression-era America. Dreiser chaired the committee in 1931 and throughout the decade continued to lend his name and support to it and other CPUSA-affiliated organizations such as the International Labor Defense, the Intellectual Workers League, and the American Committee for the World Congress against War, although he complained that the CPUSA often used his name without his knowledge, with the effect of diluting its usefulness for their work.

Dreiser's tenure as chair was particularly active. He wrote to President Herbert Hoover and labor secretary William N. Doak to protest the deportation of foreign workers and labor organizers, issued statements and appeared at mass meetings demanding the release of the Scottsboro Boys, and held hearings on behalf of striking coal miners in **Harlan** and Bell Counties, Kentucky. In the hard early years of the depression, established labor unions, particularly those grouped under the umbrella of the American Federation of Labor (AFL), had tended to backpedal on labor issues. Additionally, these unions often discriminated against black, female and other "unskilled" laborers. In 1930 and 1931, the CPUSA-affiliated National Miners' Union was attempting to organize miners in Kentucky who were not being served by the AFL-affiliated and company-sanctioned United Mine Workers of America. In this typical event in the history of American labor struggles, mine operators, local law enforcement, and hired "strike-breakers" with the complicity of city and county officials, the pulpit, and civic organizations shot strikers and journalists,

dynamited relief kitchens, and harassed starving workers and their families. The AFL remained passive while, according to the International Labor Defense, some 18,000 Americans suffered a "reign of terror" (National Committee 5).

After asking political figures such as Robert M. LaFollette, Felix Frankfurter, and Charles Taft to accompany him and being turned down, Dreiser traveled to Kentucky with fellow NCDPP members John Dos Passos, Charles Rumford Walker, Adelaide Walker, Bruce Crawford, Samuel Ornitz, Lester Cohen, and Melvin P. Levy. Dreiser also brought a woman friend along, which resulted in Bell County officials attempting to discredit the NCDPP and Dreiser by indicting him later that year on adultery charges. Dreiser and his NCDPP companions were also charged with criminal syndicalism. Since syndicalists argued that any form of state should be abolished, this was a serious charge carrying a hefty sentence. The charges eventually faded away, but the press coverage, especially of the adultery charge, had the added benefit of drawing public attention to Harlan and Bell Counties. After leaving Kentucky, Dreiser and the committee continued to collect relief funds and published, in 1932, *Harlan Miners Speak*, a collection of essays and testimony on the strike. Dreiser's Introduction to the book recounts his experiences in Kentucky, excoriates the AFL, locates the dawning of his interest in labor issues in his early newspaper days, and calls for overturning an American government based on "rapacious individualism" (16).

Further Reading

National Committee for the Defense of Political Prisoners. *Harlan Miners Speak: Report on Terrorism in the Kentucky Coal Fields.* New York: Harcourt, Brace, 1932.

Carol S. Loranger

NATURALISM. Naturalism is a late-nineteenth-century literary movement that seeks to apply scientific principles of objectivity and detailed observation to the writing of fiction. Emphasizing external forces rather than rational choices as determining factors in human lives, classic naturalism combines objectivity of presentation with a philosophical determinism that challenges or negates the possibility of free will. Through the study of individuals shaped by their heredity and environment, naturalistic writers believed that they could investigate and identify the underlying natural laws that govern human behavior. Unlike the romantic view that idealized the natural state of human beings and the beneficence of the natural world, for the naturalists all men and women were "human beasts" governed primarily by passions and instincts with only a veneer of civilization keeping their naturally brutish impulses in check.

Accordingly, naturalists tend to focus on lower-class characters since they were thought to be less influenced by civilizing forces and closer to the natural state of human beings. Subjected to the complexities of their environment, whether to an indifferent or hostile natural world or to an urban landscape of industrialism, poverty, violence, and brutal economic forces, characters struggle to overcome the obstacles that surround them, rarely, if ever, reflecting on, or discerning, the hopelessness of their effort. As it developed, naturalism faced criticism for its contradictory perspectives, such as its implicit tendency to suggest social reform instead of maintaining a much-vaunted objectivity and to imply a degree of what Donald Pizer has called "compensating humanistic value" (*Realism and Naturalism* 10) in the protagonist. Moreover, naturalistic works consistently address the impact of social and environmental forces on the individual and

implicitly express sympathy for the individual's struggle to control them, yet works such as Dreiser's **Cowperwood** trilogy or **Frank Norris's** *The Pit* (1903) betray each writer's fascination with, even admiration for, the forces of power and success that crush the individual. The writers most often called naturalists in the nineteenth and early twentieth centuries are Frank Norris, Stephen Crane, Jack London, Harold Frederic, and Theodore Dreiser, although, except for Norris, these authors did not formally identify themselves with the movement.

Nineteenth-century American naturalism borrowed ideas from a variety of traditions, including French naturalism, literary **realism**, and, most important to Dreiser, the scientific and philosophical ideas of Darwin, **Spencer**, and Huxley. Along with Edmond and Jules de Goncourt, Émile Zola was the leading proponent of French naturalism. In *Le roman expérimental* (*The Experimental Novel*, 1880), Zola proposed that writers follow the physiologist Claude Bernard's empirical model and establish the novel as a "laboratory" in which the author could subject his specimens or "human beasts" to the conditions of race, epoch, and milieu that Hippolyte Taine had argued ruled human behavior. Zola's multivolume Rougon-Macquart series, which traced the fortunes of two families through several generations and explored their inherited traits, was a practical application of his theories. Closer to home, American literary realism shared with naturalism a commitment to detailed, objective description as a technique. Since realists like **William Dean Howells** and Henry James viewed the artistic challenge of realism as making the ordinary events of a life interesting through the artist's treatment of the material, however, the realism of the 1880s focused on unexceptional middle-class lives.

Dreiser and others of the second generation saw in this earlier realism a commitment to what Howells had called the "smiling aspects of life, which are the more American" ("Editor's Study," *Harper's Monthly* 73 [September 1886]: 641) rather than a realism that was "nothing more and nothing less than the truthful treatment of material" ("Editor's Study," *Harper's Monthly* 79 [November 1889: 966). Instead, naturalist writers gravitated toward describing grotesque, violent, sordid, or sexually explicit incidents that strained the audience's identification with the characters, if not their sympathy for them. As Frank Norris writes in "Zola as a Romantic Writer," "Terrible things must happen to the characters of the naturalistic tale. They must be twisted from the ordinary, wrenched out from the quiet, uneventful round of everyday life, and flung into the throes of a vast and terrible drama that works itself out in unleashed passions, in blood, and in sudden death" (*Frank Norris: Novels and Essays*, ed. Donald Pizer [New York: Literary Classics of the United States, 1986], 1107). More significant than Zola to Dreiser were the works of Darwin, Huxley, and especially Herbert Spencer, who had applied Darwin's evolutionary principles to social processes, a practice that Huxley had earlier termed social Darwinism. Spencer's *First Principles* (1862) deeply affected Dreiser when he read the book in 1894, and Dreiser incorporated the ideas wholesale into one of his early stories, "McEwen of the Shining Slave Makers." A better-known example of Dreiser's use of Darwinian principles is the battle between the squid and the lobster in the first chapter of *The Financier* when young **Frank Cowperwood**, watching the lobster snip portions from, and finally kill, the helpless squid, deduces that the world belongs to those with strength and that "that's the way it has to be." Another ex-

ample of Dreiser's use of a biological explanation for behavior is the description of Hurstwood in Chapter 33 of *Sister Carrie*; Dreiser alludes briefly to a theory of katastates and anastates, or chemicals that cause pain and pleasure, respectively, as a biological explanation for his decline, a "scientific" explanation derived from the eccentric scientist **Elmer Gates**.

Dreiser is considered a primary proponent of American naturalism because of his interest in the world of circumstances massed against the individual, his frank representation of sexuality and the biological basis for human behavior, and his characteristic method of thorough observation and massive accretion of detail. The term "naturalism" was not always applied admiringly, however; the early and, until *An American Tragedy*, hostile critic **Stuart Pratt Sherman** called Dreiser a naturalist because realist novels are "based upon a theory of human conduct," whereas "a naturalistic novel is . . . based upon a theory of animal behavior" ("The Naturalism of Mr. Dreiser," *Documents of American Realism and Naturalism*, ed. Donald Pizer [Carbondale: Southern Illinois University Press, 1998], 196). More common are those who acknowledge Dreiser as a naturalist but find his deterministic philosophy inconsistently applied, whether because the transcendentalist part of the "divided stream" of naturalism allows for free will, as Charles Child Walcutt argued, or because the dynamic "animated field, endowed with an unconscious soul" (60) of the urban marketplace encourages gestures of free will, according to Christophe Den Tandt. As Pizer notes, maintaining fidelity to an ideal of determinism did not interest Dreiser, yet "without offering a clear-cut endorsement of the naturalistic premise that man lives in a fully conditioned universe, Dreiser buys into a qualified acceptance of portions of that premise," such as the role of physical strength and sexuality in determining fate ("The Problem" 10). As Dreiser puts it in "True Art Speaks Plainly," the purpose of literary art "may be expressed in three words—tell the truth," and the principles of naturalism or "realism," as he frequently termed it, provided the necessary framework.

Further Reading

Den Tandt, Christophe. *The Urban Sublime in American Literary Naturalism.* Urbana: University of Illinois Press, 1998.

Fisher, Philip. "Acting, Reading, Fortune's Wheel: *Sister Carrie* and the Life History of Objects." *American Realism: New Essays.* Ed. Eric J. Sundquist. Baltimore: Johns Hopkins University Press, 1982. 259–77.

Gelfant, Blanche H. "What More Can Carrie Want? Naturalistic Ways of Consuming Women." *The Cambridge Companion to American Realism and Naturalism: Howells to London.* Ed. Donald Pizer. Cambridge: Cambridge University Press, 1995. 178–210.

Kucharski, Judith. "*Jennie Gerhardt*: Naturalism Reconsidered." *Dreiser's* Jennie Gerhardt: *New Essays on the Restored Text.* Ed. James L. W. West III. Philadelphia: University of Pennsylvania Press, 1995. 17–26.

Pizer, Donald. "American Literary Naturalism: The Example of Dreiser." *The Theory and Practice of American Literary Naturalism.* Carbondale: Southern Illinois University Press, 1993. 54–68.

———. "The Problem of American Literary Naturalism and Theodore Dreiser's *Sister Carrie*." *American Literary Realism* 32.1 (1999): 1–11.

———. *Realism and Naturalism in Nineteenth-Century American Literature.* Rev. ed. Carbondale: Southern Illinois University Press, 1984.

———. " 'True Art Speaks Plainly': Theodore Dreiser and the Late Nineteenth-Century American Debate over Realism and Naturalism." *Nineteenth-Century Prose* 23.2 (1996): 76–89.

Donna M. Campbell

NEURASTHENIA. By 1980, the third edition of *The Diagnostic and Statistical Manual of Mental Disorders*, published by the American Psychiatric Association, no longer listed "neurasthenia" as a single disease. Considered by many as the predecessor to "chronic fatigue disorder," neurasthenia was displaced by the pre–World War I burgeoning of Freudianism and apparently disappeared in the early twentieth century, its specific symptoms classified as various pathologies. Historians of American culture and medicine describe the affliction as peculiarly American and peculiarly nineteenth-century. Clustering a symptomology of erratic eruptions of irritability, indigestion, backache, loss of appetite, blurred vision, headache, vertigo, palpitations, disorientation, restlessness, nervous tics, insomnia, dyspepsia, depression, emotional disturbances, anxiety, tension, and chronic enervation under the label of "neurasthenia"—"neuro" (nerve) and "asthenia" (weakness)—George M. Beard, in 1869, hypothesized a bodily economy as dependent on a limited amount of "nerve force" or nervous energy. Channeling one's energy into respectable and productive occupations and child raising would, Beard theorized, "reinvest" one's life energy. Yet turn-of-the-twentieth-century modern life, with what Beard described as its five elements of "steam power, the periodical press, the telegraph, the sciences, and the mental activity of men and women" (qtd. in Lutz 4), was, ironically, the very cause of debilitation or "dissipation." The more industrialized a society, the more civilized and thus the more vulnerable; neurasthenia was an "impressive illness for men, ideally suited to capitalistic society and to the identification of masculinity with money and property" (Showalter 135). Paradoxically, neurasthenia could also afflict those whose moral behaviors were perceived as compromised or questionable. Suspicious activities—gambling, sexual "excess," or masturbation, for example—would, Beard and his followers believed, also cause symptoms; thus, doctors could invoke this one disease to legitimate social Darwinist tenets.

By 1903, the language of neurasthenia and its representations flooded both consumer culture—magazines, fiction, and advertisements for cures, products, and spas—as well as medical literature (see Lutz, esp. 2–17). The discursive deployment of the malady served to bolster the iconography and ideology not only of class and race but also of gender arrangements. Though women were viewed as innately governed by their reproductive organs and emotionally weaker than men, white middle- and upper-class women experienced the same symptoms as men. Yet while men were often prescribed a treatment regimen that include travel, diet, and exercise, women, including Edith Wharton, Jane Addams, Winifred Howells, and Virginia Woolf, were often prescribed the "rest cure," a reinscription into the domestic sphere that also equated passivity with femininity and whose chief proponent was that specialist in women's diseases, Silas Weir Mitchell. Bed rest, typically ordered for six weeks to two months, in addition to complete immobility, supported the authoritative paternalism inherent in Mitchell's politics. Charlotte Perkins Gilman immortalized the punitive treatment in "The Yellow Wallpaper" (1891), a horrific fictional account of a woman's break with reality.

For Dreiser, a severely debilitating emotional collapse following the market failure of Sister Carrie and the abandonment of Jennie Gerhardt in 1902 culminated in a full-blown neurasthenic experience. What W. A. Swanberg describes as "The Crack-up," Dreiser narrates as autobiogra-phy in An Amateur Laborer and "Culhane, the Solid Man." Both pieces describe Dreiser's 1903 stay at **William Muldoon's** health spa, Olympia, near White Plains, New York, from 21 April to 2 June. At brother Paul's behest, Dreiser agreed to participate in a transformative regimen to cure both body and spirit. To quell deep fears of personal and professional failure, he committed to Muldoon's strenuous diet and exercise program and left the sanatorium rejuvenated. In "Culhane, the Solid Man," Dreiser appends a reflective elegy to his "liege," the "lord of the manor," and reaffirms the cultural work of Muldoon's (renamed "Culhane") reformist mission: neurasthenic men can work out and work through their physical ailments as well as psychological anxieties under the tutelage of Culhane, one "very virile, very intelligent, very indifferent, intolerant and even threatening" leader.

Further Reading

Bassuk, Ellen. "The Rest Cure: Repetition or Resolution of Victorian Women's Conflicts?" The Female Body in Western Culture. Ed. Susan Rubin Suleiman. Cambridge: Harvard University Press, 1986. 139–51.

Gossling, F. G. Before Freud: Neurasthenia and the American Medical Community, 1870–1910. Urbana: University of Illinois Press, 1987.

Lutz, Tom. "Making It Big: Theodore Dreiser, Sex, and Success." American Nervousness, 1903: An Anecdotal History. New York: Cornell University Press, 1991. 38–62.

Rotundo, E. Anthony. "The Cultural Meaning of Male Neurasthenia." American Manhood: Transformations of Masculinity from the Revolution to the Modern Era. New York: Basic Books, 1993. 167–93.

Showalter, Elaine. The Female Malady: Women, Madness and English Culture, 1830–1980. New York: Pantheon, 1985.

Kathy Frederickson

"NEUROTIC AMERICA AND THE SEX IMPULSE" first appeared in *Hey Rub-a-Dub-Dub*. Like most of the essays written for, or collected in, this volume, "Neurotic America" probes the widening cleft between ideal and real in American self-image. Dreiser's stated focus here is on American middle-class sexual hypocrisy, particularly as manifested in the middle-sized cities of the interior. The essay arrays an extensive set of contradictory behaviors enacted by individuals possessed of a "perfectly normal . . . sex impulse" yet in thrall to a cultural preference for "an infantile conception of life and its processes, unsuited to thinking men and women . . . a pretense that sex does not exist." Among the contradictions was that where prostitution is suppressed, unchaperoned public tea dances, "dashing" manicurists, and cars parked in lovers' lanes thrive. While some of these behaviors appear dated to the contemporary eye—a boy in a two-piece bathing suit arrested for indecency, *Hedda Gabler* and Rousseau's *Confessions* banned as immoral—others, including Americans' "convulsive" fascination with sex crime reports and hostility to public sex education, suggest the accuracy of Dreiser's assessment of Americans as deeply neurotic regarding all matters sexual. Along with "Life, Art and America," also included in *Hey Rub-a-Dub-Dub*, "Neurotic America" obliquely addresses the puritanical impulses Dreiser blamed for the 1916 suppression of *The "Genius."*

A focus on American sexual hypocrisy is consistent across Dreiser's oeuvre, and Dreiser breaks little new ground here, but read as representative of its historical moment—the opening two decades of the twentieth century saw both the development of the science of sexology (a term coined by W. H. Walling in 1902) and the rise of the sexual hygiene and social purity movements—this slight piece is most illuminating. In support of the normalcy and primacy of the "sex impulse," Dreiser cites Krafft-Ebing, Havelock Ellis, and **Freud**, whose most famous and controversial works on human sexuality appeared in 1886, 1897, and 1905, respectively. Dreiser seems especially indebted to Freud's vision of the dominance of the sexual drive from infancy and Freud's classic etiology of neurosis. The implications of these works were widely discussed among intellectuals despite the physical inaccessibility of some of the works themselves; Havelock Ellis's mammoth *Studies in the Psychology of Sex* (1897–1927), for example, was available only to medical professionals in the United States until 1935. At the same time, in the United States, perhaps spurred into activity by a 1906 *McClure's* exposé of the "white slave trade," organizations such as the National Vigilance Committee, the American Social Hygiene Association, the Young Men's Christian Association (YMCA), and the American Purity Alliance, among others, along with individual city vice squads, the pulpit, popular press, and U.S. Congress—which passed the Mann Act in 1910—campaigned actively against a variety of forms of sexual expression from prostitution to birth control, and sex education to coeducation. With the exception of a specific reference to the "White Slave Crusade," Dreiser only alludes in general to these organizations and movements via his criticism of their peculiar and repressive social outcomes.

Carol S. Loranger

NEW YORK CITY. Dreiser drew generously on his own experiences in New York to create novels that have become the benchmark for modern city **naturalism**, a literary genre that emphasizes environment as the predisposing factor shaping character. *Sister Carrie* became the prototype of the modern city novel, in that it depicted how newcomers are seduced by the lure of the city and its dazzling riches, only to be repelled and conquered by its heartlessness. The theme of success and failure in the big city continues to appear in other Dreiser works, particularly *The "Genius,"* a semiautobiographical novel that follows the career of a young artist from the Midwest who is initially awed by the fabulous wealth he sees there but who ultimately finds disappointment and moral defeat.

Dreiser's own first response to New York indelibly frames his view of the city as a place of unrivaled opportunity, compared to the relative placidity of the Midwest. When he first visited New York in the summer of 1894, Dreiser approached the city with a great sense of hope and expectation, overcome by the spectacle that he saw before him, later disclosing his reaction to the event in *Newspaper Days*: "Here, as one could feel were huge dreams and lusts and vanities being gratified hourly. I wanted to know the worst and the best of it." But Dreiser was quick to see that New York was not an elegant, handsome city but a self-indulgent metropolis with shocking contrasts, in which abject poverty, squalor, and moral deprivation existed alongside unimagined riches. In the discovery of these contrasts Dreiser the naturalist found fertile ground for much of his future work.

Dreiser returned to his newspaper job in Pittsburgh, determined to save enough money to move to New York. Within four months he managed to accumulate $240, arriving back in the city in the fall of 1894. Initially, he stayed with his sister Emma, who was living in a flat on Fifteenth Street with her husband, **L. A. Hopkins**, an unemployed and demoralized man whom Dreiser used as the prototype for *Sister Carrie*'s George Hurstwood. Dreiser later

moved into the Mills Hotel at Bleeker and Thompson Streets, where he paid twenty-five cents a night for a bed. In seeking work Dreiser gained firsthand experience of New York's cold indifference to newcomers, soon realizing that outsiders had little chance to succeed. After days of frustration, unable to get in to see the city editors of the *Sun*, the *Tribune*, and the *World*, he sat down at four in the afternoon on a bench in City Hall Park and looked upon the great buildings. His difficulty finding work and its accompanying depression would become part of his characterization of Hurstwood. Motivated by sheer desperation, Dreiser managed to push his way into the city editor's office at the *World* and demanded work. He was taken on as a space-rate reporter, a poorly paid position that earned him only $1.86 on his first day of work, and on some days he would make even less. Newspaper work was ideal for Dreiser's apprenticeship, for it provided him with the opportunity to gather a wealth of experience about the seamier side of the city. As he later recounted in *Newspaper Days*, revealing his perennial fascination with the spectacle of city life: "Nowhere before had I seen such a lavish show of wealth, or, such bitter poverty. In my reporting rounds I soon came upon the East Side; the Bowery, with its endless line of degraded and impossible lodging-houses, a perfect whorl of bums and failures; the Brooklyn waterfront, parts of it terrible in its degradation; and then by contrast of contrast again the great hotels, the mansions along Fifth Avenue, the smart shops and clubs and churches." Many of the memorable scenes described in *Sister Carrie* were mined from experiences Dreiser obtained going out on newspaper assignments—the desperate and hungry Hurstwood taking his place on a bread line at Fleischmann's Vienna Bakery, the Brooklyn trolley strike,

Hurstwood turning on the gas in a Bowery flophouse.

Frustrated by his efforts to earn a decent living as a newspaperman, Dreiser began to despise New York, repelled and disillusioned by its ruthlessness and indifference, describing it in *Newspaper Days* as "difficult and revolting." Later, in *The Color of a Great City*, Dreiser would express his disappointment at being betrayed by the false promises of the city: "How dare life, with its brutal non-perception of values, withhold so much from one so worthy as myself and give so much to others?" But things began to improve for Dreiser in 1895, when his brother Paul offered him a job as editor of *Ev'ry Month*, a magazine that billed itself as "The Woman's Magazine of Literature and Popular Music." As editor he wrote reviews, editorials, and a column that he signed "The Prophet." While the position provided him with a more comfortable existence, Dreiser was still not happy. In 1897 he left *Ev'ry Month* and spent the next three years as a freelance writer for popular magazines such as *Munsey's, Metropolitan, Ainslee's,* and *Success*. In 1901 he published his first short story, "The Shining Slave Makers," followed by his second, "Nigger Jeff," a story he would significantly revise for *Free and Other Stories*.

Throughout the thirty-eight years he lived in New York, Dreiser moved frequently. As soon as he was earning enough from writing popular magazine stories, he moved into the Salmagundi Club at 14 West 12th Street and then into his own apartment at 232 West 15th Street. In September 1899, Dreiser brought his new bride, Sara White, to live with him at 6 West 102nd Street, an apartment located a few steps from Central Park in which he wrote *Sister Carrie*. He also began writing *Jennie Gerhardt* here on 6 January 1901 but didn't complete it until 1911, when he was living at 608 Riverside Drive. The next year Dreiser moved to 605 West 111th Street, and then back to **Greenwich Village** in 1914, after a brief stay at 109 St. Mark's Place on Staten Island. Dreiser enjoyed the literary ambience of the Village, but he kept to himself and spent little time in neighborhood haunts. His friends knew he worked from nine to four and disliked being disturbed. When there were occasions to be celebrated, it was at the Brevoort Hotel, on the northeast corner of Fifth Avenue and 8th Street. Writers looking for a more informal place to drink met at the Lafayette Hotel, on the corner of University Place and 9th Avenue.

Dreiser was living at 165 West 10th Street in 1919, when he met Helen Patges Richardson, an actress whose grandmother was a sister of Dreiser's mother. Dreiser became romantically involved with the young woman and followed her to Los Angeles, where she wished to pursue a film career. He returned to New York in October 1922 and rented the parlor floor at 16 St. Luke's Place. The next year he moved to 118 West 11th Street, one of the houses in Rhinelander Gardens, where he completed *An American Tragedy*. Its great success enabled him to move uptown to 200 West 57th Street, his last New York City address before moving to Mt. Kisco, New York, in October 1931.

Further Reading

Edminston, Susan, and Linda D. Cirino. *Literary New York: A History and Guide.* New York: Houghton Mifflin, 1976.

White, Morton G., and Lucia White. "Disappointment in New York: Frank Norris and Theodore Dreiser." *The Intellectual versus the City: From Thomas Jefferson to Frank Lloyd Wright.* Cambridge: Harvard University Press, 1962. 117–38.

Zlotnick, Joan. *Portrait of an American City: The Novelists' New York*. Port Washington: Kennikat Press, 1982.

Joseph F. Alexander

NEW YORK SOCIETY FOR THE SUP-PRESSION OF VICE.

Founded in 1873 by **Anthony Comstock**, J. P. Morgan, and John D. Rockefeller, the New York Society for the Suppression of Vice was created to enforce the federal antiobscenity postal statutes of 1873. The rising sales of pornographic books and magazines and the large number of prostitutes at the time probably led to the aforementioned legislation. The organization had as its predecessor the Young Men's Christian Association's Committee for the Suppression of Vice; the society was charted by the New York state legislature and was supported by voluntary contributions. Its chief duties involved investigating citizens' complaints and, if an apparent violation of the law was found, handing the case to the authorities for prosecution. The society worked in cooperation with the police, district attorneys, courts, postal inspectors, the Federal Bureau of Investigation (FBI), and U.S. customs officials. Anthony Comstock presided over the organization until his death in 1915. When **John Saxton Sumner** took over as executive secretary the same year, the society enjoyed more than two decades of virtually unlimited power and authority over writers, publishers, and librarians. Sumner and the society believed that if they could rid the world of what they considered to be immoral literature, they could eliminate prostitution and venereal disease. One of the more famous cases that the society handled involved Dreiser's novel *The "Genius."* The society attempted to block its publication, citing several lewd and blasphemous passages. In July 1916, it successfully forced the **John Lane Company** to recall the book from distributors.

Dreiser fought the decision in court, but nothing came of it. Though the novel was not republished until 1923 by **Horace Liveright**, the incident did help generate interest in **censorship** and forced Americans to think about whether such an organization, other than the court system, should have such control over what an adult could read. For Dreiser, the organization was nothing less than puritanical, an impediment to artistic freedom.

Further Reading

Dardis, Tom. "Firebrand at Work." *Antioch Review* 53 (1995): 338–56.

Gertzman, Jay A. "John Saxton Sumner of the New York Society for the Suppression Vice: A Chief Smut-Eradicator of the Interwar Period." *Journal of American Culture* 17.2 (1994): 41–47.

Kevin Jett

NEWSPAPER DAYS. In this installment of his autobiography, Dreiser continued to set for himself the difficult task of absolute self-revelation. "We are all so biased in our own favor—so poetically inclined to 'color up' our side of the story," he writes to acknowledge the subjective nature of autobiographical writing while announcing his desire for objectivity. Significantly, one working title for *Newspaper Days* was *A Novel about Myself*. Like the principal characters in his novels, the younger self in *Newspaper Days* becomes an object of analysis. The scrutiny of young Theodore occurs amid the abundant description of urban setting and activity also characteristic of Dreiser's longer fiction. The personal and professional experiences he had as a young man in some of America's larger cities affected his intellectual and artistic growth. Dreiser could therefore approach his life story as he would a novel by creating a recognizable plot that depicts the rise from inexperience to experience, from naïveté to greater self-knowledge.

Although published before *Dawn*, which covers the first twenty years of his life, *Newspaper Days* is the second volume chronologically of a projected multivolume autobiography. A narration of his experiences between December 1891 and March 1895, it was first published as *A Book about Myself* by **Boni & Liveright** in 1922. The title was changed to *Newspaper Days* in 1931, when Horace Liveright, Inc., reissued the book to accompany *Dawn*. These editions present an expurgated version of the original manuscripts, whose sexual frankness and rejection of traditional moral positions made it impossible to publish as written. Dreiser's experience with **censorship** over the publication of *The "Genius"* had most recently demonstrated to him the limits of public acceptance for explicit subject matter. He therefore allowed his typist **Estelle Kubitz** to remove potentially offensive passages. H. L. Mencken, **William C. Lengel**, and **Horace Liveright** also edited the work before publication. The 1991 **Pennsylvania Dreiser Edition** restores excised material.

In producing an explicit record of his past, Dreiser followed his commitment to documentary **realism**—the depiction of "life at close range," as he put it—to identify the forces that shape the individual, but his belief in determinism and the essential "nothingness of man" did not negate his interest in the particularities of individual character. While he insists that "our passions control us," he still allows for a singular response to experience. Able to confess his flaws, the older writer retains an admiration for a unique maturation process. His romantic notion of himself appears, for instance, when he declares that "in all the matters of individual development we fare alone."

Dreiser's commitment to an inductive approach to understanding life, the notion that principles must derive from direct experience, accounts for the book's attention to sexual details. His materialist philosophy derived in part from his sexual experiences. In his numerous erotic encounters delight is always accompanied by a measure of shame. Ignorance and self-doubt caused some of this shame because he confused premature ejaculation with "impotence," and he regretted his perceived inability to satisfy his first sexual partners. Boyhood lessons about the sin of fornication, inculcated during his Catholic upbringing, also created guilt, yet, freely acknowledging his insistent desire, Dreiser recounts his affair with Lois Zahn and his attraction to Sara White, his liaisons with two of his landladies in St. Louis and with other women he met, and his transactions with prostitutes. His struggles with a sanctimonious attitude about sex generated compassion for prostitutes who were often, he recognized, victims of poverty but who provided, as he saw it, a necessary outlet that might prevent sexual crime. His commentary about marriage as a "trap" may more accurately reflect the attitude of the older man, but it does suggest the younger man's increasing sense of societal restriction. Although in these years he apparently could not prevent himself from making moralistic judgments about the women with whom he had sex, Dreiser began to accept lust as instinctive, privileging the natural condition over the social one. "Nature's way is correct," he concludes. "Her impulses are sound. . . . Old prejudices must always fall, and life must always change. It is the law."

A belief in immutable laws and a "mechanistic view of the universe" combined with his conclusion that "at its best life is unquestionably material and sensual—the idealists to the contrary notwithstanding." Both his personal experiences and his reading of Thomas Henry Huxley and **Herbert Spencer** contributed to this philosophy. *Newspaper Days* documents the evolving conviction of the mature man that life provides little autonomy and that **chance** and natural forces dominate human existence. His "exact education as to the working of life" put him in contact with "the hard reality underlying all romance." By rejecting the abstractions of conventional **religion** and society, Dreiser felt more equipped to draw conclusions from his observations and experiences. His philosophy emphasized this individual empiricism even as it tended to deny personal control over external circumstances.

The evolution of a philosophy accompanied his progress as a writer. Initially, newspaper work attracted him so intensely that he abruptly quit his job before securing his first position in **journalism** as a reporter for the *Chicago Daily Globe*. In Chicago, journalists seemed charged with the excitement of the "symphonic" city life they covered. Although eventually disabused of this romantic view of journalism, Dreiser remained enamored of the possibilities the profession offered for advancement. In an age when celebrated editors and publishers could impress their personalities on their papers, the ambitious young man gravitated toward newspaper work as a source of potential recognition. Convinced of his ability and drawn to the power represented by business tycoons and great artists, he would work for three years as a reporter in an effort to rise above the undistinguished. While fame and wealth eluded him, his newspaper days served as a literary apprenticeship. In addition to developing his writing skills, his reporting career established several lasting attitudes about his work. Among these was his lifelong acceptance of editorial assistance. Much to his gratitude, his

first editor, John Maxwell, disciplined his "turgid English." Maxwell also told Dreiser he could be a serious writer whose talent could take him beyond the newsroom.

As a chronicle of newspaper life, *Newspaper Days* provides a vivid history of a particular era in journalism. Calling the yellow journalism of the time a "slough of muck," Dreiser details the unethical methods reporters employed to get stories. In St. Louis, where he went after Chicago and where he worked for the *St. Louis Globe-Democrat* and later for the *St. Louis Republic*, he quickly learned how to manipulate sources. Newspapers, he soon observed, cared less about factual reporting and more about the dramatic possibilities of a story. To misrepresent oneself in the pursuit of a sensational tale was accepted practice, and outright fabrication of stories was often tacitly approved. Dreiser discovered that fact when he began writing the "Heard in the Corridors" column for the *Globe-Democrat*, for which he received a byline at a time when reporters' names were not commonly published. That he was nonetheless both resourceful and industrious as a reporter is apparent from his description of two of the biggest stories of his career: a railroad accident and an interview with an arrested train robber—though in the case of this latter story he felt bested by a rival who had replaced him at the *Globe-Democrat*.

When he moved to Pittsburgh, after briefly working for papers in Toledo and Cleveland, he considered himself a veteran reporter. His employment with the *Pittsburg Dispatch* took him into steel mills and slums. Although fond of his time in Pittsburgh, he was disgusted by the control the steel magnates held over the city's newspapers, which could not print stories favorable to labor. What he saw but could not report produced a keener awareness of social inequity, and he likened his own position to that of the steel industry's abused workers. He pursued greater professional freedom by leaving for New York City. His stint with Joseph Pulitzer's *New York World*, however, became the worst experience of his career in journalism. Paid very little and prevented from writing the most interesting stories he uncovered, he soon quit the newspaper life to concentrate on literature.

Dreiser ends *Newspaper Days* with the suggestion that his early career in literature might provide the subject of a future book, but, as it had for many of his contemporaries, a career in journalism amplified his literary ambitions. "No newspaper will tolerate a bad writer," he notes, and with almost every paper he proved his value, learning that his strengths lay in registering the "the larger and more tragic phases of life" while coming to doubt the service literature could lend to social reform. Yearning in these years to be a playwright or a poet, he was encouraged in his literary endeavors by certain editors and colleagues. Although at the time he considered novel writing to be beyond his ability, the novels of Honoré de Balzac and Émile Zola inspired him. America's newspapers, furthermore, insisted on publishing "sweet tales" that abstained from depicting society's harsher conditions. In New York he began to study magazine fiction in a search for models, and he found these stories equally evasive. His principal literary goal became, therefore, a more truthful and less hypocritical depiction of life as he knew it.

Despite attempting a meticulous explanation of himself, Dreiser nevertheless admitted that any individual, however carefully examined, retains some secret: "In the main, a brisk, alive human being is almost indescribable—as elusive as radium or life itself." Defying the indescrib-able, Dreiser wrote to expose the mystery of himself during a foundational period in his life, choosing documentation over self-flattery. The resulting depth and honesty of *Dawn* and *Newspaper Days* justify Richard Lingeman's assertion that these volumes belong among "the greatest American autobiographies" (Lingeman 1: 351).

Scott D. Emmert

"NIGGER JEFF." One of three stories composed in the summer of 1899 (immediately preceding the writing of *Sister Carrie* that winter) at **Arthur Henry's** seasonal home in Maumee, Ohio, "Nigger Jeff" was first published in *Ainslee's* in November 1901 before being revised and reprinted in *Free and Other Stories*. Perhaps the idyllic atmosphere of Henry's modest estate inspired the setting of the story, "a sunny spring afternoon" in which the protagonist, "one of [the] best reporters" on the staff of the local newspaper, receives an assignment from his city editor that will upset his entire worldview: travel to "Pleasant Valley" to cover a potential lynching. Although critics agree that Elmer Davies represents Dreiser himself earlier in the 1890s, the reporter-turned-editor-turned-fictionist apparently never witnessed this particular event. T. D. Nostwich has argued that the source was a *St. Louis Republic* story dated 17 January 1884. Despite its title, Dreiser's version is far less about Jeff Ingalls, accused of assaulting nineteen-year-old Ada Whitaker and who is afterward pursued by a mob, or about the victim herself than it is about the reporter who follows in their tracks and falls, like one of Melville's bachelors, from a state of insulated innocence to hard experience of the world. His editor signals the shift by sending him into the field on the promise that "[a] lynching up here would be a big thing. There's never been one in this state."

Davies had previously held the luxurious and simple belief that life operates according to "a fixed and ordered process of rewards and punishments. If one did not do exactly right, one did not get along well. On the contrary, if one did, one did." However, the idea of a summary lynching, unhampered by restraint or due process of law, sickens him because it is anomalous to his binary ideology. His wish to avoid witnessing Jeff's capture (which Dreiser softens considerably when compared to the midcentury depictions of lynchings by Richard Wright) and "just gather the details of the crime and the—aftermath—and return" is thwarted when duty compels him to accompany the mob, led by Ada's father and brother Jake. He witnesses their wresting of the captive from the sheriff, endures the sight of the "limp form plung[ing] down and pull[ing] up with a creaking sound of rope," and finally visits the Ingalls cabin. The pathos of Jeff's guiltless mother and sister, for whom Jeff has unsuccessfully risked capture by returning to bid them good-bye, becomes for Davies the epiphanic knowledge "that it was not always exact justice that was meted out to all and that it was not so much the business of the writer to indict as to interpret" events and circumstances. Among other things retroactively significant to the newspaperman and therefore interpretable has been the recurring indifference of Nature throughout the night's events: "By contrast with the horror impending, as he now noted, the night was so beautiful that it was all but poignant. Stars were already beginning to shine. Distant lamps twinkled like yellow eyes from the cottages in the valleys and on the hillsides. The air was fresh and tender. Some pea-fowls were crying afar off, and the east promised a golden moon. Silently the assembled company trotted on. . . . Young Jake, riding silently toward the front, looked as if trag-

edy were all he craved." Human depravity, then—indifference, bloodlust, rebellion—is to be found even in Eden.

Further Reading

Nostwich, T. D. "The Source of Dreiser's 'Nigger Jeff.' " *Resources for American Literary Study* 8 (1978): 174–87.
Pizer, Donald. " 'Nigger Jeff': The Development of an Aesthetic." *American Literature* 41 (1969): 331–41.

Shawn St. Jean

NOBEL PRIZE. In 1911, the British publisher **Grant Richards** planted the idea in Dreiser's mind that he could become the first American writer to win the Nobel Prize. Although Richards ended up doing little to assist Dreiser in this ambition, it remained the author's steadfast goal for almost twenty years.

In the 1920s Dreiser enlisted the help of H. L. Mencken, who may have unofficially lobbied on his behalf, but not until after the publication of *An American Tragedy* was Dreiser considered a serious contender. Capitalizing on his new critical acclaim, Dreiser embarked on an informal campaign of self-promotion with Swedish publishers during his European trip of 1926 and with members of the Swedish Academy, whose committee selected the winner. Back home, he petitioned Franklin P. Adams, a columnist for the *New York World*, and others in the reviewing establishment to promote him as a Nobel candidate, but apparently they did not do so. Dreiser did, however, deliberately work to improve his relations with European publishers, in particular his German publisher Paul Zsolnay, who was instrumental in making Dreiser a better-known author in Europe.

By 1929 it was an open secret in the United States and abroad that the next winner would be an American and that

Dreiser was locked in a tight race with **Sinclair Lewis**, who had been having a phenomenally successful run that decade with novels like *Main Street* (1920) and *Elmer Gantry* (1926). To many observers of the literary scene, these novels, which poked fun at some of the most sacred American institutions in a flamboyant, quick-witted way, endeared him to his European judges, who openly admired exposés of American hypocrisy. In the end, Lewis's clever satires won out over Dreiser's complex analyses.

The American literati's reaction to Lewis's beating Dreiser was negative, with almost everyone feeling that Dreiser had been cheated. Although Lewis was generous to Dreiser in his acceptance speech, singling him out as a pathbreaker to whom all later American writers owed an immense debt, Dreiser could not shrug off the slight by the Swedish Academy, and thereafter he nursed a lifelong grudge against Lewis (manifested at least once by a public slapping match at a New York dinner).

Further Reading

Hutchisson, James M. *The Rise of Sinclair Lewis, 1920–1930.* University Park: Pennsylvania State University Press, 1996.

Lundén, Rolf. "Theodore Dreiser and the Nobel Prize." *American Literature* 50 (1978): 216–29.

James M. Hutchisson

NORRIS, FRANK (1870–1902). Benjamin Franklin Norris Jr. was born in Chicago, but he regarded his real home as San Francisco, where his family moved in 1885. Educated first as an art student at the Julien Atelier in Paris (1887–1889) and then at the University of California at Berkeley, Norris was influenced by the evolutionary theories of Joseph Le Conte and **Herbert Spencer** as well as by the novels of Émile Zola and other French naturalistic writers.

As part of his daily assignments for a writing course under Lewis E. Gates at Harvard in 1894–1895, Norris wrote the sketches that he would later incorporate into *McTeague* (1899) and *Vandover and the Brute* (1914). After travel to South Africa in 1895 and a period of recovery from a fever he had contracted, Norris began writing for the *Wave*, a San Francisco weekly that serialized his first published novel, the adventure story *Moran of the Lady Letty*, in 1898. Published the following year and widely considered his masterpiece, *McTeague* established Norris's reputation as a naturalistic writer, and despite deviations from this pattern—*Blix*, a courtship novel, appeared in 1899, and *A Man's Woman* in 1900—for the rest of his career Norris turned his efforts toward examining the world of economic, social, and hereditary forces in his projected trilogy of the wheat: *The Octopus* (1900), *The Pit* (1903), and the never-written *The Wolf*, which were to chronicle the production, trading, and distribution of the grain. As he and his wife were about to depart on a voyage to gather materials for *The Wolf*, Norris was stricken with appendicitis and then peritonitis. His death on 25 October 1902 was the occasion for an outpouring of admiring critical retrospectives, and several of his works were published posthumously, including two volumes of short stories and the critical essays collected in *The Responsibilities of the Novelist* (1903), in which Norris promoted the West as a subject for fiction and truthfulness and sincerity as a method.

Norris played an important role in Dreiser's career when, as a reader for the New York publishing company of **Doubleday, Page**, he read the manuscript for *Sister Carrie* and recommended it enthusiastically to the company. *Sister Carrie*, he wrote to Dreiser on 28 May 1900, "was the best novel I had read in MS. since I had been reading for the firm, and . . . it pleased me as well as any novel I have read in *any* form, published or otherwise" (*Letters* 1: 52n.). Shortly thereafter he met Dreiser and witnessed the contract between Dreiser and Doubleday, Page. The subsequent publishing debacle became famous. After **Frank Doubleday** had second thoughts about publishing such a decidedly ungenteel book and urged him to take the manuscript to another publisher, Dreiser held the company to the terms of his contract and forced the book's publication. In later versions of the story, only Norris escaped blame for what Dreiser insisted was the suppression of the book; according to Dreiser, Norris "stood steadfastly" by him, urging him to stick by the terms of the Doubleday, Page contract, writing "many letters," and sending out 300 copies for review. Although Dreiser maintained that he was not influenced by Norris's *McTeague*, reading it for the first time after his manuscript of *Sister Carrie* was rejected at **Harper & Brothers's** before coming to Doubleday, Page, he soon placed it among the "few books" that constituted his "private library of American realism" (*Letters* 3: 949). Of Norris's other works, *The Octopus* also ranked high with Dreiser, who called Norris "the first novelist to produce an American novel of social protest" (*Letters* 3: 877). *The Pit* did not fare as well. Perhaps drawing on his own experiences with Frank Doubleday, Dreiser said that Norris had told him that Doubleday had asked him to change his original plan, so that what was left was, in Dreiser's words, "a bastard bit of romance of the best seller variety" (*Letters* 1: 329).

Further Reading

McElrath, Joseph R., Jr. "Norris's Attitude toward *Sister Carrie*." *Dreiser Studies* 18.2 (1987): 39–42.

Myers, Robert M. "Dreiser's Copy of *McTeague*." *Papers on Language and Literature* 27.2 (1991): 260–67.

Donna M. Campbell

NOTES ON LIFE. After the publication of *An American Tragedy* in 1925, Dreiser's literary output declined markedly, with nonfiction works constituting most of his output until the posthumous publication of *The Bulwark* and *The Stoic*. During the last two decades of his life, a great deal of Dreiser's time and effort was devoted to a massive undertaking—called at various times by Dreiser "The Mechanism Called Man," "The Formulae Called Life," "The Formula Called Man," and "Illusion Called Life"—that was intended to be a final testament of his personal philosophy and that he hoped would give him credit and status as a thinker and provide empirical confirmation of the views he had been developing ever since reading **Herbert Spencer's** *First Principles* in 1894. The work contemplated by Dreiser was left uncompleted at his death and consisted of a trove of miscellaneous materials inserted by Dreiser into hundreds of folders with titles such as "Mechanism Called the Universe," "Necessity for Repetition," "The Factor Called Time," "The Emotions," "Myth of Individuality," "Myth of Free Will," "Beauty and Ugliness," "Order and Disorder," "Good and Evil," "The Salve Called Religion," and so forth that he envisioned as individual chapters of the proposed work. Dreiser also left an outline of the projected work's contents. The folders themselves comprised a miscellany of both materials, in holograph and typescript, that Dreiser had composed (i.e., brief essays on the folder topics as well as aphorisms and commentary on developments in science and other fields that he found interesting) and materials he had compiled to stimulate his thinking and provide support for, and clarification of, his views (i.e., notes based on his readings, observations, and exchanges with scientists; and newspaper clippings and magazine articles on various phenomena, often of a scientific or pseudoscientific nature, that Dreiser had collected over the years with the help of amanuenses). Some of the materials date from the early 1920s and earlier, which is not surprising, since Dreiser acknowledged, in a letter to his friend **George Douglas**, that he had a "glimmering" of the proposed work as far back as 1915 (*Letters* 2: 718). Some of the central ideas in the work, which was published posthumously in 1974 as *Notes on Life*, were first adumbrated by Dreiser in *Hey Rub-a-Dub-Dub*, a book of essays published in 1920.

The archival materials on which *Notes on Life* is based were bequeathed to the University of Pennsylvania in 1952 by Dreiser's second wife, Helen Dreiser, who had hoped to assist in preparing the materials for publication but who was prevented by illness from doing so. The task was undertaken (with Helen Dreiser's approval) by a young Dreiser scholar, Sydney Horovitz, who died unexpectedly in 1953, bringing the project of preparing the work for publication to an abrupt halt. The project languished for a considerable period of time before being revived by **Marguerite Tjader** and John J. McAleer, by whom *Notes on Life* was coedited. Tjader, who was closely associated with Dreiser at several periods during which he was working on *Notes*, was familiar with Dreiser's thinking and intentions during the work's generation and was acutely aware of his desire to publish a definitive and final statement of his views. She played a major role in bringing about the work's publication. The title "Notes on Life" was not Dreiser's. It was apparently coined by Helen Dreiser and was used thereafter to refer to Dreiser's collection of

philosophical papers, of which *Notes on Life* represents an abridgment.

Notes on Life received scant attention upon its long-awaited appearance in print, and the notice that it did receive consisted of reviews in scholarly journals that were in the aggregate decidedly unfavorable. Joseph K. Davis stated that the *Notes* "are little more than miscellaneous fragments; and they are all too frequently pompous and awkward in composition, contradictory and reductionist in argument, and—worse—thoroughly dull in content" (*Sewanee Review* 85 [1975]: cxxvii). Observed James Lundquist in his review, "Dreiser's philosophizing leads to far more inanities than it does profundities. His interest in philosophy and his passion for science fail to compensate for his inability to think clearly for more than a paragraph or two" (*Old Northwest* 1 [1975]: 427). Donald Pizer observed that "those seeking to find in *Notes on Life* a logically organized and defended representation of Dreiser's final philosophical position will be disappointed. The book is a collection of fragments in which the reader will have to search for the connecting edges in order to puzzle out the nature and shape of Dreiser's beliefs. . . . When Dreiser expounds his ideas as philosophy, the ideas plod and stumble; they become silly and jejune and eventually resolve themselves into absurdities or platitudes" (*American Literary Realism* 8 [1975]: 365). A problem noted by reviewers is that in reading *Notes on Life* it is difficult to get a sense of the chronology of their completion, for most of the pieces are undated, and the reader is challenged to understand what period of Dreiser's thought they represent.

The range of topics that engage Dreiser's attention in the volume is truly impressive, as is the sense of awe and reverence he exhibits for the workings of the cosmos and natural phenomena. Dreiser was, as Ernest Griffin observed, "a great evidence-collector, apparently tireless in following up the latest discoveries of research professors in applied science, especially physiologists, entomologists, geneticists, zoologists and the like. He was fascinated by the habits of the lower forms of life and would relate them to the human condition" (*Modernist Studies* 2 [1977]: 77). No topic seems too small or large for Dreiser's attention, whether it is the behavior of ants, spiders, and grasshoppers; the nature of physical forces; the process of **evolution**; the birth and death of stars; the speed of calculations performed by Vannevar Bush's differential analyzer (an early computer); or research into telepathy by J. B. Rhine of Duke University. Dreiser also commented on scientific discoveries such as cosmic rays, relativity, and the uncertainty principle; trends in psychology and the social sciences such as behaviorism; and the theories of scientists such as the geneticist Calvin Bridges, whose work Dreiser had observed firsthand (and who became Dreiser's friend) in the course of his research. Often, Dreiser segues from the scientific to the purely speculative or philosophical—for example, is the attraction of the elements to one another an emotional as well as scientifically observable (chemical) phenomenon? Is there a physical basis for the emotional responses caused by different colors? In the metaphysical domain, he addresses questions such as the problem of good and evil, the problem of death, the ultimate origins of energy, whether the universe has purpose or design, and one's place in the universe.

See also "Equation Inevitable"; "The Essential Tragedy of Life"; Mechanism.

Further Reading

Furmanczyk, Wieslaw. "Theodore Dreiser's Views on Religion in the Light of His Philosophical Papers." *Zeitschrift für Anglistik und Amerikanistik* 25 (1977): 213–20.

Lundén, Rolf. *The Inevitable Equation: The Antithetic Pattern of Theodore Dreiser's Thought and Art.* Uppsala, Sweden: Studia Anglistica Upsaliensia, no. 16, 1973.

McAleer, John J. "Dreiser's 'Notes on Life' ": Responses to an Impenetrable Universe." *Library Chronicle* 38 (1972): 78–91.

Tjader, Marguerite. "Dreiser's Investigations of Nature." *Dreiser Newsletter* 11.2 (1980): 1–9.

Westlake, Neda. "Theodore Dreiser's *Notes on Life.*" *Library Chronicle* 20 (1954): 69–75.

Roger W. Smith

O

"THE OLD NEIGHBORHOOD." First appearing in *Metropolitan* magazine in December 1918, this story was included in Dreiser's second volume of short stories, *Chains: Lesser Novels and Stories*. In "The Old Neighborhood," the unnamed mechanic and inventor visits his past by going back to the apartment in which he and his wife, Marie, lived after they were first married. Through a series of flashbacks, limited to the protagonist's memory but written in third person, the reader learns of his dissatisfaction with the events of his past as he reflects upon his early struggles in life. Impoverished and burdened with two young children, he spends his nights and Sundays working on inventions and slowly begins to attain fame and wealth. But his ambition is stifled by his home life; so he can pursue his career unfettered, he wishes he were not burdened by a family and a wife who seems to him dull, soft, and clinging. Fate grants his wish: a series of ailments affects Marie and the two children until both children die, within three days of each other, from pneumonia. After the death of his children, the protagonist leaves Marie to follow his dream of wealth and success. At the time of the story, the narrator has remarried and is wealthy. He has returned to the old neighborhood to try to reclaim his past in order to be free from the guilt of losing his children and abandoning his wife in order to follow his ambition. After visiting their old apartment, the protagonist realizes that this trip into his past has done nothing to salve his conscience and that his life now, with its fame and wealth, is not all that he thought it would be.

As in several other stories collected in *Chains*, Dreiser addresses the causes of unhappiness in marriage. In "The Old Neighborhood," Dreiser suggests that ambition causes one to sacrifice a contented spouse and, ultimately, one's happiness, for the narrator's return to his old neighborhood is an effort to seek absolution for the pain he has caused Marie. That effort, the story suggests, is futile, for the narrator achieves no release for his guilt and instead learns the bitter lesson that, despite his success, getting what one wishes is not always the best thing.

Kari Lee Siko

"OLD RAGPICKER." Completed by November 1915, this one-act play was first published in *Plays of the Natural and Supernatural*. One of the two "natural" plays in the volume, *"Old Ragpicker"* is an indictment of callous attitudes toward the poor and a comment on the irony of fate. The play opens with two Irish policemen comparing their experiences working the tough streets on the Lower West Side of New York City. They come upon an impoverished old man rummaging through the ash cans for rags and tin to sell, shunned by workers on the street going about their business. When the old man ignores an old woman's offer of her coat, she turns to the others for help rather than taking action herself. "Somebody should do something," she says. She represents those Good Samaritans who preach reform but pass on the responsibility to others. When a grocery boy tells her to forget about the old man, his comment represents Americans at their most apathetic. Young children going home from school ridicule him, perhaps suggesting that our prejudices are carried on from generation to generation. As the old man rambles on, lost in his past, we discover he was once a powerful man. A former capitalist, he has lost his money, his wife, his child, his friends, and finally his identity as a consequence of the play of economic forces. Despite his losses, in his madness he has achieved a certain acceptance of his fate and an inner peace: "I'm not crazy now," he mumbles. "I got better. I live by myself now. I'm all alone where I can watch the water go." Ironically, although he cannot remember his name when the two cops prod him, he seizes upon the taunts of a passing street boy, who cries, "Look at the ragpicker!" "Ragpicker! Ragpicker!" he muses. "Now I remember. That's my name."

Although *Old Ragpicker* is the slightest play in the volume, its depiction of pathos testifies to Dreiser's ability to create sympathy for the downtrodden. In his other one-act plays Dreiser had concentrated on portraying human beings as the helpless victims of mechanistic forces; *Old Ragpicker* extends that portrayal by focusing our attention on an archetypal

victim—an old man so reduced by economic circumstances that he feeds from garbage pails, becomes the sport of boys who throw cans, and forgets his own name. By depicting "Old Ragpicker" as the product of these forces, Dreiser demonstrates his thesis that the forces that propel the universe are amoral, maintaining a rhythmic balance between those who, like **Cowperwood**, succeed and those who, like "Old Ragpicker," fail.

D. L. Anderson

"OLD ROGAUM AND HIS THERESA."
One of Dreiser's earliest stories, "Old Rogaum and His Theresa" was written in the summer of 1899; as Dreiser explained in a letter to H. L. Mencken, the story was one of a group of five stories, including "Nigger Jeff" and "The Shining Slave Makers," that he wrote just before beginning *Sister Carrie* (*D-M Letters* 1: 232). First published under the title "Butcher Rogaum's Door" in *Reedy's Mirror* on 12 December 1901, the story was revised and collected under its present title in *Free and Other Stories*.

The story centers on the kind of incident Dreiser had witnessed while living in lower Manhattan: in a working-class neighborhood watched over by Officer Maguire, Rogaum, a German immigrant, threatens each night to lock out his eighteen-year-old daughter, Theresa, if she does not return home by ten o'clock. One evening, as she lingers with her beau Connie Almerting, a seductive idler, Rogaum locks the door and refuses to open it in answer to her rattling of the handle. As Theresa leaves with Almerting, who plots to take her to the clubhouse of his gang, The Roosters, another figure slumps at Rogaum's door, this time a "blonde of the type the world too well knows" whose expensive rings and clothing reveal her to be a prostitute. The girl, named Emily, has tried to commit suicide by taking acid. As the madam of the brothel where Emily had worked tells Maguire, she met her downfall after her family had locked her out one night. Maguire finds Theresa and returns her to her father, but he warns Rogaum that the same thing could happen to Theresa. Rogaum is moved, but Dreiser undercuts this potentially sentimental ending by suggesting that little has changed; Theresa declares that she will still stay out late despite Rogaum's prohibition, and Rogaum will not stop berating her for walking the streets in the evening.

The story adumbrates several of the themes and incidents of Dreiser's later work. Like Carrie Meeber, who stands in the doorway of her sister Minnie's apartment building for the same reasons, Theresa turns her back on the staid routine of family life and looks toward the danger and excitement of the streets, an impulse that Dreiser renders as natural to those in the "thoughtless, sensory" phase of life. Nature, sexual awareness, and the city speak with one voice to Theresa, who is irresistibly drawn out to "the dark sky with its stars, the street lamps, the cars, the tinkle and laughter of eternal life." Dreiser renders this conflict between desire and duty through tactile as well as auditory images by contrasting Almerting's hold on Theresa's "soft white fingers," which makes her quiver, to her father's "fat hand" on her shoulder, the one coaxing and the other restraining as Theresa is caught between them, on the threshold of adulthood as well as the literally liminal space of Butcher Rogaum's doorway. In addition to the tension between the voices of nature and those of social respectability, the story also addresses other themes: the biologically driven separation of child from parent at the point of sexual maturity; the conflict between the Old World and the New as an immigrant family's standards of conduct clash with the American ideal of individual freedom; and the nineteenth century's uncompromising standard of female purity that recognized either virginity or prostitution with no middle ground, exemplified in the paired characters of Theresa and Emily. Dreiser uses the locked door as a metaphor for this divide; ironically, Rogaum is initially more charitable to the travelers and newsboys who sometimes seek refuge in his doorway than to his daughter, never locking the entryway against them as he does against her. The conflict between Rogaum, torn between enforcing Old World morality and his love for his child, and Theresa, whose entry into the world carries risks but also the potential for a better life, prefigures the similar relationship between **Jennie Gerhardt** and her father in *Jennie Gerhardt*.

Donna M. Campbell

"OLIVE BRAND." First published in *Hearst's International-Cosmopolitan* in May 1928 and later revised for publication in *A Gallery of Women*, this semifictional sketch is based on Dreiser's friendship with **Edith DeLong Jarmuth** during his years in **Greenwich Village**. Jarmuth had left her husband in Colorado and moved to New York, where she socialized with the artists and political radicals in the Village while studying to become a writer. Following her divorce, she married Dreiser's friend **Edward H. Smith**, a journalist with the *New York Sunday World*, whom Dreiser calls Jethro in the sketch.

The narrator-author first meets Olive at a dinner party, where he is struck by her intellect, obvious wealth, and "Castilian" appearance. Later, after learning she is "remarkably well-informed" and has an exceptional collection of books and after accepting an invitation to go with her a folk play at a Bohemian Hall, he comes to like her "very much," claiming "there was something positively inspirational about her attitude toward life, her enthusiasm for it, her sense of beauty, poetry, romance, her intense interest in those who could do anything mentally . . . as well as her real pity for those who could not." At the same time, he is disturbed by her belief in sexual freedom for women and her promiscuous lifestyle, particularly since she is being supported by a husband in Spokane, Washington.

The narrator accompanies Olive on visits to various places and events in the city and accepts invitations to her apartment, where she introduces him to the works of **Freud** and other authors in her collection. He notes, however, that he is not in love with her, and, consequently, when her actions lead him to believe that she is interested in a physical relationship, he stops seeing her. Some months later, the narrator is again drawn to Olive when he learns she has ended her financial arrangement with her husband to make her own way writing. To illustrate her talent, he quotes a long poem he has received from her, in which she reveals her strong feelings for him.

After emphasizing that the poem "led to nothing more than that warm friendship that already existed between us," the narrator later learns that Olive plans to marry Jethro. Surprised at the news because Jethro is not "a grand dramatic figure such as [Olive's] very remarkable temperament might have entitled her to," the narrator, nonetheless, sees the marriage "as a happy outcome for Olive" and serves as the best man at their wedding. Still, he believes there has to be something more than an emotional attraction between them, and, in time, he discovers that it lies in her willingness to use her writing talent to help Jethro realize his aspiration to become an author of plays, short stories, and novels. Then, just as they are beginning to be suc-

cessful, Olive quite unexpectedly comes down with a fever and is rushed to a hospital. When the narrator comes to visit her, she reminds him of the poem in which she revealed her feelings for him and tells him that, when she discovered he did not share her love, she turned to Jethro because "he needed me so." Following this conversation, her condition worsens, and, a few days later, she dies.

The narrator-author concludes the sketch with a summary of Jethro's life after Olive's death. Failing to succeed as a dramatist and story-writer without her, Jethro turned to helping a medical investigator write a book on the human glands. "But more and more," the narrator notes, "he seemed to be losing interest in life," and he began to lead a life of "drinking and partying." This lifestyle, in turn, led to problems with his health, until, while still in his forties, Jethro comes down with a cold and then dies of a high fever, spending his last days in the hospital out of his senses and talking of Olive.

Like many of the sketches in *A Gallery of Women*, "Olive Brand" has received only passing notice from reviewers and scholars of Dreiser. Slightly more attention has been paid by Dreiser's biographers, however. Both W. A. Swanberg and Richard Lingeman point out that Edward Smith was disturbed by Dreiser's portrait of his wife when, shortly before his death, he heard of, or read, the unpublished sketch and made some remarks to Dreiser for which he later apologized. Swanberg adds that despite the apology, Smith's remarks brought an end to the correspondence between the two men. Lingeman, on the other hand, closes his account of the episode by stating: "Actually 'Olive Brand' is one of the finest portraits in the book: Olive is like a female Peter McCord of

Twelve Men, an ardent, seeking temperament crushed by fate" (Lingeman 2: 328).

Frederic E. Rusch

"ON BEING POOR." "Poverty is so relative," begins this sketch from *The Color of a Great City*. "I have lived to be thirty-two now, and am just beginning to find that out." This places the sketch in 1903, when Dreiser had descended to the depths of a long slide into poverty and mental depression, which, according to biographer W. A. Swanberg, began in 1900 and lasted until approximately 1905 (94–118). Too proud to call on his successful brother, Paul Dresser, or his sister Mame and her husband for room or financial support, Dreiser, often unable to work, was reduced to staying in the cheapest lodgings he could find and often did without meals. Here he muses on the differences between his own experience and what he deems "the most dreadful and inhibiting and destroying of all forms of poverty"—poverty of mind. Dreiser defines this poverty as not so much a lack of money as a lack of taste, of understanding, of imagination, of cleanliness, of discrimination, of order, of a sense of beauty or comfort. As in most of the sketches included in *The Color of a Great City*, Dreiser maintains a distance between himself and his subject—the truly poor. He maintains that he has never felt the depth of poverty that he finds in so many thousands around him because he has been able to maintain "my own mind, my own point of view." Lacking the means to go to the theater or a good restaurant, as he would prefer, he nevertheless visits many museums, exhibits, collections and libraries open to the public, and he has retained his keen awareness of the life around him. "These are not things to which those materially deficient would in the main turn for solace," he remarks, "but to me they are substances of solace, the major portion of all my wealth or possible wealth, in exchange for which I would not take a miser's hoard." Dreiser's careful distinction between himself and those he considers truly poor is a mask to conceal his own fear of becoming like them. His rejection of "the gospel of wealth," the obsession with obtaining riches at all costs, briefly dealt with here, was later developed more fully in his novel *An American Tragedy* in 1925.

Nancy McIlvaine Donovan

"ON THE BANKS OF THE WABASH, FAR AWAY." Written, Dreiser would claim in "The Birth and Growth of a Popular Song," "in less than an hour of an April Sunday afternoon" in 1898, "On the Banks of the Wabash," together with "My Gal Sal" (1905), was one of Paul Dresser's most successful and enduring songs. The two-verse lyric combines nostalgic evocation of place—rural, riparian Indiana—with two condensed narratives of personal loss by a single speaker who appears to be, in the first verse, *on* the riverbank, and in the second, far away from that moonlit stream. Themes of lost mother and sweetheart and the longing for a lost home paired with music that intensified the sentiment form a typical subset of early Tin Pan Alley compositions, such as Williams and Van Alstyne's "In the Shade of the Old Apple Tree" (1905) or Buck and Morse's "Dear Old Girl" (1903). By 1905, songs in this mode were losing ground to ragtime and to the more urbane and witty compositions associated with Tin Pan Alley's golden age.

Popular as the song was at the turn of the century and despite its continuing status as the official state song of Indiana, "Wabash" would be of little interest to Dreiser scholars were it not for ongoing controversy about the song's authorship. Dreiser offers four varying accounts of his contributions to this song. In "Birth and

Growth of a Popular Song" (1898) Dreiser claimed to have been present during its composition. After Paul's death Dreiser's claims to joint authorship become both larger and more specific. In *A Hoosier Holiday* (1916), *Twelve Men* (1919), and his Introduction to *The Songs of Paul Dresser* (1927), Dreiser laid claim to the song's first verse and chorus. This claim remained undisputed until 1939 and was reproduced both in early bibliographic scholarship on Dreiser and by early historians of American popular music. A contradictory account attributed to Dresser's sometime arranger Max Hoffman and included in Isidore Whitmark and Isaac Goldberg's *From Ragtime to Swingtime: The Story of the House of Whitmark* (New York: Rurman, 1939) places the song's composition in a Chicago hotel room in summer, with Dresser struggling to write the lyric while Hoffman plays the chorus over and over again "for at least two or three hours," and Dreiser nowhere in sight (170). From this point until the present, the question of the brothers' collaboration on "Wabash" has been hotly contested, with musicologists tending to base their views upon Hoffman's account, and literary historians, upon Dreiser's. In 1976 the brothers' niece Vera Dreiser introduced a third party supporting Dreiser's account—Paul and Theodore's brother Ed Dreiser, who claimed to have been present as the brothers collaborated; but Ed's account, like Hoffman's, is reported at secondhand. Old newspaper clippings, letters, financial statements, and speculations about the brothers' comparative veracity, mendacity, and skill as writers have provided the bulk of the slim data upon which the debate is conducted. The song itself, particularly its unusual double narrative and inconsistent sense of place, has been examined for evidence of more than two writers. Given the self-interested nature of the three eyewitness accounts to date, the fact that all but Dreiser's are reported at secondhand, and Dresser's silence on the matter, the controversy does not seem likely to be completely resolved.

Further Reading

Loranger, Carol S., and Dennis Loranger. "Collaborating on 'The Banks of the Wabash': A Brief History of an Interdisciplinary Debate, Some New Evidence, and a Reflexive Consideration of Turf and Ownership." *Dreiser Studies* 30.1 (1999): 3–20.

Tawa, Nicholas. *The Way to Tin Pan Alley.* New York: Schirmer, 1990.

Carol S. Loranger

P

PAGE, WALTER HINES (1855–1918). Page became a partner with **Frank Doubleday** of **Doubleday, Page & Co.** in 1899 after a successful career as editor of the *Forum* and *Atlantic Monthly*. As an editor and publisher, Page was outspoken about the importance of commercial standards in judging literary work. Dreiser approached the company with the manuscript of *Sister Carrie* in May 1900, after its initial rejection from **Harper & Brothers**. He chose the new publishing house primarily because **Frank Norris**, whom Dreiser greatly admired, was a reader with the firm. Norris praised *Sister Carrie*, and his enthusiasm was influential in Page's acceptance of the manuscript, despite his reservations regarding the book's strong language. Acting on his own review of the novel as well as the judgment of Norris, Page agreed to publish the book, and by June of 1900 a contract had been signed.

In late June, Frank Doubleday returned to New York from a vacation abroad. After learning of the contract with Dreiser, he read *Sister Carrie* and found it vulgar and offensive. As senior partner, he determined that his company would not publish a book he found distasteful. Page was given the task of rescinding the offer and wrote to Dreiser to urge him to postpone publication until he had further estab-

lished himself as a writer. He encouraged him instead to submit a more suitable first novel that Doubleday, Page could support and promote. A terse correspondence ensued, with Page trying various tactics to urge Dreiser to release the firm from its contract. Dreiser firmly declined the offer, holding Page to the signed contract. Dreiser was disappointed and angered by Page's withdrawal of support for *Sister Carrie* and later wrote that Page had been intimidated by his older and more powerful partner, Frank Doubleday, and thus had not spoken up for the merit of the novel he had initially praised. Doubleday, Page finally fulfilled the contract by publishing *Sister Carrie* in November 1900 but did little to promote the novel in the literary or general press.

In November 1900 Page founded the *World's Work*, which he edited until 1913, when he left New York for London to become the U.S. ambassador to Great Britain under President Wilson. He was influential in urging America to respond to the escalating war in Europe. He left England in poor health in October 1918 and died two months later at his childhood home in North Carolina.

Further Reading

Cooper, John Milton. *Walter Hines Page: The Southerner as American.* Chapel Hill: University of North Carolina Press, 1977.

Blythe Ferguson

PATGES, MYRTLE (1894?–?). Myrtle Patges was the younger sister of Dreiser's second wife, the actress Helen Richardson, and served as the model for the sketch "Reina," included in *A Gallery of Women.* The events upon which "Reina" is based took place between 1920 and 1922. Although not yet legally married, Dreiser and Helen were living together in a common-law marriage (they did not marry until 1944, just eighteen months before Dreiser's death and two years after Dreiser's first wife, Sara White, died). From Dreiser's *American Diaries,* we learn that Helen received a letter from Myrtle stating that she wanted to leave her husband, Grell, the model for Sven, and come live with them. When she tells Helen that she needn't worry because she won't tell anyone she is her sister, Helen cries. Myrtle's letter encapsulates the tensions portrayed in "Reina," based on Myrtle's on-again, off-again marriage with Grell, and her sister's sympathy. Myrtle and, eventually, Grell do arrive in Los Angeles, and Dreiser recounts numerous pleasant outings in Grell's car with Myrtle, Helen, and Grell. In Dreiser's diaries there is little to suggest the abuse depicted in "Reina" other than the occasional note that he and Helen "roast" Myrtle for her regard for Grell. Dreiser does recount Myrtle's enjoyment of clothing, parties, and restaurants, but she doesn't seem to enjoy them anymore than Helen or even Dreiser himself does. In fact, Dreiser's depiction of their interaction sounds rather idyllic until Grell has a car accident, an event that is also pivotal in "Reina." Afterward, Grell gets a car on loan from the repair company, and the foursome take up outings as before. Still, one night Grell does not return home. The next day they learn he has disappeared, closing his bank account and leaving Myrtle with nothing. Myrtle moves in with Helen and Dreiser but eventually moves back to Portland to live with her mother. While there is some evidence of Myrtle's crassness and superficial ambition in the dairies, Dreiser seems to exaggerate her abusiveness and parasitism in his depiction of Reina.

Still, Myrtle remained a marginal figure in Dreiser's life as Helen remained a dominant one. Dreiser and Helen visited Myrtle a few times, and Myrtle and her mother came to stay with Helen at **Iroki,** Dreiser and Helen's country house, when she had temporarily separated from Dreiser. Finally, Myrtle and her new fiancé, Chester Butcher, served as the only witnesses to Helen and Dreiser's marriage on 13 June 1944.

Kimberly Freeman

PENNSYLVANIA DREISER EDITION.

In 1981, the University of Pennsylvania Press issued a radically new edition of *Sister Carrie,* the first volume of the Pennsylvania Dreiser Edition. Neda M. Westlake, curator of rare books at Penn's Van Pelt Library, was the first general editor. With the resources of the extensive Dreiser Collection at Penn available to her, she had, by the time Thomas P. Riggio succeeded her in 1986, established a "tradition of publishing authoritative texts of writings that either survive in manuscript or are not easily accessible to the specialist and general reader alike" (Riggio, Preface to *Jennie Gerhardt* xii). Each volume is a scholarly edition with historical and textual commentaries, notes, tables of emendations, and the like. In order of publication, the edition consists of *Sister Carrie* (1981), the autobiographical fragment *An Amateur*

Laborer (1983), *American Diaries, 1902–1926* (1983), *Dreiser-Mencken Letters* (1986; two volumes), the first volume of *Theodore Dreiser: Journalism* (1988), *Newspaper Days* (1991), *Jennie Gerhardt* (1992), *Dreiser's Russian Diary* (1996), and *Twelve Men* (1998). The Dreiser Edition has been a boon to Dreiser scholarship, stimulating fresh interpretations of well-known works and making available to critics and biographers alike masses of previously inaccessible material.

Controversy has arisen, however, over *Sister Carrie*, *Jennie Gerhardt*, and, to a lesser extent, *Newspaper Days*, each of which restores large blocks of text cut at the time of original publication. At issue are both the nature of authorship and the role of the textual editor.

The editors of the Pennsylvania Edition adhere to the general practice of W. W. Greg and Fredson Bowers. In this tradition, the editor's job is to choose a copy-text that most fully embodies the author's artistic intentions, to accept only those cuts, additions, and revisions made or approved by the author to further those intentions, and to use aesthetic judgment when the evidence is ambiguous. Because it represents choices from among different states of text, the result is an ideal, or "eclectic," version that never existed before in precisely that form. The Pennsylvania *Sister Carrie* and *Jennie Gerhardt* are both eclectic editions. James L. W. West III, who decided the editorial principles for both, argues that in yielding to pressure from his friends, his wife, and his publishers, Dreiser permitted the publication of collaborative, expurgated works aimed at not offending female readers. In explaining his editorial principles, West says that Dreiser abandoned his "authorial function" once he completed the original writing; he then became an "editor" whose "motives for revising and cutting" were

"sometimes artistic, but just as often . . . not" ("Textual Commentary," *Sister Carrie* 580). Following this line of reasoning, West has chosen as copy-texts the earliest complete versions—the holograph of *Sister Carrie* and the composite holograph-typescript of *Jennie Gerhardt*. For each novel, he has restored both tens of thousands of words cut during the original editing for reasons deemed nonartistic and hundreds of other early readings. When evidence of Dreiser's motive is weak or lacking, he has used his own judgment, deciding, for instance, on the original ending of *Sister Carrie* without the Balzacian coda and accepting the late addition of **Lester Kane's** confession of love in *Jennie Gerhardt*.

Many readers have greeted these editions enthusiastically for at last freeing Dreiser's work from the chains of Victorian prudery. Those who demur, however, argue that most works are at least partly collaborative and, as evidence against expurgation, point to Dreiser's lifelong reliance on friends and hired editors to help him shape his books for publication. They argue further that motives for the thousands of changes made to each novel during the process of revising and editing are impossible to sort out with any confidence and that in the absence of more compelling evidence for expurgation editors should stay with versions that have assumed an important place in literary history.

In a recent new Introduction to the Penn *Sister Carrie*, Riggio has announced a general shift in editorial policy relating to these eclectic editions. The controversy is "dated," he writes, both sides playing a "variation on themes" (ix) from arguments in the 1980s about the literary canon. Whereas West had proclaimed the edition to be "a new work of art" ("Historical Commentary," *Sister Carrie* 532) superior to the 1900 **Doubleday, Page** text and requiring fresh interpretation, Riggio asserts that it is just "a version in a continuum of composition" that, when considered with all other versions, can "give us a good idea of the complex process of writing and editing that went into making the novel" (xi). Would Dreiser approve this state of affairs? He did think that a work "carries a charge of experience" whose "potential" for realization in the observer is limited only by "the concreteness of the form" (*Notes on Life* 180). The Pennsylvania Edition has enabled us to understand the fluidity of his forms. Dreiser just might like the limitless potential for new experiences his readers now possess.

To date, no detailed comparisons of the two versions have been published for either *Sister Carrie* or *Jennie Gerhardt*. Critics who deal with both versions tend either to focus on narrowly defined issues or to select one version for analysis and use the other for passing comparison. In 2002, the Pennsylvania Edition, whose name reflects the location of the Dreiser Papers rather than the original press, found a new publisher in the University of Illinois Press. At the time of this writing, new editions are in the works for *The Financier*, *The "Genius,"* and *A Traveler at Forty*. Also under way are a collection of Dreiser's public interviews, two volumes of his previously unpublished letters, and his European diaries.

Further Reading

Brennan, Stephen C. "Freedom and Tyranny in Textual Editing: The Pennsylvania Dreiser Edition." *Journal of Contemporary Thought* 5 (1995): 157–75.

————. "The Two Endings of *Sister Carrie*." *Studies in American Fiction* 16 (1988): 13–26.

Hayes, Kevin J. "Textual Anomalies in the 1900 Doubleday, Page *Sister Carrie*." *American Literary Realism* 22 (1989): 53–68.

Pizer, Donald. "Self-Censorship and Textual Editing." *Textual Criticism and Literary Interpretation*. Ed. Jerome J. McGann. Chicago: University of Chicago Press, 1985. 144–61.

————. "The Text of *Sister Carrie*: Where We Are Now." *Dreiser Studies* 32.2 (2001): 42–48.

Riggio, Thomas P. Introduction. *Sister Carrie*. By Theodore Dreiser. The Pennsylvania Edition. Ed. John C. Berkey, Alice M. Winters, and James L. W. West III. Philadelphia: University of Pennsylvania Press, 1998. vii–xv.

West, James L. W., III. "Editorial Theory and the Act of Submission." *Papers of the Bibliographic Society of America* 83 (1989): 169–85.

Whaley, Annemarie Koning. "Obscuring the Home: Textual Editing and Dreiser's *Jennie Gerhardt*." *Theodore Dreiser and American Culture: New Readings*. Ed. Yoshinobu Hakutani. Newark: University of Delaware Press, 2000. 161–75.

Stephen C. Brennan

"PERSONALITY" appears in *Hey Rub-a-Dub-Dub* as Dreiser's attempt to explain the inherent difference between the successful man and the more common, less successful individual. Dreiser identifies "personality" as the most important determinant for success. For Dreiser there is no formula to adequately create the combination of traits that lead to success because the element that leads to success is "inexplicable to the individual himself." Personality is the key—"that unexplainable, inescapable something with which we come." Dreiser is unable to articulate more clearly what constitutes this "something," yet it is clear that for the individual, personality is innate, an "inherent capacity, a something which he cannot create for himself, try as he may." It is impossible, Dreiser concludes, for the common person to produce something truly new because individuals are socially inclined to become as similar to everyone else as possible. Therefore, Nature makes superior individuals possible by creating in them an inherent ability to surpass others.

The characteristics of personality are provided by Nature and are merely honed by life. Dreiser's emphasis on the role of Nature in determining who possesses this internal quality illustrates the influence of social Darwinism—those who are most fit by Nature will rise to the top. Dreiser compares the natural instincts of animals and the natural characteristics of humans and sees very little difference in the distribution of significant traits, such as cunning in animals and the distribution of the *successful* personality in humans. The differences between people are rooted in the differences provided by Nature: "That which places one being over another and sets differences between man and man is not alone intellect or knowledge . . . but these plus . . . the vital energy to apply them or the hypnotic power of attracting attention to them—in other words, personality."

Jennifer Marie Raspet

"PETER." The first biographical sketch in *Twelve Men*, "Peter" is about **Peter B. McCord**, a close friend of Dreiser's from his early newspaper days in St. Louis until McCord's death in 1908. Although written especially for *Twelve Men*, "Peter" was probably begun during the 1915–1916 period, when Dreiser was producing a large quantity of autobiographical material. Dreiser placed this sketch first to establish immediately the ideals that he wished to convey through this collection about men he admired; Peter embodied the sophistication and intellect that the young Dreiser wished to emulate. The sketch also served to establish clearly the narrator's youthfully subservient relationship with Peter McCord and the next five men, as opposed to his relationship of equality with the second six.

"Peter" begins in 1892 with a description of the young Dreiser coming to work as a reporter for the *St. Louis Globe-Democrat*, where he meets the witty and sophisticated newspaper artist Peter McCord. Dreiser describes their youthful adventures in St. Louis, making clear his admiration for the more mature McCord, who was only a year older. Dreiser wrote that McCord was someone "to whom I owe some of the most ecstatic intellectual hours of my life." Dreiser leaves St. Louis for New York in 1894 but is able to resume their friendship when Peter moves to Philadelphia in 1898. Though no longer a callow youth, the narrator maintains his admiration for the talented McCord. The rest of the sketch is devoted to their adventures over the next ten years. Dreiser finds everything McCord does to be fascinating, from teaching himself to make Chinese pottery to pulling off a hoax about a primitive "wild man" on a rampage in southern New Jersey. After marriage, Peter not only is the ideal husband and father but he also still maintains his vigorous enthusiasm for life. When Peter dies unexpectedly of pneumonia at the age of thirty-eight, the narrator is left with an immense sense of loss.

Robert Coltrane

PHANTASMAGORIA. Dreiser completed this one-act play in February 1918, and, after he unsuccessfully submitted it to a number of magazines, it appeared in his collection of essays, *Hey Rub-a-Dub-Dub*. Like others of his one-act plays, *Phantasmagoria* is less a play and more a philosophical discussion in dramatic form. In the first scene, "The House of Birth," A "blind, aged, and insane" Lord of the Universe creates from his mind elemental forces: first Beauty, desiring to be worshiped, and then Ambition, sinister and demanding to be obeyed. Exhausted, the Lord of the

Universe staggers and despairs but quickly births the thoughts Hate, Despair, Love, Pity, Hope, and Fear. In the second scene, "The House of Life," the Lord of the Universe dreams insane dreams in which Beauty competes with Ambition to be first in the Lord's thoughts, while the other emotions clamor for recognition. As Ambition triumphs, the Lord grows confused and sinks deeper into a mad dream. In the third scene, "The House of Death," a now thoroughly insane and destructive Lord of the Universe destroys all that he has created by recalling all of his thoughts, with Beauty, his first thought, the last to return.

As a parable of the senselessness and ironic destructiveness of the creative force, *Phantasmagoria* shares with a number of essays in *Hey Rub-a-Dub-Dub* an insistence upon the arbitrariness of meaning and value. It may also have been inspired, in part, by **Charles Fort's** notion of "autogenetic orthogenesis"—the idea that all life emanates from some cosmic mind—an idea Dreiser also depicted in his play *The Dream*.

Keith Newlin

"PHANTOM GOLD." This tale of greed and malice first appeared in *Live Stories* in February 1921. A slightly revised version was collected in *Chains: Lesser Novels and Stories*. When zinc deposits on Bursay Queeder's farm raise the value of his property, the old man envisions a life of leisure without his family. He plots against his wife, son, and daughter, planning to deny them the profits from the farm's sale. His family is just as avaricious, however, and circumstances help them to thwart Bursay's plan. Ultimately, his son beats him into signing a bill of sale and then keeps most of the money. Dispossessed of his wits and "trussed like a fowl for market," in the end Bursay is left at the mercy of his selfish relatives.

Although it may prove a point about the psychological danger of overriding desire, the story produces little sympathy for its characters, toward whom Dreiser is uncharacteristically condescending. In a style that emphasizes their lack of sophistication and base ignorance, the Queeders speak in a rural dialect that contrasts sharply with the narrator's inflated diction. At best, "Phantom Gold" avoids the simplistic equation between lack of money and superior morality that informs the better-known story of rural midwestern life, "Under the Lion's Paw" (1891), by Hamlin Garland, in which a well-to-do landlord takes advantage of a poor and hardworking farmer. But, consistent with his fatalistic philosophy, Dreiser expresses none of Garland's reformism, emphasizing instead the primacy of self-interest: "Love, family tenderness, family unity—if these had ever existed they had long since withered in the thin, unnourishing air of this rough, poverty-stricken world."

Scott Emmert

"A PHOTOGRAPHIC TALK WITH EDISON." This interview first appeared in the February 1898 edition of *Success*, a magazine founded and edited by Dr. **Orison Swett Marden**. After the magazine began publication in 1897, Dreiser published interviews almost every month for the next two years, eventually publishing a total of thirty, fifteen of which Marden later reprinted in three collections of such interviews. "A Talk with Edison" later appeared in *How They Succeeded* (1901) and again as "Hard Work, the Secret of a Great Inventor's Genius—Thomas Alva Edison" in *Little Visits with Great Americans* (1903). It can also be found in *SMA 1*. As with his other interviews, Dreiser's focuses on Edison's humble beginnings and devotion to hard work. Such themes, of course, appealed to the fantasies of a mass audience of young men hoping for similar success in their own lives, and Dreiser's questions led his interviewees to offer advice on how to improve their own lives. This audience also wanted a glimpse of the luxurious life, and Dreiser often contrasts the early hardships of his subjects' lives with their present opulence, while noting his own privileged access to this world. In this case, Dreiser provides the details of Edison's workplace and appearance and observes that the scope of his library suggests "an idea of the breadth and thought and sympathy of this man who grew up with scarcely a common school education." Dreiser's interview with Edison, however, differs from his typical pattern. Edison is unique in eschewing moderation, a well-balanced life, and thrift. Instead, he identifies success as "the ability to apply your physical and mental energies to one problem incessantly without growing weary," and rather than saving money, he says that he "devoted every cent, regardless of future needs, to scientific books and materials for experiments."

In emphasizing Edison's singular devotion to work, Dreiser's interview suggests why Edison has had a more durable hold on the popular imagination than the other tycoons whom he interviewed—their advice appears almost quaint compared to Edison's exhortations. Dreiser's interview also reveals quite a bit about his own insecurities and devotion to success. Amid the gentle irony that frames the piece, Dreiser focuses on what we can recognize as obvious similarities between Edison's life and his own. He notes that Edison's family suffered similar financial reversals that caused him to begin working at a young age and that Edison, like Dreiser, came east "with no ready money and in rather dilapidated condition" and later spent his first weeks in New York wandering "about the town with actual hunger star-

ing him in the face." Dreiser also presents Edison as the kind of pure soul that Dreiser's father always wanted his children to be; during his days as a tramp telegraph operator, Edison lived "free and easy" but avoided the "dissipations" of his companions. Edison was still on Dreiser's mind two years later, when he used him as the basis for the composite character **Robert Ames** in *Sister Carrie*. Ames possesses the devotion to success and purity of character that Dreiser saw in Edison and the interest in art and literature that he himself chose to pursue. Dreiser's complex attitude toward Edison, then, offers insights into his similarly complex attitude toward his character Ames as someone who tries to articulate a philosophy of success that brings these two sets of values together.

Further Reading

Humphries, David T. " 'The Shock of Sympathy': Bob Ames's Reading and Re-reading of Sister Carrie." *Dreiser Studies* 32.1 (2001): 34–55.

Hussman, Lawrence E. "Thomas Edison and *Sister Carrie*: A Source for Character and Theme." *American Literary Realism* 8 (1975): 155–58.

David T. Humphries

PLAYS, PRODUCTIONS OF. Dreiser's years of active playwriting (1913 to 1918) coincided with the rise of the Little Theater movement, which stressed experimental, noncommercial productions and favored the one-act play form. Soon after the publication of *Plays of the Natural and Supernatural* in 1916, Dreiser fielded a number of inquiries from little theater groups interested in staging his plays. The first to reach the stage—*Laughing Gas*, under the direction of Carl Bernhardt at the Indianapolis Little Theater on 7 December 1916—is of historic importance, for it marked the first effective use in America of expressionistic staging techniques to portray the unconscious mind. The troupe was interested in the play in part because it was then promoting the work of Hoosier playwrights, but they were also attracted to the technical challenge posed by staging Vatabeel's dream hallucinations, which are prompted by the realistic actions of the medical team. In their production, the players conveyed the simultaneous interconnection of real and dream characters through stylized, rhythmic motions of the actors accompanied by symbolic shadings of light. In an unsigned review for the *Indianapolis News*, Oliver Sayler, who would become an influential proponent of the Russian Art Theater, proclaimed, "The achievement in the effective production of 'Laughing Gas' is nothing less than revolutionary. . . . [The production] is one of the three or four creative discoveries of the little theater movement the world over" (8 December 1916: 27). Moreover, the production inspired other theater groups by demonstrating dramatically effective means of mingling conscious and dream states through methods derived from the "new stagecraft," which tended to subordinate **realism** to emotional effects conveyed through simplified and symbolic sets. With its realistic set, topical subject matter—a botched abortion amid a labor strike—and the then-sensational device of having an open coffin at center stage, *The Girl in the Coffin* proved to be the play that most interested theatrical groups. Of its six productions, the most significant was by the Washington Square Players, under the direction of Edward Goodman, on 3 December 1917. Reviewers responded enthusiastically, as did the audience; on opening night there were eighteen curtain calls and cries for the author, which Dreiser missed since he chose not to attend, fearing a poor reception. Reviewers almost universally praised the realism of situation and dialogue, which in 1917 was still not common in commercial plays. Charles Darnton of the *Evening World* wrote that "Mr. Dreiser's play is . . . so sane and true and real that it has the grip of tragedy. The characters talk and look and act like people who have felt the hard grind of labor all their days" (7 December 1917: 25) Ralph Block of the *New York Tribune* agreed: the play has "the first natural dialogue of laboring men I have heard on the stage for a long time. The speech makes use of idioms and turns of the tongue that could have been garnered only after a serious and painstaking scrutiny of the kind of life that is represented" (9 December 1917; sec. 4: 2). Reviews of performances by other theater groups also tended to focus on the play's realism; *The Girl in the Coffin* thus had a small, but important, role in training actors in realistic performance and in educating audiences about dramatic innovation.

While his one-act plays promptly interested theaters soon after publication, Dreiser's only full-length play, *The Hand of the Potter*, had a more circuitous route to production. Dreiser completed the play in December 1916 and agreed to hold off publication when theatrical producer Arthur Hopkins, then the most renowned director of serious drama on Broadway, optioned the play. When Hopkins let his option lapse, Dreiser arranged to have the play published in 1918 by **Boni & Liveright**, but agreed to delay its release when producer Charles Coburn optioned the play. But when a current Coburn production became the smash hit of the season, his plans for Dreiser's play languished, and the play was eventually published in 1919. Dreiser had meanwhile moved to Hollywood, and he engaged his friend **Edward Smith** to negotiate for a production of the play. Smith eventually interested the Provincetown Players in staging *The Hand of the Potter*, which opened on 5 December 1921 under the direction of Charles O'Brien Kennedy.

The Provincetown production stirred great critical interest because of their chutzpah in staging Dreiser's sympathetic portrait of a sexual deviate who rapes and murders an eleven-year-old girl. Although Dreiser was assured that the play would have a first-rate cast, the more experienced actors were engaged in simultaneous productions of Eugene O'Neill's *The Emperor Jones* and Susan Glaspell's *The Verge*, leaving a largely inexperienced cast to perform his play. Although many reviewers objected to the content of the play, most admired the performance of the actors, and nearly all objected to the rather windy fourth act, despite its cutting for performance, as undramatic and anticlimactic. J. Ranken Towse of the *New York Evening Post* called the play "a morbid and unsavory piece, which offers little compensation for its relentless unwholesomeness" (6 December 1921: 9). The *New York Globe and Commercial Advertiser*, while concluding that "the play should not have been written, and certainly it should never have been produced," praised the acting as "admirable" (6 December 1921: 18). And Louis De Foe of the widely read *New York World* called the play "a revolting specimen of pathological drama" that is "palpably insincere and ineffective" and clumsily structured as well (18 December 1921: 2M).

A complete list of productions during Dreiser's lifetime, with opening dates, follows:

Laughing Gas. 7 December 1916; Indianapolis: Little Theater Society of Indiana, dir. Carl Bernhardt.
The Girl in the Coffin. (1) 29 January 1917; St. Louis: St. Louis Artist's Guild, dir. A. H. Brueggman; (2) 9 October 1917; San Fran-

cisco: St. Francis Little Theater Club, dir. Arthur Maitland: (3) 3 December 1917; New York: Washington Square Players, dir. Edward Goodman; (4) 21 March 1918; Detroit: Arts and Crafts Players, dir. Sam Hume; (5) 24 January 1920; New York: Workers' Theater Guild, dir. Wayne Arey; (6) 11 July 1941; Institute: West Virginia State College, dir. F. S. Belcher.
"Old Ragpicker." (1) 30 January 1918; San Francisco: St. Francis Little Theater Club, dir. Arthur Maitland; (2) 1 June 1923; New York: Cellar Players, dir. George Bamman.
The Hand of the Potter. (1) 5 December 1921; New York: The Provincetown Players, dir. Charles O'Brien Kennedy; (2) September 1928; Berlin, Germany: Drei Masken Verlag, dir. Gustave Hartung; (3) 5 May 1938; London, England: Portfolio Players, dir. Hector Abbas.
The Blue Sphere. 4 June 1930; broadcast over radio WABC, New York, dir. Georgia Backus.

Further Reading

"Appendix 3: Productions of Dreiser's Plays." *The Collected Plays of Theodore Dreiser*. Ed. Keith Newlin and Frederic E. Rusch. Albany, N.Y.: Whitston, 2000. 331–53.

Newlin, Keith. "Dreiser's 'The Girl in the Coffin' in the Little Theatre." *Dreiser Studies* 25.1 (1994): 31–50.

———. "Expressionism Takes the Stage: Dreiser's 'Laughing Gas.' " *Journal of American Drama and Theatre* 4.1 (1992): 5–22.

Keith Newlin

PLAYS OF THE NATURAL AND SUPERNATURAL. In December 1912 Dreiser went to Chicago to gather material about **Charles Yerkes** for use in *The Titan*. While there, he went to Maurice Browne's Chicago Little Theater to see a performance of Euripides' *The Trojan Women*. He was attracted to **Kirah Markham**, who played the lead, as well as to the innovative staging of the play, which emphasized rhythmic motion and symbolic, suggestive sets rather than the customary stage **realism** of mainstream plays. He was apparently inspired by Brown's theater and by Markham, with whom he would live until 1916, for when he returned to New York, he wrote *The Girl in the Coffin*, his first completed play. Over the next two years, he wrote a number of other one-act plays, publishing six in magazines before collecting them with a seventh unpublished play in *Plays of the Natural and Supernatural*, published by **John Lane** on 18 February 1916.

Of these seven plays, only two observed any fidelity to realism. *The Girl in the Coffin*, a piece redolent with dramatic irony, discloses a strike leader's realization that he must put aside his personal grief over his daughter's death for his larger duty to his fellow strikers; *"Old Ragpicker"* enlists realistic detail to delineate the pathos of an old street scavenger's decline. The other five plays dramatize the **supernatural** and mechanical forces that Dreiser believed to be responsible for human behavior and action. *Laughing Gas* depicts a surgical patient's dream vision in which the leading characters are the Rhythm of the Universe, the gas nitrous oxide, and "Alcepheron, an element of physics." *The Blue Sphere* violates the unity of time and place as a mysterious Shadow lures a deformed child to its death under the wheels of a train. *In the Dark* conveys the melodrama of guilt and vengeance as a murderer is pursued by spirits and demons; *The Spring Recital* portrays an organist playing for various human and spectral entities; and *The Light in the Window*, an ironic study of envy and social climbing that anticipates *An American Tragedy*, depicts the poor's images of the wealthy through a kaleidoscopic montage that violates dramatic space. All depict a common theme—that despite its apparent disorder, unfairness, futility, and purpose-

lessness, life is still precious and is to be cherished.

At first Dreiser himself did not take his plays very seriously, calling them "skits" and "stunts" in his letters to H. L. Mencken, who was his chief confidant during the seven years that Dreiser tried his hand at playwriting. But as he became caught up in their composition, he began to recognize that dramatic form enabled him to address more directly than did his fiction the metaphysical questions that increasingly began to preoccupy him after the publication of *The Titan*. The plays are therefore an important resource for understanding the development of Dreiser's aesthetics.

The plays in particular suggest the melodramatic basis of Dreiser's conception of **naturalism**. If the hallmark of the melodramatic imagination is a Manichean perception of good locked into battle with evil, then Dreiser's imagination is surely melodramatic, for the conflict he delineates so frequently in his fiction and essays consistently pits people against a world of cosmic forces largely indifferent though occasionally hostile to them. For Dreiser, as for other melodramatists, people are victims, the playthings of "forces" they can rarely perceive and never completely understand. As he explains at length in "Equation Inevitable," the cornerstone of his philosophy, "Nature has supplied us with certain forces or chemic tendencies and responses, and has also provided (rather roughly in certain instances) the checks and balances which govern the same. Our puny strengths will permit us to do only so much; no more."

In these plays, Dreiser grafts a mechanistic explanation of human behavior onto melodramatic patterns of conflict between one's will to live and personifications of the forces that determine one's actions. Unlike most melodramatists of his generation, however, Dreiser locates the action within the mind rather than within the external movement of plot and character. Because they dramatize the mechanical workings of the mind, Dreiser's plays are among the first attempts to portray a psychology of character grounded in mechanistic science. Indeed, their formal innovations forecast methods of depicting character psychology that dramatists such as Elmer Rice (in *The Adding Machine*, 1923), Eugene O'Neill (in *Strange Interlude*, 1928), and Thornton Wilder (in *Our Town*, 1938) would later experiment with in their efforts to convey the inner conflicts of the mind.

When *Plays of the Natural and Supernatural* appeared, reviewers were largely appreciative, though occasionally baffled. Montrose Moses, reviewing the plays for *Book News Monthly*, thought the plays represented "a distinctly new element in playwriting in this country." Dreiser "successfully mingle[s] realism with what one might almost call a super-symbolism" to "produce such definite psychological effects" (rpt. in Salzman 266–67). What attracted Moses—as well as other reviewers—was Dreiser's innovative attempt to dramatize the spiritual and material forces responsible for human action and perception. The *Boston Evening Transcript* suggested that the volume "opens up a new vista in American play writing," for through Dreiser's art "we have been enabled to grasp a little more clearly the inner meanings of life and the subtle dependence of the material on the immaterial" (rpt. in Salzman 259). And the *American Review of Reviews* concluded, "Everyone who is interested in the progress of the American drama will welcome this new departure in the field of dramatics" (rpt. in Salzman 265). While the *San Francisco Chronicle* dismissed them as "completely unplayable" (rpt. in Salzman 261), the real-

istic *Girl in the Coffin* was staged six times during Dreiser's lifetime, and adventurous theater groups performed *Laughing Gas*, "*Old Ragpicker*," and *The Blue Sphere* once each.

Plays of the Natural and Supernatural was reprinted by **Boni & Liveright** in 1926 and by Constable & Co. (London) in 1930. The latter reprinting also includes three one-act plays appearing in *Hey Rub-a-Dub-Dub—The Dream*, *Phantasmagoria*, and *The Court of Progress*—as well as Dreiser's only full-length play, *The Hand of the Potter*. All of Dreiser's plays were collected and edited in *The Collected Plays of Theodore Dreiser*, edited by Newlin and Rusch.

See also Plays, Productions of.

Keith Newlin

POTTER, CHARLES TILDEN (1845–1930). Charlie Potter was one of the people Dreiser met and wrote about as a result of his summer in Noank, Connecticut, in 1901 with **Arthur Henry**. While talking to the villagers, Dreiser kept hearing about this totally selfless man who was locally famous for helping those in need, so he traveled to nearby Norwich, where he interviewed Potter. The result was the sketch published in *Twelve Men* as "A Doer of the Word."

Captain Charles Tilden Potter was born in Noank on 11 September 1845. He had acquired the title of "captain" when he commanded a boat of his own as a member of the fishing fleet running out of Noank. Earlier, in 1863, while serving as a ship's cook, he had survived the sinking of his ship by a southern privateer. As a young man, Potter was known as a hard drinker, but he reformed and took on the task of reforming others as an evangelical minister. He first served as superintendent of the Bradley Street Mission in New London, Connecticut, for six years. Around 1897, he opened his own mission room in

Norwich and later established the Norwich Holiness Mission on Main Street, where he conducted services and provided assistance to the needy until his death at age eighty-five on 28 December 1930. His wife, Martha, whom he had married in 1868, died in 1939 at age ninety-one. They had four children of their own, plus others (according to Dreiser's account) whom they took in as foster parents. Shortly after Dreiser's sketch first appeared in *Ainslee's* in June 1902, Potter obtained permission to publish it as a tract. In Dreiser's fiction, Potter served as the model for the Quaker jailer, Chapin, in *The Financier*.

Robert Coltrane

POTTER, ELIHU H. (1845?–1906). While in Noank, Connecticut, during the summer of 1901, Dreiser interviewed a store owner named Elihu H. Potter and wrote a sketch about him that he called "Heart Bowed Down." Despite several attempts, Dreiser was never able to sell this piece to a magazine. He later published a revised version in *Twelve Men* as "The Village Feudists," changing Potter's name to Burridge to avoid confusion with another Noank native in the book, **Charles Tilden Potter**.

Elihu H. Potter died in Noank on 23 January 1906, but neither his grave marker nor his obituary gives his age or year of birth. Since he was a corporal in Company C of the Twenty-First Infantry, Connecticut Volunteers, during the Civil War and was likely about sixteen in 1861, then he was probably around sixty when he died. Potter was not quite the social outcast Dreiser depicts; his obituary headline calls him a "Good Samaritan" and states that stores were closed and public school classes were halted during the funeral. Ships in the harbor also flew their flags at half-mast. The obituary does confirm that Dreiser's depiction of Potter's "feud" with area churches was accurate: ministers from

three different churches presided at the funeral. However, local residents recall that Potter was not as benign at dispensing Christmas treats as Dreiser describes. Instead, he mixed up pennies, candy, and syrup in a cask and poured the mixture out onto the snow so he could enjoy watching the local urchins scramble for it.

Robert Coltrane

POWYS, JOHN COWPER (1872–1963). English-born novelist and essayist who lived in the United States from 1905 to 1934, where he spent much of his time as an itinerant lecturer. Powys began his serious career as a novelist only in his fifties and is best known for his massive, quasi-mystical novels *Wolf Solent* (1929) and *A Glastonbury Romance* (1932). Powys spent his last three decades living in Wales, where he won recondite fame as a sage and continued to write long and ambitious fiction, most notably, *Porius* (1949).

Powys met Dreiser in October 1914 when Dreiser was involved with **Kirah Markham** and living at 165 West Tenth Street, and Powys was living with his sister, Marian, on West Twelfth Street. Some weeks later, Powys impressed his **Greenwich Village** neighbor by lecturing on Dreiser's work in the latter author's presence at St. Mark's Church in downtown New York City. Powys reviewed The "*Genius*" for the *Little Review* in November 1915, emphasizing the book's vitalistic rendering of the artist and Dreiser's indebtedness to Whitman, and he went on to champion the novel when it ran afoul of the **New York Society for the Suppression of Vice** by drafting protests for British writers to sign. Dreiser's portrait of **Eugene Witla** can be seen to reverberate in Powys's many portraits of energetic, yet introverted, men, although Powys never really wrote an overt *Kunstlerroman* as did Dreiser. **Frank Cowperwood** in *The Titan* surely also impacted the characterization of the industrialist Philip Crow in *A Glastonbury Romance*. Although Powys's writing style was more rhetorical in intent than was Dreiser's, his books resembled Dreiser's in featuring men driven by their will and often manifesting a contestatory or antagonistic relationship with the surrounding environment.

Dreiser, regarded by Powys as a fellow "magician," was the cynosure of Powys's American literary friendships, which also included e. e. cummings, **Edgar Lee Masters**, and Edna St. Vincent Millay, all linked by a common creativity and opposition to restrictive social protocols. Dreiser, who was also friendly with Powys's younger brother Llewelyn, admired Powys's energy as a lecturer and his sympathy for the underdog. In turn, Powys admired Dreiser as the one American writer totally liberated from Victorian and bourgeois inhibitions. In a celebrated story, Dreiser and Powys liked to arm-wrestle with each other, an activity in which neither gained the upper hand. This matched strength was generally agreed to be true of their position as novelists as well, although Dreiser achieved fame far earlier and to a far greater extent than did Powys, who was a year younger than Dreiser. Dreiser, who saw himself as more practical than the often extravagant Powys, influenced Powys to see a gastroenterologist in 1917, which led to Powys's notorious ulcers slowly coming under greater control. When Powys reviewed *An American Tragedy* for the *Dial* in May 1926, remarking that the book's seeming shapelessness was actually a kind of primordial emanation of "psychic chemistry" (rpt. in Salzman 489) from deep within the American soul, Dreiser bought Powys a rare book he had long coveted; similar acts of generosity characterized the friendship throughout.

The fictional modes of the two men were very different, for Powys was not at all a naturalist and only intermittently a social novelist, though his unorthodox religiosity did strike a common chord with Dreiser's own. Powys did, however, recognize that Dreiser's dialogue reflected the drift and babble of living speech. The two men had fewer opportunities to meet when Powys moved back to Britain in 1934, although Dreiser did visit Powys while he was living in Corwen, Wales, in 1938, when Dreiser was returning from visiting the front during the Spanish civil war. Despite their differences, Powys and Dreiser shared a friendship anchored by similar literary ambitions and equivalently titanic "life illusions."

Further Reading

Hopkins, Kenneth. *The Powys Brothers: A Biographical Appreciation*. Rutherford, N.J.: Fairleigh Dickinson University Press, 1967.

Powys, John Cowper. *Autobiography*. New York: Simon and Schuster, 1934. 503–7.

Saalbach, Robert. "Dreiser and the Powys Family." *Dreiser Newsletter* 6.2 (1975): 10–16.

Tjader, Marguerite. "J. C. Powys and T. Dreiser: A Friendship." *The Powys Review* 6 (1980): 16–23.

Nicholas Birns

"THE PRINCE WHO WAS A THIEF" is a story within a story, one of the exploitation of hopeless poverty, and the other of princely romance and riches. It was the second of Dreiser's short stories set in Arabia, reflecting his lifelong interest in Eastern themes, inculcated perhaps from his boyhood reading of *Arabian Nights*. Like the other Dreiser Arabian story, "Khat," the setting for "The Prince Who Was a Thief" takes place in the town of Hodeidah in Yemen, populated with many of the same peripheral characters. Both stories were personal favorites of Dreiser, and although neither was accepted for magazine publication, they appeared together in *Chains: Lesser Novels and Stories*. The protagonist in the story is Gazzar-al-Din, a storyteller and a beggar who is too old to be of any use to anyone. By artfully exchanging bits of his story for money, he enraptures his audience with the tale of the young thief Hussein, who uses his ingenuity to steal vast amounts of treasure from the caliph. Ultimately, Hussein disavows his thievery in exchange for winning the hand of the caliph's daughter, Yanee, after it is discovered that he is of royal blood.

In a letter to H. L. Mencken, Dreiser claimed that the idea for the story came to him "roughly sketched (nothing like it is here) among some Greek folk tales at the Public Library" (*D-M Letters* 1: 153). Unlike "Khat," a tedious Dreiserian allegory with a deterministic theme, "The Prince Who Was a Thief" was embellished with a degree of entertainment value, a departure from his earlier stories. The theme of the story noticeably shifts from the tragic consequences of life and an obsessive preoccupation with success to a romantic fairy tale of mistaken identity and lovers united. In 1951, a film version of the story, starring Tony Curtis and Piper Laurie, was released by Universal-International under the same title.

See also Adaptations, Film.

Joseph F. Alexander

"THE PUSHCART MAN." First published in the *New York Call* on 30 March 1919 before being reprinted in *The Color of a Great City*, this short essay concerns an aging, Italian-born fruit vendor whose seemingly imperturbable nature allows him to eke out a meager living under very difficult circumstances. The essay moves from a general description of the life of a street vendor, to a detailed account of one such vendor at work, and finally to a sketch of this man's living conditions (Dreiser apparently follows the man to his tenement apartment) and a brief consideration of the Pushcart Man as representative of all city dwellers. Depictions of the Italian Pushcart Man, his wife and children, and the Irish policeman are largely stereotyped and flat. When Dreiser's view tends toward the macroscopic, however, the piece is kept alive by his use of naturalistic imagery, which presents the subject as both parasite and host. Part of a general swarm of vendors who "infest" New York, the Pushcart Man is simultaneously "picked and grafted upon" by corrupt and bigoted policemen.

Most interesting is Dreiser's treatment of "success." The hardworking European immigrant character seems tailor-made for a rags-to-riches narrative. Dreiser recognizes in the man "the qualities which make for success in this world," but these qualities are not those usually associated with the American success myth. The vendor's ability to withstand patiently the endless difficulties of his day-to-day life without wishing his situation were otherwise constitutes his strength. Success for Dreiser is not defined by material or social improvement. Rather, in escaping these illusions, the Pushcart Man finds "success." This Italian-born street vendor refuses to join the majority of Americans in their "fruitless effort to be what they cannot."

Jon Dietrick

PYNE, MARY (1894–1919), the American actress and model for "Esther Norn" in *A Gallery of Women*, belongs to Dreiser's **Greenwich Village** years. A photograph shows a gentle-looking woman, with long dress, posing like a cowboy with a revolver and belt on her hip, presumably part of a stage act. Despite crippling health troubles including consumption and a heart condition, Pyne had success with acting with the Provincetown Players: in December 1915, in *Before Breakfast*, playing opposite Eugene O'Neill; in March 1917, in Irwin Granich's (Mike Gold) *Ivan's Homecoming* and Harry Kemp's *The Prodigal Son*; and in January 1918, in Alice I. Rostetter's *The Widow's Veil*. Immersed in the culture of the Provincetown Players, she was, however, unable to support herself.

After meeting Pyne in the Brevoort Hotel on 25 November 1917, Dreiser called her "a bad-good girl" in his diary and mused that her history "would make a good short story" (*American Diaries* 220). Dreiser readily assumed the role of protector for the impecunious Pyne, at the same time that he denied financial help to his own estranged wife, Sara (Jug) Dreiser, who had lost her job in the same month of November 1917. Pyne frequently stopped at Dreiser's nearby Tenth Street apartment, warming herself at his fireplace and sharing details of her life with him.

During the mid-teens, Pyne lived with the well-known poet and writer Harry Kemp (1883–1960), the Byron of the Village, who was active in the Little Theater movement. On 18 February 1918, the writer Nina Wilcox Putnam asked Dreiser to help Kemp and his Thimble Theatre. In "Esther Norn," Dreiser presents Kemp as an exploitative companion, yet Pyne's unpublished letters to Hutchins Hapgood suggest her genuine fondness of Kemp: "Harry is here now, and I feel much more animated and full of life when he's here, I catch it from him, I suppose." The anarchist writer and Pyne's friend Hutchins Hapgood similarly aroused Dreiser's sexual jealousy; Hapgood insisted that his relations with Pyne were purely platonic, although Pyne's unpublished letters to him imply otherwise.

By 1919, when tuberculosis ended Pyne's career and life, Kemp, Hapgood, and Dreiser were sporadic visitors at her bedside. Pyne's friend Djuna Barnes, the writer of *Nightwood* (1936), faithfully visited Pyne in the sanatorium, nursing her in the last months of her life. In her letters, Pyne frequently refers to "Djuna," with whom she shared an emotionally and likely erotically charged friendship. After her death, Barnes claimed Pyne's body, as well as writing an elegy. In "Esther Norn," Dreiser silenced this intense friendship and solidarity between the two women and surrounds Esther exclusively with men, evidence for Dreiser's heterosexist bias that routinely ignored gay and lesbian issues. His solicitous treatment of Pyne and simultaneous condemnation of Hapgood and Kemp show evidence of guilt about his own philandering desertion and neglect of the Pyne-like women in his life, including Jug.

Further Reading

Brevda, William. "Love's Brief Immortality: Mary Pyne." *Harry Kemp: The Last Bohemian*. Lewisburg. Pa.: Bucknell University Press, 1986. 97–105.

Hapgood, Hutchins. *A Victorian in the Modern World*. New York: Harcourt, 1939.

Herring, Phillip. *Djuna: The Life and Work of Djuna Barnes*. New York: Penguin, 1995.

Pyne, Mary. Letters to Hutchins Hapgood, ca. 1918–1919. The Yale Collection of American Literature, Beinecke Rare Book and Manuscript Library, Yale University.

Irene Gammel

R

"THE RAKE." In 1915 Dreiser began to write a novel called "The Rake," which was based on the New York murder case of Roland B. Molineux in 1899–1902. Although "The Rake" was never finished, it is an important document in the compositional history of *An American Tragedy*. Just as some details in *An American Tragedy* are based on **Chester Gillette's** murder of **Grace Brown**, much of "The Rake" is taken directly from the Molineux case. Molineux, a chemist, was accused and later acquitted of sending poison to Harry Cornish, physical director of the athletic club to which Molineux belonged. The protagonist of "The Rake," Anstey Bellinger, is also a chemist who belongs to an athletic club and seems headed for conflict with the club's physical director, Victor Quimby. The descriptions of both Bellinger and Quimby resemble newspaper accounts of Molineux and Cornish. Dreiser studied the Molineux case for use in "The Rake," saving clippings from the *New York World* and copying many pages of newspaper reports in his own hand. The descriptions of corpses, poisons, and courtroom proceedings could have been used to give "The Rake" the same kind of factual **realism** that Dreiser later created in *An American Tragedy*. The copied pages also include many descriptions of life and procedures at the Knickerbocker Athletic Club that Dreiser used in the existing fragments of the novel.

"The Rake" can be regarded as a first attempt at writing *An American Tragedy* inasmuch as it is based on a real murder, but the Molineux case, set in the world of wealthy men's athletic clubs, did not provide Dreiser with suitable material for the kind of socially and economically motivated murder depicted in *An American Tragedy*. The character Anstey Bellinger comes from a distinguished family of diminished means who can be considered poor only in comparison to the greater wealth of the new rich. Anstey complains, for example, that he cannot become a member of the yacht club along with his father because the family can afford only one boat. Anstey does not experience the true poverty of Clyde Griffiths's background. He also has the education and social standing that Clyde lacks. Anstey Bellinger is thus portrayed as an effete snob who maneuvers skillfully within the society Clyde so desperately strives to join. The parts of the manuscript that rely heavily on the facts of the Molineux case lead the plot toward a conflict between men in the athletic club, but Dreiser strays from the historical case and injects wholly original elements. In these sections, such as when Anstey dreams of a socially elevating marriage while at the same time seducing poor factory girls, Dreiser moves in a new direction, away from his source material and toward the story of *An American Tragedy*. "The Rake" was never finished, but its failure helps us better understand the novel Dreiser would eventually write.

Further Reading

Plank, Kathryn M., ed. "The Rake." *Papers on Language and Literature* 27 (1991): 45–73.

Kathryn M. Plank

RASCOE, BURTON (1892–1957). Editor, literary critic, and journalist, Rascoe wrote for the *Chicago Tribune*, the *New York Herald Tribune*, the *New York World-Telegram*, and various magazines throughout his life and was the author and editor of numerous books. His career was marked by literary militancy, especially his defense of H. L. Mencken, James Branch Cabell, and Theodore Dreiser. His first published book, *Theodore Dreiser* (1925), was also the first literary study of Dreiser, whom he hailed as the outstanding pioneer of a new American **realism** and a trumpet and a banner to all subsequent writers. The book served Dreiser by attacking his opponents and putting his work in the context of social changes in American life. Rascoe also wrote an appreciative chapter on Dreiser in a later book published in 1933 entitled *Prometheans, Ancient and Modern*. This book also included chapters on Petronious, Nietzsche, Saint Mark, and Cabell. Rascoe wrote other books of literary criticism, as well as the autobiographies *Before I Forget* (1937) and *We Were Interrupted* (1947), and he is known for his encouragement of new talent, his battles against **censorship**, and his promotion of a uniquely American literature.

Rascoe first made the acquaintance of Dreiser in Chicago in the early years of the twentieth century, during the Chicago Renaissance. Throughout his career, Rascoe saw Dreiser as the leading figure in a tough and prolonged battle to reshape American literature and as the great example of a true American genius. Dreiser was delighted with Rascoe's support of him and with the literary talent Rascoe demonstrated; he encouraged Rascoe in his efforts to champion creative freedom and to wrestle frankly with the social issues and ills of the day.

Rascoe's defense of Dreiser was frequent and took many forms. In addition to rising to his defense when Dreiser came under fire by cultural and political conservatives, Rascoe helped Dreiser in 1921 to edit *Newspaper Days* and supported his efforts in 1926 to prevent the first, weakened film version of *An American Tragedy* from being released. In 1930, while associate editor of *Plain Talk*, Rascoe published an article by Dreiser on divorce ("Whom God Hath Joined Together," April, 401–4) that had been rejected by the *New York World* because of critical remarks Dreiser had made about the Catholic Church.

While Rascoe did socialize on occasion with Dreiser, theirs was largely a professional relationship, marked by Rascoe's admiration for Dreiser's ambitious and fearless novels, especially *An American Tragedy*. In a review in the *New York Sun* in 1926, for instance, Rascoe affirmed that "Dreiser's already towering stature among modern realists increases with this tragedy" (rpt. in Salzman 450–51). Rascoe was far less supportive of Dreiser's political and philosophical ideas, which he felt had a damaging effect on his creative work. In an article about Dreiser's play *The Hand of the Potter* in the *Chicago Tribune* in 1919, for instance, Rascoe was critical of what he felt was Dreiser's preachiness and moralism, a flaw that he also suggested weakened Dreiser's fiction (rpt. in Salzman 355–57).

Rascoe was even more critical of Dreiser when he turned away from fiction altogether. Nevertheless, Rascoe's reputation is that of a gifted critic who tirelessly defended Dreiser as one of the giants of modern American literature whose work turned the country's fiction in a more muscular and frank direction and away from the domination of English literary traditions. His deep affection and admiration for Dreiser helped to strengthen Dreiser's status as the premier American writer of his era and to expand Dreiser's general readership. In turn, Dreiser encouraged Rascoe in his literary ambitions and was happy to provide him with much-needed moral and professional support in a time when the battle against the previous "genteel tradition" of literature was at its most intense.

Further Reading

Hensley, Donald M. *Burton Rascoe*. New York: Twayne, 1970.

Margaret Boe Birns

"THE REAL HOWELLS." *See* Howells, William Dean.

REALISM. The term refers generally to a mode of writing stressing the accurate depiction of ordinary human experience, behavior, and speech. In this sense of "faithful representation of reality," realism of one kind or another has been a characteristic of literary writing or a concern of literary criticism since early times. In Plato's *Republic*, for example, Socrates faults poetry for its inaccurate representation of the real, while Aristotle's *Poetics* requires that, in observance of the unities, dramatic representation of an action adhere closely to the action's actual duration. More specifically, "realism" refers to a literary movement of the latter half of the nineteenth century having specific philosophical underpinnings and arising from the powerful advance of the twin forces of industrialism and "free-market" **capitalism** in the United States and Europe.

Notable realist writers of Europe and Great Britain include **Honoré de Balzac**, Gustave Flaubert, Henrik Ibsen, Leo Tolstoy, Ivan Turgenev, Thomas Hardy, George Eliot, George Gissing, and Joseph Conrad. In the United States, the first piece of realist fiction is arguably Rebecca Harding Davis's "Life in the Iron Mills" (1861). Walt Whitman, Mark Twain, **William Dean Howells**, Sarah Orne Jewett, Mary Wilkins Freeman, Hamlin Garland, W. E. B. DuBois, Henry James, Edith Wharton, James Weldon Johnson, and Willa Cather represent the range of realist voices and topics during the period's height in the United States. Theodore Dreiser, Stephen Crane, and **Frank Norris** occupy a shifting middle ground between realism and the more pessimistic and deterministic **naturalism**, which would, thanks largely to their work, supplant realism at the turn of the twentieth century.

Opposing itself to the romanticism of the first half of the century, realism sought to record the ordinary lives of ordinary, imperfect people in the middle and lower walks of modern industrial life. As such, realism positioned itself as the literature of democracy: orphans, farmers, commercial and foundry workers, industrialists, the desperately poor, the complacent bourgeoisie, and the nouveaux riches populated realist writings, which detailed their petty ambitions and strivings, their minor flaws and virtues, and their economic hopes and social delusions. In most cases, realist writers resisted the tragic impulse, adopting by preference a pragmatic and occasionally mildly comic attitude toward their characters and situations. Stylistically, realist writers were notable for their photographic depictions of locale, attempts to record peculiarities of dialect and dress, and explicit, but studiedly impartial, delineations of character and social milieu. Hostile readers criticized the movement for its emphasis on gross physicality and its preference for characters "one would positively avoid coming into contact with in real life" (qtd. in Pizer 5). Fueling American realism was a tension between Americans' post–Civil War commitment to a future of industrial capitalism and technological progress and their rapidly dawning awareness that, in a culture devoted to acquisition of personal wealth, political corruption, cycles of boom and bust, individual want, and decay of family and community were inevitable.

Because realist writers sought to imitate life in all its minute detail, their fiction and poetry tended toward sprawl. Attention to aesthetic form—in the sense of carefully organizing and selecting textual elements with an eye toward artistic effects—was not a significant characteristic of realism, although some writers, notably, Henry James and Willa Cather, did demonstrate an aesthetic bent. In a 1922 essay, "The Novel Démeublé"—which can be read as an early document in the transition to a modernist aesthetic—Cather would criticize realists' sacrifice of aesthetics to journalistic fidelity: "If the novel is a form of imaginative art, it cannot be at the same time a vivid and brilliant form of journalism. Out of the teeming, gleaming stream of the present it must select the eternal material of art" (*Willa Cather on Writing: Critical Studies on Writing as an Art* [Lincoln: University of Nebraska Press, 1988], 40). Cather might easily have been responding to one of Dreiser's own manifestos of realism: his 1903 essay "True Art Speaks Plainly," which identified the artist's purview as "the extent of all reality . . . honestly and reverentially set down" as

"both moral and artistic." Dreiser's oft-noted sins as a literary stylist are as much a product of his commitment to vivid **journalism** and his fascination with material and mechanical processes as to his lack of classical education or propensity toward unwieldy Germanic sentences. Rejecting idealistic representations of life's possibilities led naturally to rejecting novelistic artifice in rhetoric and design.

The democratic concerns and philosophic tensions of realism are most evident in Dreiser's early novels, particularly *Sister Carrie*, whose narrator, even while offering dissertations on the moral ambiguity of American materialism, shares Carrie's unslaked admiration for the mass-produced material and luxury goods available in the novel's lovingly detailed temples of consumption: the Fair, Fitzgerald and Moy's saloon and other department stores and estaminets in Chicago, and Sherry's and Fifth Avenue in New York City. While partly suspicious of contemporary commercial culture, the realist does not, as the naturalist would, view individuals as being essentially and permanently debased by the conditions that produce them. Things are, for the realist, as they are; or, as Dreiser puts it in "True Art Speaks Plainly," "The business of the author . . . is to say what he knows to be true, and, having said as much, to abide the result with patience." Carrie's rise, Hurstwood's fall, Drouet's impervious middle status, the inability of all three to reflect beyond their intellectual capacities upon the randomness of their possible outcomes, and Dreiser's refusal to judge his characters according to any rubric not implicit within the contemporary culture of materialism situate the novel firmly within realism. In *Jennie Gerhardt*, while flouting conventional morality with yet another soiled heroine, Dreiser endows her with enough democratic leanings, optimism, and bourgeois familial affection to make her an embodiment of realist values. Even her ending, alone in a train station surrounded by Americans moving busily and cheerfully forward by the fastest transportation of the day, stresses the inevitability of progress rather than Jennie's personal losses. Despite their frankness about sex and appetite, more characteristic of naturalism than of the realism of James and Howells, both novels lack the clinical treatment of their characters as mere embodiments of animal compulsions, the selective arrangement of increasingly debasing and disintegrative incidents, and the willingness to orchestrate a tragic plot with the individual as victim to his or her compulsions essential to naturalism and more characteristic of Dreiser's later fictions.

Realism has come to be seen as synonymous with late-nineteenth-century literature, particularly the great outpouring and popular consumption of novels on both sides of the Atlantic between 1865 and 1920, but no treatment of realism would be entirely accurate without acknowledging that the movement required constant nurturing by the intelligentsia and promotion and defense by powerful columnists such as William Dean Howells and H. L. Mencken in the middle- and highbrow magazines of the era. A glance at the sales figures not only of Dreiser's early fictions but also of earlier, less earthy realists such as James, Howells, and Garland suggests that the movement had limited popular appeal. Carrying the field in popular sales and not needing periodic defense from Howells's "Easy Chair" columns were decidedly undemocratic contemporary romances such as Anthony Hope's *Prisoner of Zenda* (1894) and Thomas Dixon's anti-Reconstruction tract *The Leopard's Spots* (1902), romances of the American West, such as Owen Wister's *The Virginian* (1902), and the burgeoning genre of nostalgic historical romance, typified by Helen Hunt Jackson's *Ramona* (1884) and John Fox's *Little Shepherd of Kingdom Come* (1903). What is seen in hindsight as the impact of realism upon the development of a serious American literature might not have been entirely apparent to its own practitioners, much less to contemporary readers.

Further Reading

Bell, Michael Davitt. *The Problem of American Realism: Studies in the Cultural History of a Literary Idea.* Chicago: University of Chicago Press, 1993.

Borus, Daniel H. *Writing Realism: Howells, James, and Norris in the Mass Market.* Chapel Hill: University of North Carolina Press, 1989.

Pizer, Donald, ed. *Documents of American Realism and Naturalism.* Carbondale: Southern Illinois University Press, 1998.

Carol S. Loranger

"THE REFORMER." Dreiser's original evaluation of the motives of social reformers appeared in his collection of philosophical essays, *Hey Rub-a-Dub-Dub.* Dreiser applies **Herbert Spencer's** belief that all things tend to maintain a balance to the role of reformers in society. Reformers such as Buddha, Christ, Confucius, and Mohammed attempt to change society so that it will align with an image that is agreeable to them. The reformer therefore "seeks to represent himself to himself as a world need."

According to Dreiser, reformers are not compelled by a need for justice or goodwill. Rather, they are Nature's response to a change in the balance of society, "a chemic and psychic sign" who "is merely an individual expression of the general tendency toward balance or equation. And he will surely come when things swing too far in any given direction." Permanent attempts at reform are "ridiculous" despite the declarations of reformers, who are unconsciously reacting to a shift in the natural balance and are attempting to return to that balance rather than create any significant changes for the greater good. As it happens, often the shift to balance requires a movement toward the good of society; however, this is only an insignificant matter of circumstances. Indeed, it is also possible for the world to have shifted too far toward what is commonly believed to be good, and movement in the opposite direction will restore balance.

Dreiser describes this balance as part of the natural manner in which human lives evolve. Life has its own variations, "swing[ing] to and fro." From this natural inclination, Dreiser asks whether this balance "is an attribute of God or the life force, a conditioning attribute, and one under which it *must* express itself?" Following this relationship between a higher power and natural balance, Dreiser denies any true connection between a higher power and the reformer. Dreiser, like Spencer, gives strong credence to the unknowable and is unwilling to commit to any specific higher power, whether God, a Life Force, Nature, or the Universe. Whatever higher power(s) is at work requires both the saint and the sinner for balance, without having strong concerns for one over the other.

See also "Equation Inevitable."

Jennifer Marie Raspet

"REGINA C——." First published in the June 1928 *Hearst's International Cosmopolitan* before appearing as the first sketch in the second volume of *Gallery of Women,* "Regina C——" was based on details from the life of nurse Miriam Taylor as told to Dreiser by **Estelle Kubitz**, the companion with whom he lived intermittently from 1916 to 1919.

In the opening paragraph, Dreiser's narrator poses a question that underlies the sketch: Do those who lack morals fare as well in life as those who conform religiously and ethically? The balance of the sketch—a portrait of a woman who seemingly has it all yet who sinks into morphine addiction—is his answer. Regina C——, a graduate chemist, bacteriologist, and trained nurse, is the superintendent of nurses in a private hospital in Washington. The narrator describes her as "vigorous and dynamic" with an "almost irritating energy, which seemed not to let her rest for a moment," but her friends describe her as "shrewd and clever," as the "coldest and meanest of girls," as having "no sense of responsibility or honor," and as someone who "doesn't really care for anybody." Though the narrator admires Regina's enjoyment of life, he resists his attraction to her because he sees her as "evasive, elusive, remote," and she refrains from confiding in friends and "live[s] within herself." The narrator senses something "cynical and sinister, and at times even erratic about her."

Regina came from a good Virginia family, but her father treated her mother badly, and her mother died of a broken heart when Regina was only one year old. The home was broken up, and her two sisters and two brothers went to live with various relatives. As a result, Regina has "no family feeling." Regina delights in defying rules, and the narrator notes that she "thought and dreamed on a higher plane than most girls."

After her medical training, Regina becomes involved with a surgeon, Walter La Grange, who secures her a position as a superintendent of a hospital in New York. The narrator presents La Grange as "courteous, soft-spoken, genial," a "cautious, practical, medical man," who "still seeks to conform ethically to the tenets of his profession."

Regina experiments with drinking and drugs and eventually becomes a morphine addict. After being forced to resign from her position at the hospital, she manipulates her acquaintances to acquire morphine and steals the drug from La Grange and from the hospital, even after he steps in to revive her from a morphine-induced suicide attempt. When Regina suspects that La Grange is involved with another woman, she contacts his family, and La Grange begins to distance himself from her, though he continues to pay her bills. He also now recognizes Regina's addiction, and after La Grange pulls away from her, Regina sinks more heavily into morphine addiction.

When Regina is injured stealing morphine from a hospital, La Grange comes forward to treat her, and Regina is incarcerated in the detention ward of the hospital until her court trial. A woman from a home for "erring girls" comes to care for Regina, and after La Grange and the woman testify on Regina's behalf, the court dismisses her case.

At last sighting, Regina appears in the "poor section" of the city, and after that, the narrator never sees her again. A nurse acquainted with Regina reports that a girl fitting her description was picked up unconscious on the street, subsequently determined to be insane, and taken to Bellevue, where she died in a straitjacket. Since La Grange can find no record of Regina's commitment to Bellevue, he prefers to believe her alive; others also report having seen her alive.

The narrator's subjective judgment of Regina as "a capable but erratic soul, one who had some queer twist in regard to the affections and who seemed to think that unless life could be bent to her mood, it was not worth living, or at least, not worth

working for," offers one potential answer to Dreiser's initial question, which frames the narrative: Do those who lack morals fare as well in life as those who conform religiously and ethically? However, the open-ended nature of the sketch's conclusion and Regina's inner strength, determination, and resourcefulness suggest that Regina could just as easily be alive and well as she could be dead or addicted to morphine. Dreiser seems to suggest that an individual's success does not necessarily depend on his or her willingness to conform to societal conventions; rather, success in life relies on the interaction between fate and free will.

Amy E. Ujvari

"REINA." First published in *Century* magazine in September 1923, "Reina" is Dreiser's sketch of **Myrtle Patges**, his second wife's sister, and it opens his 1929 collection *A Gallery of Women*. From the details of the story there is not much to like about Reina; however, there is still something appreciative and sympathetic in Dreiser's portrayal. While the narrator mocks her grammar and loves to egg her on just to hear her wild ideas and funny, vulgar stories, he admires her vivacity and implies that beneath her cold, wisecracking exterior may be a sensitive, dreamy young woman, who like any "good" American aims for self-improvement. She is just rather confused about what self-improvement means. Thinking improvement to be conspicuous consumption, Reina wants the finest clothes, the best cars, and the best-situated house. As in *Sister Carrie*, Dreiser here depicts the craven hollowness and circular desire of consumer culture. Not only does Reina want the goods, but she wants to live the lifestyle of a Hollywood movie and automobile advertisement. She abhors labor of any sort and wants to spend life playing, eating out in restaurants, and motoring around Southern California. Reina becomes frustrated when her husband, Sven, cannot immediately deliver the goods she desires. She resents both the limitations of his income and the time he has to spend working. Her frustration and boredom with Sven have dominated her marriage to him. Every time she gets bored with a place, she leaves him, and he eventually follows, forsaking potentially well-paying, secure jobs. Eventually, after a pivotal car crash that sets Sven back financially, even Sven grows tired of Reina's abuse and disappointment, and he disappears, leaving her with nothing.

Yet Reina is both a particular individual and a type, affected by, and reflective of, her environment. At first, she seems to exhibit characteristics of the Pacific Northwest, but because she lives in Los Angeles, Dreiser notes that she seems particularly susceptible to the idle and parasitic mood of that city and Hollywood. In some ways, the marriage of Sven and Reina functions as a metaphor for the working class trying to survive in a city like Los Angeles. As such, Dreiser suggests that Reina's crudeness and abuse of Sven are not just an individual failing but one that reveals the struggle of individuals against the many forces, social, chemical, and perhaps metaphysical, that are so characteristic of Dreiser's work in general.

Finally, Dreiser also contrasts Reina's character with that of her sister in the portrait, Rhoda, the fictional equivalent of Dreiser's second wife, Helen Richardson (though they were not yet legally married). While Rhoda's character may seem pale in comparison to Reina, she is an infinitely patient and sympathetic character who tries to act as mediator between Sven and Reina. She continues to help Reina, who continually tests the limits of familial support. Thus, through refraction Dreiser also provides a portrait of Helen Richardson.

Kimberly Freeman

RELIGION. As a youth, Dreiser remained under the influence of his father's overzealous commitment to Catholicism, and well into his twenties, he clung to a belief in a higher being who managed a morally ordered universe anchored in justice. Eventually, he grew tired of his father's ironfisted sermonizing and his inadequacies as a family provider. In fact, Dreiser is most likely thinking of his father when he writes in his essay "What I Believe" that "religion is in itself, not wholly an evil nor yet an unmixed good, but only an illusion of the rankest character, yet which for many at least has served as a nervous or emotional escape from a condition much too severe to be endured." Dreiser's skepticism of religion only grew when his mother died. Because Sarah Dreiser worked endless hours to support the family, she spent little time in church and had not participated in confession. A local priest refused to give her last rites after she died on the grounds that she had not received absolution. Not until Dreiser's father agreed to pay $2.50 for a special mass to repose her soul did the church agree to let her be buried in a Catholic cemetery. Dreiser, who loved his mother dearly, never forgot the incident and thereafter condemned organized religion as hypocritical. Whatever religion Dreiser might have retained after his mother's death was dealt a serious blow when he encountered **Herbert Spencer's** *First Principles* (1862) while working as a newspaperman in Pittsburgh.

The writings of Spencer and **Jacques Loeb** made Dreiser doubt the existence of any type of creator and compelled him to understand the world from a mechanistic viewpoint. Humans were simply cogs in a cosmic machine—driven by forces beyond their control and thus deprived of free will. The only truth in life was that all matter, including humans, remained in constant flux and change, that life moved in a circle, in a continuous motion, but went nowhere. This constant change produced contrast, from which Dreiser developed his notion of the "equation inevitable," the idea that one force in life always brings about its opposite. In fact, knowledge could be found only in seeing life in terms of opposites. This understanding of the world caused Dreiser to lament that no God or Creator could be so indifferent to so many unfit individuals and condemn them to an ignorance of their very being. Nonetheless, he spent his entire life attempting to learn more about the universe and how humans figured into the equation. First, he relied heavily upon science, even going so far as to interview important scientists of his day in the hopes that they could answer his questions. By the mid-1930s, he went so far as to dabble in Vedanta philosophy and the *Bhagavad-Gita*.

Some critics believe that though Dreiser may have found religion to be dogmatic, ritualistic, and often hypocritical, he still adhered to the true spirit of it, namely, the teaching of compassion, mercy, and tolerance. In fact, biographer W. A. Swanberg once observed that Dreiser often "wavered between blasphemy and worship." In 1895, under the pseudonym "The Prophet," Dreiser wrote a column called "Reflections" for the magazine *Ev'ry Month* and often drew upon lessons learned from Christ's Sermon on the Mount to back his moralistic view of the world, a view that included not only a mistrust of materialism and desire but also compassion for the poor. Such compassion, derived from Christian doctrines, can be seen in his first novel, *Sister Carrie*. Rather than condemning George Hurst-

wood for stealing money from his employers and committing adultery, Dreiser instead depicts sympathy for him during his fall from grace. In one important passage, Hurstwood encounters an unnamed Good Samaritan who, without gaining anything in return, collects money for the destitute and finds them a place to sleep for the night, a character seemingly out of place in a work of **naturalism**. The novel further warns readers about the dangers of materialism. Though Carrie is not punished in any traditional sense for her adulterous behavior and, in fact, achieves monetary success, the novel ends with her tucked away in a posh hotel room feeling alone and dissatisfied. In his second novel, *Jennie Gerhardt*, Dreiser creates a character in Jennie who often places others ahead of herself, despite the cost to her reputation.

After H. L. Mencken introduced him to Nietzsche around 1908, Dreiser began to see Christian morality and puritan conventions as a distortion of people's very nature. In *A Hoosier Holiday*, he decries the arrogance of sanctimonious religious leaders: we should "[s]hut up the churches, knock down the steeples," for religion is a "weak man's shield"—an attitude that can be seen clearly in the character of **Frank Cowperwood** in the *Trilogy of Desire*. Through Cowperwood, Dreiser illustrates how survival in the cutthroat business environment means abandoning Christian principles of virtue and honesty and fighting with whatever means possible to stay alive. In *The Financier*, Dreiser purposely contrasts Cowperwood with the staunch Irish Catholic Edward Butler, who maintains an outward, sentimental attachment to organized religion in his personal life but who is just as conniving as Cowperwood in the business world. Accordingly, Dreiser reveals his admiration of an amoral man like Cowperwood for accepting reality and logically refuting Christian ethics with Darwinian precision and his condemnation of a man like Butler for wallowing in Christian hypocrisy. In fact, in "Life, Art and America," Dreiser notes that "with one hand the naïve American takes and executes with all the brutal insistence of Nature itself; with the other he writes glowing platitudes concerning brotherly love, virtue, purity, truth." Dreiser's outright rejection of religion culminated in his battle with Christian fundamentalists such as **John Sumner** for banning his novel *The "Genius"* on grounds of immorality. The struggle against Progressive moralists prompted him to angrily proclaim religion as "pure dogmatic bunk."

Despite his mechanistic philosophy, toward the end of his life Dreiser became more spiritual and acknowledged his belief in a Creative Intelligence. He began to admire the design, beauty, and aestheticism found in Nature. In his essay "My Creator," written in 1943, Dreiser admits that design, however one may feel concerning some of it, "is the great treasure that nature or the creative force has to offer man and through which it seems to emphasize its own genius and to offer the knowledge of the same to man." This tempered view of religion can be seen in the novel *The Bulwark*. Dreiser began writing *The Bulwark* in 1914, a time when he had his greatest contempt for religion. He originally intended **Solon Barnes**, the central figure in the novel, to be a tragic figure, whose stubborn and narrow-minded fixation on his religious principles would keep him from accepting reality. Thus, when Solon loses the true, humanitarian spirit of his Quaker faith and, instead, becomes entrenched in its dogmatism and prescriptive codes, he can neither understand nor accept the adverse affects of modern life on his children. However, Dreiser did not finish the novel until the early 1940s, long after his contemptuous

outlook on religion had diminished. In the final version of the novel, Dreiser allows Solon again to recognize the redeeming qualities of human compassion. Scholars often point to Solon's encounter with nature along the Lever Creek at Thornbrough, specifically his run-in with a puff adder and his watching a green fly eat a flower bud, as a key occurrence reaffirming Solon's belief in the universal presence of a Creative Force with a purpose behind the beauty, tragedy, and variety of life. Solon eventually resigns his position at the bank, shuns the American drive for wealth, and defends the poor, an ending strikingly reminiscent of Dreiser's moralistic views as "The Prophet."

See also "Equation Inevitable"; Mechanism; The Supernatural.

Further Reading

Dreiser, Theodore. "My Creator." *Theodore Dreiser: A Selection of Uncollected Prose.* Ed. Donald Pizer. Detroit: Wayne State University Press, 1977. 324–29.

———. "What I Believe." *Forum* 82 (1929): 279–81, 317–20. Rpt. *Theodore Dreiser: A Selection of Uncollected Prose.* Ed. Donald Pizer. Detroit: Wayne State University Press, 1977. 245–58.

Forrey, Robert. "Dreiser and the Prophetic Tradition." *American Studies* 15 (1974): 21–35.

Furmanczyk, Wieslaw. "Theodore Dreiser's Views on Religion in Light of His Philosophical Papers." *Zeitschrift für Anglistik und Amerikanistik* 25 (1977): 213–20.

Lehan, Richard. "The Romantic Dilemma." *Theodore Dreiser: His World and His Novels.* Carbondale: Southern Illinois University Press, 1969. 45–53.

Swanberg, W. A. "The Double Life of Theodore Dreiser." *Critic* 29 (1970): 20–27.

Zanine, Louis. "Science as Religious Quest." *Mechanism and Mysticism: The Influence of Science on the Thought and Work of Theodore Dreiser.* Philadelphia: University of Pennsylvania Press, 1993. 146–78.

Kevin Jett

"RELLA." First published in *Hearst's International-Cosmopolitan* in April 1928 before being reprinted in *A Gallery of Women*, "Rella" is a curiously fictionalized account of **Rose White**, the sister of Dreiser's first wife, Sara White. Perhaps trying to create some distance between autobiography and fiction, though he had not lived with Sara in fourteen years, Dreiser opens this sketch with a Foreword in which he claims to have heard this story one evening in **Greenwich Village** from a poet who is now dead and whose fame has faded. Whether or not he establishes such distance, Dreiser certainly strays from the facts (at least those he reports in his autobiography *Newspaper Days*), exaggerating his feelings for Rose White to create a steamy, romantic southern heroine in Rella. Like so many of the women in *A Gallery of Women*, Rella is as much a reflection of her region as she is an individual character. Continually described in earthy terms, with hair the color of corn and a body as sensuous as the Arkansas hills she inhabits, Rella's attractiveness is due in large part to her symbiotic relationship with the region. Dreiser's language, excessive and melodramatic, also reflects his attempt to create a poetic romance of the South.

Going to stay with his wife's southern relatives, the narrator plans to use his trip as a writing retreat, but he is instead captivated by the landscape, the sultry profusion of which both excites and depresses him. He is inspired but, trapped in an unhappy marriage, feels he has no object for this inspiration. Along comes his wife's seventeen-year-old niece, Rella. At first, the narrator believes the attraction is all on his part, and he is stunned to find a woman fourteen years his junior playing along. Literally playing games together, they thrill at secret rendezvous and stolen moments. (Curiously, these meetings sound more like encounters Dreiser describes with his then-future wife Sara during one of his courtship visits to her family homestead.) Eventually, the narrator's wife and other family members grow suspicious, and he must return to New York. Although the narrator fantasizes about running away with Rella, she is more practical and suggests that they wait. Back in New York, he receives a few letters from her, complaining about restraints back home and asking him to send her money so that she can come join him, but he does not have the funds. The last he hears of Rella is that she has moved to Texas, married an oil speculator, and been disfigured by a disease, destroying her extraordinary beauty before she reaches age thirty.

In addition to having fun with the southern romance tradition, Dreiser uses his sketch of Rella to expound upon the constrictions of marriage and mortality upon the individual. Describing the chemical forces that drive individuals in their attractions to each other, the narrator bemoans the bonds of marriage and social duty, seeing in them a parallel with the limits of age and death. One afternoon, wandering the hills and admiring the "living poetry" of the region, he notes that life and youth go on without us. So he and even Rella will age and die. Thus, the real tragedy is not in the end of his affair with Rella but in the fact that all things must end.

Kimberly Freeman

"A REMARKABLE ART: ALFRED STIEGLITZ." *See* "A Master of Photography."

RICE, ANNE ESTELLE (1877–1959), an American painter and illustrator whose work has recently been rediscovered within American Fauvism, is the model behind Dreiser's semifictional sketch of

"Ellen Adams Wrynn" in *A Gallery of Women*. After studies at the Philadelphia art school and work as an illustrator for magazines, Rice lived in Paris, where the inspiration of Pablo Picasso and Henri Matisse propelled her work into modernity. In 1909 she exhibited her paintings on panels in Philadelphia's Wanamaker department store. Her paintings present emotionally and erotically charged women who are in charge of themselves, their bodies displayed in daring colors and in unconventionally large sizes.

Dreiser first met Rice and her companion, the Scottish modernist painter John Duncan Fergusson (1874–1961), in Paris in January 1912 and was impressed by the couple's modern-day living arrangements: both had their own studios, an ideal system of mutual support and independence. Rice and Fergusson introduced Dreiser to the Left Bank's "*places* of amusement." In May 1913, just two months after the landmark Armory Show in New York City had propelled the American art world into modernism, Rice tried to solicit Dreiser's help for her first American exhibition in 1914 in New York City. In September 1913, Fergusson's affair with a dancer prompted the breakup of the couple's six-year relationship; three months later, in December, Rice married the critic O. Raymond Drey (1885–1977), a supportive and loving man.

In early 1914, Rice arrived in New York City and settled into a studio above Healey's Restaurant, yet her friendship with Dreiser became increasingly strained as Dreiser failed to help her with the planned exhibition. In 1915, she left her paintings with an art dealer in New York City and joined her husband in England. Thus, she missed the New York Dada movement (1915–1921) generated by the spring 1915 arrival of European vanguard artists, including Marcel Duchamp, Francis Picabia, and Jean Crotti. Dreiser "inher-

ited" Rice's paintings when her art dealer was no longer able to store them after a move to new location. A photograph held in the University of Pennsylvania Dreiser Papers shows Dreiser in his studio proudly posing with Rice's paintings, among them *La Négresse* (1910–1911) and *Nicoline* (1910–1911). Rice's paintings of erotically charged, yet powerful, women were inspiring and unsettling for Dreiser; her art and career continued to preoccupy him, even after their friendship had cooled. In the sketch of "Ellen Adams Wrynn," he translated her marriage with Drey as an admission of her failure as an artist. Yet Rice continued to paint and illustrate, producing important work, including the brilliantly red portrait of the New Zealand author Katherine Mansfield (1918) and ten colored illustrations for D. H. Lawrence's *Bay: A Book of Poems* (1919).

Further Reading

Nathanson, Carol A. "Anne Estelle Rice: Theodore Dreiser's 'Ellen Adams Wrynn.' " *Women's Art Journal* (Fall 1992/Winter 1993): 3–11.
———. "Anne Estelle Rice and 'Ellen Adams Wrynn' ": Dreiser's Perspectives on Gender and Gendered Perspectives on Art." *Dreiser Studies* 32.1 (2001): 3–35.

Irene Gammel

RICHARDS, (FRANKLIN THOMAS) GRANT (1872–1948). Grant Richards is the English publisher who encouraged the writing of *Jennie Gerhardt* and who, in 1911, helped Dreiser organize his first tour of Europe and arranged a publishing agreement for *A Traveler at Forty* with the Century Company as well as with his own firm. Born in Glasgow as the son of Franklin Thomas Richards, fellow and tutor of Trinity College, Oxford, and educated at the City of London School, he was introduced into the world of publishing by his uncle, Grant Allen, a writer, philosopher and scientist. Having opened a business of his own in 1897, he soon found his place among the most prominent publishers of his time, Chatto, Heinemann, and Lane. He was able to secure the publishing rights for major writers such as George Bernard Shaw, Alfred Housman, G. K. Chesterton, John Masefield, Samuel Butler, and Arnold Bennett, and he pioneered the World's Classics Series. Regular trips to the United States to bargain for the English copyright on forthcoming American books brought him into contact with Hamlin Garland and **Frank Norris**. While he was an aggressive and modern-minded publisher, he nevertheless hesitated to follow up on Norris's advice to publish *Sister Carrie*. Going back into business after his bankruptcy in 1905, he struck up a correspondence with Dreiser in hopes of obtaining the English rights for his next novel, *Jennie Gerhardt*, and made several minor deals using Dreiser's connections as an editor.

Meeting with Dreiser shortly after the publication of *Jennie* in 1911, he enthusiastically renewed his standing invitation to a guided tour of Europe. Richards offered Dreiser a social entrée into London drawing rooms and artistic circles as well as English country homes; he was his part-time travel companion both in Paris and on the French Riviera, and, wherever needed, he provided Dreiser with detailed travel instructions. Richards, who had a true sense of literature, impressed Dreiser with his managerial qualities and his amiable character. In many ways Richards was a kindred spirit. In his travelogue *A Traveler at Forty*, Dreiser portrays Richards as "Barfleur" and praises his "social, artistic and critical genius," his "reverence for literary and artistic ability," and "the inestimable significance of his personality."

However, the relationship of the English publisher (and writer) and the Ameri-

can author was not without its difficulties. Richards's easygoing handling of Dreiser's financial (and on occasion amorous) affairs and Dreiser's reluctance to enter into a contract with Richards for *The Financier* darkened their otherwise spirited and genial friendship. Dreiser's realistic portrayal of Richards's family, friends, and acquaintances alienated Richards. To protect them, Richards demanded enormous cuts in the text and even threatened a lawsuit, whereas Dreiser fought for a complete publication of his book. After their estrangement, their formerly lively correspondence peters out to a meager exchange of information about business matters. In *Author Hunting* (1934), though, Richards devotes two chapters to his encounters with Dreiser, gladly uncovers his disguise as Barfleur, and delights in his memories of the times they had spent together. He also admits that he "did not exactly repeat the Doubleday–*Sister Carrie* trick" but that he "certainly was not very zealous in pushing the book" (186).

After his business had flourished for two decades, Richards went bankrupt for a second time in 1927, at which time the firm was renamed the Richards Press and was directed by a board. Ten years later it was sold to Martin Secker. Richards retired to write novels, guidebooks, and his memoirs. He died in Monte Carlo in 1948.

Further Reading

Bardeleben, Renate von. "Dreiser's English Vergil." *Literature in Context*. Festschrift for Horst W. Drescher. Ed. Joachim Schwend et al. Frankfurt am Main: Peter Lang, 1992. 345–71.

Brockman, William S. "Grant Richards." *Dictionary of Literary Biography*. Vol. 112: *British Literary Publishing Houses, 1881–1965*. Ed. Jonathan Rose and Patricia J. Anderson. Detroit: Gale, 1991. 272–79.

Kinsaul, Lucia A. "The Letters of Grant Richards to Theodore Dreiser: 1905–1914." M.A. thesis, Florida State University, 1990.

Richards, Grant. *Author Hunting by an Old Literary Sportsman: Memories of Years Spent Mainly in Publishing, 1897–1925*. London: Hamilton, 1934; New York: Coward-McCann, 1934.

———. *Memories of a Misspent Youth, 1872–1896*. London: Heinemann, 1932.

———. Papers of Grant Richards. Special Collections, University of Illinois at Urbana-Champaign. See *Index to the Archives of Grant Richards*. Cambridge: Chadwyck-Healey, 1981.

Renate von Bardeleben

RICHARDSON, HELEN. *See* Dreiser, Helen Richardson.

"THE RIVERS OF THE NAMELESS DEAD." This closing sketch in *The Color of a Great City*, first published in the March 1905 issue of *Tom Watson's Magazine*, is perhaps the most poignant and most beautifully written of the collection. While Dreiser opens his book with a vibrant description of New York and the youthful dreams it holds for him and for thousands of others who flock to the city annually, he ends with the hundreds who jump or are pushed into its rivers and float, nameless, out to sea. He writes: "Scarcely a day passes but one, and sometimes many, go down from the light and the show and the merriment of the island to the shores of the waters where peace may be found." To underscore the banality of, and the indifference to, these suicides, Dreiser begins with a brief clipping from a New York newspaper. It simply reports that a man's body has been found in the North River and a brass check from the New York Registry Company was found on it. What shattered hopes that check represents can only be guessed from the sparse information provided. The man is unidentified, stripped not only of his dreams but also of his name. Dreiser describes the lure of the waters: "Such waters seem to be kind, and yet they are not so. They seem to be cruel, and yet they are not so; merely indifferent these waters are—dark, strong, deep, indifferent," much like the city itself. Dreiser suggests that perhaps these nameless dead are inevitable in a city, or a society, where great triumphs for some must lead to great defeats for others: "They have yielded themselves as a sacrifice to the variety of life. They have proved the uncharitableness of the island of beauty."

Nancy McIlvaine Donovan

ROBIN, JOSEPH G. (1876?–1929). Though referred to only as X———, Joseph G. Robin is the subject of " 'Vanity, Vanity,' Saith the Preacher," the ninth biographical sketch in *Twelve Men*. He was placed among the second six men, those Dreiser admired who were ultimately failures, in Robin's case, a failed financier. Robin was born Rabinovitch in Russia around 1876 and came to America with his parents when he was eleven. After amassing great wealth through the consolidation of several banks in New York City, he was convicted of mismanagement of banking funds in 1912 and served the following year in jail. He then devoted his efforts to the publishing business and to providing legal counseling. In the 1920s, he published two plays under the pen name Odin Gregory, *Caius Gracchus* and *Jesus, the Tragedy of Man*. On 7 April 1929, Robin died in White Plains, New York, at about age fifty-three from myocarditis, a heart condition.

Dreiser first met Robin in 1908 while managing editor of the prestigious **Butterick Publishing Company**, a position that gave him the social prominence to mingle with the wealthy. Dreiser's admiration for Robin originally resulted in large part from their similarities: both had been born poor of immigrant parents, and both had suffered nervous breakdowns when younger but had overcome adversity to rise to positions of prominence. Dreiser maintained a newspaper clipping file about Robin's financial activities for the novel he eventually planned to write. That novel became *The Financier*, whose plot was based on the life of **Charles Tyson Yerkes**. For the personality of his central character, **Frank Cowperwood**, Dreiser used that of someone similar whom he had actually known, Joseph G. Robin. Later, the newspaper clippings about Robin provided the factual basis for the sketch produced especially for *Twelve Men*.

Robert Coltrane

"RONA MURTHA." The eleventh of fifteen semifictionalized sketches in *A Gallery of Women*, is based on **Anna Mallon**, whose typing agency prepared the typescript of Dreiser's first novel, *Sister Carrie*, and who married Dreiser's close friend **Arthur Henry** in 1903. The twenty-five-year-old Rona Murtha is remarkably androgynous. Dressed in a masculine, tailored suit with tie collar and cuffs, she occupies the man's position of power: she lives in the business heart of New York City, is financially independent, pays for the meals in restaurants, and gives commands and instructions like a man. In this sketch of **gender** crossings and triangulated desire, the narrator (aka Dreiser) finds himself in an oddly feminine position as he becomes entangled in a contest with Rona Murtha for the possession of a man: the androgynously named Winnie Vlasto (Arthur Henry), a colorful poet and dreamer and the narrator's closest friend. Indeed, the title "Rona Murtha" (Murtha = M[allon] + Arthur) suggests that the sketch is as much about Arthur Henry as it is about Anna Mallon.

The two men's relationship is intimately charged, as they are connected in a collaborative writing project, a marriage of minds, whose child is a novel. As Rona draws Winnie into her orbit, however, Winnie abandons the novel and betrays the intimacy of male–male collaboration by triangulating their bond. In a conflict-charged working and holiday outing on a remote island, the narrator dwells on Winnie's lack of physical passion for Rona and Winnie's obvious preference for a triangulated relationship that includes his male friend. Seeing himself thus as the third part in this lovers' tryst, in which traditional gender positions are crossed, the narrator eventually withdraws, a little like the proverbial wife when faced with her husband's new mistress. A sense of regret and betrayal remains.

Several years later, the cycle continues. Now it is Rona's turn to be deserted, as Winnie turns to a more advantageous liaison. Winnie (the winner) is the inevitable artist-parasite, a feature that aligns this sketch with "Ellen Adams Wrynn" and "Esther Norn," where women are also exploited by parasitic artists. "Rona Murtha" is circular and open-ended; looking for a typing agency, the narrator discovers Rona's new business sign, Mrs. Winfield Vlasto. Has Rona's identity become assimilated by the cannibalistic Winnie (she has lost her own name)? Or does the name on the sign suggest the strong woman's ability to survive even disastrous and exploitative love? For the narrator, too, there is wistful mourning of his loss but also a bittersweet reminder of the parasitic exploitation that continued intimate closeness with Winnie might have entailed. Dreiser's negative portrayal is at least in part prompted by Arthur Henry's critical portrayal of Dreiser in his roman-à-clef, *An Island Cabin* (1901).

Further Reading

Lingeman, Richard. "Nancy, Ruth, Tom, and I." *Theodore Dreiser: At the Gates of the City, 1871–1907*. New York: Putnam, 1986. 312–18.

Irene Gammel

ROSENTHAL, LILLIAN (1887–1972). A graduate of the Damrosch Institute of Musical Art (later renamed the Juilliard School of New York), Rosenthal was a successful vaudevillian, singer, composer, teacher, and theatrical agent. She began life as the daughter of a prominent New York attorney and patron of the arts, Elias Rosenthal. Dreiser attended literary evenings at Rosenthal's New York apartment and became a good friend of the family. The Rosenthals took Dreiser in and gave him a room in their home after the 1910 scandal over **Thelma Cudlipp** led both to the loss of his editorial job at *The Delineator* and to the separation from his wife, Sara White Dreiser. Lillian wrote to Dreiser on 25 January 1911, after reading a typescript of *Jennie Gerhardt*. Dreiser had originally ended the novel with Jennie's marriage to **Lester Kane**. In her letter she wrote, "Poignancy is necessary in this story, and can be maintained by persistent want on the part of Jennie. The loss of Lester would assure this" (Dreiser Papers). Her letter influenced Dreiser's decision to revise the manuscript from its original "happy ending" to the more somber version (with Lester's marriage to another woman and Jennie's forlornness at his death) that Dreiser published in 1911. For a decade she and Dreiser were lovers; his portrait of Aglaia in the "This Madness" series of sketches for *Hearst's International-Cosmopolitan* is based on their relationship. After her marriage to attorney Mark Goodman in 1922, she became a well-known vocal teacher under the name of Lillian Rosedale Goodman. In the 1940s she and her husband lived near Dreiser in Los Angeles, and the couple remained good friends with him and Helen Richardson Dreiser until the novelist's death in 1945.

Thomas P. Riggio

S

"ST. COLUMBA AND THE RIVER."
Growing out of his experiences with manual labor near the turn of the century, the initial source for "St. Columba and the River," as Joseph Griffin reports, was an article Dreiser wrote in 1904 for the United Press, "Just What Happened When the Waters of the Hudson Broke into the North River Tunnel" (94). In 1917, the *Saturday Evening Post* purchased the story but, after six years, declined to publish it as a result of readers' anger with Dreiser's depiction of marriage in another story, "Free." The story was published under the title "Glory Be! McGlathery" in *Pictorial Review* in January 1925 before being collected in *Chains: Lesser Novels and Stories*.

An Irish-Catholic immigrant, Dennis McGlathery, is hired by his "fellow churchman," Thomas Cavanaugh, to dig a tunnel under the Hudson River. Three times the powerful river destroys the tunnel and drowns the "sandhogs," despite the introduction of improved tunneling mechanisms. McGlathery himself survives each disaster, although "Gargantuan" Cavanaugh sacrifices his own life with courage that both frightens and inspires McGlathery. Encouraged by Cavanaugh's example, McGlathery plugs a leak with his own body before being blown out of the tunnel up to the river's surface, thus concluding his tunneling career as a hero in the Sunday editions. Left crippled by the bends, McGlathery credits his salvation to St. Columba, a saint worshiped in his native Irish village and in the Brooklyn church where he prays devoutly; however, his experience leads him to question his faith, and he wonders whether St. Columba "did not have as much control over the river as he should or as he might like to have."

Some critics have described the story as a characteristic expression of conflict concerning Nature, technology, and **religion**, the last treated somewhat facetiously as mere superstition and hardly, as McGlathery wants to believe, triumphant. But with its vivid working scenes, the story is equally important as a narrative of work and can profitably be read in the context of such autobiographical representations of manual labor as "The Mighty Rourke" and the related *An Amateur Laborer*. As he does with factory scenes in *Sister Carrie* and *An American Tragedy*, here Dreiser demonstrates his strong affinities with an American aesthetic of industrial **realism**. His connections to the Ashcan painters and to his version of himself as a painter in *The "Genius"* are evident throughout "St. Columba" as, for example, in this portrait of workers inside the tunnel: "How they tugged, sweated, grunted, cursed, in this dark muddy hole, lit by a few flittering electric arcs. . . . Stripped to the waist, in mud-soaked trousers and boots, their arms and backs and breasts mud-smeared and wet, their hair tousled, their eyes bleary—an artist's dream of bedlam, a heavenly inferno of toil—so they labored." In addition to appearing in Howard Fast's *The Best Short Stories of Theodore Dreiser* (1947), the story was anthologized in a collection titled *Our Lives: American Labor Stories* (1948). "St. Columba" was also dramatized by Earl Robinson and Waldo Salt under the title *Sandhog*, a musical put on by the Phoenix Theater in New York in November 1954.

See also Adaptations, Stage.

Scott Zaluda

"SANCTUARY." Originally published in *Smart Set* in October 1919 and later included in *Chains: Lesser Novels and Stories*, "Sanctuary" in many respects is similar to Stephen Crane's *Maggie, a Girl of the Streets* (1893). Like Maggie, Dreiser's Madeleine Kinsella emerges from a life of poverty in the slums of New York. Despite the squalor of her surroundings, she emerges as a "flower"—an image repeated throughout the story. And like Maggie, as Joseph Griffin suggests, Madeleine is "attracted to and seduced by flashily dressed young males and [is] forced to turn to prostitution" (82).

Left alone with her mother after the death of her drunkard father, thirteen-year-old Madeleine Kinsella must find work to ensure the survival of herself and her indolent, alcohol-obsessed mother. Employed first as a shop girl and then as a domestic servant, Madeleine moves through her teen years. At age sixteen, Madeleine meets her first love. Like Maggie's Pete, he is "charming" but possesses "vanity enough for ten"; he views

young innocents as "something to be deflowered and then put aside." Falling prey to his sexual conquest and then cast to the side, Madeleine is heartbroken. Tearfully wandering the streets, she is befriended by a young woman of the streets who teaches her "how to make her way" through prostitution. Though the unseemly profession is a temporary, but necessary, means of survival, such rationalizations do not assuage the heartless detective who later entraps and arrests Madeleine, who is then sentenced to one year in the Sisterhood of the Good Shepherd. The spiritual solemnity and imposed ritualism of the institute "smacked of penance," yet Madeleine discovers a gentle peace within its "gray and bony walls." After a year Madeleine returns to society. She dreams of finding love and, after several years, meets and falls in love with Fred, whose sensuality blinds her to his addiction to gambling. When Fred's luck sours, he convinces Madeleine to return to the streets. After a year and a half of abuse, Fred ejects her from her home—used, heartbroken, and dejected. She returns to the House of the Good Shepherd, where she becomes a permanent resident; for Madeleine, it is "the only true home or sanctuary she had ever known."

"Sanctuary" portrays a woman driven by a desire for love and marriage yet at the mercy of rapacious male desire. Madeleine falsely believes that marriage is a means to achieve a loving home life, but this ideal, however traditional and sought after, is a mirage. Once again, Dreiser passes harsh judgment on marriage and critiques the conventional idea of home, suggesting that true happiness is not to be found within its bounds. While marriage seemingly offers "the sanctuary of an enveloping heart," Madeleine's frantic search for love and marriage only "cut and burned and seared and scarred." Madeleine's life is a catalog of victimization and male domination; she is maltreated by all of the men she encounters, beginning with her father and ending with her husband. Consequently, Madeleine's retreat into the matriarchal world of the sisterhood may be viewed as an attempt to escape the patriarchal world that exploits and abuses her. This chaste, all-female environment offers security and acceptance; the occupants are free from the oppressiveness of patriarchal society, and, as the story's title suggests, a life without marriage and men offers a true "sanctuary" for women.

Donna Packer-Kinlaw

SCHOPENHAUER, ARTHUR (1788–1860), was a German philosopher widely known as the father of modern Western pessimism. In his emphasis on will and sexual desire as the unconscious determining forces in human life, he was a forerunner of both Nietzsche and **Freud**. His most important work is *Die Welt als Wille und Vorstellung* (1818, revised 1844), translated in Dreiser's time as *The World as Will and Idea*. Schopenhauer was fashionable reading for fin de siècle intellectuals, often in collections like the 1912 edition of *Essays in Pessimism* in Dreiser's library. When he discovered Nietzsche in 1909, Dreiser at first thought him merely "Schopenhauer confused and warmed over" (*D-M Letters* 1: 42). It is a little puzzling, then, that Schopenhauer's influence has received so little attention from biographers and critics.

Extending Kant's transcendental idealism, Schopenhauer asserts that the object as it really is—"the thing in itself"—is unknowable since its qualities are given by the mind, yet each time our wills act on our bodies we learn something about the noumenon. The world is both will and its idea (its "representation" in more recent translations). As the blind impulse con-

tinuously generating the phenomenal world, the will is essentially the "will-to-live." As the most powerful manifestation of the will-to-live, sexual desire virtually reduces people to "concrete sexual impulse" (514); it is the greatest source of illusion and suffering, "a malevolent demon, striving to pervert, to confuse, and to overthrow everything" (534). Love is a trick played by the will-to-live in order to attain the Platonic Idea of the species, and life for most is a hellish nightmare of desire alternating with disillusionment and boredom. The only basis of morality is thus sympathy for others' suffering.

Whether expressed directly or sublimated, Schopenhauer's malevolent demon drives many of Dreiser's protagonists in pursuit of illusions—Carrie Meeber, **Eugene Witla**, **Frank Cowperwood**, Clyde Griffiths—and his famous pity for the downtrodden and his assaults on conventional morality would certainly meet with the German's approval. Moreover, Schopenhauer's aesthetics probably influenced *The "Genius"* and may even account for those troublesome quotation marks in the title. For Schopenhauer, who embraced the ascetic aspects of Eastern philosophy, contentment requires freedom from the tyranny of desire. The genius is a man (never a woman) of exquisite sensibility and passionate temperament who escapes suffering by means of a superior imagination and intellect, perceiving by the one the Platonic Idea within the particular and attaining by the other a bemused detachment from the spectacle of human suffering. He may well depict life in all its ugliness and tragedy but only to indict it and to teach the virtues of resignation. The idealist Eugene Witla is *almost* such a genius. After many years foolishly pursuing the "impossible she," girls and women whose beauty is more "in his own soul" than in their bodies, he withdraws from the world, "accusing nature" in brutal depictions of human degradation and crushing his desire for **Suzanne Dale** "[u]nder the heel of his intellectuality." Even so, because he is "prone to the old illusions," his self-mastery and "genius" remain in doubt.

Dreiser himself liked to assume the stance of the detached Schopenhauerian genius. The visible world, he wrote in 1931 at the end of *Dawn*, is a meaningless "picture," and all explanatory theories are "mere phantoms of the eternal unrest," yet, ever restless himself, he could not help following the phantom of love—and the phantom theories of science, metaphysics, and politics—the rest of his days.

Further Reading

Moroskina, Eugenia. "Dreiser and Schopenhauer: The Concept of Desire." *Dreiser Studies* 28.2 (1997): 22–33.

Schopenhauer, Arthur. *The World as Will and Representation*. Vol. 2. Trans. E.F.J. Payne. Indian Hills, Colo.: Falcon's Wing Press, 1958.

Stephen C. Brennan

"THE SECOND CHOICE" appeared first in the February 1918 *Cosmopolitan* and was then slightly revised for inclusion later that year in *Free and Other Stories*. In it, a young working-class woman named Shirley, rejected by the dashing, but footloose, man she loves, feels compelled to go back to the commonplace telegraph operator she had once planned to marry, yet in settling for her second choice Shirley is less a victim than a resourceful woman making the best of straitened circumstances.

In the first two-thirds of the story, Shirley, rejection letter in hand, thinks back over the past year—how the "masterful and eager" Arthur Bristow had created "a world of color and light . . . so transfiguring as to seem celestial" and had brought her "the perfection of love" one spring afternoon as they lay on the grass. But she also recalls her "dreadful sense of helplessness" when he talked of a future without her, "the agony of the long days" when he began to ignore her. Now, ashamed at being "the leavings of others" and fighting thoughts of "retaliation" against Arthur and men in general, she decides to take back the "faithful" Barton Williams, whom she has treated so shabbily. The story then moves forward in time as Shirley, masking her humiliation, visits the surprised and willing Barton at his workplace and returns home in disgust. "Why shouldn't I marry Barton," she asks herself. "I don't amount to anything, anyhow."

Her choice is really no defeat. Probably because her mother has always been the sustaining force in the family, marriage "was the only future [Shirley] had ever contemplated." While Arthur has ignored her hints that she would "look nice in a pearl satin wedding-dress," she knows Barton will rescue her from her monotonous life clerking in a drugstore. Even as she berates herself, she is satisfying the will to power. She knows she can "crook a finger," and Barton, who loves her as "slavishly, hopelessly" as she has loved Arthur, will come running. She has even achieved domination over the "masterful" Arthur by reducing him to "a mere memory" she can summon at will to bring back the splendor in the grass. Barton will want several children, she tells herself, but in her imagination "[I]t would be Arthur she would be loving or kissing." None of this makes for a happy ending exactly, but it makes "The Second Choice" an insightful study of the compromises one woman makes to salvage her self-respect and fulfill her deepest fantasy.

Further Reading

Brennan, Stephen C. "Sadomasochistic Fantasy in 'The Second Choice.'" *Dreiser Studies* 31.1 (2000): 43–62.

Harris, Susan K. "Vicious Binaries: Gender and Authorial Paranoia in Dreiser's 'Second Choice,' Howells's 'Editha,' and Hemingway's 'The Short Happy Life of Francis Macomber.'" *College Literature* 20.2 (1993): 70–81.

Stephen C. Brennan

"SECRECY—ITS VALUE" is an essay in *Hey Rub-a-Dub-Dub* that compares one's ability to succeed to an animal's ability to adapt to its environment. The inherent secrecy of Nature appears in humanity as one of its strongest characteristics. Secrecy functions to preserve and propagate each individual against the interest of all others, a successful adaptation of the individual to the environment. We reveal only that which may assist us, keeping our own confidences in regard to all else. Dreiser considers one's skill in secrecy itself to be an advantage in opposing the secrecy in others. Individuals can learn to discern secrets in others as an additional tool in the quest for their own protection. War provides an example of the inherent importance of secrecy when one's survival is in question. Professionals in various fields, including law, medicine, and many religions, keep their own secrets, often through obscure revelations and elite language, to secure their own futures. One succeeds as one is able to maintain one's own secrets. Dreiser does not deny that it is possible for the "rare individual born so strong, so wise, so courageous, that he needs few if any disguises" to exist in this world; however, this is the "rare" individual. Unfortunately, even this rare individual must disguise his strengths to protect himself from the jealousy of others.

Jennifer Marie Raspet

SEMPLE, LILLIAN. Modeled after **Charles Tyson Yerkes's** first wife, **Susanna Gamble**, Lillian (Wiggin) Semple is the first wife of **Frank Cowperwood** in *The Financier*. Cowperwood first encounters Lillian while working as a stockbroker for Tighe & Company at the age of nineteen; she is twenty-four and married to a shoe salesman, Alfred Semple. Immediately attracted to her waxlike beauty and soothing, delightful manner, Cowperwood begins to make frequent visits to the Semples, even buying his shoes from Alfred's store. Two years after their first meeting, Alfred dies of pneumonia, and Frank seizes the opportunity to pursue a relationship with her. She momentarily resists but soon concedes to his desire for marriage. Lillian is five years older than Cowperwood when they marry, a difference in age that Frank eventually will not be able to ignore. They have two children together, Frank Jr. and Lillian, and, for a time, live a rather uneventful existence; however, this soon changes when Frank meets the younger, more sensual **Aileen Butler**.

Critics often describe Lillian as duty-bound, maternal, moralistic, and proper. She shows no emotion and, as Dreiser writes, has "a certain placidity of soul, which came more from lack of understanding than from force of character." Her strong adherence to Victorian values and domestic ideals are probably a result of her Presbyterian upbringing. In fact, Lillian views the universe as ordered and believes that justice will always win out, as illustrated by her private, if not self-righteous, feeling that Cowperwood deserved jail time for his raiding of the city treasury. Dreiser reveals, in Lillian, how such a narrow view of the world can often render one helpless when one is either tossed into a crisis or placed in morally ambiguous circumstances. When she discovers Frank's affair with Aileen and when she realizes that he will go to prison for embezzlement, she can do nothing but wonder about the future, not knowing what to think. In addition, Lillian tends to conform to society's prescriptive codes for women, which may explain her early resistance of Frank and her feeling ashamed about her sexuality. When Cowperwood begins to compare Aileen to Lillian and notices that her beauty is giving way to age, that she lacks individuality, and that she will always accept life as it comes to her, he loses interest and turns his attentions solely to the unbridled passions of Aileen.

Further Reading

Michaels, Walter Benn. "Dreiser's Financier: The Man of Business as a Man of Letters." *American Realism: New Essays*. Ed. Eric J. Sundquist. Baltimore: Johns Hopkins University Press, 1982. 278–96.

Kevin Jett

"THE SHADOW." First published in *Harper's Bazar* in August 1924 as "Jealousy: Nine Women Out of Ten" before being reprinted in *Chains: Lesser Novels and Stories*, the story is one of several in which Dreiser depicted unhappy marriages, including "Free," "Convention," and "Marriage—for One." "The Shadow" is divided into two roughly equal internal monologues. In the first, Gil Stoddard, a dull clerk, struggles with his suspicions that his wife, Beryl, is having an affair. He thinks he sees her in a car with a strange man and is told by his acquaintance Naigly that he saw her coming out of the Deming Hotel. He suspects her of having an affair, although he can't understand why she would do so. He confronts her, and she laughs it off, but he continues to doubt.

In the story's second section, we enter Beryl's point of view and learn that she is indeed having an affair, brought on by having outgrown Gil and their life together. Her lover is Mr. Barclay, the author of a book that describes a life strikingly like her own; because of his sympathetic portrayal, she hopes he might help her somehow. Barclay recommends that she do nothing drastic till she can support herself, telling her, "Life is an economic problem." She ends the affair for fear of losing her child, Tickles. The story concludes with her hopeless wish that her life might follow the happy ending of Barclay's novel, in which the husband disappears and the heroine finds true love.

As in much of Dreiser's work, **chance** plays an important role in the story. Beryl reflects upon the coincidences that led Gil to observe her with Barclay after he took a wrong turn, that caused Naigly to see her in the Deming Hotel, that caused a car to shine its lights on her just as Gil glanced in her direction, and that led him to look at the fireplace after she had burned Barclay's letters. She feels that there must be a secret, unseen force leading Gil to her just when she least wants him there.

Dreiser, apparently intending to portray the pathetic through the mundane, succeeds only partially. The story of suspicious, self-doubting Gil manages to portray his confusion and create some tension. Beryl seems self-absorbed and generally detached; we don't see much evidence of her having outgrown her husband, we don't understand Barclay's attraction to her, and we don't feel much sympathy for her unhappy situation. The story seems a sketch of the background for the better-realized story that it could be. As Joseph Griffin points out, the two monologues are so pure that the characters are too disconnected from any worldly details for the reader to relate to them (91).

James F. Collins

SHERMAN, STUART PRATT (1881–1926). Professor of English at the University of Illinois, New Humanist literary critic, and book reviewer for the *Nation* and later for the *New York Herald Tribune Books*, Sherman's genteel standards echoed Irving Babbitt's classicism, didacticism, and privileging of ethics and values over nature and science, **Anthony Comstock's** moralism, and President Woodrow Wilson's "hyphenated Americans" nativism. Following publication of *The "Genius,"* Sherman's "The Naturalism of Mr. Dreiser"—characterized by H. L. Mencken as "a masterly exposure of what is going on within the Puritan mind," especially its "maniacal fear of the German" (*D-M Letters* 1: 211)—dismissed Dreiser's **naturalism** as embodying solely a "theory of animal behavior." Dreiser's German American background allegedly hindered his capacity for spiritual values. The first academic critic to assess Dreiser, prior to 1925 Sherman found fault with both the substance and the style of Dreiser's writings.

But Dreiser had the satisfaction of witnessing Sherman's critical transformation from New Humanist reviewer of his first five novels to formalist interpreter of *An American Tragedy*, which, in a review for the *New York Herald Tribune Books*, he credited as a "great novel," "mark[ing]" a long stride toward a genuine and adequate realism." Sherman esteemed the "artistic 'detachment' " of the narrator's point of view and praised the "masterly exhaustiveness" of character development, specifically "complete and convincing" analysis of the psychological forces driving Clyde Griffiths to his doom. Though repeating his long-standing objections to elements of Dreiser's style, Sherman commended Dreiser's mastery of novel structure and his achievement of "unexceptionable moral effect" (rpt. in Salzman 440–45).

Further Reading

Sherman, Stuart Pratt. "The Naturalism of Mr. Dreiser." *Nation* 2 December 1915: 648–50.
Zeitlin, Jacob, and Homer Woodbridge. *The Life and Letters of Stuart P. Sherman*. New York: Farrar & Rinehart, 1929.

Louis J. Oldani

"THE SHINING SLAVE MAKERS." *See* "McEwen of the Shining Slave Makers."

SHINN, EVERETT (1876–1953), was an illustrator, painter, and muralist best known for his gritty studies of the urban scene and theater subjects. After studying art in Philadelphia at the Spring Garden Institute and at the Pennsylvania Academy of Fine Arts, he worked as an illustrator, where his work regularly appeared in the *New York World* and in such magazines as *Harper's Weekly*, *Ainslee's*, *Everybody's*, and *Cosmopolitan*. Through his work for the Philadelphia newspapers, he met William Glackens, John Sloan, and George Luks and, through them, Robert Henri. After moving to New York in 1897, he exhibited his paintings in a number of galleries. In February 1908 Shinn and seven of his illustrator friends (known as "the Eight") mounted an exhibition at the Macbeth Galleries and attained notoriety as the Ashcan school, named for the group's preference for realistic studies of city life.

Shinn met Dreiser through submitting illustrations to **Broadway Magazine**, which Dreiser edited from 1906 to 1907, and working with him for a number of other magazines. The two became friends, for both shared an interest in observing and recording the spectacle presented by urban life. When Dreiser began work on the manuscript of *The "Genius"* in 1911, he based many of the details of **Eugene**

Witla's artistic career upon Shinn's (though not the personal life, which was based upon Dreiser's own experiences). In 1947, Shinn annotated a copy of The *"Genius,"* noting the correspondences to his life, and was interviewed by Joseph J. Kwiat about his friendship with Dreiser.

Further Reading

Kwiat, Joseph J. "Dreiser's The *'Genius'* and Everett Shinn, the 'Ash-Can' Painter." *PMLA* 67 (1952): 15–35.

Keith Newlin

SISTER CARRIE is Dreiser's first and best-known novel. It is the story of Carrie Meeber, a naive, small-town girl from Wisconsin who comes to Chicago seeking her fortune, surrenders her virtue in order to escape a life of boredom and drudgery, and eventually, through a parody of the Horatio Alger formula of luck and pluck, becomes a celebrated Broadway star. And it is the story of George Hurstwood, a fortyish family man and manager of a "truly swell saloon" who falls in love with eighteen-year-old Carrie, runs off to New York with her and ten thousand dollars of his employers' money, and eventually finds himself deserted and driven to beggary and suicide.

Dreiser began the novel in the fall of 1899 almost as a lark. He and his bride Sara were summering in Maumee, Ohio, with **Arthur** and **Maude Henry** when Henry began urging him to write a novel. He first tried his hand at four or five short stories before beginning the longer narrative after his return to New York in September. Work proceeded rapidly, with but one or two periods of writer's block. When **Harper & Brothers** rejected the book in April 1900 for being too long and too crude for female readers, Dreiser sent a cut and revised version to **Doubleday, Page and Co.**, which, after some legendary hos-

tile negotiations, issued the book in November.

Carrie's story not only repeats scandalous events in the life of Dreiser's sister Emma but recapitulates the rise of the Indiana hick who worked his way up from poverty to become a prominent freelancer in New York. Dreiser knew well Carrie's ache to have what she can't. He also knew what it was to have it and lose it, for after a promising early career as a reporter in the Midwest he proved unfit for the New York newspaper jungle. Sitting on a park bench on a chill December day in 1894, he later wrote in his autobiography *Newspaper Days*, he saw imaged in the derelicts thronging the area the thing he feared to be, the "nothing" that Hurstwood would become.

The book is also a "superior piece of reportorial realism," as the Harper's reader put it in his rejection letter. As a reporter, magazine editor, and freelance journalist, Dreiser had written about labor strikes, the theater, and life on the mean streets. He drew heavily on these experiences to give his fictive world authenticity, even inserting directly into his novel several manuscript pages from his recently published magazine piece "Curious Shifts of the Poor." He also inserted many details about the material and popular culture of the day. Characters wear fashionable "nobby" suits, use one of the first telephone booths, have newfangled dumbwaiters in their flats, shop at Lord and Taylor's, dine at Sherry's, live at the Waldorf, and read Bertha Clay's *Dora Thorne*.

Still, objectivity is not the book's dominant impression, for the narrator is an almost continuous empathic presence. Moreover, when most realists were eschewing authorial omniscience, Dreiser was, in the manner of **Honoré de Balzac**, freely discoursing about all manner of subjects and occasionally lapsing into sentimentality. While this mélange of styles has long been viewed as a sign of ineptitude, it now strikes some readers as what Mikhail Bakhtin calls "heteroglossia"—a carnival of styles each of which critiques the implicit ideologies of the others.

In the novel's best-known philosophical passage, Dreiser asserts that "evolution is ever in action," though the version he has in mind is not Darwin's but **Herbert Spencer's**. In his widely influential *First Principles*, which shook Dreiser to the core when he first read it in 1894, Spencer deduces from the law of the conservation of force a rhythmic "moving equilibrium" of **evolution** and dissolution, growth and decay. The two processes are never precisely in balance; from the beginning, when attracting and repelling forces began to churn the primal homogenous mass, the universe has been undergoing an advance from simplicity to complexity that will end ultimately in physical and moral perfection. Spencer's simultaneous processes are evidenced in *Sister Carrie*'s chiasmic structure, for at the center of the plot is the intersection of the protagonists' opposite trajectories: Carrie's evolution from simple country girl with a "rudimentary" mind to Broadway star reading Balzac (the "perfect Carrie," Dreiser wrote in the holograph) and Hurstwood's decline as he pursues "gnawing, luring, idle phantoms . . . until death and dissolution dissolve their power." Spencer's image of a "moving equilibrium" also informs crucial scenes: Carrie repeatedly rocks in her famous rocking chair as she yearns for change, and Hurstwood "trembles in the balance between duty and desire" when tempted to steal his employers' money. Never do "the true ethics of the situation" determine moral choices, only the chance tipping of the balance by some unconscious impulse or external force.

Since choices are largely determined, conventional moral judgments become "arbitrary." Carrie is not to blame for her sexual fall because "[a]mong the forces which sweep and play throughout the universe, untutored man is but a wisp in the wind." Chicago is the "magnet attracting" of the first chapter's title, or a "tossing, thoughtless sea" on which Carrie is set adrift. Spencer's physical-chemical psychology seemed to be verified by the experimental psychologist **Elmer Gates**, whom Dreiser interviewed during the novel's composition, so the "subtle" basis for Hurstwood's tragedy becomes the "atmosphere" created by New York's rich and powerful, which, "like a chemical reagent," permanently "discolour[s]" the mind, or, "like opium," produces insatiable "cravings."

On the positive side, Spencer, along with Darwin and other evolutionists, demonstrated the continuity of all life. Carrie is a "daisy" drawn to the light and warmth of restaurants, theaters, and men. The "radiant presence" of her first lover, Charlie Drouet, aids her blooming, while he swarms with the other "moths" to the "lamp-flower" of Hurstwood's saloon. Such metaphors contribute to a transvaluation of values rather than a denial. Spencer's belief that morals are evolving is "infantile"; there is an absolute "essence" in the heart's yearning for beauty and happiness that constitutes "the first principles of morals." The things Carrie wants—a little fur jacket, a big apartment, a joyous round of restaurants and theaters—are often meretricious, but her zest for life "raised her above the level of erring. She was saved in that she was hopeful."

Goodness also manifests itself in the spontaneous upwelling of sympathy—Carrie's pity "from the depths of her heart" at the sight of poor working girls,

Drouet's instinctively handing a dime to a panhandler. Sympathy, like hostility, is one of the novel's strongest environmental forces, for a "change of affectional atmosphere" has more influence than any words. Sympathy is also the basis of artistic "genius," as Tolstoy's neo-Christian polemics had taught Dreiser. It is not as a professional actress that Carrie shows her "emotional greatness" but as a novice in an amateurish melodrama who, immersed in her own rueful thoughts, produces "radiating waves of feeling and sincerity" that infect her audience.

Ultimately, however, *Sister Carrie* succeeds not as philosophy or moral tract but as a moving human drama played out against what Dreiser called a "picture of conditions" in America's great cities at the turn of the century. When, on an afternoon in August 1889 eighteen-year-old Caroline Meeber boards the train for Chicago in Columbia City, Wisconsin, "the threads which bound her so lightly to girlhood and home were irretrievably broken." She is hurtling into the future, into a place where "all [is] wonderful, all vast, all far removed." Here everyone is an immigrant of sorts, and both the traditional family and sense of self are under assault. A girl like her seems to confront only two possibilities: "Either she falls into saving hands and becomes better, or she rapidly assumes the cosmopolitan standard of virtue and becomes worse," but in a city of "wall-lined mysteries" and "strange mazes" the path to the "better" may not be straight and narrow, especially for a girl yearning to explore the "paths of song." Once she enters the dreary working-class world governed by the puritan work ethic, Carrie spends her days laboring for a paltry $4.50 per week in a shoe factory, where the repetitive motion at her hole-punching machine is "absolutely nauseating" and where the slang and open sexuality of the workers make the atmosphere "sordid." Evenings at her sister's are not much better, for under the influence of her husband, Sven's, "morbid turn of character" Minnie has lost her youthful capacity for joy, and all Carrie's efforts at pleasure seeking meet an unspoken resistance.

When Carrie does fall into "saving hands," they belong not to sister Minnie but to Drouet, the "brotherly" embodiment of the "cosmopolitan standard of virtue." Having tried to pick Carrie up on the train, the fast-talking traveling salesman runs into her on a street corner when she is depressed and out of work and offers her the sympathy and money that restore her wilting spirit. In the following days, he escorts her to restaurants and plays—and to the new department stores with their mazes of consumer goods. Stylish clothes especially make "[h]er woman's heart . . . warm with desire." By the time Drouet invites his friend George Hurstwood for an evening of cards at the flat where he has installed her as "Mrs. Drouet," Carrie has become not "worse" but so much "prettier" that she "might well have been a new and different individual."

Carrie is the perfect consumer in America's emerging mass-market economy. Whenever anything new and better—a modish jacket, a man—intrudes upon her consciousness, the "invidious comparison," to use Thorstein Veblen's phrase, makes her intensely dissatisfied with what she has. With his elegant clothes and manners, Hurstwood contrasts with the relatively gauche and tactless Drouet, while she seems to promise the "flowering" of Hurstwood's lost youth. Drouet fails to mention that his friend is married, and when he clumsily tramples on her feelings and makes lame excuses for not marrying her, he opens the door to his rival.

All the world's a stage, and all the actors are on the make. When Drouet is on the road, the affair develops as a kind of melodrama, Hurstwood posing as the lonely, erring man desperate for the love of a good woman and she responding with "the tenderness which virtue ever feels in its hope of reclaiming vice." Fittingly, when Carrie plays the suffering heroine in an actual melodrama put on by Drouet and Hurstwood's Elks lodge, the "fascinating make-believe of the moment" makes her seem all-desirable and leaves Hurstwood "feeling as if he should die if he did not find affectionate relief." When the affair is discovered, Carrie, seemingly abandoned by Drouet and outraged at Hurstwood's double life, recalls her success in the amateur theatrical and makes the rounds of theaters in hopes of getting an acting job, while Hurstwood is hounded by his wife's lawyers. One night, after one too many drinks with his pals, he finds the saloon's safe accidentally unlocked. Desire and fear war for mastery until, the money in his hand, "the lock clicked. It had sprung! Did he do it?" Though he tells himself, "That was a mistake," he hastens to Carrie's doorstep, tells her Drouet is injured and wants to see her, and hurries her aboard the 3 A.M. mail train to Detroit.

With extended appeals, passionate embraces, and a "flood" of emotion, Hurstwood overcomes Carrie's resistance and, during a stopover in Montreal, puts the law off his trail by returning most of the loot. He also pays a handy minister to perform a marriage ceremony so Carrie can think herself an honest woman. Still, when "Mr. and Mrs. Wheeler" step off the train in New York, their future is not promising, for Carrie feels only "a semblance of affection" heavily adulterated with pity.

For about two years following their arrival in the summer of 1890, Carrie and Hurstwood live a relatively stable, middle-class existence in the vast "ocean" of New York. With most of his remaining money, Hurstwood buys a one-third partnership in a saloon on the Lower West Side and establishes a household in a modern flat on West 78th Street. Before long, however, the two start to drift apart. Then Hurstwood's "almost perfectly balanced" state becomes a slow "sagging to the grave side." His gloomy state of mind begins to drive customers away from the saloon and to infect his home life, and the move to a cheaper flat only makes matters worse for Carrie. Once the saloon closes in early 1894 and desultory job searches turn up nothing, disgust and shame drive him first into warm hotel lobbies and then to his cozy rocker by the stove, where he escapes his troubles in the "Lethean waters" of the daily newspapers. Eventually, his penny-pinching, shabby clothes and unshaven face so "ate the heart out of Carrie" that her sympathy turns to "gnawing contempt." She has long dreamed of the stage, so as poverty threatens, she uses her good looks to hire on as a lowly chorus girl. She is now the breadwinner resenting any "infringement on her liberty"; Hurstwood, the housekeeper obsessively counting pennies. As a last expression of manhood, he signs on as a scab during the violent Brooklyn streetcar strike of January 1895. However, he is only "the least shadow" of "the old Hurstwood," and after a nearly fatal encounter with a mob, he sneaks home through the snow-crusted back streets, too ashamed even to tell Carrie of his adventure. By this time she has had enough. Not without guilt, in the early spring she cuts Hurstwood loose and moves in with Lola Osborne, a sympathetic chorus girl who has helped her learn the ropes on Broadway.

The meteoric rise that follows has little to do with Carrie's talent and everything to do with her commodification in America's emerging celebrity culture. With "characteristic perversity," a bored audience finds her performance in a bit part so hilarious that she becomes the star of a new hit comedy. "The vagaries of fortune," proclaims the reviewer the next day, "are indeed curious." As her salary makes a quantum leap and her picture is plastered across the trade papers, her name becomes suddenly "worth something"; she is given a lavish suite at the posh new Wellington Hotel for a nominal fee and is pestered with "*[m]ash notes*" from millionaires, though by now she has realized the "impotence" of men as well as money to bring happiness.

This "curious" good fortune contrasts with the "curious shifts" that keep Hurstwood alive in his last months. He spends his days standing in bread lines and eating in soup kitchens, searching discarded newspapers for "any trace of Carrie," and begging change until the "touch of philosophy" that has sustained him is replaced by "death in his heart." One evening in the winter of 1896–1897, Carrie is sitting with Lola in their "comfortable chambers at the Waldorf" while Hurstwood waits in the snow with other "dumb brutes" outside a flophouse. Once the doors have opened and the frozen mass has "melted inward, like logs floating, and disappeared," the ex-manager turns on the gas in his "dingy" and "rueful" room and with a weak " 'What's the use?' . . . stretched himself to rest."

Despite her material success, Carrie, too, is an object of pathos. In the next-to-last chapter, she reencounters **Robert Ames**, the handsome, altruistic inventor from Indianapolis who has been her "ideal" since their first meeting a few years before. Ames urges her to use her talent for the good of others, but she cannot grasp his meaning and is too comfortable to change. The effect is like "roiling helpless waters." In the novel's sentimental Balzacian coda, the narrator defends her as a romantic dreamer who has been lured down "the despised path" in her "blind strivings" after "beauty" and "soul." In a final irony, the actress who has stepped beyond the pale must ever herself be a spectator. "In your rocking chair, by your window," the narrator tells her in the novel's last sentence, "shall you dream such happiness as you may never feel."

As she was first conceived, however, Carrie feels considerable happiness. In 1981, the University of Pennsylvania Press issued an edition based on the original holograph, a text relatively free of influence from Sara Dreiser, Arthur Henry, and the editors at Harper's and Doubleday, Page. In this version, with some 30,000 words restored, there is more grit to the **realism**, more philosophizing from the author, and more contrast in the denouement, which lacks the saccharine Coda. Carrie, now "perfect . . . in mind and body," is "warm with delight" at Ames's interest and seems ready to tumble for the youthful, good looking "genius." While Dreiser suggests that this relationship, too, will suffer an inevitable dissolution, the novel ends in equilibrium, Carrie's warm, sympathetic communion with Ames being balanced by Hurstwood's cold, lonely suicide. The "unexpurgated" **Pennsylvania Dreiser Edition** appeared in the full blush of poststructuralist questioning of authority. In one of those curious vagaries of fortune, the effort to restore *Sister Carrie*'s purity has been at the cost of innocence. It has roiled the critical waters, forcing readers into a choice that can never fully satisfy.

See also Adaptations, Film; Adaptations, Stage.

Further Reading

Bowlby, Rachel. "Starring: Dreiser's *Sister Carrie*." *Just Looking: Consumer Culture in Dreiser, Gissing, and Zola*. New York: Methuen, 1985. 52–65.

Brennan, Stephen C. "*Sister Carrie* and the Tolstoyan Artist." *Research Studies* 47 (1979): 1–16.

Grebstein, Sheldon. "Dreiser's Victorian Lamp." *Midcontinent American Studies Journal* 4 (1963): 3–12.

Kaplan, Amy. "The Sentimental Revolt of *Sister Carrie*. *The Social Construction of American Realism*. Chicago: University of Chicago Press, 1988. 140–60.

Lehan, Richard. *Sister Carrie*. Gale Study Guides to Great Literature: Literary Masterpieces 7. Detroit: Gale, 2001.

Livingston, James. "*Sister Carrie*'s Absent Causes." *Theodore Dreiser: Beyond Naturalism*. Ed. Miriam Gogol. New York: New York University Press, 1995. 216–46.

Michaels, Walter Benn. "*Sister Carrie*'s Popular Economy." *The Gold Standard and the Logic of Naturalism*. Berkeley: University of California Press, 1987. 31–58.

Moers, Ellen. *Two Dreisers*. New York: Viking, 1969.

Petrey, Sandy. "The Language of Realism, The Language of False Consciousness: A Reading of *Sister Carrie*." *Novel* 10 (1977): 101–13.

Phillips, William L. "The Imagery of Dreiser's Novels." *PMLA* 78 (1963): 572–75.

Pizer, Donald. "*Sister Carrie*." *The Novels of Theodore Dreiser: A Critical Study*. Minneapolis: University of Minnesota Press, 1976. 31–95.

———, ed. *New Essays on* Sister Carrie. Cambridge and New York: Cambridge University Press, 1991.

———. *Sister Carrie*. By Theodore Dreiser. Norton Critical Edition. 2nd ed. New York: Norton, 1991.

Poirier, Richard. "Panoramic Environment and the Anonymity of the Self." *A World Elsewhere: The Place of Style in American Literature*. New York: Oxford University Press, 1966. 235–50.

Sloane, David E. E. *Sister Carrie: Theodore Dreiser's Sociological Tragedy*. Twayne's Masterwork Studies 97. New York: Twayne, 1992.

West, James L. W., III. *A Sister Carrie Portfolio*. Charlottesville: University Press of Virginia, 1985.

Stephen C. Brennan

SMITH, EDWARD H. (1881–1927). One of Dreiser's closest friends during the 1910s and 1920s, Smith was educated at the University of Jena in Germany and was a journalist and author of magazine articles and books. He began his newspaper career in Kansas and later became an assistant editor with the *Chicago Tribune* before joining the staff of the *New York Sunday World* in 1911. In the fall of 1918, he married Dreiser's friend **Edith DeLong Jarmuth**, who died nine months later, a victim of influenza. Among his interests were the theories on criminal behavior of Max G. Schlapp, a professor of neuropathology, and in the 1920s he collaborated with Schlapp on a book entitled *The New Criminology: A Consideration of the Chemical Causation of Abnormal Behavior* (1928), which summarized these theories. Also, in the 1920s he published *Release*, a play that was later produced in Baltimore, as well as numerous magazine articles, many of which focused on the schemes of confidence artists and problems in the American prison system. Some of these articles were collected in books published before and after his death from pneumonia in 1927.

An admirer of Dreiser's work from the time he read *Sister Carrie* while still in Kansas, Smith assisted Dreiser in various ways during the years of their friendship. Shortly after meeting the author at one of Edith Jarmuth's social gatherings, he became involved in the protest over the suppression of *The "Genius"* and in Dreiser's attempt to set up an organization to subsidize the publication of work of authors whose writings were too controversial or too realistic for conventional publishers. Later, when Dreiser moved to California, he followed up on Dreiser's requests for help in finding a New York producer for *The Hand of the Potter* and in dealing with some of the property he and Helen left in New York. But Smith was more than just an errand boy for Dreiser. Knowledgeable about the mechanistic theories of the time, particularly as they pertained to criminal behavior, and interested in drama, he often discussed these topics with Dreiser. And, like Mencken, he was not hesitant to offer criticism of Dreiser's work when he felt it was appropriate. For instance, in a letter to Dreiser dated 3 January 1921, he wrote, "Your plays of the supernatural rather appal [*sic*] me. I find you playing more and more with metaphysical terms and ideas—perhaps unconsciously—in much of your later work. (*Hey Rub*; one or two stories in *Free and Others*, a few phrases in your astounding introduction to Odin Gregory's play [*Caius Gracchus*])" (qtd. in *Letters* 1: 335).

In an interview of Dreiser he published in the *Bookman*, Smith included a lengthy discussion of Dreiser's personality that best captures his feelings for and about the author. Dreiser, in turn, included a detailed sketch of Smith in "Olive Brand," his semifictional account of Smith's wife, Edith DeLong Jarmuth. Naming him Jethro in the sketch, Dreiser describes Smith as "a most amazingly well-informed man" who "was not of a highly imaginative turn," and he suggests that Smith was attracted to his wife in part because her artistic talent would enable her to help him achieve his aspirations to write plays and short stories. What Dreiser leaves out of the sketch, unfairly it seems, are Smith's affection for, and admiration of, Dreiser himself, feelings that he attributes to Edith instead. For this reason, a much fairer assessment appears to be that of Helen

Dreiser, who in *My Life with Dreiser* says about Smith, "He was one of those rare few who had the capacity for deep and lasting love and friendship" (13).

Further Reading

Dreiser, Theodore. "American Tragedies." Rev. of *The New Criminology*, by Max Schlapp and Edward H. Smith. *New York Herald Tribune Books* 10 June 1928: 1–2.
Smith, Edward H. "Dreiser—After Twenty Years." *Bookman* 53 (March 1921): 27–39.
Frederic E. Rusch

SMITH'S MAGAZINE. Dreiser edited this magazine for "the John Smiths of America" from its inaugural issue in April 1905 until he left his post a year later. Published by **Street and Smith**, the dime novel company, *Smith's* billed itself as a "home magazine" that would print articles appealing to the average wage-earner's household. Under Dreiser's editorship, the magazine included regular departments such as "The Out-of-Town Girl in New York" (a report on cosmopolitan fashions with suggestions for obtaining bargains in New York stores), "The Passing Hour" (a column on society doings), and "What Americans Are Thinking." Dreiser also published conventional short stories and serials by recognized authors of the day including Mary J. Holmes, Annie Hamilton Donnell, Charles Garvice, Kate Jordan, and Mrs. Georgie Sheldon. In addition, *Smith's* featured longer articles commenting on contemporary institutions ("The Public and the Post Office," "How Our Railroads Regulate Us") and social trends. Indeed, two of Dreiser's own articles, "The City of Crowds" and "The Peace of the Thousand Islands," appeared in *Smith's* during and immediately after his tenure as editor. (They, respectively, analyzed the unthinking force represented by the amazing crowds in New York City and the sublime feelings of peace and rest vacationers could attain by retreating to upstate New York.) *Smith's* appeared during the Progressive Era, which witnessed the muckrakers exposing corporate power and government corruption. Compared to *McClure's* and other competitors, *Smith's* was cautious in its criticism of contemporary problems. In his editorials, Dreiser urged readers to "protest dishonesty wherever you see it" (March 1906), but the magazine was not an active agent for reform under his stewardship. Dreiser's work at *Smith's* attracted the attention of the new owners of **Broadway Magazine**, who offered him the editor's chair at that publication. He accepted and finished his work at *Smith's* in April 1906; the last issue of *Smith's* he oversaw was published in June 1906. *Smith's* ceased publication with its February 1922 issue.

Christopher Weinmann

"SOLUTION." This short story was published in the November 1933 issue of *Woman's Home Companion*, one of the mass-circulation magazines of the day. Its appearance marked the second consecutive time Dreiser's short fiction had found a place in a popular women's monthly, "Fine Furniture" having been serialized in the November and December 1929 numbers of *Household Magazine*.

In "Solution" Dreiser returned to an earlier subject of his, indeed to a subject common to the fiction of all languages, the youthful boy–girl relationship carried on in the face of parental restriction. The attractive and headstrong Marjorie Salter, daughter of one of bucolic Greenville's leading citizens, the widower Isaac Salter, falls in love with Walter Stone, who does not return her love. In an effort to secure Walter, Marjorie seduces him and becomes pregnant. The Great War intervenes, Walter goes off to fight, and he returns to Greenville an amputee—he has lost an arm. Now rejected by the young woman to whom he was engaged, Wanda Davison, he chooses, with the blessing of Isaac, to return to Marjorie and marry her. The story's closing paragraph sees the young couple and Salter settling down to dinner in the latter's house, Salter's blessing over their evening meal a kind of benediction on their lives together.

Dreiser had tackled the subject of youthful relationships in such earlier stories as "Old Rogaum and His Theresa," "Typhoon," "Sanctuary," and "The Second Choice." In this he was writing about what the periodicals of his day were publishing, for magazines sought stories that dealt with love, business, and especially sex. "Solution," however, breaks Dreiser's own mold, for here the problems deriving from the relationship are resolved satisfactorily. The solution springs from religious affirmation, so that it can be said that the story is more in the spirit of Dreiser's late novel, *The Bulwark*, than of its short story forebears.

One of the most interesting facets of "Solution" is the movement from a position in which Walter Stone is seen to be all but guiltless in the impregnation of Marjorie to one in which he is perceived as sharing her guilt, an escalation that suggests a larger cultural paradigm. When Marjorie confronts Walter with the fact of her pregnancy, she assumes responsibility because she has seduced him. "What you have done has hurt me and will hurt you now," he tells her. Even Marjorie's father thinks that "it was not Walter's fault but her own," before realizing that Walter "should not be permitted to sin with an erring child and then burden her entirely with the guilt." Finally, Walter himself acknowledges his complicity, setting the stage for the establishment of the new family: "And could he now truly say that she alone was to blame? And had he not shared, in part, at least—erred against Marjorie as well as Wanda, and so shared her guilt?"

Further Reading

Griffin, Joseph P. "Dreiser's Later Short Stories." *Dreiser Newsletter* 9.1 (1978): 5–10.

Joseph P. Griffin

"SOME ASPECTS OF OUR NATIONAL CHARACTER" first appeared in *Hey Rub-a-Dub-Dub*. Dreiser begins with a dismissive recounting of the myths of America's greatness and inevitability—from Columbus and the Founding Fathers to the freeing of slaves and "liberation" of Cuba from imperialist Spain—as these are firmly established in the American consciousness and seconded by schoolboy histories and the popular press. He continues with a sketch of Americans' unexamined and naive faith in their own freedom and a lengthy examination of their complicity with the U.S. government in the abrogation of those freedoms during the Great War; how is it, he asks, that public sentiment permits forced conscription, rationing, deportation of radicals, and passage of the Espionage Act in the name of making the world safe for democracy? Americans' blind worship of the Ten Commandments, the prurient moralism that leads them to hunt out private or artistic sexual expression in order to ban it, the publicly sanctioned and abetted racism, the hostility to their own genuine artists, and Americans' expansionist xenophobia, coupled with "adoration of all things foreign," are also examined as significant constituents of American character.

Throughout the piece Dreiser asserts the ever-widening gap between the ideal America—as embodied in the nation's sacred texts and mythologies—and the real. Unlike other essays in *Hey Rub-a-Dub-Dub*

that tend to focus on the general, here the focus is on specific, recent incidents: state, circuit, federal, and Supreme Court decisions permitting exploitation of child labor, the revocation of habeas corpus, and the prohibition of arbitration in labor disputes, for example, or Department of Labor Statistics and Federal Trade Commission reports demonstrating not only the widening economic gap between rich and poor Americans but, most tellingly, the widening gap in legal protection and civil rights between the same groups. That these inequities are paired with an oft-asserted cultism of the individual, Dreiser finds particularly ironic.

Dreiser falls short of predicting the utter failure of the American democratic experiment, though he reminds the reader that other, greater nations have failed. He does insist, however, that without "intelligent, artistic, accurate vision" the nation is doomed, or at least doomed to be, in the grand scope of things and in company with all its citizens, one of the world's great fools.

Carol S. Loranger

SONNTAG, WILLIAM LOUIS, JR. (1869–1898). Sonntag became one of Dreiser's close friends when they first met in New York in 1895. Both were in their mid-twenties and believed themselves to be talented and making progress toward successful careers—Sonntag as an artist and Dreiser as a writer. Sonntag's unexpected death at the age of twenty-nine served as a haunting reminder to Dreiser of his own mortality and the possibility of dying before having realized his potential. Shortly after Sonntag's death on 11 May 1898, Dreiser's sentimental poem lamenting this loss, "Of One Who Dreamed," was published in *Collier's* (28 May 1898: 2). Three years later he published in *Harper's Weekly* "The Color of To-Day," a prose elegy that he revised for inclusion in *Twelve Men* as "W. L. S." He placed this sketch last in the collection so that the extensively revised concluding lines not only offered a final commentary about Sonntag as an example of unfulfilled artistic expectations but also reinforced a theme running throughout *Twelve Men*: the quest for success is a search for fulfillment that is never attained.

William Louis Sonntag Jr. was born in New York City on 2 February 1869, son of the famous landscape artist William Louis Sonntag. He began his career in art at an early age, exhibiting a watercolor of the Brooklyn Bridge as the National Academy of Design when only thirteen. As an adult, he made his living by painting illustrations for weekly newspapers and such reputable magazines as *Harper's Weekly*, *Harper's Monthly*, and *Scribner's*. He also illustrated works by such noted writers as **William Dean Howells** and Rudyard Kipling. Dreiser first met Sonntag when he commissioned him to produce a Christmas illustration and later a title page design for *Ev'ry Month*, the periodical Dreiser was editing from 1896 to 1897. When the Spanish-American War broke out in April 1898, Sonntag went to Cuba to cover the war as a news illustrator. He died in New York the following month of a fever, most likely malaria. As Dreiser reports, Sonntag actually was descended from royalty, the Von Sonntags of Bohemia, and his great-grandfather fought in the American Revolutionary War with Count Rochambeau's troops.

Much of **Eugene Witla's** activity as a painter in *The "Genius"* is derived from Dreiser's memories of his friend Louis Sonntag.

Robert Coltrane

SPAFFORD, JESSIE (?–?). A fortune-teller in **Greenwich Village** whom Dreiser consulted for answers to questions on future prospects and for entertainment purposes, she became the model for the sketch "Giff" in *A Gallery of Women*. Dreiser's diary suggests he was both amused by her and disposed to believe her predictions. On 7 November 1917, for example, Dreiser recorded Spafford predicting that he would receive "money, success in work, beautiful women. Sees money for me by November 15th. Also a great triumph with some book, one of three" (*American Diaries* 200). Coincidentally, perhaps, two days later he entered into negotiations with Edward Goodman of the Washington Square Players for a production of his play *The Girl in the Coffin*, a deal sealed with a check for $200 on 13 November. Spafford first appears in Dreiser's diaries on 12 August 1917, when he mentions discussing her predictions for him with **Estelle Kubitz**, which sparks an argument between Dreiser and Kubitz: "At once her mood changes to one of intense depression since Spafford said I was to fall in love with some one else. She becomes so self-centered and remote that we quarrel" (*American Diaries* 180). Additionally, Dreiser's diaries note that Spafford predicted his future by reading his palm and tea leaves. He also remarks, "She was once in an insane asylum in Canada. Now plays a harp, reads palms and sings in M. E. Church for a living. Gets 25 cents an evening for singing" (200); Dreiser pays her one dollar for her readings. The last reading that Dreiser mentions in his *American Diaries* appears on 26 December 1917, during which Spafford predicts the entrance of a new woman in his life, travel, money, and his debut in national affairs; she also foresees the defeat of America in the war (239).

Amy E. Ujvari

SPENCER, HERBERT (1820–1903). A British engineer and philosopher, Spencer was the most significant single influence on Dreiser's own philosophical outlook. Although he had read and discussed Spencer with a fellow student at **Indiana University**, Dreiser did not fall under Spencer's spell until 1894, when in Pittsburgh he encountered *First Principles* (1862), a book that he claimed in *Newspaper Days* "quite blew me away, intellectually, to bits." For many like Dreiser, unnerved by the social upheaval characteristic of the Gilded Age, Spencer provided a totalizing system, a prepackaged philosophy disguised as science, which affirmed in ponderous, but calmly confident, prose the "inevitability" of moral and material progress. (Spencer's extension of Darwinism into the social realm would be particularly embraced by men such as Andrew Carnegie and Henry Ford.) Dreiser was especially captivated by Spencer's view of the universe as a machine driven by "Force" in which the fittest survive and in which individuals are not necessarily motivated by ideals or ethics but by the compulsions of desire and the avoidance of pain. He was struck also by the depiction of the individual as largely helpless, buffeted by internal and external forces beyond his or her control and understanding, a "waif amid forces" (as he would label Carrie six years later). By 1896, writing "The Prophet" column in *Ev'ry Month*, Dreiser often echoed Spencer's ideas. However, he was troubled by Spencer's equation of wealth and success with natural superiority and by what he saw as the dark underside of progress. His questioning of progress is particularly apparent in *Jennie Gerhardt*, where he points out that the human brain is ill-equipped for the complex thinking and rapid pace connected to technological development. (Any remaining faith in progress would be discarded by the mid-1920s when he encountered the writings of behaviorist **Jacques Loeb**.) In spite of these objections, Dreiser agreed with Spencer that the universe functioned under scientific laws and that scientists evince a religious instinct of their own in their pursuit of knowledge. He further echoed and extended Spencerian thought in his fiction, particularly in *The Financier* when the young **Frank Cowperwood** translates the struggle between the lobster and the squid into a recognition of society as a Darwinian jungle. Likewise, Cowperwood's eventual downfall almost certainly reflects Spencer's notion that life is a sort of tug-of-war where opposite forces struggle for dominance, canceling each other out and proving in the process that any upward drive is followed inevitably by a downward spiral; **evolution** moves toward equilibrium. Even *An American Tragedy* depicts people as **mechanisms**, controlled by chemical forces and by inherited and inescapable character traits. To the end, Dreiser remained a disciple of Spencer, and it is perhaps ironic that, for all of his rebellion against his father's Catholicism, Dreiser displayed the same sort of religious zeal as his father did (or just as Clyde Griffiths does for the worlds of the Green-Davidson and later of **Sondra Finchley**), substituting the **religion** of his father for the "science" of Spencer, exchanging the cold, punitive Old Testament God for a cold, impersonal universe.

Further Reading

Martin, Ronald E. *American Literature and the Universe of Force.* Durham, N.C.: University of North Carolina Press, 1981.

Monty Kozbial Ernst

THE SPRING RECITAL. A one-act play first published in the December 1915 *Little Review* before being collected in *The Plays of the Natural and the Supernatural*, the action takes place during an organ concert in a largely disused church. There are only four living audience members, but the vibrations of the music attract a wide variety of nonliving, spectral entities, which include dryads, a faun, hags, a bum, wastrels, various newly dead spirits, and several priests. Although all are attracted by the mysterious force of the music, the play itself functions mainly as a framing device for the religious and philosophical debate that goes on between the priests. Although some are ancient Egyptians—thousands of years dead—and some are Christians many hundreds of years deceased, none have found the "eternal reward" promised by their respective beliefs, nor, much to their chagrin, have any of them "met their makers" as these religious men assumed they would upon their deaths. They hold themselves aloof from the other entities by clinging to their former earthly status but are constantly reminded by the character of the Bum that there are no answers and that they are fools to cling to their persistent belief that there must be something more.

The truly contented characters in the play are the living lovers, who are so full of the joy of life, and the earthly elementals, manifest in the pagan dryads and the faun who simply enjoy the lure of life and celebrate the music itself. These odd creatures are unlike the religious men who are particularly dour and conflicted because they long to restore to themselves the illusions they once held while alive.

The Spring Recital is a meditation on unseen forces and the role of **religion** that anticipates Dreiser's later discussion in his collection of philosophical essays, *Hey Rub-a-Dub-Dub*. The powerful lure of life, which draws this disparate group of spirits to hover so near the living, is depicted through the mysterious power of the organ music that brings them all into the church during the recital. In the play Dreiser offers a Spencerian critique of the attempt to fathom the nature of God, and he makes a strong case that life is a force to be embraced because the sheer force of it cannot be denied.

Debra Niven

"A START IN LIFE." Although this piece, published in *Scribner's* in October 1934, was referred to as fiction on both the magazine's cover and the story's title page, it has more in common with the personal sketches Dreiser was producing during this stage of his career than with his short stories. In consecutive issues of *Hearst's International-Cosmopolitan* running from February to July 1929, his "This Madness—An Honest Novel about Love" appeared, its contents three two-part sketches of women he had known; and in consecutive numbers of *Esquire* from October 1944 to March 1945 a series of sketches of other acquaintances, "Black Sheep," was published. Other single profiles of people Dreiser knew were published in *Esquire* and the *American Spectator* in 1933 and 1934. In short, Dreiser seemed more interested during his last years in writing documentary material than in writing short fiction.

In the construct that is "A Start in Life," Dreiser recounts in the first person the biography of a young man in his thirties, Nelson Peterson "from the Dakotas," who aspires to be, and becomes, a newspaperman and writer. Drawing on accounts of his life that Peterson provides and on his own observations of his young friend, the narrator, who is called Mr. Dreiser at one point in the sketch, takes the reader through his subject's early years, his coming east to New York, his marriage, his disillusionment at Peterson's failure, his second romantic (but more down-to-earth) relationship, and his achievement of professional and artistic success. Throughout, the narrator walks a thin line between sympathy for, and critical objectivity toward, Peterson.

"A Start in Life" is essentially the tale of a romantic young man's evolution through pain to a mature and realistic consciousness. (The title is double-pronged, referring both to Peterson's callow beginnings on a western farm and to the experienced man we find at the end of the piece, more prepared in his newfound maturity to inform his writing with the stuff of real life.) The watershed in Peterson's life is his rejection by his beautiful and resourceful young wife, who abruptly and (for him) totally unexpectedly informs him one evening that she is in love with a diplomat named Rapalje and plans to divorce Petersen. Ava's family roots are more sophisticated than Peterson's, and his appeal to her is, finally, limited, for she seeks a man of the world who would provide her with more opportunity for self-development in a more cosmopolitan, affluent, and refined life.

Peterson weathers the severe hurt by leaving New York and throwing himself into hard manual work. When the narrator sees him after some time, he has embarked on a cautious relationship with Amalie, a published writer herself. The narrator senses that the old wound is still there but that now his friend "was by no means the romantic youth who had stood on the hilltop in western Dakota, looking at the grain elevator and the cities of the East."

Further Reading

Griffin, Joseph P. "Dreiser's Later Short Stories." *Dreiser Newsletter* 9.1 (1978): 5–10.

Joseph P. Griffin

STIEGLITZ, ALFRED. *See* "A Master of Photography."

THE STOIC. The final volume of Dreiser's *Trilogy of Desire* proved to be the most difficult of all of his books for the author to complete. This was not because Dreiser lacked specific materials or was hesitant about lines of action, for both of these questions had been decided by 1911, when he made his extensive research trip to London and European cities. The final stage of **Charles T. Yerkes's** career, in fact, was the most heavily documented of all, much of it reported on at length in the daily newspapers, for which both Mr. and Mrs. Yerkes had become celebrities of the first water, personalities whose every move was watched with care, individuals whose lives held promise at any moment of taking a newsworthy turn. In fact, when Dreiser finished *The Titan*, he was fully prepared to charge straight ahead into the composition of the closing volume of his trilogy.

Problems arose after he decided to publish a different novel in 1915, a book that he had already completed. *The "Genius"* was based roughly on Dreiser's own life and was replete with fictionalized incidents from his own rather full romantic life, sexual escapades even more numerous and more explicit than had been the case with *The Titan*. At this point the new ground that the author had been breaking in the presentation of sexual adventures collided with increasing pressures exerted by those who sought official **censorship** of literary works. The most powerful of these groups, the **New York Society for the Suppression of Vice**, announced its finding that the novel was obscene, citing numerous specific examples of unacceptable action and language, the majority of which involved controversial exclamations as tame to modern ears as "My God!" Making the book acceptable would mean resetting the type entirely. Publisher **John Lane**, unable to withstand the pressure, caved in and withdrew *The "Genius"* from the booksellers. The upshot was that Dreiser, intent upon proving in court that his book was not obscene, let himself in for endless legal procedures. He stopped writing novels entirely for nearly a decade, and when he resumed his trade, it was to publish his most popular novel, *An American Tragedy,* in 1925.

Meanwhile, *The Stoic* languished while other projects took precedence. During the 1930s Dreiser made a major effort to complete *The Stoic,* but in the end he failed to produce a publishable manuscript. Growing older, he found composition more difficult. Not until he was seventy-four, in the last year of his life, did the weary and ailing author again work seriously on the novel (along with desperately attempting to complete *The Bulwark,* another often-delayed story), and *The Stoic* was not published until after he was dead.

The story told in *The Stoic,* which came out in 1947, continues from the point at which *The Titan* had closed more than thirty years before, recapitulating the final years of Dreiser's model, financier Charles T. Yerkes Jr. Having lost his bid for long-term streetcar franchises in Chicago, the fictional hero, **Frank Cowperwood**, withdraws to New York and sells his Chicago properties in order to finance his last and grandest entrepreneurial plan: the acquisition of Underground lines in London and their eventual amalgamation into a profitable monopoly. Cowperwood wishes to rid himself of his second wife, the former **Aileen Butler**, but she refuses to be put aside to make room for his youthful mistress, **Berenice Fleming**, who has moved to New York.

Frank cannot afford to antagonize Aileen for fear that she may be driven by anger to institute a scandalous divorce that would permanently cripple his hope someday to enter New York's high society with Berenice on his arm. Frank employs a handsome ne'er-do-well, Bruce Tollifer, to amuse his wife and divert her attention from his dalliance with Berenice, whom he has established in an expensive house on Park Avenue. For the moment, this plan works well.

In London, Cowperwood's scouts advise him about the appropriate moment and the best method by which their boss might initiate his foray into the English traction business. Deciding to travel to London in order to be positioned at the very heart of the action, where he can direct matters personally, Cowperwood sails for England. He takes Aileen with him, but a reconciliation is not his aim, for he sees to it that Bruce Tollifer is aboard, while on another great liner Berenice and her mother travel to London. Tollifer is sent on to Paris, while not far from Windsor, along the Thames, Cowperwood leases an estate for Berenice, close enough to London so that he can travel back and forth with ease while posing as a visitor to her mother. Feigning renewed affection for Aileen, he disarms her sufficiently to throw her off her guard. Then, when Bruce Tollifer, at Cowperwood's instigation, begs Aileen to meet him in Paris, she agrees to travel to the continent to join him and resume their romance. Cowperwood's ruse works; left on his own, he takes Berenice on a tour of the English cathedral towns.

Cowperwood's business schemes move forward rapidly. Using tricks and misrepresentations, pitting rival Underground lines against one another, he schemes to divide and conquer in London. This is the work he is good at, the work for which he was born: ruthless deception and the use of any available weapon or any chicanery that will secure the defeat of his opponent and fill his own coffers with profits. He dupes Underground officials, particularly the powerful Lord Stane, with his story that all he seeks in London is a directorial position. What he actually is after—full personal control of all the Underground systems—is cunningly hidden from the men who would have much to lose under a Cowperwood-headed monopoly. In order to finance the truly gigantic plan he has in mind, Cowperwood returns to America, where he can employ all of his persuasive skills in convincing well-heeled investors from Chicago, Boston, and Philadelphia to join him in the raid on London transit.

He brings Aileen home with him, primarily to allay any suspicion that he might again be perpetrating a secret romantic alliance. Using another boat, Bruce Tollifer travels back to New York also. Berenice remains in the London area, where Cowperwood is certain that he will be returning as soon as feasible. His varied romantic life has become a juggling act that requires intricate planning and eternal vigilance, both of which Cowperwood has mastered and enjoys. But his carefully planned deception of Aileen runs aground in Baltimore when he meets Lorna Maris, a young dancer who is beautiful and accomplished and happens to be a distant cousin. Cowperwood becomes infatuated, and for a time the two become lovers. When the New York scandal tabloid *Town Topics* headlines the affair and Aileen discovers her husband's new deception, she is enraged. As a means of revenge she sends a copy of the paper to Berenice in England, hoping to derail that continuing affair. She nearly succeeds, for Cowperwood is now sixty years old, and Berenice senses that she may have to look elsewhere for long-term security. However, admitting to herself that Frank Cowperwood even in his advanced years remains infinitely more attractive to her than any other suitor, she reconciles with him.

A further personal complication develops when Aileen writes to tell her errant husband that she is contemplating an exposé of his latest duplicity in the public press. Because such a scandal could well prove ruinous to his delicate financial maneuvering, Frank returns to America and feigns repentance. A supposed reconciliation removes the threat of scandal. Because he has long planned to establish his credentials as a philanthropist by donating his immense and very important artworks to the people of New York, along with a gallery for their public exhibition, Cowperwood purchases the property adjoining his mansion with the intention of joining it with his own and remodeling it as a museum. Aileen is highly flattered when Cowperwood requests that she assume personal leadership in this significant project, and she feels somehow that perhaps he loves and trusts her once again. Actually, he is covering for his return to England, to Berenice, and to the climactic events in his campaign to control the Underground.

Cowperwood's health has suffered a serious decline, although he retains sufficient strength to push his projects toward successful conclusion. He feels triumphant in beating Stanford Drake, modeled upon American financier J. P. Morgan, in a rivalry to secure the all-important franchise from Parliament. However, sensing a lack of vigor, Cowperwood has an examination by a London medical specialist, who diagnoses his ailment as Bright's disease, a failure of the kidneys that then was considered incurable. The fatal diagnosis is confirmed by his American physician, and Cowperwood labors overtime to complete his Underground project and to have work completed on an elaborate marble tomb that he has commissioned in Brooklyn's Greenwood Cemetery. He is determined to preserve his facade of vigor, beating back persistent rumors of ill health that could jeopardize his ambitious projects by discouraging his financial backers. He hopes to have his monopoly officially organized and operating before he dies, but in five months he suffers another kidney attack, this one so serious that he books passage on a liner bound for New York. Berenice follows by the next boat.

During the voyage, another bad attack almost kills the financier, and from the dock in New York he is carried by ambulance to the Waldorf Astoria Hotel, a few blocks down Fifth Avenue from his mansion, which has been closed on account of the remodeling for the new art gallery. For this section of the Yerkes story, Dreiser possessed a wealth of data, for in 1905 reporters had met Yerkes's ship, followed his ambulance to the Waldorf, and then, sensing that a truly big story was in its breaking stage, never lessened their surveillance over him.

When **Emilie Grigsby's** ship arrived in New York and she went at once to the hotel, the reporters took note. For the newspapers the question of the day was: will Mrs. Yerkes visit her ailing husband? They crowded her Fifth Avenue door to ask. No, she would not go to the hotel. Then, discovering that the man's illness was terminal, she relented and did visit his sickroom, only to discover her hated rival, Emilie, by the patient's side. She stormed out, returned to her mansion, and locked herself in. *The Stoic* duplicates these incidents.

The dramatic events surrounding the death of Charles T. Yerkes Jr. on 5 December 1905, his interment at Greenwood, the dispersal of his vast wealth, and the subsequent death of his widow were dealt with by Dreiser with great fidelity to the printed record, in part because the intense and dramatic ironies of the story could scarcely be improved upon by a fictioneer

and in part because Dreiser, at seventy-five, was too tired and too ill to do otherwise. And so the Frank Cowperwood story proceeds, his death followed by the outraged Aileen's refusal to allow his coffin to lie in state on Fifth Avenue. His lieutenants bribe the servants, and the ponderous bronze coffin is brought in surreptitiously by dark of night. Then the funeral cortege winds its way to Brooklyn and to the Parthenon-style marble tomb where the financier is entombed.

With the reading of Cowperwood's will, his benefactions to the city are made public. The works in their art gallery will go to the city, and plans are revealed for a great charity hospital to be built in the Bronx, carrying the donor's name in honor to posterity. Universal praise arises. But wait—Cowperwood has perished before his Underground deal has been consummated. Suddenly, like vultures, hordes of creditors appear with claims upon the estate.

Legions of attorneys get into the act. The courts are heavily involved. Dreary months pass, then years, while Mrs. Cowperwood waits in vain for a fortune that will never truly become hers. Involved against her better judgment in a maze of litigation, Aileen, to obtain at last her widow's portion of the estate, is compelled to forswear everything else, even the mansion itself, and the grand house and all of its works of art are sold on the auction block. *Sic transit gloria mundi!*

Pneumonia ends Aileen's sad life, and she is interred with Frank in the tomb at Greenwood. Based on a trip that Emilie Grigsby had taken to India in 1913, Dreiser in his last days concocted a story in which Berenice, after being converted to the spiritual life by an Indian guru, decides to simplify her existence and to purify herself by using the considerable wealth given her by Cowperwood to assure that his charity hospital will become reality. Dreiser wrote *The Stoic* while literally at the end of his own life, and at this point in the action a heart attack brought his career to its close. In the novel, when it appeared in print, the story continued with an Appendix written by his widow, Helen Richardson Dreiser. In that final section, Berenice does indeed build the Cowperwood Hospital, and she devotes her life to nunlike service to indigent children, thereby achieving for herself (and perhaps vicariously for Cowperwood) a kind of redemption.

The Stoic was received by the critics politely, with reverence for Dreiser's lifetime accomplishment, but it was clear to one and all that the novel was not a strong contender. It lacked the massed detail that some had complained of but that was an important facet of Dreiser's style and a wellspring of his power as a novelist. The best sections of the book may be the final chapters, but even here Dreiser hews close to his newspaper sources, erring on the side of compression rather than expansion and at times using newspaper reports verbatim. The primary virtue of having *The Stoic* "finished" and in print is that it does serve to bring to a close the otherwise unresolved story that Dreiser began to compose in the 1910s. In so doing, the book emphasizes the ironic facets of the Yerkes story that were important considerations in the author's original decision to use it as his base for fiction. As the reader sees the financier's wealth, power, and material greatness dwindle away to nothing, the story aptly echoes that Dreiser truism first uttered by the discouraged George Hurstwood in *Sister Carrie*: "What's the use?"

Further Reading

Emmert, Scott D. "Dreiser's Metaphor: *The Stoic* and Cowperwood's Tomb." *Dreiser Studies* 30.1 (1999): 21–34.

Gerber, Philip. "Dreiser's *Stoic*: A Study in Literary Frustration." *Literary Monographs*. Ed. Eric Rothstein and Joseph Wittreich Jr. Vol. 7. Madison: University of Wisconsin Press, 1975. 85–144.

———. "Financier, Titan, and Stoic: *A Trilogy of Desire*." *Theodore Dreiser*. New York: Twayne, 1964. 87–110.

Hochman, Barbara. "Dreiser's Last Work: *The Bulwark* and *The Stoic*—Conversion or Continuity?" *Dreiser Newsletter* 14.2 (1983): 1–15.

Hussman, Lawrence E., Jr. *Dreiser and His Fiction: A Twentieth-Century Quest*. Philadelphia: University of Pennsylvania Press, 1983. 180–93.

Lehan, Richard. "*The Financier, The Titan*, and *The Stoic*." *Theodore Dreiser: His World and His Novels*. Carbondale: Southern Illinois University Press, 1969. 97–116.

Lingeman, Richard. Introduction. *The Stoic*. By Theodore Dreiser. New York: New American Library, 1981. v–xiii.

Matthiessen, F. O. "The Business Novel." *Theodore Dreiser*. New York: William Sloane, 1951. 127–58.

Mookerjee, R. N. "Dreiser's Use of Hindu Thought in *The Stoic*." *American Literature* 43 (1971): 273–78.

Øverland, Orm. "The Inadequate Vehicle: Dreiser's Financier 1912–1945." *American Studies in Scandinavia* 7 (1972): 18–38.

Pizer, Donald. "*The Stoic*." *The Novels of Theodore Dreiser: A Critical Study*. Minneapolis: University of Minnesota Press, 1976. 332–46.

Takeda, Miyoko. "The Theme of Hinduism in *The Stoic*." *Dreiser Studies* 20.2 (1989): 28–34.

Philip Gerber

"THE STORY OF A SONG-QUEEN'S TRIUMPH." This interview-sketch of world-renowned American soprano Lillian Nordica first appeared in *Success* in January 1900. It has been included in several collections, among them *SMA* 2 and Dreiser, *Art, Music, and Literature, 1897–1902*.

Not only does much of Dreiser's early magazine **journalism** address the status of women, but Dreiser was genuinely concerned about the competition in music between the sexes. The objectivity and compassion toward women that would emerge in his novels are apparent in his role as music critic as well. In "The Story of a Song-Queen's Triumph," Dreiser combines a portrait of Lillian Nordica with an incisive analysis of her character, discipline, and artistry that is a good illustration of the pattern of interviews he conducted for *Success* magazine, one that suggests that, despite temporary early disappointments, talent is usually rewarded if one combines hard work with an ability to recognize and take advantage of opportunity.

Lillian Nordica (1857–1914) was born as Lillian Norton in Farmington, Maine, and died in Batavia, Java, after a shipwreck. When she was studying voice in Milan, Italy, her teacher suggested she use the name Nordica. An immediate success, she sang in St. Petersburg, Russia, for two years and then appeared in Paris in 1882. From 1887 to 1893 she sang at Convent Garden, London. In 1894 she sang the part of Elsa in *Lohengrin* at the Wagner Theater in Bayreuth, Germany, the first American to sing there. In 1895 she made her Metropolitan Opera debut as Isolde in *Tristan und Isolde*, after which she concentrated on Wagnerian roles. From 1907 to 1908 she was a member of Oscar Hammerstein's Manhattan Opera Company, and from 1912 until 1914 she appeared only in concert.

When Dreiser interviewed her, Nordica was at the height of her career. She enjoyed the distinction of being one of the first two American women to attain international fame as an opera singer, the other being Emma Eames. Nordica was in the midst of the most brilliant operatic season the city had ever known. She lived "in sumptuous style" at the Waldorf-Astoria Hotel, as does Sister Carrie in the novel, where Dreiser met her by appointment. Discussing the philosophy of an opera

singer's success in view of its difficulties, she told Dreiser, "The material for a great voice may be born in a person,—it is, in fact,—but the making of it into a great voice is a work of the most laborious character." Nordica was critical of young American women singers, who she thought had great voices but not sufficient energy. "To be a great singer," she told Dreiser, "means, first, to be a great student. To be a great student means that you have no time for balls and parties, very little for friends, and less for carriage rides and pleasant strolls. All that is really left is a shortened allowance of sleep, of time for meals, and time for exercise." "Did you ever imagine," Dreiser asked, "that people leaped into permanent fame when still young and without much effort on their part?" "I did," she replied. "But I discovered that real fame,—permanent recognition, which cannot be taken away from you,—is acquired only by a lifetime of most earnest labor."

Yoshinobu Hakutani

"A STORY OF STORIES" is a tale lifted in 1917 from the manuscript of the yet-unpublished *A Book about Myself*. It briefly made the rounds of leading magazines but, finding no takers, was published in *Free and Other Stories* the following year. In Chapters 44 to 46 of *A Book about Myself*, Dreiser had told of his journalistic competition during 1893 with "Red" Galvin, a tough-minded, politically savvy reporter for the *St. Louis Globe-Democrat*. As Galvin was at best semiliterate, the task of ghostwriting his stories fell to others on the staff, including, humiliatingly enough, Dreiser himself when he worked for the *Globe-Democrat*. After Dreiser moved to the *Republic*, he and Galvin were often rivals, vying for the same stories. In *A Book about Myself* Dreiser narrated two episodes to demonstrate the intensity and unpredictability of that reportorial competition. In the first, a ghetto romance that ended with a beautiful Negro girl's being trapped and razor-slashed by her vengeful ex-lover, Dreiser's more fertile imagination and literary superiority allowed him to make a colorful story out of an incident that Galvin had dismissed as insignificant. The second episode involved a bandit who had single-handedly robbed a Missouri Pacific train and, having been captured, was being transported by that same line to St. Louis for incarceration. Dreiser had created the opportunity for an interview en route, but Galvin, through his aggressive nature and manipulative powers, had not only forced his way into that interview but also, upon arriving in St. Louis, maneuvered the subject to the *Globe-Democrat,* where that paper's victory over the *Republic* was photographically captured for its readers. Dreiser brooded over this defeat and its naturalistic implications, realizing how his own intellectual superiority and tactical advantages could be "superseded or set at naught by the raw animal or psychic force of a man like Galvin."

In the process of fictionalizing these episodes, Dreiser gave himself the name Augustus Binns, a "tall, college-y, rather graceful" fellow whose sartorial pretensions annoyed the city editor. Galvin became "Red" Collins. The *Globe-Democrat* and the *Republic* were the *News* and the *Star.* Beyond these name changes, Dreiser sharpened the contrast between the sophisticated, artistically talented Binns and the pugnacious, but highly manipulative, Collins; however, he did little else to distinguish "A Story of Stories" from its autobiographical source. In fact, numerous sections of the short-story text were copied virtually verbatim. According to Joseph Griffin in *The Small Canvas,* Dreiser's reluctance to thoroughly recast the material from *A Book about Myself* contributed to the

"artistic failure" (63) of "A Story of Stories." The thematic focus on Collins's animal nature, a focus suggested by the tentative title "Force," is overwhelmed by the narrative detail, and the omniscient point of view, superimposed on the first-person narration of the original telling, is inconsistent. Still, Griffin concludes, " 'A Story of Stories' effectively articulates Dreiser's fascination with the psychic, as well as his nostalgia for the excitement of the newspaperman's life" (64).

Richard W. Dowell

STREET AND SMITH. After a period of poverty and despair when he did no literary work and worked on the New York Central Railroad (as recounted in his posthumously published work *An Amateur Laborer*), Dreiser was hired in August 1904 by the publishing firm of Street and Smith as an assistant editor for various boys' books at a salary of fifteen dollars per week. He was subsequently promoted to editor of *Smith's Magazine,* a Street and Smith "home magazine" that made its debut (with Dreiser as editor) in April 1905. Dreiser spent about a year and a half in the employ of Street and Smith, where he was paid the handsome sum of sixty dollars a week as editor of *Smith's,* launching what proved for a while to be a successful career in commercial publishing. Dreiser left Street and Smith in April 1906 to become editor of *Broadway Magazine.*

Founded by Francis Scott Street (1831–1883) and Francis Shubael Smith (1819–1887), Street and Smith became one of the largest publishers in the United States of dime novels, which it began publishing in 1889 in the form of boys' "libraries," and was a pioneer in developing home magazines that provided substantial fare for the general public rather than (as was the case with older publications such as *Harper's Weekly*) being aimed primarily at an educated readership. Street and Smith made its entrée into magazine publishing in 1898 with *Ainslee's Magazine*. Dreiser was a regular and prolific contributor to *Ainslee's*, whose editor, **Richard Duffy**, became his close friend. It was probably Duffy who recommended Dreiser for an in-house position at Street and Smith.

In his autobiography *Dawn*, Dreiser recalls being an avid reader of the Street and Smith "story paper" the *New York Weekly* during his boyhood in Evansville, Indiana, and "being introduced, by some of the youths who gathered in the shade of our barn," to the spellbinding world of dime novel heroes such as Diamond Dick. The dime novels were a natural outgrowth of the story papers and featured many of the same characters, written according to strict formulas by a stable of mostly anonymous writers. They included several basic plot types: Wild West adventures, detective stories, school and sports stories, and "working-girl" stories.

The working-girl stories told of innocent girls working and living in the city for the first time who are beset by the perils of living away from home amid temptations of the city and threats to their virtue. In an unpublished portion of the *Dawn* manuscript, Dreiser describes the strong effect such stories had on him: "I just had to see what became of the poor, beautiful, struggling working girl who was seized by thugs on her way from work, bundled into a carriage and driven, gagged, and blindfolded, to a wretched shanty far out on the Hackensack meadows, where she was confronted by her lustful and immoral pursuer of the Four Hundred" (qtd. in Godfrey 66–67). This effect is clearly discernible in *Sister Carrie*, *Jennie Gerhardt*, and *An American Tragedy*, the three Dreiser novels featuring "working-girl" protagonists.

Wild West hero Diamond Dick was one of Street and Smith's most popular dime novel characters. The primary author of the Diamond Dick stories at the time of Dreiser's employment at Street and Smith was George C. Jenks, a newspaperman whom Dreiser had befriended while on the staff of the *New York World*. As seems to be indicated by internal evidence (a handwritten note by Dreiser summarizing some of this early literary experiences that is preserved in the Dreiser Papers), Dreiser probably had a hand in preparing some of the Diamond Dick stories for publication in *Diamond Dick Jr. Boys Best Weekly*. Whether he actually wrote any of the Diamond Dick or other pulp fiction stories while at Street and Smith is unknown.

In 1959, Street and Smith was acquired by Condé Nast Publications, the publishers of *Vogue* and other fashion magazines.

Further Reading

Davidson, Cathy N., and Arnold E. Davidson. "Carrie's Sisters: The Popular Prototypes for Dreiser's Heroine." *Modern Fiction Studies* 23 (1977): 395–407.

Gardner, Ralph D. "Street and Smith." *Publishers for Mass Entertainment in Nineteenth Century America*. Ed. Madeleine B. Stern. Boston: G. K. Hall, 1980. 277–94.

Godfrey, Lydia S. "The Influence of Dime Novels on Theodore Dreiser." *Dime Novel Round-Up* 52.5 (1983): 66–71.

Reynolds, Quentin. *The Fiction Factory, or from Pulp Row to Quality Street*. New York: Random, 1955.

Schurman, Lydia Cushman. "The Publishing Firm of Street and Smith: Its First Fifty Years, 1855–1905." *Dime Novel Round-Up* 57.2 (1988): 20–24.

———. "Richard Lingeman's Myth Making: Theodore Dreiser's Editing of the Jack Harkaway Stories." *Dime Novel Round-Up* 64.6 (1995): 151–68.

———. "The Sensational Stories and Dime Novel Writing Days of Louisa May Alcott, Horatio Alger, Theodore Dreiser, and Upton Sinclair." *Dime Novel Round-Up* 57.6 (1988): 84–92.

———. "Theodore Dreiser and His Street and Smith Circle." *Dime Novel Round-Up* 65.6 (1996): 183–95.

Roger W. Smith

SUCCESS was an inspirational journal founded in 1897 by **Orison Swett Marden** to promote his credo, "Unceasing struggle in adversity brings triumph." Initially, *Success* gained a wide following by featuring stories about, and interviews with, prominent Americans from all walks of life who had surmounted obstacles through the practice of virtues emblazoned on the magazine's cover: Education, Enterprise, Enthusiasm, Economy, Self-respect, Self-reliance, Self-help, Self-culture, Self-control, Work, Sagacity, Honesty, Truth, and Courage. Eventually, however, according to Marden biographer Margaret Connolly, "insidious" members of the journal's staff "secured control of the magazine" and made it an instrument of the muckraker movement sweeping the country (226–27). *Success*'s popularity declined; it went into bankruptcy; and in 1911 the magazine ceased publication. Marden, undaunted by this setback, founded a "new" *Success* in 1918 and edited it until shortly before his death in 1924.

During *Success*'s heyday, Dreiser was one of that journal's most prolific contributors, publishing thirty interviews and one poem between January 1898 and June 1900. Among his interviewees were Thomas Edison, Philip Armour, Marshall Field, Andrew Carnegie, and **William Dean Howells**. Typically, these interviews conformed to a formulaic pattern. Dreiser would establish the circumstances of his meeting with the subject, then introduce, when applicable, any barriers to success that person had overcome. The bulk of the piece highlighted the virtues that allowed the interviewee to win through to wealth and/or acclaim. Edison, for example, attributed his success to hard work and singleness of purpose; Armour, to honesty and frugality; Field, to the sagacious use of money; and Carnegie, to industry, perseverance, and thrift. Dreiser himself, for each of these tributes to ambition and enterprise, earned $100.

In view of Dreiser's criticism of the capitalistic system, both before and after his association with *Success*, scholars have sought and occasionally found hints of irony embedded in these tributes to robber barons such as Carnegie. When biographer **Robert Elias** asked about the possibility of a satirical intent, however, Dreiser responded, "If you will look at the magazine you will understand why a denunciation of Mr. Carnegie would have lost me $100" (qtd. in Lingeman 1: 187).

After an eighteen-month hiatus, during which *Sister Carrie* failed and his struggle with **neurasthenia** began, Dreiser published three more essays in *Success*. The tone of these later contributions, however, was more subdued, and the successes they narrated were more humanistic than material. "A Cripple Whose Energy Gives Inspiration" (February 1902) told the story of a physically handicapped boy whose industry, thrift, and honesty kept him economically independent amid the malaise of a commercially depressed Connecticut community. "A Touch of Human Brotherhood" (March 1902: 140–41, 176) focused on the humanitarian efforts of an ex-soldier, known as the "Captain," who solicited coins amid the glitter of New York's theater district to provide shelter for the homeless on winter nights. The "Captain" had also appeared in *Sister Carrie*. Finally, "The Tenement Toilers" (April 1902) described the deplorable living conditions of sweatshop workers whose struggle to survive in a capitalistic system taught their children "that wealth is all." These final contributions to *Success* would seem to reflect the muckraker bias that the journal was assuming.

Further Reading

Connolly, Margaret. *The Life Story of Orison Swett Marden: The Man Who Benefited Men.* New York: Crowell, 1925.

Richard W. Dowell

SUMNER, JOHN SAXTON (1876–1971). A staunch Episcopalian and Republican, John Sumner was a moral crusader who became the executive secretary of the **New York Society for the Suppression of Vice** immediately following the death of one of the organization's original founders, **Anthony Comstock**, in 1915. Sumner held this position for thirty-five years. The son of a navy officer, Sumner received his preliminary education at public and private schools in Washington, D.C. After a short stint in the brokerage business in the late 1890s, he pursued and received a law degree from New York University in 1904, a degree that would later serve him well in court when authors and publishers attempted to bypass New York's antiobscenity laws. Sumner's fear of urban decadence, combined with his belief that immigrants were the cause of such moral depravity, drove him to enforce energetically the federal antiobscenity postal statutes of 1873 and to censor or sanitize all literature that he and his organization deemed lewd and lascivious. He often labeled booksellers and publishers, as well as the lawyers and civil libertarians who defended the publication of questionable material, as un-American and un-Christian. Some of the better-known novels that Sumner banned for vulgar passages included James Joyce's *Ulysses* (1922), D. H. Lawrence's *Lady Chatterley's Lover* (1928), Edmund Wilson's *Memoirs of Hecate County* (1946), and Theodore Dreiser's *The "Genius."*

In particular, the dispute between Sumner and Dreiser over the publication of *The "Genius"* became a rallying cry for supporters of artistic freedom. Citing some seventeen profane and seventy-five lewd passages from *The "Genius,"* Sumner used his political clout to force **J. Jefferson Jones** of **John Lane's** New York office to recall all copies of the novel from bookstores in 1916. With the help of his friend H. L. Mencken, Dreiser gained the support of the **Authors' League of America**. This organization and Mencken convinced over 500 of the nation's most respected creative artists and editors to sign a protest. Legally, not much came of the incident other than Dreiser bringing suit against John Lane for breaking their contract on the grounds the book did not violate the law. However, though the book remained banned until 1923 (when it was reissued by **Boni & Liveright**) and did cost Dreiser some royalties, the incident, more importantly, made people begin to question **censorship**.

After an unsuccessful attempt to pass the Clean Books Bill of 1923, Sumner's power began to wane as entertainment and leisure time became commercialized. Dance halls, restaurants, theaters, movies, and the increased circulation of cheap books and magazines persuaded many to find Sumner's puritan values antiquated. When the American Civil Liberties Union organized a National Council on Freedom from Censorship in 1931, membership in Sumner's organization began to decline.

Further Reading

Gertzman, Jay A. "John Saxton Sumner of the New York Society for the Suppression Vice: A Chief Smut-Eradicator of the Interwar Period." *Journal of American Culture* 17.2 (1994): 41–47.

Kevin Jett

THE SUPERNATURAL. Dreiser's world-view, as is well known, was heavily indebted to many of the intellectual trends and scientific developments of his day, which are associated with terms such as **naturalism**, social Darwinism, **mechanism**, determinism, and the like. Dreiser often posited (both as an essayist and as an omniscient narrator in his novels) and portrayed (as the artificer of a fictional milieu) a world that seems bleakly deterministic or mechanistic in which characters are at the mercy of impersonal forces. Dreiser rejected his father's Catholicism and found conventional religious belief to be an anathema. In view of his desire to ground his beliefs in science, as evidenced by the extensive investigations of scientific phenomena he did in preparation for his philosophical work *Notes on Life*, Dreiser's weltanschauung would seem to exclude anything supernatural. It is surprising, therefore, that the concept of supernatural forces (not a supreme being per se) played such a large role in Dreiser's consciousness and is clearly visible in his creative output.

The supernatural manifests itself in three major ways: first, in Dreiser's own superstitiousness, his willingness to give credence to extrasensory phenomena, and an underlying psychological makeup that made factors such as **chance** and fate loom so large in his consciousness; second, in the development of Dreiser's thought, primarily ideas he took from his reading of **Herbert Spencer's** *First Principles* (and from other writers of the late nineteenth and early twentieth centuries), which led him to embrace mechanism and reject **religion** but which left him with an intellectual framework, based primarily on Spencer's concept of the Unknowable, in which it was possible to conceive of supernatural forces; and third, in Dreiser's works, in which supernatural forces (as well as superstition) often play a part, ei-

ther explicitly or implicitly. Dreiser was, as his biographer W. A. Swanberg has observed (using a term coined by the critic Eliseo Vivas), "an inconsistent mechanist. . . . Nor should any real mechanist be as superstitious as TD was" ("Airmail Interview," *Dreiser Newsletter* 1.1 [1970]: 3).

Dreiser believed in mental telepathy, hypnotism, Ouija boards, psalmists, and other occultisms; omens and spiritualism; premonitions; old folk sayings and practices; and charms. Dreiser had a lifelong fascination with fortune-telling and sympathetically portrays a **Greenwich Village** fortune-teller he knew and consulted, **Jessie Spafford**, in the sketch "Giff" in *A Gallery of Women*. Dreiser was also obsessed by the role chance or luck plays in everyday affairs and crafted such pivotal scenes as Hurstwood's theft from the safe and Clyde Giffiths's drowning of **Roberta Alden** to turn on matters of chance. Throughout his life, Dreiser advocated research in the field of psychic phenomena.

Dreiser's superstitiousness was frequently commented on by his contemporaries and is conspicuous in his diaries and memoirs. While recounting his experiences as a traveler in works such as *A Traveler at Forty* and *A Hoosier Holiday*, for example, he often takes note of, and speculates about, the possible outcomes of such occurrences as seeing a horseshoe, a cross-eyed person, or a hunchbacked man. Dreiser's superstitious beliefs and practices are one of the salient facts of his life and personality noted in the books written after his death by intimates such as Dreiser's second wife, Helen Dreiser, **Louise Campbell, Marguerite Tjader** (who attended séances with Dreiser), **Vera Dreiser,** and **Yvette Eastman.** H. L. Mencken fumed against Dreiser's superstitiousness and his credulousness, "giving a grave ear to quackeries," as Mencken termed it in *A Book of Prefaces* (rpt. in *D-M Letters* 2: 786).

Dreiser states in *Dawn* that he inherited "a deeply-rooted vein of superstition which was one of the few traits of temperament my father and mother possessed in common and which was the heritage of most of their children." In the opening pages of that autobiography, Dreiser notes several instances of supernatural occurrences that were said to be associated with his birth and the death of his parents' first three children. These include the story (told to him by his sister Mame, who insisted on its veracity later in life) that spirits in the form of "three maidens . . . garbed in brightly-colored costumes" entered the Dreiser home when Dreiser was born, and another family legend that Dreiser's mother, Sarah, had a premonition of the death of her first three children associated with three lights his mother glimpsed in a backyard before they vanished into the woods. Another tale involves an old German woman in Terre Haute, Indiana (Dreiser's birthplace), believed to have occult powers, who advised Dreiser's mother to perform a secret ritual to ensure that Dreiser, who was scrawny and weak when born, would not die in infancy. Lights forewarning imminent death such as those spoken of by Dreiser's mother are depicted in two of Dreiser's stories, "The Old Neighborhood" and "The Lost Phoebe."

In Dreiser's days as a newspaperman, he was often sent to report on performances by psychics and mediums and to investigate their claims. Sometimes Dreiser described these performances with irony and skepticism; at other times, he was greatly impressed by what he saw. These included stories for the *St. Louis Republic* on the exploits of the famous mind reader and hypnotist J. Alexander McIvor Tyndall and on the medium Jules Wallace, who

was ultimately exposed (in stories attributed to Dreiser) by the *Republic* as "an unmitigated fraud."

In a March 1897 editorial for *Ev'ry Month*, Dreiser compared psychic phenomena to the wondrous discoveries made possible by modern science. "If a telephone apparatus and wire will instantly carry the voice for thousands of miles and reproduce it to the ear of another," he asked, why should not phenomena such as telepathy be possible in which "the ether of space carry a powerful mental vision or impression through equally great space and permit it to affect the already sympathetic and harmonized mind for which it is intended?" (rpt. in *Theodore Dreiser's Ev'ry Month*, ed. Barrineau, 259). In 1909, he wrote an anonymous editorial entitled "In the Matter of Spiritualism" for the *Bohemian Magazine* in which he stated that psychic phenomena were common, everyday occurrences, the existence of which could not be denied; that scientific evidence (and support within the scientific community) for the reality of psychic phenomena was growing; and that psychic energy was just another manifestation of "the forces of life," which also included matter and energy and other phenomena within the realm of physics.

Intellectually, Dreiser was greatly influenced by the writings of the British sociologist and philosopher **Herbert Spencer**, whose work *First Principles* (1862) completely overthrew Dreiser's previous conceptions of life. In *First Principles*, Spencer argues that an ultimate knowledge of the universe is incomprehensible to human beings and that both religion and scientific inquiry ultimately lead to the same realization that there is an unknowable force operative in the cosmos. The concept of the Unknowable caused Dreiser to despair of ever finding the foundation of any sort of personal belief system or finding meaning in the universe, as Dreiser later confided to interviewer Frank Harris. Spencer's Unknowable, in other words, provided the foundation for a pessimistic view of the universe as essentially meaningless. But the Unknowable also "allowed Dreiser to maintain a belief in some sort of vague, supernatural force that controlled events in the universe," as Louis Zanine has noted (19). This has led to a curious phenomenon in Dreiser's oeuvre, what another Dreiser scholar, J. D. Thomas, has called his "supernatural naturalism," a naturalistic worldview overlaid with strong elements of supernaturalism.

Words such as "ghosts," "wraiths," and "spirits" are common in Dreiser's fiction, as are demons such as the Efrit (a genie associated with the tales of the Arabian Nights), who represents Clyde's unconscious in *An American Tragedy* and whose suggestion that Clyde can resolve his problems by murdering Roberta he cannot get out of his mind. Spirits and supernatural forces often play a role in Dreiser's short stories and plays—notably "The Hand," "The Lost Phoebe," *Laughing Gas, The Blue Sphere, In the Dark,* and *The Spring Recital.*

The "Genius," the most autobiographical of Dreiser's novels, offers an interesting portrayal of Dreiser's beliefs and their evolution in the context of the supernatural. The protagonist, **Eugene Witla**, is intensely superstitious, as was Dreiser; he is always looking for omens and signs of what fate intends for him. Eugene is also torn, as was Dreiser, by a "compulsion to accept a deterministic explanation of existence as opposed to his need to believe in a transcendent meaning" (Hussman 91). The book ends on a philosophical and somewhat optimistic note with a quotation from Spencer about the Unknowable. The passage from Spencer leads Eugene, Dreiser's alter ego, to muse both on the limitations of human thought and on the wonders of the cosmos as he gazes at the nighttime sky.

Further Reading

Dreiser, Theodore. "In the Matter of Spiritualism." *Bohemian* 17 (1909): 424–25.

Harris, Frank. *Contemporary Portraits, Second Series.* New York: Frank Harris, 1919. 81–106.

Hussman, Lawrence E., Jr. "The 'Genius.' " *Dreiser and His Fiction: A Twentieth-Century Quest.* Philadelphia: University of Pennsylvania Press, 1983. 91–112.

Lynn, Kenneth S. "Theodore Dreiser: The Man of Ice." *The Dream of Success: A Study of the Modern American Imagination.* Boston: Little, Brown, 1955. 13–74.

Ross, Woodburn O. "Concerning Dreiser's Mind." *American Literature* 18 (1946): 233–43.

Thomas, J. D. "The Natural Supernaturalism of Dreiser's Novels." *Rice Institute Pamphlets* 44:1 (1957): 112–25.

———. "The Supernatural Naturalism of Dreiser's Novels." *Rice Institute Pamphlets* 46:1 (1959): 53–69.

Townsend, Barbara Ann. "Superstitious Beliefs of Theodore Dreiser." Diss., Ball State University, 1972.

Zanine, Louis J. "Science and the Supernatural." *Mechanism and Mysticism: The Influence of Science on the Thought and Work of Theodore Dreiser.* Philadelphia: University of Pennsylvania Press, 1993. 115–45.

Roger W. Smith

T

"TABLOID TRAGEDY." One of four un-collected short stories Dreiser finished during the 1930's, "Tabloid Tragedy" was published in *Hearst's International-Cosmopolitan* in December 1933. The magazine gave the story ample showcasing, decorating its two title pages with drawings of typical tabloid headlines, illustrating it lavishly with sketches by Marshall Frantz, and setting it up with an editorial preamble that ended with the sentence: "What he did and what happened to him truly make another 'American Tragedy.' "

The "he" in question is Ralph Thompson, a successful businessman, married, and living in an otherwise unidentified Williamstown, and what he did constitutes the essence of the story. Off on a moonlight tryst with his lover, twenty-nine-year-old Marcella Dey, he and the young woman are undetected witnesses to a brutal murder that occurs a few feet from where they are. After much soul-searching and despite the misgivings of Marcella, who is fearful about the damage to her reputation if her relationship with Thompson is found out, the latter goes to the authorities and declares himself a witness to the crime. Because he misrepresents some of the circumstances surrounding the viewing of the murder in order to protect Marcella's and his own good name, his

effort to right matters turns sour; the rightfully accused perpetrators go free, Marcella loses her job, and Thompson loses both his paramour and his wife and feels obliged to leave Williamstown for good. The final paragraph finds him "confused, irritated, disillusioned towards the new life he was going to try to make." His effort to do right has failed.

The tale of the lovers' tragic outcome makes up only a portion of "Tabloid Tragedy." Large sections deal with the crime itself, its aftermath, and, of course, the principals: Frank and Tony Palmeri, the murderers; Luigi Del Papa, their victim; Rosie Palmeri, husband of Tony, and Del Papa's lover; district attorney Driscoll; and the Palmeris' lawyer, Rocco. For long stretches of the story these things become salient and virtually displace its major concerns and protagonists; what is merely the wherewithal to allow the primary story to progress becomes a major entity in itself— as if to justify the use of the word "tabloid" in the story's title.

The dilemma the well-intentioned Thompson faces and consciously articulates in retrospect, whereby he feels himself in a predicament from which there is no escape, is a familiar one in Dreiser stories and marks such earlier successes as "Free" and "Chains," the title stories of his two collections. But the seemingly inordinate attention given to the Palmeri side of events suggests that Dreiser was attempting something different from what he had done earlier. It does appear that if the Palmeri coverage satisfies the requirements of the title "Tabloid Tragedy," the more dramatically accented personal tragedies of Thompson and Marcella, in their privateness and extended ramifications—much of which are outside the interest of tabloid journalism—hold center stage and render the crime story, interesting as it is, superfluous.

Further Reading

Griffin, Joseph P. "Dreiser's Later Short Stories." *Dreiser Newsletter* 9.1 (1978): 5–10.

Joseph P. Griffin

TATUM, ANNA P. (1882–1950). On 7 November 1911 Tatum, a graduate of Wellesley, wrote to Dreiser describing the effect on her of reading *Jennie Gerhardt* and disputing part of his depiction of the novel's heroine. After an exchange of letters, they met in New York in the fall of 1912, and she told him of her devout Quaker father, whose story moved Dreiser to begin planning what would become *The Bulwark*. According to Dreiser's diary, they lived together intermittently until January 1913. He was attracted to Tatum's youth, beauty, and rebellious spirit: she smoked cigarettes in public, began to drink after she met him, had had a lesbian affair but was "a virgin, except for being a Lesbian" before she met him, and actively pursued a sexual encounter with him (*American Diaries* 207–8). Tatum worked with him on *The Titan* and helped him find a publisher after **Harper & Brothers** declined to publish it; Dreiser broke off their relationship because Tatum longed for a more exclusive commitment. In 1933, she again entered his life and typed and edited his essays

and a screenplay, but since she objected to his social theories, Dreiser asked her to edit the manuscript of *The Stoic* instead. Although she had initially objected to *The Bulwark*, fearing that Dreiser's use of the story would embarrass her family, she encouraged him to return to the long-stalled novel after her parents' deaths. Dreiser used his relationship with Tatum as the basis of the character **Etta Barnes** in *The Bulwark* and Elizabeth in "This Madness: The Story of Elizabeth," published in *Hearst's International-Cosmopolitan* in 1929.

Keith Newlin

TAYLOR, THOMAS P. (1857–1913). Taylor was mayor of Bridgeport, Connecticut, from 1897 to 1899. Dreiser first became aware of this controversial mayor when he was in Bridgeport in the spring of 1898 to gather materials for magazine articles about weapons and munitions. The impending war with Spain had created reader interest in these topics. Mayor Taylor's well-publicized efforts to fight political corruption would have found favor with Dreiser, who possibly interviewed Taylor at this time for a *Success*-type article that was never published. When Dreiser returned to Connecticut in 1901, Taylor was out of office. The interview Dreiser conducted then was sold as "A Mayor and His People" to *Era* (published June 1903). Dreiser later revised this sketch for inclusion in *Twelve Men*.

Thomas P. Taylor was born in Bristol, Pennsylvania, near Philadelphia, in 1857 and was graduated from the Packard Business College in Brooklyn, New York. He came to Bridgeport in 1877, where he worked as a bookkeeper for the Warner Brothers corset factory. He held patents on over 100 inventions and improvements for manufactured clothing items such as hose supporters and bustles. In 1892, he went into business for himself to manufacture paper boxes and women's notions. He was on the executive committee of the Republican Club and a member of the common council. In 1897, Taylor was elected mayor of Bridgeport at the age of forty. During his two years as mayor, Taylor tried to eliminate government corruption, such as requiring contractors to provide the materials and services for which they were being paid with tax dollars. His enemies sought to condemn him with the label of "socialist." In 1899, he was replaced on the Republican ticket by a party hack. Taylor returned to manufacturing and continued as a private citizen to work for the improvement of the city. He was most remembered for two traits: the frankness of his speech and his concern for the welfare of the workers in his factory. Taylor died in Bridgeport of heart failure on 25 May 1913 at age fifty-six.

Robert Coltrane

"THE TENEMENT TOILERS" concerns an underclass, 100,000 people in New York City at the end of the nineteenth century, variously called "sewing-machine workers," "tenement toilers," and "sweat-shop employees." Walking into the tenement district, Dreiser encounters "a civilization that is as strange and un-American as if it were not included in this land at all." This section, full of little stores with grimy windows, exhibits "an atmosphere of crowdedness and poverty." Adults and children alike, constantly and energetically moving around in haste and with enthusiasm, seem like ants.

Dreiser traces the development of tenement houses to reveal that shrewd, greedy Italians and those called "padrones" leased entire blocks of property from a landowner like William Waldorf Astor, the founder of the Waldorf-Astoria Hotel, and divided "each natural department up into two or three. Then these cubby-holes are leased to the toilers, and the tenement crowding begins." Focusing on a middle-aged Jewish Hungarian immigrant, his wife, and their fifteen-year-old daughter, Dreiser describes how the whole family, confined illegally in a small room with other workers, engages in the sewing work no machine worker could do. These garment workers must work so hard that they have little time for education. Adults and children alike toil for bread; children under twelve are often sent to work illegally. Although Dreiser saw some civic organizations, such as Hebrew Aid Societies and Legal Aid Societies, trying to help these people, the percentage of opportunity was small. "Nearly the only ideal," Dreiser remarks, "that is set before these strugglers, in the area still toiling here, is the one of getting money. A hundred thousand children, the sons and daughters of working parents whose lives are as difficult as that of the Hungarian portrayed, and whose homes are these unlovely tenements, are inoculated in infancy with the doctrine that wealth is all."

"The Tenement Toilers" first appeared in *Success* (April 1902), before being republished in the *New York Call Magazine* (24 August 1919). It was then reprinted as "The Toilers of the Tenements" in *The Color of a Great City*. The *Success* version was included in *SMA* 2.

Yoshinobu Hakutani

"THIS MADNESS." A series of three sketches ("Aglaia," "Elizabeth," "Sidonie") published in six installments in *Hearst's International-Cosmopolitan* from February to July 1929. The sketches are driven by an autobiographical, confessional thrust, as the author-narrator notes in the beginning: "In my own life—as I have frankly confessed these many years—sex has been understood and accepted by me for the controlling and directing force that it is."

The subheading to the first installment, "An Honest Novel about Love by the Man Who Wrote 'An American Tragedy,' " signals a fictionalizing of events in the reference to the "novel," but Dreiser leaves deliberate autobiographical clues—his nickname "Dodar," his third novel is entitled *The Financier*, and so forth—to suggest that the narrating "I" is, indeed, identical with the name of the author and that we are meant to read his sketches autobiographically.

In "This Madness" Dreiser dismantles the conventions of monogamy and marriage with a vengeance, aggressively claiming sexual varietism for himself by disclosing his sex life with three sexually liberated women during the early to mid-1910s, after he had severed his marriage bonds and had just suffered humiliating public failure in his thwarted affair with the seventeen-year-old **Thelma Cudlipp** (aka Leonore). The painful episode cost him his position at **Butterick Publishing** and heightened his need of reasserting his sexual ego. "This Madness" is the autobiographical story of the Casanova/womanizer who sexually conquers women and then moves on—unrelentingly—to the next object of desire. According to Dreiser's philosophy, this pattern is justified as part of "this great creative world-building impulse," as well as part of the convention-slashing, antibourgeois honesty in life and writing that would mark twentieth-century modernity. Life itself was epitomized in the ever-changing sex drive that refused "the stable, the fixed, the unchanging."

Yet the narrative also reveals the monomaniacal aspect of this sexual odyssey (hence the ironic and self-critical title, "This Madness"), as the author sardonically looks at himself for what he is: a middle-aged man seeking to recover his youth, his mistresses being half his age; jealous because younger rivals easily outdo him "on a tennis-court, or golf links, or in the drawing-room"; and resentfully misanthropic because of past wounds that he carries with him without ever being able to find a cure.

The autobiographical self thus emerges as far from positive. He is egotistical, selfish, exploitative, and essentially amoral, as his antibourgeois violation of conventions assaults sacred human bonds. In "Aglaia," he seduces the young daughter of the man who has invited him into his home, not unlike the Trojan Paris stealing Helen from Menelaus in his own home. He inflicts suffering on the man who has acted most generously toward him, even while admitting that his attraction to Aglaia is far from overpowering. He is offered generous gifts but remains moody, gloomy, irritated, jealous, and caustic, a characteristic killjoy figure who has difficulties forging healthy human connections. In the happy family context, he feels irritated and out of place. His psyche is ruled by the Casanova's desire to conquer, consume, and move on. This, however, does not preclude opposite impulses, as expressed in his rhapsodizing about the women he meets. Aglaia, for example, is likened to a nymph, a dryad, and a Madonna ("I see her face now, haloed by the brown leaves"). In "This Madness," Dreiser is a Sadeian transgressor who is ruthless in his philosophy of promiscuity, even while he sympathizes with his victims. The liberated woman turns martyr, a Sadeian Justine, whose psyche becomes bruised as the masochistically waiting heroine is tortured by the hero's infidelities, lies, and subtle (or not so subtle) cruelties. In all three sketches, he evokes the pathos of the ending of *Jennie Gerhardt*, the woman in love celebrated and pitied for her "capacity for suffering."

"This Madness" also matches the pattern of *A Gallery of Women*, yet is more openly sexual. The author/narrator is active *agon* more than historiographer. The women's identities are only slightly veiled by pseudonyms. "Aglaia" (from Greek "Splendor"), one of the three Graces in Greek mythology, is based on **Lillian Rosenthal**, the daughter of his friend Elias Rosenthal, who had read his novel *Jennie Gerhardt* and provided important feedback and critique. She became a musician who later gave voice lessons to Helen Richardson in Hollywood. "Elizabeth" is the second of the three Graces and makes her appearance in androgynous garb with a "somewhat mannish gray suit." Strong and intellectual, she is likened to "Diana" and "Portia." She is based on **Anna P. Tatum**, who began corresponding with Dreiser in 1911, met him in 1912, and helped edit *The Titan*. Finally, "Sidonie," who loves to dress in fantastic and artistic costumes, is based on Elaine Hyman, an actress with the Provincetown Players who assumed the name of **Kirah Markham**. Although Dreiser's double in varietism and in pleasure seeking, she, too, falls into the predictable masochistic pattern of attachment. By the end of the sketch, after separating from him, she returns yearningly to his window, unable to let go of her love.

As is customary for magazine publication, "This Madness" was tailored for mainstream consumption; a reference to Lillian Rosenthal's abortion, for instance, was omitted. The sketches were framed by advertisements for feminine body products promising healthy gums, white teeth, and hair removal, as well as Bayer Aspirin, face-powder, mouthwash, internal baths, diet books, Hawaiian vacations—and portable typewriters. The female readership presumably included typists, the very function that Dreiser's mistresses also fulfilled. Marshall Frantz's illustrations that accompanied the text were designed to sanitize Dreiser's transgressions, providing drama and glamour, conventional female beauty, and modern party culture, as well as glossing over the generational divide depicted by Dreiser. Frantz's illustrations image gender stereotypes, including women gazing up to the man. While Frantz's women are occasionally surrounded by books, none hold a pen in their hand, even though the female protagonists—like the women behind the text—were actively involved in editing and shaping Dreiser's work.

Ultimately, "This Madness" shows Dreiser's systematic sexualization of all life, including the modern woman's desire for new freedoms and artistic expressions. Through his relations with three exceptional women he also shows the darker side of the author whose psychical wounds and compulsions turned him into a precursor for Nabokov's Humbert Humbert figure. Women who sought to liberate themselves from Victorian repressions found Dreiser's view of life and sex seductive, but once in Dreiser's orbit, they also realized that they needed to distance themselves from Dreiser in order to flourish as women and as artists.

Irene Gammel

THOMPSON, DOROTHY (1893–1961). From an inauspicious start in life as the daughter of a small-town Methodist minister in upstate New York, Dorothy Thompson went on to become one of the best-known female journalists in the world. During World War II she was an unofficial adviser to Franklin D. Roosevelt and among the half dozen or so most admired women in America. Among her more notable achievements was the rare coup of being the first foreign journalist to be granted an interview by Adolf Hitler. As the Berlin correspondent for the *Philadelphia Public Ledger* in 1927, she met her future husband, the novelist **Sinclair Lewis**, and perhaps unintentionally stoked the fire of a feud between him and Dreiser by not denying rumors that she was involved romantically with the latter.

Dreiser and Thompson were both en route to Moscow as part of a group of writers, dignitaries, and members of the intelligentsia who had been invited by the new Soviet government to report on conditions there since the 1917 revolution. Dreiser fell ill; Thompson took care of him in his hotel room, with Dreiser's gratitude. Yet when Lewis appeared, Dreiser snubbed him. To make matters worse, when Dreiser's and Thompson's subsequent writings on the new Russia were published (*Dreiser Looks at Russia* and Thompson's series of articles in the *New York Evening Post*), Dreiser was accused by Thompson—who was backed up by almost everybody in the literary world—of purloining material from her articles and incorporating them, sometimes without even the most superficial changes, into his book. Dreiser responded that the government's information officers had distributed to all the reporters the same fact sheets, so it was not unusual that there should have been such repetition.

An enraged Thompson threatened to sue Dreiser. Although some legal posturing followed, no concrete action was taken until some four years later, when Lewis, recently crowned as America's first Nobel laureate, shared the rostrum with Dreiser at a dinner honoring the Russian novelist Boris Pilnyak. Lewis publicly repeated the plagiarism charge, and the two men slapped each other, with Lewis stridently defending his wife's integrity.

Thompson did not go on record about the incident, but literary history has generally awarded the mantle of virtue to her and concluded that Dreiser did, even if inadvertently, use material from Thompson's writings.

Further Reading

Kurth, Peter. *American Cassandra: The Life of Dorothy Thompson*. Boston: Little, Brown, 1990.

Sheean, Vincent. *Dorothy and Red*. Boston: Houghton Mifflin, 1963.

James M. Hutchisson

THE TITAN. In 1912 Dreiser published what he had completed of his lengthy projected novel based on the life story of **Charles T. Yerkes Jr.** That discrete volume, *The Financier*, became the opening segment of a trilogy whose future installments would continue and complete the story. Dreiser used the momentum built up during his first stint of writing to forge ahead on the second volume of what he now called *A Trilogy of Desire*. This new book, to be called *The Titan*, would follow his financial genius, **Frank Cowperwood**, through his business career in Chicago, which lasted from sometime shortly before 1880 until approximately 1894, when the financier completed his New York mansion. Fortuitously, these years again enclosed a discrete portion of the cradle-to-grave saga that was Dreiser's larger aim. A third volume would then close the trilogy by dealing with Yerkes's final years, as a flamboyant contender in the business worlds of New York and London.

In Chicago, during the late 1880s, Dreiser, as a teenage observer, had himself first encountered Yerkes, and it came about through a bitter strike by workers protesting the antilabor practices of the Chicago streetcar lines. By means both fair and foul, Yerkes had connived to combine all the local streetcar companies into a single giant, moneymaking monopoly called the Union Traction Company. Young Dreiser had wandered north from Terre

Haute, alone, to seek his fortune in the rapidly growing metropolis of the Midwest. Untrained, inexperienced, and very raw, he was finding it hard sledding to create a viable life in the economic jungle of the metropolis. The youth bounced from one commonplace and ill-paid job to another, as he sought to find an acceptable vocation. Like other working-class Chicagoans, Dreiser paid his daily nickel to commute on the Yerkes lines and in this manner witnessed firsthand the abominable conditions of the streetcars. In the summer they were stiflingly hot and in the winter freezing cold. At peak periods, Yerkes refused to send out extra cars, forcing hordes of commuters to pack into every available inch of room, standing and holding for support onto leather straps that hung from the roofs of the cars. "It's the straphangers who pay the dividends," Yerkes brazenly declared to the few investigative journalists who dared question his management of the lines. By 1890 his monopoly had brought him the wealth of Croesus as well as the hatred of untold Chicagoans, who knew his arrogant methods firsthand and at least had heard the stories of his political chicanery. In fact, around Chicago, the financier's autocratic stance had earned him the title "Baron Yerkes." This is why, when his workers finally took to the streets to plead their case for decent conditions and a living wage, the populace poured out in massed support, cheering the strikers on and even tearing up streetcar rails to prevent passage of the scab cars that Yerkes sent out from the car barns as he attempted to continue regular service along his routes.

"It is none of the public's business," protested the streetcar king, but of course he was dead wrong—for the public was the people and the people were learning slowly, if painfully, that America was very much their business. The people made certain that Yerkes understood this, even if they were powerless as yet to effect reform. All of these events young Dreiser was witness to, and while he understood little about their significance beyond the captivating drama of the moment, each new circumstance and revelation piled into his memory, where they helped eventually to shape his writerly attitudes toward social issues such as those concerning the relations between wealth and poverty, worker and employer, legislators and the governed. Such issues formed the basis for Dreiser's fiction and are a prime reason for the continuing relevance of his works.

After he left his teens and entered newspaper work as a rookie reporter in Chicago, Dreiser had a greater opportunity both to observe Yerkes and to learn about his methodology. The man very early on had established nefarious relationships with the elected aldermen who made up the Chicago City Council. Finding favor with these officials was indispensable to Yerkes because they created the ordinances that established rules for operating the city, and even though Yerkes personally owned all the streetcar lines in Chicago (a city expanding by 50,000 residents every year), he depended entirely upon civic permissions, called franchises, to use the public streets. Lacking such franchises, Yerkes would not be able to move a single streetcar out of its barn.

As political aides, the financier enlisted the services of two of the most powerful and notoriously corrupt aldermen in Chicago, "Hinky Dink" Kenna and "Bathtub John" Coughlin, masters of the art of political graft and controllers of the rampant gambling and prostitution in Chicago's "tenderloin" district. Although Dreiser in his fiction chose not to dramatize the great Yerkes streetcar strike that he had witnessed as a boy, he did deal with Kenna and Coughlin, who in the fictional telling became the characters Michael Tiernan and Patrick Kerrigan. This pair is complicit in Frank Cowperwood's successful struggle to dominate the City Council via bribery (it was widely known that Yerkes was offering Aldermen $20,000 per year to vote for measures favoring his Union Traction Company). The City Council gave the Yerkes streetcar lines many favors, including the practically free use of a downtown tunnel on LaSalle Street that had been built by civic funds. A number of local ears picked up on this chicanery, but it was rammed through the City Council nevertheless, saving Yerkes tens of thousands of dollars.

As the financier's wealth and power mounted, so did his audacity. He grew tired of needing to renew his franchises at ten-year intervals. He sought now what the opposition newspapers called "eternal franchises." These would extend his monopoly over the Chicago streets for another fifty years, and such a guaranteed franchise would make his streetcar companies of inestimable value in case he wished to market them to another owner. Secretly, he did have exactly such a plan in mind, for he was weary of Chicago, where he felt that too many of the local newspaper editors were determined to "sandbag" him. Also, the angry voters seemed slowly but steadily to be gathering power via civic reform associations—with him and his streetcar lines as chief targets. That potential threat aside, Yerkes had gotten everything he asked for except his fifty-year franchises, which could not be granted locally without a change in the state law forbidding such practices. The financier's next move was clear: he must find a way to remove this challenge.

Meanwhile, Yerkes's personal life became as notorious as his business methods, and this turmoil was duly reflected, fictionally, in *The Titan* as Dreiser portrayed the growing estrangement between Frank and Aileen Cowperwood. In shaking the dust of Philadelphia from his boots and moving to a newer, more accepting midwestern context, Yerkes had entered a world that as yet was taking shape, one where most members of society were relative newcomers. Because many were escaping from past failures and problems, few embarrassing questions were asked about any newcomer's past life. It was a new opportunity for the ex-convict from the East, which Charles Yerkes was, after all, despite his riches. Not only did he have a chance to make a fresh start in business but potentially to become a civic leader as well. Anything was possible. Yerkes had divorced his first wife, married his young Philadelphia mistress, and built a new mansion in Chicago, thereby hoping to enter Chicago society on its upper rungs. But this did not happen, in part because divorce was too much frowned upon socially and because his wife, who had been depicted as **Aileen Butler** in *The Financier*, was considered too brash, too vulgar—and too dangerously beautiful—to find ready acceptance among the older, more staid wives in the moneyed classes whose approval he sought.

Even more important perhaps was the fact that as Yerkes, a fierce competitor, forced his way up on the local business scene; he had stepped on too many important toes and worked too many shady deals against well-entrenched Chicago leaders, men who had the potential to deny him what he most craved. With triumph in business as his most immediate obsession, he had neglected personal relationships that, when he turned to the social world for approbation, turned out to be decisive. He had been overly certain that his new trophy wife would make a favorable impression on society forceful enough to override important Chicagoans' concerns about his unscrupulous business tactics. But the wives of industrial rivals whom he had whipped with underhanded or savage methods were not about to entertain the Yerkeses or to attend the lavish open-house entertainments held in the sumptuous new Yerkes home on Michigan Avenue. In Chicago the Cowperwoods, standing in fictionally for Yerkes and his wife, are frozen out.

Consequently, Frank Cowperwood comes to blame Aileen for his difficulty, feeling that she has failed to serve her purpose. In his frustration and also as a consequence of his naturally sybaritic personality, Cowperwood strays from his marriage to initiate a series of extramarital sexual affairs. Some of these dalliances rather foolishly involve wives and daughters of other business leaders, which only increases the opposition to him. Yerkes had been a notorious womanizer, and Dreiser in *The Titan* not only portrays this licentiousness but exaggerates both the number and the seriousness of Cowperwood's affairs, so much so that the literary critic **Stuart P. Sherman** was led, in a famous attack, to charge that Dreiser's novel resembled a mammoth club sandwich composed of alternating layers of business and sex. The description was not far off the mark, although it was not intended as any compliment.

The principal upshot of these numerous sexual affairs is to cause the estrangement of Mrs. Cowperwood. At one point, in fact, Aileen is so enraged with Frank's duplicity that she attacks a rival physically. Both Cowperwoods realize that their marriage is in serious trouble, and in antagonizing Aileen, Frank weakens the one bastion of support that heretofore he could depend on unequivocally. Undeterred, the financier on a trip to Kentucky meets the lovely and protected **Berenice Fleming**, the teenage daughter of a woman who keeps a brothel. Cowperwood is smitten. He now visualizes in Berenice his ideal woman. With her mother's cooperation, Berenice is put into a private school where she can be groomed for the day that Cowperwood will be free of Aileen, who has taken to drink and whom he now views as a useless failure. He plans some day to marry Berenice and with her achieve his obsessive desire to conquer the social world.

What Cowperwood schemes to do eventually is precisely what his real-life model had done: dump his streetcar lines on another entrepreneur for an immense sum and with the resultant millions invade New York, escaping to what he envisions as being far greener pastures, a place where his desire to bestride the city both financially and socially can reach fulfillment. Even before abandoning the Midwest, Yerkes had built a new mansion in New York, a palace costing $2 million. Dreiser's Cowperwood does the same. As a sop to Chicago and as a distraction from his true aims, Cowperwood, like Yerkes, gives the city an elaborate electric fountain and then the largest telescope in the world along with the observatory to house it. His wish is eventually to be known not as a robber baron but as a philanthropist. The telescope, housed in the Yerkes Observatory at Lake Geneva, Wisconsin, is the only public gift to survive Yerkes into our own time.

In his final, all-out attempt to assure long-term franchises, Cowperwood sets up an office in the state capital, Springfield, and proceeds to bribe the legislators as blatantly as he had bought the City Council in Chicago. A bill permitting cities to issue long-term franchises is passed, but it is vetoed by an honest governor, whose character Dreiser based upon John P. Altgeld, an honest politician to whom Yerkes had offered a million-dollar bribe merely to sign the bill into law. Failing to obtain his preferential law, Frank Cowperwood bulls his way ahead. Still retaining ownership of his traction companies, he carries out his plan to abandon Chicago for New York, moving with Aileen to the new mansion on "Millionaires Row." Aileen remains an unhappy, rejected spouse, and, discovering Frank's alliance with Berenice Fleming, she attempts suicide.

Meanwhile, Illinois has elected a new governor, one less ethical and more amenable to Cowperwood's wishes. He signs into law the state bill allowing municipalities to issue long-term franchises. The issue then boils down to the City Council's willingness or ability to pass an ordinance granting Cowperwood "eternal" dominion over Chicago streets. What once had seemed an easy task turns into a difficulty because of the rapid rise of citizen reform groups that join with outraged newspapers and rival financiers in opposing Cowperwood's plan to work his will through the corrupt aldermen. Cowperwood returns to Chicago, mustering all of his legal and political power for an 1898 meeting of the City Council, where the franchise issue is to be voted on. Angry citizens, sensing a new, united strength and motivated by zeal for reform, pack the visitors' galleries. Some dangle nooses from the balconies and noisily challenge their aldermen individually to vote in favor of the franchises *if they dare*. Faced with the realistic prospect of losing their elective seats, the aldermen desert Cowperwood and vote to reject his franchise ordinance. In defeat, the financier can do nothing but leave Chicago, hoping to unload his streetcar lines at a good, if not exorbitant, price. He has been beaten, but he is far from whipped and certainly is not discouraged. In his moment of need, Berenice, now of legal age, comes to join him, and he feels confident that in the not

too distant future, with her at his side in place of Aileen, he will realize all of his ambitions, financial as well as social. Again, the continuing story of Frank Cowperwood in its broad outlines and in most of its details follows the record established by Charles Yerkes.

In 1912 **Harper & Brothers** had rushed *The Financier* into print as soon as Dreiser delivered the manuscript. Not so with *The Titan*. In the two years between 1912 and 1914, the threat of official **censorship** had grown apace in America, and *The Titan*, with its extended series of close-to-explicit scenes of passion, made the publisher quake. Added to this was the fact that by 1914, although both Mr. and Mrs. Yerkes were dead, **Emilie Grigsby**, the actual "Berenice," was very much alive, had powerful allies, and was in a position to sue for libel. Harper's could not stand the pressure. Dreiser's book had been set up in print and was all but ready to be issued when the decision was made not to publish. Dreiser was in misery and did not know which way to turn when the English publisher **John Lane**, newly establishing an American branch, agreed to take *The Titan*. Only a change of title page was necessary before the novel could be bound and sent to bookstores.

Once published, *The Titan* served to confirm various emerging opinions of Dreiser as a novelist. Detractors said that the book was uncomfortable, offensive, nasty, even loathsome, but it was also said to be wonderfully complete, big and terrible in its effects, and more urbane and cultured than any of Dreiser's previous efforts. The range went from a condemnation of *The Titan* as more contemptible than pornography to a vision of the novel as a sermon. That the book helped establish Dreiser as a leading novelist is undeniable, and Allen Updegraff said in the *Baltimore News* that the writer's "big, square sentences were never piled upon each other to better effect" (rpt. in Salzman 180).

Further Reading

Gerber, Philip. "Financier, Titan, and Stoic: *A Trilogy of Desire.*" *Theodore Dreiser.* New York: Twayne, 1964. 87–110.

Hussman, Lawrence E., Jr. *Dreiser and His Fiction: A Twentieth-Century Quest.* Philadelphia: University of Pennsylvania Press, 1983. 70–90.

Lehan, Richard. "*The Financier, The Titan,* and *The Stoic.*" *Theodore Dreiser: His World and His Novels.* Carbondale: Southern Illinois University Press, 1969. 97–116.

Matthiessen, F. O. "The Business Novel." *Theodore Dreiser.* New York: William Sloane, 1951. 127–58.

Millgate, Michael. "Theodore Dreiser and the American Financier." *Studi americani* 7 (1961): 133–45.

O'Neill, John. "The Disproportion of Sadness: Dreiser's *The Financier* and *The Titan.*" *Modern Fiction Studies* 23 (1977): 409–22.

Pizer, Donald. "*The Titan.*" *The Novels of Theodore Dreiser: A Critical Study.* Minneapolis: University of Minnesota Press, 1976. 183–200.

Philip Gerber

"THE TITHE OF THE LORD." *Esquire* published "The Tithe of the Lord" in its July 1938 issue, calling it "fiction" and placing the following comment directly under the story's title: "It might have been conscience, or superstition, but some power guided Benziger after his strange contract." Thus, the unequivocally religious tone of the title is balanced by this editorial caption, something *Esquire*, with its hedonistic reputation and its stated policy of seeking from other magazine editors manuscripts "that seemed too daring or different for them to use," no doubt felt compelled to do.

For his structure in this, his last-published short story, Dreiser drew upon certain personal sketches he was writing during the 1930s, especially upon "A Start in Life," a piece that had come out four years earlier in *Scribner's*. Presented as a first-person narration by one not directly involved in the action, "The Tithe of the Lord" offers a more sophisticated version of the narrative method of "A Start in Life," increasing the number of narrators to three and having them respond in more pointed fashion to the ups and downs of Benziger's life. The story is told by a certain Lamborn, one who is "identified with shipping interests" and who recounts events as he hears them consecutively from two other acquaintances of Benziger. The first of these, an architect named Kelcey, provides the details of Benziger's life up to the point of his decision to turn to **religion**; Lamborn receives the particulars of Benziger's later experience from the banker Henneberry.

Kelcey is particularly intrigued by Benziger's conversion. The latter has been a successful businessman and happily married to Rhonda, a beautiful and undemanding wife, but when he becomes involved with Olive, the wife of his close friend Calvin Ellis, Rhonda takes her own life. Subsequently, Benziger experiences a drastic business and personal decline and finds himself in a hand-to-mouth existence. Struck by the message on a religious pamphlet and by the surprise appearance of a handsome young man who offers him food and drink before mysteriously disappearing, Benziger resolves to strike a bargain with God: if he is successful once more, he will amend his life and give 10 percent of his earnings to further the Lord's work on earth.

Henneberry chronicles Benziger's life after the conversion: his ascent to power in the Wickerware Trust; his marriage to a new wife, Rose; his attempts to be faithful to his bargain by establishing charitable works; his marital infidelities; and the troubles encountered in his business. Henneberry's tale elicits much more response from Lamborn, and the story ends with a philosophical dialogue about the implications of Benziger's conversion and second fall. There is a broad consensus between the two as to the existence of a higher force, although neither defines that force in an exact way. Dreiser's last-published short story thus has something of the religious affirmation of his final novel, *The Bulwark*.

Further Reading

Griffin, Joseph P. "Dreiser's Later Short Stories." *Dreiser Newsletter* 9.1 (1978): 5–10.

Joseph P. Griffin

TJADER, MARGUERITE (HARRIS)

(1901–1986), served as a typist, amanuensis, and love interest for Dreiser during several periods of his life after the two met in 1928 at a small dinner party in his New York apartment. At the time of their meeting, Dreiser was in his late fifties, and Tjader was in her late twenties and married to attorney Overton (Tony) Harris, whom she divorced in 1933.

In significant part stemming from Dreiser's inspiration, Tjader also became an active player in the arts and politics. She published an impressive, though since neglected, novel, *Borealis*, in 1930. Its story, set in Sweden, traces the development of its heroine, Signe, from adolescence to womanhood and from a burgeoning interest in the erotic to a series of tragic love affairs. Dreiser was favorably disposed toward Tjader's achievement in exposing, through *Borealis*, the woman's view, or at least one woman's view of untrammeled sexuality.

From the late 1930s to the early 1040s, Tjader edited a leftist, "antifascist" journal that she founded, *Direction*. Its distin-

guished list of contributing writers and artists included, in addition to Dreiser, John Dos Passos, **Sherwood Anderson**, Ernest Hemingway, Erskine Caldwell, Richard Wright, Ralph Ellison, Carl Sandburg, Paul Tillich, Berthold Brecht, Charlie Chaplin, Van Wyck Brooks, and many others. Several of the journal's rotating editors were admitted communists or "fellow travelers."

Tjader played her most significant role in Dreiser's career during its final two years. In 1944, when the novelist was living in Los Angeles with Helen Richardson, he summoned Tjader to help him finish his long gestating novel *The Bulwark*. The two worked together to complete the book for what became its posthumous publication in 1946. The editing process took a highly complicated and contentious turn with Tjader, Helen, **Louise Campbell**, **James T. Farrell**, and finally Doubleday associate editor **Donald B. Elder** exerting varying degrees of influence on Dreiser. Most critics and scholars judge Elder to have been the prime shaper of the ultimate product.

After Dreiser's death, Tjader continued to write and in 1965 published *Theodore Dreiser: A New Dimension*, a book that provided a unique perspective on the novelist's state of mind during its final phase. She argues in the book that Dreiser's late spiritual affirmation was indeed genuine and that it represented the culmination of a lifelong struggle to believe. A decade later, she collaborated with the academic scholar John McAleer in structuring and editing Dreiser's massive collection of philosophical essays and fragments, *Notes on Life*, which was published in 1974. The novelist had left this mountain of miscellany only roughly organized at his death.

Tjader also published two books on religious subjects, *Mother Elisabeth* (1972) and *Birgitta of Sweden* (1980). She spent her last years living in a carriage house on the grounds of her family's Darien, Connecticut, estate, Vikingsborg, which she had donated to an order of Swedish nuns. They had established a convent there. A short memoir, *Love That Will Not Let Me Go: My Time with Theodore Dreiser*, describing her relationship with the novelist, their work together on *The Bulwark*, his friendships with **John Cowper Powys** and others, her feelings toward Helen, and various related subjects, was published a dozen years after her death, in 1998.

To what extent Tjader influenced Dreiser's late-in-life spiritual sea change and the ultimate affirming message of *The Bulwark* has always been a matter of conjecture among Dreiser critics and scholars. She had become a Roman Catholic during the 1930s after having grown up in a Swedish American family whose head was a charismatic Free Church preacher. Richard Tjader, along with his wife, Margaret, established the Church of the Strangers early in the century in New York City. Marguerite had become quite devout in her Catholicism by the time she joined Dreiser in Los Angeles to assist in the completion of *The Bulwark*. Just how much her enthusiasm for her faith prompted her to urge Dreiser in religious directions and the degree of his willingness to be urged will probably never be known.

Further Reading

Hussman, Lawrence E. "My Time With Marguerite Tjader." *Dreiser Studies* 29 (1998): 3–17.
Tjader, Marguerite. "Airmail Interview." *Dreiser Newsletter* 2.2 (1971): 11–17.
                    Lawrence E. Hussman

"THE TOIL OF THE LABORER." First published in the *New York Call* in July 1913 and reprinted in *Hey Rub-a-Dub-Dub*, the essay is subtitled "A Trilogy" and is organized into three parts, each of which describes Dreiser's largely negative experiences as a laborer. The first section, beginning "The toil of the laborer is artless," considers the ironic absence of color and form in the labor of construction workers, who themselves create color and form. In the second section, beginning, "The toil of the laborer is thoughtless," Dreiser examines his experience working in a lumber factory to speculate about why workers seem unreflective. In this section, Dreiser also considers whether the disparity between work and rewards for workers and owners is necessary, a part of the variety that characterizes Nature. Dreiser begins the third section by noting, "The toil of the laborer is without mercy," and he describes his experiences working for the railroad. Unlike the first two sections, which are philosophical and abstract, the third section is grounded in detail and follows a narrative, as Dreiser is promoted from unskilled laborer to foreman, ultimately quitting because of his divided loyalty between the owners and workers.

Like the posthumously published *An Amateur Laborer*, from which it is reworked, "The Toil of the Laborer" originated in Dreiser's experiences during 1903, when he worked as a laborer to recuperate from a mental breakdown. Despite an uncharacteristically taut structure and style, the essay serves as a record of Dreiser's thought process during his early career. The first section emphasizes the distinction between process and product, for it is in the process of making that the worker is immersed in a colorless world of disorder, while the unseen product of his toil is itself full of "color, form, tone, beauty." Perspective here is everything; Dreiser has the broader artistic temperament to see order, which the other workers lack. Like the ants in "McEwen of the Shining Slave Makers," the workers participate in society without being able to articulate their roles, and in the third section, Dreiser, working as a foreman, describes the men working for him as "running about like ants." In the second section Dreiser again finds that despite his status as a laborer, his ability to contemplate the diversity of life gives him "the privilege of but a few." He again links society with Nature, wondering if "in spite of the seeming injustice involved in this situation, variety was as essential to happiness as so-called justice or equation, and that the very inequalities I was bemoaning were the things which I was admiring in Nature." Dreiser's decision to quit his job as foreman, however, shows his ambivalence about possessing any special privilege. Together, the three sections provide an insight into Dreiser's view of society's structure, its injustices, and his own conceptions of himself as a writer. Though he can side comfortably neither with the thoughtlessness of the workers nor with the unearned and privileged position of the owners, he struggles to bring together these differing perspectives as a way of understanding his role as a writer.

Further Reading

Brennan, Stephen C. "Theodore Dreiser's *An Amateur Laborer:* A Myth in the Making." *American Literary Realism* 19.2 (1987): 66–84.

David T. Humphries

"THE TOILERS OF THE TENEMENTS." *See* "The Tenement Toilers."

"THE TRACK WALKER." Originally published in the *New York Daily News* (3 April 1904) as "The Story of a Human Nine-Pin" before being reprinted in *Tom Watson's Magazine* (May 1905) as "The Track Walker" and subsequently included in *The Color of a Great City*, this brief sketch focuses, like "The Sandwich Man" and "The Men in the Storm" and others in the collection, on a group of people whose work is vital to the city and yet who remain mostly anonymous, scarcely noticed by those who walk or ride by them on their way to work or entertainment. Here Dreiser refers to a group in the singular, the track walker, the man who risks his life to inspect the many miles of subway rails that lie beneath the city of New York, in all kinds of weather and at great risk to himself. "If he were not watchful," Dreiser writes, "if he did not perform his work carefully and well, if he had a touch of malice or a feeling of vengefulness, he could wreck your train, mangle your body and send you praying and screaming to your Maker," yet the track walker is in continual danger of his own life. Dreiser goes on to describe the noise, the smoke, and the dim lighting that narrow his chances of hearing or seeing the next train in time to avoid it and the small pockets in the walls that sometimes provide a place of safety, yet so near the train that the dust and grime from the wheels spatter over him. But for all the power these men hold over the commuters of the city, Dreiser notes, the work they do is not considered especially valuable. The usual rate is thirty to thirty-five cents an hour, for ten to twelve hours' work each day, and when one is killed, scarcely a line or two appears in the daily papers. The sketch ends with less detachment and a stronger indictment than most in the book: "Rough necessity, a sense of duty, and behold, we are as bricks and stones, to be put anywhere in the wall, at the bottom of the foundation in the dark, or at the top in the light. And who chooses for us?"

Nancy McIlvaine Donovan

TRAGIC AMERICA. Published in December 1931 by **Horace Liveright**, *Tragic America* marks an important transition in Dreiser's progression toward communism. Though released only three years after

Dreiser Looks at Russia, in which Dreiser expressed both a sympathy for communism but also a faith in the power of economic individualism, *Tragic America* angrily condemns **capitalism** as a wasteful, corrupt, and dehumanizing construct. After visiting some of America's most economically depressed and socially troubled areas after the onset of the Great Depression, Dreiser came to believe that the only solution for America's problems was to rewrite the Constitution and to tear down the existing economic framework, with the intention of securing equitable treatment for the masses. In *Tragic America*, Dreiser aims to win converts to these viewpoints by cataloging a variety of social crises, abuses of power, and scandals and then proffering Soviet-style government as a solution.

Dreiser begins *Tragic America* by recounting his visits to the New Jersey mill towns of Passaic and Paterson. There, Dreiser found evidence of the worst kinds of capitalist oppression: a police force and a press essentially in the employ of industrialists; the deplorable living conditions of the underpaid workers; and a government, ostensibly bought out by moneyed interests, actively opposed to strike activities. Dreiser also mentions his October 1931 visit to **Harlan County**, Kentucky, during which he was indicted by local officials for adultery and for attempting to "promulgate a reign of terror." Dreiser draws from these experiences the conclusion that the ruinous influence of capitalism on the everyday lives of workers is simply unacceptable and also that attempting to fight capitalist abuses via the capitalist social structure was impossible.

Many of *Tragic America*'s chapters are dedicated to proving that the capitalist stranglehold on the conduits of power was unbreakable, and in many cases, Dreiser's chapter titles indicate the nature of his indictment of government and corporate corruption. Chapter headings such as "The Supreme Court as a Corporate-Minded Institution," "Government Operation of the Express Companies for Private Profit," and "Our Banks and Corporations as Government" convey the thrust of Dreiser's ideas. Later chapters, which discuss in greater detail the corruption of local, state, and federal police, the subterfuge of charities, and the wealthy and complaisant organized churches, round out Dreiser's portrait of an America where the common people had little chance in the face of the heartless oppression of the ruling oligarchy.

During his tour of the Soviet Union three years earlier, Dreiser had actively argued with his hosts on the behalf of the great American capitalists, such as Rockefeller and Vanderbilt, stressing the importance of their mental abilities in taming an untapped wilderness and developing the techniques of production. In *Tragic America*, Dreiser emphatically refutes these arguments, apparently strongly influenced by Gustavus Myers's *History of the Great American Fortunes* (1910), and he states that the great wealth and industrial empires built by American magnates were essentially stolen from the people. At great length, Dreiser describes how, since the very beginnings of the American nation, moneyed entities, with cooperation of the government, had obtained possession of priceless resources. Furthermore, Dreiser alleges that these same entities, evolving into corporate trusts, not only failed to pay back the debts incurred acquiring these resources but instead used their privileged positions to tax the people through price fixing and tax indemnities. Thus, the Vanderbilts and Rockefellers of American history, in Dreiser's opinion, were no longer heroes but thieves, assisted by a complicit government.

At the end of *Tragic America*, Dreiser suggests the only solution that would be able to defeat the forces of collusion and corruption: government ownership of the forces of production. Because reform via the ballot box is impossible, Dreiser claims, the masses must reeducate themselves and create an "executive power for the American working masses" that would have "as its sole motivation the well-being of all people." This executive power would abolish private property, confiscating private homes and appropriating private fortunes, and enjoy "full law-making authority, so as to be able to legislate, and quickly, as circumstances might warrant." Dreiser seemed to understand the paradox of his proposal, for he writes, "The source of this [new] government authority constitutes a very difficult problem, because by and large the people . . . let whoever will—priest, political demagogue, corporation executive, arresting and fascinating individuals out of nowhere—tell them anything or everything," yet he nonetheless insists that for any meaningful reform to take place, "the masses [must] build themselves new institutions." One grasps that Dreiser himself, despite his pleas, is not convinced such an event is likely.

Because Dreiser had written in *Dreiser Looks at Russia*, "I am an incorrigible individualist—therefore opposed to Communism," it is possible to interpret his rapprochement with communism as a repudiation of individualism. However, a closer reading of *Tragic America* indicates that Dreiser still saw himself as a champion of the individual but had decided that capitalism was the true enemy of the individual. Statements such as "the holding companies and the like grow stronger while the individual grows weaker, mentally as well as economically," show that by the 1930s, Dreiser's belief in individualism led him to oppose not communism but capitalism.

Nonetheless, Dreiser's official dealings with the radical Left remained desultory. The year before the publication of *Tragic America*, Dreiser had visited Harlan County on the request of the American Communist Party, though his application to the party had been denied. He continued to advocate a Soviet-style government for the United States and entertained the notion of organizing study groups to examine *Tragic America*, as others had studied the works of John Reed. Yet Dreiser's ongoing negotiations with publishers and production studios were scarcely the actions of a communist, the visits to labor hot spots at the bequest of the Communist Party ended, and Dreiser's next novel was not a Marxist drama, but *The Stoic*, the third volume of Dreiser's trilogy about financier **Frank Cowperwood**. If Dreiser became a communist during this period, he created his own particular brand of communism.

Tragic America was not a success for Dreiser. The book sold only 4,600 copies in its first year, there were scattered reports of **censorship**, and the critical reception was tepid. Furthermore, *Tragic America* signaled a trend toward radical politics, an unpopular subject for the newspapers and magazines that had published many of Dreiser's articles in the 1920s, and the subsequent lack of income exacerbated the financial woes that afflicted Dreiser in the 1930s.

Further Reading

Hirsh, John C. "*Tragic America*: Dreiser's American Communism and a General Motors Executive." *Dreiser Newsletter* 13.1 (1982): 10–16.

Stephen Brain

TRANSCENDENTALISM. Though Dreiser is usually regarded as a writer of **realism** and **naturalism**, it must not be forgotten (though it sometimes is) that he was also a poet—and even a transcendentalist poet. In the middle of his career, in 1926, he published a collection of poems entitled *Moods: Cadenced and Declaimed*. As Walt Whitman did with his *Leaves of Grass*, he kept revising it, enlarging and enriching it. Two other editions appeared in 1928 and 1935, which shows how much he prized it. In 1935, the title became *Moods: Philosophical and Emotional (Cadenced and Declaimed)*. In these poems, he describes social phenomena from a materialistic point of view with the detachment of a scientist, but in them he also expresses the wonder of a child or a poet before the mystery of the world. In the poem entitled "Wood Notes," for instance, he concludes a brief sketch with lines that suggest a mysterious spiritual presence in the woods and the unreality of matter: "Of what vast deep is this the echo? / Of what old dreams the answer?" And in the poem "All in All," God is present in all things and in the humblest of men: "God / To my astonishment / Is shining my shoes / He has taken the form, / In part, / Of an Italian shoe black / Who is eager to earn a dime."

Though, like Emerson, he had moments of doubt, they were only "moods," and he succeeded in transcending them; in other poems, such as "The Hidden God," he prays to the "hidden God" and worships him with the fervor of a true transcendentalist: "Yet I must pray— / Pray. / And do. / I lift up my hands. / I kneel. / I seek in my heart / Because I must— / Must, / But of whom? / To Whom? / Whom?" Like the transcendentalists, Dreiser was keenly aware of the mysterious presence beyond (i.e., "trans") appearances, of something mysterious that es-

capes his senses, as he noted in "The Image of Our Dreams": "Beyond this seeming substance / Of reality . . . / Picturing something / Seeking something / The image of our dreams." In poems like "Protoplast," the world is "[a] substance that is not flesh / Or thought / Or Reality" but is rather "[t]he dream, mayhap, / Of something that is eternal." He worships life in all its forms "as it is," to take up the very words he used to define his realism (which shows there is no fundamental incompatibility between his transcendentalism and his naturalism).

"All things," he also wrote to a graduate student in 1940, "are emanations and evolutions of cosmic forces and cosmic law. Buddha and Mary Baker Eddy affirmed an *over* or *one* universal soul, itself *being* and so *containing* all wisdom and all creative power. Modern science sees no other answer than this, but it is not willing to affirm it" (*Letters* 3: 887). In poems such as "In a Country Graveyard," Emerson's "oversoul" becomes identified with energy as conceived by modern physicists: "Energy / Color, / Form, / Tone, / Mingle and make 'Life.' " This dynamic vitalism leads to a wish to live rather than expiate, to self-reliance and the exaltation of the individual. Consequently, like Emerson, he praised "representative men": "Most people are not capable of expressing their feelings," he notes toward the end of *Sister Carrie*. "They depend upon others. That is what genius is for." His **Frank Cowperwood** is such a man, "a kind of superman," "a significant individual," "doing what his instincts tell him to do," as he writes toward the end of *The Titan*.

This resemblance between Emerson's transcendentalism and Dreiser's philosophy is not accidental. In his youth, Dreiser read Emerson's works with passion, and in 1939 he enthusiastically agreed to contribute an introduction to *The Living Thoughts of Thoreau.* As he explained to **Edgar Lee Masters**, who was similarly "presenting" *The Living Thoughts of Emerson* (1940): "I felt . . . that I had gotten together a body of real thought most valuable to me if no other" (*Letters* 3: 874).

His autobiography *Dawn* shows that he had an innate sense of the mystery and beauty of the physical world, but transcendentalism no doubt reinforced it, and his mysticism illuminates not only his poems but also his so-called naturalistic novels. It resonates even in *An American Tragedy* which is probably the most prosaic of his books. In this novel we do not always see "life as it is" but rather life as it appears to the wondering eyes of Clyde Griffiths. Reality often gives place to dreams of beauty, wealth, and pleasure. No wonder the original title of the novel was to be "Mirage," a strange title for a naturalistic study.

Dreiser, besides, is not interested in his characters as individuals but rather as forces that move forward and come into conflict with other forces, but they have no idiosyncrasies, no minor traits. They constantly aspire to something beyond the workaday world in which they are caught. They crave a fuller life, beauty, something that they cannot define but in whose existence they firmly believe. In *Sister Carrie* in particular, Dreiser again and again suggests "that constant drag to something better" that Carrie feels so strongly. She is a transcendentalist poet in her own silent way when she rocks in her chair and dreams. "Oh, Carrie, Carrie!" Dreiser apostrophizes. "Oh, blind striving of the human heart! Onward; onward, it saith, and where beauty leads, it follows." She yields to "the lure of the spirit."

Thus, Dreiser, instead of minutely describing the more or less sordid background of his characters, again and again allows himself to be carried away by his imagination, and his imagination is the poetic faculty Coleridge calls "esemplastic power" in *Biographia Literaria* and what Wordsworth describes in "Peele Castle" as "the gleam, / The light that never was, on sea or land. / The consecration, and the Poet's dream." Dreiser used nearly the same words in "The Ascent" when he referred to "The high suggestion of a world that never was / On earth or sea."

Thanks to the intervention of this quasi-mystical faculty, when we read Dreiser's novels, we are frequently reminded of the cosmic context of his characters' lives. We are not allowed to forget the presence of an infinite and mysterious universe in the background. Carrie sits in her rocking chair "looking out upon the night and streets in silent wonder." On another occasion, "she tripped along, the clear sky pouring liquid blue into her soul."

Dreiser is in several respects a belated transcendentalist in his naturalistic fiction as well as in his poems. Without this poetical power, his works would be nothing but dull, naturalistic descriptions of American life. He sings and celebrates humanity and the presence in us of irresistible forces at work in the world beyond material appearances. His transcendentalism is to a large extent the true source of his greatness.

Further Reading

Asselineau, Roger. *The Transcendentalist Constant in American Literature.* New York: New York University Press, 1980.

Frothingham, Octavius Brooks. *Transcendentalism in New England: A History.* New York: Harper, 1959.

Roger Asselineau

A TRAVELER AT FORTY. Published on 25 November 1913 by the Century Company and illustrated by William Glackens, *A*

Traveler at Forty is the record of Dreiser's first voyage to Europe and his grand tour through England, France, Italy, Switzerland, Germany, the Netherlands, and Belgium. As the reviewer for the *Philadelphia North American* observed, though a book of travel, it deals "with people rather than places" (rpt. in Salzman 147) and reveals much about Dreiser himself and European society shortly before World War I. The travelogue is thus important first as an autobiographical narrative and a realist writer's slice of life and second, although it became standard reading on transatlantic ocean liners, as a travel guide to Europe.

Arranged immediately after the publication of *Jennie Gerhardt* in October 1911, the journey from 22 November to 23 April 1912, which Dreiser later praised as "a tonic that lasted me for years" (Dudley 284), was not planned for mere pleasure but to continue his investigations of the life of **Charles T. Yerkes**, the model for **Frank Cowperwood** in *The Trilogy of Desire*, who in his final years had been engaged in trying to gain control of the London subway system. The travel book opens at this crucial juncture in the author's life, intimately acquainting the reader with its writer, his literary and philosophical views, and his financial and artistic dilemmas. At this point his English publisher and friend **Grant Richards**, who is disguised as "Barfleur" in the 1913 edition and to whom Dreiser dedicates the book, enters the scene, invites the author to accompany him to England, and proposes to organize his European tour. Richards, who owned a firm bearing his name, succeeds in helping the author to extract from **Harper & Brothers** a $2,000 advance for *The Financier* and in convincing his friends at the Century Company to commission three articles about his impressions of Europe and to offer an option on

any book Dreiser might write about his trip.

Serving two publishers and his own plans for a novel, Dreiser at times finds it difficult to reconcile the varying obligations and conflicting expectations. While the pleasant style smoothes over some of the more difficult moments in the journey and not infrequently contributes humorous and self-ironic passages, Dreiser makes use of this special situation as an underlying pattern for the book. Though seeing Europe at the age of forty, he poses as an American innocent abroad, marveling at the European sights and questioning European mores from the point of view of a much younger person. His youthful image is contrasted with the knowing, overly wise, and fatherly manner of his English friend. The book thus relies strongly on an inbred subversive opposition between child and parent, pupil and teacher, author and publisher, American and Englishman, "raw American force" and European refinement, New World and Old World. This oppositional nexus combines with a contrast of values—youth and age, curiosity and knowledge, quest and experience, experiment and established order. It informs the tenor of numerous conversations and structures Dreiser's presentation, which is never forgetful of its starting place, America. Unbiased, the traveling author emerges both as a critic and as an advocate of the manners and peoples on the two sides of the Atlantic.

The passage on board the *Mauretania* furnishes Dreiser with an opportunity to review closely the passengers on board and to provide some romantic interest by beginning an affair with a young English actress. A first-class passenger, the realist writer also descends to the lower decks of the ship and, in the manner of Zola, provides a detailed description of the steamer and its engine room and of a conversation with the chief engineer. Similarly, visits to Richards's country home (including an English Christmas) and London drawing rooms, conversations with critics, art experts, and a member of Parliament, and attendance at a court session are balanced by a morning in a public washhouse and an evening with a prostitute. The south of England is contrasted with the north as he goes to Manchester and its surrounding manufacturing towns, where he talks with businessmen and investigates the life of the workers. Here, as elsewhere in his travelogue, in a truly democratic spirit, but also with the naturalist's dissecting eye, Dreiser glances at all levels of society: he depicts a gardener, a housemaid, and an old, poverty-stricken woman as well as the gentlemen and the ladies of high society.

Together with Richards he crosses the channel to France and delights in Paris, its nightlife, its bars, its demimonde, and its art museums; his point of reference remains all the while America, especially New York. He compares the Seine to the Harlem River, and he comments on the Tuileries: "No such charm and beauty could be attained in America because we would not permit the public use of the nude in this fashion. . . . I was astonished to find how much of the heart of Paris is devoted to public usage in this manner. It corresponds, in theory at least, to the space devoted to Central Park in New York"; or on the Parisians: "We have enormous crowds in New York, but they seem to be going somewhere very much more definitely than in Paris." From such observations he later develops a distinction between the American work ethic and the French joie de vivre.

Proceeding to the Riviera with Richards and his Irish friend, nicknamed Sir Scorp (Sir Hugh Lane), Dreiser indulges in the world of gaming tables at the casinos in Monte Carlo and Nice. Alone, he travels on to Rome, where he meets Richards's mother, who is wintering there, and where he is "tremendously impressed with the wonder of a life that is utterly gone." While he learns the history of the Borgias from an American lady companion, Mrs. Q. (Rella Abell Armstrong), and "follow[s] dutifully" his Roman guide, the art historian Signor Tani, the wealth of art and historical detail taxes his capacity as a viewer. After a disappointing audience at the Vatican, since the pope pays no attention to him, he nevertheless concludes, "I was very glad I had come." The sojourn in Italy, more than anywhere else, deepens his sense of history and of the importance of individuals: "In the particular period in which Florence, and all Italy for that matter, was so remarkable, Italy was alive with ambitious men—strong, remarkable, capable characters. *They* made the wonder of the life, it was not the architecture that did it and not the routine movements of the people."

Entering Germany via Switzerland and Lucerne, he focuses his visit on three cities, Frankfurt, where he attends a concert of a London acquaintance, Madame A. (Julia Culp); Mayen, his father's hometown; and Berlin, the German capital and home of Madame Culp. Examining national stereotypes wherever he goes, Germany is presented in very ambiguous terms; for Dreiser it has "any number of defects of temperament," illustrated by the pervasive military air and "Teutonic bursts of temper," and yet it has "virtues and capacities so noteworthy, admirable and advantageous that the whole world may well sit up and take notice." The home of his ancestors, Mayen makes "a deep impression" on him: "It was like entering the shell of some great mollusc that had long since died, to enter this walled town." Berlin with its pompous architecture, "blunderheaded, vainglorious," earns his criticism, but here again he gains access to various social strata. He seeks to know the city from the point of view of a typical Prussian businessman, of an elderly housekeeper, and of the famous singer Madame Culp, but also from the story of a Berlin near-prostitute, Hanscha Jauer, with whom he has a brief and touching affair (and which he had to omit from the published book).

The trip ends with short stays mainly devoted to sightseeing in Amsterdam, Haarlem, Bruges, Ghent, and Brussels and, in full circle, a return via Paris to London and to the country home of his publisher friend. Crossing the Atlantic on the *Kroonland,* Dreiser describes the passengers' reactions to the news of the sinking of the *Titanic,* which they receive in midocean and which instills in the traveler a heightened sense of homecoming when he finds himself walking once more on Broadway.

Despite a warm reception and steady sales, the complete text of *A Traveler at Forty,* housed in the Dreiser Papers at the University of Pennsylvania, has yet to be published in full.

Further Reading

Bardeleben, Renate von. "Dreiser's Diaristic Mode." *Dreiser Studies* 31.1 (2000): 26–42.
———. "Dreiser's English Virgil." *Literatur im Kontext—Literature in Context.* Ed. Joachim Schwend et al. Frankfurt am Main: Peter Lang, 1992. 345–71.
———. "From Travel Guide to Autobiography: Recovering the Original of *A Traveler at Forty." Theodore Dreiser and American Culture: New Readings.* Ed Yoshinobu Hakutani. Newark: University of Delaware Press, 2000. 177–86.
Riggio, Thomas P. "Europe without Baedeker: The Omitted Hanscha Jower Story—from *A Traveler at Forty." Modern Fiction Studies* 23 (1977): 423–40.

Renate von Bardeleben

A TRILOGY OF DESIRE. See The Financier; The Titan; The Stoic.

"TRUE ART SPEAKS PLAINLY." This brief (450-word) essay, originally published in *Booklovers Magazine* in February 1903 and widely reprinted since then, is Dreiser's principal contribution to the debate over the propriety of **realism** that had been appearing in American magazines since the mid-1870s. When *Sister Carrie* was published in 1900, it met with a chorus of criticism for its choice of subject matter and its amoral attitude toward Carrie's "fall." Prompted in part by this criticism, "True Art Speaks Plainly" mounts a defense of the artist's choice of subject and its treatment. "[T]he business of the author," Dreiser begins, "is to say what he knows to be true, and, having said as much, to abide the result with patience." Critics who complain about the immorality of a novel under the guise of protecting the reader are really objecting to the upsetting of their "little theories concerning life, which in some cases may be nothing more than a quiet acceptance of things as they are without any regard to the well-being of the future." As a result, they prevent open discussion of social ills and thus inhibit social progress. The artist must, therefore, depict "a true picture of life, honestly and reverentially set down" if one is to render a true picture of human nature.

Further Reading

Pizer, Donald. " 'True Art Speaks Plainly': Theodore Dreiser and the Late Nineteenth-Century American Debate over Realism and Naturalism." *Nineteenth-Century Prose* 23 (1996): 76–89.

Keith Newlin

"A TRUE PATRIARCH: A STUDY FROM LIFE." First published in December 1901 in *McClure's,* this sketch of Dreiser's future father-in-law was included, with many stylistic revisions, as "A True Patriarch" in *Twelve Men*. The *McClure's* version was reprinted in *SMA* 1.

When Dreiser was a newspaper reporter for the *St. Louis Globe-Democrat* in the early 1890s, he became acquainted with **Archibald Herndon White**, an influential country politician in Missouri. Later Dreiser worked for the rival paper, the *St. Louis Republic*, which sent him to the World's Columbian Exposition at Chicago in 1893 in the company of young schoolteachers from the St. Louis area, among whom was Sara Osborne White. "On the street of a certain moderate-sized country seat in Missouri," Dreiser began the portrait, "may be seen a true patriarch. Tall, white-haired, stout in body and mind, he roams among his neighbors, dispensing sympathy and goodness through the leisure of his day." In Dreiser's "Champ Clark and His District," another magazine article about a country politician published in *Ainslee's* for June 1900, White is identified as "a sound Democrat of the old school and the oldest resident of the town." Dreiser was impressed with his skills as a politician: "When the primaries were held there, this man organized the Clark forces in such a way, and so artfully worked in the prejudices against Montgomery City, that Clark delegates were elected from the quarters."

What impressed the young reporter and future son-in-law the most, however, was White's compassionate character. His Samaritan activities reminded Dreiser of Walt Whitman and "Song of Myself." The old patriarch also reminded Dreiser of William Cullen Bryant, Dreiser's lifelong favorite American poet. Dreiser considered White to be a transcendentalist in the vein of Whitman and Bryant. Not only did White regard "everyman his brother, every human being honest," but he believed that God resided not only in heaven but on earth and in every human being. Dreiser related an anecdote in which White sought to help a terminally ill woman in White's neighborhood by offering a prayer so that she would not strangle when she died. Apparently, God answered White's prayer, for she died in peace. Skeptical of such divine power, Dreiser asked, "Might it not have been merely the change of atmosphere which was introduced by your voice and strength? The quality of your own thoughts goes for something in such matters. Mind acts on mind." "Certainly," White responded, as though there was no disagreement between Dreiser's doctrine and his own. "But, after all," he added, "what is *that*—my mind, your mind, the sound of voice. It's all the Lord anyhow, whatever you think."

Yoshinobu Hakutani

TWELVE MEN. In 1917, Dreiser began revising several early character sketches to create a collection about men he admired or considered influential in his life. This collection would be published in April 1919 as *Twelve Men*. In February 1919, Dreiser wrote H. L. Mencken that "seven of the features were done within the last 10 months" (*D-M Letters* 2: 336), but that statement is misleading. While several were composed especially for *Twelve Men*, eight already existed in some earlier version by 1904, five having been previously published. Dreiser did, however, make extensive revisions to create a consistent narrative voice so the sketches could be arranged into a thematic pattern. The earlier sketches selected for the collection and those newly written were chosen not only for their appeal to the reading public but also for their autobiographical importance. *Twelve Men* provides a record of Dreiser's years from his boyhood in Warsaw, Indiana (1884–1887), to the year before publication (1918) and a portrayal of the formative events in his life.

Four of the sketches cover the period from 1884 to 1900, when Dreiser was growing up and then began to earn his living as a journalist. Dr. **Amos Woolley** (Gridley in "The Country Doctor") was the Dreiser family doctor in Warsaw. **Peter B. McCord** ("Peter"), a newspaper artist, was Dreiser's close friend from the time they met in St. Louis in 1892 until McCord's death in New Jersey in 1908. Dreiser had befriended **William Louis Sonntag Jr.**, ("W. L. S."), another young artist, in New York City in 1895, but Sonntag died three years later. **Archibald Herndon White** ("A True Patriarch") was the father of Sara Osborne White, the woman Dreiser married in 1898.

The bulk of the sketches cover the period from 1900 to 1904, when Dreiser wrote *Sister Carrie* and then experienced a debilitating collapse that made it impossible for him to earn his living as a writer. Suffering from the disappointment of the reception of *Sister Carrie*, Dreiser joined his mentor **Arthur Henry** for a summer vacation in Noank, Connecticut, in 1901. There he interviewed various residents and produced several journalistic sketches, three later included in *Twelve Men*. One was about **Charles Potter** ("A Doer of the Word"), a man noted for his Christian charity; another was about **Elihu Potter** (Burridge in "The Village Feudists"), a former Samaritan who had become a bitter eccentric; the third was about **Thomas P. Taylor** ("A Mayor and His People"), the mayor of Bridgeport when Dreiser was in Connecticut doing research for magazine articles during 1898. In 1903, Dreiser had a nervous breakdown and was rescued by his brother Paul Dresser ("My Brother Paul"), who sent him to a sanitarium run by the famous ex-wrestler **William Mul-** doon ("Culhane, the Solid Man"). After recovering his health at Muldoon's, Dreiser worked briefly for the New York Central Railroad under foreman **Michael Burke** ("The Mighty Rourke").

The remaining two sketches cover the period from 1904 to 1918, when Dreiser worked for the first six years as a magazine editor and then once again supported himself through the sale of his own writing. "De Maupassant, Jr." is about **Harris Merton Lyon**, a promising young fiction writer whom Dreiser hired in 1906 while editor of *Broadway Magazine*. " 'Vanity, Vanity,' Saith the Preacher" is about the failed New York financier **Joseph G. Robin**, whom Dreiser met in 1908 while managing editor of the **Butterick Publishing Company**. After giving up his position as editor in 1910 and becoming a full-time writer again, Dreiser continued to monitor Robin's financial affairs, concluding the sketch with a final view of the now-ruined financier around 1918.

In ordering these sketches, Dreiser grouped them thematically rather than chronologically. The first six are about men Dreiser admired who were achievers; the second six were failures. He arranged them in an alternating pattern of Good Samaritan or talented individualist, beginning with the man he admired most, Peter McCord. Then follow the Samaritan Charlie Potter and Dreiser's talented brother Paul. The sequence continues this pattern: after Paul is the Samaritan Dr. Woolley (Gridley), followed by the individualist William Muldoon (Culhane), and then the Samaritan Arch White. Next come the failures: Harris Merton Lyon, the former Samaritan Elihu Potter (Burridge), the failed financier Joseph G. Robin, and the Samaritan foreman Mike Burke (Rourke). Dreiser had originally continued this pattern so that the talented artist who died before realizing his potential, Louis Sonntag, came next and the collection ended with the Samaritan Mayor. Dreiser decided, however, that the final paragraph of the Sonntag portrait provided a more fitting conclusion, so he switched the order of the last two sketches.

Twelve Men was published on 14 April 1919 by **Boni & Liveright**, who reprinted it a tenth and final time in May 1931. Other American printings include a Modern Library edition in 1928, a Fawcett paperback edition in 1962, a Library of America edition in 1987, and the **Pennsylvania Dreiser Edition** in 1998.

Robert Coltrane

"TYPHOON." First published in an abridged form as "The Wages of Sin" in *Hearst's International-Cosmopolitan* in October 1926, the story appeared in Dreiser's second volume of short fiction, *Chains: Lesser Novels and Stories*. A reedited version, based on Dreiser's manuscripts, appeared in the *Heath Anthology of American Literature*, vol. 2 (1990). "Typhoon" depicts the story of Ida Zobel, whose overprotective, German immigrant father has allowed her little freedom to interact with her peers. The teenaged Ida, whom Dreiser sketches as redolent with a blossoming sexuality, meets Edward Hauptwanger ("Hauptfuhrer" in the reedited version), a cad who schemes to seduce her, in part in an effort to "outwit" her father. In due course Ida becomes pregnant, and Edward begins to avoid her, suggesting he is just one of many fellows who might be responsible. Distraught and desperate, Ida pleads with her seducer to marry her and attempts to frighten him with a gun. The gun fires, Edward dies, and Ida is arrested for murder. In the ensuing weeks, the newspapers sensationalize the crime, and a wealthy socialite posts Ida's bail and cares for her until the baby is born. But Ida is unable to live with the guilt of having killed the man she still loves, and one afternoon she goes to the trees by the river where she and Edward had first made love and drowns herself.

Like *An American Tragedy*, with which it shares several themes, "Typhoon" grew out of Dreiser's file of newspaper clippings of murder cases and was based on a *Philadelphia Public Ledger* account of the shooting of Edward Lister by fifteen-year-old Helen Schultz, whom he had made pregnant. "Typhoon" is important for its concise expression of several of Dreiser's principal interests: the drama of the innocent girl at the mercy of older, calculating men; the pervasive influence of sexual impulses that one can neither control nor comprehend; the role of **chance** in determining consequences. Moreover, while Dreiser has been accused of writing in a cumbersome style, "Typhoon" displays Dreiser at his stylistic best, as, for example, with the metaphor of the typhoon representing Ida's mental tumult and confusion when she confronts Edward: "And then blindness! Pain. Whirling, fiery sparks such as had never in all her life before had she seen—and executing strange rhythmic convolutions and orbits in her brain— swift and eccentric and red and yet beautiful orbits. And in the center of them the face of her beloved, but not as it was now—oh, no—but rather haloed by a strange white light, and as it was under the trees in the spring."

Further Reading

Hutchisson, James M. "The Composition and Publication of 'Another American Tragedy': Dreiser's 'Typhoon.' " *Papers of the Bibliographic Society of America* 81 (1987): 25–35.

Keith Newlin

V

"'VANITY, VANITY,' SAITH THE PREACHER." Although referred to in this sketch only as X——, the subject is **Joseph G. Robin**, a financier whom Dreiser first met in 1908 while editor of the **Butterick Publishing Company**. This sketch was developed especially for *Twelve Men* and placed among the second six, men who had failed. It describes how Robin rose to prominence by consolidating several banks in New York City, but when he attempted to move into the increasingly lucrative street railway business, he was opposed by other more powerful financiers. Within six months, he was under indictment for banking fraud. He served a year in jail and lost his entire fortune, ending up, according to Dreiser, a broken man. The narrator concludes the sketch by saying that, after seeing Robin on the street in 1918 looking "a little worn and dusty," he had never seen or talked to him since. Dreiser did, however, correspond and meet with Robin throughout the 1920s, until Robin's death in 1929.

"Vanity, Vanity" is the weakest portrait in *Twelve Men*, consisting mostly of a narrative summary. The narrator does not seek out information from other people as in the other sketches but instead relies on reporting his own limited experience with Robin or on providing a summary of the newspaper reports published after Robin was indicted. Except for a brief conversation at the beginning, the sketch contains no dialogue. Dreiser had to some extent "novelized" Robin in *The Financier*. "Vanity, Vanity" fails to bring Robin to life not only because Dreiser did not use the techniques that made the other sketches so effective but also because he had already used Robin's personality some years earlier to create **Frank Cowperwood**.

This sketch was apparently the last written for *Twelve Men*, composed probably in late 1918 to provide an even dozen. Dreiser attempted unsuccessfully to sell it to *Red Book*, *Century*, and *Harper's* in October 1918.

Robert Coltrane

"VICTORY" is a short story that initially appeared in the *Jewish Daily Forward* on 24 April 1927 before being reprinted in the same month in *Chains: Lesser Novels and Stories*. "Victory" is unique in that each of its five sections is told from a different point of view, presenting an increasingly complex and sympathetic assessment of the protagonist, J. H. Osterman, who is ultimately described by his longtime legal adviser as "a curious combination of speculator, financier, and dreamer, with a high percentage of sharper thrown in for good measure." Section 1, made up of excerpts from a posthumous tribute to Osterman, written by a subordinate, presents the tycoon as a driven man of force and courage, yet "not always a pleasant person to be near." He was enigmatic and something of an intellectual parasite. Section 2 is taken from the reminiscences of a special investigator and counsel for plaintiffs in a suit against Osterman. From this point of view, Osterman is revealed to be a ruthless and highly manipulative man who made his vast fortune by entrapping his competitors financially, gaining control of their enterprises, and often destroying their lives. Section 3 is excerpted from a biography of Osterman published in a leading magazine. These excerpts detail the financier's bleak and loveless childhood, as well as his early struggle as a farmer, when he confronted not only the vagaries of Nature but also the dog-eat-dog attitude of his Kansas community. These early experiences left him with a bitter determination to succeed and a curious sympathy for farm boys and orphan children.

Section 4 is drawn from Osterman's "private cogitations," as he cynically reviewed his failure to succeed honestly and then the chicanery that ultimately led to his amassing a fortune that failed to bring him satisfaction. There were also flickerings of guilt over the lives he had destroyed and a decision to achieve fulfillment by leaving his estate to orphans rather than to his cold, spendthrift wife and her two wastrel sons. The climactic Section 5, narrated through the recollections of Osterman's lawyer, tells of the failure of a philanthropic plan to build "a chain of modern local asylums for orphans that was to have belted America." Death, however, struck Osterman down, pen in hand, as he struggled to sign a revised will, positioned appropriately enough on a Ouija board. In typical Dreiser fashion, Fate is "the victor."

"Victory" has generated critical interest primarily because of the parallels between Osterman and **Frank Cowperwood**, especially in the latter stages of their careers. John J. McAleer in *Theodore Dreiser* has in fact suggested that Dreiser wrote "Victory" in an effort to jump-start his flagging interest in the completion of *The Stoic*. Both of these unscrupulous entrepreneurs come to realize the emptiness of material success and were thwarted in their efforts to give their lives meaning through philanthropy. Cowperwood, however, had **Berenice Fleming** to carry on his humanitarian quest; Osterman had no one.

Richard W. Dowell

"THE VILLAGE FEUDISTS." Originally titled "Heart Bowed Down," this sketch was written in 1901 based on an interview with a local store owner named **Elihu H. Potter** while Dreiser was in Noank, Connecticut, that summer. Dreiser later revised the sketch for inclusion in *Twelve Men*, changing the title and the names of people and surrounding villages. He changed Elihu Potter's last name to Burridge because he was also including a sketch about another Noank native named **Charles Potter**.

The narrator first encounters Burridge when he goes into his store to buy provisions and is struck not only by Burridge's unusual appearance but also by the disorderly arrangement of the store's merchandise. Only the eccentric Burridge is capable of finding anything. The narrator makes inquiries in the village and discovers Burridge had once been prosperous and generous, a Good Samaritan, but his influence in the community had been destroyed when he opposed the wealthy owner of the local shipbuilding yard, Robert Palmer. Burridge then became an embittered man.

The narrative personality intrudes less into this sketch than any other in *Twelve Men*. Dreiser's own feelings of discontent at this time (1901), resulting from his unhappy experiences with **Frank Doubleday** and *Sister Carrie*, are reflected indirectly in his depiction of the adverse effect on Burridge of the "forces of authority" in the community, represented by Robert Palmer. Dreiser depicts Burridge as having once been a leading citizen of Noank who, because of his stubbornness and refusal to compromise his ideals, made enemies of those who disagreed with him. Burridge refused to conform to community standards when he believed them to be wrong, a position with which Dreiser could strongly identify. Dreiser's frustrations as a creative artist whose work was puritanically suppressed finds its strongest expression in this sketch about Elihu Burridge. When Dreiser revised this sketch some fifteen years later for *Twelve Men*, the changes he made only served to clarify, rather than diminish, the negative tone of the original 1901 version.

Robert Coltrane

THE VOICE. A brief, one-act play, unpublished in Dreiser's lifetime and first published in *The Collected Plays of Theodore Dreiser*, about the spirit of a jealous lover who cannot quite let go. Edith, grieving for her dead lover Richard, has married Harold in an attempt to move on with her life, but Richard (appearing in the play as a disembodied "Voice"), shadows Edith's every move, jealously taunting her with reminders of their deep physical attraction for each other—here presented as a fetish for Edith's white neck. Harold, insecure in Edith's love for him, is sensitive to every nuance of her movements and seeks confirmation of her continued love for Richard and her disinterest in him. When Harold's jealousy finds that confirmation in Edith's sigh over a Swinburne poem, he seizes her by the neck and begins to strangle her, while the Voice (audible only to Edith) chants, "Tighter! Tighter!" But when Harold realizes he can't bear to part from her "white body [and] white face and neck," he abruptly leaves. Edith, recognizing the truth of Harold's accusation, drinks poison and so joins her dead lover. Like Dreiser's other one-act plays, *The Voice* is of interest chiefly for Dreiser's experiments with depicting the emotional forces that prompt action. As he did in *The Blue Sphere* and *In the Dark*, Dreiser embodies in the spectral "Voice" an objectification of one's unconscious motives, in this case the manifestation of Edith's conscience prompting her to decide whom she really loves.

Keith Newlin

W

"W. L. S." *See* "The Color of To-Day."

WARREN, ROBERT PENN (1905–1989). One of the most acclaimed and versatile American writers of the twentieth century and a major figure in the "Southern Renaissance," Warren was the author of ten published novels, including the classic *All the King's Men* (1946). Justly celebrated for his social as well as literary commentary, he began and ended his career as a poet and was named the nation's first official poet laureate in 1986. Educated at Vanderbilt, Berkeley, Yale, and Oxford, Warren combined the role of man of letters with that of professional academic, and with his close friend and colleague Cleanth Brooks he brought out an influential series of textbooks that revolutionized the teaching of literature in college classrooms and served to popularize the analytical formalism associated with the New Criticism. Always an astute and practical critic, Warren made a lasting contribution to Dreiser studies with the publication of *Homage to Theodore Dreiser on the Centennial of His Birth* (1971), a relatively brief—but wide-ranging and insightful—monograph that some have argued reveals more about its author than its subject.

While Warren's freewheeling "homage" to Dreiser, however irreverent and ambivalent, is ultimately the tribute of one American master to another, it would be a mistake to dismiss it as overly subjective and impressionistic. Warren may introduce his remarks with a prefatory poem, one of his most striking, but the discussion that follows attests not only to his easy familiarity with the Dreiser corpus as a whole but to the conscientiousness with which he consulted, evaluated, and incorporated the relevant work of previous scholars and commentators, and Warren's wide and systematic reading in history and philosophy enables him to "historicize" Dreiser and his work in ways that subsequent readers have frequently found valuable and suggestive. As a vestigial "New Critic," Warren is frankly impatient with Dreiser's acknowledged offenses against taste and usage. He finds Dreiser's prose nothing short of "abominable" at times, but for all his awareness of his subject's literary shortcomings he confesses a grudging, but deeply genuine, respect for the elemental power of Dreiser's "art"—a term Warren pointedly insists upon in opposition to those critics who had dismissed Dreiser's work as essentially artless.

Not surprisingly, Warren regards *Sister Carrie* and *An American Tragedy* (and to lesser extent *Jennie Gerhardt*) as Dreiser's defining achievements, and his "close readings" of aspects of these novels are nuanced and supple, models of their kind. Subjected to the same rigorous analysis, the remainder of the canon comes off poorly, though Warren is honest enough to admit that in judging the **Cowperwood** trilogy a "failure," he may have invoked the wrong fictional imperatives. This is a significant admission, quite daring in its implications.

The value of *Homage to Theodore Dreiser* as a gloss on Warren's own work has long been recognized. Whatever residual value it holds for Dreiser studies may be disputed, but the integrity and intensity of Warren's little book will not be denied.

Further Reading

Blotner, Joseph. *Robert Penn Warren: A Biography.* New York: Random, 1997.

William Bedford Clark

WATKINS, ANN (1885–1967). Watkins was a writer and literary agent in New York with her own company at 366 Fifth Avenue and later at 210 Madison Avenue. Her 1935 stationery lists her as the president of the agency, which also included Pat Duggan, who was responsible for the play department, and Harold Matson, vice president and treasurer. According to the *New Yorker* records of literary agents files in the New York Public Library, Watkins's list of customers included Ezra Pound, Antoine de Saint-Exupery, Peter De Vries, Evelyn Eaton, Robert Gibbings, Max Miller, and Theodore White. Dreiser knew Watkins as a colleague and friend when she worked for *Everybody's Magazine* during the early 1910s. When interviewed by W. A. Swanberg in November 1962, Watkins described Dreiser as "a tremendously physical person, without conventional morals, almost ugly, and yet he had a kindliness and warmth that were magnetic" (Swanberg 133). During the early

1910s, Watkins was friends with **Thelma Cudlipp** and became a personal witness of Dreiser's unhappy infatuation as his courtship efforts were thwarted by Cudlipp's mother. Watkins described her observations of Dreiser's suicidal despair to Swanberg. Watkins was a sympathetic friend, but when Dreiser begged her to disclose Cudlipp's whereabouts in London, England, she refused to help him, although she did send Dreiser's address to Thelma Cudlipp.

Richard Lehan has identified Watkins as the model behind the strikingly beautiful, yet sexually distant, "Emanuela" in Dreiser's *A Gallery of Women* (164n). The sketch details the abduction of Watkins by the mentally unstable Fritz Krog (aka Scheib) who was infatuated with her, yet the sketch's true focus is on Dreiser's diagnosis of Watkins's "frigidity," a somewhat vindictive portrait that was likely prompted by her persistent rejection of his sexual advances and by his professional jealousy of her impressive career. Perhaps even more unforgiving was the strong female solidarity she had displayed in the Thelma Cudlipp crisis, when she protected her friend's whereabouts from the pursuing Dreiser. Dreiser's closing sentence in "Emanuela" sounds a cold good-bye: "But from that day to this I have never seen nor heard of Emanuela. It may be that she is dead—although I doubt it." Given Watkins's impressive professional network of connections among American writers, this cool ending suggests that Dreiser had actively closed the door on her.

Further Reading

Gammel, Irene. "Female Sexuality and the Naturalist Crisis: 'Emanuela.' " *Sexualizing Power in Naturalism: Theodore Dreiser and Frederick Philip Grove.* Calgary: University of Calgary Press, 1994. 83–99.

Irene Gammel

"A WAYPLACE OF THE FALLEN." This sketch from *The Color of A Great City* describes an inexpensive New York hotel that was intended to house those who were either temporarily or permanently impoverished and in which Dreiser himself had once stayed, probably about 1903. It is "a hybrid, or cross between a hotel and a charity, one of those old philanthropies . . . which were supposed to bridge with some sort of relief the immense gap which existed between the rich and the poor; a gap that was not supposed to exist in a republic devoted to human brotherhood and the equality of man." Most striking in this sketch are not so much the descriptions of the occupants but the architectural detail; here, Dreiser delineates the ways in which the space itself defines, shapes, and attempts to discipline its occupants. He begins with the exterior, a handsome building of cream-colored brick intended to fit in well with the once-fashionable neighborhood in which it was built. However attractive the outside might be, the inside of the building is stark. It consists primarily of two large courts or lounging rooms around which the floors of individual rooms are built and which rise to the glass ceilings nine stories above. These lounging rooms can be used only from the hours of 9 A.M., when the tenants must be out of their rooms, and 10 P.M. and during these times is watched over by a surly guard. Dreiser notes that those who were out of work often felt compelled to walk the streets between the hours of nine and five, when their rooms could be reoccupied, because of the distinct feeling of being unwelcome in the lounging rooms in the daytime. Thus, the lack of friendliness or comfort serves as an impetus to keep the occupants from using the hotel as though it were their own personal space or as a home during working hours. The sense of surveillance and lack of privacy are carried to the public bathrooms, with their open stalls and showers, overseen by a watchful employee, and into the bedrooms. "They were really not rooms at all," Dreiser writes, "but cells partitioned or arranged in such a way as to provide the largest amount of renting space and personal supervision and espionage to the founder . . . but only a bare bed to the guest." He describes the cells as being five feet by eight feet, with tiny windows, an iron bed, a single chair, and a very small wardrobe or closet. The walls are actually marble partitions set upon jacks two feet from the floor and three from the ceiling, thereby allowing surveillance of those in adjoining rooms. These carefully detailed descriptions suggest a prison in which the minds and lives of the inmates are entirely controlled by guards who purport to be conditioning the inmates for their own benefit. Perhaps surprisingly, Dreiser does not question the necessity of such rigid control but simply notes that "the general effect [on me] was coarse and bitter." In this sketch, as in "On Being Poor," "Bums," and others in *The Color of a Great City*, Dreiser is careful to distinguish himself, whom he considers only temporarily impoverished, from those he assumes will live in these conditions for the rest of their lives. He ends by noting, sadly, those for whom even these sparse and unfriendly lodgings are beyond their means.

Nancy McIlvaine Donovan

"WHEN THE OLD CENTURY WAS NEW" is one of five short stories Dreiser wrote during the summer of 1899, while visiting **Arthur Henry** in Maumee, Ohio—stories Richard Lingeman terms Dreiser's "finger exercises" before the composition of *Sister Carrie* (Lingeman 1: 267). It was initially published in the January 1901 issue of *Pearson's* and was reprinted in *Free and Other Stories*.

Set in the spring of 1801, "When the Old Century Was New" describes a day in the life of William Walton, a wealthy young New York merchant who has taken a rare holiday from his "counting-house duties" to engage in a variety of social activities—a high-society luncheon, an afternoon with Beppie Cruger, his soon-to-be fiancée, and an evening at the Apollo Theater. Resplendent in his fashionable attire, the jaunty Walton "is a striking example of the new order of things which had come with the Declaration of Independence." As he ambles past stately mansions and lovely gardens, meeting and chatting with such dignitaries as President John Adams, Thomas Jefferson, and John Jacob Astor, Walton is confronted by ominous signs that the beauty and gentility of the life he loves are passing. Commerce has become all-consuming, leaving the Bowling Green vacant and threatening to eliminate gardens in favor of office buildings; the recent invention of the steamboat suggests the arrival of the Industrial Revolution; the piratical attacks on American shipping, as well as the prominence of black servants, foreshadow nineteenth-century hostilities; and social conflict can be seen in the tendency of "the aristocracy, gentry, and common rabble [to form] in separate groups." The servant who jostles Walton "rudely" on the street seems a portent.

For Walton, largely impervious to these tensions, the day is a great success. He luxuriates in the elegance of the luncheon, served by two "splendid imported Africans, trained in Virginia," and vows to have such skilled servants in his future home. Later, Beppie accepts a diamond, tacitly agreeing to become his bride. Thus, the story ends with Walton's strolling the "idyllic" Bowery, dreaming of the halcyon

future he seems to have in store. "He had no inkling," Dreiser concludes, "of what a century might bring forth. The crush and stress and wretchedness fast treading upon this path of loveliness he could not see."

The critical response to "When the Old Century Was New" has varied widely. Yoshinobu Hakutani in *Young Dreiser* finds in the story evidence of Dreiser's own "joy and optimism" during the late 1890s (166). Donald Pizer and F. O. Matthiessen have seen in it little more than Dreiser's attempt to tap into the current popularity of historical romances. Pizer in "A Summer at Maumee" has termed the story "almost worthless" (*Novels of Theodore Dreiser* 6), while Matthiessen in *Theodore Dreiser* finds "nothing to distinguish it from other paper-thin period pieces" (52). On the other hand, Joseph Griffin in *The Small Canvas* reads "When the Old Century Was New" as a parody of the historical romance, written to satirize "the 'roseate' stories of the day." To take the tale at face value, concludes Griffin, is to give little credit to Dreiser's sensitivity (26).

Further Reading

Griffin, Joseph P. " 'When the Old Century Was New': An Early Dreiser Parody." *Studies in Short Fiction* 17 (1980): 285–89.

Richard W. Dowell

"WHEN THE SAILS ARE FURLED: SAILOR'S SNUG HARBOR." First published in *Ainslee's* in December 1898, this article was later reprinted in a slightly expanded version in *The Color of a Great City*. The *Ainslee's* version was reprinted in *SMA* 2. "When the Sails Are Furled: Sailor's Snug Harbor" is a portrayal of retired sailors in an urban community in the 1890s. The city is traditionally associated with evil and hell, and to many twentieth-century modernist writers it is a wasteland. John Burroughs, the sage of late-nineteenth-century America, pleaded for the value of nature and warned against humankind's overindulgence in materialism, but such warnings went unheeded. After the turn of the century, however, as shown by an architect like Frank Lloyd Wright, Americans began to absorb Nature into their consciousness. If Nature did not completely vanish from the daily activities of one's living, it became steadily accommodated by them.

In this portrayal of a small harbor near New York City, Dreiser, like Frank Lloyd Wright, draws a cityscape in harmony with nature. "As the waters flow onward," Dreiser writes, "following the trend of the shore line of Staten Island, they become less and less exposed to the winds of the sea, and soon, as they pass the northernmost end of the Island, they make a sharp bend to the west, passing between it and Liberty Statue, where the tranquil Kill von Kull separates the island from New Jersey." This environment, "a mixture of land and sea," provides old sea-weary mariners with a peaceful, comfortable retreat. The harbor was founded by Captain Robert Randall, who came to America from Scotland in 1776. His son, having no children, bequeathed much of his father's property "for the benefit of unfortunate and disabled seamen," as Alexander Hamilton and Daniel D. Tomkins drew up and signed the papers. The estate was highlighted by a statue of St. Gaudens. "Everywhere about the grounds and buildings," Dreiser describes, "are seen nautical signs, and many loving reminders of the man who willed so nobly and so well."

In the resident halls Dreiser finds a robust lifestyle, where "hundreds of old sailors [are] all hard at work, defying monotony with toil." Despite the harmony and comfort that prevailed in the living quarters, Dreiser ends this essay with a reserva-tion: "Still, there is not altogether happiness, however well appointed the scene." He senses that in their heart these pensioners wish to be elsewhere, either by traveling or by settling into private houses. Nevertheless, the Sailor's Snug Harbor "is a great institution, and indeed a splendid benefaction, but it insists on what is the bane and destruction of heart and mind and that is conformity to routine—a monotonous system." Such sentiments speak of the spirit of freedom and independence deeply ingrained in national character.

Yoshinobu Hakutani

"WHENCE THE SONG." This article about the popularity of Tin Pan Alley songwriters, illustrated by William J. Glackens, first appeared in *Harper's Weekly* on 8 December 1900. The essay was reprinted, with some minor stylistic alterations, in Dreiser's *The Color of a Great City.* The *Harper's Weekly* version was collected in *SMA 2*, as well as in Dreiser, *Art, Music, and Literature, 1897–1902.*

Popular songs are born in the parlors of a score of publishers, Dreiser explains in this essay. Into that world gather the mixed company of successful and unsuccessful authors, as well as a variety of artists who try to coordinate song making with directors of touring bands and orchestra leaders of Bowery theaters and uptown variety halls and singers. But the popularity of a song and the economic success of an author seldom last for long. Other songwriters quickly replace current ones as new melodies replace the old songs. Alluding to the fate of his brother Paul Dresser, Dreiser writes, "Oh, the glory of success in this little world in his eye at this time! . . . Outside, as he stretches himself, may even now be heard the murmur of that joyous rout of which he was so recently a part—the lights, the laughter, the songs. Only he must linger in the shadow." Years later Paul Dresser's songs, such as "Just Tell Them That You Saw Me," continued to be sung over the land, but the author's name was forgotten and his royalty payment long since ceased. "It seems wonderful," Dreiser nevertheless remarks, "that they should come to this, singers, authors, women and all; and yet not more wonderful than that their little feeling, worked into a melody and a set of words, should reach far out o'er land and water, touching the hearts of the nation."

Dreiser may not have had an ear or a taste for serious music, but in "Whence the Song" he captures the vibrancy of the music world of the 1890s as well as the democratic spirit that was beginning to manifest itself, reflected especially in the serious attention the public and critics were paying to women. In "Women Who Have Won Distinction in Music" (*Success*, 8 April 1899: 325–26), Dreiser reported that although only one-tenth of the musical manuscripts had been written by women in the past, by the end of the nineteenth century, twice as many pieces were composed by women as by men. Furthermore, composers and performers should not be viewed as types and patterns considered embodiments of tradition and convention. Instead, they should be viewed as individual artists whose songs have touched "the hearts of the nation" with "the marvel of the common song."

Yoshinobu Hakutani

WHITE, ARCHIBALD HERNDON (1831–1902). Arch White was the father of Sara Osborne White, the woman Dreiser married in December 1898. Born in 1831, he spent his life in the small village of Danville, Missouri, the seat of Montgomery County, located some seventy-five miles west of St. Louis. The White family had been living in this area since 1824, when Arch White's father moved there from

Kentucky, became a large landowner, and established himself as a man of prominence. Arch White was active in the local Democratic Party, but his only elected position was as sheriff in 1885. He was one of thirteen children and himself the father of three sons and seven daughters.

Dreiser wrote two versions of his father-in-law, the first called "A True Patriarch" and included in *Twelve Men*, and the second included in "Rella," a sketch in *A Gallery of Women*. The original portrait of Arch White, published in the December 1901 issue of *McClure's*, presents a favorable image of a man whose domineering personality is tempered by his Samaritan-like qualities. He is opinionated but likable. The revisions Dreiser made for *Twelve Men* served only to emphasize further Arch White's good qualities. Some ten years later in "Rella," Dreiser presents a different portrait, one that emphasizes all the negative aspects of Arch White's patriarchal personality. The disparity was due to the differences in purpose of each sketch and in Dreiser's personal circumstances. In 1900, when Dreiser wrote "A True Patriarch," his marriage was still a happy one. In *Twelve Men*, Arch White is placed among the first six men, whom Dreiser admired and categorized as successful. By 1929, when "Rella" appears, Dreiser's marriage was only a legal technicality (he and Sara had not lived together since 1914). In "Rella," Arch White is portrayed as the father whose old-fashioned ideas of morality stand between Dreiser and the attainment of his desires—sexual relations with his sister-in-law, **Rose White**.

Arch White died on 16 July 1902, having lived just long enough to enjoy the glory of appearing in the December issue of *McClure's*. "A True Patriarch" is carved on his tombstone.

Robert Coltrane

WHITE, ROSE (c.1870–1918). The younger sister of Dreiser's first wife, Sara, Rose White is the primary source for his short story "Rella" in *A Gallery of Women*, as well as the source of Miss W——'s sister in *Newspaper Days* and Marietta Blue in *The "Genius."* In all three works, the characterization of Rose is consistent; she is vivacious and gay, and the protagonist of each work, who is involved with her sister or her aunt, finds her irresistibly attractive, causing him to question monogamy and the institution of marriage. Dreiser first met Rose not long after he met Sara, when both sisters journeyed to Chicago for the World's Colombian Exposition of 1893. Working for the *St. Louis Republic*, Dreiser was picked to host a group of young women, including the White sisters. Attracted to Sara, as well as to one or two other women in the group, Dreiser was immediately aware that he was also attracted to Rose, who arrived a few days after her sister. During a boating excursion, Rose seemed to return Dreiser's attention; however, suddenly aware of what was occurring, Rose desisted, remembering her sister's interest in Dreiser, and she shied away from him for the rest of the trip. Later Rose wrote to Dreiser to scold him about his neglect of her sister, demanding that he follow through on his promise of marriage. Dreiser later uses this instance in *The "Genius"* when Marietta writes to the protagonist, **Eugene Witla**, urging him to marry her sister, **Angela Blue**. Her letter is effective. As Dreiser marries Sara White, so Witla marries Angela Blue. Finally, Rose is the only witness, with the possible exception of her brother, Richard, to Sara and Dreiser's elopement in Washington, D.C., on 28 December 1898.

Although there is little in Rose's behavior to suggest the character of Rella, the confusion of emotions caused by Dreiser's attraction to Rose influences the tensions of that sketch. In his autobiography *Newspaper Days*, Dreiser describes his and Sara's visit to the family homestead in Missouri, where he again realizes his attraction to Rose, thinking that Rose, more literary and more worldly than Sara, might be better suited to him. Still, Rose gives him no encouragement. Nonetheless, the situation causes him to wish that "love was not a matter of poky marriage vows and incomes and children, a whole life long of duty and drudgery, but rather one of pagan, Dionysian contact." Dreiser waxes on about love as bacchanalian revelry, concluding that marriage is "the slaughter of romance itself." Finally, he speculates that love is a burden one carries for "something which uses man as a tool." Such speculation is characteristic of the protagonist of "Rella" as well, who feels burdened by conflicting chemical and social forces.

Although Rose White remained a marginal figure in Dreiser's life, she made one other important contribution. A week after he had completed *Sister Carrie*, Rose introduced Dreiser to **Frank Norris's** *McTeague* (1899), a novel that confirmed his sense of literary direction and provided, perhaps, a model for future writing. As he told H. L. Mencken, "It made a great hit with me and I talked of nothing else for months. It was the first real American book I had ever read" (*D-M Letters* 1: 231).

Further Reading

Hakutani, Yoshinobu. "Dreiser and Rose White." *Library Chronicle* 44 (Spring 1979): 27–31.
Kimberly Freeman

WHITE, SARA. *See* Dreiser, Sara White.

"WILL YOU WALK INTO MY PARLOR?" is the longest of Dreiser's short stories and represents his only attempt to capitalize on the popularity of surprise-ending fiction. That attempt, however, was relatively unsuccessful. By 1917, the story was circulating, only to be rejected by at least eight magazines. Then, in 1918, it was published in *Free and Other Stories*.

The story's protagonist, Ed Gregory, a crusading journalist, has been collecting evidence of corruption to thwart the re-election of a figurehead big-city mayor, thereby bringing himself into conflict with a racketeer kingmaker named Tilney. At Tilney's instigation, Gregory has been the target of bribery, intimidation, and two apparent assassination attempts, but he presses forward, spurred on by his civic duty and an ambition to promote his own career. Ultimately, his wife and child being out of town for an extended period, Gregory comes under the spell of young, beautiful, and vivacious Imogene Carle, who checks into Triton Hall, the luxurious seaside hotel where he lives. Soon it becomes obvious that Imogene, aided by a coterie of coconspirators, has been planted by Tilney to lure Gregory into a sexually compromising situation. Still, intrigued by her attention and hopeful he can enlist her as a confederate, Gregory allows himself a modest flirtation, chaperoned always by his friend and confidant Frank Blount to prevent seeming improprieties. Nevertheless, he narrowly escapes a potentially damaging intrigue and in a fit of rage accuses Imogene of treachery. She admits her association with Tilney but insists that her futile love for Gregory would prevent her doing him harm. As evidence of her good faith, she seemingly puts herself in harm's way by providing him with a notarized confession of her part in the plot. Gregory—and hopefully the reader—feels that he has won a moral and political victory; thus, he grants her a final meeting and a parting kiss. Imogene, however, turns this latter noblesse oblige gesture into a passionate embrace. The preposi-

tioned cameras roll, recording this apparent infidelity for blackmail purposes. Tilney has won.

In 1934, Dreiser nominated "Will You Walk into My Parlor?" among a handful of short stories to appear in an omnibus projected but never published by Simon and Schuster. Scholars, however, have been less enthusiastic. Most do not include the story in their commentaries, and those who do tend to dismiss it as an inferior production. For example, F. O. Matthiessen in *Theodore Dreiser* pronounces the tale "dismally flat" (181). Joseph Griffin in *The Small Canvas* concurs, attributing that "flatness" to a diffuse point of view, sterility of characterization, and failure to bring the setting to life. Griffin does commend Dreiser for catching the reader off guard with his concluding reversal but suggests that after seventy pages that reader "is more relieved with the end than satisfied with the ending" (66).

Richard W. Dowell

WITLA, EUGENE TENNYSON. Protagonist of *The "Genius,"* realistic painter of urban scenes who becomes an advertising executive and publishing magnate after a neurasthenic breakdown. Drawing on how he saw himself, Dreiser depicts young Witla as sensitive, impractical, "to a notable extent artistic," and positively "mad about" women. His lustiness remains a keynote of his character, along with a more aesthetic love of beauty. Indeed, Dreiser attempts to make Witla's artistic sensibility and his promiscuity functions of each other. As the narrator says, "The artist is a blend of subtleties in emotion. . . . No one woman could have satisfied all sides of Eugene's character. . . . Beauty was the point with him."

Clare Eby

WOOD, MAUDE. *See* Henry, Maude Wood.

WOOLLEY, AMOS (1829–1899). Dr. Woolley was Dreiser's family physician when he was a boy living in Warsaw, Indiana. Dreiser's most extensive portrayal of Dr. Woolley is the sketch in *Twelve Men* called "The Country Doctor," but he also gave a summary of the treatments provided his family by Dr. Woolley in *Dawn*. Another incident is included in *A Hoosier Holiday*. The earliest published anecdote about Dr. Woolley appeared in the 16 January 1893 "Heard in the Corridors" column, which Dreiser wrote for the *St. Louis Globe-Democrat*.

Amos Woolley was born in Philadelphia on 1 March 1829, moved to Cincinnati, Ohio, with his parents when he was four, and then to Lebanon, Ohio, where he attended school until age seventeen. He joined his brothers as a blacksmith in a wagon- and carriage-making business in Miami County, Indiana, but eventually decided to prepare for the medical profession by studying under Dr. B. Henton, one of the first physicians of Peru, Indiana. After two years of study, he moved to Gilead, Miami County, where he began to practice medicine with Dr. C. Hector. In 1857, at age twenty-eight, he moved to the village of Palestine in Kosciusko County, where he practiced medicine for nine years. After marrying Martha Bunker in 1865, he enrolled at the Medical College in Fort Wayne, Indiana, from which he was graduated with honors. In 1869, he moved to Warsaw, where he practiced medicine until his death at age seventy on 3 April 1899.

The Dreisers lived in Warsaw from 1884 to 1887 and were treated for various ailments by Dr. Woolley.

Robert Coltrane

Y

YERKES, CHARLES TYSON (1837–1905). Perhaps best remembered for his "titanic" impact on the railway systems of late-nineteenth-century Philadelphia and Chicago, as well as his financial support for the establishment of the University of Chicago's world-renowned telescope, Charles Tyson Yerkes is the thinly disguised model for Dreiser's entrepreneurial wizard **Frank Algernon Cowperwood**, of the *Trilogy of Desire*—*The Financier*, *The Titan*, and *The Stoic*. The *Trilogy* follows the exploits of Cowperwood through his financial coming-of-age in *The Financier* to his death in *The Stoic*.

In 1859, Yerkes started a broker's business, bought out a bank, specialized in stocks and bonds, and commenced a rapid rise to wealth and notoriety. However, when the bond market collapsed after the 1871 Great Chicago Fire, he lost his fortune. For embezzling $400,000 of the city's money, he was sent to prison to serve a thirty-three-month term but was pardoned by the governor after seven months. While in the Philadelphia Penitentiary, Yerkes is alleged to have said, "I have made up my mind to keep my mental strength unimpaired, and think my chances for regaining my former position, financially, are as good as they ever were" (qtd. in Garfield). Yerkes left Philadelphia, divorced his first

wife, remarried, and moved to Chicago in 1881. In 1886, he acquired, with Peter Widener and William Elkins, a bare majority of stock (2,505 shares at $600 each, totaling $1,503,000) in the North Chicago City Railway and created a holding company they dubbed the "North Chicago Street Railroad Company," which became the lessee to North Chicago City Railway for all of its property for a period of 999 years. The $1.2 million in revenues were generated at no cost to Yerkes. He maintained his monopoly by doling out kickbacks and bribes while continuing to contain any competitors. In 1894, he overtook the Lake Street Elevated Railroad by colluding with Frank Underwood (perhaps the source of the moniker "Frank Cowperwood") and other major stockholders for a majority interest in the Lake Street "L."

In an attempt to streamline traffic patterns, Yerkes created a downtown terminal, signifier of the central business district—the Loop. He obtained numerous franchises and construction deadline extensions, and by 1897, the Loop was operational, coming into full service in 1900. In 1899, Yerkes's strategy to insulate his empire by trying to manipulate a 100-year, no-cost franchise failed; an angry mob stormed a City Council meeting and demanded Yerkes be held accountable for offering over $1 million in bribes (see Garfield for a chronological account of his railway dealings.)

While he was maneuvering the transit system, he was manipulated by the University of Chicago president, William Rainey Harper, and George Ellery Hale, a young astronomer who agreed to accept a professorship at the University of Chicago only if the university would construct a $250,000 observatory. Harper and Hale played up Yerkes's generosity in the newspapers, and Yerkes found himself committed to funding the construction of both a telescope and the observatory. Neither the $.5 million project nor his robber baron image, concretized in his $1.5 million mansion on New York City's Fifth Avenue, secured the social redemption he was so invested in attaining. His baronial estate, occupied in 1894, housed European art treasures, a marble staircase, and a conservatory replete with birds. Nearby, at 67th Street, his mistress **Emilie Grigsby** and her mother, the models for Dreiser's **Berenice Fleming** and her mother, enjoyed similar aggrandizement unbeknownst to Yerkes's wife, **Mary Adelaide Moore** Yerkes. Disgraced, in 1900 Yerkes deserted Chicago for a permanent residency in New York City, sold most of his holdings, and invested in the London's Underground.

In nearly "stenographer's dictation" (Gerber, "Financier" 105), Dreiser parallels the entire life. Cowperwood, like Yerkes, is the scion of Quakers and rapidly rises by his own wits. In *The Financier*, he serves an eighteen-month prison term for embezzlement and then seeks opportunities in Chicago, intending to start fresh by divorcing his first wife, **Lillian Semple** and marrying his former mistress, **Aileen Butler**. His bribing of politicians, his numerous affairs, his donation of $300,000 to the University of Chicago for the construction of the "Cowperwood Telescope," even his death from Bright's disease and interment in Brooklyn's Greenwood Cemetery create a biographical narrative that barely masks the life of this American traction king.

Because *The Titan* and *The Stoic* read, largely, as Charles Shapiro notes, as "one man's novel, in structure and in story" (27), critics have found *The Trilogy* clunky (e.g., *The Titan* alternates chapters between Cowperwood's business and amorous involvements) and "inferior" to Dreiser's other major novels because Cowperwood "turns quickly into a flat parody of Yerkes" (Shapiro 42). Yet, as Richard Lehan points out, Yerkes—"with [his] rags-to-riches caree[r] and [his] overpowering sense of materialism—represents one extreme of American consciousness" (87). Moreover, Dreiser's fascination with polar extremes—Cowperwood is the exact opposite of proletarian Clyde Griffiths—is represented in this profile of a megatycoon, one Dreiser both "admired and hated" (Lehan 43). *The Titan*'s Nietzschean superman, whose motto is ever "I satisfy myself," is a spectacle of seemingly limitless narcissism, with the power to commodify nearly every aspect of his social and personal environment.

Further Reading

Garfield, Graham. "Charles Tyson Yerkes (1837–1905)." Chicago-L.org. <http://www.chicago-l.org/figures/yerkes/>

Gerber, Philip. "Financier, Titan, Stoic: A Trilogy of Desire." *Theodore Dreiser.* New York: Twayne, 1964. 87–110.

———. "Jolly Mrs. Yerkes Is Home from Abroad: Dreiser and the Celebrity Culture." *Theodore Dreiser and American Culture: New Readings.* Ed. Yoshinobu Hakutani. Newark: University of Delaware Press, 2000. 79–103.

Lehan, Richard. *Theodore Dreiser: His World and His Novels.* Carbondale: Southern Illinois University Press, 1969. 41–44.

Lingeman, Richard. Introduction to *The Stoic*. New York: New American Library, 1981. v–xiii.

Kathy Frederickson

Selected Bibliography

Books by Theodore Dreiser

Sister Carrie. New York: Doubleday, Page, 1900.

Jennie Gerhardt. New York: Harper & Brothers, 1911.

The Financier. New York: Harper & Brothers, 1912.

A Traveler at Forty. New York: Century, 1913.

The Titan. New York: John Lane, 1914.

The "Genius." New York: John Lane, 1915.

A Hoosier Holiday. New York: John Lane, 1916.

Plays of the Natural and Supernatural. New York: John Lane, 1916.

Free and Other Stories. New York: Boni & Liveright, 1918.

The Hand of the Potter. New York: Boni & Liveright, 1919.

Twelve Men. New York: Boni & Liveright, 1919.

Hey Rub-a-Dub-Dub: A Book of the Mystery and Wonder and Terror of Life. New York: Boni & Liveright, 1920.

A Book about Myself. New York: Boni & Liveright, 1922.

The Color of a Great City. New York: Boni & Liveright, 1923.

An American Tragedy. New York: Boni & Liveright, 1925.

Moods: Cadenced and Declaimed. New York: Boni & Liveright, 1926.

Chains: Lesser Novels and Stories. New York: Boni & Liveright, 1927.

Dreiser Looks at Russia. New York: Horace Liveright, 1928.

A Gallery of Women. New York: Horace Liveright, 1929.

Dawn. New York: Horace Liveright, 1931.

Tragic America. New York: Horace Liveright, 1931.

America Is Worth Saving. New York: Modern Age, 1941.

The Bulwark. Garden City, N.Y.: Doubleday, 1946.

The Stoic. Garden City, N.Y.: Doubleday, 1947.

Pennsylvania Dreiser Edition

An Amateur Laborer. Ed. Richard W. Dowell. Philadelphia: University of Pennsylvania Press, 1983.

American Diaries, 1902–1926. Ed. Thomas P. Riggio. Philadelphia: University of Pennsylvania Press, 1983.

Dreiser-Mencken Letters: The Correspondence of Theodore Dreiser and H. L. Mencken, 1907–1945. 2 vols. Ed. Thomas P. Riggio. Philadelphia: University of Pennsylvania Press, 1986.

Dreiser's Russian Diary. Ed. Thomas P. Riggio and James L. W. West III. Philadelphia: University of Pennsylvania Press, 1996.

Jennie Gerhardt. Ed. James L. W. West III. Philadelphia: University of Pennsylvania Press, 1992.

Newspaper Days. Ed. T. D. Nostwich. Philadelphia: University of Pennsylvania Press, 1991.

Sister Carrie. Ed. John C. Berkey, Alice M. Winters, and James L. W. West III. Philadelphia: University of Pennsylvania Press, 1981.

Theodore Dreiser Journalism, Vol. 1. *Newspaper Writings, 1892–1895*. Ed. T. D. Nostwich.

Philadelphia: University of Pennsylvania Press, 1988.

Twelve Men. Ed. Robert Coltrane. Philadelphia: University of Pennsylvania Press, 1998.

Miscellaneous Collections

Art, Music, and Literature, 1897-1902. Ed. Yoshinobu Hakutani. Urbana: University of Illinois Press, 2001.

Best Short Stories of Theodore Dreiser. Ed. Howard Fast. 1947. Rpt. Chicago: Ivan R. Dee, 1989.

The Collected Plays of Theodore Dreiser. Ed. Keith Newlin and Frederic E. Rusch. Albany: Whitston, 2000.

Fulfilment and Other Tales of Women and Men. Ed. T. D. Nostwich. Santa Rosa, Calif.: Black Sparrow Press, 1992.

Letters of Theodore Dreiser: A Selection. 3 vols. Ed. Robert H. Elias. Philadelphia: University of Pennsylvania Press, 1959.

Notes on Life. Ed. Marguerite Tjader and John J. McAleer. University: University of Alabama Press, 1974.

Selected Magazine Articles of Theodore Dreiser: Life and Art in the American 1890s. Ed. Yoshinobu Hakutani. 2 vols. Rutherford, N.J.: Fairleigh Dickinson University Press, 1985, 1987.

Sister Carrie: An Authoritative Text, Backgrounds and Sources, Criticism. Ed. Donald Pizer. Norton Critical Edition. 2nd ed. New York: Norton, 1991.

Theodore Dreiser: A Selection of Uncollected Prose. Ed. Donald Pizer. Detroit: Wayne State University Press, 1977.

Theodore Dreiser's Ev'ry Month. Ed. Nancy Warner Barrineau. Athens: University of Georgia Press, 1996.

Theodore Dreiser's "Heard in the Corridors" Articles and Related Writings. Ed. T. D. Nostwich. Ames: Iowa State University Press, 1988.

Works by Others

Bibliographies

Boswell, Jeanetta. *Theodore Dreiser and the Critics, 1911–1982: A Bibliography with Selective Annotations*. Metuchen, N.J.: Scarecrow, 1982.

Pizer, Donald, Richard W. Dowell, and Frederic E. Rusch. *Theodore Dreiser: A Primary Bibliography and Reference Guide*. Boston: G. K. Hall, 1991.

Biographies and Memoirs

Campbell, Louise. *Letters to Louise: Theodore Dreiser's Letters to Louise Campbell*. Philadelphia: University of Pennsylvania Press, 1959.

Dreiser, Helen. *My Life with Dreiser*. Cleveland: World, 1951.

Dreiser, Vera, with Brett Howard. *My Uncle Theodore*. New York: Nash, 1976.

Dudley, Dorothy. *Forgotten Frontiers: Dreiser and the Land of the Free*. New York: Harrison Smith, 1932.

Eastman, Yvette. *Dearest Wilding: A Memoir*. Ed. Thomas P. Riggio. Philadelphia: University of Pennsylvania Press, 1995.

Kennell, Ruth Epperson. *Theodore Dreiser and the Soviet Union, 1927–1945: A First-Hand Chronicle*. New York: International, 1969.

Lingeman, Richard. *Theodore Dreiser: An American Journey, 1908–1945*. New York: Putnam, 1990.

———. *Theodore Dreiser: At the Gates of the City, 1871–1907*. New York: Putnam, 1986.

Swanberg, W. A. *Dreiser*. New York: Scribner, 1965.

Tjader, Marguerite. *Love That Will Not Let Me Go: My Time with Theodore Dreiser*. Ed. Lawrence E. Hussman. New York: Peter Lang, 1998.

———. *Theodore Dreiser, A New Dimension*. Norwalk, Conn.: Silvermine, 1965.

Critical Studies

Eby, Clare Virginia. *Dreiser and Veblen, Saboteurs of the Status Quo*. Columbia: University of Missouri Press, 1998.

Elias, Robert H. *Theodore Dreiser: Apostle of Nature*. 1949. Emended edition. Ithaca, N.Y.: Cornell University Press, 1970.

Gammel, Irene. *Sexualizing Power in Naturalism: Theodore Dreiser and Frederick Philip Grove*. Calgary: University of Calgary Press, 1994.

Gerber, Philip L. *Plots and Characters in the Fiction of Theodore Dreiser.* Hamden, Conn.: Archon, 1977.

———. *Theodore Dreiser.* New York: Twayne, 1964.

———. *Theodore Dreiser Revisited.* New York: Twayne, 1992.

Gogol, Miriam, ed. *Theodore Dreiser: Beyond Naturalism.* New York: New York University Press, 1995.

Griffin, Joseph. *The Small Canvas: An Introduction to Dreiser's Short Stories.* Rutherford, N.J.: Fairleigh Dickinson University Press, 1985.

Hakutani, Yoshinobu. *Young Dreiser.* Rutherford, N.J.: Fairleigh Dickinson University Press, 1980.

———, ed. *Theodore Dreiser and American Culture: New Readings.* Newark: University of Delaware Press, 2000.

Hussman, Lawrence E., Jr. *Dreiser and His Fiction: A Twentieth-Century Quest.* Philadelphia: University of Pennsylvania Press, 1983.

Kazin, Alfred, and Charles Shapiro, eds. *The Stature of Theodore Dreiser.* Bloomington: Indiana University Press, 1955.

Lehan, Richard. *Theodore Dreiser: His World and His Novels.* Carbondale: Southern Illinois University Press, 1969.

Lundén, Rolf. *The Inevitable Equation: The Antithetic Pattern of Theodore Dreiser's Thought and Art.* Uppsala, Sweden: Studia Anglistica Upsaliensia, no. 16, 1973.

Lundquist, James. *Theodore Dreiser.* New York: Ungar, 1974.

Lydenberg, John, ed. *Dreiser: A Collection of Critical Essays.* Englewood Cliffs, N.J.: Prentice-Hall, 1971.

Mathiesson, F. O. *Theodore Dreiser.* New York: William Sloane, 1951.

Moers, Ellen. *Two Dreisers.* New York: Viking, 1969.

Mookerjee, R. N. *Theodore Dreiser: His Thought and Social Criticism.* Delhi: National Publishing House, 1974.

Orlov, Paul. An American Tragedy: *Perils of the Self Seeking "Success."* Lewisburg, Pa.: Bucknell University Press, 1998.

Pizer, Donald. *The Novels of Theodore Dreiser: A Critical Study.* Minneapolis: University of Minnesota Press, 1976.

———, ed. *Critical Essays on Theodore Dreiser.* Boston: G. K. Hall, 1981.

———, *New Essays on* Sister Carrie. Cambridge and New York: Cambridge University Press, 1991.

Rascoe, Burton. *Theodore Dreiser.* New York: Robert M. McBride, 1925.

Salzman, Jack, ed. *Theodore Dreiser: The Critical Reception.* New York: David Lewis, 1972.

Shapiro, Charles. *Theodore Dreiser: Our Bitter Patriot.* Carbondale: Southern Illinois University Press, 1966.

St. Jean, Shawn. *Pagan Dreiser: Songs from an American Mythology.* Madison, N.J.: Fairleigh Dickinson University Press, 2001.

Warren, Robert Penn. *Homage to Theodore Dreiser: On the Centennial of His Birth.* New York: Random House, 1971.

West, James L. W., III. A Sister Carrie *Portfolio.* Charlottesville: University Press of Virginia, 1985.

———, ed. *Dreiser's* Jennie Gerhardt: *New Essays on the Restored Text.* Philadelphia: University of Pennsylvania Press, 1995.

Zanine, Louis J. *Mechanism and Mysticism: The Influence of Science on the Thought and Work of Theodore Dreiser.* Philadelphia: University of Pennsylvania Press, 1993.

Index

Boldface page numbers indicate the location of main entries.

About the Contributors

JOSEPH F. ALEXANDER was born in New York City and received an M.S. from Fairleigh Dickinson University. Currently, he is enrolled in the M.F.A program in creative writing at the University of North Carolina at Wilmington. His most recent story, " 'Z' as in Xylophone," appeared in the *Vermont Literary Review*.

D. L. ANDERSON, a poet, playwright, and actress, resides in Brunswick County, North Carolina, where she teaches English at Brunswick Community College. She has had plays produced in New York City, Arizona, and the Carolinas. As an actress, she has been in many theater and film productions.

ROGER ASSELINEAU, Professor Emeritus at the University of Paris–Sorbonne before his death in July 2002, is the author of a number of books, including *The Evolution of Walt Whitman* (1960–1962) and *The Transcendentalist Constant in American Literature* (1980), and coauthor (with Gay W. Allen) of *St. John de Crevecoeur: The Life of an American Farmer* (1987).

RENATE VON BARDELEBEN is Professor of American Studies at Johannes Gutenberg University of Mainz. She is the author of *Das Bild New Yorks im Ezählwerk*

von Dreiser und Dos Passos (1967) and *Studien zur amerikanischen Autobiographie: Benjamin Franklin und Mark Twain* (1981). Besides editing six collections on ethnic literature and gender studies, she has published numerous articles on Dreiser and is now finishing a new, unabridged edition of *A Traveler at Forty*.

NANCY WARNER BARRINEAU, Professor of English at the University of North Carolina at Pembroke, has published several articles on Theodore Dreiser and is the editor of *Theodore Dreiser's Ev'ry Month* (1996). She has also written about Brander Matthews, Caroline Chesebro, Mark Twain, Thomas Hardy, Lee Smith, and the American expatriate community in Paris.

BLAIR F. BIGELOW is Professor of English at Suffolk University. His doctoral dissertation was a collected edition of Dreiser's newspaper writing from 1892 to 1895.

MARGARET BOE BIRNS is an Adjunct Assistant Professor at New York University and a member of the faculty of New School University and New School Online University, specializing in modern English and American literature. She has published articles on Sinclair Lewis, Henrik

Ibsen, Anthony Powell, Agatha Christie, Lewis Carroll, and William Faulkner.

NICHOLAS BIRNS is a Lecturer in English at New School University in New York City, where he edits *Powys Notes*. He received his B.A. from Columbia in 1988 and his Ph.D. from New York University in 1992. He has published over twenty scholarly articles and has also written for general-interest periodicals such as the *New York Times Book Review* and *Midstream*.

DAVID BLAMY earned his M.A. from the University of North Carolina at Wilmington and is pursuing a Ph.D. in dramatic literature at Texas Tech University.

STEPHEN BRAIN is a Ph.D. student in the history department at the University of California, Berkeley. His M.A. thesis investigated Dreiser's trip to the Soviet Union and his subsequent writings about the U.S.S.R.

STEPHEN C. BRENNAN is Professor of English at Louisiana State University in Shreveport. He received his doctorate from Tulane University in 1979 and has published numerous articles on Dreiser. Since 1999 he has been coeditor of *Dreiser Studies*.

DONNA M. CAMPBELL, Associate Professor of English at Gonzaga University, is the author of *Resisting Regionalism: Gender and Naturalism in American Fiction, 1885–1915* (1997). In addition to the "Fiction: 1900–1930" annual essay in *American Literary Scholarship*, which includes a review of Dreiser scholarship, her recent work includes articles on Jack London, Edith Wharton, Mary Wilkins Freeman, and William Dean Howells.

ARTHUR D. CASCIATO is the Director of the Center for Undergraduate Research and Fellowships at the University of Pennsylvania.

WILLIAM BEDFORD CLARK, Professor of English at Texas A&M University, has published widely in American literary studies and is the general editor of the Robert Penn Warren Correspondence Project.

JAMES F. COLLINS is a technical writer and independent literary scholar, specializing in Gene Wolfe, Ursula LeGuin, and other literary speculative fiction. He has published articles in *Science Fiction Research Association Review* and the *Bulletin of Bibliography*, as well as numerous technical articles and manuals. He lives in Wilmington, North Carolina.

ROBERT COLTRANE is Professor of English at Lock Haven University of Pennsylvania. His dissertation research provided the information he used to produce the Pennsylvania Dreiser Edition of *Twelve Men*, published in 1998. He has also published scholarly articles on Ernest Hemingway, William Styron, and W. B. Yeats.

THOMAS F. CONNOLLY is a member of the Suffolk University English Department. He is the managing editor of the *Eugene O'Neill Review*. From 1996–1998, he was Fulbright Professor of American Literature and American Studies at the University of Ostrava, Czech Republic. His most recent book is *George Jean Nathan and the Making of Modern American Drama Criticism* (2000).

JON DIETRICK teaches English literature and composition at the University of the District of Columbia. A reformed stockbroker interested in connections between literature and economic life, he is currently at work on a book about salesmen in twentieth-century American fiction and drama.

NANCY McILVAINE DONOVAN received her Ph.D. from Miami University of Ohio. In 2000 she received the first Dreiser Essay Prize, an annual award sponsored by the Dreiser Society, for her essay "Representing Grace Brown: The Working Class-Woman in 'American Tragedy' Narratives," which appeared in *Dreiser Studies* 31.2 (2000).

RICHARD W. DOWELL is Professor Emeritus at Indiana State University. Coauthor of *Theodore Dreiser: A Primary Bibliography and Reference Guide* (1991) and editor of Dreiser's *An Amateur Laborer* (1983), he is the founder and coeditor of the *Dreiser Newsletter* (1970–1986) and of *Dreiser Studies* (1987–1989).

CLARE EBY, Professor of English at the University of Connecticut, is the author of *Dreiser and Veblen, Saboteurs of the Status Quo* (1998) and editor of the Norton Critical Edition of Upton Sinclair's *The Jungle*. She is coeditor of the forthcoming *The Cambridge Companion to Theodore Dreiser* and is editing the Pennsylvania Dreiser Edition of *The Genius*.

SCOTT D. EMMERT is an Assistant Professor of English at the University of Wisconsin–Fox Valley. He is the author of *Loaded Fictions: Social Critique in the Twentieth-Century Western* (1996).

MONTY KOZBIAL ERNST received his M.A. from Marquette University and his Ph.D. from the University of Toledo. He has taught at a number of schools including Utah State University, Fairfield University, and St. Norbert College. He is cur-

rently the McNair Research Coordinator at the University of Wisconsin at Eau Claire.

BLYTHE FERGUSON received an M.A. in English in 2002 from the University of North Carolina at Wilmington. She teaches English composition for non-native speakers at Cape Fear Community College and at the University of North Carolina at Wilmington.

DENNIS FLYNN is Professor of English at Bentley College. His most recent publications include *John Donne and the Ancient Catholic Nobility* (1995) and (with Gary Stringer et al.) *The Anniversaries and the Epicedes and Obsequies* (volume 6) and *The Elegies* (volume 3) of *The Variorum Edition of the Poetry of John Donne* (1995 and 2001).

KATHY FREDERICKSON, a graduate of the University of Massachusetts at Amherst, has been teaching in the Massachusetts Community College system since 1982. Her research interests include late nineteenth- and early-twentieth-century American literature, feminist criticism, American women's autobiography, composition and rhetoric studies, and distance learning.

KIMBERLY FREEMAN is an Assistant Professor of English at the University of the District of Columbia, where she teaches American and medieval literature and composition. She has contributed to *a/b: Studies in Autobiography* and *The Reader's Guide to Gay and Lesbian Studies* and is currently working on a book on divorce in the American novel.

IRENE GAMMEL teaches modern literature and culture at the University of Prince Edward Island, Canada. The author of *Sexualizing Power in Naturalism: Theodore Dreiser and Frederick Philip Grove* (1994), her most recent books are *Making Avonlea: L. M. Montgomery and Popular Culture* (2002) and *Baroness Elsa: Gender, Dada and Everyday Modernity—A Cultural Biography* (2002).

PHILIP GERBER is Distinguished Professor Emeritus at the State University of New York in Brockport, where in 1990 he hosted the conference on *"Sister Carrie at Ninety,"* out of which grew the present International Theodore Dreiser Society. He has published extensively on Dreiser since the 1960s, his latest book being *Theodore Dreiser Revisited* (1992).

JOSEPH GRIFFIN, now retired, taught American literature at the University of Ottawa. His study of Dreiser's short stories, *The Small Canvas*, appeared in 1985. He has also published articles on James T. Farrell, Howard Fast, and Ernest Gaines. He is now in the final stages of a comprehensive study of Edith Wharton's short stories.

YOSHINOBU HAKUTANI, Distinguished Professor of English at Kent State University, is the author or editor of several books on Dreiser: *Young Dreiser* (1980), *Selected Magazine Articles of Theodore Dreiser* (1985, 1987, recipient of a *Choice* award), *Theodore Dreiser and American Culture* (2000), *Art, Music, and Literature, 1897–1902*, by Theodore Dreiser (2001), and *Theodore Dreiser's Uncollected Magazine Articles, 1897–1902* (2002).

LAURA HAPKE is Professor of English at Pace University. Her most recent book is *Labor's Text: The Worker in American Fiction* (2001).

DAVID T. HUMPHRIES earned his M.A. from Ohio State University and is currently completing his Ph.D. at the Gradu-

ate Center of the City University of New York. He works with the honors program at Queens College and has published articles on Dreiser and Wallace Stevens.

LAWRENCE E. HUSSMAN, Professor Emeritus at Wright State University, is the author of *Dreiser and His Fiction, A Twentieth-Century Quest* (1983), and *Harbingers of a Century: The Novels of Frank Norris* (1999). He is the editor of *Love That Will Not Let Me Go: My Time with Theodore Dreiser*, by Marguerite Tjader (1998).

JAMES M. HUTCHISSON, Professor of English at the Citadel, has written widely on such American authors as Dreiser, Lewis, Poe, Chopin, and others. His most recent book is *A DuBose Heyward Reader* (2003).

KEVIN JETT is completing his Ph.D. at the University of Toledo, Ohio, where he is an instructor of freshmen writing and introduction to literature classes. He is particularly interested in the treatment of the businessman, consumerism, and corporate liberalism in American literature. His work has appeared in *Lamar Journal of the Humanities, Dreiser Studies, Mississippi Quarterly*, and *MidAmerica*.

MARC JOHNSTON is an M.F.A. student in the creative writing program at the University of North Carolina at Wilmington.

DANA STOLTE KOLLER graduated from the University of North Carolina at Wilmington in 2002 with an M.A. in English with an emphasis in critical literacy.

RICHARD LINGEMAN is the author of *Theodore Dreiser: At the Gates of the City, 1871–1908* (1986) and *Theodore Dreiser: An American Journey, 1908–1945* (1990). An abridged, one-volume paperback edition,

Theodore Dreiser: An American Journey, was published in 1993. He is also the author of *Small Town America* (1980) and *Sinclair Lewis: Rebel from Main Street* (2002). He is a senior editor of the *Nation*.

CAROL S. LORANGER, Associate Professor of English at Wright State University in Dayton, Ohio, teaches twentieth- and later-nineteenth-century American literature. Her scholarship appears in *Dreiser Studies*, *Pynchon Notes*, and *Journal of Postmodern Culture*.

JEROME LOVING, Professor of English at Texas A&M University, is the author or editor of eight books, including the biography *Walt Whitman: The Song of Himself* (1999). He is currently finishing a full-length biography of Dreiser and is the author of the Dreiser essays in the *Oxford Encyclopedia of American Literature* and Scribner's *American Writers* series.

RENEÉ D. McELHENEY is completing an M.A. in English at the University of North Carolina at Wilmington.

ROARK MULLIGAN, Associate Professor of English at Christopher Newport University in Newport News, Virginia, teaches literature and composition while directing the freshman writing program. In addition to articles on composition and pedagogical topics, he has written essays on Dreiser that have appeared in *American Literary Realism*, *English Language Notes*, and *Dreiser Studies*.

KEITH NEWLIN, Professor of English at the University of North Carolina at Wilmington, is the coeditor of *Dreiser Studies*. His most recent book is an edition of Hamlin Garland's *The Book of the American Indian* (2002).

DEBRA NIVEN is completing an M.A. in English at the University of North Carolina at Wilmington.

DONALD T. OAKES is an Episcopal priest and educator and past president of the Mountain Top Historical Society. He is the author of a children's book, *The Promise*, and the Foreword and Afterword to Arthur Henry's *The House in the Woods* and editor of the Mountain Top Edition of *Rip Van Winkle*, *A Pride of Palaces*, and *The Norman Rockwell Bicycle Tour of Stockbridge*.

LOUIS J. OLDANI, Professor of English at Rockhurst University in Kansas City, Missouri, has published on Dreiser in the *Dreiser Newsletter*, *Library Chronicle*, *Research Studies*, and *Studies in Bibliography*.

PAUL A. ORLOV is an Associate Professor of English and American studies at the Delaware County campus of Pennsylvania State University. The author of *An American Tragedy: Perils of the Self Seeking "Success"* (1998), he has published many articles on Dreiser's fiction as well as essays on Whitman, Frost, and Stephen Crane. He was the secretary/treasurer of the International Theodore Dreiser Society from 1993 to 2002.

DONNA PACKER-KINLAW is a Ph.D. student at the University of Maryland. In 2001 she was awarded the second Dreiser Essay Prize for her essay "Life on the Margins: The Silent Feminist in Theodore Dreiser's 'Marriage—for One,'" which was published in *Dreiser Studies* 32.2 (2001). She is the secretary-treasurer of the Dreiser Society.

DONALD PIZER, Pierce Butler Professor of English Emeritus at Tulane University, has published widely on late-nineteenth and early-twentieth century American literature. Among his works on Dreiser are *The Novels of Theodore Dreiser: A Critical Study* (1976), *Theodore Dreiser: A Selection of Uncollected Prose* (1977), and editions of *Sister Carrie* and *Jennie Gerhardt*.

KATHRYN M. PLANK is the Associate Director of Faculty and Teaching Assistant Development at Ohio State University. She received her Ph.D. in English from Pennsylvania State University and has written on both Dreiser and William Carlos Williams. Her research interests include literature and medicine, educational technology, faculty development, and gender issues in higher education.

JENNIFER MARIE RASPET received an M.A. in English from the University of North Carolina at Wilmington in 2002. She teaches British literature at Union High School in Sampson County, North Carolina, and composition at James Sprunt Community College.

JOHN W. REYNOLDS teaches American literature at the University of Connecticut.

THOMAS P. RIGGIO is a Professor of English at the University of Connecticut and General Editor of the Dreiser Edition at the University of Pennsylvania Library. He is currently working on a biography of Dreiser and editing a volume of letters in the Dreiser Edition, which is published by the University of Illinois Press. His edition of *An American Tragedy* in the Library of America series appeared in 2003.

IAN F. ROBERTS is an Assistant Professor of English at Missouri Western State College, where he teaches courses on naturalism, on literature and science, and on hard science fiction.

FREDERIC E. RUSCH, Professor Emeritus of English at Indiana State University, is a cofounder of the International Theodore Dreiser Society and former editor of *Dreiser Studies*. He is the coeditor of *The Collected Plays of Theodore Dreiser* (2000) and a coauthor of *Theodore Dreiser: A Primary Bibliography and Reference Guide* (1991), the standard reference book on works by and about Dreiser.

MANDY SEE graduated from the University of North Carolina at Wilmington in 2002 with an M.A. in English.

NANCY M. SHAWCROSS is an Adjunct Professor of English at the University of Pennsylvania and Curator of Manuscripts in the Rare Book and Manuscript Library, University of Pennsylvania, where she is responsible for the management of the Theodore Dreiser Papers.

KARI LEE SIKO graduated with an M.Ed. in Secondary English from the University of North Carolina at Wilmington and is currently an English teacher at Emsley A. Laney High School in Wilmington.

ROGER W. SMITH is an independent scholar living in Maspeth, Queens, New York, who has done extensive research on Theodore Dreiser. His major interests include Dreiser's early career, Dreiser's style and development as a writer, issues related to the composition of *The "Genius"* and *An American Tragedy*, and Dreiser's religious and philosophical views.

SHAWN ST. JEAN teaches world and American literature at the State University of New York in Brockport. He is the author of *Pagan Dreiser: Songs from American Mythology* (2001), an exploration of nineteenth- and twentieth-century literary reconstruction of myth and paganism. He has published articles on literature and film in *Midwest Quarterly, Massachusetts Review, Studies in Bibliography, James Joyce Quarterly, Feminist Studies,* and others.

CAREN J. TOWN is an Associate Professor of English at Georgia Southern University. She has published articles on Dreiser's representation of women in *Sister Carrie* and on narrative structure in *An American Tragedy.* She has recently completed articles on Sinclair Lewis and Anne Tyler and a monograph on female adolescents in contemporary southern literature. Currently she is at work on a study of gender in young adult fiction.

AMY E. UJVARI received her Ph.D. from Kent State University, and she is currently an Assistant Professor at Trocaire College in Buffalo, New York, where she teaches English and philosophy courses. Her publications and writings include essays about Dreiser, Simone de Beauvoir, Richard Wright, Margaret Atwood, Louisa May Alcott, H.D., and Elizabeth Siddall.

CHRISTOPHER WEINMANN received his B.A. from Haverford College and his M.A. and Ph.D. from Pennsylvania State University. His dissertation analyzed and edited five unpublished short story manuscripts written by Dreiser during his "Lost Decade."

MICHAEL WENTWORTH is Professor of English and Director of the Master of Arts in Liberal Studies Program at the University of North Carolina at Wilmington. In addition to books on Sir Thomas More and Thomas Heywood, he has published articles on Michael Drayton, Fitz-James O'Brien, Sherwood Anderson, Vachel Lindsay, Frank O'Connor, William Inge, and the teaching of writing and literature.

JAMES L. W. WEST III is Edwin Erle Sparks Professor of English at Pennsylvania State University. His scholarly editions of *Sister Carrie, Jennie Gerhardt,* and other Dreiser writings have been published by the University of Pennsylvania Press.

ANNEMARIE KONING WHALEY is an Associate Professor of English at East Texas Baptist University. Her article "Obscuring the Home: Textual Editing in Theodore Dreiser's *Jennie Gerhardt*" appears in *Theodore Dreiser and American Culture: New Readings* (2000). She has also published and presented numerous articles on Southern literature and Renaissance women writers.

SCOTT ZALUDA has published essays on Dreiser's fiction in *Theodore Dreiser: Beyond Naturalism* (1995) and in *Dreiser Studies.* His doctoral dissertation, "Between Wonder and Entanglement: Dreiser's Fictions of Community" (City University of New York, 1992), examines *Sister Carrie* within late-nineteenth-century dialogues on urban community. He is on the English faculty of Westchester Community College of the State University of New York.

MOHAMED ZAYANI has a Ph.D. in English from Indiana University. He is currently Associate Professor of Literature and Critical Theory at the American University in Sharjah, United Arab Emirates (UAE). He is the author of *Reading the Symptom: Frank Norris, Theodore Dreiser, and the Dynamics of Capitalism* (1999).